PRAISE FOR *Investing Bible*

"Today's investors can be forgiven for feeling a bit like Job, gi[ven the] setbacks the market has thrown at them. For those seeking inspiration, look no further than Lynn O'Shaughnessy's *Investing Bible*. For navigating both up and down markets, this is one very good book."

> —Don Phillips, Managing Director, Morningstar, Inc.

"So much to know, so much trouble to figure out where to find it all...until now. If you want to learn how to take control of your financial future but don't know where to turn, the *Investing Bible* is the answer to your prayers. Lynn O'Shaughnessy has done a wonderful job of pulling together and clarifying a wide variety of information across the entire investment scene."

> —Marc H. Gerstein, Director of Investment Research, Multex.com

"The *Investing Bible* is a must-read for anyone investing in funds, stocks, or bonds for their financial planning needs."

> —Alan J. Cohn, CFP, Co-Founder, Sage Online

"A must-read resource for the individual investor. The *Investing Bible* is comprehensive, objective and jam-packed full of helpful online references."

> —Sue Stevens, Director, Financial Planning, Morningstar Associates LLC

Investing Bible

Lynn O'Shaughnessy

WILEY

Wiley Publishing, Inc.

Investing Bible

Published by

Wiley Publishing, Inc.

111 River Street

Hoboken, NJ 07030

www.wiley.com

Library of Congress Control Number: 2001092753

ISBN: 978-0-7645-5380-6

Printed in the United States of America

1B/RU/QZ/QR/IN

10 9

Distributed in the United States by Wiley Publishing, Inc.

For general information on Wiley Publishing, Inc. books in the U.S., please call our Customer Care Service department at 800-762-2974.

For reseller information, including discounts and premium sales, please call our Reseller Customer Service department at 800-434-3422.

For sales inquiries and special prices for bulk quantities, please contact our Order Services department at 800-434-3422 or write to the address above.

Credits

Acquisitions Editor
Kevin Thornton

Development Editor
Maureen Kelly

Production Editor
Heather Gregory

Copy Editors
Elizabeth Kim
Heather Stith

Project Coordinator
Nancee Reeves

Graphics and Production Specialists
Joyce Haughey
Barry Offringa
Jill Piscitelli
Betty Schulte
Laurie Stevens
Brian Torwelle

Quality Control Specialist
Marianne Santy

Proofreader
TECHBOOKS Production Services

Indexer
TECHBOOKS Production Services

Cover Image
Anthony Bunyan

About the Author

Lynn O'Shaughnessy, the author of *The Unofficial Guide to Investing* and the *Retirement Bible,* has been writing about personal finance for nearly a decade. The former Los Angeles Times reporter has contributed countless articles to *Mutual Funds Magazine, Bloomberg Personal Finance Magazine, The Wall Street Journal, Forbes Magazine*'s Web site, and a variety of other magazines and online ventures. She is also a popular guest on Sage Online, a highly successful financial Internet site that has partnered with America Online for many years. Lynn, who graduated with honors from the University of Missouri's School of Journalism, worked as a reporter for the *Los Angeles Times* for nearly seven years. She lives with her husband and two children in San Diego.

To Bruce, Caitlin, and Ben.

And the rest of my family, past and present.

Contents

Part IV: Bonding with Your Investments   277

Chapter 17: Bond Basics 279

Chapter 18: Uncle Sam's Bond World 299

Acknowledgments

I t's no fun undoing what's been done. If you've ever addressed, stamped, and sealed an envelope and then realized you forgot to put the letter inside you know what I mean. Multiply that aggravation by about 100 and you'll have some idea of how I felt after Congress passed landmark tax legislation that created 441 changes to U.S. tax law. Shortly before President George W. Bush signed the bill, I had finished writing the *Investing Bible*. Suddenly, I was scrambling to revise the book before its publication.

Luckily, plenty of people were willing to help. I am very grateful for the wealth of updated tax materials that CCH Inc. swiftly provided me. In particular, I want to thank Mark Luscombe, CCH's principal federal tax analyst, and Nicolas Kaster, CCH's IRA and pension analyst. Also pitching in was Ed Slott, a CPA and IRA expert, who is always willing to check the accuracy of my work no matter how busy his schedule. I also wish to thank three certified financial planners, Fern Alix LaRocca, Susan Hodges Strasbaugh, and Sue Stevens, director of financial planning at Morningstar, as well as Peter F. McDonnell, CLU, CHFC, who shared their thoughts on how the tax changes would affect college savings.

I'd also like to single out those who helped me with my stock and bond chapters. Thanks to them, I believe that I was able to provide readers with much more than the same old tired generalizations that you often read elsewhere. I surely couldn't have written about bonds with as much confidence or depth without the help of Peter Hollenbach at the U.S. Treasury Department's Bureau of the Public Debt; my brother, John O'Shaughnessy, a CPA and investment advisor; and Kathy M. Foody-Malus, a senior portfolio manager at Federated Investors. Marc H. Gerstein, the director of investment research at Multex.com, shared his considerable knowledge as I worked on the stock chapters.

When I was tackling the investment club chapter, Ion Yadigaroglu of bivio.com and Mark Robertson of the National Association of Investors Corp., were helpful with their insights. And I was happy that Ted Benna, regarded as the father of 401(k) plans, reviewed my 401(k) chapter. When researching the chapter devoted to broker troubles and scams, I relied upon Ashley Baker of the North American Securities Administrators Association and Mark Maddox, president of the Public Investors Arbitration Bar Association. William P. Bengen, a CFP who is practically a neighbor, and Anthony Steuer, a life insurance analyst, respectively helped out with the financial planner and insurance chapters.

Meanwhile, many organizations provided me with helpful statistics that you see sprinkled throughout the book. I obtained statistics from Morningstar; Wiesenberger, Thomson Financial; Lipper, a Reuters Company; The Leuthold Group; Standard & Poor's; Morgan Stanley Capital International; AdvisoryWorld; U.S. Bancorp Piper Jaffray; and Credit Suisse First Boston.

I also want to acknowledge the people at Wiley Publishing, who helped put this book together during a time of tremendous change within the company. Thanks to Maureen Kelly, Kevin Thornton, Mark Butler, and Heather Gregory, as well as to a pair of Wiley Publishing alum, Kathy Welton and Jon Malysiak. I also appreciated the comments of the book's two technical reviewers, Douglas Gerlach, a well-known online investing expert, and Pam Autrey, president of Strategic Management Services in Austin, Texas. In addition, I appreciate the help of my agent, Daniel Greenberg of James Levine Communications.

Finally, I wish to thank my parents, Vincent P. and Jacquelin O'Shaughnessy, who encouraged my passionate love of books by taking me to the neighborhood library in St. Louis hundreds of time. I never seriously thought that some day I'd be writing my own. I'm also grateful to the support that my sisters and my other brother gave me. Berkeley and Riley, my utterly loyal Golden Retrievers, also deserve a thank you, or better yet, a milk bone. And I can't express enough gratitude to my husband, Bruce V. Bigelow, and our two children, Caitlin and Ben, who have nobly tried to adjust to living with an author. During back-to-back books, they were reminded of the unglamorous side of writing. Thanks for being such good sports!

Lynn O'Shaughnessy
San Diego

Introduction

Do you remember the first time you had to make a fairly complicated investing decision? I do.

When an information packet about my company's 401(k) plan landed on my desk years ago, I did what many do. I procrastinated. At the time, I was a young reporter at the *Los Angeles Times,* who was working long hours to keep my editors from second-guessing their decision to hire me. The prospects of spending free time grappling with my investment choices was as appealing as washing dinner dishes on Thanksgiving.

When I finally spread the paperwork on the dining room table and forced myself to focus, I was uncertain what to do. Like the typical 401(k), the plan allowed me to spread my money among stocks, bonds, and cash. I ultimately decided to evenly divide my contributions among all the choices.

I figured I had done the right thing by following the old adage—don't put all your eggs in one basket. But the portfolio that I signed off on was far too conservative for someone so young. I had blown that decision. But I was hardly alone. Millions of Americans have inadvertently made similar mistakes.

Why Do You Need This Book?

Unfortunately, Americans are under more pressure than ever before to be smart investors and avoid the kind of mistake that I made. In the past, people like you and me could have managed quite comfortably without knowing the difference between the Standard & Poor's 500 Index and the Nasdaq-100. It was traditionally our employers who worried about our financial well-being. But now fewer corporations offer pension plans that spit out a lifetime of monthly retirement checks. What have largely taken their place are those 401(k) plans, where timecard punchers are on their own.

Saving for retirement is only one of many occasions when investing smarts is mandatory. Parents struggling to save enough to send their kids to college are bombarded with more choices than ever before. Many baby boomers will have to figure out how to wisely invest inheritances. Meanwhile, saving for a dream home poses its own challenges. No matter what our financial goals are, we have to sidestep the hidden land mines that riddle our paths.

Tip   If there's a lesson to be learned from my own experience it's this: Education can defuse the financial land mines. The more we know about how to invest wisely, the more prosperous we should become.

Even if you rely upon a financial planner or a broker for assistance, knowing the basics is essential. After all, the only one who is ultimately responsible for your financial security is yourself.

Here's your edge

The *Investing Bible* will help by shortening your learning curve. Within its covers is plenty of advice for beginners as well as those who have already mastered the investing ABCs. You'll find in-depth advice on stocks, bonds, and mutual funds, as well as new and innovative ways to invest your cash. You'll also learn the latest strategies for investing for retirement and college, as well as how to prepare your children for their own investing careers. Scattered throughout the book are practical and timely suggestions that could very well enhance your investing success.

Why should you buy this book when you can receive free handouts from brokers, mutual funds, and other financial institutions? While some of their information is very good, it can be perilously incomplete. Can you really expect a brokerage firm to mention that its fees are the most outrageous in the industry? Will a mutual fund divulge that its returns have kept it locked in the basement with the other losers during three out of the last five years? Do you think that an insurer's glossy handout on variable annuities will explain that tax law makes these investments a gloriously bad choice for most people? In contrast, you can depend upon the *Investing Bible* to provide you with unbiased and independent information.

The aim of the *Investing Bible* is not to force-feed the same old superficial advice you might have heard already. What you read in many investing books can be infuriatingly vague.

Example   Plenty of Americans are intrigued by the prospect of investing in individual stocks, but they are mystified about how to proceed. Yet personal finance books, which often merely provide a cursory explanation of how to analyze a stock, often leave readers yearning for more.

The *Investing Bible* fills such information gaps, digging deep into subjects on which readers need the full scoop. An entire chapter, for instance, is devoted to explaining how any individual stock can be analyzed by using free resources.

Many personal finance books often treat bonds in the same slapdash manner, dutifully providing short descriptions of municipal, corporate, and Treasury bonds and then quickly scooting on to the next subject. The *Investing Bible,* however, not only explains how different bonds work, but also provides strategies on how they can be used most effectively.

A taste of what's to come

What's to be learned by reading this thick book? Here is a sampling of the kind of advice that you can discover inside:

- ✦ Over your investing lifetime, you can save tens of thousands of dollars or more in expenses by favoring cheap mutual funds. (See Chapters 1 & 8.)

- ✦ When evaluating a stock, know where to find key financial ratios that will make comparisons with other stocks easier. (See Chapter 15.)

- ✦ Include small-cap stocks in your portfolio; historically they have captured the honors as the best equity performers. (See Chapter 12.)

- ✦ Use free Internet tools to help you evaluate how risky your portfolio really is. (See Chapter 3.)

- ✦ Using the yield curve can help you pinpoint the best bond bargains. (See Chapter 17.)

- ✦ Be careful investing in a particular sector, such as technology, energy, and health care, if it's already experienced tremendous gains. (See Chapter 14.)

- ✦ You can identify mutual funds that are tax hogs by consulting a couple of sources. (See Chapter 25.)

- ✦ Set your child up with a kiddie Roth IRA. (See Chapter 24.)

- ✦ Investigate Section 529 plans if you're investing for your child's college education. (See Chapter 23.)

- ✦ Reduce your tax burden by putting different types of investments in retirement and taxable accounts. (See Chapter 25.)

- ✦ Explore whether the GARP (growth-at-a-reasonable-price) stock-picking strategy might be right for you. (See Chapter 12.)

- ✦ Fed up with most mutual funds? Consider index funds and exchange-traded funds. (See Chapters 10 & 11.)

- ✦ When hunting for a financial planner, whittle down your choices by calling two phone numbers. (See Chapter 5.)

The Investing Bible Quiz

If you already know a fair amount about investing, you might wonder whether you really need another book on your shelf. A quick way to help answer that question is to take this quiz. If you flub it, don't panic. After reading the *Investing Bible,* you'll know all the answers and much, much more.

1. Since the 1920s, which type of stock has performed the best?

   A. Large-cap growth stocks

   B. Small-cap growth stocks

   C. Large-cap value stocks

   D. Small-cap value stocks

2. If your investment earns an average annual return of 10 percent, how many years will it take before your money doubles?

   A. Ten years

   B. Seven years

   C. Five years

3. A bear market occurs when stocks fall this far from their peak:

   A. 10 percent

   B. 20 percent

   C. 25 percent

4. The reason stock and bond index funds often do better than other mutual funds is that they have lower expenses.

   A. True

   B. False

5. When investing in a mutual fund, this is the one variable that you can control:

   A. Expenses

   B. Portfolio performance

   C. Annual return

6. A whisper number is:

   A. An unofficial estimate of a company's future earnings that is often posted online.

B. The true price of your stock trades.

C. None of the above.

7. Who or what is Edgar?

A. He is a popular commentator on CNBC, the financial news network.

B. The nickname for the U.S. Securities and Exchange Commission's database that contains all the financial filings for the nation's publicly traded stocks.

C. It's an acronym for a type of technical stock analysis.

8. If you have $10,000 invested in a mutual fund with a 1.50 percent expense ratio, the annual fee will be:

A. $15

B. $150

C. $75

9. Tax-free municipal bonds and variable annuities are ideal investments to put into an IRA.

A. True

B. False

10. Unless you sell your mutual fund shares, you'll never have to pay capital gains taxes.

A. True

B. False

11. You won't find this in a company's annual report:

A. Income statement

B. Balance sheet

C. Stock analysts' opinions

12. How do you obtain a stock's P/E ratio?

A. You divide a stock's share price by the earnings a company generates for one share.

B. You look at a newspaper's stock tables.

C. You check a financial Web site.

D. All of the above.

13. A stock that doesn't have a price-to-earnings (P/E) ratio can usually be bought at a bargain-basement price.

    A. True

    B. False

14. The best way to describe what a Section 529 plan is:

    A. Parents who are saving for their children's education invest in these state-sponsored plans.

    B. The money in a Section 529 plan is sheltered from taxes.

    C. Both of the above.

15. Money markets are insured by the Federal Deposit Insurance Corporation (FDIC).

    A. True

    B. False

16. Contributions to a Roth IRA are not tax deductible.

    A. True

    B. False

17. U.S. Treasuries can be an alternative to certificates of deposit.

    A. True

    B. False

18. What is dollar-cost averaging?

    A. It's a tool the U.S. Treasury uses to measure the cost of money.

    B. It's a financial strategy requiring you to invest money at regular intervals, such as monthly.

    C. It's another term for the buy-and-hold strategy of investing.

19. When interest rates go up, what happens to bond prices?

    A. Bond prices drop.

    B. Interest rates do not influence bond prices.

    C. Bond and interest rates always rise together.

20. Which of the following is a sector fund?

    A. Equity-income fund

    B. Junk bond fund

    C. Technology fund

    D. Index fund

Answers

1.	D	11.	C
2.	B	12.	D
3.	B	13.	B
4.	A	14.	C
5.	A	15.	B
6.	A	16.	A
7.	B	17.	A
8.	B	18.	B
9.	B	19.	A
10.	B	20.	C

Investing Fundamentals

Part I will provide you with classic investing strategies that should carry you through both jubilant and terrifying times on Wall Street. You'll find special instructions for surviving a bear market, plus tips for establishing an all-weather portfolio. You'll also learn how to evaluate the dizzying number of brokerage choices, as well as how to choose an excellent financial planner.

Your Twelve Best Investment Strategies

✦ ✦ ✦ ✦

In This Chapter

Realizing your true
millionaire potential

Learning the 12 top
investment strategies

✦ ✦ ✦ ✦

This chapter hands you the tools that are critical for a lifetime of successful investing. You'll learn how to boost your net worth by diversifying, by avoiding investing mind games, and by being mindful of treacherous investment risks. You will also discover how to sidestep common mistakes that are often committed by those who are trying to stretch the investing envelope. Finally, you'll learn why boring investing is often best.

The Path to Riches

It didn't take glitzy prime-time quiz shows or conniving contestants stranded in the Australian outback to start Americans dreaming about becoming millionaires. Try typing "millionaire" into an Internet search engine and you'll get hundreds of thousands of hits. Our fascination with owning enough dollar bills to stuff a Brinks armored truck is practically genetic. Even kids with piggy banks instinctively know that being rich is a big deal. Americans' preoccupation with great wealth is boundless.

Despite the hype, many people assume that their only chance of attaining their millionaire stripes is if the Publishers Clearing House's Prize Patrol comes knocking on their door. But if you believe this, you're selling yourself short.

Note The Americans who can safely call themselves rich aren't necessarily the ones earning the largest paychecks. Plenty of people pulling in huge salaries plow most of their money into maintaining opulent lifestyles.

We've all read inspiring stories about ordinary middle-class folks who leave considerable sums behind to a charity, school, or some other worthy cause. The media focuses on their generosity, yet their personal finance skills were no doubt equally inspiring.

Becoming wealthy is certainly doable. Determined souls can get there without winning a game show or a sweepstakes. For 99.9 percent of us, reaching our financial goal, whether it's $1 million or some other impressive figure, requires seed money and investing smarts. This chapter can't provide the cash, but it can share classic ways to build a successful investment portfolio either from scratch or by remodeling. Later chapters outline many more specifics on how to invest wisely in individual stocks, mutual funds, and bonds. It's how you invest your money—not so much what you earn—that ultimately makes the difference

Twelve Winning Investment Strategies

When the markets are prospering, successful investors may look like geniuses. But when the markets turn surly, only the shrewd investors, who have carefully built their portfolios brick by brick, will be left standing. Use the following dozen strategies to pave your road to riches:

Strategy no. 1: Don't forget the "D" word.

Diversification might seem like a curious strategy to promote because it pretty much ensures that investors won't make a bundle of money quickly. When you diversify a portfolio, you spread your assets across a variety of investments in different sectors and industries and even different continents. Along with investing in New Economy stocks that may be pushing the technological envelope, for example, you might mix in some smokestack industries and a smattering of bonds. With diversification, a portfolio is not dominated by any one type or style of investment.

The main purpose of diversification is to protect your portfolio from extreme market volatility—and from the resulting calamitous losses. If your assets are scattered across the investment spectrum, they are not likely to collapse simultaneously. At the same time, diversification enables you to share in the spoils when particular segments of the markets are thriving. In other words, you have your bases covered.

Note   If the recent collapse of the 1990s bull market proved anything, it's that betting heavily on two or three stocks or a couple of promising industries is extremely treacherous.

Although concentrated portfolios offer the promise of explosive growth, investors with these kinds of portfolios also face greater risks of a blowout. In contrast, when money is spread among a variety of choices, the chances of hitting home runs are greatly reduced, but you have a greater potential for singles and doubles.

Looking at the whole picture

Diversifying stock holdings is only one part of the equation. Adding bonds is the other. Stock and bond returns don't follow each other like shadows. If your holdings in blue-chip stocks take a hit one year, your bonds may still be doing just fine. When bonds are depressed, stocks could be up. Of course, bonds and stocks don't always balance each other out; both could get hammered at the same time. But more often than not, the combination of stocks and bonds has historically dampened the volatility of the typical investor's portfolio.

Over the years, studies have documented that a portfolio's mix of stocks, bonds, and cash is far more important to financial success than decisions about which individual stocks and bonds to buy. So such things as market timing, the securities investors select, and even dumb luck have less of an impact than many folks think.

Divvying up your portfolio

To construct a diversified portfolio, you typically need these essential building blocks:

✦ Large-cap stocks

✦ Mid-cap stocks

✦ Small-cap stocks

✦ Foreign stocks

✦ Bonds

✦ Cash

In addition to having a mixture of investment assets, you also need to rely on a variety of investment styles: growth, value, or a blend of the two.

Cross-Reference You'll learn more about these investment styles and types of stocks in Chapter 12. Chapter 2 lists places to park your cash, and Chapters 17, 18, and 19 cover the bond world.

The percentage of your money that you should put in different types of stocks and bonds varies depending on your needs. Many experts recommend that 50 percent of a typical person's equity portfolio be dedicated to large domestic stocks, split between value and growth or a blend of the two. You may want to divide what's left among small and mid-cap stocks and foreign stocks. Aggressive investors may want to sink more money into small-cap stocks or funds. Since the 1920s, the small-cap stocks have outperformed the large-caps by a significant margin, but small-caps are far more volatile.

 Note Rather than adding a fund or individual stock to your portfolio when it grabs your attention, you should develop an investing game plan and stick with it. Never add an investment to your holdings without considering how it would affect your overall mix.

After reviewing your time horizon, risk tolerance, and financial goals, decide what assets you want in each investing category. Then try to pick solid funds or stocks or bonds within those categories (more on this subject later in this chapter).

Table 1-1 shows the kind of historical returns that various mixes of stocks, bonds and cash have produced.

Table 1-1 Rewards of Asset Allocation Historical Time Horizon = 12/1979–04/2001						
Portfolio	*Stocks*	*Bonds*	*Cash*	*Avg. Annual Return*	*Best Year*	*Worst Year*
Conservative	20%	45%	35%	9.90%	27.74%	−7.13%
Moderately Conservative	40%	40%	20%	13.78%	37.31%	−13.63%
Moderate	60%	30%	10%	15.28%	45.98%	−17.33%
Moderately Aggressive	80%	20%	0%	16.54%	54.93%	−19.63%
Aggressive	95%	5%	0%	17.28%	59.62%	−21.23%

Source: Wilson Associates International

Are You Really Diversified?

Even if you think you're diversified, you may not be. You could be inadvertently overdosing on certain stocks. During the height of the technology craze, for instance, Cisco Systems, Microsoft, and Intel were the darlings of the nation's fund managers. So if you held shares in Cisco or Microsoft and also owned a large-cap stock fund, your portfolio could have been investing too heavily in technology. Some people assume that owning several mutual funds guarantees that their money is safely spread around. But that isn't necessarily true. For instance, when the stable of Janus funds was clocking extraordinary returns in the late 1990s, many people congratulated themselves for being properly diversified if they had money in two or three Janus funds. What they didn't realize is that these funds were essentially placing bets on many of the same stocks. The funds rose and then stumbled together.

An easy way to determine whether your holdings are lopsided is to use Morningstar's portfolio manager tools (www.morningstar.com). With Morningstar's Instant X-Ray online tool, you can plug in all the funds and stocks you own, and it will break down your holdings into various investment categories. A more in-depth tool, the Portfolio X-Ray, is available to paid Morningstar subscribers, but you can sign up for a free 30-day trial membership to try this one out.

Rule of 72

Getting psyched about saving is easier if you realize how fast your money can multiply, which you can determine using the Rule of 72. This easy math formula enables you to figure out how long it'll take your money to double. Simply divide 72 by the amount of interest you anticipate your investment earning. Suppose you expect your portfolio to earn an average of 11 percent a year. If your portfolio stays on that track—of course, that's a big if— your portfolio would double in 6.5 years. (72 ÷ 11). In contrast, if you stuck your cash in a savings account earning 2.5 percent interest, the doubling incubation period would be a very long 28.8 years (72 ÷ 2.5).

The sooner you start, the faster your money can grow. If you're 35 and your money grows at 12 percent, your money will double six times by your 65th birthday.

Strategy no. 2: Set your goals.

You'd never build a house without blueprints, and you shouldn't start investing without a plan. To formulate an investing plan, ask yourself the following questions:

What are your objectives?

First, you have to establish your financial goals. How much money do you want to have when you retire? How much will you need for your child's braces or college education? Based on how much you've already saved and how much you will continue to invest, you need to calculate what kind of rate of return is necessary to meet your goals.

What is your time horizon?

Establish a financial timeline. You need to match the length of time you can afford to keep money in an investment with appropriate investment choices. If you'll need money in three or four years, for instance, you don't want to sink your cash in an aggressive growth mutual fund that's as risky as a tightrope act. You should sink cash for a short-term goal, such as buying a car, into a safe investment, such as a money market.

Playing it safe, however, can backfire if your time horizon is long. The longer you have to invest, the less you need to fret about market fluctuations. Instead, you have the luxury of investing in stocks, which historically have provided higher returns than any other type of assets. You wouldn't want to rely heavily upon ultra-safe savings bonds for a toddler's college education because you wouldn't get high enough returns. If your time horizon is at least five years, you can usually afford to sink some cash into stocks.

Need Help Setting Goals?

Setting investment goals and assembling a model portfolio is no picnic, but online asset allocation tools can make it easier. Here are a few of the sites that offer free (or partially free), interactive planning tools:

✦ **Financial Engines:** www.financialengines.com

✦ **Quicken.com:** www.quicken.com

✦ **T. Rowe Price:** www.troweprice.com

✦ **TIAA-CREF:** www.tiaacref.com

✦ **Vanguard Group:** www.vanguard.com

What is your financial situation?

What percentage of your net worth do you have invested or would you like to see invested? If you don't have an adequate amount in reserve for emergencies, you might want to be more cautious with your investments.

What is your risk tolerance?

Risk is the final piece of the puzzle. Even if you have many years to save, it can be dangerous building a portfolio that relies heavily upon stocks if you can't handle the market's wild gyrations. If you own a fairly aggressive portfolio and hard times hit, you could become so miserable that you bail out of the market and take big losses. You'll learn more about how to assess your risk tolerance shortly.

Strategy no. 3: Evaluate your risk tolerance.

If you're at an amusement park, you can easily figure out whether you can handle the roller coaster or a bungee jump. But it's harder to know if you can stomach big dips in the market. Assessing your ability to deal with financial upheaval is important because you don't want to panic when the market is spinning in a downward spiral. Many investors who bought technology stocks that had recorded triple-digit returns, for instance, weren't seriously thinking about the potential downside when they placed their orders. If they had, quite a few people, particularly those in retirement or close to it, wouldn't have placed such speculative bets.

Note   Remember that not all risk is bad. Risk is like cholesterol. One kind of cholesterol is good; the other kind chokes your arteries. The biggest risk of all is walking blindly into an investment without researching it thoroughly first.

Strange as it might seem, one of the greatest risks you can face is shying away from any risk at all. Consider what would happen if you kept all your money tied up in a money market or certificates of deposit. Your money would be safe, but the financial price would be steep. By avoiding any risks in your portfolio, you leave your money open to the devastating effects of inflation. This devastation occurs even during periods when inflation has been almost invisible. During the past 75 years, the average rate of inflation has been 3.1 percent.

Need further convincing of inflation's sneaky ways? Look at the example in Table 1-2.

Table 1-2
Inflation's Erosion of the Purchasing Power of $50,000*

Time Frame	Value of Investment
Now	$50,000
5 years	$41,096
10 years	$33,778
15 years	$27,763
20 years	$22,819
25 years	$18,756

*Inflation estimated at 4% a year.

Strategy no. 4: Squelch crazy expectations.

People who became stock investors in the 1990s clung to pretty wacky ideas about what the markets could and couldn't do. Back then, people would buy a mutual fund or a stock and expect it to blast off immediately. Gains of 20 or 30 percent were merely sniffed at. Some tech investors began to feel ripped off if their funds didn't return triple digits. Of course, the new millennium's bear market halted this temporary insanity.

Online Risk Doctor

If you'd like help evaluating your investing comfort level, a variety of Web sites can assist you. Some brokerage firms and fund companies keep risk quizzes on their Web sites. One of the most sophisticated online risk assessment tools is at RiskGrades (www.riskgrades.com). You can plug in your current portfolio and receive an online prognosis of your holdings' volatility. The Web site was created by experts who formerly analyzed portfolio risk for managers at J.P. Morgan.

Another top-notch site is Portfolio Science (www.portfolioscience.com), which measures the potential risk of your own specific holdings over certain time periods, such as monthly or yearly. You can learn more about these online tools in Chapter 3.

Whether the markets are suffering or celebrating, knowing what returns are realistic is important. Since the mid-1920s, large-cap stocks have mustered average annual returns of 11 percent; small company stocks have averaged returns of 12.4 percent. Government bonds have trailed along at 5.3 percent, and cash investments have managed a mere 3.8 percent.

Why are grossly inflated expectations dangerous? For starters, they tend to make investors antsy. They read an article about a fund that's done better than theirs and they want to abandon their current fund, possibly facing redemption fees or incurring another broker commission. What's more, using unrealistic return projections can threaten your long-term investing plans. For instance, someone who thought he could retire at age 60 as long as his portfolio returned 18 percent a year could be booby-trapping his plans.

How do you know what's realistic? In Table 1-3, you'll see how the major stock market indexes have fared during the past decade. You can compare your own funds, stocks, and bonds to these benchmarks.

Note If an investment hasn't performed well for six months or a year, it's no big deal. The truer test is how it has performed over two, three, or more years.

Table 1-3 Performance of Leading Indexes			
Average Annual Returns	*3 Years*	*5 Years*	*10 Years*
Standard & Poor's 500	5.3%	15.6%	15.2%
Wilshire 5000	4%	13.7%	14.6%
Dow Jones Industrial Average	7.4%	15.9%	16.6%
Standard & Poor's MidCap 400	12%	18%	17.3%
Standard & Poor's SmallCap 600	3.7%	11.1%*	
Russell 2000	1.4%	8.3%	12.7%
MSCI EAFE	1.7%	4.5%	6.8%
Nasdaq Composite	4.4%	12.5%	16.7%
Nasdaq-100	14.1%	22.7%	21.5%

Source: Wiesenberger

Strategy no. 5: Don't psych yourself out.

If you listen to psychologists, American investors are basket cases. When we invest, we often act irrationally. In fact, illogical investing habits have become so widely recognized in academia that there's now a branch of economics called behavioral finance. Understanding how emotions can influence our investment choices can make us smarter and more successful investors.

What are we doing wrong? Study after study suggests that one of our biggest mistakes is holding onto losers and ditching our winners. Lurking behind this dubious behavior is an innate fear of losing. Suppose you own an Internet stock that's plunged 80 percent. Even though the stock never made a profit and analysts are now decrying the company's business plan as flawed, if you're like a lot of people, you'll hang on as it sinks into the quicksand. Surely, you tell yourself, this dot-com will rediscover its glory days. And as long as a mediocre stock isn't sold, you may think, the loss isn't official. This kind of behavior, however, can wreck a portfolio.

Tip

If you stubbornly hold onto stocks or funds that have little chance of rebounding, you may surrender a good portion of your portfolio to mediocrity. Sell those sad stocks and direct the money into promising investments that could ultimately boost your net worth.

Contrast this desire to hang onto the losers with the strange way many people treat their great stock picks. They are often quick to sell them. Why? Once again, they fear calamity is about to strike. They worry that a stock that has appreciated nicely and made a profit will turn south. Consequently, they dump perfectly good stocks for fear they will crash in the future.

Trade with logic rather than emotion.

To appreciate how emotions figure in to your investing decisions, take a good look at how you treat stock successes and failures.

Do you tend to hang on to sinking stocks because you hate to acknowledge failure? In some, perhaps many cases, you are justified in holding tight. After all, stocks fluctuate in price. But what is crucial is evaluating each stock to determine whether it deserves to remain as one of your holdings. This assessment requires delving into a stock's financial reports, checking analysts' opinions, and comparing the prospects and past performance of your stock with others in the same industry. After you've completed the research, you can feel good about the well-thought-out decision you make.

Cross-Reference   You can learn how to properly analyze stocks in Chapter 15.

When agonizing about whether to shed a winner, you should follow the same strategy. All too often, when investors watch a stock climb and then climb some more, they arbitrarily pick a target sale price. An investor will decide to sell if a stock reaches, say, $50 or $60 a share, but such price targets are frequently not linked to any financial analysis. On its face, a stock's price means nothing. A stock selling for $80 a share could be fairly valued while one selling for $15 could be vastly overpriced. Once again, you have to analyze a stock's potential before deciding whether a stock's price is bloated and it's time to sell.

Big egos can mean poor returns.

Illogical trading behavior isn't investors' only emotional hang-up. Investors who swagger with self-confidence can also fall flat on their faces. A famous study conducted by researchers at the University of California, Davis, illustrates this hazard. Excess self-confidence can be harmful because it often leads to overtrading. Trading naturally triggers transaction costs, as well as potential taxes on profits, which shrink a portfolio's overall return. Flitting in and out of stocks in hopes of owning the perfect portfolio can also sabotage performance.

After poring over the stock trades of 88,000 investors during a 10-year period, the researchers concluded that men are more likely to be cocky about their investing skills than women. Men traded 45 percent more than women, but for all this extra work their returns were 1 percent lower. The numbers were even more dramatic for single men: They traded 67 percent more than single women, and their returns were 1.4 percent worse.

Strategy no. 6: Buy cheap!

Do you know how much you paid for your car? What about your house? Silly questions, right? Of course you know. But do you realize how much you're paying for your mutual funds? How about individual bonds or a variable annuity?

Couples, Money, and Investing

Nobody can escape financial hang-ups. If you're married, you probably know that no marriage is free from money tensions. Hurt feelings and resentment are sure to exist. Sharing your own attitudes about money with your partner can help as long as the discussion doesn't seem threatening. The worst thing you can do is to criticize your partner about his or her financial quirks.

The two of you can answer these questions to start a discussion about finances:

+ How do I feel about money?

+ How much is enough? Will I ever be happy with the amount that I have or will have?

+ How do I feel about our investing strategy?

+ How do I feel about my spouse's money habits?

+ What are realistic short- and long-term financial goals?

+ Are we sabotaging our investment goals inadvertently?

+ How have we reacted during turbulent times in the stock market? Is there a better way to handle the rough periods?

+ In what ways can we compromise to reduce our money conflicts?

Although Americans may drive all over town to get $25 off the price of a washing machine or dicker with a car salesman for hours, we routinely buy overpriced investments. Because many investments are equipped with ongoing expenses, choosing pricey ones can seriously erode your returns for years.

 Cross-Reference You'll learn more about avoiding costly funds in Chapter 8.

Need proof? Consider two retirement savers who both plunk $10,000 into a stock mutual fund. Saver 1 picks a dirt-cheap fund that charges a mere .18 percent a year in fees. Saver 2 selects an average-priced fund with annual fees of 1.5 percent. For the next 25 years, both investors leave their funds, which each generate a respectable 11 percent average yearly return, alone.

During those 25 years, can you guess how much more Saver 2 paid in fees? Here are your choices:

    A) $752

    B) $2,100

    C) $6,500

    D) $12,605

If you guessed D, you were right. Now you know why the financial press keeps harping on investors to stick with cheap funds. The fees for the low-priced fund totaled $2,218, compared to $14,823 for the second one. The difference in account balances is even more dramatic. After 25 years, the cheap fund is worth $129,871, while the other fund lags behind at $93,106. Why the huge gulf? Fees are automatically removed from an investor's fund each year. Because more money is extracted from the pricier fund annually, less cash is left to grow.

 Resource You can run your own numbers on the funds you own by visiting the U.S. Securities and Exchange Commission's mutual fund cost calculator at www.sec.gov. Once at the site, click on "Interactive Tools."

Strategy no. 7: Don't chase fad investments.

Chasing after eye-popping returns is a dangerous and costly pursuit. A mutual fund or stock sector that is today's top dog can quickly turn into a mongrel. The financial history books are littered with examples of hot investments turning to cinders.

Yet the temptation of fast money can be irresistible. When personal finance magazines profile a mutual fund that's performed spectacularly, reader reaction is immediate. The phones at a fund company begin ringing furiously. Viewers watching CNBC place orders for a stock before a guest has even finished explaining why he loves it.

The awful truth

Plenty of evidence suggests that performance chasing is on the rise. A study by Financial Research Corp., which tracks mutual funds cash flows, for instance, indicates that nearly $1 out of every $3 sitting in mutual funds in 2000 was yanked. Antsy investors moved a lot of this money into funds with splashier performance numbers. What's wrong with that? Plenty. Funds that enjoy tremendous returns can't sustain them forever. Inevitably, these funds sputter. Examples are bountiful. Janus Twenty, which used to be America's fund darling, soared a total of 138 percent in 1998 and 1999, but fell 32 percent in 2000 and kept falling in 2001. Berger New Generation climbed 144 percent in 1999, but it dropped nearly 39 percent in 2000 and continued the slide the next year. ProFunds UltraOTC's meteoric 233 percent rise in 1999 was followed by a drop of 129 percent during the next 16 months.

These figures can't adequately convey the pain these investors feel. After all, looking at the statistics, you might suppose that an investor in ProFunds UltraOTC is still ahead by 104 percent, right? Unfortunately, most investors aren't around for the entire ride up. People don't know about hot funds until after the media has publicized them, and the media isn't interested until the records are already phenomenal.

Caution   In its recent study, Financial Research Corp. tried to quantify the cost of fickle trading behavior and concluded that frequent trading for better results cost fund investors 20 cents for every dollar of gains they could have captured with a buy-and-hold strategy.

Returns at the mercy of an unpredictable economy

Funds aren't necessarily to blame for their hot-and-cold cycles. They often reflect what's happening in the economy. Sometimes biotechnology and emerging market stocks are on fire. At other times, large-cap growth stocks or small-cap value stocks are the place to be. But trying to predict what's going to pop is so hard that people wait around until a fund or stock is truly smoking before embracing it. These momentum investors end up abandoning investments at their lows and buying others at their peak.

Hitting a Moving Target

Stashing cash in investments that are on a roll is always tempting. The temptation was intense in 1999 when the Nasdaq stock market set a record by soaring almost 86 percent. During that year, more than 200 technology funds produced triple-digit returns.

But loading up on what's hot is dangerous. And the reason isn't simply that hot industries eventually turn cold. Even with an incredible year like 1999, it can still be difficult to pick winners. A closer look at the Nasdaq's performance in 1999 shows exactly how difficult it can be. That year, the average return of the largest 25 Nasdaq companies, which included Microsoft, Cisco Systems, and Oracle, was up 65 percent. The bottom 6,000 Nasdaq stocks, however, inched up less than 1 percent for the year.

During the past 20 years, there have been numerous examples of one year's hot investment category turning into the coldest the next year or vice versa. Table 1-4 demonstrates some historic examples of flip-flops.

Table 1-4 Flip-Flop Performances of Selected Securities			
Year	**Top-Performing Assets**	**Year**	**Worst-Performing Assets**
1983	Small-cap stocks: 28.8%	1984	Small-cap stocks: −1.8%
1988	Small-cap stocks: 24.8%	1987	Small-cap stocks: −6.8%
1991	Small-cap stocks: 48.9%	1990	Small-cap stocks: −17.8%
1993	Long-term government bonds: 18.2%	1994	Long-term government bonds: −7.8%
1999	Small-cap stocks: 26.8%	1998	Small-cap stocks: −.8%

Although the examples seem to suggest that it's primarily the pint-sized stocks that experience dramatic fluctuations, that's hardly the case. When the categories are broadened, many more wide swings are apparent. For instance, in 1992, foreign stocks performed miserably by posting a negative 12.2 percent return, but the next year the average foreign stock soared 32.6 percent. After several years of amazing performance by large-cap growth stocks, the category dropped a negative 22 percent in 2000.

Strategy no. 8: Don't try market timing.

Becoming wealthy is a long-term goal. Remind yourself of that when the stock market occasionally blows up like a spectacular Hollywood car chase scene. What happens to your investments this year won't matter 10 years from now as long as you hang tight.

What's more dangerous is pulling out of the market, even for short periods of time. Investors known as *market timers* try to pull money out of the market as it's beginning to fall or, even better, right before it reaches the cliff's edge. They jump back in right when the market shakes off its funk. This strategy sounds great, but studies repeatedly have shown that it's nearly impossible to pull off successfully. Nobody knows when the market has peaked or hit bottom until long after it's happened.

According to Ibbotson Associates, a firm that provides historical financial data, if you invested $1,000 in the stock market in 1980 and then sat on it until the end of 2000, the portfolio would be worth $18,410. But if you were sitting on the sidelines for what turned out to be the market's 15 best months during that period, your investment would have shriveled to just $4,730.

If you look back even farther in history, the hazards of market timing are more glaring. Someone who had invested $1,000 in the stock market at the start of 1926 until the end of 2000 would be worth $2.5 million. In contrast, an individual who happened to be sitting out during just the best 40 months throughout that entire period would have a mere $15,330!

Caution

Mediocre returns aren't the only hazard you face if your commitment to an investment is as short as a Las Vegas wedding. Selling a stock, bond, or fund can trigger transaction costs as well as taxes, which can dramatically erode any gains.

Strategy no. 9: Start investing now.

The sooner you begin saving diligently or boosting what you're already stashing away, the faster you'll reach your financial goal. What makes the early-bird principle so effective is the magic of *compounding,* which has been called the eighth wonder of the world. Growing at 10 percent a year, $100 would be worth $1.3 million in 100 years thanks to compounding.

The greater the head start you give your nest egg, the less you'll need to squirrel away. If this sounds like propaganda, consider Exhibit A from Ibbotson Associates: Suppose you had invested a mere $2,000 in the stock market for 10 years beginning in 1980 and then let the money ride until 2000. Your $20,000 investment would have soared to $295,400. Now suppose that your neighbor waited until 1990 to begin saving. To make up for lost time, he contributed $4,000 annually for a total investment of $40,000. Despite his greater financial sacrifice, his portfolio would be worth just $133,600 by 2000. Obviously, getting a head start is invaluable.

When you first look at these numbers, they seem to defy logic. But when you think about it, it makes sense. That's because starting early allows the compounding more time to build. Think of it as a snowball that rolls down an entire mountain instead of just one slope.

Strategy no. 10: Squirrel away even small amounts of cash.

What if you're already saving as much as you believe possible? Scrounging under sofa cushions isn't your only option. The real key is thinking small. Spotting little opportunities for additional saving is easier than trying to save one huge amount. For instance, if your child graduates from potty training, you'll no longer spend $40 or so a month for diapers. Rather than let that cash get sucked into your checking account's black hole, escort that money into a mutual fund. Even slight increases in your savings can push you much closer to your goal.

Example

If you stash away an extra $40 a month for 30 years and the money earns 12 percent interest, you'll have an additional $141,000 without much effort.

Spotting ways to save money is the easy part; not squandering it is tougher. Our tendency to spend whatever's within reach of our ATM card is the best reason to consider investing systematically. Have a certain amount automatically withdrawn from a checking or savings account each month and deposited into a mutual fund or brokerage account. Autopilot investing works wonderfully with 401(k)s, but many people don't think to use the same strategy with other investments as well.

Strategy no. 11: Don't forget about taxes.

We're all interested in how well our investments do, but many of us don't spend time investigating whether our investments are tax-friendly. However, focusing on how much money you actually get to keep from an investment, not just on a port-folio's percentage gain, is important.

Ignoring whether your investments are tax-efficient can be costly. A big mistake that is often avoidable is triggering short-term capital gains taxes. If you sell a profitable fund or stock within a year of purchasing it, you'll get clobbered with this one. You'll owe taxes at your personal income tax rate.

Example

If you're in the 30 percent tax bracket and you realize a $10,000 gain on a short-term sale, you'll owe the IRS $3,000. If you sell the investment after one year and a day, however, the tax will drop to 20 percent or much lower for those in the smallest brackets.

One nice thing about investing in individual stocks is that you can control whether you pay capital gains. If you hang onto your shares, there will be no capital gains taxes. Unfortunately, that isn't so with mutual funds. Too many funds are tax-sloppy.

Tip

One way to find out if your fund is tax-efficient is to look at your year-end 1099 tax statement that you get from your mutual fund. If you had to pay a lot of taxes on your fund distributions, you'll know that it's not a tax-friendly fund.

The U.S. Securities and Exchange Commission made it easier for investors to evaluate their funds when it recently began requiring funds to provide after-tax performance statistics in their literature. Morningstar also reports on the tax efficiency of the funds it analyzes.

Cross-Reference

You'll learn more about tax-efficient investing in Chapter 25.

Strategy no. 12: Stick with the basics.

A lot has been written and said about the secrets of successful investing. Unread doctoral dissertations and weighty books have been devoted to the topic. Newsletters that purport to have the answers charge hundreds of dollars a year. Financial news networks and radio shows spend endless hours discussing how to become wealthy. Yet what it boils down to is this: Investing should be boring. If you want to do well, you don't need to weave in and out of the market. You don't need to get into derivatives, options, futures, and other incredibly exotic stuff. And you don't need to worry about whatever utterances come out of the mouth of the Federal Reserve chairman, who wields the power to raise or lower the nation's short-term interest rates.

You can tune out all that noise. Instead, you should pick a small number of investments that offer a historical return that you can live with. These investments should also offer a level of risk that won't keep you up at night. Once that's done, leave your selections alone.

Tip Don't check on your portfolio every week or even every month. If you do, you might be tempted to make changes that you later regret.

You might be surprised at how little time you need to spend babysitting your portfolio. Checking how it's faring every quarter should be sufficient for most. If you own individual stocks, you might need to keep closer tabs. All in all, it's a very boring but successful way to get rich.

Summary

✦ Diversifying your portfolio should protect you from the most dramatic price swings.

✦ Don't let your emotions hijack a perfectly sensible investing approach.

✦ Resist the temptation to market time; it's a loser's game.

✦ Chances are good that you will get burned chasing the market's hottest stocks and mutual funds.

✦ Your portfolio will grow faster if you avoid high-priced investments.

✦   ✦   ✦

Preparing to Invest

Even if you are conscientious to a fault and you've already reduced your debt, established financial goals, and organized your finances, this chapter can provide pointers on how to wring the most yield out of money that needs to remain very safe. Whether you've pulled money out of the stock market temporarily or have established a rainy-day fund, it's worth the effort to find the most lucrative spot for it. This chapter gives you great tips on such basic but essential tasks as finding a dirt-cheap money market, locating the best CDs nationwide, and evaluating a short-term bond fund. Beginners to investing will discover what basic steps they need to take before they can feel confident about putting their money into stocks and bonds.

The Best Places to Stash Your Cash

Not all cash is created equal. That's a lesson that a lot of people forget. When people are preoccupied with playing the stock market, they often overlook what's happening to their cash. Ultraconservative investors who continue to favor bank passbook accounts are also guilty of poor financial judgment. Even those who tuck cash into money markets (more than $2 trillion is stashed in such accounts) could be losing out by picking the wrong one. Too many of us have our cash stuffed in mediocre places.

Whether you're sitting on a pile of cash for an emergency fund or you've pulled money out of a turbulent stock market, squeezing the most out of your cash can pay great dividends down the road.

The difference between a money market that offers a 5 percent yield versus a passbook savings account offering 3 percent may seem as inconsequential as the price difference between a Big Mac selling for $2.50 and a Quarter Pounder selling at $2.75. But the difference, over time, can be tremendous. The reason, as you learned in the previous chapter, is the power of compounding, which enables even a skimpy pile of money to grow exponentially. That money builds and multiplies like a snowball rolling down a mountain. Table 2-1 shows how compounding can make a huge difference even if cash is earning just a couple of percentage points more.

Table 2-1 The Effects of Compounding on the Value of a $25,000 Investment			
Years to Invest	**2%**	**4%**	**6%**
5 years	$27,602	$30,416	$33,456
10 years	$30,475	$37,006	$44,771
15 years	$33,647	$45,024	$59,914
20 years	$37,149	$54,778	$80,178

If you want to avoid incredibly anemic returns, stay away from bank savings and passbook accounts. For more than a decade, savings account rates have steadily been dwindling. For much of that time, these accounts have been paying a measly 2 percent or less. The following alternatives are much better:

✦ Money market funds

✦ Certificates of deposit

✦ U.S. Treasury bills

✦ Short-term bond funds

✦ Fixed annuities

Money market funds

Many people don't realize that money markets are mutual funds. But unlike regular mutual funds, money markets don't zigzag in price. Day in and day out, year in and year out, the price of one share should always be $1. The yield that your money generates is what varies.

Technically, money markets are not as safe as bank deposits. The Federal Deposit Insurance Corporation (FDIC) doesn't protect the money. However, no individual investor has ever lost a dime in a money market fund. The U.S. Securities and Exchange Commission tightly regulates these funds, and keeping them safe is a zealous preoccupation of the mutual fund industry. Whenever the $1 share value of any fund has faced the slightest threat, the fund company has scrambled to prop it up. The last thing the industry wants to do is to scare away customers.

You can invest in money markets through individual mutual funds companies, brokerage firms and banks. A money market is a must for anyone owning stocks, bonds or funds through a brokerage account. If you sell investments or receive dividends, for instance, the cash can be automatically swept into your money market. You can also stash cash in the money market while you're trying to decide how to invest it.

Deciding factor: Expense ratios

Choosing a money market can be like shopping for white athletic socks. The selection doesn't differ much. The SEC keeps a tight rein on what money managers can invest in their cash portfolios.

Tip   When choosing among hundreds of retail money market funds, pay close attention to expenses. The expenses largely make the difference between funds sporting high or low yields.

With competition among the funds so fierce, funds slash their fees to entice new customers. Often the funds with the highest yields have waived a portion of their fees. When selecting a fund, ask how long the firm intends to keep its fees low. Ideally, you'll want to find a money market that doesn't have to resort to waiving fees to earn its status as a top yielder.

Tip   An excellent place to find funds with continually low fees is the Vanguard Group, which is best known for its low-priced index funds. Vanguard manages numerous money market funds, including those specifically geared toward residents of California, New York, Ohio, New Jersey, and Pennsylvania. See the Resource Guide for contact information.

Today's typical money market has an expense ratio of .84 percent. The expense ratio refers to the percentage of cash in your money market that is automatically deducted each year to compensate the fund's sponsor. An expense ratio of .88 percent means that a $10,000 investment would trigger a fee of $88. Try to stick with money markets that charge well below the average. You can discover what a fund's expense ratio is by looking at its prospectus; you can order a free copy by calling the fund or brokerage firm.

Caution   Banks offer their own money markets, but steer clear of them. The rates can be laughably lower than competitive money markets, because banks have no incentive to draw money away from their own savings accounts with their puny rates. Instead, shop for money markets among mutual fund companies and brokerage firms.

Taxable versus tax-exempt money market accounts

One of the most important decisions you must make is deciding whether to go with a taxable or a tax-exempt money market. Tax-exempt funds offer a skimpier yield, but you do secure a tax break. You won't have to pay federal taxes, and in some cases, you won't have to pay state taxes either. You can skip the state taxes if you live where state-specific, tax-exempt funds are available. The following states have funds designed for their residents:

Arizona	California	Connecticut
Florida	Maryland	Massachusetts
Michigan	Minnesota	New Jersey
New York	North Carolina	Ohio
Pennsylvania	Rhode Island	

On a tax-adjusted basis, state-specific tax-free funds don't always offer better returns than national tax-free funds. These specialized funds are more attractive if you live in a state with very high taxes, such as California, Massachusetts, Minnesota, and New York.

> **Tip**
>
> A tax-free fund typically makes financial sense for investors in the higher tax brackets. Anyone in the lowest 10 and 15 percent brackets should stick with a taxable money fund.

Those in higher tax brackets must do some simple math to figure out whether a particular taxable or tax-free fund is best. Use this formula:

Tax-free yield ÷ (1 – your federal tax bracket) = taxable equivalent yield

Say you're in the 27 percent tax bracket and you're trying to decide whether a taxable fund with a 6 percent yield is a better deal than a tax-free one offering 4 percent.

You would plug in the numbers this way:

4 ÷ (1 – .27) = taxable equivalent yield

4 ÷ .73 = 5.47%

The tax-free fund's taxable equivalent is 5.47 percent, which obviously does not beat the 6 percent taxable yield. In this case, the tax-free fund is the inferior choice.

Minimum deposit

Most money markets require an initial deposit that can range anywhere from $1,000 to $25,000 for some of the highest-yielding funds. The number of checks you may write off a fund also differs between money markets. Some money markets permit customers to write as many as they please; others impose a ceiling of less than 10. Also beware that some funds don't let a customer write a check for less than $100 or $500.

Money Market Shopping List

By asking the same questions about all your prospective money markets, you can compare apples to apples. Before selecting a money market fund, you should ask these key questions:

✦ What is the current yield?

✦ Is this a taxable or tax-exempt fund?

✦ Are higher yields available for bigger balances?

✦ What is the minimum initial investment?

✦ Can checks be written off the account for any amount?

✦ What is the fund's expense ratio?

✦ Is the expense ratio scheduled to go up?

✦ Are there additional fees?

Certificates of deposit

If you can't sleep with your money unprotected by FDIC insurance, you will probably be happy with a certificate of deposit (CD). FDIC insures money invested in CDs and savings accounts up to $100,000 per person at any given bank or savings and loan. When you buy a CD, you agree to keep your money in the bank for a specified period of time. The arrangement could last for weeks, months, or years. Most CDs pay a set rate of interest, though some offer a variable rate that moves up or down depending on interest rate conditions. The interest you can expect to receive from a CD is better than the anemic amount you can extract from a savings account.

Caution

You can get stung if you pull your money out of a CD early. If you need to withdraw the money, you will forfeit some interest, which won't happen with a money market or short-term bond fund. Before selecting a CD, be sure to find out the penalties for early withdrawal.

When you are CD shopping, look beyond your neighborhood. One way to find the best rates is to hunt nationwide through a brokerage firm or by looking at the CD charts typically listed in local newspapers. Another resource is one of the Web sites that tracks CD rates, such as the following:

✦ Bankrate.com (www.bankrate.com)

✦ iMoneyNet (www.imoneynet.com)

✦ BanxQuote (www.banxquote.com)

Brokerage firms are another source for competitive rates. Brokers can scour the country for rates you might not be able to uncover on your own. Typically brokered CDs can be traced back to smaller financial institutions that don't have the resources to publicize their rates. You should not have to pay a commission to buy a CD through a broker. The firm is compensated by the difference in what it pays for the CD and what it charges you, the customer.

Brokered CDs function just like other CDs except in one respect: If you abandon one of these CDs prematurely, you could lose some of your principal. On the other hand, you could make a profit. Which way it goes depends upon interest rates. If rates have collapsed since you bought the CD, your CD will be more valuable for the next customer. The new owner will pay a premium. If rates have risen, however, no one will want to buy your CD unless it's for a discount.

Tip   Because of the fluctuating value of brokered CDs, you should not buy one unless you can hold on to it until maturity.

U.S. Treasury bills

The U.S. Treasury offers a variety of bonds that have maturities ranging from 13 weeks to 30 years. The Treasuries with the shortest maturities are called bills. You can buy bills that last for 13 and 26 weeks. (In 2001, the Treasury discontinued one-year bills.)

Some investors prefer Treasury bills to CDs because they're equipped with a built-in tax break. Federal taxes are owed on Treasuries, but you can skip the state and local taxes. If you live in a high-tax state, this tax break can be sizable.

 Cross-Reference   You learn much more about Treasuries in Chapter 18.

Treasuries are also more flexible than CDs because there is no penalty for bailing prematurely. You can sell the bills by going through the federal government's TreasuryDirect program. You may also buy Treasuries directly from the government. To obtain the necessary forms, call a TreasuryDirect customer representative at (800) 722-2678 or visit the Web site at www.treasurydirect.gov.

Tip   You can purchase Treasuries through a brokerage firm, but you will save money if you don't go this route. A brokerage firm will charge you a fee for completing the transaction.

Treasuries aren't protected by the FDIC, but you can sleep like a baby with these bills. It's preposterous to think that the federal government will ever fail to honor its bond obligations.

Short-term bond funds

Short-term bond funds invest in a hodge-podge of U.S. government and corporate bonds. They are riskier than Treasuries or money markets, but in return, you may be able to capture a little extra yield. The life span (or *maturity*) of short-term bonds typically doesn't exceed three years (which is why they're called short-term). Because these bonds aren't around long, they aren't as sensitive to interest rate hikes.

As you'll learn in Part IV, "Bonding with Your Investments," bonds are allergic to interest rate hikes. And the longer a bond's maturity is, the more a bond will get hammered if interest rates jump. The hardest hit are long-term bonds that can last for 30 years.

Consequently, you could lose a bit of your original investment when you sink money in a short-term bond fund. Those who seek greater safety should check out ultra-short-term bond funds. The bonds in one of these funds may have an average maturity of about six months.

When you are shopping for a short-term bond fund, price is absolutely critical. The potential yield advantage you'd get with one of these bond funds will likely disappear if the fund charges above average expenses.

Tip

Stick with short-term bond funds that have expense ratios no higher than .60 percent. If you can't buy a cheap fund, then consider sticking with a money market.

Also avoid buying a short-term bond fund that comes with a *load,* which is another name for sales charge. Individual brokers sometimes recommend one of these load funds over a money market because they get to pocket a commission. But a load can wreck whatever return advantage a short-term bond has. For instance, if someone sinks $10,000 into a money market with a 3 percent load, $300 will be whisked out of the fund from the start.

Consider these low-cost alternatives when you're shopping for short-term bond funds:

▸ Metropolitan West Low Duration Bond: (800) 241-4671

▸ Schwab Short-Term Bond Market Index: (800) 435-4000

▸ Fidelity Short-Term Bond: (800) 635-1511

▸ Vanguard Short-Term Bond Index: (800) 662-7447

d annuities

.. ..ic lineup of cash candidates, fixed annuities are the most overlooked alternative. Annuities are offered by insurance companies and come wrapped with a certain amount of tax protection. Although variable annuities have been a hot investment in recent years, the fixed annuity has been forgotten. This is unfortunate. A fixed annuity can make a practical addition to the ultraconservative portion of a portfolio.

With a fixed annuity, you receive a guaranteed rate of return for your investment. The rate of return can never slip below the guaranteed floor set at the time of purchase. While the floor doesn't change, the actual rate may fluctuate as often as every month. Whether the rate inches up or down depends upon such factors as the prevailing interest rates and the performance of the insurer's conservative investment portfolio of corporate and government bonds. While some people feel safe with the guarantee, there's no assurance that a fixed annuity will keep up with inflation.

Cross-Reference See Chapter 22 for details on annuities of all kinds.

The interest rate for a fixed annuity can be significantly higher than Treasury bills and CDs. What's more, the fixed income annuity grows tax-deferred. The tax is owed only when the money is withdrawn. In contrast, CD and Treasury investors must pay taxes annually on the interest. You can't, however, expect the same flexibility that you enjoy with a money market.

Caution Like variable annuities, you'll be charged a surrender fee if you pull money out of a fixed annuity before a certain period of time has elapsed. Find out the length of this period and the penalty before making your investing decision.

Compared with variable annuities, fees aren't as big a factor with fixed annuities. That's because the fees have already been subtracted from the rate that an insurer quotes. So if a fixed annuity is offering 6.5 percent, that's what you will get after fees. The fixed annuity guarantees the same rate for a set period of time. Once that period has expired, the insurer can increase or lower the rate depending upon a variety of factors.

Caution Be wary of an insurer pushing a fixed annuity that offers what seems to be an incredibly generous interest rate. This rate could be a teaser introductory rate that will vanish quickly.

To make the hunt for a fixed annuity easier, two publications provide a huge amount of data on countless numbers of annuities:

✦ *Comparative Annuity Reports,* (916) 487-7863,
   www.annuitycomparativedata.com

✦ Fisher Annuity Index, (800) 833-1450

Insurers' Financial Strength

When buying a fixed annuity, customers often take for granted an insurer's financial strength. They shouldn't. Insurance companies do fail, and when it happens, it can create an unbelievable nightmare for those left behind. Sticking with the highest-rated companies is important because insurance customers have no FDIC protection. In a worst-case scenario, your money could vanish if an insurance company collapses. Quite a few insurers have been taken over by government regulators in the past few years, so it's best not to be complacent.

A handful of rating services evaluate whether an individual insurer should be able to meet its obligations. In most cases, the information is free. You should also be able to find what you need at a good library reference department or by using the Internet. Here is the contact information for these rating services:

✦ A.M. Best at (908) 439-2200 or www.ambest.com

✦ Fitch IBCA, Duff & Phelps at (800) 853-4824, ext. 199 or www.fitchratings.com

✦ Standard & Poor's at (212) 438-2400 or www.standardandpoors.com/ratings

✦ Moody's Investors Service at (212) 553-0377 or www.moodys.com

✦ Weiss Ratings at (800) 289-9222 or www.weissratings.com

Six Simple Steps to a Financial Foundation

Finding an ideal spot for your cash isn't the only step you need to take to lay a solid financial foundation. When the markets are behaving, investing is fun. But sinking money into stocks and bonds can be premature if you haven't dealt with the basic financial tasks of filling up an emergency fund and decreasing debt. Tasks such as evaluating your finances, setting financial goals, and finding a safe place to stash your cash are less than glamorous, but they are essential nonetheless. Laying a good foundation for your investing career should increase your chances of financial success in the years ahead. It may also soften the blow if a financial disaster strikes.

You'll start off on the right foot if you can check off all six items on this list:

Step no. 1: Establish an emergency fund.

Once you've settled on the best spot for your cash, you have to establish how much you should set aside for a financial cushion. This money is for all those potential emergencies that make you wake up in a cold sweat: Someone in your family is hospitalized for weeks, you lose your job, you are sucked into an expensive lawsuit. The scenarios are endless.

Financial experts suggest that you set aside three to six months' worth of your living expenses in an ultrasafe place, such as a bank account or money market. However, most people are not going to refrain from investing in stocks and bonds while they slowly and faithfully accumulate a significant slush pile of cash. If your income is $60,000, for instance, you'd have to stockpile up to $30,000 before the personal finance wizards would say it's safe to venture into the financial markets. If you set aside $400 a month for your reserve, it would take you six years to come up with the dough.

Not many of us have this kind of financial self-control to save for a rainy day. If we did, there wouldn't be so many Americans leasing new cars because they don't have the down payment to buy one outright. What this rigid hurdle can do is discourage would-be investors from ever sticking their toes in the starting blocks. And if you never get started, you'll never appreciate how rewarding investing can be.

Of course, somebody without a dime in the bank should definitely not put his next paycheck in the stock market. It's wise to maintain a safe cash reserve for the inevitable aggravations, such as when your engine needs an overhaul, your property tax is due, or the stove burns its last batch of cookies. Just how much you should stash away depends on your situation.

Tip One month's salary is a reasonable beginning savings goal for most people.

How much is enough?

The amount of money someone should set aside in an emergency fund varies dramatically from person to person. Before setting an amount, ask yourself these questions:

+ Is my job at risk because of corporate mergers or downsizing? Is my work seasonal with periods of unemployment?

+ Does my household rely on one income?

+ Am I self-employed, a small business owner, or heavily dependent on commissions?

+ Do I lack disability insurance?

+ Is my medical insurance inadequate if someone in my family contracts a catastrophic illness?

If you answered yes to any of these questions, you might want to keep more money on hand for emergencies.

Turbocharging your emergency fund on Wall Street

After tucking away a month's salary in a safe place, such as a money market, think about putting additional contributions to your emergency fund into a conservative stock or bond fund with an excellent pedigree. Because most people aren't going to have a big lump sum to invest all at once anyway, consider gradually building up this secondary emergency fund through monthly or bimonthly deposits into a mutual fund.

Tip If you don't have the discipline to write those regular checks, establishing an automatic withdrawal plan is an excellent way to start.

Automatic withdrawal plans are the ultimate in convenience. Once the paperwork is finished, the mutual fund automatically withdraws an agreed-upon amount from your bank account each month on a designated day. This money is deposited into your fund, and you receive a statement with your deposit duly noted.

By sinking money regularly into a more aggressive rainy-day fund, you should, over the years, enjoy greater returns than a money market or Treasury bills can offer. And with a mutual fund, you will eventually earn enough money for just about any emergency.

Note Don't casually dip into this rainy-day fund money, because this savings strategy brings the most benefit when the shares are bought and held.

Some will consider sticking money that needs to remain safe into the stock market financial heresy. Critics might suggest that putting reserve money into the market can be risky if your timing is exquisitely bad. Think back to October 19, 1987, when the stock market lost 20 percent of its value within just a few hours. If you desperately needed to pull money out the next day, you were in bad shape. The meltdown of the stock market in 2000 and 2001 provided its own even more graphic horror story.

But if you choose a mutual fund that has demonstrated an unwavering ability to ride out tough times in fine fashion, this risk should be far less of a worry. Believe it or not, some excellent funds have enjoyed impressive returns even during tumultuous periods on Wall Street.

Cross-Reference Chapter 7 provides the names of five solid funds that have not posted a losing year during the 1990s or since the start of the new century.

Step no. 2: Make sure you are adequately insured.

Evaluate your need for a variety of insurance coverage, including life, disability, long-term care, and personal liability umbrella policies. If you already have life insurance, you should periodically review your coverage amount. All sorts of life changes, including divorce, a birth, and a change in net worth, can affect the amount of coverage you need. After you retire, for example, you can probably scale back the amount of coverage.

Cross-Reference You'll find a great deal of information on insurance in Chapter 28.

Step no. 3: Draw up an estate plan.

Most individuals, unless they are living as hermits in a cave, need some type of an estate plan. You don't need to be worth a great deal of money to require some planning. For instance, a young couple with few assets still needs a will to designate whom they'd like to step in as their children's guardian if they both die. Once again, when major life changes occur, you need to revisit your estate plan.

A source for inexpensive do-it-yourself legal documents and a great deal of free information is www.nolo.com, the Web site for the legal publishing firm Nolo. You may also want to obtain a copy of the *Retirement Bible,* which provides considerable information on estate planning and trusts.

Step no. 4: Get organized.

Financial organization is important because it pinpoints where your starting line is and helps you determine a logical plan of action. Many people make financial decisions in an information vacuum. As a result, you might buy a whole life insurance policy from a neighbor, an annuity from a persistent broker, or a mutual fund online after reading a gushing article about it in a magazine—and yet you never spend time thinking about whether your investments work well together. In order to figure out whether your holdings mesh nicely, you must have a sense of what your underlying financial foundation is. To do that, you need to have a clear understanding of your cash flow, insurance coverage, debt load, savings track records, and your net worth. Only after you figure out where all your money is and what it's doing can you move into the more fun stuff, such as picking stocks, bonds, and mutual funds.

It need not take long to fill in the blanks: You can jot down a do-it-yourself portfolio outline on a legal pad or in a spreadsheet in an afternoon and keep that outline with your financial records for quick access. When your brother's broker wants to sell you one more mutual fund, you can consult this list to determine whether you really need it and how it would fit into your overall plan. This process also helps you determine your net worth, because you must tally up your assets and debts. Subtract your debts from your assets and you'll know what your net worth is.

Assets

Common assets that you need to keep track of include cash, investments, real estate, retirement assets, personal assets, and loans you have made that you expect to be repaid. Cash assets include the following types of accounts:

✦ Checking accounts

✦ Savings accounts

✦ Money markets

✦ Certificates of deposit

Investments include the following:

✦ Stocks

✦ Bonds

✦ Mutual funds

✦ Variable annuities

Real estate assets include your home and any other property you own. Retirement assets include the following:

✦ Vested interest in company pension or profit-sharing plan

✦ 401(k) plan

✦ Other retirement plans

When totaling your personal assets, you need to determine their fair market or replacement value. Such assets would include the following items:

✦ Cars

✦ Jewelry

✦ Antiques

✦ Furniture

Debts

The following are common sources of debt:

✦ Mortgages on your home and other real estate

✦ Vehicle loans

✦ Bank loans

✦ Credit card balances

✦ 401(k) loan

✦ Student loan

✦ Outstanding judgments

Step no. 5: Reduce your debt.

Debt can be like a sore tooth. If you ignore it, chances are it's only going to get worse. Credit card debt is the most insidious kind because it often doesn't appear too bad, but looks are deceiving. If you pay only the minimum on your credit cards, it could take you decades and tens of thousands of dollars in interest to pay it off. All this money that's getting wasted on credit card interest could be put to much better use in a decent mutual fund.

Papers to Keep

The following list includes the documents that you or your heirs will need at some point. Keeping all the documents together, perhaps in a safety deposit box, is the easiest way to stay organized. At the very least, write down the location of all your important papers and make sure someone else knows where they're kept.

✦ Birth certificates

✦ Life insurance policies

✦ Other insurance policies

✦ Lease documents

✦ Mortgage papers

✦ Car titles

✦ Pension, profit-sharing, and other retirement plan documents

✦ Marriage certificate

✦ Divorce or separation agreement

✦ Employment contracts

✦ Social Security card

✦ Military service records

One way to shed debt is to put yourself on a money diet. Your first step is to figure out just where you are hemorrhaging money.

Getting the exact figures for some expenses should be easy. For instance, you probably know how much your mortgage, car payment, children's tuition or day care, and various insurance premiums are each month. By pulling out your canceled checks, you can get a good handle on utilities, property taxes, telephone, and other such expenses. If you're a heavy credit card user, checking past statements should fill in a lot of the remaining blanks. And your bank statement will tell you how often you are hitting up the ATM for cash.

Cross-Reference The warning signs of debt overkill are explained in Chapter 27.

Look closely at your discretionary spending: the $2.75 lattes that have become a daily habit, the fast food lunches twice a week that cost you $45 a month, the impulse stop at the record shop that leaves you $35 poorer (even if two compact discs richer). If your checking account is hemorrhaging, it may well be due to a bad habit of giving yourself a bigger latte or cigar allowance than simple math allows for. If this sounds suspiciously like your situation, lose your ATM card and challenge yourself to live off a set amount of cash that you withdraw once a week. Such a tactic will force you to pay attention to where your money is going. Once you know how your cash vanishes, you're in a better position to go to the next step: reducing unnecessary spending.

Step no. 6: Scale back spending.

If you are saving the yearly maximum in your workplace retirement plan and an Individual Retirement Account, maintaining an adequate emergency cash fund, and socking away money for college tuition and other financial goals, congratulations! On the other hand, if you're stumped on how you can find extra money to save, you may need to do some belt tightening. Here are some ideas:

Obtain a free copy of 66 Ways to Save Money by sending a self-addressed business envelope to the Consumer Federation of America at CFA Publications, 1424 16th St. NW, Suite 604, Washington DC 20036-2211. Or download it from the federation's Web site at www.consumerfed.org.

✦ **Ignore a raise.** When you receive a raise, pretend that you never got it. Invest that extra money instead of letting it disappear into your checking account's black hole.

✦ **Pretend you still have a car loan.** When your car is paid off, keep making those payments to yourself. Assume that you just paid off a $190-a-month car loan. By setting aside that money each month in an account earning 7 percent, you'd have nearly $7,600 in three years.

✦ **Don't buy on impulse.** If you fall in love with something at the store, wait 24 hours. Chances are that once you're home, that must-have item won't look so alluring.

✦ **Don't spend your tax refund.** Stick the cash in an Individual Retirement Account instead.

You'll find other money-saving ideas in Chapter 27.

Summary

✦ Avoid bank savings accounts; they provide a miserly rate of return that won't keep up with inflation.

✦ You can squeeze more yield out of your cash holdings by investigating such alternatives as CDs, short-term bond funds, or fixed annuities.

✦ When shopping for a money market, keep in mind that the best ones are usually the cheapest.

✦ If you invest in a fixed annuity, make sure the insurer is highly ranked by outside rating services.

✦ Getting organized financially is crucial to an investor's success: Keep track of what you have and what you need.

✦ Pay off credit cards so the interest you'd owe can be invested instead.

Surviving in a Bear Market

Making money in a bull market is easy: Almost everything you buy seems to increase in value. Bear markets require special handling, however, and this chapter teaches you how to do it. In the next few pages, you'll learn how to hunt for bear-proof mutual funds, soften your losses with diversification, and pick through the financial wreckage carefully. Because occasional bear markets are inevitable, it's crucial to pay close attention to your portfolio's risk; this chapter directs you to online resources that can help you quickly estimate where your holdings sit on the risk spectrum.

The Nature of the Beast

Which animal is stronger, a bull or a bear? In the financial world, the bull is known for its endurance, but the bear can draw blood with its sharp claws. This kind of imagery is perhaps why Americans spend a great deal more time worrying about bears than appreciating the bulls. During a bull market, investors tend to obsess about when the market will self-destruct again. During bear markets, investors mostly just lick their wounds and worry that the pain will never vanish. Studies have repeatedly shown that investors feel their losses much more keenly than their wins.

No doubt about it, bear sightings in the stock market can be frightening. Yet even if the stock market drops 5 percent, 10 percent, or even 15 percent, it is technically experiencing a *correction,* which is a rather innocuous word to describe a flash flood of red ink. The market doesn't officially enter bear territory until a major index, such as the Dow Jones Industrial Average, plummets 20 percent from its high.

A bearish mood doesn't have to strike the entire market at once. Recently, for instance, the worst bear rampage in modern times mauled the Nasdaq Composite Index. About a year after reaching its historic peak in March 2000, the Nasdaq index, which is packed with marquee technology stocks, had plunged by 60 percent. During the same period, the Dow wasn't bludgeoned nearly as badly. The fact that different parts of the market take their licks at staggered times can be a key to protecting your portfolio from massive losses.

How can you shelter yourself from inevitable bear markets? First, try declawing your worst bear fears. When your money is trapped in a bear market, it may seem that the bear market is never going to end, but it will. As Table 3-1 shows, bear market recoveries don't drag on forever. As you can see, they also aren't nearly as frequent as the bull runs. Since the conclusion of World War II, 11 complete bear markets have come and gone. Since 1900, there've been 20 bear markets.

Table 3-1
Bear Markets in Modern Times

Bear Market	Percentage Drop	Length of Time to Break Even
1946–49	–30%	41 months
1956–57	–22%	24 months
1961–62	–28%	17 months
1966	–22%	15 months
1968–70	–36%	27 months
1973–74	–48%	45 months
1976–78	–20%	4 months
1980–82	–27%	23 months
1987	–34%	21 months
1990	–20%	9 months
1998	–19%	4 months

Source: Leuthold Group

During the past 100 years, the median bear market has lasted 2 years and 3 months. The longevity of the bear markets after World War II have tended to be shorter than that; the median length of time has been 21 months.

Eleven Ways to Beat a Bear

For a long-term investor, a bear market need not be catastrophic. But even those who have the luxury of riding out the market's fits and starts don't want to stand by helplessly and watch the value of their portfolios temporarily wither away. You can fight back by using these 10 strategies to bear-proof your portfolio:

Strategy no. 1: Invest in evergreen funds.

During bear markets, some mutual funds are hit harder than others. But what many investors overlook is that certain funds barely get nicked. The trick is to find one of these lucky charms and keep it in your portfolio.

Funds that flourish in good and bad times tend to be conservative ones that favor value stocks. The value universe includes a lot of beaten-down stocks that have been overshadowed by the flashier high-flyers. Although value stocks are more gravity bound, they don't fall as hard during turbulent times. In fact, many value stocks shine when growth stocks are being battered.

You don't have to do your own research to find these bear-proof funds. What follows is a list of six amazing evergreen funds. Five of the funds in this elite group did not experience a losing year in the 1990s. And they pulled off this feat while posting above average historical returns. So far, they have repeated this accomplishment in the new decade. A sixth fund, Third Avenue Value, dropped 1.4 percent back in 1994, but it hasn't experienced a losing year since. While their track records are impressive, keep in mind that there is no guarantee that these funds will continue to perform well in the future.

- ✦ Dodge & Cox Stock at (800) 621-3979 or www.dodgeandcox.com
- ✦ Dodge & Cox Balanced at (800) 621-3979 or www.dodgeandcox.com
- ✦ Haven at (800) 850-7163 or www.havencapital.com
- ✦ Longleaf Partners at (800) 445-9469 or www.longleafpartners.com
- ✦ Royce Total Return at (800) 221-4268 or www.roycefunds.com
- ✦ Third Avenue Value at (800) 443-1021 or www.mjwhitman.com

 Cross-Reference You'll learn a lot more about risk in your mutual fund portfolio in Chapter 6.

Strategy no. 2: Take a pass on bear-style funds.

Listen to fans of bear-style funds, and you'll assume you've found the perfect hedge against turbulent times. Responding to investors' natural fears, the mutual fund industry in the 1990s unveiled *market-neutral funds*. These funds were designed to do well in both bull and bear markets. The managers of these specialized funds don't care if stocks go up or down because they've hedged their bets for either direction. They've invested in stocks they believe will climb in value, and they've *shorted* other stocks that they suspect will fall. (When a stock is shorted, an investor borrows stock from a brokerage firm and then roots for the stock price to decline. If it does, the investor can buy cheaper shares and return the borrowed stock for a profit.)

Caution Unfortunately, market-neutral funds haven't lived up to their hype. They've generally been mediocre performers during both good and bad times, so stay away from these gimmicky funds.

Strategy no. 3: Resist market timing.

When you're watching the value of your investments sinking, it's only natural to want to yank your money out of the market. Unless you need the money soon, however, staying put is often the better strategy. Why? No one knows when the market will hit bedrock. The market bottom is easy to identify only months after the market has left the basement. If you're sitting on the sidelines when the market rallies, you will be hurt doubly. You've already lost money, and now you're watching the rally leave without you.

Cross-Reference If you doubt the danger of market timing, flip back to Chapter 1. It reveals the financial hit you'd have taken if your money had remained out of the market for just a few months during a 20-year period.

A look at the notorious bear market of 1973 and 1974 bolsters the argument against market timing. After hitting its low in October 1974, a rejuvenated stock market generated a 14.6 percent annual return during the next 20 years.

What you shouldn't do, however, is hold onto your investments simply out of loyalty. If you invest in mutual funds, review their performance once or twice a year no matter what's happening in the market. If a fund hasn't performed as well as others in the same category for a couple of years, you may want to reconsider your investment.

In doing the analysis, compare apples to apples. A small-cap value fund, for instance, must be compared with the small-cap value universe. The exercise becomes meaningless if you compare a small-cap value fund with a small-cap growth fund or an investment-grade bond fund with a junk bond fund. They have very different investing mandates and styles.

Bear Market Resource

If you want to know more about surviving in a bear market, read *Bear Market Survival Guide,* which is a free publication distributed by the Vanguard Group, the mutual fund company. You can obtain a copy at its Web site (www.vanguard.com) or by calling (800) 992-0855.

Online Bear Tracks

Want to immerse yourself in bear market commentary? Try these bear-oriented Web sites:

✦ **Beartopia at** www.beartopia.com

✦ **iTulip.com at** www.itulip.com

✦ **Fiend's Super Bear Page at** www.fiendbear.com

 Resource   An easy way to compare a fund's performance with its own investment category is to check out Morningstar's fund evaluations. Each fund's profile contains performance statistics for its investment category.

Individual stockholders need to be even more vigilant. A good time to review stocks is every three months when a company must issue its quarterly earnings report. During rough market conditions, you probably should keep an even closer eye. Compare your stocks to the appropriate indexes and other companies in the same industry.

Strategy no. 4: Stay diversified.

A diversified portfolio won't eliminate losses, but it should limit them. Bear markets can be highly choosy about who they attack. Technology and natural resource stocks, for instance, have traditionally been favorite bear prey. In contrast, other investments, such as U.S. Treasuries and investment-grade corporate bonds are often spared the worst bloodshed. During tough times, value stocks, as mentioned earlier, often fare better than growth stocks.

If you overdose on one market niche, however, your portfolio might not rebound as fast as your neighbor's. Obviously, the recent technology and telecommunications meltdown comes to mind, but the phenomenon is hardly a new one. Investors tend to invest in whatever happens to be the hottest stocks and funds around. Unfortunately, by the time the average investor sinks money into whatever sector of the market is red hot at the moment, it often signals that whatever is popular is about ready for a cool down. Just look at what happened to shareholders who piled into the Fidelity Select Technology Fund, which was a tremendously popular fund in the early 1980s. By mid-1983, the fund had soared 162 percent during the previous year. But during the next 12 months, the fund plunged nearly 25 percent, and the carnage didn't end there. Throughout the rest of the 1980s, the fund gained less than 1 percent a year while the Standard & Poor's 500 Index, which is a popular market benchmark, advanced nearly 21 percent a year. Someone who overloaded on this fund 20 years ago has likely never forgotten the experience. The fund, by the way, went on to perform spectacularly during the 1990s, but once again, it hit a wall early in the new decade.

Tech investors aren't the only ones who have enjoyed feasts and famines. Glance at the historical record of any sector in the market and you'll spot booms and busts. In 2000, for instance, utility stocks were hot and attracted tons of cash, but for most of the 1990s, utilities were bottom dwellers. In the same vein, healthcare stocks were excellent performers in the mid- to late 1980s, but after President Bill Clinton's inauguration, the sector was pummeled for a couple of years.

Unfortunately, no one can accurately predict the market's mood swings. Consequently, holding a broad array of assets is the best way to soften the blow when the market gets ugly. The typical well-balanced portfolio will include stocks, bonds and cash. But it's also important to diversify within assets classes. A mutual fund stock investor, for instance, should spread money in funds that specialize in value and growth stocks, as well as large, medium and small-sized companies.

Diversification is essential because it's impossible to predict the boom and busts cycles. Table 3-2 shows that guessing which type of investment is going to emerge as the year's winner is pointless. Table 3-3 demonstrates that predicting the year's big losers is just as impossible. In 2000, for example, if you were holding a healthy dose of small-cap value stocks, which jumped nearly 23 percent, you wouldn't have felt as bad about technology stocks, which were experiencing their worst drubbing ever.

Table 3-2 Yearly Investment Winners		
Year	*Asset Class*	*Percentage Gain*
1981	Small-cap value stocks	14.85%
1982	U.S. bonds	32.65%
1983	Small-cap value stocks	38.63%
1984	U.S bonds	15.15%
1985	Foreign stocks	56.14%
1986	Foreign stocks	69.46%
1987	Foreign stocks	24.64%
1988	Small-cap value stocks	29.47%
1989	Large-cap growth stocks	36.4%
1990	U.S. bonds	8.96%
1991	Small-cap growth stocks	51.18%
1992	Small-cap value stocks	29.15%
1993	Foreign stocks	32.57%
1994	Foreign stocks	7.78%
1995	Large-cap growth stocks	38.13%

Year	Asset Class	Percentage Gain
1996	Large-cap growth stocks	23.97%
1997	Large-cap growth stocks	36.52%
1998	Large-cap growth stocks	42.16%
1999	Small-cap growth stocks	43.09%
2000	Small-cap value stocks	22.83%

Source: Callan Associates, Inc.

Table 3-3
Historic Investment Losers

Year	Asset Class	Percentage Gain or Loss
1981	Large-cap growth stocks	−9.81%
1982	Foreign stocks	−1.86%
1983	U.S. bonds	8.19%
1984	Small-cap growth stocks	−15.84%
1985	U.S. bonds	22.13%
1986	Small-cap growth stocks	3.59%
1987	Small-cap growth stocks	−10.48%
1988	U.S. bonds	7.89%
1989	Foreign stocks	10.53%
1990	Foreign stocks	−23.45%
1991	Foreign stocks	12.14%
1992	Foreign stocks	−12.18%
1993	Large-cap growth stocks	1.68%
1994	U.S. bonds	−2.92%
1995	Foreign stocks	11.21%
1996	U.S. bonds	3.64%
1997	Foreign stocks	1.78%
1998	Small-cap value stocks	−6.46%
1999	Small-cap value stocks	−1.48%
2000	Small-cap growth stocks	−22.43%

Source: Callan Associates, Inc.

Of particular interest to risk-sensitive investors is an asset class that is missing from the winner and loser lists in Tables 3-2 and 3-3. During the time period covered, large-cap value stocks were incredibly steady performers. Among the eight different asset classes, large-cap value almost always earned a spot in the top half. This is a testament to the advantages of including rather boring stocks in a portfolio rather than exclusively chasing the hot stock du jour.

Strategy no. 5: Don't behave impulsively.

When the stock market is behaving erratically, it's only natural to feel panicky. But resist any urge to act immediately. (This advice is just as valid during bull markets when investors are giddy about their paper gains.) Don't let your emotions dictate changes in your portfolio. Hasty decisions could only aggravate your losses. In fact, it's often best to limit portfolio tinkering when the market is depressed. Say you've decided that you can't handle the volatility of a portfolio that's heavily invested in stocks, and you want to shovel some of that stock money into bonds. Consider limiting the amount of holdings you move around.

Example

For example, if you limit your changes to 15 percent of your holdings, you could still nudge your portfolio from an 80 percent stocks/20 percent bonds combination to a mix of 65 percent stocks and 35 percent bonds.

Strategy no. 6: Consider buying inflation-fighting bonds.

An excellent way to hedge your portfolio against the occasional stock slides is to invest in inflation-fighting bonds. The U.S. Treasury Department has cooked up two flavors: Treasury Inflation-Protection Securities (TIPs) and the I Bond, a newer type of savings bond. The I stands for inflation-indexed.

Unlike stocks and other bonds, these bonds are designed to thrive during inflationary times. When inflation is unrestrained, stocks can stumble because money is pouring into ultrasafe investments, such as certificates of deposit, that can now offer attractive yields.

These inflation bonds are a nice hedge because they share a very low correlation with stocks and other bonds. That is, when stock and bonds are getting hammered when inflation is on the rise, TIPs and I Bonds shine. Inflation bonds could substitute for other traditional and arguably less reliable inflation hedges such as gold, real estate, and commodities.

Cross-Reference

You can learn much more about inflation bonds in Chapter 18.

Strategy no. 7: Dollar-cost average.

If you're a long-term investor who practices dollar-cost averaging, a bear market need not be frightening; in fact, a bear market can work to your advantage. When you *dollar-cost average,* typically you invest a certain amount of money automatically each month. When you buy in a bear market, this money stretches farther, and you're more likely to snatch up shares in stocks and funds at bargain prices.

The easiest way to dollar-cost average is to sign up with a brokerage firm or fund company. Each month (you can often choose the day), cash is automatically withdrawn from your checking or savings account and deposited into a mutual fund. Often the minimum monthly investment is only $50.

Strategy no. 8: Invest in your own assets.

The stock market isn't the only game in town. If you're too nervous to invest, consider other solid options. One possibility is paying down your mortgage. Making one extra mortgage payment a month can reduce a 30-year mortgage dramatically. Another alternative is to trade in a 30-year mortgage for a 15-year one. By doing this, you can ultimately save tens or hundreds of thousands of dollars in interest over the loan's lifetime. If you are wondering how much you could save, there's no need to do the calculations yourself; countless mortgage calculators are available online. Here are a few to check out:

✦ Bloomberg at `www.bloomberg.com`

✦ Hugh's Mortgage & Financial Calculators at `www.interest.com/hugh/calc`

✦ Smart Money Magazine at `www.smartmoney.com`

✦ FinanCenter.com at `www.financenter.com`

An admittedly less gratifying move is paying off credit card debt. The typical American household is facing a total credit card balance of roughly $7,500, while recently the average credit card was charging a 17 percent interest rate. Banks can afford to charge these outrageous interest rates, even when interest rates are low, because they are well aware of Americans' addiction to plastic. You can potentially save yourself thousands in interest payments by wiping out your debt, thus freeing up more money for investing when the market inevitably bounces back into your comfort zone.

Strategy no. 9: Take your portfolio's pulse.

When the markets are behaving, fewer people worry about their investment risks. Balancing the potential risks and rewards of a portfolio, however, is a crucial exercise during all market conditions. Why is this exercise important? When there are safer ways to attain the same investment results, taking extreme risks is pointless.

Suppose you were hunting for a promising mid-cap growth fund. You ultimately eliminated all but two candidates: Janus Enterprise and MAS MidCap Growth. Both funds sport similar three-year track records, but the Janus pick is far more volatile. In 2000, for example, the tech-heavy Janus Enterprise lost nearly a third of its value, and the slide continued in 2001. In contrast, MAS fund dropped only 7.3 percent. How could the two funds have similar track records when one has fallen harder? In 1999, Enterprise soared by nearly 122 percent while MAS's fund jumped about 68 percent. Obviously, Enterprise's swings are much more dramatic than the MAS fund.

The average investor is probably much more comfortable sticking with a fund that isn't a heart stopper. Consequently, when you've narrowed your choice to promising candidates, choose the one with the safer risk profile. Unfortunately, getting a handle on an individual stock or fund's risk profile is more difficult than determining how well or poorly an individual stock or a fund is faring. Fortunately, you can get help online.

Resource   Three Web sites, RiskGrades (`www.riskgrades.com`), Portfolio Science (`www.portfolioscience.com`), and Morningstar (`www.morningstar.com`) can help you figure out an investment's risk profile and fortify your portfolio for the next bear siege.

RiskGrades

The software at the free RiskGrades Web site (`www.riskgrades.com`) can analyze the potential volatility of your portfolio. Using RiskGrades provides a convenient way to understand the underlying risk of each investment in your portfolio as well as how well your investments mesh together. RiskGrades gives your overall holdings a numerical risk grade and assigns grades to individual securities in your portfolio as well. The numbers range from 0 to 1000. A cash investment would sit at the bottom of the range while a technology startup could be at the top of the charts.

RiskGrades can help identify your portfolio's potential trouble spots. For instance, you may be overly concentrated in certain sectors, such as financials or healthcare stocks. The software's RiskImpact function can evaluate how your portfolio's risk profile will change if certain assets are removed. The software also can compare the risk your portfolio is assuming versus the risk of leading benchmarks, such as the Standard & Poor's 500. Many investors already compare their yearly portfolio performance with benchmarks, but comparing the risk you are assuming is invaluable. Finally, for those who may need to withdraw money in the near future or who worry that they might panic during another meltdown, the XLoss function determines how much money you could lose due to extreme market movements.

Tip   Using RiskGrade can also help you tackle this important question: Should you try to match an index's performance or attempt to beat it? Once you compare your risk with a benchmark's, you can determine whether there are less volatile ways to attain your investment goals.

The RiskGrades software was developed by RiskMetrics, which is a spinoff of J.P. Morgan. More than 5,000 financial institutions around the world use this company's risk measurement products.

Portfolio Science

Another free site, Portfolio Science (`www.portfolioscience.com`) assists you in getting a handle on the level of your portfolio's risk. You can receive an instant risk diagnosis by typing in the ticker symbols for an individual stock, a mutual fund, or an entire portfolio. In calculating the volatility of a fund or stock, the software compares it to major indexes, such as the Standard & Poor's 500. The site's sophisticated software can express the potential for securities fluctuation as a dollar amount or as a percentage, basing estimates on a daily, monthly, or yearly basis.

Morningstar

The typical mutual fund investor knows all about Morningstar's five-star grading system. Yet every fund that Morningstar analyzes also includes a risk assessment. You can find the analysis of roughly 1,700 funds in *Morningstar Mutual Funds,* which is circulated in many libraries. The same information is on its Web site (`www.morningstar.com`).

Most discriminating investors spurn any fund that hasn't earned four or five stars. These same folks, however, routinely ignore Morningstar's category ratings. If yo-yo performances make you anxious, make sure you take a close look at category ratings.

The category rating is a quantitative measure of a fund's risk-adjusted returns. Analysts determine how well a fund has balanced risk and return relative to the other funds in the same category. As with the star rating, a 5 is best, and a 1 is the worst. For a raw look at a fund's risk level, review the fund's category risk, which evaluates a fund's downside volatility relative to similar funds. The 10 percent of funds that experienced the fewest drops during the past three years earn a "low" risk rating. The 10 percent of funds that have experienced the biggest cardiac plunges rate a "high" risk designation. In between these ratings fall three additional risk categories.

Risk Quizzes

Plenty of Web sites offer risk quizzes, in which you fill out an online questionnaire and learn something about your own investment comfort level. You'll find risk quizzes at these sites:

✦ Fidelity Investments at `www.fidelity.com`

✦ CNBC on MSN Money at `www.money.msn.com`

✦ Vanguard Group at `www.vanguard.com`

Of course, if you've been invested since the start of the new decade, you already know what your reaction would be to an extreme bear market: You've experienced one first hand.

Strategy no. 10: Seek help.

When the stock market is on a roll, we can easily feel like investing geniuses. But when markets turn surly, our confidence can disappear as quickly as a Las Vegas hot streak. Because investment losses are often felt much more keenly than gains, sometimes calling in an objective outsider to provide a fresh prospective can be worthwhile. You may want to consult a Certified Financial Planner, who can review your asset allocation and see whether adjustments are necessary. You'll learn how to find a financial planner in Chapter 5.

Strategy no. 11: Buy on dips only with caution.

In the recent past, investors minted money by snatching up premiere stocks when their price dropped temporarily. (During volatile markets, a stock may drop 5 percent, 10 percent, 15 percent, or more on a single day.) Investors have historically considered this an ideal time to buy stellar stocks at discount prices. When optimism gripped the market, those stocks shot back up, and dips were regarded as temporary market insanity.

During such times, investors congratulate themselves on buying dirt-cheap shares in popular stocks. But you should be careful when purchasing shares of wounded companies whose stock price has dipped, as the examples in the following sections show.

Tech market maulings

Is buying big-name stocks when their prices drop a valid strategy during bear markets? It obviously was a disastrous approach for many Internet stocks during the dot-com debacle. The tiniest Internet startups to the mightiest, including Amazon.com and Yahoo!, caved in spectacular fashion. In many cases, Internet stocks that were priced above $100 a share ended up selling for the price of a couple of Krispy Kreme doughnuts.

Example

Just ask any bargain hunter who began nibbling at Yahoo! after it began dropping from a high of around $250 down to $12 and change. What might have seemed like a bargain at $150 a share looked like a costly mistake a short time later.

Blue-chip busts

We now know that the business models of too many Internet companies were as substantial as marshmallows, but what about the blue chips? Can it be worthwhile to buy a brand-name stock after a scary free fall? A study conducted by the Leuthold Group, a stock research firm in Minneapolis, suggests you need to tread very carefully if you're contemplating this move. In its study, the firm explored what happened to a group of big-name companies, such as Office Depot, Oracle, Xerox, Compaq Computer, Waste Management, and Veritas Software, which had experienced a one-day price drop of 20 percent or more. The study's time period stretched from January 1999, near the peak of the bull market, until mid-October 2000.

Overall, the picture was not pretty. After one year, the median stock in the lineup of 85 corporations lagged behind the Standard & Poor's 500 Index by 12 percentage points. The median stock also trailed the S&P 500 and Nasdaq Composite at other time periods, such as 6, 9, and 15 months after a disastrous fall.

Although the study concluded that most stocks continue to do poorly after a precipitous drop, a few stocks performed superbly. In the study, for instance, Veritas Software, which had plummeted 20 percent during a spring day in 1999, had skyrocketed by 639 percent a year later. During roughly the same period, Oracle, which had dropped 22.5 percent in one day, bounced back 451 percent.

The bottom line

What's the lesson to be learned? Don't buy a stock simply because it's dropped suddenly. It may represent a great buying opportunity, but don't rush into the purchase. As the Leuthold study suggests, most of these stocks aren't going to rebound quickly, so you have the luxury of methodically researching your decision before placing an order. Analyze why the stock dropped and how it will affect the corporation's future earnings and growth prospects before you commit any cash. Also keep this in mind: A stock that has plunged dramatically could still be significantly overpriced.

Cross-Reference

You will learn how to analyze stock fundamentals in Chapter 15.

Hedging with Options

An *option,* which is a contract, gives an investor the right to buy or sell a stock for a specified price within a preset period of time. With options, an investor can bet that the market, or an individual stock, will go up or down.

Options sound risky, and they can be. In flush times, daredevils who want to leverage their money for a greater exposure to the market snap them up like buttered popcorn. But ironically, when cautious investors deploy options effectively, they can be used as a form of insurance to protect the value of their stock portfolios.

Online Options Primer

Because options are complicated, you must thoroughly understand how they work before buying them. Your broker must give you a copy of a booklet entitled *Characteristics and Risks of Standardized Options* before you invest in options. You also can download the booklet from the Web site of the Chicago Board Options Exchange (www.cboe.com). A section of this Web site is dedicated to educating potential options investors and includes a list of software products. The CBOE site also enables you to get your feet wet by creating a simulated options position.

Options to the rescue

How can options be used defensively? A classic strategy is purchasing a *put* on a stock you own. A put gives you the right, but not the obligation, to sell a stock at a specified price, known as the *strike price,* by some future date. Buying a put allows you to determine in advance the maximum loss you'd be willing to take on a stock. Suppose your stock is priced at $50, and you buy a $50 put for 100 shares. A short time later, the stock drops to $40, but you can sell shares at $50 each instead of $40. If your stock jumps up instead, you'll still own the stock, but your gains won't be as much if you calculate the price you paid to purchase the put.

Covered calls at work

You can also provide limited downside protection for an individual stock by writing (selling) a covered call option. The opposite of a put, a *call* gives an investor the right to buy a specific number of shares of a stock at a certain price by a fixed date. It's considered a *covered call* when you sell call options while simultaneously owning an equivalent amount of that stock.

Here are the mechanics of this transaction: Say you're an investor in Home Depot stock and you're worried that the stock price seems too richly valued, but you don't want to dump it. Instead, you sell someone else the right to buy your Home Depot stock at a specified price by a certain date. By doing this, you pocket an upfront fee from the buyer, which is called a *premium.* The pricing of premiums is based on such factors as the time period, the strike price, and a stock's volatility.

Note   A stock with a long expiration period commands a higher premium, as does an option where the strike price is closer to the current price. That's because there's a greater likelihood in these cases that the owner will have to sell his shares.

If the Home Depot stock rises to the preagreed strike price before the expiration date, the investor who bought the call has the right to buy your shares. On the other hand, if the stock price remains stagnant, the call will simply lapse. You, however, will be better off financially because you keep the premium. How would writing a covered call help if the Home Depot stock plummets? If the stock does fall, the premium you earned would reduce your losses.

Beware of Naked Calls

Stay away from writing calls on stocks you don't even own. These calls are referred to as *naked calls.* This strategy is extremely perilous because you could potentially lose a tremendous amount of money. Suppose you write a call on IBM. As long as IBM doesn't rise above the strike price, you're ahead. But if IBM does soar, you'll have to buy your shares at the steep price so you can deliver the shares to the purchaser who bought the call. Naked puts are also a bad idea.

Covered calls have other potential benefits. Using covered calls has been a popular strategy among some conservative income investors who desire a better return than what they can expect from ultrasafe investments such as money markets and certificates of deposit. The strategy can be an ideal one for a stock that is stuck in a limited trading range. Instead of being frustrated that a stock is moving sideways, an investor can write a covered call and collect a premium. An investor can continue to write covered calls as long as the person on the other end of the transaction doesn't exercise the option.

Caution Of course, writing covered calls has its downside. If you relinquish your stock just when it's starting a long upward climb, you'll miss out on the growth. You will also face potential capital gains taxes on your profits.

Summary

✦ Protect your portfolio by investing in a mutual fund with a bear-proof track record.

✦ Diversifying your portfolio could help you avoid wide price swings.

✦ Invest through dollar-cost averaging and you'll eventually profit from the depressed prices.

✦ Understand your portfolio's risk level to better protect your investments during stormy times.

✦ If you lose confidence in your investing abilities, consider asking an outside expert to evaluate a portfolio.

✦ Consider using options to reduce your portfolio's risk.

✦   ✦   ✦

Picking a Broker

I n this chapter, you will learn how to intelligently evaluate your current brokerage services. If a change is necessary, this chapter provides the necessary tools to enable you to select a more attractive alternative. This chapter also details the tremendous changes the brokerage industry is undergoing and how you can take advantage of these developments.

Tumbling Down a Rabbit Hole

When Alice wandered into Wonderland, everything she saw was turned topsy-turvy. What's going on in today's brokerage industry doesn't include flying tea cups and a Mad Hatter's party, but Alice would no doubt find it equally perplexing. The business of buying and selling stocks is not what it used to be.

The traditional, stuffed-shirt brokerage firms are busting their buttons to act like their more nimble online competitors. These full-service brokers are slashing prices, welcoming do-it-yourself investors into the fold, and embracing online trading. At the same time, ambitious discount brokers are trying hard to ape the mainline Wall Street firms. No longer content to be one-note services where investors can only trade stocks, discount brokerage firms are offering an impressive lineup of services that includes wealth management, investment advice, portfolio tune-ups, insurance, credit cards, and mortgage loans.

Note As a sign of the tremendous changes taking place in the brokerage world, Charles Schwab, which was the industry's biggest discounter for many years, now has recast itself as a full-service broker. While it has its roots as a discounter, it now has many of the attributes of a full-service brokerage firm, including branches, fee-based advisors, and wealth management services.

The brokerage industry's eagerness to contort itself into new shapes shows no signs of ending. If anything, brokerage firms began feeling increased pressure to offer new services to customers when the fuel gauge on the overheated stock market hit empty. Independent investors, who considered themselves brilliant stock pickers during the 90s' bull market, began second-guessing their ability to manage their own investments when their portfolios started hemorrhaging. Many of these folks, who discovered they couldn't handle heart-stopping risk, are now looking for reassurance and dependable second opinions.

Complicating the matter is the media blitz generated by brokerages. You can get a pretty warped view of what's happening in the brokerage industry by watching television. Not long ago, firms were bankrolling some pretty entertaining commercials that made it look like all you needed to become independently wealthy was a brokerage account. Yet all that someone could truly conclude from these sorts of advertising onslaughts is that the brokerage industry spends phenomenal amounts of money trying to hook you. Whether a particle of truth exists in the glitzy hype is harder to determine.

It's no wonder then that finding the right brokerage firm can be as exasperating as securing the best cellular phone plan. To help with the research, this chapter outlines the key strengths and weaknesses of both full-service and discount brokerage firms and explains how the big changes in the brokerage industry affect you.

Considering Full-Service Brokers

For decades, full-service brokers operated pretty much the same way. Customers relied upon an individual broker to place stock, bond, and mutual fund trades and make investment recommendations. Clients wouldn't be surprised if they received eager calls from their brokers urging them to buy shares of Coca-Cola or Procter & Gamble. These stock picks were typically generated by the firm's huge network of economists and analysts located around the world. The stockbroker for a firm such as Merrill Lynch or Morgan Stanley Dean Witter was simply the messenger for this massive collection of brainpower.

Of course, this mother lode of investment wisdom came at a price: Customers paid a stiff commission, which could reach into the hundreds of dollars, each time they followed a broker's advice to buy or sell. Paying big commissions to trade didn't seem unreasonable when no alternatives existed, but the emergence of scrappy discounters threatened this arrangement.

When discounters hit the scene, they began furiously kneecapping the big guys by tantalizing investors with rock-bottom pricing. Of course, they could afford to because they didn't have to pay for the upkeep of mahogany-lined offices at prestigious addresses or the networks of offices from Portland, Maine to San Diego, California. Because discounters largely conducted business in telephone service centers and by computer, the overhead cost far less.

Full-Service Broker Lineup

The following list includes the names of some of the nation's best-known full-service brokers. You can find the office nearest you by looking in the phone book or by visiting a broker's Web site.

✦ **Merrill Lynch:** www.ml.com

✦ **Charles Schwab:** www.schwab.com

✦ **Morgan Stanley Dean Witter:** www.msdw.com

✦ **UBS PaineWebber:** www.ubspainewebber.com

✦ **Salomon Smith Barney:** www.salomonsmithbarney.com

✦ **Prudential:** www.prudentialsecurities.com

✦ **A.G. Edwards:** www.agedwards.com

✦ **Edward Jones:** www.edwardjones.com

Investors might do a double-take seeing Schwab included in this list of full-service brokers. But the San-Francisco-based brokerage firm is now offering many of the services that the full-service boys have traditionally provided. In fact, Schwab no longer considers itself a discount broker.

Picking from your new account options

For a long time, the brokerage titans rebuffed the interlopers, but ultimately they were forced to rethink their time-honored business models. Their eventual goal was to broaden their client base and stop the defection of their cost-conscious customers. At the same time, the firms tried to make their higher fees more palatable by providing additional advisory services. What ultimately occurred was the creation of a wide variety of pricing schedules. Consequently, potential customers should definitely scrutinize the different plans before signing on.

Online trading accounts

What do the changes at full-service firms mean for the skinflint investor? You can now sign up for a no-frills online trading account with a Merrill Lynch or a Morgan Stanley Dean Witter and pay for stock trades that are in the same fee ballpark as prominent discounters, such as Fidelity Investments. Recently, you could trade stocks for $29.95 a pop at some of the full-service shops. But often you'll receive little else in exchange for these fairly modest commission rates. Having one of these budget accounts doesn't entitle you to your own broker. You may also be shut out of the brokerage firm's huge wealth of analyst research.

Note To evaluate these self-directed accounts, ask the same kind of questions about services that you'd ask discount brokers, which are covered later in this chapter.

Fee-based accounts

Frankly, the full-service brokers these days are much more interested in retaining and attracting new customers through their fee-based pricing plans rather than through the traditional arrangements with personal brokers. With a fee-based account, a customer pays a certain percentage of his assets each year for the privilege of maintaining an account.

Caution Small-fry accounts can be dinged proportionately higher fees because brokerage firms typically charge a minimum yearly fee, such as $1,500.

Heavy traders benefit most

Fee-based accounts don't appeal to everybody. If you're a buy-and-hold investor who rarely tinkers with your portfolio, being obligated to skim off a percentage of your net worth each year might be galling. Thanks to the minimum yearly fee, a fee-based arrangement would be tantamount to financial suicide for modest portfolios. In contrast, a frenetic trader who has previously absorbed steep full-service commissions on each transaction could welcome the new arrangement.

The brokerage firms have tried to sweeten the deal by tossing in extra advice. Customers who sign up for fee-based accounts are entitled to a wealth of advice on everything from retirement planning and college savings to exercising stock options. In other words, your money gains you an entree into the type of services that a traditional financial planner provides. This kind of service might sound wonderful, but you need to enter into this kind of relationship with your eyes wide open.

Example Suppose you invest $100,000 with a firm that charges an annual 2.25 percent fee (which is on the high side). You'll pay $2,250 per year to park the account at the brokerage firm whether you trade heavily or just let your portfolio grow moss.

A question of credentials

Fee-based accounts have triggered criticism from consumer groups such as the Consumer Federation of America as well as certain quarters of the securities industry. The crux of the debate centers on the qualifications of the people who are providing all this great counseling. A lot of the responsibility is falling upon the broker's shoulders. In advertisements and literature, firms are referring to brokers as financial advisors and consultants. Some larger firms organize what amounts to broker teams, with the head of a group having extra credentials. But in reality, many team members, who tend to field most clients' questions, are young or relatively inexperienced.

If you call a dog a duck, does that make it one? That's essentially what the critics are asking. If you call a broker a financial advisor or planner, does that make him one? Millions of investors who have relied upon their brokers' financial advice might be shocked to learn that brokers don't undergo the type of training necessary to be financial planners.

Brokers are not and never have been bona-fide investment advisors. Brokers are salespeople who are trained to conduct transactions.

Securities regulators don't require brokers to be licensed as investment advisors because any financial counseling they provide is considered incidental to their real job, which is handling investment transactions. With customers now expecting more from their brokers, their professional qualifications are even more critical.

Some brokers do seek extra credentialing that demands additional education.

Some brokers have gone the extra mile and become Certified Financial Planners (CFP), certified public accountants (CPA), chartered financial analysts (CFA), chartered life underwriters (CLU), and chartered financial consultants (ChFC). But many are solely *registered representatives,* which is another term for stockbroker.

Note

Charles Schwab, which built an enviable track record by charging low trading commissions to its original base of do-it-yourself customers, is now experimenting with fee-based accounts. Financial advisors, employed by Schwab, will provide investment counseling and other services for clients who prefer professional investment advice.

Commissioned-based accounts

If you prefer a full-service broker, you can stick with the traditional way of paying a sizable commission with each trade in return for the broker's advice. Your broker can provide you with a wealth of information on just about any investment that you're interested in. If you want to see reports about individual stocks or about the overall economy, you can get them free of charge.

Choosing a Financial Planner Over a Broker

Full-service brokerage accounts may be a suitable choice for investors who require hand-holding, such as those who have no clue about the mechanics of investing and don't have the desire or time to learn. An alternative for such individuals, however, is hiring a Certified Financial Planner, who can make investment decisions and manage their accounts. Many CFPs maintain their clients' accounts at Charles Schwab, as well as some discount brokerage firms, where they can secure the best transaction prices. Because CFPs operate their own high-volume business, the brokerage fees are far lower than customers could obtain themselves. Planners are often entitled to the fees that are reserved for institutional customers, which include endowments and pension funds.

Just as with a fee-based brokerage plan, you typically pay a CFP an annual fee to oversee your portfolio. But you may find that the cost is much less than what you'd end up paying at a deluxe brokerage firm. See Chapter 5 for the best way to find the ideal planner.

Caution One of the age-old drawbacks of this traditional way of doing business is that it creates potential conflicts of interest. With a commission-based account, a broker doesn't profit unless you make a change in your portfolio, and portfolio changes are not necessarily in your best interest.

Brokers can also be tempted to push certain products because firms may reward their sales staff for selling in-house mutual funds and other investment products. Brokerage firms have touted their fee-based plans as a way to avoid perceived conflicts.

Some brokerage firms use a hybrid of commission and fee-based plans. They may provide access to a "money manager" through a fee-based arrangement, but charge you a commission for any holdings not with the manager.

Choosing a personal broker

The search for a full-service individual broker can be tricky, because you will be establishing a personal, long-term relationship with this person. The conventional wisdom is to ask friends, relatives, business acquaintances, your accountant, or somebody else for a recommendation. The key here is to solicit referrals from people who know a lot about investing and have been successful at it.

Look for a broker with at least several years of experience. Don't assume that a middle-aged broker has been in the business a long time. With fewer new college grads aspiring to be brokers, the ranks are being filled with those looking for a second career. It's also better to find a broker whose training goes beyond trading securities.

Before signing on with a full-service broker, confirm that he or she has a clean record with securities regulators. Get a copy of the broker's Central Registration Depository (CRD) report by contacting NASD Regulation, a subsidiary of the National Association of Securities Dealers, the industry's self-regulatory organization, at (800) 289-9999 or www.nasdr.com. The report is also available from your state's securities department. You can track down that number by calling the North American Securities Administrators Association, which is a national organization of state regulators, at (202) 737-0900 or www.nasaa.org.

Cross-Reference For more information on playing detective, see Chapter 26.

Whittling down your choices with rankings

If you don't want to do the grunt work required to find the ideal brokerage firm, plenty of worker bees will do it for you. It's hard to open up a personal finance magazine without seeing a feature that ranks brokers. An hour in a public library or on the Internet should uncover more rankings than you possibly could need.

One of the curious things that you'll notice about rankings is that they all differ. That's because each organization uses its own standards for its financial beauty contest. Consequently, you should look carefully at the measurements. For instance, if a magazine anoints a broker as the source of the cheapest commission rates, you'll want to know whether this cut-rate price applies to all stock trades. Chances are it doesn't. Market order trades, which means that an investor is willing to trade a stock immediately at the best available price, typically result in lower fees than trading with a *limit order*. An investor submitting a limit order names the price he or she is willing to buy or sell a stock for. A brokerage firm waits until that price or a better one is reached before making the transaction. For instance, if a stock is currently selling for $30 a share, an individual might instruct the broker to buy if shares dip to $27 or lower. If magazines ranked brokerage firms by the more costly limit order pricing, some of the winners could appear to be losers.

You can find evaluations of brokerage firms in these magazines and other sources:

✦ *Money Magazine* at (800) 633-9970 or `www.money.com`

✦ *Smart Money* at (800) 444-4204 or `www.smartmoney.com`

✦ *Business Week* at (800) 635-1200 or `www.businessweek.com`

✦ *Kiplinger's Personal Finance* at (800) 544-0155 or `www.kiplinger.com`

✦ American Association of Individual Investors at (312) 280-0170 or `www.aaii.org`

✦ Gomez Advisors at `www.gomez.com`

✦ CyberInvest.com at `www.cyberinvest.com`

Also, check out the "What Works" column in TheStreet.com (`www.thestreet.com`). The columnist, with helpful feedback from brokerage customers, writes her take on the strengths and weaknesses of specific brokerage houses. Another helpful source is a Web site maintained by Don Johnson, a former history professor who has been tracking discount brokerage firms since the late 1980s. You can read his no-nonsense insights at `www.sonic.net/donaldj`.

You may also find it valuable hearing the experiences of fellow investors. A source for spirited debates on brokerage firms is the Motley Fool (`www.fool.com`). Consider reading a few weeks' worth of posted comments from these brokerage customers about what they like and loathe about specific firms.

Note Don't accept anything you read as the final word. To remain competitive, brokerage firms continue to fine-tune their services and prices. You can get the latest information from many brokerage houses at their Web addresses.

Choosing a Discount Brokerage Firm

A crucial difference between a discount brokerage firm and a full-service one is this: Brokers aren't on the discounters' payrolls. Discounters have never needed commissioned brokers because, traditionally, they haven't been in the advice business. Customers were expected to be self-starters who picked their investments. The firm simply processed the orders, using employees who typically receive salaries rather than being compensated by commissions. Even as discounters ventured into the advice arena, brokers haven't appeared.

Beyond the taboo on brokers, discounters can differ tremendously. Consequently, the ideal brokerage firm for your neighbor or colleague might not be the best one for you. An individual's investing style can be as unique as a thumbprint and so can his or her brokerage needs. Someone who invests primarily in mutual funds won't want to patronize a discounter with a small inventory of funds. But this brokerage firm might be ideal for a stock jock who insists upon low stock commissions and access to initial public offerings.

Know thyself

Your first step in analyzing your current broker or shopping for a better one is to evaluate what kind of investor you are. Are you experienced or a novice? Do you own a sizable portfolio or are you barely able to scrape up the minimum cash necessary to open an account? Are you a buy-and-hold investor or a frequent trader?

Beginning investors will probably feel most comfortable with a full-service discounter. Firms such as Fidelity Investments maintain satellite offices throughout the United States for people who don't like conducting all their business by phone or computer. E*Trade has begun establishing outposts in Target stores. Brick-and-mortar discounters hold free educational seminars on a variety of investment topics from retirement saving to estate planning and may even provide one-on-one sessions for customers, who aren't sure how to trade online. You can drop into one of these offices and get your questions answered.

Online Trading Misconception

Only a day trader needs an online brokerage account, right? A surprising number of people assume that trading online is strictly for day traders, those folks who buy and sell rapidly to try and beat the market. But it's absolutely not true. Online trading simply refers to the method an investor uses to buy stocks, bonds, and mutual funds. With an online trade, you place an order by using your computer modem to log onto a broker's Web site. You can conduct transactions and monitor your holdings online regardless of whether you are a discount or full-service brokerage customer.

More sophisticated investors, who have concluded they need some professional guidance, are also gravitating to full-service discounters. The firms provide different levels of assistance. Fidelity offers professional money management for clients with at least $50,000 in assets. Both Fidelity and E*Trade can help customers find their own private money managers. Another option is Schwab, which, of course, has forsaken the discount label. Schwab, which maintains offices throughout the country, also offers managed accounts through its private client services.

Note

It's impossible to discuss outside financial planners and brokerage firms without mentioning Schwab. Schwab pioneered the idea of linking brokerage customers with third-party advisors. Today, Schwab through its AdvisorSource program can hook up a client with one of hundreds of fee-only financial advisors and money managers, who are located throughout the country. For those who only desire a second opinion on their holdings, Schwab also provides a portfolio consultation for a flat fee.

In an effort to be one-stop financial shops, the full-service discounters offer the gamut of financial products from mortgages to life insurance, as well as credit cards and ATM access.

Other investors, however, value rock-bottom commissions above all else. They are more likely to find them at cut-rate discounters, which cater to hard-core stock traders. These discounters provide cheap trading and little else. You can't expect any hand holding from these firms. They tend to attract experienced investors who value such things as real-time portfolio updates, after-hours trading, low-margin interest rates, and access to initial public offerings.

Another option is to establish a discount brokerage account with a mutual fund company that you like. Some of the major no-load fund companies, such as Vanguard, T. Rowe Price, Strong and American Century, operate their own discount brokerage arms. Through these fund companies, investors can trade stocks, bonds and invest in thousands of mutual funds. You are not limited to a fund family's own in-house fund lineup. Typically, the stock commissions are in the $20 range.

Tip

Regardless of which brokerage firm you choose, ease slowly into the new relationship. Consider depositing the minimum amount of money necessary to open an account and see how it goes for a couple of months. If you are happy with the service, transfer as much as you'd like into the account.

Researching brokerage firms

Finding a brokerage firm that makes a comfortable fit is definitely worth your time. Here's what you need to keep in mind when you're analyzing brokerage firms:

Commission structure

Understand a firm's commission structure. That's important whether you are gravitating toward a full-service or a discounter.

Keep in mind that advertised rates that brag about brokerage commission that cost about the same as a couple of McDonald's value meals don't reveal the whole story. A commission of $8 or $9 or less might be reserved for big customers who trade in large blocks of, say, 1,000 or 5,000 shares. Or they might be reserved for clients who maintain a minimum account balance or make a certain number of trades during a month or year.

Trading with a limit order usually costs more than trading with a market order. The advertised commission rates are commonly reserved for market orders. Placing a market order usually enables an investor to purchase shares within a couple of seconds or less after placing the order online. Typically, a brokerage firm charges a commission that is several dollars more for a limit order.

Once again, you have to evaluate what kind of an investor you are when determining how heavily commission rates should play in your deliberations. If you rarely trade, a few dollars difference will be inconsequential.

Customer service

Customer service is one of the more important areas to evaluate. How easy is it to invest through a given brokerage firm by phone or online? If you are primarily an online investor, start by navigating around a broker's Web pages. Is the Web site laid out intuitively or does it take many minutes and countless clicks of the mouse to find information? If you aren't sure what to hunt for, try to find the broker's fee schedule, its list of available mutual funds, and its phone number.

Also call a broker's toll-free number at different times of the day and note how long you're stuck on hold. Once you reach the firm, ask questions to determine how helpful the individuals are. Unless you intend to invest exclusively online or by phone, find out where a firm's offices are nearest you. If you're a night owl, you'll want to know whether the brokerage firm keeps the same hours as a 7-11.

The brokerage industry comes under considerable criticism during those occasional periods when everybody is anxious to trade at the same time. During periods of tremendous market volatility, thousands of people are trying to trade simultaneously, which strains a broker's infrastructure. What can you do to protect yourself? Probably not much. You just have to keep dialing (or clicking).

Tip   Consider maintaining an account at more than one firm. That way, you increase your chances of getting through during a trading traffic jam when you feel your trade is absolutely essential.

Mutual fund selection

Although most of today's investors own mutual funds, brokerage customers often overlook scrutinizing a broker's mutual fund services. This oversight can be a horrible mistake. If you primarily invest in mutual funds, a broker's fund policies could be a real deal breaker.

Note   A broker's fund pricing can be much more critical and costly than stock commissions.

A logical question to ask up front is the number of funds a broker carries. Some brokerages offer more than 10,000 while others keep 1,000 to 2,000 or even fewer on the shelves. Sheer numbers, however, shouldn't necessary impress you. What's more important is whether the funds you desire are included in the inventory. Does the broker offer the most popular and well-regarded fund families? Although fund aficionados will argue about who belongs on the list, they no doubt would include such no-load fund families as Vanguard, Fidelity, Janus, American Century, Invesco, T. Rowe Price, and Oak Associates. Some brokers offer all these fund families while others do not.

Tip   Some brokerage firms, such as Merrill Lynch, Schwab, E*Trade, and Fidelity, list all the mutual funds in their inventory, or at least all the fund families, on their Web sites for visitors and customers alike. These postings can greatly speed up your research.

Find out about fees.

Just as importantly, you want to determine what a particular broker charges for mutual fund trades. Some brokers offer certain funds gratis; you don't pay anything. These funds are sometimes referred to as NTF, which stands for "no transaction fee." Getting something for nothing is great, but some funds don't get this free ride. In many cases, you, the customer, are charged for buying shares though a broker's fund network. In some cases, the cost may seem pricey.

Example   Recently, Schwab was charging customers a percentage of a fund's purchase price to handle the transactions for funds that weren't in its NTF program. The minimum price for a fund trade was $35, but the cost could go as high as $149. In contrast, Datek was charging a flat $9.99.

The fund transaction fees can hurt your investing plans. Suppose you're a big fan of Vanguard and want to invest each month in the Vanguard Total Stock Market Index Fund through your Schwab account. If you proceed, you're committing financial suicide. Why? Because Schwab and every other brokerage firm will charge you for each Vanguard purchase. Vanguard, which is a stickler for keeping expenses low for its shareholders, doesn't compensate any broker for playing middleman on trades. Because the Pennsylvania fund company doesn't reimburse brokerage firms, customers must compensate them.

Don't dollar-cost average when fees are triggered.

Here's the bottom line for brokerage customers: Don't use dollar-cost averaging to invest in a fund that triggers transaction fees. If you have your heart set on regularly investing in such a fund, invest directly with a fund family where every purchase is free. That's certainly what you should do if you want to invest automatically in a Vanguard fund. Call up Vanguard through its toll-free number and establish an account.

For an explanation of dollar-cost averaging, see Chapter 3.

Redeem yourself by avoiding redemption fees.

One more mutual fund fee is relevant to hyperkinetic traders: Brokers reserve the right to charge a redemption fee if an investor exits a fund too quickly. For example, some brokers charge a fee if a fund isn't held for at least a year. Others rely upon a six-month holding period. In contrast, some brokers don't penalize even the most fickle fund investor.

Note Redemption fees are not necessarily a bad thing. Frequent trading has never proven to be a successful investment strategy, and these fees certainly discourage it.

Miscellaneous fees

Some brokerage firms excel at nickel-and-diming investors. You can be charged for wire transfers, transferring assets out of an account, account inactivity, and IRA maintenance. You may also be hit with an annual account fee and charged for duplicate statements or trade confirmations. To prevent the fees from piling up, you first need to be aware of what they are. Uncovering miscellaneous fees is another good reason to read all the fine print when you sign up with a brokerage firm.

Bell and whistles

Some brokerage firms have no interest in offering anything but the basics. Imagine a car dealer who wouldn't sell automobiles that come with leather seats, sunroofs, and other nonessentials. If the extras are important to you, find out which firms offer what features. What follows are some of the additional features that are available. You'll want to ask what the costs are, if any, for these extras.

Private money management

An increasing number of affluent investors are seeking the services of professional money management firms. Usually a person must be worth several million dollars for a firm to express interest. But wealthy individuals who use brokerages as intermediaries can get in the door with much smaller amounts, say $100,000 or $200,000. The full-service brokerage firms typically refer to their matchmaking services as *wrap programs*. Schwab links some of its high-net worth customers with U.S. Trust Corp., a traditional wealth-management enclave, which it recently acquired. Find out what you can expect from these services and what the investing track records and fees are.

Financial planning matchmaking

Some brokerage firms, including Schwab and E*Trade, hook up customers with financial planners in their area who meet or exceed a firm's standards. Meanwhile, Fidelity is just now getting into the field. The Schwab AdvisorSource program, which is the oldest, requires that a financial advisor, who pays a fee to participate, oversee at least $25 million in assets, and all advisors must shun commissions. If you are a full-service customer and are being provided a financial advisor, it's important to know what his or her qualifications are. Learn what the acronym's on an advisor's business card really means.

Trusts and estate planning

Historically, even people who preferred the discounters tended to move their money elsewhere when their net worth increased considerably and their financial lives became more complicated. Full-service brokerage firms have specialized in catering to the very wealthy, who typically need help with more complicated estate and trust needs. Major discounters are trying to retain rich clients by offering trust, estate planning, and private banking services.

Stock research

Brokers offer a wealth of stock research from both in-house and independent sources, such as Standard & Poor's, First Call, Argus Research, Lehman Brothers and Vickers. For some investors, this research is free. Whether a customer qualifies to receive these extra services often depends upon how much money he or she has stashed at the broker. For discount brokerage firm investors, better research and other perks typically begin when portfolios reach $100,000. The next big improvement in services typically occurs at the $500,000 mark. Active traders who have smaller accounts often qualify for the upgraded services as well.

Tip   A husband and wife can total up all the money they have invested at a discount brokerage firm in various accounts (such as IRAs, college funds, and a joint account) in an effort to qualify for red carpet treatment.

Tax services

Some brokers are quite helpful to investors at tax time. Fidelity, for instance, provides customer with year-end tax statements in addition to the required 1099 forms. Some discounters provide 1099 forms online. Meanwhile, certain brokers track the cost basis for funds or stocks that are transferred from other firms. This information comes in handy when an investor is ready to sell. E*Trade and Fidelity allow online investors to identify which specific stocks and mutual fund shares they want to sell online. (In Chapter 25, you'll learn why identifying shares for sale can dramatically shrink your capital gains tax obligations.) Some brokers, however, permit investors to do this only if they call the their toll-free numbers. Incredibly, other brokers don't allow investors to identify specific stocks or funds for sale at all.

Banking services

Some people no longer maintain a checking account with a bank. They prefer conducting all their financial dealings through a brokerage account. If this prospect appeals to you, find out what a prospective broker offers. Can you write checks, use automatic bill pay, and obtain credit and ATM cards just as you could through a bank? How much do check privileges cost and what are the annual expenses of the firm's money markets? If you get the right answers from the brokerage, you may be able to kiss your bank good-bye.

Note Encroaching even further on bank territory, some discounters and full-service brokers now make home loans.

Wireless trading

Some brokerage firms offer wireless trading, which requires such devices as Palm Pilots, Web-enabled cell phones, and two-way pagers. Wireless trading works the same way as online trading. You can buy or sell stock and mutual funds, obtain stock quotes, retrieve financial news and manage your portfolio by using a handheld device. Because wireless trading is relatively new, services can vary significantly. For instance, while some brokerage firms permit mutual fund and options transactions, others may not. The amount of financial data you can obtain on a stock will also vary.

Summary

✦ When evaluating brokerage firms, look at how outside sources have rated the candidates.

✦ Determine whether you want to sign on with a full-service or a discount brokerage firm.

✦ Scrutinize a brokerage firm based on services you consider important.

✦ Always check the background of any broker or brokerage firm that you are considering.

✦   ✦   ✦

Finding the Best Financial Advice

In this chapter, you will discover what choices are available if you
need financial guidance. Even though hundreds of thousands of
people call themselves financial advisors, whittling down your choices
to a handful of promising candidates is relatively easy. You just have to
know where to look and what questions to ask. This chapter also provides tips for finding attorneys who specialize in estate planning.

What Can a Planner Do for You?

All too often, we wear blinders when we look at our investments. We may obsess about whether we should sink money
into a promising telecommunications stock or a safer value
play, but it doesn't occur to us to examine how that investment would affect the mix of assets we have stashed elsewhere. We may focus on saving for a child's college years but
fail to consider how saving for college expenses might jeopardize our retirement goals. Or we may make investment decisions without thinking about the tax consequences.
Ultimately, our investments end up scattered like puzzle
pieces in a box. A good financial planner gathers the scattered
pieces and snaps them into one big picture.

A planner not only examines how you should be investing
your money, but also evaluates whether you are spending
your cash wisely. Before making any recommendations, a
good planner will want to know a lot more about you than
about your folder full of financial documents. A planner is like
a family physician: Although a cardiologist is concerned only
with your heart, a general practitioner checks you out from
head to toe.

A financial planner commonly provides the following services:

✦ Helps identify your investment goals

✦ Determines your risk tolerance

✦ Recommends appropriate investments

✦ Monitors your holdings and keeps you apprised of their performance

✦ Provides you with independent analysis of your investments from such organizations as Morningstar, Value Line, and Standard & Poor's

✦ Stays in touch via periodic written reports and telephone calls

✦ Teaches you the fundamentals of investing

✦ Troubleshoots

Finding a Qualified Financial Planner

If you conclude that you could use some outside advice, the first hurdle will be deciding whom to call. The choices can seem overwhelming. Depending upon whom you ask, anywhere from 100,000 to 200,000 people classify themselves as financial planners or advisors. Unlike some other professional fields, financial planning is still in its infancy. Consequently, these folks are not uniformly trained or regulated as doctors, lawyers, beauticians, or even undertakers are. Among those who call themselves financial planners or consultants are stockbrokers, insurance agents, tax preparers, accountants, money managers, and lawyers.

You can narrow the field considerably by limiting yourself to looking for a Certified Financial Planner (CFP). The CFP designation is not easy to earn, and it comes as close to a badge of honor for the profession as any other designation.

To qualify for the CFP designation, an individual must have three years of financial planning experience and pass a rigorous two-day exam. The test's pass rate is a mere 63 percent. In addition, to maintain certification (and to keep from getting rusty), CFPs must meet continuing education requirements.

The Certified Financial Planner Board of Standards oversees the CFP licensing process. This nonprofit regulatory group was started in the mid-1980s out of a frustration that no uniform standards existed for the profession. By 2001, 36,307 planners were licensed to use the CFP mark.

 Resource

Before selecting a planner, request a free Financial Planning Resource Kit from the CFP Board of Standards at www.cfp-board.org or (888) CFP-MARK. The materials in the kit include questions you should ask a prospective financial planner, as well as reasons why you may need a financial planner's services.

Double-checking on a CFP

Cynical as it might sound, don't assume that prospective advisors are CFPs just because they say they are. Double-check with the CFP Board of Standards to discover whether a planner really is a CFP and whether he has been the target of the board's disciplinary arm.

You should also contact the board if you think a CFP has been unscrupulous. The board, which requires its members to follow a strict code of ethics, will investigate your complaint. Since 1987, the board has taken disciplinary action against nearly 1,500 CFPs.

Sources for CFPs

After you determine that you need a CFP, your next step is to flush out CFP candidates. CFPs belong to different professional organizations, but two main groups exist. Either will be glad to provide you with a list of CFPs in your area.

National Association of Personal Financial Advisors

The National Association of Personal Financial Advisors is by far the most exclusive group. Almost all of its 700-plus members are CFPs; only advisors who work as fee-only planners can qualify for membership. (Later in this section, you learn why working with a fee-only planner may be advantageous.)

One reason for the small membership is the tough entrance requirements. For starters, the group refuses to accept any planner who takes commissions, which eliminates the majority of CFPs from consideration. What's more, an outside expert (the current one is a former state securities official) scrutinizes the documents a planner must file with the Securities and Exchange Commission or her state of residence. In addition, an actual financial plan, pulled from a planner's own files, must pass a NAFPA review. The continuing education requirements are high as well. You can contact NAPFA at 355 W. Dundee Rd., Suite 200, Buffalo Grove, Il 60089; (888) FEE-ONLY; www.napfa.org.

Financial Planning Association

The Financial Planning Association (FPA) is the nation's largest organization of Certified Financial Planners. But not everyone in this massive association of 29,000 members is a CFP. Membership is also open to stockbrokers, lawyers, money managers, planned giving consultants, accountants, and other financial professionals.

The FPA has made it easy to wade through the hodge-podge of professionals by providing folks searching for a financial planner with names of CFPs only. Right now, the organization's referral database holds information on 4,000 CFPs. You can obtain these names by contacting the FPA at (800) 282-PLAN or www.fpanet.org.

CPAs and Financial Planning

A growing number of certified public accountants, who have often been thought of strictly as tax experts, are getting into the personal finance field. If you would like to find a CPA who specializes in personal finance, contact the Personal Financial Planning Division of the American Institute of Certified Public Accountants (AICPA) at 1211 Avenue of the Americas New York, NY 10036; (888) 999-9256; www.aicpa.org.

One way to gauge whether a CPA is committed to financial planning is to ask whether she has extra certification. A CPA specializing in financial planning can earn a designation of personal finance specialist (PFS) through the AICPA. To become credentialed, a CPA must have devoted at least 250 hours to financial planning work each year for the past three years. A candidate must also submit six references to substantiate the work experience and pass a rigorous exam. About 3,000 CPAs have earned the PFS designation.

Understanding planner compensation

How a planner gets paid is more important than you may realize. Financial planners are compensated in three ways:

✦ Commissions

✦ Fee-only

✦ Fee-based

Commissions: Conflict of interest?

Commissioned planners earn money by selling you investments. The more your planner buys and sells on your behalf, the more money he makes. The planner is paid by the financial institution, such as a mutual fund firm or an insurance company, that offers the product—but ultimately this money comes from you.

Caution   Working with a commission-based planner might seem like a great way to get free financial advice, but proceed with caution. The arrangement can create a worrisome conflict of interest for your planner.

If the planner expects to earn money, she will have to recommend investments wrapped with loads or sales charges. The loads, which can run as low as 1 or 2 percent or as high as 8 or 10 percent or more, provide the money that generates the commission.

To customers, it appears as though they are paying nothing for their financial makeover. After all, the planner doesn't present his customers with an invoice after the work is completed. But those customers do pay a price nonetheless. In fact, they could end up paying for the planner's advice many, many years after parting company with him.

Example

Suppose a planner selects mutual funds that carry an average upfront load of 5 percent. If $100,000 is invested in these funds, a total of $5,000 is pulled from the account to compensate the planner. The client's "free" financial plan end up costing him $5,000.

An even greater financial hit lies in wait if the planner recommends *level load* mutual funds. With a level load or *C shares,* there is no upfront or back-end sale charge if the shares are held for at least 18 months on average. Unfortunately, these funds have become incredibly popular among investors, who believe they are gaining access to funds without a load. But the costs for these funds are considerable because the funds carry higher annual expenses than do other funds, and you pay these higher costs for as long as you hold the fund.

Caution

If a financial planner recommends that you buy level load mutual funds or C shares, question him or her closely. Typically, C shares are the most expensive investment option.

By necessity, commissioned planners often ignore great investment opportunities if they don't provide a commission. For instance, these planners are unlikely to recommend buying a Vanguard index fund because Vanguard won't pay a cent for the referral. Or a planner might select a technology fund that carries a load rather than buy shares in the Nasdaq-100 Index Tracking Stock, an exchange-traded fund that is commonly referred to as a *Qube* (so named for its QQQ ticker symbol), which provides instant exposure to technology stocks at a minimal price. On the other hand, a planner hungry for a big commission might be tempted to recommend a whole life insurance policy that can provide a 100 percent load during the first year when all the client needs is a cheap term life insurance policy.

Tip

Funds that carry upfront loads, or *A shares,* are usually preferable. Ask the planner for a long-range expense comparison of different types of shares, as well as the historical performance statistics of each load alternative.

The potential conflict of interest doesn't mean that commissioned planners can't be ethical advisors who make good investment choices. Many of them are. But you have to keep in mind that your universe of potential investments will shrink if you rely upon one of these planners.

Fee-only: Financial press favorite

Fee-only planners bill you for their service, just as a doctor or dentist would. They don't make money through commissions. Some planners charge a flat rate for a comprehensive financial plan; others charge a percentage of the assets they manage for you. If a planner manages your portfolio, you may end up paying .5 percent to 1.5 percent of the value of your assets for the service.

Tip

If you have a relatively simple financial decision to make, such as whether to buy or lease a car or how to save for a college education, a planner may charge by the hour for the specific advice. Fees vary by geographic area.

The financial press clearly favors the fee-only planner. In theory, these advisors can recommend the best investments because you, not an investment firm, are paying for the advice. These planners are free to make wise investment recommendations without worrying about their own livelihood. Because they don't accept commissions, they won't be tempted to tinker with a portfolio just to generate income for themselves. With you paying the bill, these planners aren't limited to a smaller universe of investments that generate commissions.

However, a major source of angst among fee-only planners is what constitutes an appropriate fee structure. Many of these planners charge a percentage of the assets for portfolios they oversee. For instance, if a planner is managing a $150,000 portfolio for a 1 percent annual fee, the charge will be $1,500. Say the same planner has another client with a $1 million portfolio who also pays the same 1 percent fee. The richer client's yearly tab is $10,000. But what if the planner devoted the same amount of time to both accounts? Is it fair that the richer customer had to fork over an extra $8,500?

Another potential drawback for fee-only planners is that some have become downright snooty. As the practices of the more successful planners have grown, the type of clients they accept narrows. Some take on new prospective clients only if their investments total in the mid to high six figures or more. Because there are fewer fee-only planners, it can be more difficult, but certainly not impossible, to find one.

Tip   If you use a fee-only planner, be sure to negotiate on price. The fatter your portfolio, the bigger the price cut should be. A planner who charges a 1 percent annual fee to oversee smaller accounts should be willing to slash that fee for a larger portfolio.

Fee-based: Not necessarily the best of both worlds

With the media noisily steering customers to fee-only planners, the industry is responding. Many commissioned planners would like to kick the commission habit, but it's difficult to do so without jeopardizing their near-term business.

Consequently, an increasing number of planners are trying to have it both ways. So-called fee-based planners earn their living through a combination of fees and commissions. These planners might charge a reduced rate to draw up a comprehensive plan. They will then select mutual funds and other investment products, some of which carry a load and will reimburse the planners for the work. These same planners may agree to work on a fee-only basis for you.

But combining fees and commissions can be a tricky situation. Because such planners spend more of their time recommending commission products, they'll probably do the same for you even though you are paying for their advice. Even if a fee-based planner does recommend no-load products, he or she might not be as familiar with them. This arrangement may also make it difficult for you to understand how the compensation works. A planner's ADV Form (covered in the next section) should shed some light on the compensation structure.

Financial Planning Versus Estate Planning

Although a CFP can assist you with a great many of your financial needs, there are limits to what a CFP can do. You may find you'll also need a tax attorney, a CPA or some other type of expert. If you haven't prepared an estate plan, which can be a critical component of your overall financial plan, you'll need to seek the help of an estate planning attorney.

Ideally, you'll want to hire a lawyer who specializes in trusts and estates. These attorneys are more likely to keep up with the frequent changes in this area of the law. An excellent resource to contact is the American College of Trust and Estate Counsel. This group invites only attorneys who have substantially contributed to this field to join. A prospective member must have at least 10 years of estate-planning experience. Contact the American College of Trust and Estate Counsel at 3415 S. Sepulveda Blvd., Suite 330 Los Angeles, CA 90034; (310) 398-1888; www.actec.org.

Another resource is your own state bar. Some bars, such as those in California, Texas, and North Carolina, issue estate-planning certification for experienced estate-planning lawyers. To receive the credentialing, an attorney typically must be a veteran in the field, pass periodic exams, and regularly satisfy continuing education requirements.

Although your state or local bar associations can provide names of lawyers practicing estate planning, they can't recommend specific attorneys. You must whittle down the choices. These two Web sites can provide the appropriate link for your own state bar:

✦ Findlaw.com at www.findlaw.com

✦ California State Bar at www.calbar.org

Another excellent source is Martindale-Hubbell, which compiles voluminous information about attorneys and law firms in 160 nations. You can hunt for an attorney practicing estate planning, or some other specialty, in your area by visiting Martindale-Hubbell's Web site at www.martindale.com. By using the "Lawyer Locator," you can discover many handy things, such as where certain attorneys attended law school, what their specialties are, and whether they hold memberships in various bar associations.

Checking Out Your Candidates

Before you hire a financial planner, do some digging. Pore over a candidate's ADV Form, which can be obtained from either the U.S. Securities and Exchange Commission or your state securities department. (ADV is short for advisor.) A planner files this paperwork with the SEC if he or she manages at least $25 million in client assets. Those overseeing smaller amounts file their ADV Form with their respective state securities departments. You can find the appropriate phone number for a state agency by contacting the North American Securities Administrators Association. Here is the contact information for both agencies:

Software Razzle-Dazzle

Don't be instantly impressed if your financial advisor or broker provides you with a binder full of glossy charts, all seemingly geared toward your own personal needs. Looks can be deceiving. With financial planning software that's dirt cheap and abundant, a lazy or mediocre advisor can create what looks like a detailed, personalized plan within a few minutes. A *Consumer Reports* journalist derisively called these glossy printouts McPlans.

✦ Securities and Exchange Commission, Office of Public Reference, 450 Fifth St. NW, Room 1300, Washington, DC 20549; (202) 942-8090; www.sec.gov

✦ North American Securities Administrators Association, 10 G St. NE, Suite 710, Washington, DC 20002; (202) 737-0900; www.nasaa.org

Although the ADV Form isn't the easiest document to read, it can be a treasure trove of information about an individual advisor. Here's what you can find in the document:

✦ Education

✦ Professional history

✦ Disciplinary record

✦ Lawsuits and arbitration proceedings

✦ How the advisor is paid

✦ Types of investments the advisor recommends

✦ Potential conflicts of interest

You can request a copy of the ADV Form from your potential advisor as well. Note that the ADV Form consists of two parts, but any juicy stuff is in Part I. Ironically, an investment advisor is legally obligated to provide you only with Part II. If a financial planner hasn't filled out this form or doesn't want to provide you with a copy, cross that candidate off your list. Be sure to read both parts.

 Resource   Another excellent resource is the Martindale-Hubbell Law Directory, which maintains profiles of hundreds of thousands of attorneys and firms worldwide. You can reach its Web site at www.lawyers.com.

Questions to Ask a Financial Planner

Your job isn't over once you obtain a list of names of financial planners. Talk to a few of these planners to get a sense of who would make the best fit. If you think this process could turn into an expensive fishing expedition, don't fret. Many financial planners do not charge anything for an introductory meeting. If the planner insists on billing you, request that the fee be applied to the development of your financial plan later. Obviously, you'll lose this money if you ultimately choose someone else.

Once you're in the candidate's office, ask these key questions:

- ✦ What is your professional background and credentials?
- ✦ How much experience do you have in this field?
- ✦ How many continuing education classes have you taken in the past year?
- ✦ What kind of financial planning services do you provide?
- ✦ Do you specialize in a particular area, such as estate planning, high net-worth individuals, retirement planning, employee benefits, or divorce?
- ✦ How are you paid? Do you negotiate on price?
- ✦ Will you provide a written analysis of my financial situation, along with recommendations?
- ✦ Do you have a particular bias towards an investment style, such as value or growth? (See Chapter 12 for an explanation of these two styles.)
- ✦ Do you recommend specific investments?
- ✦ Can you show me a sample financial plan?
- ✦ Will I maintain control of my assets? Where will my assets be held?
- ✦ Are most of your clients individuals? What is the typical size of your clients' accounts?
- ✦ What do you need to know about me?
- ✦ Can you provide me with professional references?
- ✦ Have you ever been disciplined by a regulatory body or professional organization?
- ✦ What is your investment track record?

Even if a prospective planner answers all your questions satisfactorily, you have to feel comfortable with him or her. If the planner is haughty or incapable of explaining investment concepts in plain English, look elsewhere.

Bailing Out

Once you've begun working with a financial advisor, you should never continue the relationship if you feel uncomfortable with it. Plenty of evidence points to a lot of unhealthy relationships out there. A study by the AARP, for instance, concluded that many older persons don't understand their investments and feel pressured to buy financial products. In the survey, one-third of these investors said they didn't understand the brochures and other written materials that their financial advisors handed them. What's more, one in five said they felt pushed by their advisor to invest in something they didn't want or comprehend. Here's another worrisome sign: One in four advisors and brokers didn't explain to their clients how much they'd be paying in transaction fees. Remember, it's your money, and you should take it elsewhere if you don't receive simple and satisfactory explanations.

Summary

✦ If you need a financial makeover, consider seeking help from a Certified Financial Planner.

✦ Be clear on how your planner's compensation structure affects the structure and value of your portfolio.

✦ Before hiring a planner, scrutinize his or her ADV Form.

✦ Don't ignore your estate planning needs, a crucial element of any financial plan.

✦ If you aren't completely comfortable with a planner once you've begun to work with him, find one who does inspire confidence.

✦   ✦   ✦

All Flavors of Funds

In the next six chapters, you'll be introduced to mutual fund investment strategies, a list of recommendations and a primer on the nuts and bolts of trading funds. You'll also learn why exchange-traded funds, a cross between mutual funds and stocks, are generating so much interest.

Mutual Fund ABCs

✦   ✦   ✦   ✦

In This Chapter

Understanding how
mutual funds tick

Appreciating the pros
and cons of mutual
funds

✦   ✦   ✦   ✦

In this chapter, you learn how mutual funds work and how they fit in your portfolio. Not only does this chapter cover the pros and cons of investing in mutual funds, but it also helps you choose between growth and value funds. Finally, this chapter provides an ideal mutual fund source for any cash-strapped investor.

How a Mutual Fund Works

A mutual fund pools the money of thousands of different shareholders just like you. You might send in a $2,000 check, and on the same day, the mailbags emptied at a fund's offices will contain hundreds of other checks, some as small as $50 and others many times that amount. Other investors who want their money invested more quickly send still more money to the fund electronically. On any given day, millions of dollars can gush into the most popular funds.

By some measures, mutual funds have never been so popular. Nearly 8,300 mutual funds exist today. In recent years, investors have poured cash into funds with all the fervor of slot-machine addicts depositing dollars in Vegas. The cash that's sitting in these funds has swelled to more than $6.6 trillion. Today, 88 million Americans—nearly half of all American households—own shares in a mutual fund.

What happens to all this cash? The fund managers spend their days investing your money in stocks, bonds, or other assets. The beauty of this arrangement is that you can own a tiny piece of a huge portfolio of individual stocks or bonds just by holding a few fund shares, which means your investments are diversified.

How's Your Fund IQ?

Have you mastered the art of mutual fund investing? If you aren't sure, visit the Vanguard Group's Web site (www.vanguard.com). Every year, the fund family conducts a mutual funds quiz with *Money* magazine. Despite the media blitz on mutual funds, most Americans do poorly on the test. Vanguard has posted quite a few quizzes on topics ranging from asset allocation to mutual fund and taxes. To see the complete list, type **quizzes** into the Web site's search function.

Diversification in action

Suppose you invest $3,000 in Bridgeway Aggressive Growth, a successful fund that can cherry pick companies of any size. Your money is spread thinly across all the stocks in the Bridgeway portfolio. Recently that would have meant that you owned Ford Motor Company and Chevron, along with some volatile tech companies, such as Advanced Micro Devices and JDS Uniphase. Your investment would also give you a stake in some off-beat picks, such Salton Inc., the appliance maker that makes indoor grills that former boxer George Foreman hawks on infomercials.

Chances are it would never occur to you to invest in such a jumble of different corporate sizes and styles. Even if it did, you most likely would not possess the knowledge to pull off such an investment combination successfully. Of course, if you were investing just $3,000, your money wouldn't stretch very far anyway. You'd be lucky if the money could buy 100 shares of any of the previously mentioned stocks.

Drawbacks of single stocks and bonds

Why is investing in many companies preferable to betting on just one? One stock is going to be a lot more volatile. Consider the stock performance of JDS Uniphase, one of the stocks in Bridgeway portfolio. During a recent 12-month period, the stock plunged from a high of $140 a share to $13. Most investors would have a hard time handling that kind of volatility. But if you own a mutual fund, JDS Uniphase's misfortune is theoretically neutralized by other companies in the portfolio that are doing just fine. A fund's built-in diversification reduces your risk.

Shareholders of bond funds enjoy the same diversification. If you want to own individual bonds, you need at least $50,000 to $100,000 to develop a well-rounded, fixed-income portfolio. After all, just one municipal bond can cost $5,000, and some bonds can require a commitment of at least $25,000. A bond fund, on the other hand, contains dozens or even hundreds of different bonds. If one bond issuer's credit rating slips or the bond issuer defaults, the impact isn't nearly as devastating for a bond fund investor as it is for an individual who sunk all of his or her cash into a small clutch of bonds.

Mutual Funds Pros and Cons

As you'll learn later on in the chapter, mutual funds are feeling the heat from more experienced investors for a variety of reasons. For the foreseeable future, however, mutual funds will play an integral part in most investors' portfolios, with good reason. However, mutual funds do have their drawbacks, and those are covered in this section as well.

Mutual fund advantages

Here are the best arguments to be made for investing in mutual funds:

Your money is managed professionally.

Invest in funds and you don't have to be a financial wizard. Professional money managers strategize about the best ways to invest your cash, so you don't have to. These folks slavishly work long hours to uncover the best investments and are aided by many resources to help shape and monitor the fund's portfolio. In addition, fund managers can react quicker to changing market conditions than you ever could hope to do.

Caution

Of course, you want to select a fund that is run by a seasoned manager. With one or two new funds being launched just about every day, untested managers can be thrust into starring roles.

You have a wide variety of funds to choose from.

No one can accuse the fund industry of failing to provide investors with enough choices. The sheer number of funds is vast, but so too is the variety. Funds can satisfy just about any investing desire from wireless networking stocks to overseas bonds. Stock funds are, by far, the most popular choice for Americans, and the runaway leader of the pack has recently been the large-cap stock fund, which invests in America's biggest companies. The major types of funds are listed here:

For stock investors:

- ✦ Large-cap funds
- ✦ Mid-cap funds
- ✦ Small-cap funds
- ✦ Index funds
- ✦ International funds

✦ Sector funds, including

technology, utilities,

telecommunications, natural resources,

health care, retail,

financials, consumer durables,

gold, and real estate

For bond investors:

✦ Treasury bond funds

✦ Mortgage-backed securities funds

✦ Municipal bond funds

✦ Intermediate bond funds

✦ Investment-grade corporate bond funds

✦ High-yield (junk) bond funds

✦ Multisector funds

✦ Global bond funds

For stock and bond investors:

✦ Asset allocation funds

✦ Balanced funds

For an explanation of such stock-related terms as *large-cap, value investing,* and *index,* see Chapter 12. For a quick primer on bond terms, see Chapter 17.

You can pick a fund with the appropriate investing style.

Funds also provide a variety of different investing approaches. You can choose an investing style that meets your comfort level.

Differences in investment style are most notable with stock funds. Stock funds come in three main styles:

✦ Growth

✦ Value

✦ Blend, which is a mix of the other two

Growth funds

Growth funds typically invest in corporations that are experiencing rapid growth in sales and earnings. They may specialize in large or small companies or some combination of both. Usually, large-cap growth managers gravitate to stocks that most people would instantly recognize, such as Oracle, Intel, and Wal-Mart. Throughout the past decade, growth and value funds have taken turns posting better year-end records, but growth has generated more robust returns overall during this period.

In recent years, a significant portion of the typical growth fund's edge could be traced back to a heavy reliance upon technology stocks. Growth funds, which tend to gravitate to riskier stocks, can fall harder during a bear market.

Note Growth stocks tend to plow profits back into their companies to fuel further expansion. You won't see these companies spinning off generous dividends to stockholders.

Value funds

Managers of value funds share something in common with garage-sale scroungers: They like bargains. They are always on the look out for cheap stocks. Value managers tend to snap up shares in unglamorous stocks in mature industries that boast only modest growth prospects. Value fans also favor turnaround plays, which are companies that may be experiencing financial problems, perhaps even bankruptcy, but are expected to recover. Often value funds contain stocks that are simply undervalued compared with the underlying assets of the companies. Typically these stocks offer higher than average dividends.

Is Your Fund Creepy?

Pinpointing whether a fund invests in growth or value can be tricky. A study by the Schwab Center for Investment Research analyzed a common phenomenon that's called *style creep*. During a four-year period, researchers discovered that 25 percent of growth funds and 3 out of every 10 value funds changed their style. The biggest shift was spotted among actively managed blended funds, which are blend funds that don't track an index. In contrast, index funds remained true to their style mandate.

The study's findings aren't surprising. Until recently, the U.S. Securities and Exchange Commission (SEC) required that a fund devote at least 65 percent of its money into investments that match its published mission, a figure that granted fund managers great latitude. Consequently, a value fund would still have room to stock up on Internet stocks if it desired, or a government bond fund could conceivably sink a big chunk of money into risky junk or overseas bonds.

In 2001, the SEC began requiring that a fund devote at least 80 percent of its cash to investments that stick to its stated goal. Thanks to some exemptions to this rule, wiggle room still exists. If a fund's investing style is a moving target, how can you find out what you have? Check with Morningstar, an independent fund rating service and typically a reliable source. (Its contact information is in the Resource Guide.)

Note   During the past 20 years, the average value fund has exhibited only 75 percent of the volatility of the typical growth fund.

However, value funds can be less reliable during an economic downturn. During the 1990 recession, for instance, large-cap value funds lost 6.4 percent while growth funds dropped only 2.4 percent, according to Morningstar. This fact might seem surprising because value plays are considered less volatile, but value companies are much more likely to be classified as cyclicals, which makes them more sensitive to the nation's economic hiccups. Table 6-1 shows the track record for growth and value in the last decade.

Table 6-1 Performance of Value and Growth Funds		
Year	*Value*	*Growth*
1990	−7.7%	−4.2%
1991	29.9%	47.8%
1992	12.2%	7.9%
1993	14.5%	13.3%
1994	−.8%	−1.5%
1995	30.7%	33.7%
1996	21.7%	18.6%
1997	27.3%	20.8%
1998	7.5%	21.6%
1999	6.7%	52.7%
2000	10.4%	−9.2%
2001*	1.8%	−11.3%

* Performance through April 2001.

Source: Morningstar

Blend funds

Blend funds contain a mixture of growth and value plays. Sometimes a fund may be more heavily weighted toward value, and at other times it may be more biased toward growth. Most stock index funds fall into the blend category. For example, an index fund that mimics the Standard & Poor's 500 index contains tortoises, such as Eastman Kodak and J.C. Penney, as well as hard-charging stocks such as Applied Materials and AOL Time Warner.

Choosing value, growth, or somewhere in between

Should you buy a growth or a value fund? It doesn't have to be an either/or decision. When you're selecting a core fund to build a portfolio around, consider choosing a large-cap stock fund that blends both investing styles. By investing in both growth and value, you hedge your bets no matter which style is currently in vogue. An index fund linked to the Standard & Poor's 500 or the Wilshire 5000, which covers the entire market, is an excellent choice because it covers both investing flavors. To be properly diversified, investors should definitely include both value and growth in their portfolios.

Getting started is easy.

You need little cash to begin investing in a mutual fund. Fund companies really want your money, and many don't seem to care how little you have. Some fund families even let you start with no money down if you enroll in an automatic savings program. To enroll in such a program, you fill out simple paperwork that allows a fund to withdraw an agreed-upon amount, say $50 or $100, on the same day each month from your checking or savings account. The money is then invested in whatever fund you've selected.

Note Although some funds require minimums of $3,000 or $5,000, those minimums are often waived if you are establishing an Individual Retirement Account or a custodial account for your child's education.

Even the most exclusive funds may let you in if you just know what door to knock on. Institutional funds, which have historically catered to such deep-pocket clients as pension funds and endowments, have imposed minimum investments of $250,000 or much higher. But you can buy many of these funds for as little as $2,000 if you purchase them through a discount broker.

One of the most attractive features of institutional funds is their extremely cheap cost. Your investment can grow much faster when you aren't shelling out a lot of cash every year to pay a fund's expenses. This money, by the way, is pulled out automatically so most investors are unaware of how much they really are paying in annual fees. But like all funds, the quality of institutional funds varies. As with any investment, you need to do your homework before making a decision. Morningstar provides coverage of many notable institutional funds.

Mutual fund companies are solid institutions.

You can make the case that fund companies are safer than banks and savings and loans. After all, plenty of banks have failed over the years. But since the passage of the Federal Investment Company Act of 1940, which regulates the industry, not a single fund company has gone under. However, the money in your mutual funds is not protected by Federal Deposit Insurance Corporation (FDIC), which insures bank deposits. But when your mutual fund loses money it is because the underlying investments are doing poorly, not because the fund manager absconded with cash.

Ideal Funds for the Cash-Strapped Beginner

What if you want to get started in mutual funds, but you have little cash? An ideal source for beginning fund investors is TIAA-CREF (Teachers Insurance and Annuity Association-College Retirement Equities Fund). TIAA-CREF is a financial institution that traces its historic roots back to the philanthropist Andrew Carnegie, who launched it in 1918. TIAA-CREF, which operates the world's largest private pension system, has been successfully managing retirement money for millions of college professors and other educators since its inception. It wasn't until 79 years later, in 1997, that it opened its doors to the general public.

If you like the low cost and high quality of the Vanguard Group's mutual funds, you'll also appreciate TIAA-CREF. Vanguard's minimum initial investments range from $3,000 to $25,000, but the minimum investment for all TIAA-CREF funds is a mere $250. Subsequent investments can be as little as $25.

Another plus is that some of the funds, which enjoy solid performance records, can serve as core holdings for bond and stock holdings. Here are the candidates:

✦ TIAA-CREF Growth & Income

✦ TIAA-CREF Growth Equity

✦ TIAA-CREF Managed Allocation

✦ TIAA-CREF Bond Plus

The goal of both TIAA-CREF Growth & Income and TIAA-CREF Growth Equity is to outperform their respective benchmarks: the Standard & Poor's 500, which includes 500 of the America's largest corporations, and the Russell 3000, which represents America's 3,000 largest companies. Both funds try to outperform the indexes by a combination of indexing and active stock picks. (You'll learn how indexing works in Chapter 10.)

Meanwhile, the TIAA-CREF Managed Allocation fund invests 60 percent in its own stock funds, including some international exposure, and the rest is put in its bond fund. Bond Plus tracks the popular Lehman Brothers Aggregate Bond Index.

For more information about these funds, contact TIAA-CREF at (800) 223-1200 or www.tiaacref.com.

Mutual fund disadvantages

When you are considering investing in a mutual fund, take into account its weaknesses as well as its strengths.

Mutual funds can be tax nightmares.

Suppose you sank $10,000 in a stock whose value then goes through the roof. If you hold onto your shares, will you owe the government any capital gains taxes? The answer is most definitely no. What if you sunk the same amount of money into a mutual fund and the fund duplicates the performance? Will you owe taxes? You certainly may.

This ugly reality has soured some investors on mutual funds. Unlike with individual stocks, the IRS doesn't care if you hold onto your mutual fund shares—it's focused on what your fund manager does. If he or she trades stocks in the fund's portfolio, you will be liable for the fund's realized profits.

Note Strange as it may seem, a fund can post a negative return for the year and its shareholders could still be liable for capital gains taxes.

Why can funds be so tax inefficient? One reason is performance. To generate flashy short-term performance statistics, some managers feel compelled to frequently jump in and out of stocks. Trigger-happy trading, which is measured by what's called *portfolio turnover,* tends to generate more taxes. Up until the mid-1960s, portfolio turnover in the average mutual fund was roughly 15 percent year, which is quite low. Today the turnover has ballooned to 90 percent. That means fund managers are essentially selling nearly every stock they own in just a year's time.

Cross-Reference You'll learn how to evaluate a fund's tax efficiency in Chapter 25.

Fund companies can be expensive.

According to the Securities and Exchange Commission, mutual fund fees have climbed 19 percent during the past 20 years. This increase is truly remarkable if you remember the lessons from Economics 101: As demand increases, the cost of doing business decreases. The fund world, in other words, is defying economic logic. Fees should be going down, not up.

Caution High expenses can sabotage a fund's return. The SEC estimates that a 1 percent increase in fees over 20 years can reduce a long-term investor's ending fund balance by 18 percent.

Fund expenses are insidious. You aren't mailed a bill each year to pay for the fund's management services; the money is automatically taken out without any notice. Consequently, most people are unaware of the tab. In 2001, the SEC urged fund companies to share with investors how much they are paying each year in fees in real dollar figures rather than in percentages. The General Accounting Office, which is the investigative arm of Congress, went a step further by suggesting that fund companies send investors quarterly statements that list the fees in dollar figures.

Cross-Reference Plenty of low cost funds are available; you just need to know where to look. For more information on buying funds and on typical fund expenses, see Chapter 7.

Your investment goals may conflict with fund manager's.

By now, most people understand that they shouldn't invest in a mutual fund if they can't sit on the money a long time. Investing in a stock mutual fund, for instance, is a bad idea if you need the money to buy a house in three years. But although many shareholders have their eyes trained on the horizon, fund managers are often forced to act more like impatient short-term traders.

With the competition for dollars so intense, portfolio managers are squirming under intense pressure to turn in outstanding performances every quarter and year. This pressure can lead to dubious investment moves, such as dumping promising stocks near year's end and replacing them with the current hot picks, which may be horribly overvalued. When the year-end stock holdings are revealed in fund literature, the manager will look like he or she had been smart enough to invest in the market's leaders, a practice called *window dressing* within the industry. In reality, all this trading can sabotage returns rather than inflate them.

Funds can change owners.

You may have been happily sitting on a fund for years. You like the portfolio management, the fees are reasonable, and the returns have been good. Then one day, you get a letter announcing that another financial institution has purchased the fund. Such fund purchases have been happening with increasing frequency. Well-regarded fund companies such as Stein Roe, Acorn, Scudder, and Mutual Series have been gobbled up by firms that covet their former competitor's prestige name or stable of shareholders.

Caution   These business decisions dramatically impact the shareholders. Portfolio managers might leave, investment practices can change, funds that had been closed to new investors may be reopened. A push by the new owners to increase assets can harm the existing shareholders if portfolios become too large.

Another phenomenon that's even more disruptive is the disappearance of mutual funds. More than 200 funds have been disappearing each year. When a fund shuts down, a shareholder's money is returned or is transferred to another fund within the same company. If a fund really stinks, it could deserve to die. But critics say the practice of shuttering mediocre funds makes the industry's overall performance statistics look better than they really are. Imagine wiping 200 strikeouts from the record of baseball great Mark McGwire. That would make him look like even more of a baseball genius.

Summary

✦ Mutual funds are a solid way to diversify no matter how much money you have to invest.

✦ Stock fund investors need exposure to both growth and value investing styles.

✦ You should choose funds that charge low expenses and are tax efficient.

✦   ✦   ✦

All-Star Mutual Funds

This chapter will help you cut down on the hours it takes to assemble a first-rate mutual fund portfolio. Whether you want to dabble in overseas investing, find a top-notch bond fund, or focus on socially responsible funds, you need to know what types of funds are available and are appropriate for a well-rounded portfolio. Also included here are two handy investor cheat sheets: One lists top-performing funds in the major categories and the other outlines a yearly fund checkup to perform.

Pick Your Flavor: Stock Funds

Americans are confronted with so many demands that monopolize their free time that it's hardly surprising that many of us procrastinate when it comes to our finances. The prospects of sifting through thousands of fund choices can discourage even the most motivated investor. Consequently, assembling a well diversified portfolio is likely to be pushed down to the bottom of the to-do list.

You can simplify your search by finding out what kind of funds suit you and your portfolio. The following sections provide an overview of what's out there.

Cross-Reference If you're unsure of stock terminology, check out Chapter 12 or the Glossary as needed.

Large-cap stock funds

Just as you'll find salt and pepper shakers on most dinner tables, you'll find a core large-cap fund in many investors' portfolios. These funds are stuffed with many of America's best-known and oldest corporations. Typically, these corporations are more stable and less volatile than smaller outfits, which is one big reason why they are often used as a core holding. Companies such as Johnson & Johnson and Tootsie

Roll, which have been profitably selling Band-Aids and candy for generations, are generally going to reward investors while running a smooth ship.

Tip   If you're a long-term investor, building a portfolio around a large-cap stock fund is a smart idea. These funds are a perfect fit whether you are bankrolling a college education, saving for retirement, fattening an inheritance, or stashing away a year-end bonus.

Studies have shown that your best bet is putting most of the money in the large-cap stock category into an index fund. An index fund tends to hold all or many of the stocks that are contained in a specific stock benchmark, such as the Standard & Poor's 500 Index. You'll learn much more about index funds in Chapter 9.

Small-cap funds

Small-cap stock funds invest in corporate minnows. Typically they sink money into domestic companies that have market caps of $2 billion or less. Most small-cap stock funds invest in American companies, but small-cap foreign funds exist as well.

Historically, small-cap funds have experienced more heart-stopping moves in price than their large-cap peers. If you think about it, this makes sense. The little corporate players must fight and scratch just to survive. Many of them will ultimately fold, and only a few will truly hit the jackpot to join the ranks of the nation's corporate titans, such as General Electric and Wal-Mart. Because of the hazards, only long-term investors who can afford to let their money ride for at least several years should embrace them. Ironically, however, individuals who can tolerate the cardiac plays have been richly rewarded. Historically, small-cap stocks have performed significantly better than the more established large corporations. For more on this phenomenon, see Chapter 12.

Tip   To properly diversify, long-term investors need to include smaller companies in portfolios stuffed with corporate giants.

If you own a small-cap stock fund that's performed well for years, congratulations. You should feel like a lottery winner. Small-cap funds that consistently perform well have been more rare lately than you might think. For starters, the small-cap fund universe is much tinier than the large-cap stock fund universe. Why? Throughout most of the 1990s, large-cap funds regularly whipped funds specializing in the little guys. Consequently, fund companies felt no great urgency to roll out small-cap funds when few investors were clamoring for them.

The perils of publicity

In addition, small-cap funds are more fragile. When an obscure small-cap fund manager compiles an excellent record for a couple of years, the financial press starts salivating. Journalists write glowing stories, and the publicity spreads from magazine to magazine and Web site to Web site. The hype, however, can endanger a fund. Arguably, that's what happened to the Fasciano Fund, a small-cap growth fund.

After the financial press began raving about it, its assets soared dramatically. The manager became overwhelmed, and the cash started piling up rather than being invested. Inevitably, the stellar performance lagged, and a competitor eventually bought the fund.

Popularity can hurt one of these funds in a less obvious way as well. When a fund's assets grow, it's harder to continue placing bets on nimble small companies. What happens? The fund manager might feel compelled to invest instead in mid-cap stocks. Over the years, this is what happened to American Century Ultra, which originally was in the small-cap category. Its excellent performance attracted new customers and new cash, which prompted the fund to set its sights on medium-sized companies. Ultimately, that approach was abandoned as the fund, which today is one of the nation's largest, was forced to specialize in the biggest corporate names.

Best small-cap strategies

What can you do? Although you should try to avoid a fund without a proven track record, sometimes this strategy isn't practical with small-cap funds. When a respected fund company rolls out a small-cap fund with a successful manager, you might want to jump in.

Another possibility is settling for a fund that vows to close its doors when assets reach a certain threshold. A small-cap fund that will turn away new business when assets reach $1 billion or so could be a great find. If you've uncovered such a fund but it's already closed, be patient. Many funds don't stay closed forever. Another solution is to just stick with a small-cap index fund, which is better equipped to cope with an avalanche of new cash. (See Chapter 10 for details on index fund investing.)

Mid-cap funds

Although many appreciate the importance of large-cap and small-cap funds, the funds in the middle are often overlooked. That's a shame because these funds have the potential to outperform the others. Mid-cap funds invest in medium-sized companies that generally have a market capitalization between $2 billion and $10 billion.

Corporate giants sometimes have rigid bureaucracies, but medium-sized companies are less likely to have calcified management; their leadership tends to have more of an entrepreneurial spirit. On the flip side, large-cap stocks that have floundered sometimes end up slipping down into the mid-cap territory. A recent example of this phenomenon is R.J.R. Nabisco.

Note   Because many mid-cap companies have little if any foreign sales, the ups and downs of the Euro (the European currency) or other foreign travails don't have much of an impact on their value.

These stocks may also enjoy significant advantages over smaller companies. Middle-sized companies are typically more secure with proven product lines, veteran management, and established markets.

During the past 10 years, the Standard & Poor MidCap 400 Index, a well-known mid-cap bellwether, has outperformed the nation's biggest companies. In this period, the MidCap 400 has generated an annual 17.3 percent—compare that to the Standard & Poor's 500 Index's15.25 percent. Perhaps even more impressive, mid-cap stocks have outperformed small-caps during the past 20 years, and they've accomplished this performance with less volatility.

Balanced and asset allocation funds

Can't figure out the right mix of stocks and bonds? You might want someone to make the decision for you. If you'd prefer to obtain stock and bond exposure in one place, either a *balanced fund* or an *asset allocation fund* can do just that.

A balanced fund is simply a conservative mutual fund that attempts to provide current income as well as growth with a portfolio of stocks, bonds, and cash. A balanced fund can be ideal for a more conservative investor who is leery of having too large an exposure to stocks. Such a fund can also be a solution for someone who wants exposure to bonds and stocks, but doesn't have enough money to open two funds. In contrast, balanced funds may also attract aggressive investors who have sunk just about everything they own into stocks. A balanced fund gives them a smidgen of bond exposure as a modest hedge against a stock market meltdown.

Note   Balanced funds tend to be less volatile than stock funds because of the bond holdings. For that same reason, they'll never be ranked among the great gangbuster funds.

The other auto-exposure option, the asset allocation fund, maintains a mix of stocks, bonds, and cash in order to provide instant diversification. Some of these funds keep the amounts of different assets fairly constant; others adjust the mix to capitalize on economic changes. Because they come in different varieties, it's important to know how the different types function so you can choose the one that's most appropriate for you.

One type of asset allocation fund relies upon the manager to decide the portfolio's weighting of stocks, bonds, and cash. One fund's manager may have a huge chunk of a portfolio sitting in cash; another may have most of the assets in bonds or stocks. One of the frustrations of this type of fund is finding out what holdings the fund has at any given time. It's hard to make comparisons or analyze fund performance when the underlying assets can shift regularly.

Caution   The manager-run funds are designed to soften the blow of a market slump. If trouble is looming, for instance, a manager can quickly sell off stock and convert it into cash. That sounds great, but many managers are no better than the rest of us in predicting market corrections. Arguably, this is the least attractive option.

Another type of asset allocation fund, which has been marketed as ideal for retirement savings, is the life cycle fund. This type of fund, which is often offered on 401(k) menus, becomes more conservative as the shareholders age. In other words, the bond exposure increases as the number of years before a shareholder's retirement decreases. Fidelity, Vanguard, and others have developed evolving life cycle funds that are tied to future retirement dates such as 2010, 2020, and 2030. Some funds offer conservative, moderate, and aggressive life cycle funds.

Tip Make sure you understand each fund's investing style before you choose. One fund family's aggressive life cycle fund may resemble another's moderate fund.

Funds within funds

Major fund families and some brokerage firms, such as Fidelity, T. Rowe Price, Schwab and Vanguard, offer what amounts to a fund of funds. With one fund, you can attain instant diversification domestically and overseas. T. Rowe Price Spectrum Growth Fund, for example, owns positions in eight of the fund family's other stock funds. True to its name, the Fidelity Four-In-One Index Fund is composed of four Fidelity index funds that collectively invest in large and small domestic corporations, overseas companies, and bonds. Vanguard Star invests in nine Vanguard funds that cover the gamut from long-term bonds to large-cap value stocks.

This type of fund is best reserved for beginner investors or those who don't have the time to properly diversify their holdings. With one of these funds, an investor doesn't have to fret about choosing their own mix of bonds and stocks—it's done for them. More advanced investors often won't want to surrender this control to others.

Foreign funds

Sometimes it might seem like the world revolves around the United States, but Wall Street isn't the center of the universe. The U.S. stock market represents less than 40 percent of the world's stock market capitalization. If you don't invest in foreign stocks, you will miss most of the globe's stock-picking opportunities.

Tip If you want to invest internationally, start with a large-cap foreign fund and devote no more than 15 to 20 percent of your portfolio overseas. Because of the extra volatility, you may wish to invest in a foreign fund through dollar-cost averaging.

Advocates of foreign funds say that adding overseas exposure is a smart diversification move because these markets don't move in lock step with American stocks. An increasing number of experts, however, are now suggesting that more correlation exists between domestic and foreign stocks than was previously thought. This correlation is particularly true, they suggest, among blue-chip stocks, regardless of what continent they call home. Consequently, investors might not be as diversified as they think because many foreign funds tend to invest in the same marquee names, such as Royal Dutch Petroleum, Sony, and Nokia, as large-cap domestic stock funds.

Note   According to Morningstar, foreign funds have a 68 percent correlation in performance with domestic stock funds. Foreign funds that specialize in small and mid-sized corporations have less of a link with domestic funds.

Investing in a global fund makes less sense. This type of fund permits the portfolio manager to park his or her money anywhere in the world, including the United States. This kind of fund is not a pure foreign play because a large chunk of money might never leave the United States. If you already own funds that invest in American companies, you could be duplicating your efforts. Stick with a straight international fund instead.

Emerging markets funds

If you like casinos, emerging market funds may be appealing. By investing in one of these funds, you might end up owning a tiny piece of a Malaysian newspaper chain or an Indian fertilizer company. In the past, stocks from developing countries have delivered both stupendous and disastrous returns. These funds can be extremely erratic.

If you plan to own just one foreign fund, don't choose one that concentrates in the developing world. Bottom line: If your time horizon is very long and you have a strong stomach, consider putting no more than 2 or 3 percent or so of your money into an emerging market fund.

Yearly Fund Checkup

Once you've assembled your fund portfolio, ask yourself these questions annually:

✦ How is my portfolio divided among stocks, bonds, and cash? Am I comfortable with the percentages?

✦ Do my funds overlap or do they represent distinct investing styles?

✦ Are my funds divided appropriately among large, medium, and small companies?

✦ Do I understand the holdings in my bond funds and their average maturities and durations?

✦ Is the money manager who originally attracted me to the funds still running the show?

✦ How does the total return of my funds compare to the rest of their peer groups for one, three, and five years? And how have my funds performed in comparison with their respective benchmarks, such as the Standard & Poor's 500 and the Russell 2000?

✦ Are my stock funds tax-efficient?

✦ Are the annual expenses that my funds are charging below average?

Cross-Reference Sector mutual funds, which specialize in a particular industry or sector, are another risky play. Sector funds are covered in Chapter 14.

Socially responsible funds

Like Rodney Dangerfield, socially responsible funds used to get no respect. They were viewed as funds for bleeding heart do-gooders who cared more about making the world a better place than earning a buck. But socially responsible funds no longer prompt snickering. In a survey it conducted, Morningstar determined that more than one out of five socially responsible funds had earned its vaunted five-star rating, which is twice the rate of the overall fund universe. In addition, fewer of the socially responsible funds were stuck in the ratings cellar.

What separates socially responsible investing (SRI) funds from the rest of the pack is their managers' conscious decisions to avoid investing in companies they feel are poor corporate citizens. The definitions of just what constitutes an acceptable investment vary; different funds use different screening criteria. Some religious funds, such as Amana Growth and Timothy Plan, screen out stocks that offend particular religious tenets. Other SRI funds, for instance, might avoid defense stocks, but will consider companies that rely upon animal testing. The following list contains some of the major categories that SRI funds commonly avoid:

- ✦ Defense/weapon stocks
- ✦ Tobacco stocks
- ✦ Alcohol stocks
- ✦ Gambling stocks
- ✦ Nuclear power stocks
- ✦ Companies that perform or rely on animal testing

Some SRI funds search out companies that are good corporate citizens, such as those that invest in local neighborhoods. These funds evaluate companies not only on their economic performance, but also on their community involvement, environmental record, and their handling of labor relations and human rights issues.

Socially responsible investing has its drawbacks. For starters, developing a well-diversified portfolio is harder because the pool of funds is small. What's more, because many SRI funds come from small fund shops, their fees can be higher than average.

Tip Two investing giants, Vanguard and TIAA-CREF, have recently challenged the traditionally high fee scale by unveiling their own low-cost SRI funds.

If socially responsible investing interests you, you might want to consider these SRI candidates:

✦ Domini Social Equity is a large-cap index fund. The phone number is (800) 762-6814; Web address is www.domini.com.

✦ Vanguard Calvert Social Index is also a large-cap index fund. Call (800) 635-1511 for more information; Web address is www.vanguard.com.

✦ TIAA-CREF Social Equity is another large-cap index fund. The phone number is (800) 223-1200; Web address is www.tiaacref.org

✦ Pax World Balanced is a large-cap balanced fund. The phone number is (800) 767-1729; Web address is www.paxworld.com.

✦ Citizens Emerging Growth is a mid-cap growth fund. Call (800) 223-7010 for more information; Web address is www.citizensfunds.com.

To learn more about socially responsible investing, consider contacting the non-profit organization Social Investment Forum at 1612 K St. NW, Suite 650, Washington, DC 20006. The phone number is (202) 872-5319, and the Web address is www.socialinvest.org.

All-Star Fund List

At this point you may be thinking to yourself, "Just tell me what the good funds are." Okay, the following recommendations are for anybody who loves top 10 lists. But first a caveat: These recommendations are by no means a definitive list of all the wonderful funds out there. For starters, only no-load funds made the list. As you'll learn in Chapter 8, the fund universe is divided among load and no-load funds. If a fund comes with a *load,* a sales charge is built into it. These are typically sold through full-service brokers and commissioned financial advisors. A no-load fund doesn't carry such a charge. If you are capable of selecting your own funds, you don't need to buy one that's saddled with a load.

The funds on this list have rarely disappointed. Over the years, they've outmuscled the competition by posting above-average returns. What's truly impressive and important about these funds is their consistency. They might never be hot enough to make a top 10 list, but they also haven't crashed and burned like many of yesterday's highest flyers.

One reason for the consistency is that these funds are largely run by veteran fund managers. This quality is a definite plus in an era when successful portfolio managers are acting more and more like athletic free agents. Another bonus is that the listed funds are not fee hogs. They charge below average annual expenses, which is extremely important.

Caution

Of course, there is no guarantee that the funds will continue to perform well. All too often landing on a recommended list is a kiss of death for a mutual fund. That's why it's important to research any fund before investing in it. Skipping this step is reckless indeed.

The following lists of funds that you might want to include in your portfolio are broken down by investment category. Prefacing each name is the fund's investment style.

Index funds:

✦ Blend: Vanguard Total Stock Market Index at (800) 635-1511 or www.vanguard.com

✦ Blend: Vanguard 500 Index at (800) 635-1511 or www.vanguard.com

✦ Blend: Fidelity Spartan Total Stock Market Index at (800) 544-8888 or www.fidelity.com

✦ Blend: Schwab 1000 at (800) 266-5623 or www.schwab.com

Large-cap stock funds:

✦ Value: Ameristock at (800) 394-5064 or www.ameristock.com

✦ Blend: Fidelity Dividend Growth at (800) 544-8888 or www.fidelity.com

✦ Growth: White Oak Growth Stock at (888) 462-5386 or www.oakassociates.com

✦ Value: Selected American at (800) 243-1575 or www.selectedfunds.com

✦ Value: Dodge & Cox Stock at (800) 621-3979 or www.dodgeandcox.com

Aggressive growth and small-cap funds:

✦ Growth: Bridgeway Aggressive Growth Fund at (800) 661-3550 or www.bridgewayfund.com

✦ Growth: Managers Special Equity at (800) 835-3879 or www.managersfunds.com

✦ Value: Third Avenue Value at (800) 443-1021 or www.mjwhitman.com

✦ Value: Royce Opportunity at (800) 221-4268 or www.roycefunds.com

Mid-cap stock funds:

✦ Growth: T. Rowe Price Mid-Cap Growth at (800) 638-5660 or www.troweprice.com

✦ Value: Muhlenkamp Fund at (800) 860-3863 or www.muhlenkamp.com

✦ Value: Weitz Value at (800) 232-4161 or www.weitzfunds.com

✦ Value: American Century Equity Income at (800) 345-2021 or
www.americancentury.com

✦ Growth: Turner Midcap Growth at (800) 224-6312 or www.turner-invest.com

International stock funds:

✦ Large-cap blend: Masters' Select International at (800) 960-0188 or
www.mastersfund.com

✦ Large-cap blend: Artisan International at (800) 344-1770 or
www.artisanfunds.com

✦ Large-cap value: Harbor International at (800) 422-1050 or
www.harborfund.com

Bond Terms (and Funds) to Know

Need bonds? One of the first decisions you must make is whether you require a
bond fund or should invest in individual bonds. Relying upon bond funds makes
more sense for most people. As a general rule, the greater amount of cash you wish
to invest in bonds, the more attractive individual bonds will be. (For the pros and
cons of bonds and bond funds, see Chapter 17.)

Choosing a bond fund can be trickier than selecting a garden-variety stock fund. In
the investment world, the professionals who trade bonds and understand their per-
mutations were often the kids who aced all their math courses. Don't worry, you
don't need a Ph.D., but intelligently choosing a bond fund requires you to look at a
number of variables.

At the outset, ask yourself these five questions:

✦ What is the bond fund's average maturity and duration?

✦ What is the bond fund's average credit rating?

✦ What is the bond fund's expense ratio?

✦ What type of bonds does the fund invest in?

✦ What is the fund's total return?

You can find all the answers to these questions by examining a bond fund's annual
or semi-annual report and prospectus. You can order these free reports through a
fund's toll-free number, or you might be able to download them from a fund's
Web site.

Bond fund maturity

A bond's *maturity* refers to its lifespan. A bond with a 10-year maturity would typically make interest payments to its owner for one decade. Once the maturity date is reached, the initial investment, or *principal,* would be returned. A bond fund, obviously, holds many bonds, but the fund calculates what the average maturity of its holdings is.

Why does maturity matter? Blame it partially on the prospects of high interest rates, which are the scourge of bonds. When rates jump, bond values fall. It's not hard to understand why. Suppose you own a bond generating an interest rate of 6.5 percent and rates spike. To remain competitive, the newest crop of bonds starts offering better rates, perhaps in the 7 percent range. The value of your bond drops because it compares poorly with the higher payouts. On the other hand, bonds flourish when interest rates tank. That's because, in this hypothetical case, your 6.5 percent looks awfully attractive compared to, say, a 5.5 percent or 6 percent bond. (If you hold onto an individual bond until maturity, any price fluctuations are irrelevant since you won't be selling.)

Note   Duration is an even more precise way to measure how sensitive a bond or bond fund is to interest rate changes. See more on duration in Chapter 17.

However, all bonds and bond funds aren't equally affected by interest rate swings. Fluctuations in price depend heavily upon the length of a bond's maturity. In general, the shorter the average maturity of your fund (or bond), the safer your investment is. When choosing a bond fund, you have three broad maturity ranges to choose from:

- ✦ Short-term maturity
- ✦ Intermediate-term maturity
- ✦ Long-term maturity

Short-term bond funds

Short-term bond funds are the safest because they are best equipped to deflect interest-rate fluctuations. By choosing a short-term bond fund, you accept some risk of losing money because of interest rate moves, but it's not too likely. In theory, even money markets pose some risk, though no individual investor has ever lost a dime investing in one.

Tip   Because the yield on short-term bond funds is often slightly higher than a money market, they can be an excellent place to park money that you'll need in two or three years. The key, however, is to pick a fund with very low expenses.

Consider these short-term bond fund candidates:

✦ Metropolitan West Low Duration Fund at (800) 241-4671 or `www.mwamllc.com`

✦ Montgomery Short Duration Government Fund at (800) 572-3863 or `www.montgomeryfunds.com`

✦ Vanguard Short-Term Bond Index Fund at (800) 635-1511 or `www.vanguard.com`

Intermediate-term bond funds

For most investors, funds that invest in bonds that mature in 5 to 10 years are the most sensible. Historically, the total return for these intermediate-term funds isn't quite as high as the long-term variety, but many investors are happy to give up a smidgeon in potential return in exchange for far less volatility.

Note   Intermediate-term bond funds are traditionally used as a core holding in the fixed-income portion of an investor's portfolio.

These intermediate-term bond funds are worth investigating:

✦ Dodge & Cox Income Fund at (800) 621-3979 or `www.dodgeandcox.com`

✦ Vanguard Total Bond Market Index Fund at (800) 635-1511 or `www.vanguard.com`

✦ Fremont Bond Fund at (800) 548-4539 or `www.fremontfunds.com`

✦ Harbor Bond Fund at (800) 422-1050 or `www.harborfund.com`

Long-term bond funds

Long-term bond funds are, by far, the most volatile. These funds hold debt that might not mature for 10 to 30 years. Investors in these funds expect to be rewarded for their bravery with better returns.

Note   Compared to short- and intermediate-term funds, long-term bond funds often provide the highest yields and the greatest chance for price appreciation, but they also can fall the hardest.

Active investors who like to speculate favor these bonds. When they believe interest rates are going to drop, they often scoop up long-term bonds, especially zero coupon bonds that originate at the U.S. Treasury (which are covered in Chapter 18). Although long-term bonds can provide higher total returns, the advantage isn't great enough to make them more enticing than intermediate-term bonds.

Bond fund credit risks

Because bonds are loans, you must pay attention to how reliable the borrowers are. U.S. Treasury bonds represent the ultimate in safety. On the other extreme, the credit quality of corporate junk bonds, which are also referred to as high-yield corporate bonds, can be shaky.

Mercifully, nobody expects you to judge the creditworthiness of the bonds in a fund. Funds list the average credit quality of the bonds in their portfolios in their annual reports. These ratings are provided independently by such prominent ratings services as Standard & Poor's and Moody's Investors Service. Chapter 17 provides a breakdown of the credit quality ratings.

Bond fund expenses

When you purchase a bond fund, expenses are critical. You want the best bond fund for the cheapest price. If you've never noticed whether your fund imposes high or low fees, it's understandable. A fund doesn't present its shareholders with invoices each year for its management services. The fees are automatically taken out of each shareholder's account.

/ **Note**   Because bond funds can't generate the robust returns of stock funds, expenses eat up a more significant amount of your potential return.

Frankly, the expenses are often what separate the best bond funds from average or mediocre ones. Consequently, if you focus on finding the cheapest bond funds, you are likely to simultaneously compile a list of the best picks. If you find that hard to believe, this example illustrates how much money a fund can hemorrhage if the expenses are simply average. Recently, the expense ratio for the typical general bond fund was 1.13 percent. The expense ratio refers to how much money you pay a fund each year. So if you have $10,000 in this typical bond fund, you will pay $113. A shareholder with $1,000 in the fund would pay $11.30. That doesn't sound outrageous, but the costs over time will probably shock you.

Suppose that two shareholders invest for 20 years in a bond fund that provides an average return of 7 percent. Our first investor sinks his money into Vanguard Total Bond Market Index fund, which charges a miniscule .2 percent. It would be extremely difficult finding bond funds that are priced any cheaper than that. Our other investor sticks with the average fund carrying the 1.13 percent expense ratio.

At the end of the two decades, our cheapskate investor would have paid $857 in fees, but investor no. 2 would have paid a whopping $4,349. But that doesn't tell the whole story. Our Vanguard investor's shares would now be worth $37,178, but investor no. 2's would be worth just $30,829. Why the huge gulf? The second investor's account couldn't expand as fast because each year more money was pulled out to pay expenses, which left less to continue compounding. Even more eye-opening are the differences in account values when a high-priced fund is added to the mix. Suppose you invested in a bond fund with a 1.5 percent expense ratio. Assuming the same scenario, your portfolio, at the end of 20 years, would be worth a mere $28,602.

 How can you tell how expensive your own funds are? You can plug in your own expense statistics by visiting the U.S. Securities and Exchange Commission's Web site (www.sec.gov) and using their mutual funds cost calculator.

The SEC installed a mutual funds cost calculator on their site out of concern that Americans aren't aware of how much they're paying for funds. To find out the expense ratio of your stock and bond funds, use each fund's toll-free number and ask. The expense ratio is also listed in each fund's prospectus, which is free for the asking.

 The expense ratio isn't the only fee to scrutinize. If you work with a full-service broker or a financial advisor, you could very well end up paying a sales charge or load, which will dramatically erode your return even more.

Types of bond funds

Bond funds aren't just characterized by their average maturities. They are also grouped by the kind of bonds they invest in. This section is a short synopsis of the main type of bond funds. You'll find more detailed explanations in Chapters 17, 18, and 19.

Treasury bond funds

The federal government backs U.S. Treasury bonds, which makes them the ultimate in safety. Realistically, there is no chance that the bonds in one of these funds will default. Treasuries come in three flavors based on the length of their maturities:

✦ Treasury bills: 13 weeks and 26 weeks

✦ Treasury notes: 2 to 10 years

✦ Treasury bonds: 10 to 30 years

Although you can buy Treasury bond funds, buying individual Treasuries direct from the federal government is easier and cheaper.

Other Treasury choices

Not long ago, the U.S. Treasury rocked the bond world (it's not hard to get a rise out of these folks) by unveiling a new type of bond: the Treasury Inflation-Protection Security, or TIPS. This type of bond is intended to protect its owners against inflation, the scourge of the fixed-income world. Because these bonds are fairly new, there aren't a lot of available funds yet. These two fund families offer them:

✦ Vanguard Inflation-Protected Securities Fund at (800) 635-1511 or www.vanguard.com

✦ American Century Inflation-Adjusted Treasury Fund at (800) 345-2021 or www.americancentury.com

The pickings are even smaller if you're interested in the U.S. Treasury's zero coupon bonds. American Century is the only fund company that specializes in this niche. Unlike regular bonds, zero coupon bonds don't pay out regular interest. Instead, you buy the bond at a discount and get the full value when it matures. Because zero coupon bond funds react dramatically to interest rate movements, these funds are favored by aggressive investors who like to place bets on which way interest rates are going.

Resource To learn more about investing in Treasuries, contact TreasuryDirect at (800) 722-2678 or www.treasurydirect.gov.

Mortgage-backed securities funds

Both federal agencies and quasi-government entities also issue mortgage-backed securities. The agencies and federally chartered companies create these securities by bundling home mortgages from lenders into huge packages that are sold primarily to institutional investors.

Each month, investors in these securities, either directly or through a fund, receive interest income and principal from the underlying mortgages. Mortgage-backed securities typically provide a better yield than regular Treasuries, but interest rate movements affect them more.

Municipal bond funds

State and local governments use municipal (muni) bonds to build big-ticket items like water treatment plants, prisons, and roads. The most alluring feature of a muni bond fund is the tax break. Invest in a muni fund or an individual bond and you won't pay federal income taxes on the interest that's generated. If you choose a muni fund that invests solely in bonds in your own state, you avoid state and possibly local taxes as well. Although muni bonds aren't as creditworthy as Treasuries or other federal bonds, they are generally considered safe. What's more, the majority of the muni bonds, which don't already enjoy high bond ratings, are insured.

These bond funds aren't appropriate for every fixed-income lover. If you are in the 10 or 15 percent tax bracket, your tax break won't be worth the lower yield that these muni funds typically provide. The only sure winners are Americans in the highest tax brackets. It can be a toss-up whether these funds make financial sense for somebody in the 27 percent bracket.

Intermediate bond funds

Okay, this heading might seem confusing. On the surface, the fund name seems to refer strictly to a bond's maturity. But this name is used to refer to bond funds that have a mandate to invest in a wide variety of bonds. These funds enjoy latitude in snatching up whatever looks good, whether that be corporate bonds, government bonds, or mortgage bonds. These funds make for good core holdings.

Corporate bonds

Corporate bond funds can invest in investment-grade corporate bonds or the high-yield variety. High-yield funds accumulate bonds that are issued by corporations with shakier credit histories. It's not unusual to see these funds alternate on the best and worst lists of bond fund performers.

 Tip   Although plenty of junk bond funds exist, there aren't a lot of funds dedicated to high-grade corporates. Those who want a heavy dose of corporate bonds should instead take a look at intermediate bond funds.

Beware bond fund bombast

As you review your bond fund choices, don't assume too much by looking at a fund's name. On its face, for instance, a municipal bond fund might seem safe. But even a muni fund can sprinkle its portfolio with junk munis. (Yes, there is such a thing.) Some managers gamble on speculative munis to tweak the yield. These shaky muni issuers must offer a more tantalizing yield to attract customers to make up for the credit risk.

If a bond fund's performance seems much greater than its peers, beware. This fund might not be the bond fund of your dreams, but your nightmares. That's because the fund manager might be taking far greater risks than is appropriate. In a case like this, examining the bond fund closely is even more crucial. Look at the bonds sitting in the fund's portfolio.

Tip   Funds are obliged to release their holdings only twice a year, but you may get a more updated listing by visiting a fund's Web site. Also look at the past performance statistics; wild swings in performance over the years are a red flag.

Summary

✦ A large-cap stock fund often serves as the cornerstone of a portfolio.

✦ Invest in small-cap and/or mid-cap stock funds to properly diversify your portfolio.

✦ Asset allocation funds can be appropriate for investors who don't want to create their own mix of stocks and bonds.

✦ Consider using an intermediate-term bond fund as a core fixed-income holding.

✦ Expenses can make or break your bond fund's returns: Stick with bond funds that charge very low expenses.

The Smart Investor's Fund Strategies

I n this chapter, you learn how to develop and maintain a solid portfolio of mutual funds. At the same time, you discover how to avoid common fund mistakes. The chapter also explains how to measure the riskiness of your funds. Also included are guidelines on when to sell your funds.

Mutual Funds Then and Now

Not long ago, mutual funds were being toasted as the darlings of Wall Street. Mutual funds gave people who had been hiding behind the safety of their bank passbook accounts the courage to invest in the stock and bond markets.

As trillions of dollars poured into mutual funds, a cottage industry sprung up to instruct us on where to direct these boatloads of cash. Web sites, books, and magazines made it their mission to instruct us on the nuances of fund investing. The more successful fund managers were celebrated like famous chefs and Super Bowl quarterbacks. Portfolio managers were in such high demand by financial news networks that fund companies built television studios inside their headquarters. In just the past two decades, the number of funds skyrocketed from 564 to nearly 8,300. Just about every conceivable industry from racecar driving to the funeral business has had mutual funds devoted to it.

However, the love affair is fading a bit. Some of the same people who were celebrating mutual funds are now trashing them. They point out that mutual funds can be expensive and cause tax nightmares. In addition, mutual funds' overall performance statistics can be utterly underwhelming.

Today, the traditional mutual fund faces competition from innovative alternatives. Exchange-traded funds are de rigueur, and online investment companies, such as FOLIOfn (`www.foliofn.com`), Netfolio (`www.netfolio.com`), BUYandHOLD (`www.buyandhold.com`), and ShareBuilder (`www.sharebuilder.com`), enable investors to build their own stock portfolios in new ways. Meanwhile, some investors who cut their teeth on mutual funds are turning to professionals to manage their own private cache of stocks. At the same time, stock commissions have dropped so dramatically that it's now economically feasible for small investors to buy their own stocks.

Even though the fund industry must confront its own foibles, mutual funds remain an excellent way to invest for millions of Americans. The key for investors is to avoid the considerable number of funds that rightfully trigger the wrath of the financial press for being mediocre, expensive, and tax-inefficient.

Top Mutual Fund Strategies

The fun part of investing in mutual funds is picking them out. But even selecting great funds won't guarantee great investment returns. By taking the 10 steps presented in this section, you can assemble and maintain a solid fund portfolio.

Tip no. 1: Know what type of funds you need.

Plenty of smart people own wonderful funds but have lousy portfolios. They pick funds the way impulse shoppers buy clothes. If it looks good, they grab it. What people forget to ask themselves is whether they need that seventh pair of blue jeans or their tenth highly rated mutual fund.

How you fare as an investor greatly depends upon the mix of stocks, bonds, and funds you hold. If you own too many similar funds, your portfolio assumes too much risk. Many people don't even know they possess lopsided portfolios. But it can easily happen if you've accumulated shares in several top-performing funds.

Note

> Winning funds tend to gravitate to the same type of stocks. Before the tech bear market, for instance, the nation's 25 top-performing funds had, on average, sunk 60 percent of their assets into technology stocks.

Make sure you're diversified

Why is diversification important? It wouldn't be necessary if the markets always favored technology stocks, or small-company stocks, or the biggest corporate marquee names. But the markets are fickle. Sometimes technology stocks are king, and other times they're dogs. Large-caps can enjoy a phenomenal run and then hit a drought. Utilities can be sleepy investments until some event, such as deregulation, creates new opportunities. A portfolio that contains a wide variety of investments can better survive the unpredictable market cycles and take advantage of sudden run-ups in certain segments of the market.

Many people mistakenly think they've diversified if they hold several funds. But numbers alone don't ensure diversity. For instance, when the Janus family of funds was extremely popular, people figured they were safely diversified if they held three or four Janus funds. But what many investors didn't realize is that these aggressive funds often held big stakes in the same companies.

Determine your ideal portfolio

Your first big step toward assembling a diversified portfolio is determining what an ideal fund portfolio should contain. Whether you are just beginning to invest or have been investing for many years, take a moment and ask yourself these questions:

✦ What are my investment goals?

✦ What is my time horizon for each of these goals?

✦ How much risk am I comfortable with?

✦ Will I be investing in a retirement or taxable account or both?

✦ How are my investments allocated now?

Resist the temptation to look at your holdings through a pinhole. For example, the object isn't to diversify just your 401(k) among the funds available in your workplace. You need to look at all your holdings, including a 401(k), IRAs, and taxable accounts. By doing this, you can patch holes in your portfolio. Suppose your 401(k) menu doesn't offer a small-cap fund. You can compensate for this omission by investing in one of these funds in an IRA or some other account.

Gather up your account statements and spread them on the table and see if all your holdings mesh together nicely like a jigsaw puzzle. If you're married, a spouse's accounts need to be thrown into the mix at the same time.

X-ray your portfolio on the Internet

If you're having trouble fitting all the pieces of your portfolio together, you can analyze your portfolio with handy Internet tools. One reliable resource is Morningstar's Instant X-Ray. You type in your holdings at Morningstar's Web site (www.morningstar.com), and the software dissects your portfolio and alerts you if it detects a heavy concentration in a particular sector, such as technology. The service is free, but you can receive a more in-depth analysis by signing up for a complimentary 30-day premium membership.

Financial Engines (www.financialengines.com) is another portfolio helper. The brainchild of a Nobel Prize winner, Financial Engines analyzes your portfolio and speculates on whether it can ultimately meet your investment goals. Once again, some of the analysis is free, but more involved help is not.

Tip no. 2: Limit the funds in your portfolio.

Too many mutual fund investors behave like the hound dog that chases after every truck that whizzes down the street. The dog can't help running after trucks, and the investors can't stop collecting mutual funds. Fund junkies always stumble across funds they believe are superior to the ones they already own. On the day a magazine containing a glowing profile of a fund hits the newsstands, readers start flooding the fund's phone lines. Some excited would-be investors can't even wait until daybreak to call. This kind of behavior can lead to disastrous results.

How many funds should you own? That question troubles a lot of investors. Although it may be impossible to collect too many baseball cards or state souvenir spoons, it's easy to collect too many funds.

Knowing your asset classes

For many people, a basic long-term fund portfolio includes these four asset classes:

- ✦ Large-cap stocks
- ✦ Small-cap and/or mid-cap stocks
- ✦ Foreign stocks
- ✦ Bonds

The centerpiece of the equity portion of a portfolio is one or more large-cap stock funds. This large-cap fund could represent up to 50 percent of someone's holdings. The other half may be divided among foreign and small- and mid-cap stock funds. The most daring investors may want to add a sprinkling of sector funds, which specialize in one niche, such as healthcare, technology, or financial stocks. Whether bonds are appropriate depends upon your age. People who are in their 40s or younger may desire only a token amount of bonds in their portfolio, if they have any at all.

Tip   Nearly all investors should have a large-cap stock fund in their portfolios; even retirees need exposure to stocks.

Relying on index funds: One apiece

Will one fund in each of the four asset classes do, or is it better to have more? It depends upon what kind of funds you choose. For some, the simplest solution is to turn to index funds. By its very nature, an index fund includes all or many of the stocks in a specific benchmark, such as the Standard & Poor's 500 or the Wilshire 5000. (See Chapter 10 for details on index fund strategies.) You can select an index fund for each asset class and be finished with four funds.

This model index portfolio uses funds from Vanguard, the indexing leader:

- ✦ Vanguard 500 Index (large-cap stocks)
- ✦ Vanguard Extended Market Index (small- and mid-cap stocks)

✦ Vanguard Developed Markets Index (foreign stocks)

✦ Vanguard Total Bond Market Index (bonds)

Another portfolio suggestion combines low-cost index funds offered by Fidelity and Charles Schwab:

✦ Schwab 1000 (large-caps and mid-caps)

✦ Schwab Small Cap Index (small-caps)

✦ Fidelity Spartan International Index or Schwab International Index (foreign stocks)

✦ Fidelity U.S. Bond Index or Schwab Total Bond Market Index (bonds)

Going with traditional funds: The three or less rule

Your choices won't be so cut and dried if you prefer actively managed funds. With one of these traditional funds, a manager selects companies for his or her portfolio rather than simply choosing all the stocks within a particular index. Not long ago, researchers at Charles Schwab conducted a study to try to determine the optimum number of funds to hold. A good guideline, they concluded, was to hold no more than three actively managed funds per asset class. That would mean, for instance, that three large-cap funds would ideally be the maximum an investor should have.

What's the harm in collecting an overabundance of funds? By investing in too many of the same type of funds, you harm your chances of beating the market. Holding too few funds is dangerous as well. If you own only one actively managed fund, your chances of striking it big increase, but so does the possibility that you'll severely underperform the market. In other words, sticking with just one fund dramatically increases your risks.

The Schwab study's advice was a bit different for bond and index fans. The researchers suggested that investing in just one diversified bond fund was sufficient. Schwab also concluded that one index fund per asset class was sufficient for index fund lovers. Of course, another option is to mix and match index and actively managed funds.

Tip no. 3: Refuse to be a return worshiper.

Far too many investors buy funds based on short-term performances. You should never select a fund just because it shoots to the front of the pack for one year or, heaven forbid, for just one quarter. Unfortunately, however, cash gushes most heavily into whatever funds are declared the winners of the latest quarter. If you chase leaders, you could end up with a fund like the American Heritage Fund, which posted an impressive 1997 return of 75 percent. During the next three years, however, the fund floundered in negative territory. The worst performance was in 1998, when it sank 61.2 percent.

The Problem with Popularity

Investors tend to bunch up in the same funds. According to Financial Research Corp., which tracks money in and out of funds, an amazing 90 percent of the money sloshing around in mutual funds was recently held by just 10 percent of funds. Investors tend to put their money in recent top performers that are offered by well-known fund families, such as Vanguard, Fidelity, and Janus.

As a result, the most popular funds can become grossly overweight, and all that extra weight can drag down returns. Fidelity Magellan Fund provides the most famous example of this phenomenon. While Peter Lynch, the fund world's equivalent of basketball's Michael Jordan, was at the helm from 1977 to 1990, Magellan was smoking. It finished the 1980s as the decade's top-performing fund. This incredible performance was not a secret. With so many investors eagerly signing on, Magellan swelled into America's biggest fund. That was great for Fidelity, but not so great, as it turned out, for its customers. The fund, which recently had $87 billion in assets, could no longer be nimble with that much cash in its belly. With so many billions to invest, Magellan couldn't rely upon just a few nifty stock ideas; it needed hundreds of fabulous stocks.

Here's another way to look at this dilemma: Naming the five most special people in your life is much easier than naming your 1,000 favorite people.

Not surprisingly, Magellan's returns began lagging, and Lynch's successors found themselves unable to come close to duplicating his feat. Ultimately, Fidelity, in a move that acknowledged that the fund was too big, finally closed Magellan to new investors in the 1990s, after it had several years of underperforming the market (the fund was reopened in late 2000). Magellan isn't an aberration. Plenty of other funds have ended up choking on too much cash.

A huge asset base tends to be a much bigger problem for funds that specialize in small companies and, in particular, growth stocks. If you're an investor in a small-cap stock fund that's closed, count your blessings and hope that the managers don't reopen the doors.

The market's love affair with Internet stocks provides even more amazing examples. Kinetic Internet Fund, for example, soared 245 percent in 1999 and plummeted 54.2 percent the next year. Just about every Internet fund experienced the same debacle. Meanwhile, the Janus family of funds, which became the toast of the investor world after posting unbelievable performance numbers in the late 1990s, cratered in 2000 and 2001. Many investors, who came late to the party, lost half of their money.

Tip Stick with funds that have maintained an above-average return for the past three to five years. Also check to see how a fund has performed during both bear and bull markets.

Tip no. 4: Narrow your choices intelligently.

Finding great fund prospects for your portfolio may be the easiest and most enjoyable part of your mission. While you conduct your search, don't get caught up in the media hype that permeates personal finance magazines and Web sites. Keep in mind that although print and electronic publications can provide a valuable service by pinpointing funds with enviable track records, there's no guarantee that these funds will continue to please.

Prospects in print

One way to find great funds is to browse issues of personal finance magazines, such as *Mutual Funds, Bloomberg Personal Finance, Smart Money,* and *Money,* and see what funds they recommend. Just remind yourself that these magazines tend to profile the latest money magnets, whether it's technology or biotechnology funds, aggressive growth or value funds, or whatever else has captured the public's imagination. Use these publications as a tip service. Once you gather some names, you'll need to research the candidates. Never buy a fund based solely on a media recommendation.

Caution

Remain highly skeptical of any story that's hyping its list of the best funds for the upcoming year. No one, not even a personal finance journalist, can accurately predict what funds will do well in the future.

As burned market timers can attest, no one can accurately predict next year's market performance. Veteran financial journalists, after covering the fund industry for a while and seeing so many sizzling funds fizzle, tend to become big believers in index funds, which, by their very nature, can produce only average market returns.

Online fund screeners

Another tool to help you winnow down your choices is the online fund screener. When using this software, you choose the characteristics of the fund you're looking for, and the software locates those funds that match up from its huge database. These sites provide access to this free tool:

✦ CNBC on MSN Money at www.money.msn.com

✦ Morningstar at www.morningstar.com

✦ Kiplinger's Personal Finance at www.kiplinger.com

✦ CBS MarketWatch at www.cbsmarketwatch.com

✦ Money Magazine at www.money.com

Brokerage firms can also be helpful during your scavenger hunt. Charles Schwab, Fidelity, E*Trade, and TD Waterhouse, among others, provide fund screeners on their Web pages (their Web addresses are in the Resource Guide). Again, you can plug in the type of fund you desire, and the software will spit out a list of possibilities.

Caution After gathering names, you need to do more research. Don't invest in a fund simply because a screen kicked out a name.

You can typically plug these kinds of variables into fund screening software:

- ✦ Investment focus
- ✦ Performance record over 1, 3 or 5 years
- ✦ Morningstar star rating
- ✦ Morningstar risk rating
- ✦ Manager tenure
- ✦ Expense ratio
- ✦ Minimum initial purchase
- ✦ Load/no-load fund
- ✦ Bond credit quality (for bond funds only)
- ✦ Bond duration (for bond funds only)

Tip no. 5: Look for low-cost funds.

All of us know how much we paid for our homes. No doubt, most of us remember the price we negotiated for the cars parked in our driveways. But how many people know how much they are paying each year for their mutual funds? Unfortunately, most people don't bother to look at a fund's expenses. Frankly, the mutual fund industry counts on investors who don't complain. Fees for the fund industry have been getting heftier because customers are largely oblivious that they are being overcharged.

Note Fees can have a tremendous effect on a fund's performance. In many cases, the funds charging the lowest expenses are also the ones sporting the best returns. Why? Because low fees give funds a huge built-in advantage.

Understanding expense ratios

You can determine how much your fund is charging you by looking at its expense ratio. The expense ratio refers to the percentage of your investment that is automatically taken out of your fund each year to pay for management services and other costs. For example, if you have $7,000 in a fund that has a 1.5 percent expense ratio, your tab will be $105. As your investment grows, your bill will, too. If your fund grows to $10,000, your tab for the year will be $150. The typical expense ratio today is 1.4 percent, but expense ratios range from as little as .15 percent to well over 2 percent.

The expense ratio includes a management fee, overhead, and sometimes a *12b-1 fee*. The 12b-1 fee pays for a fund's marketing costs, as well as commissions to brokers who sell the fund. If a fund charges such a fee, think hard before choosing it. Why should you pay a premium so that mutual funds can pelt prospective investors with slick, unsolicited junk mail or pay for television commercials? Believe it or not, fund companies have even advertised during Super Bowl games.

Obviously, you want to favor funds that charge less than the average expense ratio. Table 8-1 provides the average expense ratios for different fund categories:

Table 8-1	
Average Mutual Fund Expense Ratios	
Stock Mutual Funds	*Average Expense Ratio*
Large-cap growth	1.46%
Large-cap value	1.44%
Mid-cap growth	1.54%
Mid-cap value	1.49%
Small-cap growth	1.61%
Small-cap value	1.58%
S&P 500 Index	.66%
Equity income	1.36%
Balanced	1.29%
Science & Technology	1.69%
Health/Biotech	1.73%
Real estate	1.68%
Utility	1.42%
Gold	2.06%
International	1.69%
Global	1.76%
Emerging markets	2.14%
European funds	1.78%

Continued

Table 8-1 *(continued)*

Bond Funds	Average Expense Ratio
Municipal bond	1.12%
General bond	1.13%
Corporate bond	1.08%
High-yield bond	1.3%
Treasury bond	.77%
GNMA bond	1.08%
Ultra-short bond	.64%
Money market	.84%

Source: Lipper, a Reuters Company

The range of expense ratios might appear insignificant. The difference between many funds, after all, is just one percentage point or so. But even this seemingly small variation can make a huge difference over time. The following example may convince you to become a penny-pinching fund investor.

Table 8-2 charts the progress of three different funds which each grow 11 percent annually, the historic growth rate of the stock market. Each of these funds starts with $20,000. Fund A passes along very low expenses, which is typical for index funds. Funds B and C generate average expenses, but fund C also charges an initial 5 percent load. If you buy a fund through a broker or a financial advisor, who lives off commissions, you will probably pay a sales charge or *load*.

Table 8-2
Long-Range Look at Expenses and Loads

	Fund A	Fund B	Fund C
Initial investment	$20,000	$20,000	$19,000 (5% load deducted)
Expense ratio	.18%	1.4%	1.4%
Total Fund Fees:			
Five years	$247	$1,876	$2,782
10 years	$661	$4,823	$5,582
15 years	$1,353	$9,451	$9,978
20 years	$2,507	$16,718	$16,883

The fees alone, however, don't illustrate just how much these three funds are really costing. Even though the cost gap between the cheap fund and the average-priced ones looks tremendous, it doesn't reveal the entire story. Actually, investors who favor average-priced and expensive funds are paying even greater cost. That's because more money is being drained each year for expenses, so there is less left to continue to grow over time.

When we look at our three fund examples again in Table 8-3, you'll see an even more dramatic difference in their value over time. Obviously, the lesson to be learned here is to buy cheap funds with impressive track records.

Table 8-3 The Impact of Expenses and Loads on Returns			
	Fund A	*Fund B*	*Fund C*
Value of Fund in:			
5 years	$33,398	$31,407	$29,836
10 years	$55,774	$49,320	$46,854
15 years	$93,140	$77,451	$73,578
20 years	$155,539	$121,626	$115,545

Uncovering expense ratios

If you aren't sure what your funds are costing, don't chide yourself. Cost is often a mystery because we don't write yearly checks to our fund companies. Without fanfare, the fees are automatically deducted from our accounts. You can find out what the expenses are by reading a fund's prospectus, which can be ordered through the fund company. The U.S. Securities and Exchange Commission requires funds to disclose their assortment of fees in a table near the front of the document.

Several Web sites can help you pinpoint what you are paying in expenses for your own individual funds. You can also use these sources when comparing how expenses would cut into potential returns for funds you are contemplating buying. Perhaps the best of the bunch is sponsored by the U.S. Securities and Exchange (www.sec.gov). SEC officials have expressed concern that investors don't know how deeply costs can cut into fund profits. When you visit the SEC site, click on "interactive tools," and you will see a link for the mutual fund cost calculator.

Here are two other Web sites to check out:

✦ Personal Fund (www.personalfund.com)

✦ Quicken (www.quicken.com)

Beware of Flashy (and Misleading) Ads

Whether you're replacing your computer or buying new tennis shoes, you probably consult ads before making a final decision. But relying upon ads to buy mutual funds can spell disaster. The ads can be misleading. During the holiday season in 2000, for instance, fund companies relied upon advertising to crow about their technology funds' phenomenal returns. This tactic was indeed curious because technology stocks had been pummeled throughout that year.

Nevertheless, American Century was bragging about one of its tech-heavy funds. During the past 12 months, according to the ad, the American Century Vista returned 108 percent. At the time the ad appeared, however, American Century Vista's 12-month return was not quite 15 percent. So the performance figure was inflated by 93 percentage points. Other fund families, including Fidelity, AIM, T. Rowe Price, and Scudder, were also bragging about impressive returns in ads similarly flawed by gaps between the advertised performance and reality.

How could the funds be advertised this way? To figure it out, you'd have to look at the fine print. The returns were for the year ending in September, the latest full quarter. Technology had taken its greatest beating for the year after that quarter ended. Federal regulations, however, don't require fund companies to include the latest fund statistics in their advertisements.

The moral of this story is: Don't be wowed by flashy advertisements. Check the fine print. What's more, you should always be suspicious of short-term gains. What really count are a fund's long-term performance figures. Place the most stock in three- and five-year performance figures.

Tip no. 6: Consider a fund's potential volatility.

Investors are only human. They gravitate to funds with the best returns. But a fund that soared to the top of the heap one year can be hiding a dirty little secret. The fund can be as volatile as a bottle rocket. Funds that shoot to the top often assume greater risks, possibly loading up on initial public offerings, derivatives, junk bonds, and other speculative investments.

While the bull market was merrily breaking one record after another, people didn't fret much about the volatility of mutual funds. Funds seemed to know only one direction: up. Eventually that changed. The market no longer was able to routinely defy gravity. During tougher times, people tend to worry about investment volatility.

Note   Whether the market is a bull or a bear, you should know how risky your funds are. You don't have to avoid mercurial funds, but you should judge in advance whether you have the stomach for what may lie ahead.

Risk evaluation

When you are evaluating a fund's risk profile, don't do it in a vacuum. A fund's risk measurement is meaningless unless you compare it to similar funds. Suppose that you've narrowed your search for a perfect small-cap fund to a handful of choices. If the funds all have similar performance statistics, a way to break a tie is to look at each fund's risk profile. Ideally, you want a fund with the highest returns and the lowest risk.

To understand how risky your funds are, you should understand such terms as beta, alpha, and standard deviation, all of which are explained in this section. Which risk measurement is better? In a study, the Schwab Center for Investment Research suggested that the use of a particular risk tool isn't that important; all of the risk tools often lead to the same conclusions. The key is using at least one of them.

Don't worry, though, you don't need to make your own calculations; Web sites can do the calculating for you.

 See Morningstar's Web home page (www.morningstar.com) or its printed materials for risk measurements for many individual funds. Helpful resources for evaluating the risk of your entire portfolio are RiskGrades.com (www. riskgrades.com) and Portfolio Science (www.portfolioscience.com).

Beta

Beta is probably the easiest risk measure to understand. *Beta* compares a fund's volatility with that of a benchmark, such as the often-used Standard & Poor's 500 Index.

A fund with a beta of 1 is considered no riskier than its corresponding index. Index funds, such as the Vanguard 500 Index (which is the nation's second largest mutual fund), often have betas that are close to 1. The higher a fund's beta is, the riskier the fund is. Conservative funds that don't make a lot of risky bets can sport a beta that's even lower than 1.

Example Dodge & Cox Stock Fund, a large-cap value fund that is well respected in the fund industry, has a beta of just 0.72, making it quite conservative indeed.

If a beta is higher than 1, the percentage point gives a rough indication of the fund's rate of fluctuation. A fund with a beta of 1.2, for instance, has historically fluctuated 20 percent more than the index. Firecracker funds that are considered extremely volatile have betas of 1.5 or higher.

Believe it or not, the following mutual fund companies have designed their funds to intentionally magnify their betas. Some sport betas of 1.5 and higher:

✦ Rydex Funds at (800) 820-0888 or www.rydexfunds.com

✦ ProFunds at (888) 776-3637 or www.profunds.com

✦ Potomac Funds at (800) 851-0511 or www.potomacfunds.com

Rydex Nova Fund, for instance, doesn't want to match the S&P 500: It attempts to zoom right past it, no matter whether the benchmark is on its way up or down. The fund's beta is 1.5. So every time the S&P 500 jumps up, say, 10 percent, Rydex Nova should theoretically leap 15 percent. Of course, when the S&P 500 stumbles, Rydex Nova is the one that sprains its ankle: A 10 percent correction in the popular benchmark could very well erase 15 percent of Rydex Nova's value. With a 20 percent rout in the market, 30 percent of Nova's value would be rubbed out like a discarded cigarette butt. These funds are best left to the most intrepid investors who don't fear losing a huge chunk of their investment in a nanosecond.

Note   Beta isn't a foolproof tool. Some types of funds, including foreign and sector funds, don't correlate well. Gold funds have a low beta, but they may fluctuate wildly because of changes in the price of gold.

Alpha

Alpha tries to make beta more meaningful. *Alpha* measures a fund's beta with its actual performance. For example, if a fund's performance matches its beta, its alpha is zero. If a fund's alpha is positive, it means the fund exceeded the performance predicted by its beta. A negative alpha means the fund did worse than the beta suggested.

Standard deviation

The *standard deviation* measures how far a stock or bond fund's more recent performance has strayed from its long-term average. Often statisticians figure standard deviation based on how a fund's monthly returns have varied over a period of time, such as 36 or 60 months.

Standard deviation can be used to calculate how far a fund's performance can stray from its expected, or average, return. Suppose a fund has enjoyed an average return of 14 percent, while it has a standard deviation of 6.0. Based on this standard deviation, the fund's return should vacillate between 8 percent and 20 percent, two-thirds of the time. (You just add and subtract 6 from 14 to get the range.) Technically, this is called a "one standard deviation." There is more certainty with a two standard deviation. Ninety five percent of the time, the return for this particular fund, using a two standard deviation, should vary from 2 percent to 26 percent. (You add and subtract 12 [6×2] from 14 to get the range.)

When you are buying a fund, it's helpful to know whether it tends to swing wildly. The lower the standard deviation, the less volatile the fund should be.

Note   According to Morningstar, the average stock mutual fund's standard deviation is about 25. Not surprisingly, the standard deviation of the average bond fund is much lower at just under 4.0.

Sector funds are among the most volatile. For instance, Firsthand Technology Value, one of the nation's most popular tech funds, recently sported an eye-popping standard deviation of 86.2. In contrast, the far more sedate Dodge & Cox Stock's standard deviation was 19.7.

Market-Neutral: The Cowardly Funds?

No matter what kind of shape the stock market is in, you can count on professional doomsayers to predict that the worst is yet to come. Responding to that fear, a few mutual fund firms unveiled "market-neutral" funds back in the 1990s. The funds were designed to do well in both bull and bear markets. The mandate of these funds prompts the managers to root for stocks to go up as well as down. The managers have hedged their bets for either direction. They've invested in stocks they believe will climb in value, and they've *shorted* other stocks they suspect will fall. When a stock is shorted, a manager or an individual investor essentially borrows stock shares and promptly sells them on the market. They then root for the stock price to drop so when they buy back the shares to repay the borrower, they'll be able to pocket a profit.

How have these market-neutral funds done? For the most part, miserably. Stay away from them.

Morningstar category risk ratings

Investors rarely see past Morningstar's famed five-star fund rating system. Often overlooked is the extremely helpful, and arguably more important, category rating. Morningstar includes this rating on each one of its fund analyses. The category rating attempts to determine how well a fund balances risk and return compared with other funds in the same category. The risk ratings range from 1 to 5, with 5 being the best.

Tip   Stick with funds that Morningstar has awarded with a 4 or 5 category rating.

Tip no. 7: Beware of the revolving door.

Make sure that the person who is running the fund is the one responsible for the great performance. Fund managers who are blessed with a golden touch are often recruited by competitors to perform their magic there, too. That's fine and dandy unless you're stuck at the old fund with an untested new replacement. Avoid a fund with a new manager unless that manager's record is equally good.

Resource   You can obtain the background of a manager by contacting the fund company. Morningstar (www.morningstar.com) is another source.

Tip no. 8: Sell the lame funds, not the nimble.

Selling a fund can be tougher than buying one, and you can blame it all on your psyche. If a fund has been nothing but a curse for years, you might be tempted to hang on until you can break even. This strategy is not a good idea, but it happens all the time. According to researchers at the University of California and the University of Michigan, investors are 2.5 times more likely to sell winning mutual funds rather than the stinkers.

Quick Checklist for Fund Shoppers

Before you commit yourself to any fund, know the answers to these 10 questions:

✦ What is the fund's three- and five-year track record?

✦ How does the fund's performance compare with its peers?

✦ What is the fund's investment style?

✦ How long has the fund manager been in charge?

✦ How risky is the fund?

✦ Is the fund too crowded?

✦ Does the fund come with a built-in sales charge?

✦ What are the fund's annual expenses?

✦ Is the fund tax-efficient?

✦ Does the fund fit in with my investing time horizon?

Although dumping a loser is difficult—after all, losses are only on paper until a fund is sold—selling winning funds and keeping the losers is a dubious approach for a couple of reasons. First, if you sell a fund and lock in a big profit, you will owe capital gains taxes. For many investors, the long-term capital gains rate is 20 percent. At the same time, your returns can suffer if you insist on keeping the mediocre funds. Other research has shown that the funds at the bottom of the heap tend to remain laggards.

Tip   If you lose money when you sell a fund, you can deduct the loss on your annual tax return. See Chapter 23 for details on investment tax strategies.

These signals mean it's time to sell the fund:

✦ **Poor returns.** Your fund has posted mediocre returns for a couple of years while similar funds have done much better.

✦ **The manager who produced great results has left the fund.** Not only will you face the loss of a manager who may have engineered a superior record, you face the possibility of the fund generating extra taxes. This situation can occur when a new manager overhauls the portfolio by tossing out stocks he or she doesn't like. Those sales can trigger capital gains headaches for loyal shareholders. These same taxes can be generated if many investors head for the exit when the old manager leaves. Paying off these fleeing investors may force the fund to sell stocks.

✦ **The investment style has changed dramatically.** Funds enjoy investing latitude, but you don't want to stick with a fund that changes its mandate, such as a value fund that starts loading up on technology stocks. Funds sometimes abandon or dramatically alter their investing style to chase more tantalizing returns.

✦ **The fund has grown too large.** With too much money in the fund's pockets, fund managers can't find enough good picks to spend it all. As a result, returns can suffer. This is more of a problem for small- and large-cap growth funds than the value variety.

Tip no. 9: Remain patient.

Investors used to be far more patient than they are today. In the 1960s, by one estimate, investors unloaded about 7 percent of their funds each year, with a typical holding period of 14 years. But recently, some industry fund watchers say 40 percent of funds are being dumped yearly. That would mean that the typical person is holding a fund for about 30 months.

Caution

Academic research has repeatedly shown that jumping in and out of investments typically produces dreadful results.

Even if you are a patient investor, you could be harmed by those who confuse fund investing with musical chairs. That's why you shouldn't shy away from funds that charge an *exit* or *redemption fee.* A redemption fee is leveled against a shareholder if he or she sells shares in a fund within a short period of time. The fee is typically 2 percent or lower.

Tip

Just the presence of a redemption fee discourages some market timers, who like to jump in and out of investments. As a result, the fee works to the advantage of buy-and-hold investors.

Market timers can be extremely disruptive to the rest of the shareholders because large swings in a fund's asset base can create havoc. If enough active traders bail, a manager may be forced to sell stocks to pay them off. This trading can create a tax bill for the shareholders who remain. Problems can also occur when market timers pile into a fund. A manager may choke on all the new money and may be unable to promptly put it all to work. This situation could ultimately jeopardize a fund's performance.

Bottom line: Once you're in a fund, stay in, unless the fund has two lousy years. But even then, you should tough it out if the other funds in the same category are suffering, too. That's when it's likely that other factors, such as inflation, overseas turmoil, or a bear market, are keeping a lid on returns.

Summary

✦ Establish your investing goals before you begin constructing a mutual fund portfolio.

✦ Limit the number of mutual funds in your portfolio to a manageable number.

✦ Use personal finance publications and fund screening tools to narrow your search for ideal funds.

✦ Learn how to evaluate the potential volatility of your funds by using risk measurement tools.

✦ Don't hold onto a fund for the wrong reasons; look for red flags that indicate it's time to sell.

The Art of Buying and Selling Mutual Funds

◆   ◆   ◆   ◆

In This Chapter

Sticking with no-load funds

Evaluating fund supermarkets

Buying shares in a closed fund

◆   ◆   ◆   ◆

In this chapter, you learn the best way to buy and sell mutual funds, plus a variety of ways to invest money in funds. The chapter covers the mechanics of fund trades, as well as typical investment minimums and ways to circumvent them.

Loading Up on the Best Shares

Picking the ideal mutual fund is hard, right? Well, maybe it's not so tough after all. An astounding number of Americans have managed to find and invest in many of the nation's top funds. Well-known fund companies that consistently produce sterling results are swimming in dough. In contrast, many of the funds hamstrung with mediocre performance records are rightfully lonely.

Although Americans have absorbed a great deal about the art of mutual fund selection, many remain perplexed about the art of buying shares. Far too many investors are losing significant amounts of money by investing in the wrong types of fund shares. The greatest confusion occurs among investors who buy load funds. Although different types of loads are available, the most popular option is, ironically, usually the costliest.

Load versus no-load funds

Every mutual fund is either a load or a no-load fund. Which type you select can significantly impact how well your fund performs in the future. So at the outset, you need to know which variety to pick.

Buying into a load fund means the shares come with a sales charge. You can compare it to valet parking. Just as you tip the valet who parks your car, you pay an extra built-in fee to have a stockbroker or financial planner choose your fund. After all, this person expects to be compensated for assisting you.

Note The average load is 4.8 percent. The fund that recently charged the highest load was Templeton Capital Accumulator with its whopping 9 percent charge.

No-load funds, as the name suggests, never charge a sales commission. These funds don't rely upon brokers or commissioned planners to sell their funds. The funds have to attract their own customers. No-load fund companies sell their funds directly or through fund networks offered primarily through discount brokerage firms. Later in the chapter, you'll discover how the brokers' fund networks operate.

Tip If you are comfortable selecting your own funds, stick with no-load funds. Paying a commission is pointless if you are doing the choosing. Your investment will have a head start if no commission is deducted.

In the past, the lines were clearly drawn between fund firms that sold load funds through middlemen and the no-load shops. But in recent times, the lines have blurred. No-load fund companies began questioning the financial wisdom of directly selling all their funds. In the cacophony of market noise, even decent fund companies sometimes have a hard time attracting much attention. Consequently, some now offer their funds with sales charges to entice brokers into pushing their products. T. Rowe Price, American Century, Janus, and PBHG, for instance, have tacked an extra fee on certain versions of their funds to pay middlemen. At the same time, some well-respected no-load fund companies, including Acorn, Scudder, and Mutual Series, were bought by competitors, who transformed some or all funds for new shareholders into load products.

Note You can buy a load fund by calling up a fund company directly, but you'll still be forced to pay the load even though no one gave you advice.

Types of load shares

Sticking with no-load funds could be impossible if you rely upon a commissioned advisor to help construct your fund portfolio. Most will steer you to load funds. If you decide to go with load funds, you'll want to understand how commissions affect the three classes of shares.

Class A shares

Once upon a time, the Class A share, or *front-end load,* was the only one that existed. With these shares, you pay the sales charge up front. For instance, somebody who invests $10,000 into a fund with a 5 percent load pays a $500 commission. Because the broker keeps the $500, your initial investment drops to $9,500, so you are in the hole at the start.

Day-old bread is more popular today than A shares. In one respect, it's easy to see why. Investors want to avoid sales charges even if they use a broker. And the thought of losing 5 percent or 6 percent of their money instantly is unbearable.

Class B shares

Among investors, a B share, or *back-end load,* is chosen more frequently. With B shares, the load kicks in when you sell your mutual fund. And if you hold B shares for several years, you might skip paying any load at all. For a buy-and-hold investor, that situation might sound great, but the fund makes sure these folks don't enjoy a free lunch.

 Caution   Investors who congratulate themselves for dodging the sales charge bullet are paying higher annual fees. This extra expense can be as high as 1 percent.

The additional charge is tucked into what is called a 12b-1 fee. (It received its name from federal legislation passed back in 1940.) The optional fee allows a fund company to charge up to 1 percent to pay for its marketing expenses, which include broker compensation. One industry commentator has suggested that this additional fee burden is like running a 100-yard dash while carrying a 200-pound anchor.

 Tip   If you are wondering whether you are paying the 12b-1 fee, you can easily find out. Call your fund company and ask. The fund's yearly prospectus also lists all the fees.

Class C shares

Class C shares have become increasingly popular. Once again, many investors apparently believe these shares aren't burdened by a sales charge. Unless you look hard, you might not spot it.

Class C shares, which are sometimes referred to as *level load shares,* typically charge a 1 percent ongoing fee to compensate the broker. It's just not called a load. Yes, you guessed it, it's that darn 12b-1 fee again. This fee is like an unwanted houseguest: It never goes away. So if you buy Class C shares from a broker and hold the fund for 10 years, that broker will continue to be compensated each year for that long-ago fund recommendation.

Caution   Another C share hazard: If you bail out of Class C shares within the first 12 to 18 months, you will probably be charged a redemption fee.

Questions for a Broker

Most funds sold in this country still come with a load and are often sold through full-service brokers. There is nothing wrong with relying upon a broker's advice to pick funds, but a healthy amount of skepticism is advisable.

Because you'll be paying a bundle for load funds, your advisor, who will benefit from your purchase, should explain the different types of loads available in plain English. Ask him or her to show you how the different loads have affected the performance of a fund over several years.

If you are depending upon a broker to pick your funds, make the broker work for his or her commission. If a broker is raving about a fund, tell him or her that you want to see the one-page analysis of the fund from Morningstar or Value Line, the independent rating services. Both firms provide an easily understandable summary of countless funds, as well as many measurements of past performance. Also ask your broker how Lipper and/or Wiesenberger, which rank mutual funds by statistical performance, rate the recommendation.

The best shares

Which type of share is the better load share? In the vast majority of cases, A shares are clearly the superior choice. Most Americans spurn them, however, because they think they save money by skipping that initial upfront commission. Yet because B and C shares can hit you with higher expenses for a long, long time, sticking with A shares, which have lower yearly costs, is far cheaper in most circumstances.

Want proof? Just examine the performance statistics of funds that are marketed with different share classes. You can find countless examples of this phenomenon in the mutual fund listings in the newspaper. The evidence is also contained in the funds' annual reports. Inevitably, you will see that A shares perform better. For example, A shares of PIMCO Capital Appreciation recently had a three-year annualized return of 9.2 percent percent. But B and C shares lagged behind by nearly 1 percentage point.

What's more, the load on A shares can shrink if you invest a lot of money. In contrast, B and C shares don't offer a price cut for sizable investments.

Note Buying C shares might be preferable in one instance. Some people choose C shares if they buy an aggressive fund, such as a biotechnology or Internet fund, that they don't intend to stick with for the long haul.

Supermarket Fund Investing

For many years, you had just two ways to buy mutual funds: directly from the fund company or through a broker or financial advisor. But in the early 1990s, Charles Schwab invented a third choice: the fund supermarket. Today every self-respecting discount brokerage firm operates its own fund network. A few full-service firms also provide the one-stop service through their online accounts.

To understand how revolutionary the idea of a fund supermarket was, you need to appreciate how fund purchasing used to be.

Imagine what it would be like if you could buy milk at one store, but not peanut butter. Another store carries carrots, but not ice cream. Still another store sells you cheese, but you have to go elsewhere for cereal. Hardly convenient, but that's how the mutual fund industry used to function. If you wanted shares in Janus fund, you had to call the Denver fund family directly. If you liked a fund offered by the American Century fund family, you contacted the Kansas City firm. No mutual fund company could sell you more than their own fund lineup. But now you can shop for funds the way you shop for food at a grocery store: all in one place.

You can buy nearly any fund you could possibly want through many brokerage firms. If you wish to purchase funds from a variety of different fund companies, you can do so through dozens of brokerage firms, such as Schwab, E*Trade, Merrill Lynch, Morgan Stanley Dean Witter, TD Waterhouse, or Accutrade. Each broker offers its own menu of outside funds. Some maintain a better selection than others, but you should be able to buy the nation's most popular funds at all or nearly all of them.

Note Anxious not to be left behind, some big fund families that also maintain a brokerage arm, such as Fidelity, T. Rowe Price, Strong, Dreyfus, and Vanguard, also sell competing funds through their own brokerage services.

Although fund supermarkets have made investing easier, pitfalls do exist. Here are the pros and cons of fund supermarkets:

Supermarket strengths

Investing in funds through a fund supermarket definitely has its advantages. Here are the major ones:

Supermarkets are extremely convenient.

Fund networks truly provide one-stop fund shopping. With one phone call or visit to a brokerage firm's Web site, you can request all the information you need about thousands of funds. When you're ready to buy or sell funds, you can accomplish this with one phone call or trip to a broker's Web address. You can transfer money between one mutual fund and another just as easily.

Note To take advantage of this convenience, you need to open a brokerage account. (See Chapter 4 for tips on how to select a brokerage firm.) Once you've established an account, you can trade funds, stocks, individual bonds, and other types of investments.

One of the beauties of investing this way is that it cuts down on paperwork, which makes it easier for you at tax time.

After all, if you own shares in more than three or four different fund families, the paperwork can require its own filing cabinet. Also, if your accounts are spread out, it's harder to keep track of what you have, which can be a disadvantage when you're trying to properly diversify. But if you own several funds through a discount brokerage firm, all your investments are listed on one consolidated statement. You can look at your whole portfolio by examining your statement or by visiting the Web site. The technologically savvy investors may also be able to download their holdings to portfolio-tracking software.

Supermarkets provide a wide range of choices.

In fund supermarkets, you'll find funds of every variety, from the safest short-term bond funds to the most heart-stopping emerging market funds. And the shelves at these supermarkets are getting more crowded by the day. Many brokerage firms offer thousands of funds. At TD Waterhouse, for instance, the menu exceeds 10,000; Ameritrade has nearly that many as well.

You'll probably recognize the names on this short list of some of the fund families sold through supermarkets:

American Century	Oak Associates	USAA
Firsthand	Harbor	Warburg Pincus
Janus	Vanguard	PBHG
Legg Mason	Fidelity	Van Wagoner
Dodge & Cox	Invesco	Royce
Strong	Brandywine	Bridgeway
Artisan	T. Rowe Price	Gabelli
Rydex	Marsico	Profunds

Tip Load funds also sit on the supermarket shelves, but you should avoid them if you are a do-it-yourself investor. There's no reason to pay the extra sales charge.

At many fund networks, you can find promising *boutique funds* that most people have never heard of. These undiscovered funds, which originate at small firms, might not have enough assets yet to qualify for inclusion in newspapers' agate listings.

Lower minimums make it easy to get started.

Every brokerage firm has its own minimum investment requirement to open an account. Although some firms welcome new customers for as little as $500 or $1,000, more exclusive funds can frustrate beginners by setting minimum investments that can range from $3,000 to $10,000 to $25,000 or even higher. Institutional funds can impose even steeper entry hurdles: It's not unusual for these funds, which cater to pension funds, endowments, and millionaires, to have the entry bar set at $250,000 or $500,000. But supermarket funds allow you to ignore those minimums. When you invest through a brokerage firm's fund menu, an exclusive fund's minimum investment often shrinks to $1,000 or $2,000.

Example

The minimum for the MAS Mid Cap Growth Fund, managed by the highly regarded institutional money management firm of Miller Anderson & Sherrerd, is $500,000. But you can invest in shares of this fund at some brokerage houses for as little as $1,000.

When you deal directly with a fund company, you can skirt stiff minimum investment requirements in another way. Some fund firms eliminate the entry hurdle for investors who agree to set up a $50-a-month (or higher) automatic investment with the fund. In addition, initial investment minimums are often lower for an Individual Retirement Account or an account you establish for a child.

Researching funds can be easier.

With brokerage firms offering thousands of fund choices, your first instinct might be panic. After all, who could possibly wade through all that information? The firms have anticipated that fear. Many of them offer their own lists of recommended funds to ease investors' homework. E*Trade, for instance, maintains an all-star list of funds that it compiled with the help of Morningstar. Schwab, Fidelity, and others provide similar recommendations.

Meanwhile, fund-screening tools are a ubiquitous feature on many brokerage firms' Web sites. With this software, you can hunt for your own dream fund by plugging in your requirements.

Example

With screening software, you could hunt for a tax-efficient fund with above-average returns and low expenses that is overseen by a veteran fund manager. The software will scan thousands of choices to pinpoint only those funds that fit the bill.

Supermarkets decrease the time and effort of trading shares.

If you own funds through individual fund companies, making changes in your portfolio can result in regrettable down time for your cash. There's a time lag between getting the redemption check from the old company and sending it off to the new fund. You don't have to worry about this delay with the discounters because the money can move quite swiftly.

First, let's see what could happen if you've invested directly with a fund company. Suppose you decide to close out one fund and use it to buy shares in a fund located thousands of miles away. If you are lucky, the fund company will let you cash out your holdings with a phone call or via its Web site. Some companies, though, insist that you make your request in writing. If you must send in a written request, you'll need to include your name, address, account number, fund name, and the dollar amount or number of shares you want to redeem. If you and your spouse's names are on the account, you both need to sign the letter. To validate your redemption request, some funds even require that you get a signature guarantee from a bank, which is a real pain.

Note A *signature guarantee,* which means that your signature is authenticated by a third party, must be obtained at a bank or a New York Stock Exchange brokerage firm. Silly as it might seem, a notary public cannot provide a signature guarantee.

Once you've accomplished all that, you have to wait for the company to receive your instructions to close out the fund by mail. Then you wait a few more days until your mail carrier delivers your redemption check. A fund can take up to seven days after it receives your redemption request to send your money.

In the meantime, you must contact the new fund firm and request an application. Once you cash your redemption check, you need to wait for it to be credited to your account. Finally, you'll be able to write your own check and mail it to the new fund company to start your account. Sound exhausting? Definitely. It can also be infuriating if the price of the fund that you want skyrockets while you are bogged down with this paper rigmarole.

Holding Tank for Fund Cashouts

When you cash in a mutual fund, there are two likely places to store the proceeds, at least until you have pinpointed your next investment. Chapter 2 has more details on selecting places to stash your cash, but this sidebar provides a quick look at the two big options.

Money market

Whether you sell a fund through a fund company or a brokerage firm, you may want to have the cash deposited into a money market account. Larger fund families typically offer them as a convenience to their customers, and they are a fixture at brokerage firms. The cash can sit in the money market until you decide how to invest it. Because check-writing privileges come with a money market, you can make withdrawals fairly easily if you choose.

Bank account

If you prefer to stash the money in your bank account, the fund company or brokerage firm can mail you a check. Some people who are in a hurry for the money have it sent by wire. If you make the request before 4 p.m. Eastern Standard Time, you can usually have the money deposited in your own bank account the next day.

To take advantage of this quick method, you have to make arrangements in advance. The best time to do this is when you are purchasing a mutual fund. The paperwork you fill out typically asks if you want to be able to wire any proceeds to your bank. (You can wire deposits, too.) If you want this feature, you fill out your bank account information and send along a voided check with your account number on it. Check with your bank to find out whether there is a fee for the wire service.

How would this scenario be different if you went through a broker's fund network? Here's what would happen: You would call your brokerage firm and instruct it to sell shares in mutual fund A. Then you would request that the proceeds be deposited into mutual fund B. You would be off the phone in less than five minutes with no muss and no fuss. The process should be even quicker if you use the Internet.

Note The day the fund receives your sell order isn't necessarily the sale date. If the request is received on a weekend, holiday, or after the stock market closes, the sale is posted on the next business day.

Supermarket weaknesses

There are downsides to the supermarket investing. Here are the drawbacks:

Easy access encourages market timing.

If you are prone to making impulsive investing decisions, using a fund network might be a disaster. Fund networks can encourage bad habits because the convenience can be mesmerizing. Because there's no paperwork or other hassles involved in trading through these one-stop fund sources, some investors trade too often. You have to remember to keep your eyes focused on your long-term investing goals.

If you like to flit in and out of funds (which is not a good idea, by the way), you'll want to know what a brokerage firm's policy is on that kind of behavior. Fund companies and discounters often treat fund investors who practice the dubious art of market timing about as warmly as rattlesnakes.

 Example Schwab and Fidelity, for instance, charge higher fees when an investor bails out of a fund within 180 days. Fidelity recently charged $75 for these short-term trades, except when they were for its own Fidelity funds. The tab was potentially even higher at Schwab.

Supermarkets aren't always free.

By now you might be asking yourself, "What's the catch? What is this convenience going to cost me? Surely it isn't free." The short answer is, "Yes, you can get something for nothing." But the more complicated answer is, "Nothing is completely free."

Many of the funds that you purchase through a discount broker are free. You can trade certain funds and never trigger trading costs. These funds are often referred to as "no-transaction fee" funds. When you are researching the funds available through a brokerage firm, you want to determine which ones can be bought and sold for free.

Typically, however, most funds in a brokerage firm's menu trigger a transaction fee. At TD Waterhouse, for instance, only 1,400 funds out of a universe of more than 10,000 carry no transaction cost. The fee for buying funds outside the no-transaction-fee universe can cost in the neighborhood of $10 to $75 dollars a trade. In other words, purchasing these funds is like accumulating stock through a broker, it triggers a commission. The costs can be much higher than a stock commission.

Tip Your first inclination might be to stick exclusively with the free funds, but that isn't always prudent. If you do so, you'll rule out many excellent choices.

The cost of doing business

Why can't you buy all funds for free? It boils down to how individual fund firms decide to charge their customers. Strange as it may seem, the funds that cost extra are often the guys wearing the white hats.

Here's why: When you buy a fund without paying a fee, somebody has to compensate the brokerage firm for handling the sale. After all, E*Trade, Ameritrade, and the rest of the brokerage firms aren't charities. The fund company ends up paying the brokerage house for every trade its customers make. So where does that money come from? It's ultimately extracted from the pockets of every fund customer, even those who don't buy their shares from brokerage firms, in the form of higher annual expenses. And higher expenses erode a fund's performance.

Certain fund companies, including Vanguard, T. Rowe Price, and others that pride themselves on rock-bottom fund expenses, refuse to play this game. They want their funds available in supermarkets, but they decline to pay brokerage firms for peddling their funds. How is this standoff resolved? Enter the transaction fee. The customer pays the cost rather than the fund.

To fee or not to fee

Fund shoppers face trade-offs. If a fund is top-notch and charges very low annual expenses, it might be better to pay a transaction fee. If a fund is an excellent performer, charges below-average annual expenses, and doesn't carry a transaction fee, it's even better.

In some circumstances, a fund that triggers a commission is inappropriate no matter how dazzling it is. Suppose you are a Charles Schwab customer and you have your heart set on purchasing Vanguard Total Stock Market Index fund as a core holding in your portfolio, even though you have to pony up a $35 transaction fee for the buy. As a one-time purchase, that's okay. But say you also want to contribute $100 a month into the fund. With each contribution triggering a $35 fee, you'd sabotage your own investment.

Tip If you want to invest regularly in a certain fund, establish an account directly with the fund firm. A fund company will not charge its direct customers a transaction fee.

Bringing All Your Funds Together

Consolidating funds through a broker may sound great. But how do you do that if your funds are scattered at individual fund companies from Boston to San Francisco?

Your first step is to establish an account with a brokerage firm through its toll-free number or Web site. While you're at it, request account transfer paperwork. On the form, list the names of your current funds, the account numbers, and the amount of shares you want transferred. The new firm takes on the responsibility of contacting all your fund companies and notifying them of your request. When your old funds have been transferred, your new brokerage firm will let you know.

Keep in mind that a firm will accept only funds that it already carries in its inventory. If you own shares in proprietary Merrill Lynch or UBS PaineWebber funds or any other funds sponsored by full-service brokers, for instance, you may not be able to transfer them. If you want that money moved, you'll have to sell those shares.

Before you commit yourself, find out what a brokerage firm's transaction fees are and also what funds each of these discounters offer. Don't assume that the discounters offer all the major funds. Ameritrade and Datek, for instance, don't offer Fidelity's funds. Call the toll-free number for each brokerage firm and ask for their no-fee supermarket literature or check out the brokerage firms' Web sites.

Opening the Door to Closed Funds

Not all funds want your money. Some of the great ones have already closed their doors to new investors. Would-be shareholders are often turned away when a fund starts drowning in cash because a frustrated fund manager may feel that he or she no longer has enough great stock ideas to go around. If the fund doesn't spurn new money, performance could seriously falter.

A popular fund may close for only a year or so to give the portfolio manager breathing room. But in other cases, the door stays locked for a very long time. The Sequoia Fund, for instance, has remained shuttered since 1982. Some of America's most respected funds, including Janus Twenty, Janus Fund, Vanguard Primecap, and Longleaf Partners Small-Cap, are all closed.

Options and opportunities

Is there any way to unlock these doors? Sometimes. You may need only to convince one person to sell or give you a solitary share of a closed fund. Some frustrated investors publicize their search for solitary shares on Internet message boards where fund junkies hang out, such as Morningstar (www.morningstar.com) and Brill's Mutual Funds Interactive (www.brill.com). Typically, a closed fund permits its existing shareholders to continue pouring more money into it. If you own as little as one share, you'd enjoy the same privilege.

However, some fund families have erected roadblocks to stop this practice. Vanguard, for instance, only permits transfers of at least $3,000. Bridgeway Funds, a successful boutique firm in Houston, only allows transfers to family members living in the same home.

There are other possible solutions. Sometimes you can buy shares in a fund that's off limits if you invest through a financial advisor. Meanwhile, some fund companies try to appease frustrated investors by launching a clone fund. When Fidelity Contrafund was temporarily closed, for instance, Fidelity Contrafund II was born. Vanguard Windsor begot Vanguard Windsor II. The offspring sometimes fare better than the parent because the spin-off funds are less likely to be choked with cash.

Of course, plenty of shuttered funds, including Fidelity Contrafund, Fidelity Low-Priced Stocks, and Third Avenue Value, reopen. When a popular fund once again welcomes new customers, should you rush in? Not necessarily. Once an invitation is extended, a flood of money can create obstacles.

Caution   A manager may not be able to nimbly handle all the new cash in a reopened fund. The money may sit on the sidelines uninvested, which is hardly desirable when you meant to invest in a stock fund, not a money market.

In general, small-cap funds are more likely to be hurt by a bloated asset base. That's because shares of small companies tend to be less liquid, which means it's harder to find eager traders who will snap up or unload large blocks of shares. Consequently, a fund manager sitting on a pile of cash may find it extremely difficult to trade stock in small fry without triggering significant rises and falls in price. If a fund invests in large-caps, it won't make as much difference if it begins accepting new money.

Making the call

From an existing shareholder's perspective, it's better to be sitting in a closed fund. If it reopens, investors will have to decide whether to bail, and investors who were initially shut out need to decide whether to jump in.

If a closed fund reopens and you have a hard time deciding whether to jump in (or bail out), find out why a fund is seeking new shareholders. Are there big opportunities that a manager now wants to take advantage of? Or does it appear that the fund company just craves more investor money? After all, the more money it pulls in, the more money it pockets in fees. Finally, does the manager promise to close the fund in the future if assets become too unwieldy again? Call the fund's customer service line to find out where you can get answers to these key questions.

Summary

✦ Investors who buy shares in load funds should typically stick with front-end or A shares.

✦ Buying mutual funds through brokerage firms can be the simplest way to invest.

✦ Investors should evaluate a brokerage firm's mutual fund menu and commission schedules before choosing the most appropriate one.

✦ If you're interested in a mutual fund with a high investment minimum, there are ways to skirt this hurdle.

✦ Look for clones of popular funds that are closed to new investors; the clones may perform better than the original.

✦ Before you invest in a newly reopened fund, find out why the fund was reopened.

✦   ✦   ✦

Index Fund Investing

In this chapter, you discover how index funds work and why they often can outperform other types of mutual funds. You'll also learn how to intelligently use index funds in your own portfolio. In addition, this chapter includes recommended guidelines on mixing index and actively managed funds.

The Ascent of the Average

The mutual fund industry was just a financial flyspeck back in 1976 when a financial visionary in Valley Forge, Pennsylvania had the audacity to introduce a radical new way to invest in funds. Ignoring considerable ridicule and laughter, John C. Bogle, who later became the patron saint of cost-conscious investors, introduced the first retail index fund.

When this financial oddity rumbled off the conveyor belt, many in the financial world scoffed. They called index funds sheer folly and insisted that investing in them would condemn investors to mediocre returns. These skeptics were completely off the mark. Today the maligned fund that started all the commotion is America's second most popular mutual fund: the Vanguard 500 Index Fund. This granddaddy of all index funds recently was sitting on an $80 billion stockpile of cash.

Origin of Indexes

Indexes were originally created at the behest of institutional investors. With millions or even billions of dollars at stake, endowments, corporations, and other major investors wanted to know how well their own in-house or outside money managers measured up. Because the stock market is so large and unwieldy, it was compartmentalized into smaller components so the institutional powerhouses could get a better idea of whether their hired helpers were earning their keep.

But Bogle's grand experiment wouldn't have been nearly as celebrated if it had simply meant that indexing would ultimately turn the Vanguard Group into a financial powerhouse. More importantly, the indexing strategy, which took decades to truly catch on, has changed the way millions of individuals invest. By embracing indexing, investors tacitly agree that aiming for average returns is okay. This is a remarkable concession for Americans who are, after all, programmed to win big, whether it's at a Friday night poker game, a soccer scrimmage, or a presidential election. Settling for an average pediatrician, an average SAT score, or an average meal at a restaurant is unappealing to most people. Yet what even many of the skeptics ultimately concluded was that shooting for average Wall Street returns is a lot better than earning mediocre ones.

Ironically, although critics initially predicted that indexing would be a short-lived fad, some experts are now suggesting that the indexing movement, thanks to both index funds and exchange-traded funds (a topic covered in the next chapter), may someday endanger traditional mutual funds.

Anatomy of an Index Fund

Skeptics continue to believe that indexing is a flawed strategy because it condemns investors to a lifetime of average returns. To understand the argument—and find out why most of us are lucky to achieve the average—you need to appreciate how index funds function and understand how indexes work.

Index funds at work

An index fund isn't supposed to do any better or worse than the benchmark it tracks. An index fund that shadows the Standard & Poor's 500 Index, for instance, isn't designed to outperform the popular benchmark; its sole mission is to match the index's results as closely as possible. A manager accomplishes this objective by buying and holding all 500 corporate Goliaths in the index. If the committee that oversees the index drops a company from the lineup, the fund will, too. When the index replacement is announced, the fund moves money into that stock. Consequently, the fund should be a spitting image of the index.

Other index funds work similarly. A small-cap index fund linked to the Russell 2000 or Standard & Poor's SmallCap 600 Index should mimic the performance of the benchmark. Yet sometimes an index is too large to make it practical for a fund to hold every stock. That's true with index funds that track the Wilshire 5000, which contains roughly 7,000 publicly traded stocks. Instead, a fund will hold a representative sampling of the stocks in the index. Fidelity Spartan Total Market Index Fund, for example, holds around 2,300 stocks, and Vanguard Total Stock Market Index Fund keeps roughly 3,440 stocks in the portfolio.

The passive indexing approach remains an alien concept for most mutual funds. In actively managed funds, money managers try to outwit the market by trading stocks or bonds. Unlike their index colleagues, these managers don't want to just match the index: They want to pulverize it. That sounds great, right? The problem is that most managers can't do it.

Note The vast majority of professional fund managers can't regularly beat the indexes with their stock picks. Most funds don't even come close.

Popular indexes

Before you can intelligently pick an index fund, you should know what the indexes contain. Keep reading to learn about the most popular ones.

Standard & Poor's 500

The Standard & Poor's 500 index is packed with—surprise, surprise—500 companies. Most of the nation's blue-chip corporations are included in this handpicked list. These Goliaths represent about 77 percent of the market capitalization of all American stocks. Recently, the index's biggest member was General Electric; the smallest was American Greetings.

Wilshire 5000

By tracking more than 7,000 American companies, the Wilshire 5000 is the nation's broadest stock index. Although this index includes corporations of every size, blue chips still dominate as they do in the S&P 500. Over the decades, the returns of both benchmarks have been remarkably similar. However, the Wilshire 5000 should perform slightly better than the S&P 500 during periods when small-caps shine.

Tip The Wilshire 5000 can be a godsend for investors wanting to put all or part of their stock portfolios on autopilot. You can gain exposure to the entire stock market by investing in an index fund tied to the Wilshire 5000.

Dow Jones Industrial Average

The Dow Jones Industrial Average, which is the granddaddy of all indexes, is America's best-known benchmark. Charles H. Dow, a journalist and cofounder of *The Wall Street Journal,* unveiled The Dow in 1896. The Dow, which is printed in a separate box each day in *The Wall Street Journal,* tracks the performance of 30 of

America's largest and best-known corporations. (See Table 10-1.) When newscasters recap what's happened on Wall Street each day, they recite The Dow's numbers.

The owners of *The Wall Street Journal* periodically shuffle companies in and out of the Dow Jones Industrial Average so that it better reflects the U.S. economy. During the last change, which occurred in 1997, Westinghouse, Texaco, Bethlehem Steel, and Woolworth were evicted, and Hewlett-Packard, Johnson & Johnson, the Travelers Group, and Wal-Mart were invited in. Although this index generally mirrors the health of the entire market, the Standard & Poor's 500 Index is considered a better benchmark for the overall market.

Table 10-1 The 30 Corporations in the Dow Jones Industrial Average		
Alcoa	Exxon Mobil	J.P. Morgan
American Express	General Electric	McDonald's
AT&T	General Motors	Merck
Boeing	Hewlett-Packard	Microsoft
Caterpillar	Home Depot	Minnesota Mining & Manufacturing (3M)
Citigroup	Honeywell	Philip Morris
Coca-Cola	IBM	Procter & Gamble
Disney	Intel	SBC Communications
DuPont	International Paper	United Technologies
Eastman Kodak	Johnson & Johnson	Wal-Mart

Russell 2000 and Standard & Poor's SmallCap 600

The Russell 2000 index is made up of 2,000 companies that are considered small by financial standards. Add up all these stocks and they represent less than 8 percent of the total market's capitalization. You can use this benchmark or the Standard & Poor's SmallCap 600 to compare the performance of small companies or funds. Recently, the market value of all 600 handpicked stocks in this index did not equal the stock valuation of General Electric. Experts quarrel about which index is better, but institutional investors seem to prefer S&P's version.

Standard & Poor's MidCap 400

While the S&P 500 comprises about 77 percent of the total stock market, the Standard & Poor's MidCap 400 index represents the next largest 6 percent slice of the market. While mid-cap stocks are often overlooked by investors, they historically have performed almost as well as small-cap stocks, but with much less volatility.

Nasdaq Composite and Nasdaq-100

The Nasdaq Composite contains all the corporations, both domestic and foreign, that are listed on the Nasdaq stock market. Recently, about 70 percent of the index's total stock valuation could be traced to tech stocks, but only financial stocks are intentionally kept out of the mix. (The financial stocks have their own index.) Some of the nontechnology companies that are included in the index are Staples, Bed, Bath & Beyond, and Starbucks. The Nasdaq-100 includes the biggest and most popularly traded companies in the Nasdaq stock market. (Table 10-2 lists the biggest names in the Nasdaq-100.)

Note During the past 10 years, the Nasdaq-100 has out performed all the major domestic and foreign indexes.

Table 10-2
Twenty Largest Corporations Listed on the Nasdaq-100

1. Microsoft	11. Applied Material
2. Intel	12. Xilinx
3. Cisco Systems	13. Maxim Integrated Products
4. Qualcomm	14. Linear Technology
5. Oracle	15. Gemstar-TV Guide International
6. JDS Uniphase	16. WorldCom
7. Amgen	17. Immunex
8. Veritas Software	18. Check Point Software Technologies
9. Dell	19. Altera
10. VoiceStream Wireless	20. Siebel Systems

Morgan Stanley Capital International Europe, Australasia and Far East (EAFE) Index

Morgan Stanley Capital International Europe, Australasia, and Far East Index (MSCI EAFE, pronounced *Ee-feh*) is the most popular foreign index. It tracks foreign corporations in developed nations, such as Germany, France, Great Britain, Japan, Italy, and Singapore. Investors use this index as a benchmark for comparison with their own actively managed foreign funds.

To learn more about the various indexes, visit these Web sites:

✦ Standard & Poor's indexes: www.spglobal.com

✦ Dow Jones Industrial Average: http://averages.dowjones.com

✦ Russell 2000: www.russell.com

✦ Wilshire 5000: www.wilshire.com

✦ Nasdaq indexes: www.nasdaq.com

✦ MSCI EAFE: www.msci.com

Advantages of Index Funds

Most investors should consider indexing a portion of their portfolios. If you're unsure why, here are the major reasons:

Index funds demonstrate steady, superior performance.

Because of their mandate, you won't spot index funds included on the lists of the year's best-performing mutual funds. But then again, you won't spot them sitting in the basement with the true dogs. What you will often find, however, is that index funds outperform most actively managed funds over a several year period. This steady performance, as boring as stock kamikazes might consider it, has embarrassed the rest of the fund world. As you can see in Table 10-3, regular funds have had a devilish time beating the Standard & Poor's 500 Index, which is a barometer for the market, and the index funds associated with it.

Table 10-3 Percentage of Actively Managed Stock Funds that Underperformed the S&P 500 Index			
Year	Percentage	Year	Percentage
2001*	52.1%	1993	40%
2000	39.1%	1992	46%
1999	47.5%	1991	45%
1998	86.3%	1990	64%
1997	89.5%	1989	82%
1996	75%	1988	59%
1995	85%	1987	76%
1994	78%		

* through April 2001

Source: Lipper

Historical Returns of Leading Indexes

Here are historical performance figures for the major indexes:

Average Annual Returns	3 Years	5 Years	10 Years
Standard & Poor's 500	5.3%	15.6%	15.2%
Wilshire 5000	4%	13.7%	14.6%
Dow Jones Industrial Average	7.4%	15.9%	16.6%
Standard & Poor's MidCap 400	12%	18%	17.3%
Standard & Poor's SmallCap 600	3.7%	11.1%*	
Russell 2000	1.4%	8.3%	12.7%
MSCI EAFE	1.7%	4.5%	6.8%
Nasdaq Composite	4.4%	12.5%	16.7%
Nasdaq-100	14.1%	22.7%	21.5%

Source: Wiesenberger, Thomson Financial

Note

In the late 1990s, Wiesenberger, a fund tracking service, looked back 15 years to find out how many funds had beaten the S&P 500 Index in each of those years. Guess what? Not a single fund had. Only one came close: Davis New York Venture beat the index 12 out of the 15 years.

The steady performance of index funds, however, doesn't mean that the volatility has been wrung out of them. When the market is tanking, index funds tank too. But here is a reassuring thought for nervous Nellies: Historically, the stock market, despite extremely rough patches that can last for years, has managed to continue marching onward and upward. Because index funds link their fate to the market's, that fact bodes well for long-term investors.

Note

As you'll learn later in the chapter, the indexing edge is particularly pronounced with large-cap stocks. Investing in large-cap stocks through an index fund is an easy call to make.

Diversifying is easy with index funds.

With an index fund, you can own a stake in a huge chunk of the U.S. stock market for as little as $2,000 or $3,000. That modest investment can buy instant exposure to the mightiest of blue chips all the way down the food chain to aggressive Internet plays.

Index funds can resolve a dilemma faced by individuals with modest amounts of money to invest. If someone doesn't have enough cash to spread among funds that specialize in small, medium, and large companies, as well as in the growth and value style of investing, plunking money into an all-purpose index fund can be a wonderful solution.

For nearly any type of investor, an index fund makes an excellent core holding. An ideal core index fund would be one linked to the S&P 500 or perhaps even better, the Wilshire 5000, which is a broader index.

The variety of choices is wide.

Today, investors have more than 200 index fund choices. Most of these index funds are linked to the S&P 500. The rest are devoted to a hodge-podge of other indexes. You can buy index funds that are tied to the fortunes of technology, real estate, utilities, and emerging markets. There's even e-commerce and Internet index funds. Mutual fund firms, which never dreamed they'd be swept up in the indexing biz, are scrambling to offer their own indexing creations.

Even though the indexing choices aren't vast in comparison to the number of actively managed funds out there, wading through your choices can still be challenging. Consider beginning your research with the index fund candidates in the following lists:

Standard & Poor's 500 Index funds:

 ✦ Vanguard 500 Index: (800) 635-1511

 ✦ Fidelity Spartan 500 Index: (800) 343-3548

 ✦ T. Rowe Price Equity Index 500: (800) 638-5660

 ✦ Bridgeway Ultra-Large 35 Index: (800) 661-3550

Total Stock Market index funds:

 ✦ Fidelity Spartan Total Market Index: (800) 343-3548

 ✦ Schwab 1000: (800) 266-5623

 ✦ Vanguard Total Stock Market Index: (800) 635-1511

Small-Cap and Mid-Cap index funds:

 ✦ E*Trade Extended Market Index: (800) 786-2575

 ✦ Schwab Small Cap Index: (800) 266-5623

 ✦ Vanguard Small Cap Index: (800) 635-1511

 ✦ Vanguard Extended Market Index: (800) 635-1511

 ✦ Fidelity Spartan Extended Market Index: (800) 343-3548

Morgan Stanley EAFE index funds:

- ✦ Fidelity Spartan International Index: (800) 343-3548
- ✦ Schwab International Index: (800) 266-5623
- ✦ Vanguard Developed Markets Index: (800) 635-1511

Bond index funds:

- ✦ Vanguard Total Bond Market Index: (800) 635-1511
- ✦ Schwab Total Bond Market Index: (800) 266-5623
- ✦ Vanguard Intermediate-Term Bond Index: (800) 635-1511
- ✦ E*Trade Bond Index: (800) 786-2575

Index funds are cheap.

When you buy shares in an index fund, you get a Mercedes on a Hyundai budget. While your index fund should generally do better than most of the competition, it can deliver those kinds of returns for a fraction of the other guy's costs.

Note

A chief reason why index funds are so successful is because they are cheap. The average expense ratio for an index fund is .66 percent while the average stock fund charges 1.4 percent.

The expense spread might not seem like a big deal, but in the competitive mutual fund world, a 1 percent or 2 percent point advantage can make a huge difference. Imagine an Olympic sprinter having to start the 100-yard dash 10 feet behind everyone else. That sprinter is not likely to win the race. That's the kind of disadvantage actively managed funds face. If your fund returns 9 percent and the expenses are 1.5 percent, expenses eat up fully 16.6 percent of your gain. In contrast, if expenses are just .5 percent, 5.5 percent of the gain vanishes.

Tip

Don't settle for average when it comes to expenses. Cheaper is usually better.

The cost advantage is even more important in the bond universe. Even the most talented, ambitious fixed-income genius is going to find it extremely difficult to pull away from the pack. With stock funds, some funds post negative returns in the same year that other peers are enjoying gains of 10 percent, 20 percent, or more. In contrast, the performance range is quite cramped for bond funds. Typically, the bond funds that charge investors the lowest expenses are the ones that creep ahead of the pack.

Example

The annual expenses for the Vanguard Total Bond Market Index Fund are almost a whole percentage point below the average competitor. In the bond world, this gulf is as wide as the Grand Canyon.

Don't Ignore Bond Index Funds

If you are contemplating investing in a bond fund, think index. Bond index funds are a true hidden treasure. Many investors don't know they exist because stock index funds have hogged the limelight.

For the broadest fixed-income exposure, invest in a fund that tracks the Lehman Brothers Aggregate Bond Index, which is divided among Treasuries, government and corporate bonds, and mortgage-backed securities. You can also invest in index funds that focus on short-, intermediate-, or long-term bonds.

You don't have many bond index funds to choose from: Less than three dozen exist. They are, however, worth tracking down. During the past decade, bond index funds have nudged out actively managed bond funds for the top performance title. The bond index fund enjoys the major advantage of having much lower expenses.

Index funds are tax efficient.

Most investors are fixated on a mutual fund's performance. Fund companies are famous for using ads in magazines, newspapers, and even on television to brag about superior returns. If marketers roll out a successful ad campaign, cash from new investors will gush in. A fund's advertised performance, however, isn't the most important number you need to know. What's more critical is how much money you can keep after taxes. (See Chapter 25 for tried and true techniques to outmaneuver taxes.)

However, most fund firms have historically been silent on the topic of taxes. You could scour a fund's literature and never read a peep about a fund's tax efficiency. The U.S. Securities and Exchange Commission has finally put an end to this information blackout by requiring firms to supply after-tax numbers in their literature. In addition, Morningstar provides after-tax statistics on the funds it covers.

Note   Tax efficiency in mutual funds is crucial because, unlike individual stocks, you can't avoid capital gains taxes by simply holding onto a fund.

The awful truth about mutual funds and taxes

Even if you wouldn't dream of selling your fund shares, you may still face yearly taxes. That's because you and every other investor are liable for your fund manager's trading activity. If a manager dumps a lot of winning stocks that have skyrocketed in value, guess who is liable for all these gains? The fund investors, who receive the money in capital gains distributions, are liable. Pocketing this kind of windfall might sound great, but there is a catch. Although investors do indeed receive their share of the profits, the price of each of those fund shares is reduced accordingly. In other words, you own more shares, but each share is now worth less. The whole transaction would be a wash, if it weren't for the tax bill. The IRS expects you to pay capital gains taxes on any distributions. Depending upon how long the manager held the stock shares, you might be hit with short-term (the worst) or long-term capital gains taxes.

Index funds as a tax solution

Why does this nasty tax dilemma make index funds appealing? In the fund world, index funds are the model of tax efficiency because of their buy-and-hold mission. An index fund manager does very little trading because the goal is to just hang onto the stocks in the benchmark. Many stocks in the Standard & Poor's 500, for example, have belonged to the index for decades. Index fund managers will still have stocks like General Motors, Pfizer, and General Electric in their portfolios in the decades to come. With this little trading, there will be few if any capital gains distributions to worry about.

Tip   The most tax-efficient index funds encompass the entire stock market.

Index funds that are tied to the S&P 500 are extremely tax efficient. Index funds linked to small companies aren't quite as accomplished as tax busters because there is more movement of companies in and out of the small-cap indexes. Pint-sized companies that have outgrown their benchmarks are booted out of the index, and replacements are found. This kind of change requires index fund managers to tinker more with their portfolio and ultimately sell stocks. Despite this drawback, even small-cap index funds are generally far more tax-efficient than actively managed small-cap funds.

Tip   Because of their tax efficiency, index funds are considered ideal for taxable accounts.

If you invest in a retirement account, it doesn't matter if one of your funds is a poster child for sloppy tax managing. Remember that if the investment is in an IRA, a 401(k), or other retirement vehicle, you aren't liable for any taxes. You won't owe taxes until you pull money out of a retirement plan.

Disadvantages of Index Funds

A cloud or two lurks behind the silver lining of index funds. Here are potential problems you should be aware of.

Index funds don't come in every flavor.

Index funds aren't appropriate for every investing need. If you are interested in investing in a particular sector, such as healthcare, financial stocks, utilities, real estate, or even technology, you don't have much of a selection. Although about 200 or so index funds are on the market, almost half of them are linked to the S&P 500.

Tip   Exchange-traded funds or mutual funds that specialize in certain sectors can provide a better way to gain exposure in the market's smaller niches.

Not all index funds are cheap.

One of the most compelling reasons to invest in index funds is their cost, but some index funds only masquerade as bargain-basement picks. So before you invest, carefully read a fund's prospectus to discover what the fee schedule is. (To obtain a copy, call a fund's toll-free number.)

The industry's low-cost leader has traditionally been the Vanguard Group. Index funds offered by brokers such as Schwab, Fidelity, and E*Trade also keep expenses down. But when interest in index funds began soaring in the late 1990s, other institutions jumped into the arena. Not all of these newcomers are as rabid as Vanguard is about keeping costs low.

Some of the newest index funds are outrageously overpriced. The annual expense of the Vanguard 500 Index is a mere .18 percent, yet some of the other S&P 500 funds charge five or six times that amount. The bloated pricing is certainly bold considering that the same 500 stocks are in both the cheap and expensive portfolios. And the gouging doesn't end there.

Caution   Some index funds are sold with a sales commission, which is commonly referred to as a load. These funds can come gift wrapped with a sales load of 5 percent or more.

Finding index funds as cheap as Vanguard's is tough, but it's not impossible. For instance, Schwab's retail index funds cost a bit more, but the institutional versions of its funds are comparable. To qualify to buy Schwab's institutional shares, you need to be a large investor or use a financial planner who has established a relationship with the discount broker. Vanguard also offers even cheaper institutional shares for its large clients.

Indexing isn't always superior.

It's pretty much a given that placing indexing bets on large-cap stocks works. But the jury remains deadlocked on the merits of small-cap and foreign indexing. Many experts believe that actively managed funds in these two areas enjoy an advantage because these markets are quirkier. (Economists prefer to call them "inefficient.")

The market for large-cap American corporations is considered efficient because hordes of analysts follow these stocks, making surprises rarer. Any news on these giants is swiftly reflected in the stock price. In contrast, analysts often ignore smaller corporations and many overseas companies, particularly in Asia and the emerging markets. Shrewd stock pickers can flourish in this kind of vacuum. By selecting the gems among the universe of under-followed companies, a smart fund manager can pull ahead of the competition, as well as the appropriate index.

Arguably, the foreign index funds are the least attractive. Throughout most of the 1990s, for instance, actively managed overseas fund managers walloped their index brethren. During that time, two-thirds of actively managed funds beat their respective index, due in part to the downturn in the Japanese market. Actively managed funds could dump Japanese stocks, but index funds could not.

Recent developments, however, should hearten investors who would like to index overseas. Morgan Stanley Capital International is broadening its foreign indexes to include more corporations. The overhaul of the indexes was expected to be completed by the spring of 2002.

Index funds can be extremely volatile.

Some of the indexing hype has obscured this reality: You can lose money with index funds. The biggest index fund, Vanguard 500 Index, dropped 9.1 percent in 2000 after sterling performances throughout most of the 1990s. (The Standard & Poor's 500 Index plunged a negative 10.1 percent in 2001.) This volatility, however, shouldn't discourage you if you're a long-term investor who can stay on the market's roller coaster.

Swinging with small and specialized companies

Index funds that are stuffed with smaller companies can be even more volatile. A good example is Vanguard Extended Market Index Fund. This fund is linked to the Wilshire 4500, which represents the broad stock market, with the exception of the corporate giants in the S&P 500. This index is stuffed to the gills with fast-growing technology, biotechnology, and communication stocks that have yet to generate much if any earnings. Dominating this index are corporations such as Ciena, VeriSign, Genentech, and Ebay. When technology stocks do well, this fund shines, but when the tech world catches a cold so does this fund.

Specialized index funds can provoke even wilder rides. Niche funds that track such things as Internet companies, utilities, and technology are now being peddled.

 Note   Keep in mind that the narrower a fund's focus is, the greater the possibility of extreme volatility.

Losing your head with leveraged index funds

Some index funds have been intentionally designed to be incredibly volatile. You will see these funds referred to as *leveraged index funds.* These index funds were quite popular when the markets seemed to be defying gravity, but anyone without an iron stomach should stay away.

These funds, which are typically linked to the Nasdaq-100 and the S&P 500, are intended to perform much better or worse than their underlying indexes. For example, ProFunds UltraOTC, which tracks the technology-heavy Nasdaq-100, is supposed to be twice as volatile as its index. So if the index jumps 15 percent, ProFunds UltraOTC should soar about 30 percent. The same principle applies when the market is floundering. If the Nasdaq-100 drops 20 percent, this fund should plummet 40 percent. ProFunds offers the most extreme funds; other fund families, such as Rydex and Potomac, offer slightly less volatile versions.

These leveraged funds initially appealed to market timers and financial advisors. But as these funds began appearing on the annual lists of the best-performing funds during the late 1990s, average Joe investors began sinking money into them. ProFunds UltraOTC, for instance, drew phenomenal amounts of new cash when it skyrocketed 184 percent in 1998 and then repeated the feat with an astounding return of nearly 230 percent in 1999.

Caution   These firecracker funds are a terrible choice for retirees, risk-averse investors, or anyone with a short investing time horizon.

Leveraged funds may be appropriate, in small doses, for very aggressive, long-term investors who have the guts to hang on during scary periods. If you'd be tempted to flee if one of these funds dropped, say, 74 percent in one year, don't go near these funds. If you're thinking that debacle could never happen, think again. That was ProFunds UltraOTC's return in 2000.

Cross-Reference   Individuals who are interested in socially responsible investing will be pleased to learn that index funds that specialize in this niche are now available. See Chapter 7 for the names.

Indexing Your Portfolio: When Enough Is Enough

By now, many investors appreciate that investing in index funds is a smart idea. It's hard to go wrong with using an index fund that tracks the S&P 500 or the Wilshire 5000 as the cornerstone of a portfolio. But how much indexing is enough? Sure, you could index your entire portfolio and be done with it. But is that necessarily wise?

Even Vanguard, indexing's most prominent cheerleader, thinks it's possible to over-dose on indexing. The Pennsylvania fund family has traditionally recommended that 50 percent to 60 percent of a typical investor's portfolio should be allocated to index funds. The fund family declines to provide any specific guidance on how to divide up the pie because it believes no magic formula exists.

Reckoning with the research

The Schwab Center for Investment Research, a division of Charles Schwab & Co., Inc., examined the historical performance of thousands of hypothetical fund port-folios to see whether they could determine an ideal ratio. The analysts explored whether investors would be better off with an all-index portfolio, a strictly actively managed portfolio, or a combination of the two. The asset allocation breakdown of each portfolio was large-caps (40 percent), small-caps (25 percent), international (30 percent), and cash (5 percent).

Cross-Reference   For an explanation of stock lingo, see Chapter 12.

The researchers came to the following conclusions:

✦ A combination of index and actively managed funds has a better chance of outperforming the market than pure indexing. Two-thirds of these combo portfolios beat the all-index approach's total return of 19.3 percent.

✦ A mix of index and actively managed funds was 57 percent less volatile than portfolios using no indexing.

✦ An investor increases his or her chances of beating the market by combining a large-cap index fund with actively managed international and domestic small-cap funds.

In screening for the best investment combinations, the Schwab Center for Investment Research arrived at what they considered to be the optimum mix of index and actively managed funds during the 1995 to 1997 time period. In the performance race, the researchers concluded that it was tough improving upon a large-cap index fund. In contrast, international and small-cap index funds didn't perform nearly as well as their actively managed peers. In these two areas, the Schwab experts suggest that investors use indexing more sparingly.

The proportions in Table 10-4, according to Schwab's research, could represent the best opportunity to beat the market while underperforming it by the smallest percentage during turbulent times.

Table 10-4 Schwab Asset Allocation Recommendations		
Type of Fund	*Index Percentage*	*Actively Managed Percentage*
Large-cap stock	80%	20%
Small-cap stock	40%	60%
International stock	30%	70%

Mediocre funds need not apply

There is one thing you should know about the Schwab research. The study only included actively managed funds that were above average and were available through the brokerage firm. The experts readily acknowledge that if mediocre funds had been included in the study, index funds would have looked even more attractive. The Schwab researchers defended their decision to use only attractive funds because many investors gravitate to the most highly rated funds.

Summary

✦ Consider using an all-purpose index fund as the cornerstone of your portfolio.

✦ Buy only low-cost index funds.

✦ Many index funds are tax-efficient, which makes them attractive for taxable investment accounts.

✦ Invest in both index and actively managed funds.

◆   ◆   ◆   ◆

In This Chapter

Learning ETF basics

Considering the good
and bad about ETFs

Getting the skinny on
HOLDRS

◆   ◆   ◆   ◆

The New Contender: Exchange-Traded Funds

I n this chapter, you learn about exchange-traded funds, which combine some of the best features of both stock and mutual fund investing. You'll discover the kinds of choices available to you, and by the end of the chapter, you'll have some idea about whether exchange-traded funds would make an attractive addition to your portfolio.

Exchange-Traded Funds: An Investing Hybrid

Critics mocked the creation of the first index mutual fund back in the 1970s, but the introduction of the initial exchange-traded fund (ETF) was thoroughly ignored. ETFs, which were launched by the American Stock Exchange back in 1993, attracted only yawns until the late 1990s. Since then, however, interest in ETFs has grown tremendously. During the past year, money gushing into ETFs has nearly doubled. It is no longer surprising when a handful of these funds end the day as the most actively traded issues on the American Stock Exchange, where many of them are listed.

Investors have been swept up by the media hype swirling around exchange-traded funds. But is it justified? ETFs can indeed be a valuable addition to many portfolios, but it would be dead wrong to assume that they are uniformly superior to index funds. Unfortunately, the financial press, caught up in the excitement of this new investing phenomenon, is inadvertently spreading misconceptions about ETFs. There is no one-size-fits-all answer as to whether ETFs belong in your portfolio. Whether they are a logical fit for you depends to a large extent on your investing habits. After learning more about these funds, you'll have to make that call yourself.

What is an ETF?

An exchange-traded fund (ETF) is a Wall Street hybrid. It trades like an individual stock, but it behaves similarly to an index fund. (See Chapter 10 for more on index funds.) Like an index fund, an ETF typically holds a basket of stocks that make up a given benchmark, such as the Standard & Poor's 500, the Dow Jones Industrial Average, or the Nasdaq-100. Other ETFs are linked to narrower slices of the market, such as the Russell 1000 Value Index or the Dow Jones Utility Average. If you own ETF shares, your return should be nearly the same as the underlying index. The return won't be identical, in part because you will have to absorb some annual expenses.

Why are ETFs selling so well?

Investors snatch up shares in ETFs for some of the same reasons that they buy index funds:

✦ Low cost

✦ Tax efficiency

✦ Instant diversification

Another advantage is that exchange-traded funds can take the guesswork out of picking individual stocks. Perhaps you're torn between Apple Computer and Dell Computer or Bed Bath & Beyond and Staples. Buy a stake in an exchange-traded fund that contains all these companies and you can avoid the rigors of picking stocks.

Pros and Cons of Exchange-Traded Funds

There are many reasons why you might want to invest in exchange-traded funds, but there also are other reasons why you may want to keep walking.

ETF advantages

Here are the major strengths of exchange-traded funds.

Favorite Exchange-Traded Funds

The most prominent ETFs remain those that were among the first to be launched:

✦ **Qubes (stock symbol QQQ):** Officially known as the Nasdaq-100 Index Tracking Stock, this ETF is linked to corporations in the Nasdaq-100. These corporations are the biggest and most actively traded on the technology-dominated Nasdaq stock market. The Qube portfolio includes exposure to such corporations as Microsoft, Sun Microsystems, Cisco Systems, Oracle, Amgen, Worldcom, and Amazon.com.

✦ **SPDR or Spiders (stock symbol SPY):** The name is an acronmym for Standard & Poor's Depositary Receipts; often this ETF is called a Spider. Spiders contain holdings in all the stocks in the S&P 500 Index. Certain Spiders focus on sectors of the S&P 500, such as consumer staples, financials, utilities, and healthcare.

✦ **Diamonds (stock symbol DIA):** Shadowing the 30 corporations in the Dow Jones Industrial Average, these funds include American Express, General Electric, Home Depot, Disney, DuPont, General Motors, and Intel. A complete listing of these stocks is printed daily in *The Wall Street Journal*.

✦ **iShare MCSI funds:** The original lineup of ETFs also included a smattering of funds that specialized in foreign countries. Originally referred to as WEBs (world equity benchmark shares), they've been renamed iShare MSCI funds. These exchange-traded funds track the indexes maintained by individual nations such as Japan, Canada, Australia, Italy, Germany, Hong Kong, and the United Kingdom.

Here's a newer ETF to watch: The Vanguard Group, which is best known for its family of index mutual funds, launched its first exchange-traded fund in 2001. This ETF, which is called the Vanguard Total Stock Market VIPER, tracks the Wilshire 5000 Index. Vanguard expects to roll out more VIPERs in the future. You can get a Vanguard educational guide on ETFs by calling (800) 890-8507.

ETFs make diversifying easy.

Someone intent upon building a portfolio of individual stocks would need, at a minimum, tens of thousands of dollars. Although conventional wisdom suggests that 20 stocks are necessary to properly diversify, some recent academic research insists that 50 (or more) is a safer number. Even if money weren't a consideration, how many people could keep on top of that many companies?

Invest through an exchange-traded fund and that huge cash outlay or time commitment isn't necessary. Just as with a mutual fund, you can obtain broad diversification with very little money in an ETF and put a big chunk of your portfolio on autopilot. Such an investment could be used as a portfolio's cornerstone.

Tip

Sophisticated investors might want to use more specialized ETFs to focus on certain sectors, such as real estate, utilities, and natural resources. Investing in these niches through an index fund is difficult, but ETFs can rise to the occasion.

Exchange-trade choices continue to multiply as an increasing number of financial institutions develop and peddle these products. At the moment, the two big players are State Street Global Advisors, which created SPDRs and streetTRACKS ETFs, and Barclays Global Investors, which markets its own proprietary ETF product called iShares.

Note   Only stock investors have been able to invest in ETFs so far, but this situation should change soon. Barclays plans to launch several ETFs that specialize in bonds. Meanwhile, John Nuveen, a big fixed-income mutual fund source, has announced similar plans.

ETFs are traded like stocks.

You can buy and sell ETFs inside a brokerage account throughout the trading day. ETFs are priced like stocks. Each one sports a different price, depending upon the value of its underlying basket of stocks. If an exchange-traded fund is selling for $30 a share, you could buy 100 shares for $3,000. Half that amount would cost just $1,500.

The price of an ETF, just like any other stock, fluctuates during market hours. In contrast, the vast majority of mutual funds are priced only once daily, after the market closes. No matter what time investors place their orders to buy a regular mutual fund, they are locked into one daily price.

Once-a-day pricing isn't necessarily bad, and it doesn't matter at all if you're a long-term investor. However, aggressive investors are attracted to the potential of naming their own price when purchasing ETFs. Individuals can buy ETF shares through a market order, which ensures they pay the best price available at the time the order is processed. They also use another common trading technique by setting a limit order. With a limit order, you stipulate the price at which you would like to buy the security. You don't buy the security if shares never meet or drop below your price target.

Cross-Reference   Chapter 13 thoroughly explains such trading mechanics as limit orders.

Speculative investors also appreciate that they can *short* ETFs, which is impossible to do with mutual funds. When you short a stock or ETF, you essentially borrow shares from your broker with the expectation that the stock price will drop by the time the borrowed shares must be replaced. Investors typically short a stock when they think its price is outrageously expensive and they expect it to crumble.

You can try out sector investing with ETFs.

Maybe you want to invest in a couple of technology or utility stocks, but you're puzzled about which are the best. Instead of choosing one or two stocks, you can invest in a basket of stocks in the same industry with ETFs. For instance, iShare Dow Jones U.S Telecommunication Sector Index Fund invests in nearly five dozen companies, including AT&T, Worldcom, and SBC Communications. The iShare fund devoted to financial services includes Citigroup, Wells Fargo, Merrill Lynch, and American Express in its top 10 holdings.

Tip Although mutual fund families have long offered sector funds, their typically high annual costs can significantly cut into your returns. Exchange-traded funds can provide exposure to a wide variety of industries and sectors more cheaply.

The following lists show just a few of the sector plays you can now invest in through ETFs.

Select Spiders:

✦ Basic industries (stock symbol XLB)

✦ Consumer services (stock symbol XLV)

✦ Consumer staples (stock symbol XLP)

✦ Energy (stock symbol XLE)

✦ Financial (stock symbol XLF)

✦ Industrial (stock symbol XLI)

✦ Technology (stock symbol XLK)

✦ Utilities (stock symbol XLU)

Cross-Reference You can learn much more about sector investing in Chapter 14.

iShares sector funds:

✦ Dow Jones U.S. Chemicals (stock symbol IYD)

✦ Dow Jones U.S. Consumer Cyclical (stock symbol IYC)

✦ Dow Jones U.S. Non-Cyclicals (stock symbol IYK)

✦ Dow Jones U.S. Industrial (stock symbol IYJ)

✦ Dow Jones U.S. Energy (stock symbol IYE)

✦ Dow Jones U.S. Internet (stock symbol IYV)

✦ Dow Jones U.S. Healthcare (stock symbol IYH)

✦ Dow Jones U.S. Technology (stock symbol IYW)

✦ Dow Jones Telecommunications (stock symbol IYZ)

✦ Dow Jones Financial Services (stock symbol IYF)

Caution With some of these funds, the top three holdings may represent a third or even more of the fund's assets. This concentration dramatically increases the volatility of your investment. Look over a fund's literature to determine what stocks sit in the portfolio and in what percentages.

Exchange-traded funds can be inexpensive.

If you use a discount broker, a T-bone steak may cost more than an ETF's annual expenses. Because ETFs are passively managed, the ongoing expenses can be minuscule. The annual cost for a $10,000 investment could be as low as $10 a year. In contrast, a $10,000 investment in the average-priced stock mutual fund would cost more than $150 a year. As you can see in Table 11-1, the yearly cost of a Spider, one of the most popular ETFs, is far cheaper than the average index or stock mutual funds.

Table 11-1
Comparison of Investment Costs

Type of Investment	Average Yearly Cost of a $10,000 Investment
A Spider	$18
Average S&P 500 Index fund	$66
Average stock fund	$140

However, the rock-bottom price isn't universal, which is why you need to do your research. The cost of an iShare that invests in the noncyclical consumer sector, for example, is .6 percent. A $10,000 investment for this fund, which includes Procter & Gamble, Coca-Cola, and Philip Morris among its biggest holdings, would be $60, and the total cost during the first three years is projected to reach $194. (This projection assumes that the fund grows at a 5 percent clip. If it does better, the price tag would increase, too.) Compare that amount to iShare S&P 500 Index, which has projected costs of $9 the first year and a total of $31 for the first three years. The fees for some ETFs, most notably the ones that specialize in overseas investments, can be nearly 1 percent.

Caution   When you compare an ETF with the lowest-priced index mutual funds, such as the ones offered by Vanguard and a few discount brokers, the ETF price advantage can vanish.

ETFs can be tax-efficient.

ETFs can be extremely tax-efficient because they sit on buy-and-hold portfolios; there isn't as much call for stock selling. (Exceptions exist, which you'll learn about in this chapter.) Stock trading is of course one of the major triggers of annual capital gains taxes.

ETFs also don't have to worry about a big headache for traditional mutual funds: fleeing shareholders. If a critical mass of investors pulls out of a regular mutual fund, a manager could be forced to sell stocks to generate cash to pay off its fair-weather friends. Yet selling stock can trigger those pesky capital gains distributions for the remaining loyal investors. This nightmare can't happen with ETFs. Thanks to the way ETFs are internally structured, the funds don't have to dump stocks. Instead ETFs pass huge blocks of the fund to institutional investors, who provide the cash that in turn can be used to pay off the little investors.

ETF weaknesses

Here are the drawbacks you may encounter with exchange-traded funds.

ETFs can generate capital gains taxes.

Many media reports suggest that ETFs are more tax-efficient than index funds, but that's not always true. Although some ETFs excel at dodging capital gains taxes, others do not. For example, capital gains taxes can be generated when a stock sitting in an ETF must be sold because it's been removed from its underlying index. (Institutional investors can't bail out a fund in this circumstance.)

Example

Suppose a company has grown too large to remain in the Russell 2000, a benchmark for small-cap stocks. The index will eliminate the stock and so will any ETFs tracking this benchmark. This move can trigger capital gains distributions for ETF shareholders.

The potential tax liability can be a bigger headache for ETFs that are tied to the small-cap indexes. Those indexes are far more likely to become a revolving door for corporate small fry that outgrow their pond. Consequently, you can't expect an ETF like iShare Russell 2000 Growth or iShare S&P SmallCap 600 to be as tax-efficient as the Spider, which is linked to the S&P 500.

An ETF can also be forced to sell stock when its stake in a company reaches 25 percent or more of its portfolio. That's what happened with iShares MSCI Canada Index when it was compelled to shed some of its position in Nortel Networks. iShares MSCI Sweden Index experienced a similar dilemma when it had to dump stock in Ericsson Telephone, the Swedish telecommunications giant. Investors in both of these funds were stuck with stiff tax bills.

Investors can also expect to pay yearly taxes on any dividends that the corporations within an ETF spin off. The tax is equal to the rate of a person's income tax bracket. This tax burden isn't limited to ETF investors, though. The tax is owed regardless of whether someone holds a stock individually, in a mutual fund, or in an ETF. Even a very tax-efficient ETF or index fund triggers this tax.

ETFs can be guilty of imprecise sector slicing.

An ETF's name isn't completely reliable. Select Spiders, for instance, aren't grouped as precisely as you might assume. For example, there's no sector Spider devoted to retail stocks, so retail plays like Wal-Mart and the Gap are dumped into the Cyclical/Transportation Spider. Somebody wanting to load up on stocks such as Ford Motor and Delta Airlines probably wouldn't expect (or necessarily want) exposure to retailers.

Select Spiders could also frustrate investors who want to sink money into the telecommunications sector. Traditional phone companies such as Verizon and SBC Communications have been pigeonholed into the Utilities Sector Spider, which includes a lot of electric utilities, but AT&T was shoehorned into the Select Spider dedicated to technology.

Some ETFs lack liquidity.

Although ETFs have attracted plenty of media attention, investors are treating most ETFs like wallflowers. Just two ETFs, Qubes and Spiders, were recently pulling in 70 percent of investors' cash. On a recent day, for instance, when 59 million shares of Qubes traded hands, a measly 1,200 shares of the iShare devoted to Australia stocks were bought and sold. The streetTRACKS Dow Jones U.S. Large-Cap Value Index Fund drew even less interest, with the volume peaking at 400 shares.

Why should this matter? The reason can be summed up in one word: liquidity. Investors prefer that stocks, as well as ETFs, enjoy the interest of many buyers because ultimately it can reduce the price they must pay to buy these investments. Tepid market interest could lead to undesirable "bid/ask" spreads, which is the difference between the highest price a buyer is willing to pay and the lowest price a seller is willing to accept. A big spread translates to higher trading costs for investors.

 Caution   With even more ETFs expected to be launched in the future, the chances of many funds remaining stuck in obscurity seem good.

ETFs are impractical for dollar-cost averaging.

Focusing simply on an ETF's low annual expenses ignores another cost: transaction fees. Purchasing an ETF triggers a commission from your brokerage firm. Even if you are able to trade stocks for as little as $7 or $8, this fee can add up if you are investing in an ETF regularly.

For that reason, exchange-traded funds aren't practical if you intend to invest modest amounts by *dollar-cost averaging,* the practice of sinking money into an investment on a regular basis. Every time you put money into an ETF, you trigger a brokerage transaction fee. Obviously, this cost would be untenable if you were investing, say, $100 or $200 at a monthly clip. Traditional mutual funds are much better equipped to handle this slow and steady way of investing.

Information on ETFs is hard to find.

If you haven't heard about ETFs yet, you might appreciate this drawback. Obtaining background on these funds is difficult. While the financial press is constantly churning out stories about mutual funds, ETFs, with the exception of the most prominent ones, are stuck in an informational black hole. A major source of information is each fund's prospectus, which contains such things as costs, the investment objective, and risks. Although poring over these documents is important, the language is dry and sometimes hard to penetrate.

After reading the official material, an investor might be dying to know what experts think. But finding commentary on these funds, especially the dozens of obscure ones, can be challenging, if not impossible. Luckily, some independent sources of information on exchange-traded funds do exist:

✦ **IndexFunds.com:** A worthy source of information for both veteran and novice investors, this site archives articles on investing techniques, features fund profiles, and provides links to the online addresses of popular indexes (www.indexfunds.com).

✦ **Morningstar:** In recognition of the exchange-traded phenomenon, Morningstar dedicated a section of its Web site to exchange-traded funds. Meanwhile, the site maintains a very active electronic chat forum for Vanguard shareholders, who are big indexing proponents (www.morningstar.com).

✦ **TheStreet.com:** This site keeps visitors up-to-date on ETF developments: Each Saturday, it publishes a report that details which ETFs have fared the best and worst during the previous workweek (www.thestreet.com).

You can obtain prospectuses and other ETF literature through your brokerage firm. Meanwhile, you can download or order prospectuses as well as obtain current performance statistics online through these three sources:

✦ American Stock Exchange at (800) THE-AMEX ext. 1 or www.amex.com

✦ Barclays Global Investors at (800) 474-2737 or www.ishares.com

✦ Nasdaq stock exchange at www.nasdaq.com

The Nasdaq Web site is particularly helpful because it enables visitors to compare ETFs by providing current and historical performance statistics, annual costs, and tax efficiency data. On the iShares Web site, you can also obtain condensed fact sheets on each of Barclay's funds, as well as lists of the stocks that each fund portfolio contains.

 For those who don't have access to the Internet, ETFs are listed, just like other stocks, in newspaper stock tables. You can find the vast majority of ETFs under the AMEX's listings.

HOLDRS: Exchange-Traded Funds with a Twist

The popularity of ETFs has created a stampede among financial institutions to manufacture their own exchange-traded clones. Merrill Lynch, the brokerage firm, was one of the first to create its own product, HOLDRS, which stands for Holding Company Depositary Receipts. (Yes, the *E* is missing.)

HOLDRS, which are trying to cash in on the ETF craze, are different from the rest of the ETF crowd in a major way. Qubes, Spiders, and other ETFs invest in stocks in their respective indexes, but HOLDRS are more selective. Each HOLDR contains a basket of no less than 20 stocks handpicked by Merrill Lynch investment professionals. They are not required to replicate any index.

Each of the HOLDRS is devoted to a sector or industry, such as biotechnology, pharmaceuticals, telecommunications, and a variety of Internet categories. One newer HOLDRS fund invests in 50 of the largest European companies that trade on an American stock exchange.

Caution   Because HOLDRS are pure sector plays, they are inherently more volatile than the typical mutual fund or an exchange-traded fund that's linked to the broad market.

The following funds are a sampling of the HOLDRS that are available:

✦ Biotech (stock symbol BBH)

✦ Broadband (stock symbol BDH)

✦ B2B Internet (stock symbol BHH)

✦ Internet (stock symbol HHH)

✦ Pharmaceutical (stock symbol PPH)

✦ Regional bank (stock symbol RKH)

✦ Semiconductor (stock symbol SMH)

✦ Telecom (stock symbol TTH)

✦ Utilities (stock symbol UTH)

Resource   You can download a prospectus, as well as find out more about this investment alternative, by visiting Merrill Lynch's Web site devoted to HOLDRS at `www.holdrs.com`. The same literature is available at your brokerage firm.

HOLDRS strengths

HOLDRS can be an attractive investing alternative for the following reasons.

They are cheap.

Once you pay a stock commission to buy into a HOLDRS, the costs are minimal. The annual fee on HOLDRS is just eight cents per 100 shares. And this fee is waived if there aren't enough dividends distributed from the underlying stocks to cover the cost.

They are tax-friendly and flexible.

HOLDRS are extremely tax-efficient. Bailing out of a HOLDRS is not a taxable event. When you sell HOLDRS, you receive actual shares of the underlying stocks in your brokerage account. You simply own the 20 or so individual stocks. At this point, you can unbundle the stocks and decide whether to sell all or any of them. You can use this flexibility to your advantage at tax time. For instance, you may want to sell a winning stock, which could trigger a huge capital gains tax bill, but offset it by ditching another stock in the old HOLDRS portfolio that has suffered losses.

HOLDRS weaknesses

Here's why some investors should stay away from HOLDRS.

They come with potentially high trading minimums.

Unlike individual stocks or ETFs, you must buy HOLDRS in lots of 100 shares, which is known as a round lot. This requirement can make certain HOLDRS unaffordable for some individuals. The Internet HOLDR, for instance, was recently trading at close to $54 a share, which would put the minimum investment at nearly $5,400. Picking up 100 shares of Biotech HOLDRS would cost more than $15,000, but an equal number of shares in the B2B Internet HOLDRS could recently be had for little more than $1,800.

In addition, you can cash in a HOLDRS only in round lots of 100 shares. The cost of selling 100 shares is $10. Of course, once you sell your shares, you aren't rid of the investment. You have essentially traded in your compact investment for a bevy of individual stocks. Some investors won't want to clutter their portfolios in this way. Getting rid of all or some of these stocks could generate significant trading commissions.

They rely upon on subjective stock picking.

ETFs are appealing to many investors because their index link eliminates subjectivity. With HOLDRS, Merrill Lynch decides what stocks to place in the basket. If the assortment is flawed, you could end up with a poorly performing investment that is hard to unload.

The portfolio choices are inflexible.

Stock selection for a HOLDRS portfolio is a one-time event: Stocks can never be added to the portfolio, nor can any be dropped unless they no longer exist. So if a HOLDRS fund contains stake in the software provider Red Hat, for instance, and that stock loses 90 percent of its value, it will still remain in the portfolio.

Thanks to the inflexibility, investing in a HOLDRS can be far more volatile than sinking money into a passively managed index fund. If a few stocks implode in an index fund, which may be composed of hundreds or thousands of stocks, it won't necessarily impact the return much. But if one or two stocks in a far more concentrated portfolio blow up, it could sabotage the performance.

Dogs of the Dow

For decades, investors have searched for a sure-fire way to win on Wall Street without perspiring. Fans of the Dogs of the Dow believed they had found the answer. With this stock-picking strategy, an investor can spend more time mowing the lawn than assembling a stock portfolio.

Although many variations exist, the Dogs of the Dow essentially works in this way: You purchase equal dollar amounts of the 10 highest dividend-yielding stocks from the Dow Jones Industrial Average. Determining the identity of these Dow stocks is easy because The Wall Street Journal lists all 30 Dow stocks each day in a separate box in the stock tables. They are called dogs because typically they are the Dow's underperformers. The lineup often includes corporations such as Caterpillar, International Paper, and Eastman Kodak. You hold onto these 10 stocks for exactly one year and then you reshuffle so that you once again hold only the top 10 dividend yielders. You sell any stocks that no longer make the cut and add those that do. To follow this approach, you don't have to start January 1-any day will do. If you picked your stocks on September 27, 2001, for instance, you would reshuffle your holdings one year later.

During much of the 1990s, the Dogs of the Dow did phenomenally well. Among the biggest cheerleaders of the strategy were the two brothers who created the Motley Fool, the phenomenally popular financial Web site. The brothers touted the strategy in their books and Web site. But as growth stocks dominated Wall Street, Dow stocks that were more of a value play faded. Even the Motley Fool abandoned their advocacy of the strategy in late 2000. You can read their reasoning by visiting the Motley Fool Web site at `www.fool.com`. The following table shows how this strategy performed in the late 1990s. Note that although it did very well in 1996 and 1997, it did not beat the average of either the S&P 500 or the Dow Jones Industrial Average over the course of five years.

Benchmark	Five year Average	2000	1999	1998	1997	1996
Dogs of the Dow	11.98%	6.4%	4%	10.7%	22.2%	28.6%
Dow Jones Industrial Average	15.58%	−4.9%	27.2%	18.1%	24.3%	28.8%
S&P 500	15.97%	−10.1%	21.1%	28.6%	33.3%	22.9%

Dogs of the Dow was a flawed concept. Flagging returns are just one concern. If you faithfully follow the Dogs of the Dow approach, you must sell stocks yearly, and generate potential capital gains taxes. If you want to learn more about Dogs of the Dow, you can sate your curiosity by visiting a Web site devoted to the topic at `www.dogsofthedow.com`.

HOLDRS versus unit investment trusts

Because a HOLDRS's portfolio is fixed, HOLDRS have been compared to unit investment trusts. UITs, as they are called, are quirky investments that have languished in the backwaters of the financial world. Just like a HOLDRS, a UIT can contain a fixed basket of stocks or bonds that are selected by the sponsoring brokerage firm.

The UIT investor, however, isn't locked into a portfolio forever. Unlike a HOLDRS, each UIT eventually expires. Investors are told before they invest what the maturity date is. Bond UITs often last 10 to 30 years, though some mature earlier. Stock UITs often mature in one to five years. When a UIT is disbanded, capital gains taxes on any profits are owed.

Tip If you are intrigued by the concept, owning HOLDRS can be preferable to owning UITs because HOLDRS are cheaper and more tax-efficient. Keeping tabs on HOLDRS is easier as well because they are traded on Wall Street.

UITs have historically been most popular with bond investors. But the investment product enjoyed its 15 minutes of fame in the 1990s when investors were enchanted with the Dogs of the Dow. The Dogs of the Dow strategy was devised as a way to beat the market by investing in the most downtrodden stocks within the Dow Jones Industrial Average. UITs were launched that contained Dogs stocks. As true believers in the strategy dwindled, so did interest in UITs.

Whether a UIT contains stocks or bonds, it works in the same way. The sponsoring brokerage firm decides what stocks or bonds should be kept in the UIT. Analysts at a firm like UBS PaineWebber or Salomon Smith Barney typically recommend stocks they think have the best chance of appreciating in the next few years. Equity UITs are often designed to capitalize on some theme, such as the New Economy or Information Age stocks. You can also invest in such sectors as healthcare, global telecommunications, and biotechnology. Fixed-income UITs often contain portfolios of municipal bonds.

Stock slams

Like a HOLDRS, stocks or bonds are selected for UIT portfolios, and then those selections are frozen. In most cases, no one can tinker with the investment lineup. Investments can't be dropped, nor can they be added. This inflexibility can dynamite a static portfolio.

Example If a UIT holds a stake in Philip Morris, which gets hammered with horrific punitive damages in some legal action, the UIT still can't unload its tobacco stock.

Bond bruising

The inflexibility of UITs can be just as harmful to bond investors. Fixed-income fans who gravitate to UITs do so because they want a steady stream of income. This move sounds great in theory, but the reality can be harsher. The bonds are not guaranteed to stay in the portfolio. Why? Because many types of bonds are callable. That means that the borrower, whether it's a state or local government or a corporation, can repay its debt early.

Borrowers love to call back their bonds when interest rates are inching down. They are eager to repay their bonds so that they can issue new ones that capitalize on the skimpier interest rates. When this happens in a UIT, no attempt is made to reinvest this money into other bonds. Instead, the money from the repaid bond, which is referred to as the principal, is proportionately returned to the shareholders. Once the money is returned, you're stuck finding a new investment to stash it into.

High price, low liquidity

Another disadvantage to a UIT is the price. Although the continuing costs can be low thanks to the passive investment approach, the admission price is hardly cheap. You will pay a stiff load that could range from 2.75 percent to 5 percent. What's more, a UIT can be difficult to unload. UITs aren't traded on the stock exchanges, which also means that you can't check on their valuation in the newspaper.

When you weigh the pros and cons of UIT investing, it's obvious why these investments are wallflowers. There is no compelling reason to own one. Most of the investors were probably sweet-talked into buying one by a full-service broker or a financial planner who lives off commissions.

Summary

✦ Exchange-traded funds can be an alternative to index funds and individual stock picking.

✦ Investing in exchange-traded funds through dollar-cost averaging is often impractical.

✦ Finding information on exchange-traded funds can be challenging, but independent sources of information do exist online.

✦ Before investing in HOLDRS, understand how they work.

✦   ✦   ✦

Stocking Up: Techniques and Technology

No one ever said that successful stock investing was easy. You will boost your chances of success, however, if you understand how Wall Street works and how you can intelligently analyze individual stocks. The next five chapters will help you learn to do just that.

A Stock Primer

In this chapter, you will learn the major types of stocks available on the market and discover their strengths and hazards. Meanwhile, you'll receive a crash course in the two major investing styles—value and growth—as well as an investing strategy called growth at a reasonable price. This chapter also shares the latest research results suggesting that the conventional wisdom on international investing may be wrong.

A Little Background: Bull Meets Bear

For many years, the United States seemed to be the epicenter of brilliant stock pickers. Millions of American investors, who appeared blessed with phenomenal financial wisdom, watched their stock portfolios grow and grow.

The most amazing bull market in history, which some suggest started as long ago as 1982, made a lot of investors look like Wall Street geniuses. Then fortunes changed suddenly, when the bear came to town. No longer could fast money be made by throwing darts at the stock tables. A market meltdown of historic proportions disintegrated investors' self confidence, as did every nightly news report of another catastrophic drop on Wall Street.

Note During a *bull market*, stock prices increase for an extended period of time. In contrast, *bear market* describes a period of prolonged decline in the market, specifically a period in which stock values decrease at least 20 percent or more.

Investors began questioning their own investing approaches. Were their portfolios too heavy in this and not heavy enough in that? Should they have taken bonds more seriously? Did they trade too infrequently, or perhaps too much? At a time when more Americans own stock than at any other period in history, all this introspection is understandable and even healthy. Americans shouldn't assume that stocks are the only way to make money.

Auto-Pilot Stock Investing

It takes hard work to assemble a first-class portfolio of stocks that can weather the hard periods and flourish in the good times. After that, an investor needs to monitor his or her holdings and make tough decisions about when to buy and sell. Perhaps the only angst-free way to invest in stocks is through an index mutual fund. By sinking money into an index fund, you instantly obtain exposure to a broad swath of the market, whether it's the Standard & Poor's 500 Index or the entire stock market. You will do about as well or as poorly as the broader market, but since stocks historically have averaged an 11 percent return each year, over time you should do quite well indeed.

But some historical perspective is necessary too. It's true that equities have jilted stock lovers many times before. Anybody who was invested in the market in 1987 will remember the heartache. The pain was even greater during the brutal bear market siege in 1973 and 1974. Yet over time, stocks have amply rewarded those who remain loyal. Throughout the years, stocks have performed far, far better than bonds, certificates of deposit, and the lowly savings account.

The ABCs of Stocks

Let's start with the basics. When you buy stock, you're purchasing a tiny piece of a company. The emphasis is on the word "tiny." Suppose that you buy 100 shares of American Express. By doing so, you join the ranks of other American Express owners. How many are there? The number of shares outstanding, which means the number of shares investors own, is 1.3 billion.

Corporations issue stocks to raise money. Usually companies turn to stocks when they've outgrown private sources like venture capital. In more recent times, untested, fledgling companies made the leap more rapidly because investors were in a far more speculative mood. Opening the door to the broader market can generate vast sums of cash for a company. The other major way that corporations raise money is to issue bonds, which are discussed in Chapters 17 though 19. While bondholders get a fixed rate on their investment, stock shareholders can't know for sure what they will receive.

Your financial stake in a company is proportional to the amount of stock you own. What do you get for your financial commitment? If the stock price appreciates, you enjoy the ride up. If you decide to cash in on your good fortune, the difference between your original price and the final one is called a *capital gain*. A capital gain is characterized as either a short- or long-term gain.

Cross-Reference As you'll learn in Chapter 25, it's better to sell stocks for a long-term gain, since the tax bite won't be as great.

In addition to price appreciation, some corporations, usually larger and older ones, issue *dividends*. Dividends represent a portion of a company's profits that are paid out as cash. A shareholder can either cash an actual check or instruct his or her broker to automatically reinvest this money to buy more company shares.

Investing 101: Resources

Investing in individual stocks can be a bewildering experience. Wall Street is great at generating hot stock picks, but for investors who wish to make their own reasoned and researched decisions, there is often no helping hand. Sources exist, however, to help serious investors who want to learn how to select stocks or strengthen their stock picking skills.

✦ **American Association of Individual Investors.** The aim of this nonprofit organization is to make its members smarter investors. Members receive a monthly magazine that is dreadfully dry, but the information is first rate. Contributors are well-respected members of the investment community. The AAII also holds investment conferences open to nonmembers throughout the year in major cities. In addition, the organization oversees many local chapters. At (800) 428-2244, or www.aaii.org.

✦ **National Association of Investors Corp.** This is the umbrella group for tens of thousands of investment clubs operating around the country. You don't have to belong to a group, however, to use NAIC's educational materials and software. For much more on investment clubs, see Chapter 16. At (877) 275-6242, or www.better-investing.org.

✦ **Investor's Streaming University.** This unique site was born as a collaborative effort of the American Association of Individual Investors and the National Association of Securities Dealers. You can view 5- to 8-minute videos (or read the transcripts) of lectures given by experts on subjects such as whisper earnings, free cash flow, and the use of margin accounts. Lectures are added regularly to the site. At www.streamingu.org.

✦ *Bloomberg Personal Finance.* This ain't no *Money* magazine. Its audience is affluent investors who already know the basics. Contributors to this sophisticated magazine include veteran journalists from the Bloomberg financial information empire, as well as high profile and prominent experts such as Burton G. Malkiel, Chuck Carlson, John Dorfman, and Laszlo Birinyi. At (888) 432-5820, or www.bloomberg.com.

✦ **Briefing.com.** This site's Learning Center contains dozens of articles on such topics as technical analysis basics, hedging techniques, important market indicators, tracking stocks, preferred stocks, and investing strategies. At www.briefing.com.

✦ *A Random Walk Down Wall Street,* **W.W. Norton & Co., June 2000.** This classic investment guide, which was written by Burton G. Malkiel, a professor at Princeton University, has been updated numerous times since it was released in the 1970s.

Growth Versus Value Versus GARP

While thousands of stocks trade on stock exchanges, they can be divided into two broad investment classes: growth and value. For most of the 1990s, the value stock was treated like a penny on a sidewalk. It was ignored. Instead investors worshipped growth stocks and the demand inflated their prices to unbelievable heights. Both types of stock, however, belong in a diversified portfolio. Investing in both ensures that you won't get left behind when one or the other dominates the market for what can be long stretches. What many stock investors don't appreciate is that there is a third alternative. As you'll learn, "GARP," or growth at a reasonable price, represents a compromise between value and growth.

Appreciating value stocks

Value investors would feel at home at a yard sale. They love to buy bloodied, beaten-down stocks for a song. Value stocks are often priced cheaply because investors are not enthusiastic about a company's future earnings prospects. Sometimes stocks have been hobbled because of poor management or because an entire industry, such as chemicals, heavy manufacturing, or steel, faces a downturn.

Other times something else causes companies to stumble. When this happens, you can see prominent stocks like IBM, Worldcom, and Wal-Mart slip into the value category.

Example

Philip Morris hit the skids for a while when big legal guns were aimed at the cigarette maker. Investors who sank money into the beleaguered company had reason to celebrate as the stock took off after the company settled one of its legal troubles.

What's tricky about value stocks is that many of them aren't at all valuable. Some stocks deserve their lowly prices because their chances of rebounding are slim. The ideal value strategy is to find bruised stocks that don't deserve the beating. In early 1999, for instance, investors punished oil stocks when the price of crude hit a 20-year low. Prices, however, began to rebound and some of the major oil companies began scouting for acquisition and merger possibilities. This consolidation move was just the boost that oil stocks needed. Bottom feeders who spotted this catalyst and bought oil stock for cheap were rewarded.

Tip

While growth stocks tend to grab headlines and monopolize investor enthusiasm, value stocks have historically been the market's best performers by a wide margin.

For alert investors, value stocks can be extremely lucrative, if not glamorous. You can see just how huge the gulf is in Table 12-1.

Table 12-1
75-Year History of Growth Versus Value Investing

Type of Stock	Average Return	Ending Investment Value of an Initial $1000
Small-Cap Value	14.2%	$16 million
Large-Cap Value	12.4%	$5.1 million
Large-Cap Growth	10%	$1 million
Small-Cap Growth	9.4%	$727,000

Source: Ibbotson Associates

It's true, however, that value and growth tend to swap places as market conditions and sentiments change. In the latter half of the 1990s, growth reigned supreme, but then value became top dog again. Even during this time of growth domination, which was largely fueled by technology stocks, value remarkably held its own. You can see for yourself in Table 12-2.

Table 12-2
Value Versus Growth Investing 1990 to 2000

Type of Stock	Average Return	Ending Investment Value of an Initial $1000
Large-cap growth	18.1%	$5,290
Small-cap value	17.5%	$5,020
Large-cap value	16.1%	$4,460
Small-cap growth	14%	$3,690

Source: Ibbotson Associates

Tip   Value stocks are attractive for another reason. Choosing wisely should reduce your portfolio's overall risk. Since a value stock is inherently cheap, it can't fall as far as a growth stock that's selling at an exorbitant price.

Signs of a value stock

How do you spot an undervalued stock? One big tip-off is a low *price-to-earnings ratio* (P/E) compared with the rest of the market. The P/E ratio, which is listed next to each company's name in a newspaper's financial listings, is determined by dividing the current price of one share of stock by the earnings generated by a single share of stock. In the summer of 2000, the average P/E for stocks in the Standard & Poor's 500 Index was 28.5, which was historically quite high.

A higher than normal dividend can sometimes provide another clue that a stock might be worth a closer look. Value investors also salivate when they spot a stock with an attractive *price-to-book value.* This figure essentially tells an investor how much the company would be worth if it sold all its assets for cash.

Cross-Reference

You will learn more about the price-to-earnings ratio, as well as other important financial ratios, in Chapter 15.

Extra attention needed

As in any healthy relationship, you can't just ignore your portfolio and assume it's all working out. Value investing can be especially challenging because stocks can move in and out of the value category. Consequently, value stocks typically aren't the kind you can put in a lock box and forget about.

Caution

When the market spots a sleeper and its price escalates, the reason for continuing to hold the stock may disappear. For this reason, you'll need to monitor value stocks closely.

Investing in growth stocks

It is easy to love a winner. Who wouldn't enjoy watching a stock that you own streak to the top of the stock charts? When growth stocks are hot, many people forget alternatives. And it's no wonder that investors were fixated on growth for so long when stock returns looked more like typos. During the rah-rah '90s, Dell Computer, the nation's best-performing stock, catapulted 90,772 percent. Following close behind were CMGI, the Internet incubator (84,797 percent); EMC (81,131 percent); and Cisco Systems (68,624 percent).

Traits of a growth stock

What qualifies as a growth stock? Investors have formulated their own lists of traits. A common criteria, however, is that a stock has increased its earnings for three or more consecutive years. Whether a stock meets that hurdle can be determined easily by flipping through a corporation's annual reports.

Resource

You can easily find earnings figures by visiting Multex Investor (www.multexinvestor.com), which provides historical data on individual stocks.

Growth investors also prefer stocks that analysts expect to do well in the future, such as those that appear capable of growing at least 10 percent to 15 percent or much more for the next three to five years. Some growth fans focus on companies that should produce earnings that are at least twice the growth rate of the typical corporation in the Standard & Poor's 500 Index. (Growth stocks can come from the ranks of both large and small companies.)

Note

Gangbuster growth, whether it materializes or not, is often going to cost you. Investors typically have to pay more for growth stocks because their futures seem so bright.

One way to judge if a stock is expensive is by comparing its price-to-earnings ratio to its projected growth rate. If the growth rate is much less than the P/E ratio, the stock is considered richly valued. For example, if growth is 20 percent and the P/E ratio is 40, that's a growth stock. In this case, investors are willing to pay $40 for every dollar of earnings the company has generated. In contrast, a value investor may only be willing to pay $10 or $11 for each dollar of a company's earnings.

Tip Don't become so infatuated with growth stock that you are willing to pay any price. The bigger the premium you pay for a stock, the harder it potentially can fall later on.

A growth stock's premium depends upon more than just its financial performance. The economy also plays a role. Investors are less likely to balk at pricey growth stocks when interest rates are relatively low or falling. Why? Because safe investments, such as certificates of deposit and money markets, don't seem like great investments when their yields are so meager. In contrast, the P/E ratios for growth can falter when interest rates are rising and a certificate of deposit offering 8 percent interest may look like an attractive sure thing.

Risks of growth stocks

While growth stocks can be enormously rewarding, they are riskier than their value peers. Here are the big reasons:

✦ **Lack of cushioning dividends:** High fliers typically aren't going to divert excess cash into dividends. They sink their profits into expanding their business or developing new products. Large growth companies are more likely to generate dividends, but often they are only token amounts. Without dividends, a stock's free fall will have absolutely no cushion.

✦ **Greater potential for loss:** Investors demand a lot from their growth picks. Since they typically pay a premium for these stocks, they want the earnings celebration parties to continue forever. When growth stocks falter they are punished more brutally than pedestrian stocks.

✦ **Missteps:** Sometimes stocks can't live up to their reputations. Even companies with hot products can cool if they don't remain at the head of a competitive industry. Sometimes the setbacks are temporary, which can make for excellent buying opportunities. Other times a corporation's competitive edge, especially among small companies, never recovers.

Who should invest in growth stocks or growth-oriented mutual funds? Anybody with a long-term investing horizon who can handle volatility. Growth stocks are certainly appropriate for someone saving for college, retirement, or some other lengthy goal.

Growth Stock Free Falls

Gory examples of Wall Street floggings are plentiful. When the Nasdaq recently suffered its very worst bear market, maimed stocks littered the trading floors. During a 12-month stretch, Intel's stock dropped 60 percent, Oracle plummeted 56 percent, and one of the market's favorite young darlings, JDS Uniphase, watched more than 84 percent of its share price evaporate. But hit-and-run casualties aren't confined to the tech sector. During the same tortuous period, Charles Schwab plunged 59 percent; Home Depot, one of Wall Street's perennially favorite retail stocks, lost a third of its value.

Moving to the middle ground: Growth at a reasonable price

Growth stocks can be hair-raising. Value can be stodgy. Is there no middle ground? Yes. It's called *growth at a reasonable price,* or GARP for short. GARP investors want it all—high quality growth companies, like Cisco Systems, Home Depot, and Sun Microsystems, without paying too much. The GARP style allows value lovers to invest in growth opportunities at the same time it discourages the growth worshippers from chasing the more outrageously priced firecrackers.

While sidestepping the hottest stocks, GARP investors look for promising stocks that won't necessarily pay off with fat returns in the next few months or year. This approach contrasts with the style of pure growth fans, who may not flinch at buying growth at any price, and with the value approach, which prefers undervalued stocks. The GARP approach sits in the middle of the risk spectrum.

Definition of a GARP stock

For GARP investors, the PEG ratio is key to uncovering promising stocks. PEG is short for *price-to-earnings-growth ratio.* Here's how the PEG ratio is calculated: First you find a company's trailing P/E ratio. (It's listed in the newspaper.) Next you divide it by the company's expected growth rate. For the growth rate, you use analysts' consensus for say, a three- to five-year span. (You can find these projections at many online financial Web sites, such as Zacks Investment Research [www.zacks.com], and Yahoo!Finance [http://finance.yahoo.com].) Say a company has a P/E ratio of 20 and analysts expect the company to grow at an annual 35 percent clip. Its PEG ratio is .57.

If the PEG ratio is 1.0, a stock is assumed to be fairly valued. The lower the PEG ratio creeps below 1.0, the more it's assumed to be undervalued. A GARP investor will typically see a PEG ratio of less than 1.0 as a buy signal.

There is no need to calculate your own PEG ratio, unless you want to plug in your own growth projections. Yahoo!Finance includes the PEG ratio for the stocks it follows.

One caveat

Is there an Achilles heel in this strategy? Sure. Remember, there is no sure thing on Wall Street. Skeptics point in particular to the GARP strategy's reliance upon analysts' projections. Those earnings predictions must be plugged into the formula. Analysts, as you'll learn in Chapter 15, tend to be an overly optimistic bunch.

Stocks of Every Size and Shape

Stocks not only come wrapped in different investment style categories; they are also packaged in different-sized boxes. Here are your choices:

✦ Large-cap stocks

✦ Mid-cap stocks

✦ Small-cap stocks

✦ Micro-cap stocks

Large-cap stocks

These are the big guys—America's largest companies. You'll see them referred to as large-cap stocks, which is short for *large capitalization.* The capitalization of a company is determined by multiplying the current share price by the number of shares investors hold. While definitions vary somewhat, a stock is generally labeled as large if its market cap is greater than $10 billion.

Many of these monster stocks are considered *blue chips.* Why the name? In poker, the blue chips are considered the most valuable. Companies like Johnson & Johnson and Tootsie Roll, which have been profitably selling Band-Aids and cheap candy for generations, are generally going to continue running a smooth ship, though there is no guarantee.

Note As a general rule, blue chips are considerably less risky than small-cap stocks.

You'll find the biggest collection of these corporate giants in the Standard & Poor's 500 Index. Table 12-3 shows a recent lineup of the 10 biggest.

Table 12-3
Largest Stocks on the Standard & Poor's 500 Index

Company	Market Capitalization
1. General Electric	$460 billion
2. Microsoft	$314 billion
3. Pfizer	$283 billion
4. Exxon Mobil	$281 billion
5. Citigroup	$276 billion
6. Wal-Mart	$223 billion
7. Intel	$192 billion
8. AOL Time Warner	$190 billion
9. American International Group	$190 billion
10. Merck & Co.	$184 billion

Mid-cap stocks

Like the middle kids in a large family, mid-cap stocks are often overlooked, partly because people aren't familiar with them. A kindergartner knows the names of large, prominent American corporations, like McDonald's and Hershey Foods, but you can stump even an experienced investor by asking for the names of a few prominent mid-caps. These stocks typically have market caps of between $2 and $10 billion.

Tip Don't overlook mid-caps. They represent an opportunity to boost your portfolio's total return and at the same time reduce its overall risk. When buying individual mid-cap stocks look for market leaders since they have the broadest customer bases and therefore should be more stable.

You'll find a hodgepodge of corporations in this middle zone. Some of the companies in this category used to be small-cap companies that have done phenomenally well. They have moved up the food chain. On the other hand, the territory is also inhabited by former large-cap stocks that have experienced a prolonged bout with lackluster stock returns. Table 12-4 shows a sampling of stocks in the Standard & Poor's MidCap 400 Index, which tracks the mid-cap universe.

Table 12-4	
Companies in the Standard & Poor's MidCap 400 Index	
Washington Post	RJ Reynolds Tobacco
E*Trade	Abercrombie & Fitch
Jones Apparel Group	Scholastic
Global Marine	Dreyer's Grand Ice Cream
American Standard	Dunn & Bradstreet
Smucker	Williams-Sonoma
Oxford Health Plan	Wind River Systems

Why should mid-caps capture your interest? Results. Mid-caps tend to be steadier and more stable than the small-caps. They've been doing something right to get to where they are so far. The risk level for the typical mid-cap stock falls in the middle range between the more volatile smaller companies and the safer big giants. Yet while mid-cap stocks aren't as risky as the little guys, they are rewarded with returns that are nearly identical if you look back 75 years. (As a general investing rule, the greater risk you assume, the greater your potential reward. Small-caps are characterized as the riskiest stock category and, sure enough, historically, they have been the best investing category.)

Mid-caps historically tend to outperform other types of stocks during bear markets. For instance, in 2000, when large-cap stocks were getting eviscerated, mid-cap stocks enjoyed a nice rally. The same thing happened during the recession of 1974.

Why are big caps less risky? Having survived toddlerhood, a medium-sized company's financial condition can be on more solid footing. In a better position to raise more cash, a company should be able to bankroll even more growth. What's more, since mid-caps are less apt to be operating overseas than big companies, they aren't exposed to the volatility of foreign currency and markets.

The lower volatility has been coupled with impressive returns. During the past 20 years, mid-cap stocks have outperformed small- and large-caps. A mid-cap stock category has captured the top performance crown in three-, five- and 10-year periods. See Table 12-5.

Table 12-5
Stock Performance By Category

Category	3 years	5 years	10 years
Mid-cap value	8.32%	13.15%	14.13%
Mid-cap growth	11.18%	10.20%	13.17%
Large-cap value	5.48%	12.52%	13.40%
Large-cap growth	6.62%	12.18%	13.12%
Small-cap value	5.59%	11.90%	13.77%
Small-cap growth	9.95%	8.70%	13.33%

Source: Morningstar

Small-cap stocks

As the name suggests, these stocks are the market's small fry. A company is considered small if its capitalization roughly ranges from $1 billion to $2 billion. Table 12-6 shows a few of the stocks in the Standard & Poor's SmallCap 600 Index.

Table 12-6
Household Names in Standard & Poor's SmallCap 600 Index

Ethan Allen Interiors	La-Z-Boy Chairs
Pier 1	OshKosh B'Gosh
Jack in the Box	Roper Industries
Zale	Orthodontic Centers of America
Cymer	Atmos Energy
Eaton Vance	Smithfield Foods

Why invest in the market's small potatoes? Historically, they've performed better than large-caps. Since 1925, small-cap stocks have averaged yearly returns of 12.4 percent. If someone had sunk $1,000 in the typical small-cap stock back then and held it until the end of 2000, that investment would have mushroomed to $6.4 million. During that same period, large-cap stocks maintained an average yearly growth of 11 percent. That seems quite respectable until you look at Table 12-7 and see the difference that 1.4 percent can make.

Table 12-7
75-Year Performance of Stocks, Bonds and Cash

Type of Stock	Average Return	Ending Investment Value of an initial $1000
Small-cap stocks	12.4%	$6.4 million
Large-cap stocks	11%	$2.5 million
Government bonds	5.3%	$49,000
Treasury bills (cash)	3.8%	$17,000

Why have small-caps outperformed the giants? A little company with an innovative product or service has a greater earnings potential than a lumbering giant. And the market rewards fast growers. Small-caps can also be nimbler and may be able to react more quickly to new opportunities and changing market conditions.

Hang on for a wild ride.

While small-caps have been the superior performer over time, they can be incredibly infuriating. They may poke along for years as they lag the market and then they'll take off unexpectedly. When this happens, the increase in small stock prices can be explosive. One amazing period came between 1978 and 1982, when small-caps provided annual returns in excess of 29 percent. The small fry enjoyed another wild and profitable ride in the early 1990s.

Note

Small-caps often flourish when the country has shaken off a recession and the economy is gaining momentum. On the other hand, small companies tend to do worse when the economy begins to struggle or a recession is expected.

Small-caps are riskier by nature. It's not hard to see why. Often in business for decades, huge companies have proven the Darwinian theory of survival of the fittest. Through the years, these giants have nurtured a loyal following and attracted more and more customers. There is a sense of predictability about what these companies can do. It would be hard to imagine, for instance, shoppers hesitating before reaching for a tube of Coppertone suntan lotion.

Many small-cap stocks can only hope to attain the same level of consumer confidence that Coppertone's large-cap drug manufacturer, Schering-Plough, enjoys. They are still fighting it out with the other Lilliputian competitors for the right to survive. These companies also have to cope with economic demons. Increasing interest rates, for example, can hobble a young company with expansion plans, because borrowing money will become far too costly. Many smaller companies can also inadvertently sabotage their plans when they grow too fast and begin to let quality slip or mismanage growth in other ways. Because the fortunes of small-caps can change very quickly, you can't adopt a laissez-faire approach with small-caps.

Buyer Beware: Initial Public Offerings

Initial Public Offerings (IPOs) are Wall Street's version of debutantes—privately held companies that have decided to "go public." These companies are offering stock shares to investors on a stock exchange for the first time.

Small investors need not apply

IPOs that do stupendously initially attract a lot of media attention, but they are almost always best to avoid. The only investors who typically make out like bandits are those who are guaranteed shares at the opening day price. Those investors usually are favored customers of the *underwriters,* the investment firm or group of investment firms that are shepherding the company through the process. Such favorite clients typically include mutual funds, pension plans, other institutional investors, and high-net-worth clients. It is very difficult for a small individual investor to get a piece of this. When the markets are hot, the price of an IPO will spike on the first day, allowing the professional players to sell their shares for a quick buck. It's often the less-sophisticated individuals who buy high and then see the value of their hot little numbers cool down.

Survey says: 5 percent return

In one notable study, researchers pored through 20 years worth of IPO stock prices in hopes of determining whether they are worth the gamble for the average investor. They concluded that the average return someone can expect from an IPO is a measly 5 percent. Hardly worth the trouble, and extremely risky. Even if you are offered an opportunity to get in on the ground floor with an IPO, you should probably pass. Ask yourself why all those folks at the top of the food chain weren't interested in this particular IPO, making it available to smaller investors.

That said, not all IPOs are flashes in the pan like Pets.com. On occasion very large, privately held companies or corporate spin-offs go public. Here is a list of the biggest IPOs in U.S. history, according to Hoover's Online:

1. AT&T Wireless Group
2. United Parcel Service
3. Verizon Wireless
4. Conoco
5. Agere Systems
6. Goldman Sachs Group
7. Charter Communications
8. Lucent Technologies
9. Metropolitan Life Insurance
10. Infinity Broadcasting

Resources for more information

To keep on top of the fast-paced IPO market, check out TheStreet.com (www.thestreet.com). It provides frequent commentaries on individual IPOs, as well as trends. Also check out IPO.com (www.ipo.com) and Hoover's Online IPO Central (www.hoovers.com).

Another interesting site is iporesources.org (www.iporesources.org), where a finance professor at Yale University has archived a variety of materials on IPOs and provided many handy links. The site, however, hasn't been updated in a while.

Less publicity means more opportunity.

Another hazard and, ironically, one of the benefits of fishing for small fry is that fewer people pay attention to these stocks. These little guys are so busy trying to inch up the food chain, they don't have time to court Wall Street. And Wall Street, quite frankly, isn't interested in many of them. While there can be dozens of highly paid analysts shadowing every move that an IBM, General Electric, or Microsoft makes, there are often no more than one or two experts following the small companies. And sometimes nobody is watching at all.

This black hole can present buying opportunities if you discover a great little company that hasn't shown up on Wall Street's radar. At the same time, you'll find it tougher to obtain information on the smaller stocks because fewer institutional investors are monitoring them.

Tip
Because analyzing and selecting small-cap stocks can be tricky, especially in the science and technology field, many investors fare better if they rely upon mutual funds to invest in the corporate Little League.

Pros and Cons of Dividend Stocks

Remember dividends? They are largely forgotten when growth stocks are hogging the limelight, but appreciated when the market is ailing. Put simply, a dividend is a payment of a portion of a company's earnings to its investors. The board of directors determines the dividend amount, which is paid in cash. You will see a dividend referred to as a dollar amount per share. The yield is determined by dividing the dividend by the share price. Consequently, a $20 stock that pays an annual $1 dividend has a dividend yield of 5 percent. The yield will obviously fluctuate as the stock price changes.

Investors can pocket the dividend payout, which is what a lot of retirees living on a fixed income do. They can receive the check in the mail. Other investors, who don't want the money just yet, opt to reinvest dividends to buy more shares. When purchasing shares of a stock with a dividend, you can direct your brokerage firm to automatically reinvest the dividends.

Advantages of dividends

Here are reasons why some investors like dividend-yielding stocks.

They provide a buffer during rocky times.

Conservative investors love stocks that pay dividends because they can provide a cushion during times when the stock market turns surly. When these stocks start caving, the dividend usually remains dependable. That knowledge can give investors the courage to hang on tight during a rocky ride.

Dividend Reinvestment Plans (DRIPs)

It's possible to invest in companies that spin off dividends through dividend reinvestment plans (DRIPs). To participate in a DRIP program, you must already hold one share of a company's stock, which means you'll need a broker for that first share. After that, however, you can often buy stock directly from a corporation, as well as reinvest any dividends your shares earn. An increasing number of companies, however, will sell you that initial share directly. You often see these programs referred to as *direct purchase plans.* The number of companies offering direct purchase plans continues to grow.

DRIPs are geared toward small investors, who want to occasionally invest small amounts of money into a stock. You may be able to invest as little as $10 or $25 at a time into a company using one of these plans. Some people like these plans because they don't trigger broker commissions, but many companies are now instituting their own fees.

To learn more about DRIPS, visit these two Web sites:

   ◆ Netstock Direct at www.netstockdirect.com

   ◆ DRIP Investor at www.dripinvestor.com

Example

Imagine what could happen to a $20 stock that pays an annual $1 dividend (5 percent) when the market slumps. The stock price may drop by 15 percent to $17, but the dividend cuts the loss to 10 percent.

Corporations that pay a regular dividend tend to experience less volatility in a turbulent market than companies that don't. Of course, when a stock does climb in price, a dividend will boost its total return.

Dividends can boost growth.

Over time, reinvested dividends can dramatically enhance a stock's total return, which includes the dividend and any price appreciation or decline. Looking back at the past two decades, dividends accounted for 49 percent of the S&P 500's total return.

They outpace inflation.

Historically, dividends have grown faster than inflation, which helps investors preserve the buying power of their income. During a recent 20-year period, dividends paid by companies in the Standard & Poor's 500 rose an average of 5.6 percent yearly, while during this same period inflation averaged 4 percent.

Dividends offer a more stable source of income.

When interest rates dip, fixed-income retirees can suffer because rates on safe investments, such as certificates of deposits and money markets, will drop too. This can be a hardship for a retiree, who is looking for an investment with a good yield alternative while a CD or bond is maturing. Stocks offering dividends may be a more attractive option.

Disadvantages of dividends

Here are reasons why some investors scorn dividend-yielding stocks.

The hot stocks don't pay dividends.

Corporations tend to pay dividends when their explosive growth years are behind them. With operations no longer expanding rapidly, less money is needed internally, so a company gives some back to its shareholders. The so-called Old Economy stocks, which are often value plays, are the dividend generators. Growth players, such as Oracle, Amgen, and EMC, prefer to plow every loose dollar back into their operations. What's more, smaller companies also tend to rely less on dividends.

Caution Consequently, if you favor companies that dole out dividends, you'll find yourself owning a lopsided portfolio, one that could be stuffed with bank and utility stocks.

Dividend amounts have stagnated.

When corporate earnings and stock prices were skyrocketing, companies didn't feel pressured to bolster their dividends or begin offering them, so the yield remains paltry. Recently the typical dividend yield offered by a corporation in the Standard & Poor's 500 Index was a measly 1.55 percent. But that's a slight improvement over 1.27 percent, which is what the yield averaged during the past five years. The last time the S&P 500's dividend yield reached 3 percent was back in 1990. That year the average yield was 3.73 percent. You'd have to push the clock back to 1981 to find the last time the average dividend yield reached 5 percent.

High dividends can signal corporate problems.

Trawling for the fattest dividends can be a dangerous strategy. Sure you want a decent dividend, but you don't want the highest. Why? These dividends could be masking severe corporate problems. Remember, the dividend yield increases as the stock price drops. So a beleaguered company that's had its stock hammered, perhaps for very solid reasons, will have its dividend automatically pumped up.

Pacific Gas & Electric and Edison International, two public utilities in California, provide an excellent cautionary tale of this phenomenon. Thanks to the state's deregulation of the power industry, the two utilities were slammed by price caps on what they could charge consumers and by exorbitant prices from outside power providers. When their pair of stocks plummeted, the yields were pushed above 8 percent. Under the circumstances, these are definitely not the kind of high-yielding stocks you'd want to buy for safe income.

 Resource If you want a safe income from your investments, avoid a distressed stock. A quick look at the stock chart on Yahoo!Finance or BigCharts (www.bigcharts.com), can tell you instantly if the stock has suffered.

Another indicator is a company's dividend payout ratio. The payout ratio represents the percent of earnings paid to shareholders as dividends. Most corporations, with the exception of many utilities, pass along less than 50 percent of their earnings in dividends, and the rest is reinvested back into the company. The greater the payout, the greater the risk for investors because if earnings falter, a company may be forced to scale back its dividend.

 Resource   You can find any company's dividend payout ratio by typing in a stock ticker symbol at Multex Investor (`www.multexinvestor.com`).

Dividends can increase tax pain.

Unfortunately, the Internal Revenue Service doesn't give dividend lovers a break. Dividends, regardless of whether they are spent or reinvested, are taxed each year as ordinary income. This means that you will owe tax based upon your individual tax bracket. If you're in the 27 percent tax bracket, for example, and you have a $1,000 dividend, the federal tax on this money is $270. The higher the tax bracket, the worse the pain.

In contrast, an investor who sold a stock for a $1,000 profit faces a smaller tax bite. This same individual would face a 20 percent federal capital gains tax if the stock were held more than a year.

Quarterly checks are disappearing.

While retirees have come to depend upon regular dividends, many companies, including Walt Disney, McDonald's, and Waste Management, have ditched the historic quarterly payment schedules. These corporations and others have concluded that mailing checks just once a year can save considerable money. Theoretically this switch should boost profits. It's expected that the majority of companies will switch to annual dividends within the next few years. The adjustment could be painful for those on fixed incomes.

Looking for Dividends?

Interested in dividend-paying stocks, but not sure where to find them? Try an online stock screener. Plenty of financial sites have prescreened lists of high-yielding stocks. For instance, CNBC on MSN Money (`www.money.msn.com`) allows you to screen for the highest-yielding stocks in the Standard & Poor's 500. Recently, the screen included utilities, banks, a steelmaker, a manufacturer of electronic components, and a timber company. At Quicken.com (`www.quicken.com`), a screen that scours for the highest yielding stocks uncovered a long list of real estate investment trusts (REITs).

Aren't plugged into the Internet? No problem. Visit the resource section of your library for a copy of Value Line, which analyzes a universe of roughly 1,700 large companies. One of the features of the weekly publication is a list of stocks yielding solid dividends.

Adventures Abroad: Foreign Investing

If you invest overseas, you probably do so for the same reason that you floss your teeth: It's good for you. At least that's the gist of the argument that financial experts have strenuously made for decades. Americans have traditionally been urged to embrace foreign stocks because they've been regarded as an excellent way to diversify. This diversity was supposed to lower a portfolio's risk because overseas markets, whether in Malaysia, Spain, Brazil, or some other time zone were often lousy at correlating with the returns of our domestic market. In other words, it's the yin and yang principal. When Wall Street is drowning in bad news, you hope that stocks in Hong Kong and France or some other nation are prospering.

Even if you're leery of investing overseas, you probably already have foreign exposure. You will have indirectly invested overseas if you have exposure in multinational corporations, either as a stock or fund investor. When the market for hamburgers, diapers, and soft drinks was saturated at home, domestic corporations set their sights on conquering the rest of the world. After all, how many more Big Macs do Americans need? Overseas is where millions, if not billions, of potential customers are waiting.

The experts have often suggested that we devote anywhere from 20 percent to 30 percent of our stock portfolios or more to foreign holdings. Many Americans, however, have never bought the global argument. By one recent estimate, Americans had a mere 2.3 percent of their money tied up abroad.

Current trend: Nations losing out to sectors

In a stunning turnaround, academics and some influential strategists at leading financial institutions have changed their minds about how big a role foreign stocks should play in anyone's portfolio. As it turns out, the doubting Thomases now believe that foreign stocks aren't such a great diversification panacea after all. Institutions like Merrill Lynch, U.S. Trust Co., and J.P. Morgan Chase were recently advising clients to scale back their foreign exposure.

What happened? The latest research suggests that foreign stocks aren't as nifty a diversification tool as previously assumed. One widely discussed study, conducted by two finance professors at the Michigan State and Illinois State universities, suggests that the foreign hedge against a turbulent market in the U.S. shrivels just when it's needed most. In other words, foreign stocks behave very much like the U.S. stocks when times are really bad. When stocks are getting clobbered here, chances are the same thing is happening in much of the rest of the world.

Perversely, the study found that foreign stocks were far less likely to mimic American stocks when Wall Street is booming. Obviously, you want foreign stocks to behave like Wall Street's identical twin during prosperous times. But the correlation is less than half that of declining markets. Only during tranquil times when the market isn't making big moves in either direction was there little correlation between domestic and foreign equities.

Resource   If you want to read the entire study on global diversification, you can download a copy from Kirt Butler, who teaches at Michigan State University (`http://courses.bus.msu.edu/fi/fi860`).

The biggest change is not whether but *how* experts are investing abroad. Instead of trying to identify the year's most promising countries and then finding the best stock picks within those borders, money managers are increasingly betting on global sectors. The manager of a global healthcare mutual fund, for instance, would pick the best drug and medical stocks from around the world. The same strategy would be used for worldwide funds that specialize in technology, telecommunications, financials, and other sectors.

Note   While enthusiasm for foreign stocks has tempered, the experts aren't suggesting that international stocks be abandoned. After all, if you invest exclusively in the U.S, you eliminate half of the world's stocks.

Checking in with the most popular overseas index

The best way to assess how the foreign portion of your portfolio is doing is to check the Morgan Stanley Capital International Europe, Australasia and Far East Index (MSCI EAFE). MSCI EAFE (pronounced *Ee-feh*), tracks foreign companies located in 21 developed nations, such as Great Britain, Germany, France, Italy, Japan, Ireland, and Singapore. The benchmark was originally created in the 1960s as a way for institutional investors to gauge how their overseas holdings were faring.

You can find this index in the business section of newspapers alongside other major benchmarks such as the Standard & Poor's 500 Index and the Dow Jones Industrial Average. You can also track dozens of Morgan Stanley's foreign indexes, including those of individual countries and global sectors, at its Web site (`www.msci.com`).

Getting around the risks of foreign investing

If you do invest overseas, regardless of your commitment, you'll face these hazards:

✦ **Hazier financial data.** Accounting and financial disclosures can vary dramatically from nation to nation.

✦ **Currency fluctuation.** Foreign exchange rates fluctuate constantly, which will enhance or decrease the dollar value of a stock even when its price doesn't budge.

✦ **Trading costs.** Investing in foreign stocks can be more costly.

Tip   For adventurous investors, there are ways to invest abroad without encountering the hassles or inconvenience of going through a foreign stock market. The easiest way to invest in the rest of the world is through mutual funds.

Another way around the hassles of foreign investing: You can purchase American depositary receipts (ADRs), which are certificates of ownership of foreign shares that are held by American banks. ADRs are traded in dollars on the U.S. stock exchanges.

Here's how an ADR works: Say you want to buy 500 shares in Nokia, a Finnish telecommunications corporation. You contact your brokerage firm that, in turn, contacts a French counterpart, who makes the purchase. The 500 shares, however, never leave France. Instead the French broker deposits the shares in a French branch of an American bank. The bank issues the receipt or ADR to your American broker.

More than 1,600 ADRS are now available from roughly 60 countries. Recently, these were the most popular foreign-traded stocks:

1.	Nokia	Finland
2.	Ericsson Telephone	Sweden
3.	Vodafone Group	United Kingdom
4.	BP Amoco	United Kingdom
5.	Telefonos de Mexico	Mexico
6.	Royal Dutch Petroleum	Netherlands
7.	Telebras Holding Co.	Brazil
8.	Alcatel	France
9.	STMicroelectronics	Netherlands
10.	Telefonica	Spain
11.	Elan Corp.	Ireland
12.	Koninklijke Philips Electronics	Netherlands
13.	ASM Lithography	Netherlands
14.	Sony	Japan
15.	Terra Networks	Spain

Resource To find out more about ADRs, including current prices, check out the Web sites of J.P. Morgan (www.adr.com) and the Bank of New York (www.adrbny.com).

Summary

✦ A well-balanced stock portfolio includes both growth and value investment styles.

✦ Consider using the growth-at-a-reasonable price (GARP) approach when assembling a portfolio.

✦ Don't overlook mid-cap stocks when overhauling a portfolio.

✦ Owning stocks with dividends can dampen wild price swings.

✦ Steer clear of risky initial public offerings.

✦ There are reliable sources for the motivated investor who wants to learn more about selecting individual stocks.

✦ You may want to reevaluate how much foreign exposure you desire in your portfolio.

Stock Strategies for the Successful Investor

✦ ✦ ✦ ✦

In This Chapter

Using the best tactics
to build a winning
portfolio

✦ ✦ ✦ ✦

In this chapter, you'll become familiar with strategies that smart stock investors have followed for years. At the same time, some tried-and-true strategies that have been accepted as gospel truth will be reexamined, such as the conventional buy-and-hold mantra and what's considered an acceptable level of stock diversification. In addition, the chapter provides advice on how you can use the market's major indexes to evaluate the success of your own portfolio and use online stock screens to uncover hidden gems.

Top 10 Strategies for Boosting Your Stock Portfolio

In the 1990s, Cisco Systems soared 68,624 percent. During the same period, investors in Best Buy, the electronics retailer, and Charles Schwab, the brokerage firm, watched as their stocks skyrocketed 9,750 percent and 8,246 percent, respectively. The performance figures for quite a few stocks were equally unprecedented. These dazzling numbers encouraged millions of Americans to do something they wouldn't have dared to do in the past: They began buying individual stocks.

Wall Street encouraged the stampede into individual stocks by making it easier and cheaper to invest in the market. In recent years, discount brokers led the way by dramatically shrinking stock commissions, which made trading far more economical. At the same time, online trading exploded in popularity while access to sophisticated stock information that used to be off limits to all but institutional investors was opened up to anybody with a computer modem. In this environment, it was perhaps inevitable that a generation of stock pickers was born.

While Americans are now fascinated with stock investing, not everyone possesses the know-how to succeed. During prosperous times, mistakes can sometimes be made without serious consequences, but when the markets are gripped by turbulence, errors can be disastrous. You will boost your chances of succeeding if you follow these 10 strategies.

Strategy no. 1: Evaluate your motivations.

If you're contemplating investing in individual stocks, join the crowd. An increasing number of fairly sophisticated investors are giving it a whirl. Before doing so, however, take a moment to explore your own motivations. Here are reasons why you might want to take a look at investing in individual equities:

 Cross-Reference You can learn much more about tax strategies and investing in Chapter 25.

Stocks are more tax efficient than mutual funds.

By holding individual stocks, an investor controls when he or she triggers taxes on the profits. Stock shareholders, who hang onto their shares, won't owe capital gains taxes, even if a stock soars 50 percent, 100 percent or 10,000 percent. The sky's the limit. As long as the stock isn't sold, the Internal Revenue Service receives nothing.

In comparison, mutual fund investors get a raw deal. Every year, many mutual funds generate taxes. And guess what? Even if investors don't sell a single fund share, they can get walloped with yearly capital gains taxes. What's truly appalling is that hapless investors who own a fund that's lost money during a calendar year can still end up with a fat tax bill.

Note Holding individual stocks can also be cheaper because after a commission is paid, a stock doesn't trigger annual charges like a mutual fund does.

They offer potentially greater returns.

Unfortunately, most mutual funds, over time, underperform the stock market. Some ambitious investors believe they can do better by selecting individual stocks or mixing stocks with funds. Yet an investor who buys only individual equities doesn't necessarily have to choose all winners. It's possible that a few well-placed picks can more than make up for the losers. But assembling an enviable portfolio requires considerable time and enough money to properly diversify across many sectors. The typical mutual fund, in contrast, offers almost instant diversification.

Stocks are intellectually stimulating.

Some people relish challenges, and assembling a first-class portfolio falls into that category. With the playing field nearly leveled for the little guys, few artificial impediments still exist to prevent individuals from becoming successful stock jocks. One danger, however, has lingered. Some people discover that picking stocks is great fun, but monitoring them becomes tedious. Keeping track of your holdings is essential, even if it's less glamorous than making the initial purchase.

 Caution Consider avoiding investing in individual stocks if you think you'll end up obsessing about the portfolio's performance. Investors who check stock prices every day or every hour online and agonize about a stock's short-term price movement may become too emotionally involved to hold stocks.

Strategy no. 2: Decide how many stocks is enough.

How many stocks should you own? Nobody knows for sure. Or rather, nobody can agree on a nice round figure. Those who find comfort in conventional wisdom believe an investor can be safely diversified by holding anywhere from 12 to 20 stocks. But don't be too sure. This rule of thumb is being vigorously challenged by many academics and professional money managers, who insist that holding any less than 50 or 60 stocks or, in some cases, 100 or more, may be foolhardy.

Option 1: Less is more.

The "less is more" crowd has some impressive headliners in its camp. The most prominent is Warren Buffett, the mastermind behind Berkshire Hathaway, whose corporate portfolio has performed spectacularly with a relatively small number of stocks. Another celebrated believer is Burton G. Malkiel, who wrote the classic investing book, *A Random Walk Down Wall Street.*

Supporters of the minimalist approach suggest that the fewer stocks in a portfolio, the greater the chances it will outperform the overall market. One prominent study that looked at 12,000 different portfolios over a long period of time concluded that a 15-stock portfolio had a one in four chance of beating the market, while the odds slipped to one in 50 for a portfolio crammed with 250 stocks.

Note Amazingly, research has suggested that when 15 or 20 stocks are spread across a variety of industries, a portfolio's risk can be nearly identical to that of the broader stock market.

The studies trickling out from this camp have been compelling enough for mutual fund companies to roll out dozens of concentrated funds, which aim for outsized returns by generally holding no more than two dozen or so stocks. (See Chapter 14 for more on concentrated funds.)

Note   Those who believe investors would be better off with fewer stocks insist that the key to pulling off this strategy is diversification in different industries, a concept covered further in this chapter.

Option 2: More is better.

The opposing camp scoffs at the bare-bones portfolio approach. They insist that a handful of stocks, no matter how intelligently selected, can't possibly be a prudent approach for someone who wants to do better than his or her neighbors, much less Wall Street. This is especially true, they say, as the volatility of individual stocks has been rising over the years. The contrarians observe that too much focus in this numbers-game debate has been centered on whether a relatively small stock portfolio can pose no more of a risk to its owner than a humongous one.

Note   These experts say portfolio volatility isn't the only risk involved here. The other important risk, they suggest, is underperforming the market.

William J. Bernstein, the author of a book, entitled, *The Intelligent Asset Allocator,* made a stab at quantifying this risk in some recent number crunching. He randomly formed 98 portfolios, with 15 stocks from the Standard & Poor's 500 Index in each. He then compared how these portfolios fared against the index. The results weren't pretty. During a 10-year period, three-quarters of the portfolios failed to beat the index. Some of the portfolios lagged the index by as much as 5 percent to 10 percent a year.

Bernstein found that the portfolios didn't do as well if they failed to contain what he called a "super stock." These were stocks like Dell Computer, which was the best performing stock of the 1990s. He concluded that the risks involved in trying to outsmart the market are so considerable that it's better to own the whole thing. This, of course, can be accomplished with an index mutual fund.

Resource   You can read Bernstein's study, as well as some of his others, at his Web site (www.efficientfrontier.com).

Strategy no. 3: Mix up stocks and mutual funds.

Holding dozens of stocks is hardly practical for any person expected to take out the trash, cart kids around, earn a living, and perform all the other chores that fill a lifetime of to-do lists. However, don't assume that stock picking is an all-or-nothing proposition. A logical compromise is to hold mutual funds plus a smattering of stocks. Owning funds can help you venture out into the stock world and can provide diversification while you test the waters.

There are countless ways to mix and match. Someone, for instance, may keep the core of his or her holdings in an index fund that provides exposure to the broad stock market, thus reducing the potential volatility of the portfolio. Vanguard Total Stock Market Index Fund and Fidelity Spartan Total Market Index Fund are two candidates that cover the entire market. On the fringes, an investor could buy a mix of stocks of various sizes. The goal would be to improve upon the performance of the index fund, which by its very nature isn't equipped to beat the market.

Another alternative is to use a mutual fund for your small-cap investing. You may want to consider such indexing candidates as Vanguard Extended Market Index or Fidelity Spartan Extended Market Index funds. With an index fund providing your small- and mid-cap exposure, you can select your own individual large-cap stocks.

 Tip　If index funds leave you cold, consider a core holding of an all-weather mutual fund that has performed well in both rocky and exuberant markets. A list of such honor roll funds is in Chapter 3.

Strategy no. 4: Question the buy-and-hold mantra.

Warren Buffett is famous for his allegiance to many of his stocks. He doesn't just buy his stocks, he practically marries them. He's grown old with stocks like American Express, *The Washington Post,* and Coca-Cola.

The Nebraska billionaire's track record seems to validate what a lot of mere mortal investors have tried to practice. They've concluded that their ticket to financial paradise depends upon following the buy-and-hold strategy that's observed by Buffett and many other experts. (Truth be told, Buffett does dump stocks on occasion.)

The wisdom of the buy-and-hold philosophy is rarely questioned, even by those who sheepishly don't practice it. But conventional wisdom isn't necessarily always right. Even the most venerated blue chips can fail spectacularly. What happened in the early 1970s and was eerily repeated in the new century provides a cautionary tale.

Downfall of the Nifty Fifty and the tech market

In the early seventies, the Nifty Fifty dominated the stock market. These were 50 growth stocks that Wall Street adored. The roster included companies like Xerox, Polaroid, Digital Equipment, Upjohn, Kmart, Simplicity Pattern, and a smattering of drug stocks. They were supposed to be the no-brainer stocks for the rest of the 20th century. Holding them for a lifetime would surely make the owners wealthy. But there was one worrisome footnote in this fairy tale. The stocks were lavishly overvalued. Money managers, however, didn't blanch at the princely prices because they believed these firecrackers would never fizzle.

Many of the finest minds on Wall Street miscalculated. After peaking in late 1972, the Nifty Fifty was anything but. All of a sudden, investors couldn't ditch their shares fast enough. The Nifty Fifty plummeted, as did the rest of Wall Street. The struggling stock market did not reach its 1973 peak for another nine years.

Go Slow with Stock Selection

Picking stocks isn't that different from graduating from a tricycle. Staying balanced on a two-wheeler that is careening down the street isn't something you know instinctively. Neither is stock investing. If you want to pick individual stocks, go slow. When you're compiling a portfolio of stocks, there's no need to rush.

Do you see parallels to what happened to some of America's premiere stocks in recent times? If you do, you aren't the first. Stocks like Cisco Systems, Dell Computer, Yahoo!, AOL Time Warner, Intel, and Microsoft were even more popular than the stocks captivating Americans back when Richard Nixon was president. You could find stocks like these in many of the most successful mutual fund portfolios. Money managers and individuals alike dismissed the extremely high valuations as acceptable because the so-called New Economy had allegedly changed the rules on Wall Street.

These stock darlings, however, got hammered once the 1990s faded from view. Some of these stocks are recovering from their concussions and will ultimately prove they have staying power. That's exactly what stocks like Johnson & Johnson, Walt Disney, and Merck, all Nifty Fifty alumni, did. But others may disappear, get swallowed up, or just tread water.

The rest of the story

Historical research by the Leuthold Group, a prominent money management firm, suggests that blindly sticking with yesterday's popular stocks is not always prudent. The firm examined the fate of 25 Nifty Fifty companies with the most expensive price tags in the early 1970s. From 1972 to 1982, these 25 former stars gained just 2 percent. If an investor had sunk $1,000 into each of these stocks in 1972 and held on until June 2000, the portfolio would have been worth $445,148. That may look impressive until you see how much the investment would have been worth if it had been sunk into an index fund that tracks the Standard & Poor's 500 Index. It would have reached $752,603.

The bottom line

History strongly suggests that sure things don't exist on Wall Street. Buying a stock and forgetting about it for years can be dangerous. No matter how well regarded a stock in your portfolio is, it needs to be monitored on a regular basis. Ask yourself if the reasons you initially picked a stock are still valid.

Strategy no. 5: Find stock ideas in the right places.

Stock ideas can come from many sources. You can find them in magazines, online stock screeners, financial news shows, or a neighbor. You can discover decent leads by flipping through an annual report of your favorite mutual fund. Inside these updates, you'll find an entire listing of a fund's equity holdings. Some managers helpfully explain why they are thrilled with certain stocks and why they have jettisoned others.

Trend alert

If you believe Peter Lynch, a legendary stock picker who used to run Fidelity Magellan Fund, you can generate solid ideas by just staying alert to trends. You might notice that your daughter and every other impressionable teen is wearing the same fashions and that most of it is coming from the same manufacturer. Or maybe a national pet supply chain has gobbled up the store where you buy your golden retriever's chew toys, as well as other outlets in your city. Hmmm. Maybe there's a growth opportunity there.

Personal and professional expertise

Lynch and others suggest that you can profit by investing in your own area of competence. If you're a banker, you should have a leg up on analyzing banking stocks. A retailer would have a better eye for determining whether a hot clothing retailer is a flash-in-the pan or a legitimate investment opportunity. Investors can also do a good job following companies in their own region. Local newspapers will cover regional companies much more closely than those outside the area. So if you live in St. Louis, you'll read a lot about Anheuser Busch and Emerson Electric, while someone in Minneapolis can easily keep up with Target, Pillsbury, General Mills, and Northwest Airlines.

Tip To obtain a national perspective on prospective companies, consider subscribing to *Barron's* or *Bloomberg Personal Finance Magazine.*

While more people are familiar with *Barron's* sister publication, *The Wall Street Journal, Barron's* is better appreciated for its market commentary and insightful analysis of individual corporations. Its reporting is often considered ahead of the curve. *Bloomberg Personal Finance Magazine* is another sophisticated publication for those interested in learning more about individual stocks as well as stock picking strategies.

Stock screens

Want a more organized way to unearth gems? Try stock screeners. Many online sites allow you to develop your own list of promising stocks by picking and choosing from dozens of variables. Based on the variables you select, the software spits out names of potential candidates for you. For investors with less experience, you can rely upon prescreened models that search for the best stocks in particular categories, such as:

✦ Income stocks

✦ Contrarian plays

✦ Growth at a reasonable price

✦ Momentum stocks

✦ Stocks with accelerating earnings

✦ Safe large-cap stocks

✦ Inexpensive small-cap stocks

One of the strengths of stock screeners is that they can usher you into a universe of companies that you didn't know existed. This is especially valuable if you desire to invest in small- and medium-sized stocks. While magazines, newspapers, and other financial sources tend to focus most of their attention on traditional headline grabbers, which are often blue chip companies like Wal-Mart, Exxon Mobil, Ford Motor, and Citigroup, mainstream media generally doesn't provide much coverage of the corporate Little League.

Here are some stock screeners to check out:

✦ Multex Investor   (www.multexinvestor.com)

✦ CNBC on MSN Money   (www.money.msn.com)

✦ Hoover's Online   (www.hoovers.com)

✦ Morningstar   (www.morningstar.com)

✦ Quicken   (www.quicken.com)

Each stock screener has different strengths and weaknesses. Some are geared toward sophisticated investors, who don't need much information on the meaning of the screen variables, while others are geared to the beginner. Multex Investor, for example, has an extensive lineup of preestablished screens. You can click the hyperlink for income stocks and watch a list of stocks with high dividends scroll onto the screen. Multex Investor's more sophisticated screening tools, meant for experienced investors, are available for a monthly fee.

If you've got a stock in mind, Quicken has its own one-click scorecard that allows you to instantly see how four well-known stock strategies would rate your candidate. Your prospective stock will be assessed against the stock-picking strategies used by the Motley Fool; the National Association of Investors Corp., the national investment club organization; billionaire investor Warren Buffett; and Geraldine Weiss, a prominent value investor.

Caution   Don't automatically assume that the stocks generated by a software program are winners. Screening is best used for whittling down choices. After that, it's up to you to evaluate the survivors until you discover a winner.

Strategy no. 7: Consult the indexes.

So how is your stock portfolio doing? Just by looking at the raw numbers, you won't necessarily know. If your portfolio is down 5 percent for the year, you might chide yourself, but if the market has sunk 12 percent, you'd actually be doing better than most. On the other hand, if your holdings have jumped 10 percent but the rest of the market is clocking gains of 20 percent, you've fallen behind. To really know how your investments are doing, you need to measure the gains or losses of your stocks and mutual funds against the relevant indexes.

Tip As you compare your holdings with the appropriate index, remember that the shorter the time frame you use for a reference, the less relevant it is. Two, three, and five years are the more meaningful time frames when measuring performance.

Today, literally thousands of indexes dissect the markets in innumerable ways. The typical individual investor, however, can focus on the major ones. The following list describes indexes that you should know.

Dow Jones Industrial Average

This index tracks 30 of the largest and some of the most highly regarded blue chip corporations in America. The 30 Dow stocks, which include such corporations as Microsoft, Merck, DuPont, American Express, and Disney, are listed each day in *The Wall Street Journal.*

Note The Dow Jones Industrial Average, which is more than a century old, was designed to mirror the health of the entire market, but the S&P 500 and the Wilshire 5000 are considered better measures.

Standard & Poor's 500

This index is composed of 500 of America's largest corporations. Many of the companies in this index are instantly recognizable, such as Hershey Foods, AOL Time Warner, Chevron, Kellogg, Yahoo!, and General Electric. You will want to compare the performance of any large corporations you own with this index.

This is also the index that is used most frequently to compare the performance of stock mutual funds. Again, when making comparisons between your stock and the index, use the long-term track records, such as three- and five-year performances.

Wilshire 5000

By tracking the performance of more than 7,000 American companies, this is the broadest domestic index of them all. The range of stocks included in the Wilshire 5000 is vast, from tiny companies with stock worth less than $1 million to Goliaths with individual market values reaching $460 billion.

 Cross-Reference Chapter 10 contains more information on all of the indexes described in this chapter.

This index is the widely used barometer of broad trends in the overall stock market. Even though the index is stuffed with thousands of tiny companies, it's ironically still most heavily influenced by the largest corporate members. The Wilshire 5000 should perform slightly better than the S&P 500 during times when small company stocks are enjoying great success. The long-term performance of both indexes is remarkably similar.

Indexing Data Galore

You can find up-to-date index statistics, as well as more background on the indexes, at these Web addresses:

- ✦ Standard & Poor's   (www.spglobal.com)
- ✦ Wilshire Associates   (www.wilshire.com)
- ✦ Morgan Stanley Capital International   (www.mscidata.com)
- ✦ Frank Russell Co.   (www.russell.com)
- ✦ Nasdaq   (www.nasdaq.com)
- ✦ Barra   (www.barra.com)
- ✦ IndexFunds.com   (www.indexfunds.com)

Nasdaq Composite and Nasdaq-100

The Nasdaq Composite, which was created in 1971, contains all the American and foreign companies that are listed on the Nasdaq stock market. The list of companies exceeds 5,000. The Nasdaq has become synonymous with technology for good reason. About 70 percent of the composite's total stock valuation can be traced to technology stocks. Most young companies, tech or not, end up listing on the Nasdaq.

Both of these benchmarks can be used to gauge the performance of the technology portion of your portfolio. They are widely considered to be a proxy for the so-called New Economy stocks.

Russell 2000 and Standard & Poor's SmallCap 600 Index

The Russell 2000 contains 2,000 small companies, while the S&P SmallCap 600, as its name suggests, doesn't cast as wide a net. Those that make the S&P cut are slightly bigger companies than what you'd find in the Russell 2000. While experts debate which index is superior, institutional investors seem to prefer S&P's version.

Tip   If you continually find that the benchmarks outperform your collection of stocks, it's time to reevaluate your strategy. Perhaps your talents do not lie in stock picking, in which case mutual funds or exchange-traded funds are a better bet.

Strategy no. 8: Know the signs to sell.

Buying stocks is fun. Contemplating a sell is agonizing. When selling stocks, many investors fly blind. They may sell because a stock isn't growing fast enough, it's stuck in a holding pattern, or perhaps it's free falling. But the decision is often based more on emotion than on a critical analysis. That's why when some investors sell, they continue to follow their old stocks in an attempt to second-guess themselves.

Tip

When you buy a stock, write down what has attracted you to it. Pretend you must convince a roomful of skeptics, who need to be won over before you can place an order. When you are tempted to sell, revisit your original arguments for comparison to the stock's current situation.

You can short-circuit some of the angst by developing sound sell guidelines. No one correct strategy exists, but before selling, spend as much time researching your move as you hopefully did before buying the stock. Here are some factors to consider:

Cockroach phenomenon

Every quarter, publicly traded companies are required to file their latest earnings with the U.S. Securities and Exchange Commission. Earnings season is a very big event on Wall Street as analysts try to anticipate a corporation's earnings. If a company does better than the Street's projections, its stock can enjoy a nice pop. If a company falls short, its stock may be crushed. Although any company can experience a lousy quarter, all too often bad earnings news isn't an isolated event. When a corporation reports disappointing earnings, there could be more bad news in future quarters. This is sometimes referred to as the cockroach effect, since cockroaches rarely travel alone.

The release of quarterly earnings is a good time to revisit the reasons you bought the stock and if those same reasons still exist. You'll want to determine whether the company is flourishing or being threatened by such things as increased competition, an empty pipeline of new ideas, product obsolescence, or a change in business strategy, or whether it's in an industry that has become less attractive.

Cross-
Reference

You'll learn more about interpreting quarterly earnings releases in Chapter 15.

Accounting hanky panky

This one is a stock's kiss of death. Wall Street abhors any corporation that has fiddled with the books. When federal regulators announce an investigation of a corporation's "accounting irregularities," expect a stock free fall. That's what happened to Cendant Corp., whose brand-name businesses include Avis, Coldwell Banker, and Ramada. In 1998, the government accused the corporation of inflating its earnings for at least a decade. When the news reached the financial media, the stock plummeted.

Obviously, it's best to look for worrisome clues before the Securities and Exchange Commission steps in. What are some potential red flags?

✦ **The corporation uses an obscure accounting firm to handle its financial audits.** While smaller firms can be ethically honest, the nationally known accounting firms have their invaluable reputations on the line. They may be less prone to wink at some fiscal impropriety. You can find out who is auditing the financial records by looking at the corporation's annual report and the SEC financial filings.

✦ **The auditors must play musical chairs.** It doesn't look good if a company regularly replaces its outside auditors.

✦ **A chief financial officer's tenure is short-lived.** A CFO is the keeper of a company's financial secrets. If they don't like what they see, they aren't going to hold a press conference, but they might quietly move on.

Inflated stock price

Is a stock that doubles in price overvalued? What about a triple-bagger? Gazing at a price chart of a stock won't provide any clues. (Investors who favor technical stock analysis, however, will quarrel with this.) In fact, a stock that's soared 30 or 40 percent may still be a screaming bargain compared to an overvalued stock that's just been treading water.

If stock price can't tell you anything, what can? One indicator is the *PEG ratio,* which is the P/E ratio divided by the estimated rate of growth in the future. (P/E ratios are defined in Chapter 12.) Here is the equation:

P/E ratio ÷ future growth rate = PEG ratio

If a company's P/E ratio is 30 and analysts expect the company to grow an average of 15 percent for the next few years, the PEG ratio is 2 (30 ÷ 15). A stock is generally considered fairly valued if its PEG ratio is 1.0. You can find this ratio for any stock at Yahoo!Finance (`http://finance.yahoo.com`).

Applying the PEG ratio

To see how the PEG ratio works, look at two little-known stocks, which did phenomenally well during the infamous technology stock implosion. By the summer of 2001, Apollo Group, which owns a string of private colleges, and SCP Pool, the world's largest swimming pool supply company, had respectively soared 72 percent and 68 percent during the previous 12 months. Time to sell both of them? Maybe not.

The stock price of Apollo, which operates Phoenix University branches, climbed for a variety of reasons. The company generated big earnings, the education sector was thriving, and investors concluded that the business was insulated from recessionary worries because laid off workers would need to return to school to make themselves more marketable. SCP, which has POOL as its stock ticker, is a darling of institutional investors, who love the Louisiana company's steady sales and earnings progress. Look at a five-year chart of the company and you see very few dips.

When you compared the PEG ratio of the two stocks, however, SCP Pool looked like a better stock to keep. Its PEG ratio was .92. This means that relative to its anticipated future earnings, the stock was 8 percent undervalued. In contrast, Apollo's PEG ratio was 1.68. This means the stock, according to the ratio, is 68 percent overvalued.

Selling Out

Selling a stock doesn't have to be an all-or-nothing proposition. An investor who remains torn even after doing the research can decide to sell just a portion of a stock. If shares drop later, revisit the stock and see whether it is worthwhile to reinvest.

Keeping the PEG in perspective

You shouldn't treat the PEG ratio as gospel truth. That's because the formula relies upon analysts' predictions of future earnings. If the earnings estimates change, the PEG ratio could change dramatically. Consequently, you should be conservative when looking at PEG ratios, whether you're buying or selling. If you're particularly interested in picking up shares in a small or medium-sized company, a PEG ratio should ideally be well below 1.0.

You will learn much more about financial ratios and analysts' earnings projections in Chapter 15.

Negative analyst sentiment

Analysts hardly ever trash a stock publicly. Sell ratings are about as rare as meteor showers. Consequently, if an analyst or two are bold enough to issue a "sell" recommendation, this can be a very ominous sign.

An easy way to discover analyst rankings on any stock is to visit Zacks Investment Research at www.zacks.com.

Strong insider trading

If company insiders such as board members, the chief financial officer, and chief executive officer dump lots of stock, this is a worrisome sign. Large stock sales can suggest that the top people running a company know something bad is brewing. Investors may also assume that the insiders don't have much confidence in their stocks. Plenty of cases surfaced of insiders at tech companies, who sold massive amounts of their stock before the tech plunge began in 2000.

What's tricky is that stock sales don't automatically mean that executives are pessimistic about their company's future. With a great deal of their net worth tied up in the fortunes of one stock, they naturally want to diversify into other investments. That's why you should look for patterns of broad selling.

The amount of stock that high-ranking executives own is most critical at smaller companies where remaining competitive and innovative is crucial to staying alive. If a company's top management and board own at least 30 percent of the stock, that's often a good sign. It's harder to pinpoint an ideal percentage for major corporations, but it's better if the executives' compensation is tied to meeting the corporation's goals rather than to how well its stock price does.

You can keep track of insider stock ownership at these major financial Web sites.

✦ Securities & Exchange Commission   www.sec.gov

✦ Edgar-Online   www.edgar-online.com

✦ CBSMarketwatch   www.cbsmarketwatch.com

✦ Yahoo!Finance   http://finance.yahoo.com

Strategy no. 9: Understand the mechanics of stock trading.

If you're going to invest in individual stocks, you'll need to know how to execute your order. Unfortunately, people's trading mistakes have cost them dearly. Here are your main choices:

Market order

If it's important to buy or sell stock immediately, this is the way to go. By placing a market order, you instruct your broker to make the trade at the best available price at the time. With a market order, you can often pick up shares or dump some within seconds after placing an order. This is by far the most popular way to trade stocks, and it's also the cheapest.

Limit order

The limit order is favored by investors, who hope to trade shares at a specific price. For example, suppose that General Motors is selling at 54 but you don't think it's a good value unless it inches down to 50. If you place a limit order at 50, you won't own General Motors unless the price drops that low or lower. With limit orders, however, you run the risk of never making a trade. For instance, if General Motors only dips down to 50.25, the shares won't be bought.

Note   Using a limit order can be a good idea when the markets are especially volatile. Limit orders, however, typically cost more money than trading stock on a market order.

Stop orders

Stop orders are designed to protect gains or limit the losses. When the markets are edgy, stop orders might help restless investors sleep soundly. Worried about further turbulence of technology stocks, you place a stop sell order on your Applied Micro Circuits stock for $20 when the price is at $28. If the stock tanks, you know what your worst loss will be. The stop order, however, won't ensure that your stock will be sold at the exact price you set. In a fast-declining market, your shares could be executed at a lower price. Some investors place stop orders that are 10 percent below the current value of their shares. Ask yourself if you want to be a seller when prices are plummeting.

Stock Splits

Would you rather buy 50 shares of stock at $100 a pop or wait until you can snatch up 100 shares of the same stock priced at $50? Either way, your investment would be worth $5,000. What's the catch? Welcome to your first lesson in stock splits.

On its face, a stock split is a wash. Suppose you own 100 shares of a $40 stock. If the corporation decides to split its shares in half, you'd own 200 shares of a $20 stock. This 2-for-1 split is a common way that corporations divide shares when they want to attract more investors. A stock that's priced at $40 looks more affordable than one that's trading at $80 or $120; psychologically, investors like cheaper stocks. Some companies prefer a 3-for-1 split. With one of these splits, a shareholder with 100 shares priced at $100 a piece will ultimately own 300 shares at $33.33 a piece. Another possibility is a 3-for-2 split.

Investors are often thrilled when their stocks split. Splits can signal that a company is feeling confident about its future prospects. After all, a company probably isn't going to voluntarily shrink shares if it believes Wall Street will soon punish its stock. That's one of the conclusions made by a pair of Rice University professors, who examined more than 3,000 stock splits during a 10-year period. In their study, the researchers discovered that in the year following a split announcement, a company outperformed similar corporations by an average of nine percentage points.

A corporation doesn't split shares overnight. It must announce its intentions prior to the move. Because split announcements are greeted with such enthusiasm, the possibility of a split can boost a stock. In fact, a stock often enjoys a run up when the Street speculates that a company is a prime split candidate. Ironically, once the announcement is made, a stock may surrender some of its gains—the cash rushed in when anticipation of a split tantalized investors; after it is officially announced, some investors are looking around for the next promising stock.

Buying shares in rumored split candidates is risky business. But some Web sites encourage the practice by keeping abreast of split developments. Since splits are preannounced, it's possible to buy into a stock before it happens. Here are sites that maintain stock split calendars listing what companies have announced splits and when the splits will take effect.

- ✦ SplitTrader.com   (www.splittrader.com)
- ✦ StockSplits.net   (www.stocksplits.net)
- ✦ Briefing.com   (www.briefing.com)
- ✦ The Online Investor   (www.theonlineinvestor.com)

Tip   You can place a stop or limit order for just one day or you can keep it in effect indefinitely. The latter are referred to as *good-till-canceled* orders.

Strategy no. 10: Get a second opinion.

Even if you've done your homework, the best stocks will, on occasion, blow up. If you find yourself agonizing over stock losses, consider calling a Certified Financial Planner for an outside assessment of your portfolio. If you're on the right track, you will be relieved to hear this from an expert. On the other hand, if your portfolio really is a mess, it's best to hear the grim news from somebody who can help with the damage control. In Chapter 5, you can find out how to locate an ideal planner.

Summary

✦ Analyze the reasons for investing in individual stocks before committing yourself.

✦ Combining mutual funds and individual stocks in a portfolio can be a sensible investing approach.

✦ Don't automatically assume that you can safely hold any stock forever, no matter what its pedigree.

✦ Gauge your stock-picking abilities by comparing your portfolio's performance with the appropriate benchmarks.

✦ Develop a sound strategy for selling stocks in your portfolio.

✦   ✦   ✦

Sector Investing: Too Hot to Handle?

In this chapter, you'll learn about the perils and rewards of sector investing, which describes an investment strategy that narrows in on just one sliver of the stock market. If you decide sector investing is for you, you'll learn how to do so wisely. You'll discover how to evaluate sector choices and avoid the financial hemorrhaging that often afflicts those who chase hot sectors. The chapter also discusses which sectors generally prosper under various economic conditions, which could help you to better time your sector bets.

A Little Background

Be honest. Have you secretly wished that you owned a piece of the year's hottest investments? In the late 1990s, just about any investment that claimed kinship with the dot-com mania was a winner, even though the earnings of many of these companies were less than a teenager's summer earnings at McDonald's. By 2000, Internet stocks were toast, but health-care stocks and energy stocks were wowing Wall Street.

This game of sector musical chairs is nothing new. Back in the early 1990s, biotechnology stocks seemed invincible—until they disappeared into a fog bank. Farther back, the clear winner at one point was the energy sector, till it lost its crown to consumer staple stocks. During the so-called "tronics boom" of the early '60s, electronics stocks were smoking, but many of them quickly saw most of their value disintegrate.

Despite the hazards, Americans are embracing sector investing like never before in history. And the money trail confirms it. Throughout much of the 1990s, petty cash trickled into sector mutual funds. But that changed dramatically in 1999, when more than $2 out of every $10 found its way into a sector fund. The next year, an astounding 33 percent of the new cash was earmarked for these specialty funds.

Tech sector popularity

Of course, a big reason for the sector mania was technology's recent dominance of the stock market, which excited investors from retired widows to teenagers, who now clamor for online brokerage accounts before they're old enough for a learner's permit. Indeed, a great deal of this hot money has been sunk in technology.

Do all the people placing bets on slivers of the stock market know what they are doing? Probably not. But just because many individuals are chasing the most phenomenal returns doesn't mean sector investing should be debunked.

Note Sinking money into sectors can be appropriate for a thoughtful investor who appreciates the rewards and risks. In contrast, it's the knee-jerk investors who can and often do get burnt.

Conventional wisdom suggests that most individuals should keep a safe distance from sectors. If you were one of the many investors who poured money into an Internet fund and then watched in horror as your account balance shrunk by 60 percent or 70 percent or more, you understand. But, as this chapter reveals, recent research from leading academics has strongly suggested that there is a place for sector investing in the mainstream.

New opportunities in all sectors

If sector investing sounds promising to you, you're in luck. There's never been such a bountiful selection of investing techniques for investors who desire to push the envelope. For starters, the number of sector mutual funds, which have been the traditional way to invest in sectors, has jumped significantly. Today, you have several hundred choices. And of course, another option, though labor intensive, is selecting individual stocks.

Now, however, you can open door no. 3 for another alternative: exchange-traded funds. This investment hybrid shares characteristics of both stocks and funds and has generally made it easier and less expensive to invest in sectors.

Cross-Reference Chapter 11 is devoted to exchange-traded funds.

Financial institutions as diverse as the American Stock Exchange and Merrill Lynch have created these funds that offer exposure both to broad sectors, like technology and healthcare, and to such subspecialties as broadband and biotechnology stocks. Bringing up the rear is another new trend that's catching fire—focused mutual funds, which may invest in less than two dozen stocks. Technically they aren't sector funds, but they can be just as rewarding, as well as treacherous. This chapter contains more information on these types of funds as well.

Sector ABCs

Just what constitutes a sector will differ depending upon your financial source. No definitive list of sectors, which are groupings of similar stocks, exists. The major sector trackers, including Standard & Poor's, Wilshire Associates and Morningstar, can only agree on three sectors—technology, financial, and utilities. Some of these firms say there are as many as 13 sectors, while others insist there are as few as nine. Obviously, carving the market into pieces is subjective.

It's possible to compartmentalize the market into far tinier boxes. The financial gurus, who oversee the Standard & Poor's 500 Index, for instance, have carved up the benchmark into 87 industry groups. Dow Jones, which is the owner of *The Wall Street Journal,* maintains dozens of industry groupings within its 10 sectors. Under the heading of Dow Jones' consumer cyclical sector, for instance, are such industries as advertising, carmakers, airlines, casinos, and restaurant stocks. Within the Dow Jones industrial sector are such industries as defense, heavy construction, pollution control, trucking, and building materials.

Sector mutual fund managers, ignoring nearly the entire universe of stocks, concentrate on just one market niche, whether it's technology, healthcare, financial stocks, or utilities. Some managers are even more focused, specializing within sectors on smaller industry groups such as e-commerce, Internet architecture, or electrical equipment.

By its very nature, sector investing can be a wild ride. After all, the thinner the investment pie is sliced, the greater the potential payoff, as well as the chance for financial indigestion. Investing in a fund that focuses on wireless telecommunication stocks, for instance, is going to be more volatile than going with a broader utility fund. A fund mandated to invest only in brokerage stocks will be riskier than a stock fund that invests in the entire financial industry.

Sector Origins

Long before you or I were born, Dow Jones launched the original three sector indexes to track industrials, transportation, and utility stocks. The number of sectors that institutional and individual investors watch closely today far exceeds the original trio.

Portrait of a sector investor

Is sector investing right for you? Read over the following investor profiles to see whether sector investing falls within your comfort zone.

◆ **Self-starter.** If you are an experienced, enthusiastic stockpicker, sector investing could work for you. This type of investing requires much more attention and expertise, than say, sinking money into an all-purpose index fund. Picking sector plays requires you to know something about economic cycles and why certain industries do better at certain times. You may also need to act quickly to move in or out of a sector.

◆ **Eagle Scout.** If you are as conscientious as a Scout in following the cardinal rule of investing (diversify!), you can more confidently venture into the wilds of sector investing. If you've already assembled a well-balanced portfolio, you'll benefit from the protection it can provide when your sector investment is getting pummeled.

◆ **Risk-averse conservative.** Anyone who couldn't handle losing 50 or 60 percent of their fund's value or more should stay off the sector investing roller coaster.

◆ **Performance chasers.** Sector investing attracts a lot of wannabe millionaires. They hope to strike it rich and they think shoveling money into a sector that's already skyrocketed will do the trick. Studies show, however, that Johnny-come-latelies do poorly. Unfortunately, most investors don't get interested in a sector until its performance has already peaked. If you love to chase the hot money and haven't done your due diligence by first building a diversified portfolio, avoid sector investing.

Caution
If you consider investing as enjoyable as flossing, forget about sector investing—it's a high maintenance activity.

Ways to play the sector game

For those who see merit in sector investing, you can easily buy into a promising industry by picking up shares in a mutual fund or exchange-traded fund, as is explained here. For tips on building a sector section of stocks in your portfolio, see Chapter 15 for details on evaluating individual stocks within a given sector.

Sector mutual funds

The mutual fund industry has gone gaga over sector plays. It would be difficult to find an industry that a fund firm somewhere hasn't specialized in. Some might suggest that the fund world has gotten carried away. Besides the popular technology and healthcare funds, you can invest in funds that specialize in golf, the funeral business, and yes, even water.

Today investors can choose from among several hundred sector mutual funds. Here is just a partial list of the sectors and industries that you can invest in through specialized funds:

Healthcare	Regional banks
Wireless communications	Biotechnology
Electronics	Natural resources
Gold	Retailing
Insurance	Energy
Utilities	Consumer products
Transportation	Internet
Defense	Basic materials

While mulling over your fund choices, pay close attention to the manager in charge of your investment. You want somebody who knows the sector inside and out, and who has been running the fund for preferably two or three years. If the fund has an excellent track record, make sure the fund manager responsible for it is still there.

When selecting a sector fund, you should also evaluate a fund's performance, as well as its annual expenses. (Chapter 7 describes typical fund expenses.) Unfortunately, sector funds are inherently more expensive because they generate more costs.

Tip   You can gain an edge by sticking with fund families that specialize in sector investing. (There aren't that many.) For example, you don't want to buy into a technology fund from a fund company that specializes in value investing.

Here's the list of four major sources of sector funds. The fund companies that can claim the longest sector track records are Fidelity and Invesco. Rydex and ProFunds are new players in this specialty.

✦ Fidelity Investments at (800) 343-3548 or www.fidelity.com

✦ Invesco at (800) 675-1705 or www.invescofunds.com

✦ Rydex Funds at (800) 820-0888 or www.rydexfunds.com

✦ ProFunds at (888) 776-3637 or www.profunds.com

Fidelity Investments maintains the largest selection of sector funds. The Boston fund family recently offered 40 sector funds (7 sector funds and 33 industry funds). Because of the big menu of Fidelity Select funds, the fund family is able to sharpen the focus of its funds more finely than competitors. Fidelity, for example, not only offers a technology sector fund, but also manages subspecialty funds within that category that cover such industries as computers, electronics, networking, infrastructure, and software and computer services. It's the same story with its financial sector fund. It has four funds devoted to banking, home finance, brokerage/investment management, and financial services.

Note   Fidelity imposes a 3 percent load and a fee of .75 percent for some redemptions. In contrast, Invesco doesn't slap loads on its funds, but its sector menu isn't as broad.

ProFunds, a fund family, which specializes in ultra aggressive funds, has recently muscled its way into the sector pack. ProFunds Ultrasector funds are far more volatile than its peers. That's because the funds are designed to produce returns that are 150 percent better or worse than underlying Dow Jones sector indexes. It's hard to justify this kind of volatility even for the most speculative investor.

Example   If the Dow Jones biotechnology index shot up 20 percent, ProFunds UltraSector Biotechnology should jump roughly 30 percent. Of course, if the fund value slid 20 percent, the investor's loss would be magnified to 30 percent.

Exchange-traded funds

You may not have heard yet about exchange-traded funds (ETFs). They are a cross between individual stocks and mutual funds. An ETF is bought and sold like a stock, but it also shares characteristics with an index fund. (See Chapters 10 and 11 for more on index and exchange-traded funds.)

An ETF, just like an index fund, contains an inventory of stocks that constitute a given benchmark, such as the Standard & Poor's 500 or the Russell 2000. Other ETFs are linked to sector and such industrial groupings as consumer services and energy. In fact, the nation's second most popular exchange-traded fund, the Nasdaq-100 Index Tracking Stock, is a sector fund since it's largely stuffed with technology stocks.

Note   If you own ETF shares, your return should be nearly the same as the underlying index. The return won't be identical, however, because you have to absorb some annual expenses.

Another type of exchange-traded fund that was created by Merrill Lynch works somewhat differently. *HOLDRS,* which stands for Holding Company Depositary Receipts, specialize almost exclusively on niche market plays such as Internet architecture and business-to-business companies. Rather than rely on passive indexes, Merrill Lynch selects at least 20 promising stocks for the HOLDR portfolios. HOLDRs, however, are static investments. Additional investments are not added to the mix, and rarely are stocks booted out of a HOLDR's portfolio.

Historical Stock Sector Performance

Wondering how different sectors have done in recent years? Here is a performance snapshot:

Sector	3 years	5 years
Consumer Durables	8.01%	9.69%
Consumer Staples	−1.02%	13.35%
Energy	9.73%	17.32%
Financials	8.74%	22.76%
Health	8.72%	21.28%
Industrial Cyclicals	14.75%	15.28%
Retail	19.93%	32.33%
Services	5.67%	15.52%
Technology	24.97%	35.56%
Utilities	10.11%	14.93%

Source: Morningstar

Here's a sampling of some exchange-traded sector funds, which you can purchase through your broker:

✦ Nasdaq-100 Index Tracking Stock (Stock symbol QQQ)

✦ Select Sector SPDR—Technology (Stock symbol XLK)

✦ Select Sector SPDR—Energy (Stock symbol XLE)

✦ iShares Dow Jones U.S. Energy Sector Index (Stock symbol IYE)

✦ iShares Dow Jones U.S. Healthcare Sector Index (Stock symbol IYH)

✦ HOLDRs Semiconductor (Stock symbol SMH)

✦ HOLDRs Pharmaceutical (Stock symbol PPH)

✦ Select Sector SPDR—Financials (Stock symbol XLF)

Sector Investing Pros and Cons

If you're not sure whether sector investing is for you, find out the strengths and weaknesses before plunging in.

Strengths of sector plays

Here are reasons why individuals consider investing in sectors.

Sector investing is becoming mainstream.

Mutual fund managers often give the same answer when they're asked what investment strategy they follow. "I'm a bottoms-up stock picker," most of them will say. These professionals search for the brightest stocks that show the best potential for beating the market no matter how the economy is behaving now or in the near future. The bottoms-up strategists believe that a great individual company can shine no matter what's happening in its respective industry.

It used to be rare to run across a portfolio manager who picked stocks from the top down. Someone advocating this strategy is keenly interested in general economic trends. Only after reaching conclusions about where the economy is headed, will they choose stocks that could benefit. For instance, if an investor believes inflation will remain low, he or she might accumulate retail stocks, like the Gap, Target, Costco, and Wal-Mart. Why? Because consumers are more likely to spend more when inflation isn't eroding the dollars in their wallets. On the other hand, when the nation appears to be heading into a recession, health-care stocks and companies specializing in consumer staples, such as food, soft drinks, tobacco and personal care products, tend to flourish.

While the bottoms-up camp has clearly been the vocal majority, an increasing number of professional investors talk like traitors. Thanks to influential academic research, more of the pros are beginning to believe that picking the right industries to invest in—before any thought is given to individual stock picks—can make a powerful difference.

Red Light, Green Light: Sector Timing

A study by Wiesenberger, a mutual fund tracking service, also highlights the rewards of picking the right sectors. Researchers set out to see how an investor with $1,000 would have done if he or she had selected the top sector for 16 consecutive years. If the right bet was made each time, the initial investment would now be worth more than $250,000. In contrast, if someone had put $1,000 into an index fund linked to the Standard & Poor's 500, it would have grown to $14,305. If a hapless investor had picked the very worst sector each year, however, he or she would have just $166 left.

Academic advice

Prominent researchers suggest that choosing the right industries will naturally lead to the most opportune stocks. While professors at the University of Chicago and UCLA back this hypothesis with statistics, there is plenty of supportive anecdotal evidence. Look at the industry groupings in the Standard & Poor's 500. In 1999, for example, the dozen or so companies in the communication equipment industry, including Qualcomm that soared 2,600 percent, all did well. In contrast, all the insurance stocks in the index's industry grouping were shellacked.

Industry groupings have become more relevant, some argue, because the companies have become more streamlined. Corporations are less likely to want to be all things to all people. In recent years, many corporations have shed ancillary businesses. Sears Roebuck, for instance, jettisoned its real estate and insurance businesses so it could focus on its department stores. Without as many conglomerates around, the industry groupings are more representative of an industry's true state.

Institutional intuition

Some institutional money managers now even suggest that a sector-based approach to investing is superior to the more traditional way of carving up a portfolio, in which an investor decides between value and growth stocks. In fact, some research suggests that value and growth investing, if you peel away the veneer, is simply being driven by sectors. Technology, for instance, recently represented 50 percent of a popular growth benchmark—the Standard & Poor's/Barra Growth Index. Meanwhile the financial sector, which is made up of banks, brokerage firms, and other financial institutions, made up about 30 percent of the Standard & Poor's/Barra Value Index.

 Cross-Reference You can learn more about value and growth investing in Chapter 12.

You can make fast profits.

Sector investing can provide higher returns over a relatively short time frame, and sometimes over the long haul, too. If you choose wisely, sector bets can make you wealthy ahead of schedule. A stock portfolio that earns 10 percent a year, which is in line with historic performance, will take seven years to double in value. Had someone invested in technology, healthcare or financials—the top sectors of the past decade—the wait would have been squeezed down considerably.

In any given year, sector mutual funds usually hog space on the lists of the best performing funds. During the past decade, an amazing 17 out of 20 top mutual funds were sector funds. In this period, the top sector fund winners specialized in technology and healthcare. Until technology thudded into the wall in 2000, the average technology stock had not experienced a negative year since 1984, which represents the longest winning streak among all fund categories. Between 1991 and 1999, the average tech fund clocked a total return of more than 1,200 percent.

Caution

There is an ugly side to this story. Concentrated bets can unleash financial disaster, and sector funds can fall hard, which is why you will often see their heavy representation in the worst-performing lists as well.

Sector plays can be suitable for the most patient investors.

Sector funds tend to attract market timers, but there's also a place for buy-and-hold investors who stick with the most promising long-term sectors, such as healthcare, financial services, and technology. Healthcare, for instance, has been the best sector performer in 5 of the past 12 complete years. Technology comes in second place, and financial services third.

Best & Worst Sectors

Sectors come and sectors go on the financial hit parade, as this table attests.

Year	Best	Worst
1984	Utilities	Precious metals
1985	Healthcare	Precious metals
1986	Precious metals	Technology
1987	Precious metals	Financial services
1988	Financial services	Precious metals
1989	Healthcare	Financial services
1990	Healthcare	Precious metals
1991	Healthcare	Precious metals
1992	Financial services	Precious metals
1993	Precious metals	Healthcare
1994	Technology	Precious metals
1995	Healthcare	Precious metals
1996	Energy & natural resources	Precious metals
1997	Financial services	Precious metals
1998	Technology	Energy & natural resources
1999	Technology	Real estate
2000	Health/biotechnology	Technology/communications
2001*	Precious metals	Technology/communications

Source: Wiesenberger
*April 2001

Disadvantages to sector investing

Here are some sensible reasons to stay away from sector bets. (Note that there are more disadvantages than advantages.)

Expect volatile returns.

Sector investing can be extremely risky because it doesn't provide the diversification to soften the blow when things are going terribly wrong. Sector funds have been known to implode by losing a third or even a half of their value in a matter of months. During a 12-month period ending in May 2001, for instance, the Nasdaq-100 Index Tracking Stock, which is heavy in big technology companies, lost nearly 46 percent. Many sane investors, upon serious reflection, conclude that the risks are too monumental to invest this way.

Investors don't necessarily know how badly sector funds are capable of performing because the ones with the rottenest records are quietly buried. In the early 1990s, for instance, the biotechnology sector became a money magnet. This was a heady time for biotech since the growing AIDS epidemic fueled the demand for research money for new drugs. One of the field's most magnificent producers was Oppenheimer Global Biotech, which one year produced a triple-digit return. But when it became obvious that young biotechnology firms had underestimated how hard it would be getting FDA approval for their drugs, biotech's momentum collapsed. One of the ultimate victims was the Oppenheimer fund, which became a mediocre also-ran. The fund was eventually merged into another one and Oppenheimer ditched the sector business.

You risk jumping aboard too late.

Human nature makes sector picking even more treacherous. That's because most people don't jump into a sector until its momentum is petering out. Some contrarians swear that a reliable way to determine if a sector's momentum is waning is to look at what the fund world's marketing departments are doing.

Why that advice? When a smoking sector inevitably captures the attention of casual investors, fund companies, sensing a lucrative opportunity, rush to create funds that capitalize on the latest fund du jour. By the time this happens, the sector has probably peaked. Look what happened with technology in recent years. When technology looked like the golden goose, investors couldn't get enough of it. The number of technology funds soared. Yet sure enough, at the height of this sector fund frenzy, technology—at least temporarily—tumbled. The same thing played out recently with telecommunications. But this isn't just a recent phenomenon. From 1991 through 1993, for instance, Fidelity's automotive sector fund soared 163 percent, which was almost triple what the Standard & Poor's 500 Index managed to make. But most investors didn't jump on board until 1993—just in time to get walloped by the fund's negative 13 percent return in 1994.

Note

Another hazard of chasing the hottest sectors is the lost opportunities. While investors are piling into hot sectors, they fail to notice the ones ready to blossom.

A new study by Financial Research Corp., which tracks mutual fund flows, estimated that chasing hot funds can reduce your returns by as much as 20 percent. They looked at average mutual fund returns during a 10-year period ending in 2000. Then they compared the returns with what they have estimated is the typical fund holding period—2.9 years. Researchers then calculated what the mean three-year annualized return for funds were. The return was 10.92 percent, but based on the investors' typical holding period, investors realized a return of 8.7 percent. That represents a 20 percent drop in performance.

Sector plays threaten your diversification.

You might think your portfolio is a model of diversification, but chances are it isn't. Why? Your all-purpose stock funds might be heavily weighted in their own sector plays. Recently, for example, the average large-cap growth fund had more than 40 percent of its money devoted to tech stocks. So if you owned the typical stock fund and added a technology fund, you'd be exposing yourself to far more volatility than you imagined. Later in this chapter, you'll learn how to analyze your portfolio to prevent sector overlaps.

They require more of a time commitment.

With some investments, complacency isn't fatal. For example, even if you ignore an index fund for years, your portfolio shouldn't suffer. You will do nearly as well as the overall market without any effort.

When you're invested in sectors, however, you can't be blasé. Sector plays are high maintenance since they can require a great deal of financial reconnaissance. If you aren't a committed buy-and-hold investor, you'll probably want to react quickly to market conditions. To protect your investment, you'll need to be mindful of market trends, including interest rate movement and Capitol Hill legislation. Keeping track of the political climate is just as crucial. If you don't, you can face a long performance drought.

Example

During the early days of the Clinton presidency, healthcare reform was a top priority—and investors were so worried about potential government interference that they punished the sector. Drugs and other medical stocks languished from 1992 to 1994.

Reading the newspaper can also alert you to buying opportunities, but you have to know how to interpret political and economic news. Let's use drug stocks as an example again. When economic uncertainty and recession fears are scaring Wall Street, it's usually the consumer staple and drug stocks that thrive. And that's exactly what happened in 2000. Health funds were one of the two top performing sector funds that year.

Why Interest Rates Matter

The stock market loathes interest rate hikes. That explains why Wall Street fixates on every speech made by the Federal Reserve Board chairman. The Federal Reserve has the power to raise or lower short-term interest rates. If the Fed's board members think the economy is overheating, it approves an interest rate hike. By doing this, the board hopes to fight off any signs of inflation.

Why do higher interest rates hurt some companies? You can blame a trickle-down effect. When rates rise, banks make it more expensive for corporations to borrow money. Corporations typically pass along this extra cost to their customers by raising prices. But when the price tag on a bicycle or a microwave jumps, fewer people are inclined to buy it. In the worst-case scenario, a company's profit drops, which often results in a lower stock price.

Sectors react differently to interest rate hikes. Retail stocks tend to get pummeled because it's easy to resist buying that 10th pair of shoes or another silk tie. Certain other types of stocks, such as financials, insurance, electric utilities, and telecommunications, also wilt when interest rates begin to spike up.

In contrast, drug stocks are more immune to inflationary periods because consumers keep taking their prescription medications, whether a month's supply costs $20 dollars a bottle or $40. Other industries, such as oil, chemicals, and metal stocks, also do quite nicely.

Sectors react just as differently when the economy slows and rate hikes cease. Financial services and utilities, for instance, tend to do well under these circumstances because they typically offer higher-than-average dividend yields, which appeal to investors unnerved by a faltering economy. In 1995, for instance, after the Federal Reserve stopped raising interest rates, financial stocks soared 49 percent.

Your gamble might not pay off.

Conventional wisdom suggests that the higher the risk, the greater the potential for better long-term returns. While this adage applies to the broader stock market, it isn't relevant with sector investing. It's not unusual for some sectors to underperform for many years. Technology can make certain sectors obsolete and mature industries may not be able to expand rapidly.

In other words, patience won't reward all sector disciples. If you choose a gold fund, for instance, don't expect to make phenomenal amounts of money. During the past 10 years, precious metal funds have posted a *negative* annual return of nearly 3 percent. Gold has traditionally been a favorite of conservative investors, who crave a hedge against inflation and turbulent market conditions. Today, investors wisely hedge their portfolios with exposure to REITs (real estate investment trusts), utilities, and natural resources stocks, which include such commodities as oil, natural gas, coal, and timber.

Painful tax bills are a possibility.

Investors who flit in and out of sectors may end up suffering from a tax migraine. Here's why: If you hold a sector fund in a taxable account for a year or less, you'll get hit with short-term capital gains taxes. According to some estimates, the typical investors who put money into the Nasdaq-100 Index Tracking Stock, an extremely popular exchange-traded fund, intend to pull their cash out in just a few days for a quick profit.

Yet quick profits get hammered the worst by the Internal Revenue Service. If you hold onto a winning stock for exactly one year or less, the gains are taxed at your income tax bracket. So if you're in the 30 percent bracket, almost one-third of your profits will disappear by April 15. In contrast, if you can hang on for at least a year and a day, the tax bill significantly drops. The highest long-term capital gains tax is 20 percent. For those in the 10 or 15 percent tax brackets, the tax is an even lower 10 percent.

Tip   You can sidestep these capital gains tax obligations if you confine the trading to a tax-deferred retirement account. Within an IRA, for example, you can trade stocks or funds as frequently as you'd like without triggering any taxes.

Sector Strategies

If you're ready for sector investing, here are strategies to improve your chances of success.

Start with a solid base.

Before seriously plunging into sectors, make sure you have a solid core portfolio. One way to achieve this is by selecting a low-cost index fund or exchange-traded fund that's linked to the Standard & Poor's 500 or the Wilshire 5000 as your portfolio's cornerstone. An excellent proxy for the broad market is the Vanguard Total Stock Market Index Fund.

Don't go overboard with sector exposure.

Use sector funds for seasoning in a portfolio, not the main course. A little cayenne is good, but too much can spoil the food. It's usually best to devote no more than 5 percent or 10 percent of your portfolio to sector plays.

Caution   It's much easier to overdose on sector plays than you might think, because so many tech firms have earned places in the major indexes.

Suppose, for instance, that the core stock fund in your portfolio is linked with the Standard & Poor's 500 Index. The index contains 500 of the largest corporations in America. Defense contractors, cereal makers, beer and soda companies, retailers, grocery chains, and plenty of other industries are stuffed in this grab bag. Because the index is so diverse, you might feel safe supplementing it with a technology fund. Do this, however, and you would be overloading on technology. That's because the S&P 500 is currently heavily concentrated in technology with 27 percent of the benchmark devoted to tech companies. When technology stocks were being treated like royalty, the tech concentration in the index was much heavier.

You can encounter the same problem when holding an all-purpose stock fund. Not too long ago, the typical stock fund had about $1 out of every $3 invested in technology. Even somebody who diversifies with multiple funds can run into trouble. The overlap can be particularly pronounced for investors who cherry pick their funds from the annual lists of best funds. Often these funds skyrocket to the top because their portfolios are nearly clones.

Online tools can detect sector overlaps in your holdings. Morningstar, as well as some brokerage firms, including Charles Schwab and Fidelity, offer portfolio analyzers via the Internet.

In fact, Morningstar has two online portfolio evaluators: Portfolio X-Ray, a service for paid subscribers, and the Instant X-Ray, which is free to any registered visitor to the site. These tools can break down your portfolio into 10 industrial sectors, so you can see how many of your holdings fall within certain sectors. The software can also analyze your portfolio by stock type and compare your holdings to the Standard & Poor's 500. For instance, you can compare how much exposure you have in healthcare or utilities, versus that industry's concentration in the benchmark index. As you might guess, Portfolio X-Ray offers many more features than the free Instant X-Ray; for example, after analyzing all your investments, the software can list your top 15 stock holdings—which can be the biggest eye opener of the evaluation. You may be stunned, for instance, to see how much General Electric or Cisco Systems you have since these two companies are popular mutual fund holdings.

Tip Although Morningstar's Portfolio X-Ray service is available only to paid online subscribers, you can sign up for a free 30-day membership by visiting the Web site at www.morningstar.com.

By visiting the Standard & Poor's Web site, you can also evaluate how diversified your portfolio is by comparing it to the Standard & Poor's SuperComposite 1500. This index contains the S&P 500, the S&P MidCap 400, and the S&P SmallCap 600. It encompasses 87 percent of the total domestic stock market capitalization. Table 14-1 contains a recent breakdown (a more detailed version of this table is available on S&P's www.businessweek.com Web site).

You can get information about a variety of major S&P indexes, as well as historical performance figures, at the Standard & Poor's Web site, www.spglobal.com.

Table 14-1
Standard & Poor's SuperComposite1500 Index
Industry Sector Weightings*

Sector	Percentage of Index
Consumer Discretionaries	13.14%
Consumer Staples	7.24%
Energy	6.78%
Financials	16.97%
Health care	12.87%
Industrials	11.5%
Information technology	19.14%
Materials	2.7%
Telecommunication Services	5.41%
Utilities	4.24%

* As of June 15, 2001

Source: Reprinted by permission of Standard & Poor's, a division of the McGraw-Hill Companies, Copyright (c) 2001.

Don't chase the hottest sector.

Of course, your goal is to double your money as quickly as possible. If you're too greedy, however, your plan can backfire. As mentioned earlier, sector picking all too often blows up for investors because they arrive at the party too late.

Play contrarian.

It actually may pay to cuddle up with the dogs. At least that's the recommendation of Morningstar. Its studies have shown that the worst performing sectors won't always stay that way. Every January, Morningstar determines the three most unpopular fund categories of the previous year. It recommends that an investor buy a fund from each category and then hang onto it for three years.

If you had followed Morningstar's advice since it began this experiment in 1996, you'd be smiling. (Morningstar also back tested the strategy back to 1987.) You'd have had a 78 percent chance of beating the average stock fund during those three years.

Pay attention to industry trends.

The best way to protect yourself from self-destructing sectors is to pay attention to the markets. You may not be able to predict whether the wireless industry is going to get beaten up in the next few months or years, but experts should be able to provide guidance. This section presents some key sources of information on sectors and industries.

Value Line

Beyond reading your local newspaper, *The Wall Street Journal,* and other financial publications, you'll want to review what industry analysts are saying. The weekly publication *Value Line* is a traditional source of "timeliness" ratings for dozens of industries. Timeliness refers to a stock's potential for a short-term increase in value. *Value Line* provides analysis on roughly 1,700 stocks and each company is rated for its timeliness. Stocks that are ranked "1" are believed to show the most promise for stock appreciation in the next 6 to 12 months. Stocks assigned the lowest "5" rating, in *Value Line*'s opinion, have little chance to gain ground. Equally helpful in each survey is a timeliness ranking of 94 industries, as well as commentaries on them.

You can order *Value Line* by calling (800) 634-3583 or visiting its Web site at www.valueline.com. A 10-week trial subscription is $55, but you can find the publication in many libraries.

Brokerage firms

Customers of full-service brokers can easily obtain mountains of reports on a variety of industries. That's one of the perks of paying for deluxe service. The discount brokers also provide materials on industry trends. You don't always have to be a customer, though, to take advantage of it. Fidelity investors can download the most recent copy of Standard & Poor's *Sector Dynamics,* which makes buy, sell, and hold recommendations on a variety of industries and sectors. Also available to investors is Fidelity's *Select Portfolios Update,* which includes some of its sector fund managers' commentaries on highlighted sectors.

Online resources

You may also want to check out the Web site of Ed Yardeni, the chief investment strategist at Deutsche Banc Alex. Brown (www.yardeni.com). He posts a weekly stock sector commentary and stuffs the site with numerous reports on such things as interest rates, inflation, global economic trends, and stock valuations.

Another nifty place to research industries is a section of Yahoo!Finance that can be reached at http://biz.yahoo.com/research/indgrp/. Yahoo!Finance carves up the market into more than six dozen industries from cosmetics and toiletries to glass products, publishing, and textiles. What can be extremely helpful are the rankings of corporations within an industry grouping. You can instantly see what the stock analyst community thinks of each company's growth prospects by the ranking it receives.

You can also access this information by pulling up an individual stock in Yahoo!Finance's stock research section. Click on the research function and you will see its ranking within the industry. You can then be linked to listings of the stocks in the group.

 Resource   Another source for analysis of American industries and sectors is a federal Department of Commerce publication *U.S. Industry & Trade Outlook,* released annually. You can purchase and download individual chapters on the Internet. For more information, visit this Web address: `www.ntis.gov/product/industry-trade.htm`.

Consider dollar-cost averaging.

Because sectors can be so volatile, you may be able to sleep better if you invest through *dollar-cost averaging,* which means you invest a certain amount of money every month or quarter. This strategy is more practical if you're investing in a mutual fund because you can often avoid a sales charge or transaction fee, especially if you invest directly with the fund family. Dollar-cost averaging can free you from any angst you may feel when your sector is sitting in the cellar or reaching a new high—no matter what the market is doing, you automatically invest.

Buy into sectors through mutual funds.

The easiest way to invest in sectors is through mutual funds and exchange-traded funds. Here's a brief snapshot of key sectors along with tips for selecting the best ones. You'll also see some fund suggestions to get you started. It's important, however, to research any fund thoroughly before investing.

Technology

No doubt about it, technology has been the best performing sector during the past decade. Technology stocks, as well as consumer cyclicals and transportation stocks, generally do well during economy expansions. Technology obviously benefited from a phenomenal economic cycle that had enough gas to last throughout the 1990s.

Note   The life expectancy for the nation's typical economic cycle is about five years, which makes the tech stampede of the nineties all the more spectacular.

Despite the flood of technology funds available today, it's tough to find technology funds that have been around for more than three years. According to Morningstar, less than two dozen tech funds have a five-year track record, while even fewer have the same manager on board as they did five years ago.

Tip   When investing in technology-oriented mutual funds, ideally you'll want a manager who has specialized in technology for a few years.

As with other sector funds, you'll need to judge how narrow a fund's focus is. Some hold a broad range of tech stocks, while others concentrate on niches, such as semiconductors. You'll also want a feel for whether a fund holds primarily small- or large-cap stocks or a combination of both. By using data from Morningstar, you can compare the volatility of different funds. (Chapter 7 explains how.)

Tip   If two funds have each performed admirably, it's better to choose the one that has done so by assuming the least risk.

You don't need to rely exclusively on funds or individual stocks for tech exposure. What have caught the fancy of many tech heads are technology exchange-traded funds. As mentioned earlier, exchange-traded funds hold a fixed basket of stocks and are generally cost- and tax-efficient.

Investment suggestions

- ✦ Dresdner RCM Global Technology at (800) 726-7240 or `www.drcmfunds.com`

- ✦ Fidelity Select Technology at (800) 343-3548 or `www.fidelity.com`

- ✦ Exchange-traded fund: Nasdaq-100 Index Tracking Stock (Stock symbol QQQ)

- ✦ Exchange-traded fund: Select Sector Spider—Technology (Stock symbol XLK)

Healthcare

Investors who have sunk money into healthcare over the long haul have been richly rewarded. During the past 40 years, for example, the major drug stocks have, on average, outperformed the S&P 500 62 percent of the time. Historically, investors have tended to pay more for these stocks because their earnings have been very stable.

If you want to make a concentrated bet on healthcare, first determine whether you want a diversified healthcare exposure or a pure dose of biotechnology. Obviously, a broader healthcare fund is a safer move. A general fund can spread money among blue chip pharmaceutical names, medical insurers, health maintenance organizations, and medical technology suppliers, as well as mercurial biotechnology plays.

Caution   A mutual fund's name alone won't always provide a clue to what's inside a health-care portfolio. If a healthcare fund, for example, boasts of a return that far exceeds its peers, it's probably stuffed with biotechnology names.

If you hanker for a biotechnology fund, the portfolio will most likely be crammed with smaller companies. While most biotech firms still aren't making a profit, an increasing number are, which should encourage investor interest. With a large number of biotech products moving through the pipeline, it can be extremely difficult to evaluate biotech firms. Consequently, it may be wise to choose a biotech fund that's managed by a physician, given that a physician may be in a better position to determine the usefulness of a firm's bio-products.

Investment suggestions

- ✦ Vanguard Healthcare at (800) 635-1511 or www.vanguard.com

- ✦ Dresdner RCM Biotechnology at (800) 726-7240 or
  www.dresdnerrcmglobalfunds.com

- ✦ Fidelity Select Biotechnology at (800) 343-3548 or www.fidelity.com

- ✦ Exchange-traded fund: iShares Dow Jones U. S. Healthcare Sector Index, Stock
  symbol IYH

Utilities

The utility sector has traditionally encompassed electric, gas, telephone, and water
companies. When utilities were heavily regulated, these stocks were considered
appropriate for the widow and orphan crowd. The stocks were slow but steady
growers and offered above average dividends.

Of course, active traders also gravitated to utilities, but they were more likely to be
fair-weather friends. These investors traditionally snapped up shares in a utility
that had tumbled in price because a regulatory body denied its rate hike request or
in some other way ruled against the utility. If the regulator's action ultimately
caused undue hardship, a regulatory solution would be found, the stock would
snap back, and speculative investors would bail with their profits.

Utility deregulation, however, is changing the strategy. In a deregulated environment, regulators will no longer be setting rates. This means, for instance, that an
electric utility or independent power provider won't have to chafe at a regulatory
cap, but on the flip side it won't have the bureaucrats bailing it out if it encounters
financial trouble.

Investment suggestions

- ✦ American Century Utilities at (800) 345-2021 or www.americancentury.com

- ✦ Vanguard Utilities Income at (800) 635-1511 or www.vanguard.com

Communications

Essentially a spin-off from the utility sector, the bulk of communications stocks
used to be telecommunications companies that paid big dividends, such as long
distance and local carriers. But plenty of dicier players are now sharing space in
this field, including wireless voice-and-data transmission businesses and media
companies such as cable, broadcasters, and online providers. While some mutual
funds continue to rely most heavily upon the old-style telecommunication stocks,
others invest in telecom upstarts here and abroad that have little or no earnings,
high debt, and tremendous growth rates. Check out a fund's portfolio to determine
how a manager has drawn the line between old-style companies like AT&T and new,
less familiar names.

Investment suggestions

✦ Invesco Telecommunications at (800) 525-8085 or www.invesco.com

✦ Gabelli Global Telecommunications at (800) 422-3554 or www.gabelli.com

Financials

The financial sector includes banks, savings and loans, insurance companies, brokerage firms, and consumer credit providers. Many financial mutual funds concentrate in a particular niche, such as the brokerage industry or regional banks.

While over time the financial sector has done very well, performance can be choppy. For instance, great returns in 1997 were followed by two dismal years, but patient investors were once again amply rewarded in 2000, when the Federal Reserve Bank signaled that it was finished raising interest rates. Mergers of financial institutions also boosted stock prices.

Tip   Avoid buying financial stocks when the Fed is boosting rates.

Financial stocks usually do better when the economy has slowed down. These stocks typically offer higher dividends that become more attractive to skittish investors, who are fretting about economic conditions. At the same time, falling interest rates, which occurred in 2001, often energize bank stocks.

Investment suggestions

✦ T. Rowe Price Financial Services at (800) 638-5660 or www.troweprice.com

✦ Invesco Financial Services at (800) 525-8085 or www.invesco.com

✦ Select Sector Spider—Financial Stock symbol XLF

Real estate

The easiest and safest way to invest in commercial real estate is through a mutual fund that specializes in real estate. These funds often invest heavily in real estate investment trusts (REITs). REITs (pronounced *reets*) are publicly traded companies that acquire, own, and manage income-producing real estate, such as apartment buildings, hotels, warehouses, factory outlets, golf courses, and office towers.

During some rocky periods in the 1990s, the commercial real estate industry reeled from self-inflicted wounds—namely its propensity to overbuild. It then suffered mightily from the excess. But some experts suggest that the industry has ditched its unprofitable behavior. Because the industry is now receiving its cash from the capital markets instead of from banks, partnerships, and other sources, it is far less likely to overbuild. In fact, the vacancy rates for commercial property lately has been low, and the pipeline of new projects has been subdued.

Tip   Before proceeding, stifle any temptation to pick a realty fund with abnormally impressive returns. If you examine the portfolios of the highest fund flyers, you'll see aggressive and highly combustible stocks that traditional REIT fund managers scorn.

For instance, not long ago some funds were sweetening their returns by holding stock in Frontline Capital Group, an Internet startup incubator spun off by a traditional REIT. In a recent 12-month period, Frontline soared as high as $63 per share but then sank to $9.

Investment suggestions

✦ Security Capital U.S. Real Estate at (888) 732-8748 or www.securitycapital.com

✦ Columbia Real Estate Equity at (800) 547-1707 or www.columbiafunds.com

✦ Vanguard REIT Index at (800) 635-1511 or www.vanguard.com

Consider investing in concentrated funds.

Concentrated funds believe less is more. While a traditional mutual fund might hold 100 or more stocks in its portfolio, the manager of a concentrated fund may invest in only two dozen stocks or less. With no need to fret about diversification, concentrated funds can invest heavily in one sector or spread their bets more evenly across the market. These funds are inherently more risky. The motto of this new breed of funds could be this: If you want to get rich in life you have to focus.

A harsh reality behind diversifying

What's so compelling about a portfolio that's light on stocks? Imagine compiling a list of 20 friends. That might not be so tough. But you'd probably struggle if you were required to name 100 friends. It's not any different for portfolio managers. It should be easier for a fund manager to find 20 stocks that he truly loves. But if he's compelled to find five or six dozen stocks, for the sake of diversification, he could be forced to accumulate stocks that he's not quite as enthusiastic about.

Certain academic studies support the rationale behind focus funds. Some researchers believe that investors who own anywhere from 8 to 20 stocks can achieve the optimal balance between risk and reward. Other experts, however, insist the ideal number is much higher.

The jury's still out

Concentrated or focus funds are a fairly new phenomenon so it's hard to gauge whether these claims will pan out over the long haul. Many of these funds have a short track record, which makes it difficult to determine whether you want to jump aboard. Your best bet is to look for an experienced portfolio manager. When launching a focused fund, some fund families appoint one of their brightest stars to run it.

Since a lot of these funds were born during the technology boom, many have been heavily invested in technology. When the tech sector got bloodied, these concentrated funds got hammered too. In contrast, concentrated funds that specialize in value stocks, such as Oakmark Select, which is now closed to new investors, Clipper, and Longleaf Partners, have excellent track records.

You can find out a fund's holdings by looking at its annual or semi-annual report. Even better, some funds post updated portfolios on their Web sites. Another place to check is Morningstar's Web site (www.morningstar.com) or its fund publication, which can be found in many public libraries.

Caution Keep in mind that a focus fund can run into just as much trouble as a sector fund, again due to the lack of diversification.

An extreme example is what happened to American Heritage Fund, once the darling of the fund world. The manager's propensity to hold just a handful of stocks, however, caused the fund to self-destruct. In 1997, for instance, the fund plummeted by 75 percent, making it the worst performing fund of the year. The fund's colorful fund manager had devoted most of the portfolio to two stocks—an obscure medical device company in New Jersey and a British biotechnology firm.

Here are some concentrated funds to investigate:

✦ Longleaf Partners at (800) 445-9469 or www.longleafpartners.com

✦ Strong Growth 20 at (800) 368-1030 or www.estrong.com

✦ Clipper at (800) 776-5033 or www.clipperfund.com

Summary

✦ It's usually best to limit your sector investments to just 5 percent to 10 percent of your portfolio.

✦ Be careful to avoid investing in a sector after it's already experienced tremendous gains.

✦ If you become an active sector investor, confine these trades to a tax-advantaged retirement account.

✦ Keep in mind the tax consequences of trading heavily in sectors.

✦　　✦　　✦

Identifying Winning Stocks

✦   ✦   ✦   ✦

In This Chapter

Understanding the basics

Researching a stock inside and out

Knowing what to make of analysts' predictions

Keeping up with institutional investors

✦   ✦   ✦   ✦

This chapter presents the basics of fundamental stock research, including tips on dissecting the critically important tell-all documents that every corporation must regularly file with the government. You'll also find out how to use financial ratios with confidence as you analyze a stock candidate, and how to listen for *whisper numbers*. Also explored is the role of Wall Street analysts. You'll appreciate why you shouldn't automatically assume that stock analysts only praise the winners.

Getting Ready: Stock Analysis Fundamentals

Studying a stock used to be a lonely pursuit. You sat down with the documents that a company is mandated to file with the U.S. Securities and Exchange Commission and crunched numbers.

Today, plenty of assistance is available and you're privy to the same information, at the same time, that the Wall Street professionals enjoy. For the first time in history, the playing field has been nearly leveled. The best and easiest way to access the crush of information is through the Internet. Here is some of what you can obtain within seconds after logging onto your computer:

- ✦ Stock research reports
- ✦ Analysts' earnings projections
- ✦ Financial ratios for individual stocks
- ✦ Financial comparisons with other stocks in the same industry and sector
- ✦ Sector outlooks
- ✦ Archived financial materials on corporate Web sites

✦ Access to corporate conference calls through Web casts

✦ Stock investing tutorials

✦ Historical stock performance data and charts

✦ Message boards on individual companies and industries

✦ Corporate press releases

Some of the information in this tidal wave of data will be extremely helpful. Other tidbits, such as the messages posted routinely on stock message boards, can be misleading and even harmful.

Doing your due diligence

Researching a stock is a lot like putting together a puzzle. There are many ways to do it. Some people start with the straight edges, others begin in the middle. It doesn't matter which method is used since the puzzle will look identical in the end. It's the same with evaluating stocks. There are different approaches, and if you hang in there, you'll find the one that's right for you.

Playing the stock market may seem glamorous, but stocks can be awfully fussy and demanding. Whether you plan to hold a stock for decades or just briefly, it's necessary to thoroughly research it before committing yourself. If you own individual stocks and you've never pored through a dreadfully dry document called a 10-K, you probably aren't analyzing stocks as carefully as you should.

Caution If your idea of stock research is flipping on CNBC and writing down stock symbols as the guests hype stocks, you could be setting yourself up for a painful financial lesson. Cracker-jack stock pickers buckle down and do their own grunt work.

Finding the financials

Much of what you'll need to answer your questions is revealed in a company's financial statements (which are thoroughly explained in the next section). You can call a company and obtain its financial statements, just like in the good old days, but it's a lot quicker getting the documents online through the SEC's Web site. The SEC's stock database is referred to as EDGAR, which stands for Electronic Data Gathering, Analysis, and Retrieval system. In addition, an increasing number of corporate Web sites archive their own SEC filings and annual reports.

Here are places to find these statements:

✦ Securities and Exchange Commission: www.sec.gov

✦ EDGAR Online: www.edgar-online.com

✦ 10-K Wizard: www.tenkwizard.com

✦ EDGARScan: www.edgarscan.com

Questions to Ask

While compiling a list of stock possibilities, ask yourself these key questions:

✦ Does the company produce high-quality products or services? Would you want to be a customer?

✦ Is the stock reasonably priced?

✦ Is the stock priced competitively compared with other companies in the same industry?

✦ What are the company's future earnings prospects?

✦ Has the company's earnings continued to improve?

✦ What do the important financial ratios say about the corporation's prospects?

✦ Does the company have a clean balance sheet?

✦ Does the corporation's cash flow statement set off any warning bells?

✦ Are there any time bombs ready to go off, such as extensive lawsuits, expiring patents, or aggressive competitors?

✦ Does a company have patents, government regulations or other barriers to keep rivals or potential competitors at bay?

✦ What percentage of the company is owned by insiders? What kind of insider trading activity has occurred in recent months?

✦ What percentage of stock is owned by institutional investors?

After reading this chapter, you'll appreciate why scouring for the answers is essential.

Required reading

At the start, you should be familiar with the financial data that the federal government requires all publicly traded corporations to file. Here is the lineup:

10-K

This document, which provides an overview of the past year's activities, contains all the figures included in a corporation's annual report and more. It's duller reading than an annual report—there aren't any smiling pictures of executives or customers, nor is there any hint of the marketing department's purple prose—but these yearly reports are far more substantial. In addition to the financial figures, the SEC requires management to candidly talk about important developments that occurred during the past year, whether good or bad. You can learn a tremendous amount about a corporation, including its successes and challenges, as well as the competitive structure of a company's industry, by reading this invaluable document.

10-Q

Companies are expected to file this quarterly report after the first, second, and third quarters. The 10-K takes care of the last quarter's data. The 10-Qs are primarily intended as updates for existing shareholders because they don't provide a comprehensive perspective on the corporation.

Form 14A (Proxy statement)

You probably don't know how much your neighbor earns, but you can see how much the head guy at General Motors is making. Proxies give you the scoop on what the corporate honchos and the board of directors are making and how they are compensated. A stockholder would rather see a chief executive officer's pay tied to performance goals rather than a very large base salary. A proxy can tell you how compensation is determined. You'll find information on the top executives' pay, bonuses, and stock options.

8-K

This document needs to be filed if a corporation experiences a *material* (or significant) event that should be shared with investors. It can be good or bad news. A corporation must submit an 8-K, for instance, if it is proposing a merger with another company or if it expects its earnings to dip significantly in the future.

Getting a helping hand

Analyzing a stock can be intimidating. That's why beginners and even more experienced investors can use help. Here are three online sources to turn to:

CNBC on MSN Money (www.money.msn.com)

This site, which was formerly known as MSN MoneyCentral, has been expanded to include CNBC's financial Web site. For the beginning stock investor, the most helpful feature of this popular and now much larger Web site is the Research Wizard. It takes you by the hand and guides you through these five stock-analysis steps.

1. Fundamentals: It describes the company's business, and indicates whether it's growing and fiscally sound.

2. Price history: It shares the price history for the past 3, 6, and 12 months.

3. Price target: It conveys what analysts think might happen to the stock price in the next one to two years.

4. Catalyst: It discusses what product or products can fuel the company's expansion.

5. Comparison: It explores how a company compares to others in the same industry.

Technical Versus Fundamental Analysis

This chapter gives you the basics of *fundamental analysis,* which requires poring through a company's financial filings. In contrast, practitioners of *technical analysis* use charts of a stock's past performance to formulate opinions of where the stock is headed next. Investors who pick stocks using technical analysis techniques exclusively don't necessarily need to know anything about the company. In fact, they don't even need to know the name, as long as they have the stock ticker.

Some investors dismiss technical analysis as stock-picking voodoo. To a newcomer, it certainly can smack of black magic. Even if technical analysis isn't your thing, it can be worthwhile to at least familiarize yourself with the basics. Many people who favor fundamental analysis will glance at some technical indicators before making a decision on a stock. You can learn a lot about technical analysis by visiting TheStreet.com (www.thestreet.com) and ClearStation (www.clearstation.com), which is a subsidiary of E*Trade.

Multex Investor (www.multexinvestor.com)

Multex Investor is an invaluable resource for all the ratios discussed in this chapter and throughout the book. In addition, Multex Investor provides income statements, balance sheets, and statements of cash flow, as well as historical financial data, for more than 10,000 companies. The Web site includes helpful primers on how to interpret the avalanche of data you can find there. What's more, it highlights stocks that its own screening software has detected as potential buys. Plus, you can buy analyst reports on thousands of companies that are produced by countless third parties.

Motley Fool (www.fool.com)

This Web site is devoted to making its visitors smarter and more analytical investors. Here you'll find oodles of tutorials on such things as interpreting financial ratios and evaluating companies. Motley Fool has also encouraged an active grassroots investing community that shares its own analysis of individual stocks.

Unearthing a 10-K's Financial Nuggets

When analyzing a company, a good place to start is with a copy of a company's 10-K. You will want to look at its four key sections:

✦ Income statement

✦ Statement of cash flow

✦ Balance sheet

✦ Management's discussion and analysis

Part 1: Income statement

How fast has a company been growing? That's a biggie that any smart investor will want answered. You can pinpoint the growth—or lack of it—by reading the 10-K's income statement, which is also referred to as the *consolidated statement of operations*. Here are the figures you need to look for:

✦ **Revenue (Sales):** You'll find this figure at the top of the income statement. What you're searching for is steady growth. If historic yearly sales are plotted on a bar chart, the sales ideally resemble a staircase, with each succeeding year representing a higher step. The 10-K or annual report lists only three years for comparison. You can obtain a longer historical perspective by getting older documents from the company or through the SEC's Web site.

✦ **Selling, General and Administrative (SG&A) Expenses:** This figure sums up how much it cost a company to stay in business during the past year. A hodgepodge of expenses is tossed into this category, from payroll, rent, advertising, travel, and utilities, to the year's worth of Scotch tape and paper clips. What you want to see is a company that can keep its costs under control. Search for trends as you look at past years' expenses.

✦ **Cost of goods sold:** This refers to the costs of all the materials and expenses related to actually making the products that a corporation sells. For instance, a retailer wouldn't put the cost of rented space in this category, but the money paid to stock a store with dresses and pants would be in this category. Once again, you'll want to know that a company has costs under control. You'll also see this referred to on the income statement as *cost of revenue*.

✦ **Net income:** Net income is what's left after expenses, depreciation, and taxes are deducted from a company's total revenues. You'll find this figure at the bottom of the income statement. Some companies enjoy ever increasing sales, but the true test of their worth is the amount of cash that ends up as profit. It's an encouraging sign if a corporation is producing steadily higher profits.

✦ **Operating income:** While net income is important, many investors put more weight on a company's operating income. You will sometimes see operating income abbreviated as *EBIT,* which stands for *earnings before interest and taxes.* This figure excludes money that a company makes from its own investment portfolio, including only income from operations, which many experts consider more meaningful. Operating income is used to determine the *operating margin,* which is expressed as a percentage. You want to see an operating margin that's better than a corporation's competitors and that grows over time.

Further, operating income is calculated before a company pays taxes. Excluding taxes can generate a more realistic number because tax rates can vary from year to year. In fact, always check a corporation's tax rate: The earnings might look great in part because the tax rate is low.

Note

You might assume that it's better to favor companies with low tax rates, but think again. Over time most corporations end up paying the average rate for their industry. You can compare a corporation's current tax rate with its historic one, as well as the rate of its respective industry, at Multex Investor.

Profit Hunting with the Newspaper

With online stock screens you can hunt for companies with large profit margins, but it's also possible to narrow the field with the newspaper. Look in the business section of your local newspaper for the daily corporate earnings table. If it doesn't carry quarterly earnings briefs, get a copy of *The Wall Street Journal* or *Investor's Business Daily*. Both of these newspapers carry earnings announcements each day. In a newspaper, a corporation's earnings report is shrunk to a size that's smaller than a cartoon panel, but it contains the two numbers you need—total revenue and net income—to obtain the profit margin.

Using the income statement's related ratios

With the information given on the 10-K's income statement sheet, investors can break down the numbers into ratios. This allows investors to easily compare a corporation's financial figures to other companies, particularly those in the same industry and sector. Some figures crucial to the decision-making process are:

✦ Net profit margin

✦ Earnings per share

✦ Price-to-earnings ratio

Luckily, there's no need to do your own math. An excellent place to obtain key corporate ratios is Multex Investor, which you can access at www.multexinvestor.com or through Yahoo!Finance (http://finance.yahoo.com). Runner-up CNBC on MSN Money (www.money.msn.com) also provides ratios.

Net profit margin

You can get a better handle on how impressive or underwhelming a company's profit is by calculating its net profit margin. To do this, divide the net income by the company's revenue.

Example

A company's net income is $14 million and its revenue is $70 million (14 million ÷ 70 million). The corporation generated a 20 percent profit margin. That means 20 cents of every dollar in sales is pure profit.

When hunting for stock candidates, try to stick with companies that have a net profit margin of at least 10 percent and preferably more. But there's a caveat. Some industries maintain historically low net profit margins, such as grocery stores, while others, such as software producers, generally enjoy much higher ones. Be sure to compare a company's net profit margin with those within the same industry.

Earnings per share

You generally won't hear investors or financial journalists chatting about a corporation's net income, which can soar into the millions or billions of dollars. Instead a company's profit is presented in a more digestible way as *earnings per share,* a figure calculated by dividing a corporation's net income by the number of common stock shares investors hold. So if a company's profits were $10 billion and 10 billion shares were in circulation, the earnings per share would be $1. With earnings broken down this way, it's easier for investors to make comparisons. Fortunately, the earnings per share figure is contained in a corporation's annual and quarterly reports.

 Example

Target, the discount chain, had earnings per share of $1.38 in 2001 and $1.26 the year before. So, in this example, Target's earnings jumped 9.5 percent.

Earnings are crucial in judging whether a corporation is prospering and ultimately whether a stock is worth buying, holding, or dumping. What investors love to see are yearly earnings superior to the previous annual figures. Even better is when a company's earnings are rising faster than its sales. That suggests that a company is squeezing more profit out of the money it's taking in.

Smoke & Mirrors at Earnings Time

While corporate earnings are crucial for evaluating a company, they aren't always what they seem. Knowing that underachievers can be severely punished by Wall Street, corporations will sometimes resort to accounting tricks to enhance their profits on paper.

For example, a corporation may use a one-time sale of a building or other property to boost its operating profits. Some tech Goliaths like Intel, Oracle, and Microsoft, which have maintained huge investment portfolios of other technology companies, have boosted their earnings in the past by including investment gains. Excess surpluses from massive corporate pension funds have also been used to massage earnings. In fact, critics have accused some major corporations of denying its retirees periodic cost-of-living pension increases because they want to claim pension excesses as corporate profits.

A strong argument can be made that using a pension fund, which belongs to employees, or gains in an investment portfolio that could disappear tomorrow, can skew a corporation's financial picture. The true test is whether the earnings are coming from what a company does, whether that's selling computers or shoe laces.

Another strategy companies use at times is puffing up less important financial figures in their press releases, which are widely distributed to online financial sites. The point of the story—disappointing earnings—is often buried at the very end.

While not every investor will be able to spot accounting tricks, read the financial press's coverage of a corporation's earnings reports. Analysts will often spot accounting shenanigans and wave the red flag, which the savvy investor will heed. The bottom line: It's the quality of earnings that count.

Note When comparing quarterly earnings figures, compare the earnings of the same quarter a year ago. So an investor would contrast Intel's third quarter earnings in 2002 with its third quarter earnings in 2001.

Why are quarterly earnings compared year over year instead of to the closest quarter? Many corporations experience seasonal sales cycles. For instance, retailers like the Gap and Wal-Mart enjoy great sales volume at Christmas, so the earnings during that quarter aren't comparable with sales during the dog days of summer. When reviewing comparable quarters, the greater the percentage increase in earnings, the better.

Price-to-earnings ratio (P/E ratio)

Earnings are sliced and diced in another way to create the most famous ratio of them all: the price-to-earnings ratio. To obtain the P/E ratio, the current price of one share of stock is divided by the earnings generated by a single share of stock. A P/E of 12 means a company has $1 in earnings for every $12 in share price. Put another way, you are paying $12 for each $1 of profit the company generates. You will also hear people refer to a P/E as a *multiple*. In this example, the company is trading at a multiple of 12.

You'll see the price-to-earnings ratio listed alongside a company's price in newspaper stock pages. In fact, the P/E ratio is the most important nugget on the stock page. A company's P/E ratio can also be found at countless financial Web sites. Many investors use the ratio to help decide whether they want to buy or sell a stock.

In fact, two P/Es can exist for the same company because there are two ways to calculate it. The newspaper stock pages typically list the *trailing P/E,* which is determined by using the past year's earnings. A *forward P/E* uses the analysts' best guess on what earnings will be for the next year.

Example Say a company last year earned $1 a share for its stock that's selling for $20 a share. The trailing P/E is 20. However if the company is expected to boost its earnings to $2 a share in the coming year, the forward or projected P/E is 10.

Don't evaluate a company's P/E in a vacuum.

A company is usually considered fairly valued if its P/E equals its growth rate. So a company that is growing at 15 percent a year is reasonably priced if its P/E is 15. If the P/E far exceeds a company's growth rate, you should proceed cautiously. Why? Because even the stock of a wonderfully managed and profitable company can be extremely overpriced. In other words, you may love filet mignon, but you're not going to pay $50 a pound for it.

Some stocks, such as large pharmaceuticals and certain other blue chips, typically trade at a premium, even during market turbulence. Before buying a stock for a premium price, check to see if it's a reasonable one. A good way to do this is to compare a stock's current P/E with its historic P/E ratios. Once again, a fast way to accomplish this is by visiting Multex Investor's Web site. The site provides the trailing P/E ratio, as well as a company's previous high and low P/Es during the last five years. It also includes these same figures for the stock's industry and sector groupings, as well as the Standard & Poor's 500.

Resource For those without a computer, *Value Line Investment Survey,* which can be found at many libraries, also carries historic P/Es for 1,700 individual companies.

In the summer of 2001, for example, the P/E ratio of Pfizer, which is America's largest drug company, was 47, while during the previous five years, it had ranged as high as 91 and as low as 28. Because Pfizer is among the bluest of the blue chips, its stock has typically carried a pricier valuation than many other pharmaceutical makers. During the same time period, the high and low P/E ratios for the major drug industry were 58 and 24, respectively.

Put the P/E in perspective.

Value investors, who aim to spend as little as possible on promising stocks, scorn companies with high P/Es or even fairly valued ones. During bear markets, it's much easier to spy the bargains value investors love. Sometimes the market overreacts and punishes a wonderful company because it happens to be in a sector that's currently in the doghouse.

Finding a company with an anemic P/E, however, isn't always the same as discovering gold in a prospector's pan. Logical reasons can explain why some of these companies appear dirt-cheap. Sometimes the financial soundness of a corporation is actually as flimsy as a Hollywood sound set. For instance, a business might be drowning in debt, or perhaps its pipeline of new products has dried up. A company can run into trouble when its livelihood is dependent on just a handful of corporate customers. Or a high-flying company's brand name might not be as prized as it once was.

Example Back in 1997, Nike's sales were crushed when fickle teens decided the swoosh was no longer a badge of hipness. The stock price and the P/E plummeted. During the past five years, Nike's P/E was as high as 71 but recently was at a historic low of 14. The stock has yet to completely recover from its 1997 free fall.

Stocks Without P/Es

Not every stock has a P/E ratio. Why? Because a company has to generate earnings to have one. If there is no profit after all the costs of business are deducted, there can be no P/E. Many young biotech, Internet, and telecommunications companies, which excel at burning up cash, fit into this category. Investing in a company without earnings is extremely speculative. Because it can be so tricky, it's often best to invest in these industries through mutual funds.

Part 2: Statement of Cash Flow

Even though lots of investors never read this section of the 10-K, avoid the temptation to skip it. In fact, many sophisticated investors look first at this statement, which pinpoints how a company generates and uses its cash. Ultimately, the figures in this statement reveal whether a company is a cash cow, which is Wall Street's favorite animal. The more cash a company can generate for future uses, the better.

Every statement of cash flow is divided into these three parts:

✦ **Operating section:** This section shows the cash that's used for a company's daily operations. Pay attention to the level of working capital, which keeps a business humming. Also check the total cash figure at the bottom of this section. Ideally, you'll want to see the operations generating increasing amounts of money each year.

✦ **Investing Section:** Here's where you find out how a corporation is investing excess cash and how it's expanding its business (a figure called *capital expenditures*). Money that's plowed into modernizing equipment, expanding into new products or pursuits, replacing worn-out plants, and buying property, is included. If a corporation has invested in other companies, that's also mentioned here.

It's typically a good sign if capital expenditures are growing steadily, which signifies that a company is reinvesting in itself. As a rule of thumb, the capital expenditures should roughly equal the company's depreciation, which is a line item that can be found in the operating section.

✦ **Financing section:** Here's where you can find out if a company repurchased shares of its own stock or issued more shares. It's generally considered a positive move when a company rebuys its own shares. Investors often interpret this as a sign that a corporation is bullish on its future and believes its stock price is too low. In contrast, you won't be thrilled if a company issues more shares to generate cash for its operations—introducing additional shares will dilute the earnings for existing shareholders. This section also indicates whether the company has borrowed money.

Net change in cash: The bottom line

Near the bottom of the cash flow statement is one more important figure, the *net change in cash.* To get this figure, accountants add up the total cash from the operating, financing, and investing sections. You hope the number is positive. This means that a company, after investing in its operations and paying any applicable dividends, still has a pile of cash left. Cash presents a company with a multitude of options. Ideally, this cash can be used to bankroll expansion plans or to buy back stock shares. If a company doesn't have free cash flow it might have to resort to borrowing more money, selling assets, or issuing more stock shares.

Ideally, the cash on the bottom line increases each year, but don't dismiss a stock if it doesn't happen every time or if the number is occasionally negative. The figure might be negative, for instance, if a company is ramping up a major capital expenditure drive.

 Caution   If a company maintains a negative number in this column for too long, such as three consecutive years, shareholders should be concerned.

Cash flow ratios

The statement of cash flow generates its own ratios. Two important ones are the *price-to-cash flow* and *price-to-free-cash flow* ratios. Experts consider the latter ratio the more important of the pair. Obviously, there is a formula to calculate each one. For instance, the price-to-free-cash flow ratio is determined by taking the current price and dividing it by the free cash flow per share. Looking at the cash flow statement, free cash flow is calculated by subtracting capital expenditures and any dividends paid from cash from operations. It's far easier to obtain the ratios by clicking the "comparison" hyperlink on Multex Investor after you've typed in a stock symbol. The lower the ratio numbers, the better.

As with all ratios, it's important to compare the current figures with the previous year's ratios and the five-year average. You'll also want to see how the ratios compare with a corporation's own industry. For instance, recently Johnson & Johnson, the drug company, had a price-to-cash flow ratio of 47.24 while the drug industry's was 70.58. This means Johnson & Johnson was more attractively priced.

Part 3: Balance sheet

A lot of investors, who fixate on a company's earnings, often don't linger at the balance sheet. The income statement may be sexier, but the balance sheet should never be ignored. The balance sheet, which serves as a snapshot of a corporation's finances, lists a company's assets and liabilities. Assets include such things as cash, property, equipment, its investments, the value of its inventory, and the accounts receivable. The liabilities include such things as long-term debt, unpaid bills, lease obligations, and accrued taxes.

After subtracting the debt from the assets, what's left—if anything—is called *shareholder equity,* which is also referred to as *book value.* You'll find the shareholder equity listed near the very bottom of the balance sheet. As you'll learn momentarily, the shareholder equity figure is used to calculate another crucial measurement, the return on equity ratio.

The balance sheet looks authoritative but it won't be as accurate as you might assume. When you're selling your home, you can get an appraisal that pinpoints your house's worth. But the appraisal process is much trickier for a company. That's because many of the figures in the balance sheet are based on historical numbers—the assets won't reflect any increase or decrease in their value over time. If a company, for instance, bought its headquarters and land back in 1955, its worth could appear to be a fraction of what that land would sell for on today's open market. Some assets that would be hard to measure are left out of the balance sheet entirely. For instance, Coca-Cola wouldn't report the value of its instantly recognizable red-and-white logo. Still, balance sheet data is necessary to calculate the following key figures:

✦ Price-to-book ratio

✦ Return-on-equity ratio

✦ Financial strength measurements

✦ Asset management measurements

Price-to-book ratio

The number that has historically attracted the most attention on the balance sheet is a company's book value. Some value investors use book value as a rough guide to determine if a stock is on sale. Once again, it's easier to get a handle on the book value by converting it into the price-to-book ratio. Here's the equation:

Shareholder equity ÷ common stock shares outstanding = price-to-book ratio

Conveniently, you don't have to hunt for the number of shares held by investors, which is referred to as *shares outstanding,* because it is listed right under the shareholder equity figure on the balance sheet. If a company had $200 million in shareholder equity and 26 million stock shares, the price-to-book ratio would be 7.7. The lower the number, the more value investors salivate.

Some experts, however, suggest that this ratio isn't as relevant as it once was because heavy manufacturing is no longer the main engine fueling the nation's economy. Why would that economic shift matter? Corporations that require a lot of factories and extensive equipment tend to sport better price-to-book ratios. For instance, the ratio for USX-U.S. Steel Group was recently a mere .72. That means an investor would, in essence, pay 72 cents for every $1 worth of assets. Contrast that with the price-to-book ratio for Oracle, the Silicon Valley software giant, which is 18.55. In other words, an Oracle investor would have to pay $18.55 for every $1 worth of assets. With these fundamental differences between industries, confine any comparisons you make between companies based on the price-to-book ratio to companies in the same industry.

Example

You wouldn't want to compare a company like Anheuser-Busch, with a price-to-book ratio of 10 (alcoholic beverage industry average of 8.73) to Federal Express with a 1.93 price-to-book ratio (air courier industry average 2.36).

Return-on-equity ratio

Return-on-equity (ROE) is one of the most important financial ratios. It provides a quick measure of how well a company's management is squeezing profits out of the shareholders' equity. To calculate this ratio, you need to extract a figure from both the balance sheet and the income statement. Here's the equation:

Net income ÷ shareholder equity = return-on-equity ratio

Tip   Since most of us aren't going to get the opportunity to size up the top brass during heart-to-heart discussions, checking the ROE is the next best thing to assessing the management team.

Some investors like to see an ROE of at least 20 percent before they become interested in a stock. Once again, you won't know if a company's return on equity is cause for celebration or tears unless you compare the company's historic ROE, as well as the ROE of similar companies. For instance, a company sporting an ROE of 20 percent will look really good, until you notice that the company's ROE for the previous five years was 30 percent.

ROEs vary significantly from industry to industry so make sure you compare your stock candidate with the appropriate industry ROE. For instance, Wrigley recently had a five-year ROE average of 28.05 percent, compared with the food processing industry's 26.72 percent. After the comparison, Wrigley's ROE looks even more impressive. In contrast, Tootsie Roll's five-year ROE average was a weaker 17.13 percent.

Financial strength measurements

Financial strength ratios, which are generated from balance sheet numbers, indicate how much risk a company is assuming and whether it's really strong enough to handle it. A financially strong company can weather difficult business conditions more easily and may be able to avoid drastic cuts, such as massive layoffs, which could delay a rebound when the economy recovers.

Here are four related ratios to pay attention to:

Current ratio: This ratio takes a company's current assets, which includes cash, inventory, and accounts receivables, and divides it by liabilities, such as outstanding bills and expenses. The ideal ratio is around 1.5, but the range will differ among corporations and industries. Recently, the average company in the Standard & Poor's 500 had a current ratio of 1.63. If the ratio dips below 1.0, it may signal that a company could experience troubles paying its short-term bills. On the other hand, a ratio that's too high can suggest that the company's inventory is bloated or that the assets are not being used effectively.

Quick ratio: A quick ratio (also known as an *acid test*) takes the current ratio and subtracts inventory from the equation. This more conservative ratio is supposed to give a more realistic idea of what kind of cash resources can be drawn upon in an emergency. A quick ratio of 1 or better is preferred. A ratio of .85, for example, indicates that the company's cash reserve can cover 85 percent of expected liabilities in the year ahead.

Total-debt-to equity and **long-term debt equity ratios:** A heavily indebted company can be ripe for disaster if tough times hit. A company may cut back on certain expenses, but some, such as the interest on its loans, won't disappear. It's generally assumed that the higher the debt, the greater the risk, but conventional wisdom won't always work. Companies in industries with stable cash flows can handle more debt than others. Currently, the total debt-to-equity ratio for the typical S&P 500 corporation is just .61. That doesn't mean, however, that American corporations are frugal. It just means that they are relying upon issuing more of their own stock to finance their needs.

Asset management measurements

The last pair of ratios that can be extracted from the balance sheet examine how efficiently the company has managed its assets. They can also tip off an investor that a business's fundamentals are eroding:

Inventory turnover ratio

Inventory refers to a corporation's finished products, the goods that may be packed in boxes and sitting on shelves in its warehouses. Investors don't like it when huge amounts of products are sitting around. Dell Computer's success in the 1990s was partially due to its founder's insistence that computers were not meant to gather dust. Michael Dell revolutionized the idea of making a computer only after the company had received an order from an individual customer. When a corporation's inventory backlog grows, it ties up valuable cash.

What you don't like to see is inventory piling up beyond its normal levels, unless there's a mighty good reason. If inventory is increasing faster than sales, that could signal that customers no longer love a company's video games, cell phones, or soda crackers. An exception might be a company that's stockpiling in advance of a new product launch.

Of course, inventory won't be an issue for some industries such as advertising, consulting, and education. But if it is relevant, look at a company's inventory ratio and compare the current inventory levels with previous years and quarters. The inventory turnover ratio shows, on average, how often a company sells and then replaces its inventory each year. The higher the inventory ratio, the better.

Note   As with other ratios, don't compare apples to oranges. Each industry maintains its own inventory average.

For instance, the average inventory ratio for the household and personal products industry was recently 5.46. Proctor & Gamble, Colgate-Palmolive and Newell Rubbermaid nearly match that average. In contrast, the average inventory ratio for the restaurant industry is a much higher 34.91. McDonald's (113.2) and Tricon

Global Restaurants (53.56), which operates Pizza Hut, Taco Bell, and KFC, over-shoot that figure considerably.

Accounts receivable ratio

Accounts receivable refers to the money that customers owe the company. Corporate customers typically buy on credit, which means the seller must wait to be paid. The shorter that wait is, the better. A sharp rise in accounts receivable can be a worrisome sign. It could indicate that the company is handing out credit too easily or is not doing a good job of collecting in a timely manner.

In the worst-case scenario, a company must write off uncollected bills as bad debt. Because occasionally selling to deadbeats is an unavoidable part of doing business, on a balance sheet you will see a company's allowance for bad debt. In setting aside money for unpaid bills, some corporations are much more conservative than others. If this allowance isn't enough, a company may be forced to take a write off to get the bad debt off its books.

This ratio attempts to pinpoint how fast a corporation collects its money. The higher the number the better. Recently, Kellogg had a receivable turnover ratio of 9.32. By dividing the number of weeks in a year by the Kellogg's turnover ratio, you'll discover that it takes about 5.5 weeks for the cereal maker to pocket its money. That's just about the average for the typical large American corporation.

Part 4: Management's discussion and analysis

After slogging through all the numbers and ratios, the management's discussion and analysis section of the 10-K will be a relief. In this narrative, the SEC expects the company to candidly share its successes and its dirty laundry. This discussion cannot be a heavily censored missive with all the bad news airbrushed out. Rather, it is supposed to be a candid portrayal of the company's successes and failures in the previous year. A corporation is mandated to discuss material developments that have hurt or helped its profitability. This section is also supposed to discuss where executives hope to take the company in the next year and what difficulties they foresee in reaching their goals.

Anheuser-Busch, for example, discussed one year how rising aluminum prices had increased its packaging costs, why the company reduced its massive inventory as part of a fresh beer campaign, and how higher beer excise taxes hurt. If you kept reading, you'd have also learned that Busch's theme parks, including Sea World, experienced record growth despite an unusually ominous hurricane season.

Analyzing Analysts

So far, this chapter has shared what you can do on your own to interpret a corporation's financial statements. But in your deliberations, you should take into consideration how Wall Street has sized up a company.

The opinions of analysts, who spend their days evaluating companies and talking with management, are watched carefully because they are considered the experts. What analysts think about a company's earnings prospects, in particular, can make a stock sink or soar.

Overachievers get the prize

Analysts aren't content to wait around for a company to release its latest quarterly earnings, but instead expend a lot of psychic energy trying to predict what the figures will be. Traditionally, corporations have tried to guide these number crunchers in the right direction. In a quarterly ritual, corporations generally aim to slightly beat the analysts' estimates. When a corporation pulls this off, it's considered a positive earnings surprise. The extra earnings, which may amount to just a penny or two more per share, can set off jubilation in the market. The stock price will normally immediately increase based on this great news.

The flip side to a positive earnings surprise is a negative surprise or an accurate prediction. A stock might stumble if a corporation simply hits the target, which is referred to as "meeting expectations." Especially during turbulent times, a corporation that falls short of analysts' predictions can experience a body blow to its stock price. For instance, when Intel warned that its third quarter profits for 2000 would miss analysts' projections by 5 percent, the stock price tanked 45 percent.

Earnings disappointments are scary for another reason. Some call it the cockroach phenomenon. When earnings disappoint, there can be more nasty earnings surprises ready to scurry into the daylight in future quarters. Conversely, when a company surprises analysts with more robust profits, it often repeats those pleasant bombshells. This is not, however, a hard and fast rule.

Reaching a consensus with ratings

Not too many years ago, it was difficult for individuals to glean what analysts thought about a particular company. Now this information, which used to be readily available only to institutions, is free on the Internet. Services gather up earnings projections from individual analysts scattered across the country and produce a consensus. Here are some sources for earnings estimates:

✦ Zacks Investment Research: www.zacks.com

✦ Multex Investor: www.multexinvestor.com

✦ Yahoo!Finance: http://finance.yahoo.com

✦ CNBC on MSN Money: www.money.msn.com

Whisper Numbers

Sophisticated investors aren't content with just knowing Wall Street's earnings predictions. They're more focused on what's been nicknamed *whisper numbers,* because they are supposed to provide the off-the-record scoop. Whisper numbers come from a variety of sources. Analysts, on the sly, might provide numbers that differ from their official estimates, while regular investors and employees of a company can make their own estimates. Thanks to the Internet, it's much easier for these whisper numbers to be compiled and publicized.

Whisper numbers are a fairly recent phenomenon, but their influence on a stock's price can be tremendous because they are often more accurate than the official earnings predictions of analysts. In fact, stocks can get pummeled if they don't meet a higher whisper number.

Here are some sources for whisper numbers:

✦ WhisperNumber.com   (www.whispernumber.com)

✦ EarningsWhispers.com   (www.earningswhispers.com)

✦ TheWhisperNumber.com   (www.thewhispernumber.com)

Don't be surprised if a stock you're researching doesn't have a whisper number. Many don't. Whisper numbers are most common with large-cap stocks and tech names.

Typically, you'll see analysts' recommendations ranked on a scale of 1 to 5. Here's what the numbers indicate:

1 = Strong buy

2 = Moderate buy

3 = Hold

4 = Moderate sell

5 = Strong sell

The recommendations are averaged for a consensus number. For instance, if three analysts recommend a stock as a moderate buy and one concludes it's a strong buy, the consensus number would be 1.75.

The dark side of analysts

As a group, analysts are arguably better brown-nosers than Eddie Haskell on *Leave it to Beaver.* Analysts are roundly criticized for censoring any pessimistic thoughts they might harbor about a company, and instead speak only in glowing terms. In their world, most stocks are buys. A sell recommendation from an analyst is almost as rare as a UFO sighting. A ridiculously low number of stock recommendations— about 1 percent—urge investors to sell. A major reason for this is the analysts' inherent conflict of interest.

Many analysts are employed by brokerage firms that depend upon corporate America for business. These firms receive a lot of valuable investment-banking business from corporations. Consequently, an analyst who bad-mouths a corporate client or prospective client shouldn't take his or her job security for granted. If an analyst's firm is engaged in investment-banking business with a corporation that he or she is following, it's best to disregard the coverage.

Because analysts tend to be too optimistic about corporate prospects, consider deflating any analyst's recommendation. For instance, treat a strong buy recommendation as a buy and a hold or neutral rating as a sell.

Tip Resist buying a stock strictly on analysts' recommendations. When researching a stock, it's important to know what analysts think, but this should be only one of many factors. Far more important than the one-word recommendation is the research that went into formulating the opinion. Reading an analyst's report can be enlightening.

With tarnished reputations, should analysts be believed? In some cases, yes. Studies have suggested that investors can make money following analysts' advice. One massive study that examined some 360,000 recommendations over 11 years showed that the stocks garnering the strongest analyst support enjoyed an annual return of 18.8 percent versus 5.8 percent for the stocks the analysts panned.

Tip Ignore the future price targets that analysts set for stocks. Institutional investors never take these price projections seriously, and neither should you.

Getting the scoop on analysts

As investing has grown into a national pastime, analysts have morphed into celebrities. Throughout the day, financial news anchors prod analysts for their favorite stock picks. Analysts enjoying a lucky streak are profiled in glowing magazine and newspaper accounts. No longer are all analysts anonymous grunts, who spend their workdays hunched over dry corporate financial reports and spreadsheets. In fact, one study not long ago suggested that the hours these experts spend on analysis are slipping.

Note According to one study, the time devoted to fundamental research has dropped to less than 40 percent, and that percentage was expected to drop further. What are analysts doing instead? They are spending more time schmoozing with brokerage firms' important institutional clients.

With thousands of analysts offering their opinions, the noise level can be deafening. But how do you know that the guy spouting off on CNBC has really done his homework? It used to be nearly impossible to determine if an analyst knew his stuff or not. Once a year, *The Wall Street Journal* publishes a list of all-star analysts in various industries along with their favorite future picks. If you missed that issue, you were out of luck. *Institutional Investor* also conducts its own highly regarded annual study, but that's not a publication that many individuals read.

Investors and Fair Disclosure

Analysts have historically enjoyed a huge advantage over the average investor: access. They could chat with a company's chief executive officer, the chief financial officer, and other bigwigs while the rest of us couldn't. Surely every individual stock investor has experienced the feeling of being left out—a stock suddenly drops significantly but there is no news to explain it. The investment community knew why it was happening, but we didn't.

Not long ago, the SEC decided that the access advantage was an unacceptable one. The government decided to abolish the inside track with something called *Regulation Fair Disclosure* or *Reg FD.* Thanks to the SEC's big stick, corporations became much more accommodating to mom-and-pop investors. They have to release information to the general public at the same time that the institutional investors receive it.

Here's one of the biggest consequences of Reg FD. The general public is now being invited to eavesdrop on the conference calls held between a corporation and analysts. Many companies, upon releasing their latest earnings, hold a conference call. Top executives field calls from analysts and money managers from around the nation and answer questions about their earnings and future growth prospects. In the old days, individual investors were largely shut out of these conference calls. Back in 1999, for instance, about 80 percent of corporations banned individual investors from listening in on the discussions. Now investors can access these conference calls live either by telephone or through Web casts.

You can discover when a corporation has scheduled a conference call by contacting its investor relations department or visiting its Web site. Another resource for conference call calendars is BestCalls.com (www.bestcalls.com), which can direct you to sites where you can access a conference call. What's more, it can alert you by e-mail when a company schedules an unexpected announcement or conference call.

Before eavesdropping on a conference call, be prepared. You'll be able to make more sense of the discussion if you've read through previous conference call transcripts. See if you can get those through a company's Web site or by calling its investors relations phone number.

During a conference call, pay attention not only to the company executives, but also to the analysts. You can get a good sense of their feelings about the earnings release by the questions they ask and their tone of voice.

Despite this new era of investor glasnost, it could be a while before all corporations are conditioned to be as open as possible. Until then, the media continues to report instances where companies have excluded individuals from receiving some critical piece of news. The SEC is also happy to investigate cases where shareholders have been shut out.

A scorecard for number crunchers

A Web site has made it its mission to independently evaluate analysts. BulldogResearch.com (www.bulldogresearch.com) tracks more than 3,000 analysts, who work at more than 350 research firms. The online service measures an analyst's earnings forecasts and stock recommendations and compares them with actual results. The site pinpoints the three best performing analysts for any given company and industry. The rankings are updated quarterly.

Example

To determine which experts have been most accurate with their earnings predictions for Home Depot, type in Home Depot's stock symbol.

The site is infuriating in one respect. It leaves a visitor clueless as to the actual predictions of these high-caliber analysts. Once you know who these brilliant analysts are, you must go elsewhere to discover what they're saying. You have to purchase the research reports written by the analysts from the brokerage firm or third party sources.

While less comprehensive, TheStreet.com provides its own analyst scorecard in dozens of industry categories. To find the yearly rankings, type "analyst rankings" in the financial site's search function. Once again, TheStreet.com does not share what the recommendations are.

Your one-stop site for rating the analysts

Another Web site, however, can help flesh out the sterile numbers that TheStreet.com and BulldogResearch.com provide. Validea.com (www.validea.com) follows stock recommendations made in the media by analysts, money managers, and others. After you've collected names of promising analysts at the other two Web sites, you can see what these analysts have been saying publicly about the stocks that they like or hate.

Considering analyst research reports

Unfortunately, while massive amounts of corporate information are free, research reports, which contain an analyst's thoughts on a company's prospects, remain pricey. One of the perks of being the customer of a full-service broker is free access to the broker's own in-house research. If you have a full-service brokerage account, you can wallpaper your house with all the accessible research.

Discount customers can also typically expect a wealth of research if they've invested enough assets. Typically, the service improves for customers with at least $100,000 invested at a firm.

Resource

Even if you don't have an account with a full-service brokerage firm, you may be able to sample its research for a few weeks. For instance, Merrill Lynch allows you to sign up for free 30-day access to its bottomless pit of research reports at www.askmerrill.com.

Do-It-Yourself Research

Thanks to greater investor access, corporate Web sites have also become a better source of investor information. Nearly all corporate sites post a copy of their latest annual report for cyber visitors, while the majority archive previous annual reports so you can make year-to-year comparisons. Here are some goodies you can expect on an increasing number of corporate sites:

✦ Quarterly reports

✦ Investor-oriented fact books

✦ Audio files or written transcripts of corporate executive speeches and presentations

✦ Question and answer sessions with senior management

✦ E-mail alerts on company news and important dates

✦ Stock quote alerts

✦ Press releases

✦ Monthly and sometimes weekly sales figures for certain industries, such as retail and airlines

Another option is to buy research reports. Much of this research is not cheap. You may pay $10, $25 or more for a report on a company or industry that could be a couple to dozens of pages long. Here are some one-stop online sources that sell research reports from countless sources:

✦ Multex Investor: www.multexinvestor.com

✦ Thomson Financial Securities Data: www.tfsd.com

✦ Zacks Investment Research: www.zacks.com

In addition, you can obtain research reports directly from independent firms that don't have business relationships with companies they cover. Here are three options:

✦ **Morningstar:** Much of the stock information on its Web site is reserved for premium subscribers, but you can obtain a free 30-day trial membership. The firm also produces a monthly newsletter entitled *Morningstar StockInvestor.* Contact them at (800) 735-0700 or go to www.morningstar.com.

✦ *Value Line:* As mentioned earlier, you can find *Value Line Investment Survey* in many libraries. This survey analyzes America's better-known and larger companies, while *Value Line Extended Survey* covers another 1,800 or so small companies. Call (800) 634-3583 or go to www.valueline.com.

✦ **Standard & Poor's:** Standard & Poor's sells its company research reports over the phone through its "Reports on Demand" service. The reports are faxed to you. New customers can receive a free demonstration report. Call (800) 292-0808.

The Other Opinion Makers: Institutional Investors

Analysts aren't the only outsiders whose opinion of stocks matter. When you are conducting your research, you'll want to know the sentiments of institutional investors. These are investment managers who oversee huge portfolios for mutual funds, corporate treasury departments, trusts, pension funds, and other major clients.

The impact of institutional trading

Because institutional investors devote their waking hours to following the market, their confidence or lack of it in a company is important. Since a great deal of the trading activity in many stocks can be traced back to these professionals, they can significantly impact a stock's price. If institutional investors flee a stock en masse, the price can crater. Of course, the reverse can happen if the big hitters decide they love a stock's prospects.

If institutions own a large percentage of the shares in a stock you like, you may assume that's a good thing. Great minds, after all, think alike. But this is not happy news. Institutions can cause a lot of damage if they leave, selling off huge chunks at once. At the same time, if institutions have already jumped aboard and they control most of the stock, a main catalyst for the stock price moving ever higher has vanished—once all the big guns have made their purchases, there isn't a comparable number of individual buyers left out there. Boosts in stock prices typically happen when there's a lot of interest.

Tip   Some experts suggest that, ideally, it's best to own shares in a company that has no more than 20 percent of its shares held by institutions.

If it's a solid company, it should eventually attract institutional interest, which should in turn boost the stock's fortune. Such a low level of institutional ownership, however, isn't going to be feasible with major corporations that have already been "discovered." In cases like these, try to find a company where institutional ownership is below the industry average.

Reading institutions' minds

How do you know what the professionals are thinking? First, you'll want to see what percentage of a stock's holdings is owned by institutions. You can find this information at Yahoo!Finance and Multex Investor.

You can also find out what institutions are collectively thinking by checking their most recent quarterly trading activity for an individual stock. Yahoo!Finance compares the institutional trading in an individual stock for the most recent quarter with the previous one. Yahoo!Finance also lists the biggest institutional investors of a stock, along with the number of shares each owns. It also breaks out the mutual funds that hold the largest number of shares. If you spot funds that you particularly admire as investors in a company, this can be a good sign.

Summary

✦ When reading a 10-K, analyze the figures contained in the income statement, cash-flow statement, and balance sheet. Then pour over the management's discussion and analysis.

✦ Never invest in a stock in a vacuum; compare its performance with other stocks in the same industry.

✦ When evaluating a stock, check a company's financial ratios at Multex Investor (www.multexinvestor.com).

✦ Knowing a corporation's whisper numbers can be just as important as traditional earnings estimates.

✦ Take what analysts are saying with a grain of salt.

✦ Know the level of institutional money in a stock before buying.

✦   ✦   ✦

Investment Clubs in the Online Age

I f investment clubs intrigue you, in this chapter you'll learn not only how clubs are evolving, but also whether you should join one. If the answer is yes, you'll discover how to start your own group or track down a club with a vacancy. You'll also find out how to use the Internet to make the mechanics of club life much easier than in the past. And you'll become acquainted with investment club myths and with the NAIC stock-picking strategy, which has helped to fuel the success of the investment club movement for half a century.

Investment Clubs in the 21st Century

It wasn't too long ago that people who knew anything about investment clubs had heard of the Beardstown Ladies. You might remember them. They shared casserole recipes, clipped coupons, baby-sat grandchildren and, yes, analyzed stocks. Through a fluke, the elderly women, who hail from Beardstown, Illinois, became overnight media sensations. At the height of their popularity, they were known for repeatedly embarrassing some of Wall Street's shrewdest money managers with their investment club's spectacular stock market returns.

The homespun stock pickers were staunchly committed to trading stocks that were as all-American as the Corn Belt. They loved blue chip companies that sell the kinds of products you find if you open your kitchen drawers or medicine cabinet, stocks like Quaker Oats, Newell-Rubbermaid, and Colgate-Palmolive.

They cashed in on their fame with a phenomenally popular book in the 1990s that shared their investing secrets. Today, however, that book is out of print. The women's investing wizardry was no more than an illusion. You can blame the whole sad story on the club's befuddled treasurer. Instead of generating impressive annual returns of more than 23 percent during a 10-year stretch, the club had done no better than 9 percent. That kind of return certainly wasn't going to make their books fly off the shelves. In fact, the ladies would be richer today if they had stayed home and invested in an index fund.

The grandmothers caught the imagination of wannabe investors because they didn't look or behave like Wall Street investors. They made decisions around a dining room table. They still don't use a computer. But times have clearly changed. The world of investment clubs, which may strike some as a quaint artifact of an age when small investors had little access to stock data, is trying to adapt and flourish in the 21st century.

Investment club boosters suggest that the need for investment clubs has only increased in this more complex investing world. There has never been so much stock data, so much news, and so many issues to understand and think about. The glut of information can totally overwhelm the individual investor. Although cheap and accessible brokerage services have grown exponentially, the number of resources for investing education and advice hasn't kept up.

Electronic advances

The Internet is helping the investment club movement usher in its biggest changes. Today, individual clubs can track their portfolio performance on the Internet much as professional mutual fund managers do. The Internet has also morphed into a Lonely Hearts matchmaker for wannabe club members. If you're in Pittsburgh, Atlanta, Salt Lake City, or anywhere else, the Internet can help you find a group to join. The Web also cultivates online clubs that welcome investors across the world. No longer do you need to be in the same city, much less the same time zone, as other investors to form a club.

The Web also provides valuable tools for investment clubs, such as free accounting software, as well as top-notch cyber advice on club nuts and bolts. Younger Web-savvy club enthusiasts are trying to breathe new life into the movement, which stalled when the Beardstown Ladies were dethroned.

NAIC staking its claim

The cyber tremors are clearly being felt by the grande dame of the investment club phenomenon, the National Association of Investors Corp., which is the umbrella group for many of the nation's investment clubs. The 50-year old umbrella organization, which has harnessed tremendous volunteer energy, is trying to evolve with the times as well. The nonprofit is slowly trying to shake its stodgy image of an organization chock full of Beardstown Ladies clones. The median age of NAIC members is 50 years old.

Investment Club Beginnings

While the oldest known investment club is believed to have started 100 years ago in Texas, the modern investment club movement can be traced back to 1940. In that year, Frederick C. Russell, a college grad who couldn't find a job, launched the Mutual Investment Club in Detroit in hopes that it would help him generate cash to start his own business.

One of the first young men to begin contributing the $10 monthly dues was Thomas O'Hara. When he and some other club members were drafted during World War II, O'Hara stayed in touch with letters filled with stock news. Some of the military censors who read the correspondence wrote back asking if they could join.

That first club, which is still in business, spawned others after the GIs returned to America. While millions have been withdrawn from the original club, today the portfolio is worth more than $7 million. Over its lifetime, the club has enjoyed an annual rate of return of 13.7 percent, which is slightly better than the Standard & Poor's 500 Index. More important than the impressive record is the investment club phenomenon that the Detroit group started in motion.

From the start, O'Hara was in charge of the organization that was named the National Association of Investors Corp. Under his leadership, the organization has grown to more than 545,000 members and 34,700 clubs. By far, the biggest fans are women, who make up 67 percent of the membership.

Today, at annual NAIC meetings, the octogenarian creates as much excitement among NAIC followers as Tiger Woods generates on fairways. The investment club movement, concluded *Smart Money Magazine* in a flattering profile, cemented O'Hara's reputation as "one of the most influential people in the stock market."

The NAIC is claiming its own territory on the Web. It's encouraged thousands of its clubs to establish online outposts even if they continue to hold meetings in person. For investors who are leery of cyberspace, the NAIC, in conjunction with Yahoo!, has established a model online club to help investors get their toes wet.

At the same time, the NAIC is pushing the idea that you don't need a living room full of other investors to follow its stock picking guidelines. Use the NAIC's stock-selection software and forget about the kaffeeklatsch. At your own convenience, you can invest when and where you want—with a group or solo.

What is an investment club?

An investment club is really no more than a miniature mutual fund. With a mutual fund, all the money that shareholders invest is pooled together. A professional money manager makes all the investing decisions on behalf of the shareholders. Just how much an investor makes or loses in a fund ultimately depends upon how many shares he or she owns.

An investment club also pools its money into one pot. Instead of a professional manager at the helm, however, the members make the investing decisions. A stock can't be added or deleted from a portfolio unless the members approve. Typically, this takes a majority vote. Traditionally, it's been the treasurer's duty to keep track of assets, provide monthly portfolio valuations to the members, and place trade orders.

Like a mutual fund, a member's stake in the portfolio depends upon how many shares he's accumulated. The more cash someone deposits into the club coffers, the more shares that he or she owns. If the underlying stocks in the portfolio are flourishing, these shares will escalate in value. Of course, if the portfolio is loaded with poorly performing stocks, the shares can take a tremendous hit. The volatility isn't supposed to trigger panic. That's because the credo of most investment clubs is buy and hold.

Caution   When members leave a club, they take their money with them—but getting the check could take two or three months, depending upon a club's bylaws. (In contrast, a mutual fund redemption can sometimes be executed in a matter of hours.)

Typically, the people who form an investment club know each other. Some clubs are formed with family members. Other clubs get started with co-workers, friends, or church members, or with people who socialize through sports or hobbies, such as golf. When a vacancy occurs, many clubs try to fill it by inviting people they know. Typically, a newcomer is asked to attend a couple of meetings to assess whether the club would be a good fit. The club members then vote on whether to accept a club candidate.

Investment club philosophies

An investment club can develop any stock-picking strategies that it desires. A group can decide it wants to place heavy bets on initial public offerings, or high-flying technology or biotechnology companies that haven't issued a single positive earnings report in their lifetimes. Other conservative clubs may favor blue chips and lean even more heavily toward corporations that generate dividends. A club may also invest in mutual funds, but that would defeat the purpose of investors banding together to analyze stocks.

This freedom to invest in any stock sporting a ticker symbol can be overwhelming. To shrink the stock universe to a more manageable level, clubs typically adopt their own stock-picking guidelines. Of course, this probably sounds like a lot of work, too. It certainly can be, which is why hundreds of thousands of people have joined the NAIC. The organization prides itself on the stock-picking strategy that it developed for investors, whether they invest individually and or through investment clubs. These stock selection guidelines, which were first developed as worksheets and then adapted into software, allow a group to follow a detailed stock-picking regimen. Later in the chapter, you'll learn more about how stocks are evaluated using this method.

You can reach the National Association of Investors Corp. at P.O. Box 220, Royal Oak, MI 48068, (877) 275-6242, or www.better-investing.org.

Reasons to consider an investment club

There are many reasons you might want to join an investment club. Here are the major ones:

You don't have to learn alone.

The amount of information on stocks can be dizzying and too many people invest in the market after hearing a neighbor or talking head rave about a company. Stock tips can whipsaw. Chasing hot tips without knowing how to analyze a company's fundamentals is a sure way to lose money. A club can help you impose discipline on your stock picking. It's even easier if the club follows the NAIC's stock guidelines, which have been used by well over 1 million investors since the 1950s.

A club can provide motivation.

If Americans were a motivated bunch, there'd be far fewer of us running to the post office on April 15 to mail in our tax returns. Some goals, such as mastering stock investing, are noble but easily postponed. It's harder to blow it off, however, if you join a club. If you exercise at a gym but can't get motivated to do it at home, you'll understand the concept. It can be easier to commit to demystifying the stock market if you're doing it with other people.

You can get started with little money.

You don't need much money to begin. Many clubs will allow you to invest as little as $25 a month. Obviously, it's impractical for an individual to start sinking such small amounts of money into stocks. Since an investment club pools its money each month, its buying power can be considerably greater. Some clubs do impose a much higher minimum contribution on its members, though.

Note The need to pool money through a club to make stock investing economical isn't as big a factor anymore. Discount brokerage commissions can be as cheap as a couple of McDonald's value meals.

Clubs provide an excuse to socialize.

Many people join investment clubs to learn about stocks, but the clubs aren't just for amateurs. Members often remain in clubs long after they've absorbed investing strategy because it's fun to socialize with people who enjoy talking about stocks. Instead of hanging out at a sports bar and talking about the Yankees, you can meet others who get a kick out of chatting about Cisco or AT&T.

There's strength in numbers.

You may not feel confident sinking money into Motorola, Home Depot, or Juniper Networks, but it won't necessarily feel so scary if you proceed with a group. Often, once people get the hang of stock analysis, they move on and begin trading stocks in their own accounts. Clubs are a way to share successes in good times and to share losses in tough times.

Clubs can provide a forum for investor expertise.

Seasoned stock traders can share expertise in areas that other veteran investors don't know much about. A club member who is a doctor can share observations about the health-care industry, while somebody in the high-tech world might be conversant in trends in the networking or semiconductor fields. Hence, a club may provide valuable tips on potential stocks that you'd like to research and possibly include in your own portfolio.

Debunking Investment Club Myths

Certainly investment clubs have a lot to offer. That explains why NAIC investors pour millions into the stock market every month. But before you get too excited, acquaint yourself with the investment club myths and the truths behind them. The articles and books written about investing clubs make them look fun and easy. Actually, they can be hard and tedious work and the dynamics of an individual club can make Thanksgiving with the in-laws seem like a cinch.

Here are the myths you need to know about:

Myth no. 1: I'm going to get filthy rich.

It's easy to see why so many people believe this. The NAIC's press clippings certainly promote this. For instance, NAIC has calculated that the average club, which responded to its survey, has a lifetime annual total return of 31.4 percent. The vast majority of professional money managers couldn't possibly pull this off.

A lot of people don't understand, however, that these numbers come only from clubs that send in their results. During the most recent survey, less than 1,000 clubs out of approximately 34,700 responded. And human nature being what it is, most of the clubs that participate have something to brag about. If your club lost, say, 20 percent of its value in one year, do you think you'd want any outsider knowing about it? Not likely.

Kenneth Janke, the NAIC's CEO and treasurer of the original NAIC club, acknowledges that he's not George Gallup. The surveys are not scientifically valid. Yet it's those amazing returns that help lure newcomers into the fold. All too often, eager new members fully expect that they'll make a fortune thanks to the stock-picking prowess of their clubs. Here's a more realistic picture of what can happen: Assume that you belong to a club of 15 members, who each invest $20 a month. At the end of five years, a club that follows the guidelines can expect to be managing a portfolio of about $22,000—a respectable sum, but certainly not enough to change anybody's lifestyle. (Of course, the club's assets will grow faster if members contribute more each month.)

Bivio.com, an excellent online resource for investment clubs, created an index in January 2001 to attempt a scientific measure of the stock picking abilities of clubs, tracking the overall performance of roughly 7,000 investment clubs. Unlike the NAIC surveys, this index does not depend upon responses from individual clubs. However, the index is too new to be able to draw any conclusions yet.

Are Investment Clubs Worth It?

During most of the 1990s, investment clubs seemed to be blessed with the Midas touch. The media and such major league fans as Peter Lynch, the legendary mutual fund manager, praised the investing smarts of grassroots investors. The Beardstown Ladies blowup, however, disrupted the love fest and prompted a more critical analysis of investment clubs. One study, in particular, seriously questioned whether investment clubs enjoy an investing advantage over everybody else.

Two nationally known researchers at the University of California, Davis, concluded that investment clubs may actually perform worse. Terrance Odean and Brad M. Barber, who are finance professors, examined the trading records of 166 clubs by using data from a large discount brokerage firm. During a six-year period ending in January 1997, investment clubs enjoyed a 14.1 percent return versus 16.4 percent for individuals and 17.9 percent for the broad market.

Why the tepid performance? The experts all have their own pet theories. A Harvard researcher, for instance, suggests that clubs sometimes feel compelled to buy a stock because they don't want to hurt the feelings of a member, who is lobbying for the buy. The California professors point to brokerage costs as a key factor. In the study, the commission costs were 7 percent for the purchase and sale of a single stock, versus a 5 percent cost for the typical individual investor. The costs are higher because investment clubs typically buy small numbers of shares, which boosts the price.

Does this mean investment clubs are a waste of time? No. In fact, Terrance Odean, one of the study's authors, suggests that investment clubs can indeed be worthwhile. Investment clubs, after all, are mainly educational forums. Club members keep most of their assets in their own portfolios, where the amounts are larger and the commissions don't impact the results in the same way. The NAIC estimates that 9 out of 10 investment club members establish their own individual stock accounts.

Who Belongs to Investment Clubs?

Investment clubs share something in common with Oprah Winfrey. Women love them. Among NAIC members, 54 percent are women, while 46 percent are men. What's more, 54 percent of all NAIC clubs accept only women members. In comparison, just 8 percent of clubs are all-male clubs.

About 73 percent of members graduated from college, while the typical member's median income is $81,000. The average NAIC portfolio is worth $106,000. Keep in mind, however, that these figures are extrapolations from past NAIC member surveys, which are not scientific.

Myth no. 2: Clubs can invest in the entire universe of stocks.

Realistically, this doesn't happen. Nationally, the 100 top holdings of investment clubs are dominated by blue chips. One reason for this embrace of the Goliaths is that newcomers feel more comfortable buying into something they know. After all, a lot of us wear Nike shoes, drink Pepsi or Coke, pass out Tootsie Rolls at Halloween, and buy fast computers powered by Intel's chips. But beyond this natural instinct, the NAIC setup favors the big boys.

One reason is the heavy reliance upon the stock-rating publication, called *The Value Line Investment Survey,* which provides a statistical analysis of roughly 1,700 large corporations in more than 90 industries. That survey still leaves out the vast majority of publicly traded companies. *The Value Line Investment Survey Expanded Edition* covers another 1,800 smaller companies, but this publication doesn't include such things as analysts' commentaries or future earnings estimates. The extended edition also isn't in a lot of libraries, unlike the basic edition. Consequently, if *Value Line* doesn't evaluate a stock, many investment clubs don't bother to do the legwork themselves.

Note Investment clubs don't snub small-cap stocks entirely. Clubs tend to accumulate shares of smaller regional companies in their own areas.

Myth no. 3: If I don't belong to a club, I can't benefit from the NAIC's materials.

Plenty of people join the NAIC solo—about 50,000. There's no reason somebody can't follow the organization's guidelines, use the software, and do quite well picking stocks solo.

Myth no. 4: Following the NAIC's guidelines won't be hard.

In media accounts, club investing may sound easy. But, especially at the start, it won't be. You'll find the stock-picking guidelines spelled out in minute detail in the book *Starting and Running a Profitable Investment Club,* by NAIC officers Kenneth S. Janke and Thomas E. O'Hara. This book, which is carried in bookstores, is crammed with page after page of deadly dull text. While the advice is informative, the writing, once again, is plodding. Later in this chapter, however, you'll find an explanation of NAIC stock-picking essentials. Reviewing these basics can give you a good idea of whether you agree with the NAIC approach, which is followed by many clubs.

Finding or Starting a Club

With tens of thousands of clubs in the United States, you might assume that it should be relatively easy to find one to join. Guess again. It can be more of a hassle than you imagine.

NAIC information freeze

Say you live in Los Angeles and want a list of nearby club contacts. If you call up the NAIC chapter in Los Angeles and ask for a list of groups with vacancies, you won't get any names. Contacting the headquarters in Michigan won't help either. Why the stonewall? NAIC officials are worried about violating U.S. Securities and Exchange Commission regulations. All securities are regulated by the SEC and the states. The issue is whether membership interest in an investment club constitutes a security or not. If not, the SEC and state regulators aren't involved and clubs can freely advertise. Was the SEC thinking about grassroots investment clubs when they wrote the regulations? Hardly. The rules are aimed at mutual fund companies and other professional investment firms that market their financial products to you and I. These firms must obviously be regulated, which requires securities attorneys, red tape, and headaches.

In its own cautious interpretation of the rule, the NAIC has concluded that SEC rules effectively prohibit it from playing matchmaker. While it seems a stretch to believe that clubs with folksy names like Money Mavens, Stock it To Me, and Million $ Belles could possibly arose the ire of the SEC, the NAIC isn't taking any chances.

Not everyone, however, has put the kibosh on recruitment. Plenty of investment club directories now exist on the Internet. These directories will link you to the Web pages of clubs throughout the United States. To make searches easier, the clubs are typically broken down by state. Just because a club makes its e-mail or Web address available, however, doesn't mean it's looking for new members. But it certainly is a place to start.

Online versus traditional clubs

No one knows how many online clubs exist, but the number is surely growing. Since they are a fairly new phenomenon, it's hard to know how quickly online clubs, which conduct their meetings over the Internet, will catch on. Some experts predict that the vast majority of clubs will be online someday and conduct most of their business that way too. What seems far more certain is that traditional clubs, which prefer holding meetings in person, will use Internet tools to make the whole buying and accounting processes easier, and will perhaps store their financial records and meeting minutes on their own Web sites.

Members of online clubs can communicate a variety of ways. They can conduct business through group e-mails or through real-time chats through Yahoo!. Some clubs establish their own Web sites where they communicate and store their records. An even easier way to launch a cyber club is to piggyback with another Web site like bivio.com or Yahoo!, the search engine.

Yahoo! has teamed up with the NAIC to create a virtual community for any interested club. Through Yahoo, a club can track its portfolio, receive market news and research specific to its holdings, conduct private discussions on its own message board, and engage in a real-time chat. On its Web site, Bivio allows clubs to create their own private cyber communities where they may store club documents, exchange e-mail and enjoy daily portfolio updates.

Online club pros

Here are the main reasons investors seek out or start online clubs.

✦ **You can live anywhere and still be in the club.** With an online club, members can live anywhere, which is particularly handy for folks who must reluctantly quit traditional clubs when they move. One peril of traditional clubs: The club sometimes shuts down when members leave, particularly if one or two departing members owned a big chunk of the assets.

✦ **Online clubs are flexible.** Finding the perfect meeting time isn't an issue with a cyber club. A member in Manhattan can be sleeping while a colleague can be critiquing a stock in Honolulu. Members can sign on anytime and present a stock evaluation, hype a potential stock, and buy or vote on a stock trade.

✦ **They encourage online research.** Clubs that conduct meetings online will probably feel quite comfortable researching stocks that way. The wealth of information you can obtain online is much greater and easier to access than what you can obtain in a library. Consequently, the quality of the research efforts may be greater.

Online club cons

Here are some of the drawbacks to online clubs:

✦ **It's hard to create a personal bond.** Many people are attracted to clubs because of the chitchat. They can munch snacks and gossip before, after, and even during the meeting. This social bond, which encourages club commitment, can be more difficult to nurture by computer. Some experts recommend that cyber clubs try to meet in person every year or 18 months. Your meetings can be more enjoyable if you can at least place names with faces.

Tip The club can schedule an in-person meeting to coincide with the annual NAIC meeting or some other investment conference, such as the ones sponsored by the American Association of Individual Investors.

✦ **Chatting online can cause writer's cramp.** Frankly, it can be easier chatting about a stock in person. If you conduct meetings online, you'll have to type in all your responses. This can involve quite a time commitment on your part if you've analyzed a stock and want to make a presentation.

Starting your own club

If you can't find an already established club that meets your wants and needs, here's a checklist of what needs to be done to start your own:

Do your homework.

To find out what you're getting into, visit the Web sites devoted to investment clubs listed later in this chapter. Read the materials and prowl message boards. You may wish to read the handful of books that are devoted to investment clubs. Here are three to start you out, including the book mentioned earlier in the chapter that was written by two leading members of the NAIC:

✦ *Starting and Running a Profitable Investment Club,* by Kenneth S. Janke and Thomas E. O'Hara

✦ *Getting Started in Investment Clubs,* by Marsha Bertrand

✦ *Investment Clubs: How to Start and Run One the Motley Fool Way,* by Selena Maranjian

Ask friends, relatives, or coworkers if they're interested.

Give potential members background material on investment clubs that you've downloaded from various Internet sites. You may want to copy the first chapter of *Starting and Running a Profitable Investment Club,* which summarizes the organization's investment philosophy.

Hold an informational meeting.

If there's an NAIC chapter in your area, invite the local club organizer as a guest speaker. The speaker can provide an overview of what's involved in starting a club. After the meeting, ask those who attended if they'd like to join.

If there's enough interest, write the club's bylaws and partnership agreement.

At least two people should be assigned to this task. You can get a sample copy of typical bylaws and the partnership agreement from the NAIC. The partnership agreement is a legal document that establishes the legal obligations of each member. You can find sample copies of both these documents at the NAIC's Web site (www.better-investing.org).

The bylaws, which are more flexible than the partnership agreement, can be extremely helpful in resolving disputes later on. For instance, the bylaws can dictate what actions a club can take if a member is frequently absent from meetings. Here are just a few of the issues that the bylaws should address:

✦ Should voting rights be based on the value of a member's account or should every member have one equal vote?

✦ Should someone be fined a token amount for missing a meeting? If so, how much?

✦ At what point can a club demand the resignation of a member who rarely shows up?

✦ When someone quits, how quickly must the investment club cut a check to the departing member?

✦ Should a member be limited to owning no more than 20 percent of a club's holdings? (This is an NAIC recommendation.)

✦ Should a redemption fee be imposed for any member who is cashing out?

✦ If a member moves away, can he or she remain in the club?

✦ How long should the club officers' terms last?

✦ How frequently should the club meet?

✦ Should the club require a minimum investment?

✦ Should the club admit new members on a unanimous vote?

✦ How will partial withdrawals be handled?

Settle the basics at the first few meetings.

Once the group comes together, it will need to address practical issues first. Discuss potential names for the group. Review and approve the bylaws and partnership agreement. Develop a mission statement that outlines what the club's stock-picking philosophy will be. If the club decides to join the NAIC, collect dues and send off the enrollment forms. Elect a president, vice president, secretary, and treasurer. Choose a brokerage firm to handle your trades.

Note   You might assume that membership in the NAIC is required if you want to start or belong to an investment club, but there is no obligation to join the national group, though many club members do.

Another key task is dividing the workload. Once a club begins buying stocks, a "stock watcher" will be needed for each of your holdings. For instance, if a club owns IBM, someone will need to keep track of how the stock is doing and arrive at each meeting with any important news. A stock watcher will also be responsible for sharing the news about a stock's quarterly earnings report.

Resource   Keeping track of a stock is much easier with the Internet, since you can easily find out what's been happening to a stock. A quick place to find news is Yahoo!Finance.

Other members may prefer to hunt for new stock ideas. They will be expected to analyze a stock before the club votes on whether to add it to the portfolio. Members may also want to take turns making an educational presentation on topics like growth versus value investing or a close look at a particular sector or industry.

Sizing Up a Club

If joining an investment club sounds like fun, remember your money will be on the line. Sure, at the beginning you won't have much in the kitty, but your investment will grow. And pretty soon, you'll be talking about real money. Consequently, it's important to hook up with people you trust. What follows are questions to ask yourself before joining a traditional and an online club:

✦ Are the financial statements, which include the holdings of each member, the value of the club portfolio, and recent financial transactions, available at each meeting? Can they be accessed at any time online?

✦ Are the meetings run professionally with an agenda?

✦ Does the job of treasurer rotate among members?

✦ What is your gut instinct about the club?

To better protect yourself, don't join a club impulsively. Attend two or three meetings before making up your mind. (Of course, the club will have to approve your membership.) If you're scouting out an online club, consider delaying your decision for a few months. By then you'll have some sense of the members and whether the club is clicking. Ask the members to send a brief bio of themselves.

Request a tax identification number.

The Internal Revenue Service will consider your club a business. The club treasurer will need to fill out IRS's Form SS-4 to obtain a tax ID. You can obtain the form by calling the IRS at (800) 829-3676. Your club's broker will need that tax ID number to report the club's purchases and sales.

Fixing Investment Club Bloopers

Every club makes mistakes. Here's how to sidestep the biggies:

Tip no. 1: Be firm about attendance.

Joining a club is easy. Staying committed is the hard part. It's only human nature that interest will eventually wane for some members. In fact, the NAIC estimates that 40 percent of clubs disband within the first two years.

Delinquent members are a problem for a couple of reasons. Absentees can endanger a quorum. If your club has 10 members and only four or five show up, the group can't conduct a meeting because there isn't a quorum. No-shows can also create resentment among members who are doing most of the work.

Some attrition is to be expected; people move away, become bored, or conclude it's too much work. One way to discourage dropouts is to require an initial investment up front. It may be $100 or considerably more. An established club with considerable assets may require prospective new members to pony up much more.

Tip   You can also discourage escapees by imposing a redemption fee on the back end. You may want to charge a departing member 1 percent or 2 percent of his or her assets.

Your bylaws should establish how quickly the club must come up with the cash. This probably won't be a problem until your club's assets have grown considerably. A club that's been around a few years can have departing members who are owed $10,000 or more. You don't want to be stuck paying them off in just 30 days.

Tip no. 2: Be patient.

A club's first year or two is a lot like a new marriage. It's tough and you'll be tempted to dissolve the group. But with any luck, once you survive a potential rocky beginning, your club will achieve a reasonable balance of yin and yang. You may discover that picking stocks is the easiest part. Working as a group with clashing personalities can pose your biggest challenge. It's for this reason that it's best to form a club with compatible people.

Beating the Accounting Blues with Bivio

It's fun to buy stocks, but it's a chore keeping track of the books. Many investment clubs fail because no one wants to tackle the grunt work. Help, however, has arrived. Bivio.com, an ambitious Internet site, is making investment club bookkeeping easy. The accounting software is the same type used by mutual funds and partnerships. Best of all, the site's software, which keeps track of such things as members' payments, capital gains, and dividends, is free.

In important ways, Bivio's software is an improvement upon the NAIC's. Bivio, for example, automatically updates each club's holdings daily. In contrast, NAIC software requires a treasurer to do this manually. As a practical matter, treasurers who rely upon the NAIC software only revise the valuations monthly. When a treasurer misses a meeting, members can go a couple of months without a club accounting. In contrast, any club member can log onto Bivio and look at the books. This easy access to the finances, suggests Bivio's founders, should encourage confidence and peace of mind. What's more, at tax time, individual club members can visit the site and print out their own K-1 tax forms, after the treasurer has completed the paperwork.

While club's financial books are kept on the site, only club members have access to it. Each club has its private section within the site, and so far over 7,000 have signed up. In this private area, you can maintain a club message board, post club Web pages, and store stock research files and club minutes.

If your club already uses NAIC software, switching to Bivio should be nearly effortless. Both types of software are compatible. The NAIC software has a function that allows it to be easily transferred to Bivio. Because the software is easy to use, a club won't need someone with an accounting background to serve as treasurer.

At this point, you're probably wondering what the catch is. The NAIC, after all, charges for its software. In fact, Bivio makes its money by signing up site sponsors. Two prominent ones are Merrill Lynch, as well as BUYandHOLD.com, which is a contender among a new crop of Internet companies trying to revolutionize the way investors buy stocks.

Bivio has also begun selling a fancier software product that links a club's holdings to its brokerage firm. Consequently, if a club buys 100 shares of Intel in its E*TRADE brokerage account, Bivio will instantly update that change in the club's portfolio. The price tag of this service was recently $95 per year.

Tip no. 3: Keep your treasurer happy.

One huge reason clubs dissolve is that their treasurer quits. The treasurer is truly the club's cement. He or she places the buy and sell orders, deposits money in brokerage accounts, and prepares the club's monthly financial statements. Each spring, he's stuck with the thankless task of preparing each member's tax form.

In some clubs, members designate that a small fraction of their monthly contribution go towards buying their treasurer extra stock. You might try this, especially if members are reluctant to take on the job.

Tip
Even if your treasurer declines the offer of a little compensation, broach the subject a couple of times a year—the treasurer might feel too sheepish to share that he or she is feeling unappreciated. Plus, members should pitch in to buy the treasurer a gift during the holidays or for a birthday.

NAIC tried to lighten the treasurer's responsibility by selling accounting software. This dramatically reduces the burden. Bivio.com, an investment club support site, offers similar software for free (see the following sidebar).

Tip no. 4: Keep a lid on membership.

The number of members varies tremendously from club to club. You'll want enough members to assume all the tasks necessary to keep the club humming. The average NAIC club has 14 members, which is just about right. When a club accumulates a portfolio, you'll need a stock watcher for each holding. Each club also requires a treasurer, a secretary to keep the minutes, and a president to set the agenda and run the meetings. You'll also want enough members to generate stock ideas.

If you have two dozen members or more, you could face a logistical nightmare. Notifying people of meeting changes or simply agreeing on a meeting time can be difficult. If your club is too big, you can also encounter trouble finding a place that can accommodate everybody.

Club resources in cyberspace

Is your club in the intensive care unit? Maybe your group is confused about its accounting procedures? Perhaps your portfolio gets creamed year after year. Or maybe you're flirting with the possibility of starting a club and want to avoid making the usual mistakes. Luckily, there are plenty of Internet resources no matter what your needs might be.

Here's a rundown of club resources on the Net.

Bivio (www.bivio.com)
Perhaps more than any other site, Bivio is revolutionizing the club movement. Naming the club Bivio, by the way, is an illustration of what happens when all the good dot.com names have been claimed. Bivio, which derives from the Latin word for road intersection, is also the name of a beautiful Swiss village whose two founders discovered it independently of each other.

Luckily, the mission of the site makes more sense than its name. With its free accounting software, Bivio has turned the thankless chore of keeping track of a club's finances into a breeze. Bivio also tries its hand at club matchmaking by introducing individuals who wish to form both traditional and online clubs.

Another strong Bivio asset are its columnists, who answer questions posted on the site. Two veterans of the investment club scene, a certified financial planner and an airline pilot, respond to just about any question imaginable regarding investment clubs. Another columnist, who belongs to multiple clubs, offers tips on such topics as keeping interest in a club alive, online club dos and don'ts, jettisoning inactive members, and avoiding club con artists. Another feature is Club Cafe, where Bivio members can chat about investment club topics.

Yahoo!Finance (`http://yahoo.finance.com`)

Yahoo has plunged into the investment club business. In conjunction with the NAIC, an individual club can now establish its own virtual community on Yahoo!, where it can engage in real-time chats, track its portfolios, use its own private message board, keep abreast of market news, and view recent club actions. Several thousand clubs now take advantage of these virtual goodies. Visiting Yahoo! can also give you a better idea of how a model online club operates. A club that includes some leading members of the NAIC welcomes outsiders to watch the proceedings during live meetings and also to check out their archived research.

Tip The easiest way to access the site is to click on the Yahoo! club logo at the NAIC Web site.

ICLUBcentral (`www.iclub.com`)

IClubcentral goes beyond merely listing the Web sites and e-mail of clubs located across the country. The site also contains educational material on investment clubs, maintains club message boards and portfolio file storage for individual clubs, and provides online investing tools.

Wild Capital Investment Club List (`www.wildcapital.com`)

This investment club in Columbia, Missouri, can very well represent the ultimate in investment club directories. Its exhaustive list of clubs includes strictly online clubs as well as those overseas. The clubs are divided by state so it should be easy to find any in your area.

Motley Fool (`www.fool.com`)

The Motley Fool provides in-depth tutorials on what lies ahead if you've caught the investment club bug. If you want moral support, whether you're a new or old club member, visit the Fool's investment club active message board.

About.com

Deep within the bowels of this site are articles on a variety of club issues from club accounting to bylaws. You can also find plenty of links to other helpful club resources by visiting About.com. To find the investment club section of this vast Web site, type "investment club" into the search function.

NAIC Stock Picking Guidelines

While investment clubs aren't required to join the NAIC or use their stock picking guidelines, so many clubs do both that you should familiarize yourself with them before joining or starting a club to determine whether these guidelines are compatible with your investing style.

The NAIC's stock picking philosophy is not flashy. The goal is not to make a quick profit on initial public offerings or other hot stocks. If you expect to bounce in and out of stocks a lot, this isn't your kind of crowd. NAIC clubs hold onto a stock an average of six years. The NAIC also isn't enthusiastic about buying cyclical stocks, such as automobiles, steel, and oil stocks, since timing the trades of these manic stocks can be tricky. Rather, the NAIC steers club members to Wall Street's steady growth performers.

Here's a rundown of NAIC's stock-picking guidelines:

Stick with long-term performers.

The NAIC loves a company that can brag about its solid long-term track record. And the organization does mean long term. When you analyze stocks the NAIC way, you find yourself plugging in financial data for the past 10 years (if the company has been publicly traded that long). A club is expected to look at sales and earnings per share data as well as stock prices to make a quick determination if the stock is worthy of further study.

If it is, a club member digs in to examine sales and earnings per share trends, as well as pre-tax profit margins and return on shareholder's equity (ROE). Someone analyzing stocks through the NAIC method will also need to estimate how high and low the stock might sell in the future. In doing this, it's assumed the economy will undergo one recession and one business boom every five years.

> **Note**
>
> If all this sounds intimidating, it doesn't have to. A lot of the number crunching can be done using NAIC's stock analysis software, and you can pull most of the numbers you need off a one-page *Value Line* analysis of a stock you're interested in.

You'll need to make some subjective calls—such as what you project future rates of revenue and earnings will be. But even then you can at least partially rely on the opinions of Wall Street analysts. You can find analyst community's growth projections at numerous sites on the Internet, including Yahoo!Finance (`http://finance.yahoo.com`) and Zacks Investment Research (`www.zacks.com`).

Once the numbers are typed in—it should take about 20 minutes after you've done a couple of them—the software will signal whether a stock is in the buy, hold, or sell range. If a stock is bought, this exercise should be repeated quarterly.

Stick with growth companies.

The NAIC recommends that its members hunt for the best-managed companies in rapidly growing industries. These gems are usually the ones with the highest profit margins and return on shareholder's equity.

The NAIC is particular about the growth stocks it favors. For instance, it shuns companies that don't produce earnings. Consequently, a club following the NAIC guidelines wouldn't be interested in a young telecommunications or biotech company that's growing like crazy but is operating in the red.

Overall, a club should look for stocks that can double its money every five years. If a club can pull this off, that performance breaks down to a 14.9 percent compounded annual growth rate. Perhaps that's not a flashy figure if we're in the midst of an overheated bull market, but it's certainly superior to the historical 11 percent returns that stocks have enjoyed since the 1920s.

Diversify.

The most popular stocks among clubs nationally include some of the biggest corporate names in the world. But the NAIC really wants its stock pickers to branch out. According to the NAIC, the ideal portfolio is more or less equally divided among large, medium, and small companies and a range of industries. Many new clubs buy 8 to 12 stocks in their first year. After that, they may dump the losers and add to their positions of the solid performers.

Table 16-1 lists the most popular stocks held by NAIC investment clubs in the year 2001:

Table 16-1
Favorite Investment Club Stocks

1) Cisco Systems	11) PepsiCo	21) Diebold
2) Intel	12) Wal-Mart	22) ADC Telecommications
3) Lucent Technologies	13) Oracle	23) Amgen
4) Home Depot	14) EMC	24) Coca-Cola
5) Microsoft	15) Motorola	25) Dell Computer
6) Pfizer	16) Disney	26) Clayton Homes
7) General Electric	17) AT&T	27) Walgreens
8) Avaya	18) Nokia	28) Wendy's International
9) Merck	19) Johnson & Johnson	29) Medtronic
10) AFLAC	20) McDonald's	30) RPM

Since 1986, the NAIC has been tracking the performance of its member clubs' favorite 100 picks. The universe of the 100 most popular stocks is also heavily invested in Blue Chips. About 26 percent of the portfolio is devoted to technology stocks, while the three closest sectors are financials (19.2 percent), consumer staples (12.8 percent) and capital goods (11.2 percent).

As you can see in Table 16-2, the annual performance track records of these 100 stocks compare quite favorably to more popular and well-known indexes.

Table 16-2
NAIC 100 Index

Time Period	NAIC Top 100	S&P 500	Dow Jones Average
3-year total return	9%	5.3%	7.5%
5-year total return	19.1%	15.5%	16%
10-year total return	16.3%	15.2%	16.7%

Stick with top-flight management.

If the NAIC has a mantra, it could be this: "It's the management, stupid." Investing in a company with poor management is sacrilege to the folks at the Michigan head-quarters. Stick with companies run by top-fight managers and you should do all right financially.

Of course, you might think that characterizing management is subjective. After all, a baby-faced CEO might seem like a genius if the company's initial public offering made a huge splash on Wall Street. And how could somebody living in California, for instance, know if the highest-paid executives at Coca-Cola in Atlanta are really earning their cushy salaries. Chances are you'll never meet these guys, but there are ways to confront the question quantitatively by using the NAIC's Stock Selection Guide, which is often referred to as a SSG.

In judging management, the NAIC loves to see the following:

✦ Sales, earnings per share, and profits are trending upward.

✦ The pre-tax profit margins and return on equity are consistent, or they are also moving up.

✦ The level of profit margins and return on equity compare favorably to those of the company's competitors.

Invest regularly.

If a club tries to time the market by guessing when Wall Street's on the verge of a collapse or a wild ascent, it will fail most of the time. Instead, members are encour-aged to regularly pump money into the market no matter what kind of shape it's in. And no investment, by the way, is too small. Nationally, the average club member contributes just $46 a month. The NAIC encourages regular investing in worthwhile companies at good prices, regardless of whether the market is prospering or in a free fall.

Reinvest all earnings.

This is pretty obvious. If a club wants its portfolio to grow through compounding, it needs to reinvest. Clubs are supposed to sink their dividends, as well as any capital gains, back into stocks. Of course, in today's market, healthy stock dividends seem more like a quaint artifact from a bygone era. But even modest dividends can help soften the blow when a stock skids.

Summary

✦ Know what to expect before joining a club, particularly if it's an online club.

✦ Try to find compatible investors when forming a new club.

✦ Take advantage of stock analysis and accounting software to cut the club's workload.

✦ When researching stocks, use the Internet to make the job easier.

✦ Don't join a club if you think it's a way to get rich quick.

Bonding with Your Investments

✦ ✦ ✦ ✦

In the next three bond chapters, you'll find the answers to many questions, including:

✦ Why are Treasuries popular during times of economic turmoil?

✦ When is the right time to buy bonds?

✦ Is a bond's yield important?

✦ Which type of yield is most crucial?

✦ Does a bond's total return matter?

✦ When are bonds overpriced?

✦ Why does the yield curve matter?

✦ What are the criteria for buying individual bonds?

✦ How do you select a bond fund?

✦ What are the pros and cons of different types of bonds?

Bond Basics

In this chapter, you'll discover how bonds work and how they can help dampen your portfolio's volatility. You'll learn the different ways you can invest in bonds and by the end of the chapter, you'll know how to identify good bond buys. Before you can appreciate whether a bond is a good value, you'll have to understand how the yield curve works and how to interpret a spread.

The Tamest Investment You'll Ever Love

Bonds are a snooze. Isn't that secretly what many of us thought for many years? Perhaps you still do. After all, during the nineties bull market, stocks were defying gravity while bonds were plodding along down here on earth, clearly bound by the rules of physics.

They're the quiet type.

Even if you ignore the stock market's most spectacular romp in recent years, bonds have historically lagged behind the splashier equities. Any economist will tell you that the historical return for bonds, during much of this century, has trailed several percentage points behind stocks. That doesn't mean you should boycott bonds, however. Americans have been squirreling them away since the 1790s, when our forefathers issued millions of dollars' worth of bonds to help eliminate the Revolutionary War debt, and for good reason.

Note The compelling story that bonds have to tell rarely gets heard. You won't hear the guests on the financial news channels hyping the day's hottest bond pick, even when stocks are getting pummeled.

Part of the information blackout can be attributed to the bond world's peculiar characteristics. Even though the amount of bonds outstanding dwarfs the number of stocks—investors are holding onto roughly $15 trillion worth of bonds—there aren't any fixed-income celebrities to divert investors' attention away from growth stocks like AOL Time Warner, Enron, and Applied Materials. It's hard to get excited about Cuyahoga (Ohio) County's hospital bonds or the debt being peddled by the Denver Airport Authority even if you do get wind of them.

Who's afraid of big bad bond lingo?

The lack of visibility is just one of the handicaps. To many outsiders, bonds are intimidating. The fixed-income world depends upon its own terminology, which it abbreviates to even more cryptic shorthand. Deciphering the jargon can be as frustrating as interpreting baby gibberish.

Even when the experts revert to plain English when discussing bonds, it's still hard to figure out. For instance, when bonds "rally" (their prices increase), is that good for the average Joe investor? It really depends upon whether Joe is shopping for a bond during this jubilant time or whether he already owns a fistful. Whether Joe should be happy, sad, or indifferent will depend upon whether Joe intends to hold his bonds until they mature or whether he is, instead, an active trader.

If you're not sure how you'd fare during a bond rally, you're not alone. In fact, most people probably don't have a clue. In contrast, everybody who owns stocks can safely and enthusiastically root for a stock rally. No ambiguity there. Fixed-income investors need to master many such basic concepts before they can feel comfortable investing in bonds.

Four Great Reasons to Love Bonds

Not sure whether you should bother with bonds? Here are the major reasons bonds can make a valuable addition to your portfolio:

Reason no. 1: Reduce portfolio volatility

Bound together in a portfolio, bonds and stocks can behave like yin and yang. For anxious stockholders, bonds can serve as a form of insurance, possibly helping to reduce the losses when the inevitable bear markets maul stock investors. Adding bonds to your cache of stocks lowers your portfolio risk because bonds not only fluctuate in value less, but their returns traditionally haven't been perfectly in sync with stocks. Since 1926, for instance, intermediate bonds earned a profit in 18 of the 20 years when stocks lost money.

Tip   Stashing money into historically less volatile bonds can smooth out some of the zigs and zags of equities.

Bonds have also enjoyed long periods of time when they were top banana. Few people remember that bonds outperformed the Standard & Poor's 500 Index during an amazing 21-year span that began with the Great Stock Market Crash of 1929 and ended with the start of the Korean War. The feat was repeated in the 1970s when both Treasury bills and corporate bonds outmuscled stocks. More recently, the returns for stocks and bonds in 2000 were nearly mirror images. The entire bond market, as measured by the Lehman Aggregate Bond Index, returned 11.63 percent, while the entire stock market, as measured by the Wilshire 5000 Index, dropped 10.99 percent. U.S. Treasury bonds performed even more spectacularly in 2000 by producing a total return of 20 percent.

Reason no. 2: Generate income

Income is another significant reason for investors to gravitate to bonds. Retirees like the regular income checks that the interest from their bonds can provide. Investors who hold individual bonds typically receive checks twice a year. Bond mutual funds usually distribute income monthly to their shareholders. Still other investors, who need to stash cash for a fairly brief period, will turn to short-term bonds to capture a higher yield than they could get with a certificate of deposit or a money market.

Reason no. 3: May provide tax-free income

The affluent have historically embraced municipal bonds to shield themselves from onerous taxes. Municipal bonds generate income that is free from federal taxes. Some munis also avoid state and even local taxes too.

 Cross-Reference You'll learn more about municipal bonds in Chapter 19.

Reason no. 4: Might fight inflation

The rap against bonds has always been that they are dreadful at protecting investors against inflation. During periods when inflation is raging, the buying power of a bond's modest income shrivels. But as you'll learn in Chapter 18, two types of bonds now exist that were expressly designed to fight inflation—Treasury Inflation-Protection Securities (TIPs) and I Bonds. While institutional investors and economists are excited about these inflation-fighting bonds, which were created by the U.S. Treasury in the 1990s, most individual investors have never heard of them.

Bond Nuts and Bolts

At its simplest, a bond is an IOU. When people buy bonds, they are loaning money to the issuers of the bonds (borrowers). Who creates bonds to raise cash? The federal government is a colossal debtor. At its auctions, the U.S. Treasury has been issuing about $2 trillion in debt each year to finance its many functions. Meanwhile, state and local governments also need cash for such worthy causes as buying park land, improving roads, strengthening bridges, and building libraries. Not to be left out are corporate borrowers: They range from the most solid of corporate citizens like Johnson & Johnson and United Parcel Service (UPS) down to shaky telecom startups, which may not survive as long as your car loan.

Coupons

When you purchase a bond, the specific sum of money you lend the debtor is called the *principal.* The bond's face value is referred to as *par:* The par of a $1,000 Treasury bond is $1,000. Of course, no one would be interested in buying a bond without a payoff. The carrot that most bonds offer prospective investors is a *coupon.* The coupon is the rate of interest that a buy-and-hold investor can expect after purchasing a bond. A $1,000 bond with an 8 percent coupon will annually pay $80 in interest. Since interest checks are typically paid semiannually, the bondholder would pocket two $40 checks a year. You can easily determine the amount of interest a bond will generate annually by multiplying its coupon rate by its face value.

Coupon rates vary widely. At one point in 2001, for instance, a 10-year U.S. Treasury note was yielding 5.2 percent, while *junk bonds* (those issued by less financially secure companies) were desperately trying to tantalize buyers with 13 percent coupons. Why the huge gulf? It's partly based on the borrower's reputation. Which would make you feel uneasier? Lending money to an Internet retailer with a hot idea but no track record, or lending money to the federal government, which has never defaulted on its bond obligations? The answer is a no-brainer. Consequently, the Internet retailer is going to have to dish out a much higher coupon to attract those fearless investors willing to take a chance on its future.

Bond yields

While a bond's coupon is usually fixed, its actual *yield* can stray from the coupon rate. If a person holds a bond until it matures, the bond's yield will indeed match the coupon's interest rate. But if the investor sells a bond early, the next owner may get a different yield from what the original investor would have gotten over the full term. How's that work? When a bond is sold, the yield can be either higher or lower than the original coupon depending upon what price the bond commands.

Example   Suppose you bought an older corporate bond with a 7 percent coupon for $950. Since you purchased it for less than its $1,000 face value, you got a discount. Consequently, you've captured a yield of 7.36 percent. On the other hand, if somebody spent $1,050 for that same bond, the yield would slip to 6.66 percent.

You might rightly wonder why anybody would pay a premium to buy a bond. Actually, this occurs frequently. If interest rates have plummeted since a bond's original purchase date, its value has increased.

Don't yield to temptation.

Most bond lovers are yield hogs. They collect bonds for their yield, enamored of a return that seems as solid as concrete. The financial markets may be getting whip-sawed by inflation, lousy corporate earnings reports, or just plain jitters, but that sacred bond coupon is a sure thing. Brokers and mutual fund firms like to exploit what seems to be a sure thing, but in fact it's not a sure thing for *all* bondholders. If you invest in a bond mutual fund, the yield that's advertised in glossy handouts and advertisements is meaningless. That's because fund managers aren't going to hold bonds until maturity. You may be a buy-and-hold investor, but your fund manager is not.

Caution

Bond fund managers trade bonds whenever they want, affecting the portfolio's overall yield and its total return, which is calculated by adding together the interest plus any price appreciation. Even if you hold onto a bond fund for a lifetime, the yield will certainly not be the same as it was the day you signed on.

Chasing the highest yield, whether you buy bonds individually or through a mutual fund, can be a dangerous hobby. If you pursue the hottest yields, your portfolio better be lined with asbestos. The highest-yielding bonds could very well burn a hole in your brokerage account.

What's the danger? A bond fund with an unusually attractive yield can be tweaking it by loading its portfolio with speculative junk bonds, high-yield municipal bonds, bonds of emerging nations, or other risky choices. Even a fund that markets itself as "investment grade" (a term used for bonds sold by solid blue chip corporations) can be stuffed with junk. Consequently, you can own a fund that temporarily sports a high yield, but the fund itself can end a year posting an overall negative return.

Look for the red flags.

How do you know if you've signed on with a swashbuckling fund manager? A potential warning sign is that your bond fund's yield is noticeably higher than the rest of the pack. If your muni bond fund is yielding 6.5 percent and most are yielding 5 percent, find out why.

You can uncover the answer by examining a fund's latest annual or semiannual report. These reports can be obtained by calling a fund's toll-free number. Inside these reports, you'll find a listing of the fund's holdings.

Tip

If you're lucky, a fund company's Web site will post a list that's even more current. Hunt for surprises.

If you're investing in a government bond fund, for example, check to see if there are corporates tucked in to juice the yield. Is your intermediate bond fund, which investors often use as a core bondholding, loaded with a heavy dose of junk or foreign bond? What about your municipal bond fund? Believe it or not, there are plenty of junk muni bonds. A lot of riskier munis are issued by nonprofit health-care agencies, which have been struggling financially in recent times.

If this detective work sounds like it's beyond your ability, relax. Each fund company should provide a percentage breakdown of the credit quality of the bonds, as well as the types found in the portfolio. You may be comfortable with a fund that pushes the yield envelope, but you should know up front how it's being run.

Tip

> To protect yourself, never invest in a fund without looking at the latest fund hold-ings. And read a fund's prospectus, the document which specifies the types and percentages of bonds the manager is free to invest in. The SEC requires that 80 percent of a bond fund's holdings must conform to its stated investment style.

Total return

If yield is not the best yardstick for a bond fund's performance, what is? Check a fund's *total return*. The total return encompasses not only the income that a fund is generating for its investors, but also any price appreciation the bonds in the port-folio enjoyed. Admittedly, bonds don't increase as much in value as stocks, but it still happens. Ideally, you want to invest in a fund with a decent yield and an impressive record of price appreciation.

Tip

> An easy way to determine a bond fund's total return is to read the fund's annual report. Another source—and this one is updated daily—is to check the performance stats of popular bond funds at Morningstar's Web site (www.morningstar.com).

Is total return important for individual bondholders? It certainly can be if you're not a buy-and-hold investor. Imagine all the investors across the nation who bought 30-year Treasuries at the start of 2000 and watched their bonds perform spectacularly. The price of these Treasury bonds jumped 13.2 percent in value. When you include the income from these Treasury bonds—another 6.85 percent—that brings the total return up to a whopping 20 percent. If a retiree who bought the bond for income before the rally holds onto it, then the Treasury bond rally is meaningless. He'll col-lect regular income checks and at the end of 30 years, he'll get his original invest-ment back.

But the Treasury rally was welcome news for aggressive investors, who like to spec-ulate in bonds. That is, they like to accumulate bonds they think are ready to appre-ciate in price and then unload them for a profit. Those who invested in Treasuries with longer maturities in early 2000 and then sold them later made a tidy profit.

Bond maturities

Bond yields are partially dependent upon the length of a bond's life, which is referred to as its *maturity*. While the definition of what qualifies as short, intermedi-ate, and long term varies, here's a common rule of thumb:

✦ Short term: 1 to 3 years

✦ Intermediate term: 3 to 10 years

✦ Long term: More than 10 years

Duration 101

Bond maturity isn't a hard lesson to master. But many investors struggle with a more prickly risk measurement—*duration*. In its simplest form, duration measures how quickly a bond-holder will get his or her money back. The shorter the time lapse, the less risky the investment. How soon a bond matures and its coupon rate is taken into account to calculate duration. Bonds with longer maturities typically have longer durations. On the other hand, the higher the coupon, the lower the duration. That's because the greater the interest income, the sooner you'll recoup your investment. Calculating a bond's duration is muddied up if the bond issuer can call in the bond before its maturity date. A bond that has such a call provision will have a shorter duration than one that can't be recalled.

Even more than a bond's maturity, duration alerts you to how sensitive a bond's price is to interest rate changes. If your bondholdings have a long duration, the more likely their value will be whipsawed during rising interest rates. On the other hand, a bond fund with a low duration will hardly be rocked at all. Risk takers who want to speculate on interest rate volatility will embrace bonds with the longest duration. For these folks, the wildest ride is zero coupon bonds. You'll learn about zero coupon bonds in the next chapter.

Duration is more than a math exercise for bond geeks. You should match your investing horizon with the duration of your bondholdings. If you'll need your money in, say, a couple of years, pick individual bonds or bond funds with a two-year duration. If you need the money in several years, look for a duration of five or six years. For long-term goals like retirement, you can feel comfortable going with a duration of 10 years or more.

A bond fund's literature will be able to tell you what its average duration is. If you are buying an individual bond from a discount or full-service broker, ask the firm for the bond's expected duration. You'll want to know what the duration is based on the bond's first call date.

A bond's term ends on what is called its *maturity date*. When a bond is held until maturity, the bond is repaid in full. Say you buy a $1,000 bond with a 10-year maturity that's offering 6 percent interest. Every year, you pocket $60 in interest. When your bond matures at the end of the 10th year, you receive your $1,000 back. By that time, you'll have earned $600 in interest.

Holding longer-term bonds is riskier. That's because you are locking in a coupon rate for a sizable period of time. Since nobody can predict where interest rates are headed, buying a long bond is considered a gutsier move. Consequently, investors who accumulate bonds with longer maturities are typically rewarded with higher yields for their bravery.

Example

Suppose you buy a 30-year Treasury with a 7 percent coupon, and five years later, identical Treasuries are offering 10 percent coupons. You're going to feel miserable. On the other hand, if interest rates crumble, you're going to look like a genius.

Tip   It's generally better for buy-and-hold investors to stick with bonds of intermediate maturity. They typically provide nearly as much yield as a long-term bond but with far less volatility.

The risky side of bonds

Bonds are safer than stocks. You won't find a high-quality bond losing 50 percent of its value in a short period of time as mighty blue chips like Intel, Procter & Gamble, and Worldcom have done when the market was rocky. But bonds still pose their own risks. Here are the major ones:

Inflation and interest rate risks

To most bondholders, inflation, which often triggers interest rate hikes, is the most dreaded bogeyman. When interest rates are rising, the value of your bond could shrivel, making your bond about as appealing as a day-old doughnut. Why? Say you're holding a bond with a 6 percent coupon when inflation hits. If you continue to hold your bond, you miss out on more attractive bonds with higher yields. But if you decide to dump your bond, you take a hit. After all, who would want to pay full price for your 6 percent coupon when the current crop is advertising more generous interest rates of 7 percent or 7.5 percent? Some investors may be willing to buy your bond, but you'd have to sell it at a discount.

While most bonds are allergic to interest rate hikes, most thrive when interest rates are disintegrating. If you own a bond with an 8 percent coupon when new bonds issuers are only offering 6 percent, your bond is much more marketable. The value of your bond increases because other investors are wiling to pay a premium for what you're holding.

Inflation poses a danger in an insidious way as well. When the price of movie tickets, toothpaste, your electric bill, and many other necessities is climbing, the real value of your bonds withers. The steady income payment you may be depending upon doesn't buy as much anymore.

Call risk

Many bonds have an irritating habit you should know about. Whether it's a bond issued by Ford Motor or the Port Authority of New Jersey, the lender may have the right to ask for its bonds back. When this is allowed, the bond is considered *callable.* Unfortunately for us, most bond issuers enjoy the freedom to pay off their loans prematurely, which is referred to as *calling back* the bond. This makes sense if you think about it. If your state highway department sold bonds for bridge construction when the going interest rate for a municipal bond was 7 percent and now they could float the same bonds for 5 percent, you can imagine that the politicians and taxpayers would love the savings in interest payouts to bondholders.

Note   U.S. Treasuries aren't callable, but most municipal and corporate bonds feature call provisions.

How Bond Funds React to Interest Rates

As you see in this chart, the bonds with the longest maturities are hit the hardest when interest rates jump, but they profit the most when rates are shrinking. This example shows the effect of interest rate changes on a $1,000 bond.

Length of time	Rates fall 1 % and bond's bond maturity value rises to:	Rates rise 1% and bond's value drops to:
3 years	$1,027.50	$973
5 years	$1,044	$958
10 years	$1,078	$929
30 years	$1,154.50	$875

* Assumes a 6% coupon, some figures have been rounded off.

Source: T. Rowe Price Associates

Bondholders hate call provisions because the debtor inevitably makes the call at the worst time, when interest rates have dropped. By canceling their old debts, a borrower can issue new IOUs at a cheaper interest rate. When a bond is called, the lender is forced to relinquish the bond for a predetermined price. This price is spelled out when the bond is originally issued. Of course, this leaves a bondholder looking for a better deal at a terrible time. Chances are a replacement will offer a punier yield unless you're willing to buy a riskier bond.

To protect yourself, always check how quickly a lender can renege on the deal. A callable bond will stipulate the dates when the bond can be redeemed and the call premium, if any. The interest rates offered may vary with each potential call date. You should understand these yields:

✦ **Simple yield.** The simple yield equals the coupon rate. If you buy a $1,000 bond with a 6.5 percent coupon, for example, the simple yield would be 6.5 percent.

✦ **Current yield.** Once you buy a bond, its value fluctuates and this movement determines the current yield. To obtain the current yield, you divide the bond's annual income by its current market price. If the price of your original $1,000 bond with a simple yield of 7 percent slipped to $850, for example, the current yield would rise to 8.2 percent ($70 divided by $850).

✦ **Yield to maturity.** If your bond can be called, this measurement may not be especially relevant, because it represents what you'd earn if you held onto it until the bitter end. This yield assumes the bond is held until maturity and factors in the semiannual coupon payments you'll receive and earnings on the reinvestment of those coupon payments (it's assumed you will reinvest for a similar rate of return).

✦ **Yield to call.** This is a more realistic measure of the impact of a bond's call provisions. It is calculated the same as yield to maturity, but it assumes that the bond will be called at the first opportunity. If the yield to call is considerably smaller than the bond's yield to maturity, search for a more attractive bond.

Credit risk

Because bonds are loans, anybody buying one needs to check the debtor's creditworthiness. You wouldn't loan money to just anybody who asks, would you? In the financial world, not all debt is alike. A wide gulf separates the best borrowers from the marginal ones.

Buying a U.S. Treasury bond is like lending money to your mother. These bonds are backed by the "full faith and credit" of the federal government. No matter what your opinion of the crowd running Washington, D.C., the chances of the government collapsing into chaos and defaulting on its obligations is nil. On the other extreme of the risk spectrum are junk bond issuers you may have never heard of, which could be on the brink of defaulting on what they owe.

Fortunately for bond shoppers, independent bond-rating services, such as Moody's Investors Service and Standard & Poor's, evaluate the financial health of the issuers and give them a letter grade. If the rating firms think a company or a governmental issuer's chances of honoring its obligations are lousy, they receive a lower rating. Typically, issuers with mediocre ratings have to pay higher rates of interest to lure investors. See Table 17-1 for a rundown of bond ratings.

Note Not all bonds receive a rating. You need to be especially cautious with these unrated bonds. They can be highly speculative and potentially disastrous.

Online Bond Value Calculators

Are you debating whether to buy a tax-free muni bond or a taxable corporate? Maybe you are agonizing over some other fixed-income question. Let the mother of online financial calculators run the numbers for you. Financenter.com, which provides many personal finance sites with calculators, maintains a dozen bond calculators. Here are just some of the questions it can answer:

✦ How will interest rate changes affect my bond's current value?

✦ What is my return if I sell today?

✦ What is my current yield on coupon income received?

✦ What price should I pay?

✦ Should I buy a zero coupon bond?

✦ Should I buy a tax-free or taxable bond?

Table 17-1
Credit Quality Ratings

Moody's	Standard & Poor's	Description
Investment Grade Bonds		
Aaa	AAA	These top ratings are enjoyed by Treasuries and federal agency bonds, which are considered to offer the highest quality with the lowest risk.
Aa	AA	Bonds with this rating are also of excellent quality; they're just a step below the very best.
A	A	This rating is bestowed on high medium-grade bonds.
Baa	BBB	This rating is the lowest for investment-grade bonds. A bond with this rating is characterized as a medium-grade bond; such a bond is creditworthy, but it has a moderate risk.
Junk Bonds		
Ba	BB	A bond with this rating has a moderate chance of remaining safe. Bonds that receive this grade and those ranked lower are considered speculative; that's why they're called junk or high-yield bonds.
B	B	The chances of your principal and interest payments continuing uninterrupted could be small if you purchase bonds with this rating.
Caa	CCC	The bond issuer for bonds of this poor quality might need favorable business and economic conditions to meet its obligations.
Ca	CC	Highly speculative bonds, they are often in default or close to it.
C (their lowest rating)	C	These bonds at this rock-bottom grade could be in default or teetering toward it.
	D	Bonds in default.

Whether you buy individual bonds or stick with bond funds, credit risk matters. When shopping for an individual bond, a broker can tell you the credit ratings. But you shouldn't stop there. Credit ratings can slip or improve. You'll want to know if a debtor is on *credit watch*—in danger of having its credit rating downgraded.

You can find out what a borrower's credit rating is, as well as credit watch information, by calling the ratings desk at either Standard & Poor's or Moody's Investors Services. You may also be able to obtain some information on the pair's Web sites.

   ✦ Standard & Poor's at (212) 438-2400 or www.standardandpoors.com

   ✦ Moody's Investors Services at (212) 553-0377 or www.moodys.com

Shopping with the Yield Curve

When setting out to buy a bond, most of us are filled with questions about which route to take. Is now the right time to buy municipal bonds? What about mortgage-backed securities? Are junk bonds looking attractive? To answer these questions, you should look at the Treasury *yield curve,* which tracks the yields of U.S. Treasuries.

You can find this all-important curve published every day in *The Wall Street Journal.* It doesn't look like much—a toddler could draw it. But the bond world depends upon it for its very livelihood. That's because you can't determine whether a bond is desirable until you consult the curve.

Note In the traditional curve, the yields are puniest for the fast-maturing Treasury bills. The biggest payoffs are reserved for those willing to bet on the bonds with the longest maturity: Investors who buy long bonds get compensated for holding on so patiently.

The textbook Treasury curve looks like a sloping mountainside. The left side of the curve reflects the yields that the shortest-term Treasuries are commanding. The middle of the curve is reserved for the intermediate Treasuries, while the right side of the curve belongs to the 30-year bonds.

Some Periods Are Curvier than Others

Sometimes the curve dramatically changes its shape. At its most extreme, the curve inverts. This happened in the late 1970s and early 1980s. During times like these, an investor choosing a short-term Treasury will capture a better yield than somebody favoring intermediate or long-term Treasuries. In 1980, for instance, the yield on a three-month Treasury was an amazing 16 percent, while the 30-year Treasury was yielding just 12 percent. This phenomenon usually happens when economists warn of looming inflation and a hike in short-term interest rates. Investors, not wanting to miss out on this potential interest rate hike, siphon money out of long-term bonds and funnel it into the short-term bonds.

By glancing at the yield curve, you'll know immediately which Treasury maturities are offering the highest yields. You'll need to know this no matter what type of bond you are in the market for. Why is the Treasury curve so important to all bond investors?

The yield curve: Bond world benchmark

No matter what bond you buy, its price is linked to U.S. Treasuries. Treasuries have always served as a benchmark for all bonds, just as the Standard & Poor's 500 Index has for stocks. The standard benchmark currently is the 10-year Treasury. When shopping for any kind of bond, you need to figure out the *spread,* which is the difference between the yield of a Treasury and the yield of another type of bond. You'll hear brokers and financial planners refer to these spreads as *basis points.* A basis point equals one hundredth of a percentage point. One hundred basis points equal 1 percent.

Tip

Bond investors get especially excited when the spread between Treasuries and other types of bonds is greater than usual. That's when you can find the best bargains among non-Treasuries.

If you look at Table 17-2, you can see that an investment-grade corporate bond's typical spread is a bit over 100 basis points, or 1 percentage point. Consequently, if corporates offer a yield that's 150 or 200 basis points better than a Treasury, that's considered a bargain.

Table 17-2
Historic Bond Spreads With Treasuries *

Type of Bond	Average Spread
Mortgage-backed bonds	118 basis points
Investment-grade corporate bonds	72 basis points
High-yield (junk) corporate bonds	416 basis points
Municipal bonds**	Yield traditionally equals 80% to 85% of Treasury yield

*Historical yield spreads during past 10 years

**A muni bond's performance can't be characterized as a spread, but is measured by how the muni yield stacks up to the Treasury.

The yield spread can stray significantly from the average, so it pays to stay alert. For instance, during the past ten years, the highest spread between Treasuries and mortgage-backed bonds has been nearly 200 basis points. At other times, the spread has narrowed to as little as 74 basis points. During the same time period, the spread between Treasuries and investment-grade corporate bonds has ranged from 36 basis points to as much as 167 basis points.

New Benchmark: And the Winner Is . . .

In the bond world, the 30-year Treasury bond has always been the top banana. Professionals have long used it to gauge the price of all other bonds. In 2000, however, something remarkable happened. The 30-year Treasury was dethroned by the 10-year Treasury note.

Why the switch? The yield on the 30-year Treasury bond had become too unreliable. Its price began soaring when the federal government concluded that it no longer needed to issue so many of them. With Washington running a budget surplus for the third year in a row, the government didn't need to remain such a voracious borrower. The government not only slowed down its borrowing, but it began buying back some of its outstanding 30-year bonds from institutional investors.

With fear spreading that the 30-year Treasury would someday become extinct, bond traders quickly snatched up the available 30-year Treasuries that hit the market. Their hoarding jacked up the price of these bonds and shrank their yields.

However, the disappearance of the 30-year Treasury isn't a sure thing. If the budget surpluses disappear, thanks to an economic slowdown or the gigantic tax cuts approved by Congress in 2001, the government could crank up its borrowing. But for now, when you want to compare the yield spread between any type of bond and a Treasury, the 10-year Treasury is the one to use.

Factors affecting spreads

You can't search for fat spreads with blinders on. A premium yield might indicate skeletons in a corporate closet. When junk bonds approached historic spreads in 2000, these bonds were defaulting at alarming rates. At one point, more than 6 out of every 100 issuers were defaulting on their debt obligations. The default rate hadn't approached that level since the beginning of the 1990s. Consequently, investors were assuming an unusually high risk by investing in junk bonds.

Sometimes, however, the bond market overreacts. While many junk bonds were getting what they deserved in 2000, you could argue that the investment grade corporate bonds of blue chip companies were being penalized unfairly. These corporations, which enjoy sterling bond ratings, almost never shirk their obligations to their lenders. By one measure, the default rate for investment-grade corporate bonds in 2000 was an infinitesimal .04 percent.

Note   Sometimes the yield spread can't be traced to anything inherently wrong with a bond category. Sometimes Treasuries are simply more popular, which drives up their price and decreases their yield.

Some investors look for significant yield spreads in an attempt to make a quick buck. They might buy corporate bonds, for instance, when the yield spread is great, and then trade out for a profit when the spread for new corporates has tightened.

How do you know what the spreads are? Besides looking at the yield curve in *The Wall Street Journal,* find the average bond yield in various bond categories in the WSJ's daily Money & Investing section. You can calculate a spread by comparing a Treasury's yield with a different type of bond.

Bonds Versus Bond Funds

One of the first issues someone venturing into the fixed-income world must decide is whether to invest in individual bonds or bond funds. Many sophisticated stock investors decide that it makes more sense to own a portfolio of individual equities rather than funds. That's not necessarily true on the fixed-income side. For most people, bond funds make more sense, but there are notable exceptions. Below are the pros and cons of both approaches.

Bond fund advantages

There are many reasons someone might want to purchase shares in a bond fund rather than buy individual bonds. Here are the major reasons:

They provide quick and easy diversification.

Getting started in a bond fund can cost as little as $500 or $1,000. You can also add money in dribs and drabs—say $50 or $100—any time you please. By purchasing an all-purpose bond fund, like Vanguard Total Bond Market Index Fund or Harbor Bond Fund, you enjoy instant diversification.

 Recently, for instance, Harbor Bond Fund held bonds from such diverse sources as the Government National Mortgage Association (Ginnie Mae), the Federal National Mortgage Association (Fannie Mae), Daimler Chrysler, Citicorp, United Airlines, and Nabors Industries, an oil driller.

In contrast, purchasing just one municipal bond can require a minimum of $5,000, and the admission price for a single Ginnie Mae can be $25,000. At that rate, you'll need at least $50,000 to $100,000 (and some experts suggest the total is much higher) to diversify your portfolio. Yet diversification is necessary to keep your risks lower.

Funds are convenient and flexible.

To withdraw money from your bond fund, you can write checks off it or redeem by phone. Selling an individual bond can be harder and more costly, especially since professional bond dealers may prefer trading in huge blocks. Somebody wanting to unload an individual bond may also face problems with *liquidity*—meaning there is little or no demand for the bond. Without liquidity, the owner may have to accept a far smaller price for the bond.

Historical Total Return of Bond Mutual Funds

Here are the historical performance figures for a variety of different bond fund categories:

Type of Bond	Average Annual Total Return		
	3 yrs.	5 yrs.	10 yrs.
Ultra short-term bonds	5.5%	5.8%	5.22%
Short-term bonds	5.77%	6.02%	6.4%
Intermediate-term bonds	5.25%	6.46%	7.39%
Long-term bonds	4.17%	6.42%	7.64%
Municipal bonds	3.76%	5.09%	6.21%
High-yield corporate	−2.8%	3.13%	8.3%
Multisector	.95%	4.98%	7.55%
International Bond	1.58%	3.65%	5.33%
Emerging Markets Bond	.62%	8.26%	NA
Convertible securities	7.63%	11.26%	12.56%

Source: Morningstar, Inc.

They offer professional management.

Do you really want to spend your free time analyzing a casino junk bond or a muni offering from West Virginia? Or how about figuring out the currency implication of a German bond? Let the fixed-income professionals, who get really jazzed about bonds, do the research for you. Professional bond managers are far better equipped to search nooks and crannies for undiscovered bonds with great potential. All you have to do is find the right fund. This won't be hard if you stick with fund companies that are well known for their razor-thin expenses, such as the Vanguard Group.

Interest is distributed monthly.

Bond funds distribute their interest income to shareholders in monthly checks. If you own an individual bond, however, interest checks are usually issued twice a year.

Bond funds give you the option of automatically reinvesting that monthly payout, which is an ideal arrangement if you don't need the regular income. If you hold individual bonds and want to invest rather than spend, it's up to you to find a place to invest it.

Funds boast high liquidity.

If you want to bail out of a bond fund, it's easy to do. You can often sell shares online or with a quick phone call. Your shares will be redeemed at whatever the closing price or *net asset value* (NAV) of the fund is at the close of the trading day. If you own individual bonds, especially if they happen to be in disfavor at the time, it could be hard unloading them. You might be forced to sell them at a far lower price than you expected.

Funds make it easier to arrange tax losses.

Each December, investors start contemplating ways to minimize taxes for the year. One traditional strategy is selling stocks and bonds at a loss since the loss can be written off on the yearly tax return. It's easy to follow this approach with bond funds. Suppose bonds have been hammered and you've got a paper loss on your Vanguard Total Bond Market Index Fund. You can sell your shares to capture the loss on your tax return and then transfer the money into a similar bond fund, such as Schwab Total Bond Market Index Fund. The federal government doesn't mind the swap and you'll pay less taxes for the year. Making the same move with individual bonds can be costlier and a greater hassle. You'll have to find replacement bonds, as well as pay commission costs.

Individual bond advantages

Here are the reasons you might want to stick with individual bonds instead.

Your income stream is predictable.

When you purchase an individual bond, you know up front what your interest payments will be. This can be especially important if you're retired and living on a fixed income. An investor can also purchase an individual bond, such as a U.S. Treasury zero coupon bond, that matures on a target date, such as the year a child is heading off to college. In contrast, a bond fund manager typically doesn't hold bonds until maturity so the amount of a fund investor's income checks varies each month.

Capital gains taxes are controllable.

Since you decide when or if to sell your bond, you are in control of your own tax destiny. If you hold a bond until maturity, you will not owe capital gains taxes. Even if you hold onto a bond fund, however, you may still be stuck with yearly capital gains taxes. These unwelcome taxes can crop up when a fund manager unloads bonds that have appreciated in value.

You know what you own.

If you own individual bonds, you'll know what's inside your portfolio. Okay, that's obvious, but consider the alternative. If you've invested in a fund, you can't know for sure what bonds the fund holds. By the time you see the fund's semiannual report, the actual portfolio could be quite different. (A fund is required to report its holdings only twice a year.) This wouldn't be a problem if fund managers stuck to their investing mandate, but some managers find it tempting to stray. A manager of a conservative bond fund, who is looking to burnish its performance stats, for instance, may try to turbo-charge its portfolio with risky bonds.

Individual bonds can be cheaper.

The debate centering on whether funds or individual bonds are cheaper may never be resolved. But the research arm of Charles Schwab, the brokerage firm, has tackled the question. Not surprisingly, the research found that the cost of building an individual bond portfolio decreases as the amount of the investment increases. The study was helpful in pinpointing a break-even point. The researchers concluded that if you invest $50,000 in individual bonds, the costs, in most cases, will be cheaper than most bond fund alternatives. The study, however, assumed that investors held the individual bonds until maturity.

Tip   If you aren't a buy-and-hold bond investor, you may do better with a bond fund.

Schwab calculated the cost of building a $50,000 portfolio of either Treasuries, investment-grade corporate bonds, or municipal bonds of various maturities. Here are the breakdowns of what each of these portfolios of individual bonds could cost the investor each year:

✦ U.S. Treasury bond portfolio: 0.13 percent of total assets a year ($65)

✦ Corporate bond portfolio: 0.11 percent of total assets a year ($55)

✦ Municipal bonds: 0.21 percent of total assets per year ($105)

Schwab compared those costs to those of bond funds, available through the brokerage firm, that charge either average or low annual expenses, and concluded that buying individual bonds versus funds is a much closer call if you make the comparison with the very cheapest bond funds. Table 17-3 shows the results of the comparison.

Table 17-3 Average and Lowest Costs for Bond Mutual Funds		
Type of Fund	*Average Cost Mutual Fund*	*Lowest Cost Mutual Fund*
Treasury	$385	$75
Corporate Bond Fund	$370	$100
Municipal Bond Fund	$340	$95

Fund Bargain Shoppers

If you buy shares in a bond fund, make sure you aren't paying too much. Here's a breakdown of average expense ratios for various types of bond funds. Never invest in a bond fund that passes along above-average costs. In fact, the cheaper the better. (See Chapter 5 for a definition of an expense ratio.)

Fund Categories	Average Expense Ratio
Junk bonds	1.3%
Global income	1.39%
Investment-grade corporate bonds	1.04%
GNMA funds	1.06%
U.S. government funds	1.21%
U.S. Treasuries	.77%
High-yield municipal bonds	1.22%
Municipal bonds	1.1%
General bonds	1.01%

Source: Lipper, a Reuters Company

Resource To get a free copy of the complete report, entitled *Fixed-Income Investing—Should You Own Individual Bonds or Bond Mutual Funds,* order by phone at (800) 435-4000 or visit the mutual fund section of Schwab's Web site at www.schwab.com/funds. Once there, click on "Investment Topics."

You can hedge your bets with a bond ladder.

Everyone appreciates that it's difficult to know when it's the right time to buy a particular stock. This same indecision can grip fixed-income investors too. Smart investors like to accumulate longer-term bonds when interest rates are poised to drop so they can enjoy high yields when other bonds are offering stingy yields. If rates are on the verge of rising, investors know to scoop up short-term bonds because they can keep capturing higher rates as these bonds mature during inflationary times.

There is just one thing wrong with this strategy. Nobody knows for certain where interest rates are heading. You might be congratulating yourself for scooping up a high-yielding Treasury, but there's no guarantee that Treasuries in a few months or a year aren't going to look much better.

So what's the solution? If you want to buy individual bonds, consider building a *bond ladder.* With this strategy, you invest equal amounts of money in individual bonds with maturities of varying lengths. Each rung of the ladder contains one or more bonds that mature at roughly the same time. This strategy works best with Treasuries. You can build it in different ways, but here's one suggestion. You purchase equal amounts of Treasuries that mature in 2, 4, 6, 8 and 10 years. (The average maturity of this portfolio is 6 years.) When a rung of Treasuries matures, you replace them with new 10-year Treasury notes. One significant benefit from laddering a portfolio like this is that interest rate fluctuations won't be a big threat because bonds are regularly maturing and you're regularly buying new ones. Laddering helps minimize interest rate fluctuations just as dollar-cost averaging helps smooth an investor's exposure to price volatility with stock and mutual fund investments. Laddering should produce a higher return than you'd typically get if you kept a stockpile of short-term bonds.

Summary

✦ As with any investment, understand the risks that bondholders face.

✦ Calculate the yield spread between Treasuries and other bond categories before investing.

✦ The average investor usually fares better investing in most bonds through a mutual fund.

✦ Don't be buffaloed by a bond fund that offers an unusually high yield; it could be harboring risky investments.

✦ Consider laddering your bonds to reduce your portfolio's risks and help provide a dependable income stream.

✦   ✦   ✦

Uncle Sam's Bond World

I n this chapter, you'll learn about U.S. Treasuries and other bonds that are linked to the federal government. You'll also discover how a new generation of bonds that fight inflation works and whether they are appropriate for your portfolio. A primer on savings bonds is also tucked inside this chapter. Finally, you'll learn about mortgage-backed securities, which march to the beat of their own drummer.

U.S. Treasuries: The Safest Bonds on the Planet

Remember what your mom used to give you when you got a cold? She probably rummaged in the kitchen cabinet for a can of Campbell's Chicken Noodle soup. Or if you were really lucky, she threw a chicken in a pot and cooked her own.

While chicken soup is an elixir for runny noses and pounding sinuses, government bonds are the financial market's comfort food. When a political conflict breaks out in the Middle East or a currency crisis spreads like spilt milk throughout Southeast Asia, the stock market often starts sliding. At times like these, investors intuitively flock to U.S. Treasuries. Knowing that the federal government backs these bonds with a 100 percent guarantee can make the most skittish investor relax. With its unbeatable guarantee, the federal government is regarded as the world's most reliable borrower. The sun will rise each day and so too will the federal government pay its debts.

Yet Treasuries attract a variety of investors, from the most conservative, who feel secure with the government's sterling credit history, to the most daring, who buy Treasuries to speculate on interest rate movements. Treasuries offer a wide range of maturities, making them suitable for many different purposes and portfolios. Here's the Treasury lineup:

✦ U.S. Treasury bills: Nicknamed T-bills, they have maturities of 13 weeks and 26 weeks. (The one-year bill was discontinued in 2001.)

✦ U.S. Treasury notes: Maturities range from 2 to 10 years.

✦ U.S. Treasury bonds: Maturities range from 10 to 30 years.

Except for Treasury bills, which are bought at a discount, Treasuries are purchased at face value, in multiples of $1,000. So if you want to buy $10,000 worth of Treasury notes, you'll write a check for $10,000. You make your money through the notes' regular interest payments. If your clutch of 10 Treasury notes came with a 5.5 percent coupon, you'd pocket $550 a year in interest.

 Note
There are actually two categories of Treasuries. The marketable ones—bills, notes and bonds—greatly interest Wall Street, while savings bonds usually just sit in safety deposit boxes and desk drawers across the country.

Advantages of Treasuries

Here are the most appealing features of Treasuries:

There's the safety factor.

These bonds, which are issued by the federal government, win the prize for the highest credit rating. There are no safer bonds on the planet. If you invest $10,000 in a 30-year Treasury today, you can be sure that you'll receive a total of 60 interest payments evenly spread throughout the next three decades. And when the bond matures, your $10,000 will be returned.

Why You Don't Need a Treasury Bond Fund

There are plenty of excellent reasons to invest in bonds through mutual funds, but there is one glaring exception. For many investors, it makes little sense to invest in Treasuries through a fund.

One of the charms of a bond mutual fund is that it reduces your credit risk. If you're gung-ho on junk bonds, investing in a mutual fund is prudent because it should be safer having a professional cherry-picking the bonds. If you buy a handful on your own, you won't necessarily own enough to protect yourself against a financial disaster, if for instance, one or two of your bonds default. However, if an individual bond in a fund portfolio self-destructs, it may barely make a ripple. But this credit risk isn't a concern with Treasuries because Treasuries aren't going to default.

Another reason why a Treasury bond fund isn't necessary is because individual Treasuries can be bought at no cost. In contrast, a fund will pass along yearly expenses.

You get a break from state and local taxes.

The interest paid on Treasuries is exempt from state and local taxes, but holders still owe federal taxes. Treasuries are especially popular in areas with high state and local tax rates such as New York City.

Treasuries provide a safe haven during tumultuous times.

When a toddler bruises his knee, the only place he wants to be is on Mom's lap. Grown-up investors don't behave much differently. In times of economic volatility, nervous investors want certainty and they get it with Treasuries. This phenomenon isn't hard to spot. When the stock market took a dramatic stumble in 2000, for instance, Treasuries experienced an impressive rally. In the late 1990s, when Asia and Russia were experiencing tumultuous times, Treasuries once again were phenomenally popular.

Savvy investors have made lots of money by capitalizing on the market's rush to quality. These investors react quickly to economic calamities throughout the world and in our own backyard. They attempt to snatch up Treasuries before the hordes of worried investors start the Treasury stampede. The eventual rush to buy Treasuries inflates their prices, which provides speculative investors with an opportunity to sell them at a tidy profit.

Treasuries can boast of excellent liquidity.

If you must sell a Treasury prematurely, it's an easy process. That's because Treasuries enjoy what in bondspeak is called *liquidity,* which means they can easily be sold for cash. There are always plenty of buyers willing to snap up your Treasuries at the market price.

The cheapest way to buy or sell Treasuries is through TreasuryDirect. Once you've established an account, you can purchase Treasuries on the Internet or by phone. The government will also sell Treasuries for you, after soliciting three bids, to the highest bidder. You will be charged $34 per issue for this service.

To get started, you'll need to fill out a form that can be downloaded from the TreasuryDirect Web site (www.treasurydirect.gov) or by calling the TreasuryDirect toll-free number at (800) 722-2678.

Buying and selling Treasuries without a broker is very beneficial for individual investors. One of the big knocks against buying many types of individual bonds is broker transaction costs. In fact, such costs can sometimes be a real deal buster. With Treasuries, it needn't be a consideration.

Treasuries can't be called.

Unlike many other type of bonds, once you buy a Treasury, you need not worry that the government is going to rain on your parade when interest rates change. Treasuries are not callable. (There is an exception for some Treasuries issued before 1985).

In contrast, many other bond issuers reserve the right to pay back their IOUs if they can obtain better lending arrangements in the future. For instance, a corporation might issue bonds offering an 8 percent coupon, but years later might pay off the loans when it can now borrow money for 7 percent. Understandably, this leaves bondholders in the lurch.

Treasuries can substitute for cash.

Treasury bills can be a substitute for certificates of deposit and other cash investments. It wasn't that long ago that a $10,000 minimum investment, made T-bills an impractical cash haven for many. But today you can buy T-bills in multiples of $1,000.

Tip   Unlike CDs, Treasuries offer that tax break and you won't be hit with an early withdrawal penalty if you want to sell before maturity.

Weaknesses of Treasuries

Treasuries do have some drawbacks. Here are the two major ones.

Lower yields.

Because Treasuries are super safe, the yields you can expect typically won't be as great as with other types of bonds. As you'll learn in this chapter, for instance, other government bonds, which are a tad riskier, typically offer a yield that is a bit more than one percentage point higher. The spread between junk bond yields and Treasuries is far higher. As an investor, you have to decide whether sacrificing a potentially greater return is worth sacrificing the extra safety.

Before buying a Treasury, you should compare its yield to those of other bonds. If the spread between the yield on Treasuries and other types of bonds is greater than usual, you might consider these alternatives. This can happen, for instance, when Treasuries are in great demand because of some overseas turbulence. When the price of a Treasury is driven up, its yield drops. Table 18-1 shows the annual average returns Treasury investors have received.

Table 18-1
Annual Average Returns of U.S. Treasuries*

Type of Bond	5 Year Average	10 Year Average
30-year Treasury	7.05%	7.99%
10-year Treasury	7.24	6.71%
2-year Treasury	6.13%	5.93%

*This includes the yield and price appreciation

Volatility can cause a loss.

Treasuries are safe, but that doesn't mean you can't lose money. You won't suffer financially, however, as long as you hold onto a Treasury until it matures. But if you need to sell a Treasury prematurely, you might have to sell at a loss or, if you're lucky, a profit. Of course, the price volatility appeals to bond traders. Just like stock investors, adventurous bond speculators try to profit from Treasury price fluctuations.

Zero Coupon Bonds

Just like Treasuries, zero coupon bonds can be traced back to the U.S. Treasury Department. As with the plain vanilla Treasuries, the creditworthiness of these bonds, which are sold through brokerage firms, is as sturdy as the Rock of Gibraltar.

Note   Zero coupon bonds act quite differently from regular Treasuries, which is why they are the most volatile of all federal government securities.

These bonds got their name because the bondholder doesn't receive a regular semi-annual interest payment. As explained in the previous chapter, coupon is another name for the rate of interest a bondholder can expect. You will see Treasury zeros referred to as STRIPS. As you'll soon learn, zero coupon investors make their money in a different way.

Strengths of zeroes

Zeroes offer these attractive reasons to invest:

They are affordable.

The cheap admission price makes zeroes alluring to many. Investors buy zeroes at a deep discount to their face value, and get a payoff for the full face value of $1,000 when the bond matures. The difference between the amount paid up front and the payout at maturity is the profit. The longer the maturity, the greater the up-front discount; you get that little perk because your money is tied up longer.

In contrast, most bonds are bought at full face value. If you purchased a 10-year Treasury bond, for instance, you'd pay $1,000 up front and earn money through the regular interest checks.

They pose no reinvestment danger.

Zeroes can be a logical choice for bond lovers, who don't require the regular income that other bonds spin off. Receiving steady income checks when you don't need them can be a real dilemma. You may struggle to find a spot to park this income that offers a comparable rate of return. That hassle is avoided with zeroes since you don't receive any interest checks throughout the life of the bond.

Zeroes can be ideal for fixed investment goals.

Zeroes are favored by investors who know they'll need a fixed amount of money in a certain year. For instance, if your child is heading to college in 10 years, you can buy a zero that matures when your valedictorian graduates from high school. (Of course, if you've got that long of a horizon before college, it's best to put most, if not all, of this cash in the stock market.)

Tip
Some parents prefer to use zeroes once a child is in or approaching high school since investing in stocks can become too risky with college just around the corner. Instead, they buy zeroes that will mature right before the fall semester to cover the first year's tuition and expenses. You can continue to do that for each year.

Weaknesses of zeroes

Naturally, you must explore the downside of zeroes before investing.

Zeroes are potentially volatile.

Zeroes can be as safe as the spare change sitting on your dresser. That assurance, however, only applies if you hold onto a zero coupon bond until maturity. If you want to bail prematurely, watch out. Holding zeroes can be a lot like getting stuck on the 30th floor of a skyscraper during an earthquake: You're going to experience a lot of sway.

Caution
A zero coupon bond is far more sensitive to changes in interest rates than are other bonds. The price of a 30-year zero coupon bond, for instance, is about three times more sensitive to interest rate fluctuations than the 30-year Treasury bond.

Say you hold a 30-year Treasury that pays 7.04 percent interest and a 30-year zero with an interest rate of 7.27 percent. The worst happens—at least from your perspective—and interest rates during the course of the year increase two percentage points. Oops. The total return for your Treasury is a negative 13.12 percent. But that's nothing compared to what happens to your poor zero. It skids a negative 38.22 percent. Why is the zero more allergic to interest-rate hikes? Because it doesn't provide biannual income. Without that regular income cushion, the bonds react violently to even the slightest hiccup in interest rates.

Note
On the other hand, an investor can make a quick fortune with zeroes if interest rates sag, which is why speculators who like to bet on the movements of interest rates adore zeroes.

These aggressive investors snatch up zeroes with the longest maturities when they see interest rates declining such as when they feel the nation is heading into a recession. They try to dump them right before interest rates start heating up.

You can't buy zeroes directly.

Unlike U.S. Treasuries, zeroes can't be purchased directly from the federal government. You'll have to buy from a broker and pay a commission. The markup is included in the price you're quoted by a full-service or discount brokerage firm.

Tip   The difference in commissions can vary significantly, so if you buy individual zeroes it's best to check the price at more than one brokerage firm.

An alternative is investing in a mutual fund devoted to zero coupons. The place to go is the American Century mutual fund family. Amazingly, in a universe of thousands of mutual funds, this fund family just about has a monopoly on the niche. You select the fund based upon the year of maturity you desire, ranging from 2005 to 2030. American Century Target Maturities Trust: 2030, for example, contains a portfolio of bonds that mature around the year 2030.

 Resource   Contact American Century at (800) 345-2021 or www.americancentury.com.

Not surprisingly, the American Century funds with the longest maturities are the most volatile. These funds are very popular when interest rates flag. When rates fall, the zero coupon funds with the most distant maturities can rocket onto the list of the year's best bond performers. In 1995, when interest rates plunged, for instance, American Century Target Maturities Trust: 2020 zoomed past the pack by soaring 61.34 percent. On the flip side, the zero coupon funds with the longest maturity can fall apart when interest rates climb. When this happened in 1999, American Century Target Maturities Trust: 2025 returned a negative 20.8 percent.

Note   American Century funds with the longest maturities often make either the year's best or worst bond fund lists. In 2000, for instance, a trio of American Century zero coupon funds claimed the titles of the no. 1, 2, and 3 best performing bond funds of the year.

Unlike traditional mutual funds, an American Century zero coupon bond fund will shut down when its portfolio of zeroes matures. Investors are informed of this up front. A future target redemption amount is established each time one of these funds is created.

There's the tax pain.

With zero coupons, you must pay federal taxes on the interest that accrues on the zero each year, even though you don't actually receive any of it until your zero matures. Do you really want to pay taxes on money that you won't be able to enjoy for 20 or 30 years? Not likely.

Tip   If you tuck your zeroes into an IRA, you won't get hit by those yearly tax bills.

TIPS and I Bonds

You will run across very few show-stopping events in the world of bonds. There certainly aren't any initial public offerings (IPOs) to shake things up, as the stock world has. But the Treasury Department managed to generate some excitement among bond wonks in the latter 1990s by unveiling two new types of bonds. The latest bonds in the federal lineup are the Treasury Inflation-Protection Securities, (TIPS), and the I Bond, which is a new type of savings bond. The "I" stands for inflation indexed.

Surfing the waves of inflation

While investors yawned during the rollouts, economists recognized the new bonds' virtue: their ability to protect against inflation. As any bondholder knows, inflation, which tends to boost interest rates, is public enemy no. 1. When interest rates spike, investors pour money into certificates of deposit and other safe cash investments that can promise a higher interest rate. This leaves bondholders earning lower yields than offerings from the local bank. If they abandon their bonds and join the stampede to cash investments, they'll discover that their bonds are worth far less on the open market. When interest rates are high, bonds are also hit with another body blow. Inflation eats away at the real value of the bond's interest and principal payments.

TIPS and I Bonds are intended to prevent this ugly carnage by increasing in value during inflationary times. Investors who buy either type will prosper if inflation hits. The bonds, however, won't perform as well if prices remain flat and inflation just doesn't happen. When inflation was rampant in the 1970s, TIPS, for instance, would have outperformed almost any other financial investment. During the 1990s, however, these bonds would have provided mediocre returns. In 1997, the year TIPS were launched, the regular 10-year Treasury returned 10.5 percent versus 1 percent for the TIPS.

> **Note**   Everybody on Wall Street, as well as individual investors, call these bonds TIPS, but officially the Treasury Department has a different name—Treasury Inflation-Indexed Securities or TIIS—which no one ever uses.

Using I Bonds and TIPS to your advantage

Since mere mortals can't accurately predict interest rate movements, fixed-income investors, who desire a hedge against inflation, can start here. These inflation bonds serve as an excellent inflation hedge because they share a negative correlation with stocks and other types of bonds. That is, when stocks and bonds are getting pummeled during inflationary periods, TIPS and I Bonds will shine. Adding inflation bonds to your portfolio will reduce your overall investment risk. Because of lower risk, you may decide to scale back on your overall bond holdings and bump up your exposure to stocks.

Savings Bond Resources

Want to brush up on your savings bond IQ? Here's where to turn for help:

✦ **Bureau of the Public Debt:** The Bureau's Savings Bond Calculator can help you determine such things as the value of your bonds now and in the near future, as well as when bonds will stop earning interest. Those who prefer making these calculations offline can download the Savings Bond Wizard. The site also explains the difference between I Bonds and Series EE bonds. Call (304) 480-6112 or the automated line at (800) 4US-BOND. The Web site address is www.savingsbonds.gov.

✦ **Savings Bond Customer Service Unit, Federal Reserve Bank of Kansas City Customer:** Service reps can answer all your savings bonds questions, including what the redemption values of your bonds are. The phone number is (800) 333-2919. There are also service centers in Buffalo, NY, Richmond, VA, Pittsburgh and Minneapolis. See Resource section.

✦ **Morningstar:** Would you love to see people argue about the merits of I Bonds versus TIPS? You'll be surprised how many knowledgeable investors pontificate on subjects like these in Morningstar's forums. Most of the conversations about savings bonds and TIPS take place in the Bond Squad and Vanguard Diehards forums. Go to www.morningstar.com.

✦ **Savings Bond Informer:** You receive regular statements for your checking, brokerage, and mutual fund accounts, but the federal government doesn't provide this convenience for its savings bond customers. Sign up with the Savings Bond Informer, for a fee, and you'll receive a customized analysis of your savings bond inventory that can help you track and evaluate your holdings. Through this private bond service, you can also order the book *Savings Bonds: When to Hold, When to Fold and Everything In-Between* (Sage Creek Press, $19.95). Call (800) 927-1901 or go to www.bondinformer.com.

Tip Inflation bonds can substitute for other traditional and less reliable inflation hedges such as gold, real estate, and commodities.

TIPS and I Bonds both share a tantalizing advantage over other investments: the borrower. As you know, there isn't a more creditworthy borrower than the U.S. Treasury. Beyond that, the two bonds work differently.

Note Because of how these bonds are taxed, TIPS are better kept in a retirement account; I Bonds have built-in federal tax deferral.

Getting specifics on TIPS

Before deciding whether an inflation-fighting bond deserves a place in your portfolio, you need to understand the workings of each kind in these basic categories:

- ✦ interest rate calculations
- ✦ tax implications
- ✦ investment minimums
- ✦ maturities
- ✦ selling implications

Starting with TIPS, here's the scoop:

Interest rate calculations

Just like regular bonds, you are guaranteed a coupon or interest rate when you buy TIPS. Say you bought a TIPS that carried a 4 percent coupon. As long as you hold onto the bond, you're guaranteed that 4 percent no matter what happens. Even if inflation disappears or a period of deflation grips the nation, that 4 percent is secure.

The reliability of the initial coupon rate is also shared by traditional bonds, but TIPS go one step further. If the federal government's economists detect inflationary signs, your interest payments will increase. The value of the bond's principal is adjusted twice a year to reflect changes in the federal Consumer Price Index-Urban Consumers (CPI-U). This index measures the price changes of a basket of goods that includes food, clothing, gas, drugs, housing, and doctor bills.

Example

Say inflation inched up 1.5 percent during the first six months after you bought $10,000 worth of TIPS with a 4 percent coupon. Normally, your interest payment would be $400, but when your TIPS are adjusted to reflect inflation, your principal is adjusted upward by 1.5 percent to $10,150. So the interest payment is calculated upon $10,150, bumping it up to $406.

Tax implications

Like regular Treasuries, a TIP investor doesn't have to worry about paying state taxes, but there is a tax hitch. Remember how the principal of a TIPS bond grows when inflation is present? Well, you don't get to pocket that extra principal until you redeem the bond. The Internal Revenue Service, however, won't wait that long to get its cut.

Caution

You'll owe yearly federal income taxes on the inflation-adjusted boost in the value of your principal. This can be particularly galling to investors since they must pay taxes on an investment gain they may not actually touch for 10 to 30 years.

The higher your tax bracket, the worse the tax pain. The income taxes affluent investors could be forced to pay on the phantom principal gains could exceed the interest income checks they receive twice a year. And all TIPS investors will owe federal income taxes on the semiannual income checks they receive.

Tip To skirt the tax dilemma, stick TIPS in a retirement account. The taxes are deferred as long as the TIPS remain there.

Investment minimums

The sky's the limit. Realistically, you can buy any amount of TIPS you'd like. (For most individuals, the limit is $5 million per issue.) You can buy these bonds easily through the TreasuryDirect program. They are issued in $1,000 increments. (See the contact information given earlier in the chapter or in the Resource Guide.) They can also be purchased through brokerage firms, though this will trigger a commission.

You can also purchase exposure to TIPS through mutual funds. If you choose this route, invest in a no-load fund with cheap expenses. Here are two to consider:

✦ Vanguard Inflation-Protected Securities at (800) 635-1511 or www.vanguard.com

✦ American Century Inflation-Adjusted Treasury at (800) 345-2021 or www.americancentury.com

Since you can buy TIPS without a commission directly from the federal government, you might wonder why you'd want to invest in a mutual fund. After all, funds charge yearly expenses. There are two chief reasons to consider investing in TIPS through a fund.

1. **Convenience.** Some investors might find it easier purchasing TIPS through a mutual fund rather than establishing an account with TreasuryDirect. Selling could also be easier through a fund.

2. **Tax relief.** Investing through a fund can address the phantom tax issue that haunts individual TIPS holders. Vanguard, for instance, will not only distribute the regular coupon payments to investors, but also the inflation-adjusted portion of the principal. If you hold individual TIPS, you can't pocket this money until the bond is redeemed or it reaches its maturity. Vanguard shareholders have the option of reinvesting this money back into the fund to buy more shares. In fact, if the principal is not plowed back into the fund, the investment will not grow with inflation.

 Resource For more information on how TIPS and other types of investments are taxed, order IRS Publication 550. Call (800) 829-3676.

Tip

Buying TIPS exposure through a mutual fund isn't a good idea unless you choose a no-load fund that charges very low expenses. The annual expenses for Vanguard's low-priced TIPS fund, for instance, is .25 percent. That means it would cost you $25 a year for a $10,000 investment.

Maturity

Currently, TIPs are sold in two maturities—10 and 30 years.

Selling implications

If you wish to unload your TIPS, you won't find as many willing buyers as for regular Treasuries. TIPs, while they have been popular with institutional investors, haven't captured individual investors' imaginations yet. In comparison to the regular Treasuries, TIPS aren't as liquid. Even so, however, you won't have trouble getting a quote from a broker. When there isn't a robust market of eager buyers, you're less likely to capture a decent price. The bid and ask spread (the difference in the buy and sell prices) can be significant.

What's more, if you sell a TIPS before maturity, you may receive less than what you originally paid due to fluctuations in its market value. (This is the same danger that all bondholders face if they sell bonds prematurely.)

Understanding how I Bonds work

I Bonds differ in some key ways from TIPS but can still be a handy way to stash some cash. Here's how they work:

Interest rate calculations

The I bond's interest rate is generated two different ways. Twice a year, the government sets a base interest rate on its latest batch of I bonds. Every May and November, the government unveils this new rate. In May 2001, for instance, the rate was set at 3 percent. No matter what happens, the I Bond customers who bought a savings bond during the next six months are guaranteed that 3 percent fixed rate for the 30-year life of the bond. What many investors don't appreciate is that this base rate is actually the real rate of return. In other words, the bondholder will enjoy this rate of return even after taking into account the effects of inflation.

How is this possible? In addition to the base rate, there's an inflation rate calculated every six months for all outstanding I bonds, resulting in a little extra interest. That extra interest is added to the bond's value monthly and paid when the bond is cashed in. As with the TIP, this bonus rate is linked to the federal Consumer Price Index-Urban Consumers (CPI-U), which is sensitive to price hikes for such things as gasoline, housing, medical bills, and food. For half of 2001, the inflation adjustment for I bonds was set at 3.62 percent. Consequently, the actual total rate for I bonds issued in May 2001 was an impressive 5.92 percent.

Of course, if inflation disappears, the savings bond customers can forget about this extra return until inflation is officially measured again. As a practical matter, though, the CPI-U almost always detects some inflation. The last year the CPI-U registered no inflation was during a six-month period spanning 1982 and 1983.

Tax implications

Just like TIPS, the interest is subject to federal tax, but not state and local taxes. But here's a key difference: As long as you hold onto an I Bond, taxes aren't a consideration. You will owe nothing until you redeem the bond or it reaches maturity—whichever comes first.

Caution

Of course, the I Bond, unlike the TIPS, doesn't kick off semiannual interest payments. You'll only get your money back, with interest, after you cash it in. If you depend upon income to live, the I Bond can't help.

Investment minimums

A ceiling exists on how many I Bonds you can accumulate, but this won't impact the majority of investors. Each individual can buy up to $30,000 worth of I Bonds a year. This is double the limit imposed on regular EE savings bonds, which you'll learn about shortly. Overall, I Bonds are practical for smaller investors, available in face amounts of $50, $75, $100, $500, $1,000, $5,000, and $10,000.

You can order I Bonds at just about any financial institution. You'll be expected to fill out a form and pay for the bonds, which will arrive in the mail within three weeks. I bonds are also available through some employer-sponsored payroll savings plans.

Maturity

I Bonds earn interest for 30 years. Since the bonds are bought at face value—unlike traditional Series E and EE savings bonds—you needn't be concerned about how long they will take to reach face value.

Tip

Consider buying more bonds in smaller increments, a practice that gives you added flexibility when the time comes to liquidate some of your holdings.

Selling implications

You don't have to hassle with selling an I Bond. You simply redeem the bond at any financial institution. You are prohibited from redeeming one during the first six months after a purchase. If you cash in your I Bond before five years elapse, you'll forfeit three months of interest.

Note

Because they are still fairly new, don't be surprised if a bank clerk seems flustered when you ask to redeem an I Bond.

Traditional Savings Bonds

While financial experts have been touting the advantages of I Bonds, many conservative investors have yet to discover them. Although EE savings bond sales have been slipping, large numbers of small investors continue to sink money into them. More sophisticated investors with greater amounts of money to invest tend to prefer the I bonds. They are using I bonds as an inflation hedge, as well as to diversify a well-rounded portfolio.

A major reason customers continue to stockpile EE bonds is that they don't know of the alternative. The federal government, unlike brokerage firms and mutual fund families, don't mail out glossy literature touting their newest products. Consequently, millions of savings bonds investors haven't even heard of the I Bond.

Caution   The preference for the old savings bond is clearly unfortunate. In many cases, the I Bond is the wiser choice because of the inflation hedge.

Common features of I Bonds and Series EE bonds

As you can see from this list, I bonds and EE bonds share a lot in common, but the differences are critical.

✦ Both earn interest for 30 years.

✦ Both are *interest accrual* bonds, which means the interest a bond generates steadily accrues. The interest is added to the bond, but the investor doesn't pocket it until the bond is redeemed or matures. The bond owner also doesn't have to pay taxes on the gains until the end.

✦ Bonds increase in value each month and interest is compounded twice a year.

✦ Three months of interest is forfeited if a bond isn't held for at least five years.

✦ A bond can't be cashed for at least six months after purchase.

✦ If certain conditions are met, both types can be used tax free for education.

✦ Bonds can be purchased through most financial institutions.

Lost Savings Bonds?

Don't despair if your savings bonds are lost or destroyed. The Bureau of Public Debt replaces them free of charge as long as it can establish that the bonds were not cashed. To safeguard your investment, keep records of the bond serial numbers, issue dates, and registration in a safe place, separate from the bonds. You can download the form from the federal savings bond Web site or call for a copy. The completed form must be mailed to the Bureau of Public Debt in Parkersburg, West Virginia 26106-1328. You can also call (304) 480-6112 or go to www.savingsbonds.gov.

I Bond and Series EE bond differences

The two major differences between the two types of savings bonds lies in how the Series EE bond is originally bought, as well as how its interest rate is calculated. Unlike the I Bond, which is acquired at face value, the Series EE bond is purchased at half its face value. If you bought a $100 Series EE bond, for instance, you'd pay $50. Over the years, the interest on this bond would gradually build up to the point where it was actually worth $100.

The interest on a Series EE bond is based upon 90 percent of the five-year Treasury note yield and while there is no direct inflation protection, the rate is adjusted every six months. Frankly, the way savings bonds increase in value has lead to a great deal of confusion about what those savings bonds that your aunt brought to your baby shower are worth.

EE bonds versus I Bonds

When inflation is present, I Bonds are clearly the better choice. Of course, no one knows for sure when inflation will appear or disappear. This reduces us to an educated guess.

Tip

Daniel J. Pederson, the creator of the Savings Bond Informer, says his research suggests that an I Bond should outperform a Series EE bond if its original base rate is set at 3.25 percent or higher.

Know when to fold 'em

Strange as it may seem, Americans are holding more than $5.3 billion worth of old savings bonds that have stopped paying interest. If you discover that bonds sitting in your desk drawer no longer pay interest, redeem them. See Table 18-2 to determine where your bonds fall.

Table 18-2	
Bonds No Longer Paying Interest	
Bonds	**Stop Paying Interest:**
Bonds issued in November 1965 and earlier	After 40 years
Bonds issued in December 1965 and later	After 30 years
Series HH bonds issued in December 1965 and later	After 30 years
Any Series HH bonds	After 30 years

Source: Savings Bond Informer

Mortgage-Backed Securities

Treasuries attract most of the limelight, but a hodgepodge of federal government agencies and government-sponsored enterprises package their own debt. The Federal Farm Credit System, the Resolution Funding Corporation, and the Tennessee Valley Authority are some of the entities that slap their own names on bonds.

However, the agency debt that generates the most interest is classified as mortgaged-backed securities. The chief purpose of these securities has always been to promote home ownership by ensuring investor demand for home mortgages. Back in the early 1960s, the federal government dreamed up a way to encourage banks to issue home loans by creating a new type of investment that would bundle massive amounts of individual home loans together. The process of packaging these huge pools of mortgages for sale to investors is called *securitization,* hence the name mortgage-backed securities.

The mortgage-backed securities are issued by these three entities, which are almost always referred to by their nicknames:

✦ Government National Mortgage Association (Ginnie Mae):
   www.ginniemae.gov

✦ Federal National Mortgage Association (Fannie Mae): www.fanniemae.com

✦ Federal Home Loan Mortgage Corporation (Freddie Mac):
   www.freddiemac.com

Each of these mortgage bundlers has a slightly different mandate and background. Ginnie Mae, which is a division of the federal Department of Housing and Urban Development, is charged with pooling mortgages that are guaranteed by the Federal Housing Administration and the Veterans Administration. Fannie Mae and Freddie Mac are a little trickier to explain. Both were created by federal charter and have some board directors appointed by the government, but they are publicly traded corporations. In fact, the stocks of these two corporations have traditionally been quite popular with investors and are common holdings of mutual funds. The pair package low-income and conventional mortgages for sale to outside investors.

Strengths of mortgage-backed securities

Here are reasons you might be interested in investing in mortgage-backed securities:

They sport excellent credit ratings.

While mortgage-backed securities aren't as creditworthy as U.S. Treasuries, they come incredibly close. In fact, they enjoy the highest rating issued by the private credit rating agencies, such as Standard & Poor's and Moody's Investors Service. Only a tiny handful of corporate borrowers, including General Electric, Johnson & Johnson, and Pfizer, share this sterling bond rating.

Ginnie Mae is technically considered slightly safer than Freddie Mac and Fannie Mae. Because Ginnie Mae is a federal agency, its bonds are backed by the "full faith and credit" of the federal government. Fannie Mae and Freddie Mac don't enjoy the same rock solid guarantee, but there is an implied federal backing. The financial markets consider Fannie Mae and Freddie Mac nearly equivalent in safety to Ginnie Mae.

Note — The trio guarantees the prompt monthly payments to its investors, whether or not homeowners in the pools have paid their mortgages. Investors can expect to receive what is owed them even if mortgages in the pool have defaulted.

They offer better yields than Treasuries.

During the past decade, mortgage-backed securities have offered an average yield that's 118 basis points (100 basis points equals 1 percent) better than 10-year Treasuries. In that same time period, the yield spread has ranged from 74 basis points to 197 basis points. In late 2000, for instance, the spread between Treasuries and Ginnie Maes widened to 180 basis points. That's a tantalizing difference when you consider that you won't assume much extra risk for the bigger yield.

 Resource — To see the current yield spread, check *The Wall Street Journal* or *Barron's.*

They're a solid choice when interest rates are stable.

Ginnie Maes and other mortgage-backed securities thrive when interest rates are mired in a holding pattern. When rates are stable, homeowners prepay their mortgages at a much slower rate. Consequently, you can pretty much expect payments that are based on a stable ratio of principal and interest.

Weaknesses of mortgage-backed securities

Mortgage-backed securities have their downsides as well, which investors should be aware of.

Principal is being returned all along.

These securities don't behave like a run-of-the-mill bond. What's treacherous is that many bondholders don't appreciate this until it's too late. Most bonds pass along interest income twice a year for their investors, but mortgage-based securities generate monthly checks. This could be a plus for someone who is living off the investments' income. But too many investors are stunned when they discover that all the checks they've cashed over the years represent not only interest but a return of principal as well. That makes sense since homeowners pay both interest and principal when writing their monthly mortgage checks. What shocks novice investors is that they don't receive their principal back after their bonds mature. It's been distributed in dribs and drabs already.

Tip   Investors of mutual funds that specialize in mortgage-backed securities won't face this rude surprise. The principal payments are automatically plowed back into the fund shares. Their monthly checks contain only the interest distributions.

Declining interest rates can hurt investors.

When interest rates decline, homeowners rush to refinance their mortgages. This hurts mortgage-backed fans because more of their principal is returned. (Ironically, for most bonds, falling interest rates are a good thing.) If investors wish to reinvest this unexpected cash they probably won't find a comparable yield because of the lower interest-rate environment.

Skyrocketing interest rates are like alien intruders to mortgage-backed holders. Prices of these securities fall to earth because newly issued mortgage-backed securities pay higher yields.

Because of interest rate fluctuations, the chance of holding onto a 30-year Ginnie Mae for three decades is just about nil. Homeowners will typically repay their loans long before that. They will do that either by buying a new home and paying off the old mortgage or refinancing the one they've got. In fact, the bond community uses the 10-year Treasury note as a benchmark for Ginnie Maes and other mortgage-backed securities since it considers a decade a more realistic time frame for these bonds.

Tip   Some investors mistakenly believe that the government backing of the mortgages in these pools extends to the price of an individual bond or a bond fund. It does not. The prices of the mortgage-backed securities and the funds that invest in them will vacillate.

There's a tax disadvantage.

While you can avoid state taxes when investing in Treasuries, that's not possible with mortgage-backed securities. You will owe income taxes on the interest these bonds generate. Consequently, taxes can wipe out some of the yield advantage they hold over Treasuries.

Note   State taxes won't be an issue if you live in a state like Texas, where there aren't any. Taxes also won't be an immediate liability if you keep your mortgage-backed securities in a tax-advantaged retirement account.

You face high minimums.

For buyers and sellers, mortgaged-backed bonds aren't as user-friendly as Treasuries. You can't buy these bonds directly from the government. And on the open market, the markup to trade these bonds can be stiff. What's more, these bonds are complicated and the minimum investment can be $25,000. Consequently, your best bet is to invest in a low-cost mutual fund.

Here are two candidates to investigate:

✦ Federated GNMA Institutional: (800) 341-7400

✦ Vanguard GNMA: (800) 662-7447

Summary

✦ U.S. Treasuries are the safest bonds you can buy.

✦ If you want to invest in U.S. Treasuries, it's easy to buy them directly rather than go through a broker or mutual fund.

✦ Explore investing in zero coupon bonds if you need a set amount of money by a specific date.

✦ Consider hedging your portfolio inflation-protected bonds.

✦ Cash in your savings bonds once they no longer generate any interest.

✦ Evaluate investing in mortgage-backed securities when interest rates are holding steady.

✦   ✦   ✦

Corporate, Municipal, and Junk Bonds

◆ ◆ ◆ ◆

In This Chapter

Weighing the advantages of municipal bonds

Understanding corporate bonds

Evaluating the pros and cons of junk bonds

◆ ◆ ◆ ◆

When the Middle East is rocked by threats of war, the Russian ruble is in trouble, or the Japanese economy suffers, American investors rush to scoop up U.S. Treasuries, which can be as reassuring as a baby's blanket during uncertain times. But Treasuries won't always be the best fit. Other bonds, whether from the private sector or state or local governments, can serve as a smart addition to many portfolios.

In this chapter, you'll learn the ins and outs of bonds beyond the orbit of the federal government. In the next few pages, you'll learn about these three common types of bonds:

✦ Municipal bonds, which are heavily favored by affluent investors and provide tax-free income.

✦ Investment-grade corporate bonds, which can usually beat Treasuries on yield with just a bit more risk.

✦ Junk bonds, which can provide a higher yield than other corporate bonds, but can be significantly more treacherous.

Municipal Bonds

Look around when you drive down the highway and you'll see the concrete results of municipal bonds. State and local governments, as well as quasi-governmental agencies, issue municipal bonds to build such things as sewage systems, airports, bridges, prisons, freeways, hospitals, and other big-ticket items.

The nation's municipal bond market is gigantic. Investors hold roughly $1.5 trillion worth of muni bonds that are issued by more than 50,000 state and local governments. The Bond

Market Association, an industry trade group, estimates that it would take 90 newspaper pages to list all the outstanding muni bond issues. Chances are you know somebody who owns muni bonds either directly or through a mutual fund. More than 5 million Americans have invested in them.

Before you can decide whether muni bonds are appropriate for your portfolio, you need to appreciate their strengths and weaknesses.

Muni Bond Advantages

If you're in a high tax bracket, muni bonds could be of great interest. Here's a rundown of their advantages.

They offer a tax break.

The big draw for municipal bonds is the tax break. Muni bonds are one of the few sure-fire methods to shelter interest-generated income from taxes. This is why they are often referred to as tax-free bonds. Here's how the tax break works: Say you sink $10,000 into a municipal bond issue offering a coupon (or interest rate) of 6 percent. Each year, your investment generates $600 in interest. You pocket the cash, but don't owe federal taxes on this amount. In contrast, if you held a corporate bond with a 6 percent coupon, you'd pay taxes on that $600. If you were in the 35 percent tax bracket, the tax would consume $210 of your profit.

Municipal bonds can assist investors in skipping state taxes too. Of course, to take advantage of this extra layer of tax protection, you must live in the state issuing the bonds. If you live in California, for instance, and own munis issued in the Golden State, you avoid paying state taxes as well. Triple tax plays are also possible for bonds issued by local municipalities, assuming the local government taxes the income.

Tip Most muni mutual funds invest in bonds throughout the country. Investors, however, can take advantage of the potential state tax break by buying into single-state funds, which buy bonds issued within a state's own borders.

Here's a partial list of the states for which single-state muni bond funds are available:

Arizona	Massachusetts	North Carolina
California	Michigan	Ohio
Connecticut	Minnesota	Pennsylvania
Georgia	Missouri	Tennessee
Kansas	New Jersey	South Carolina
Maryland	New York	Virginia

New Tax Brackets

Think you know your tax brackets? Perhaps you don't. When Congress passed its sweeping tax legislation in 2001, one of the major features was a gradual reduction in tax brackets. This chart outlines the old brackets and the accompanying new ones:

Year	Federal tax rate				
2001 (Prior to July 1)	15%	28%	31%	36%	39.6%
July 1 2001–2003	15%	27%	30%	35%	38.6%
2004–2005	15%	26%	29%	34%	37.6%
2006+	15%	25%	28%	33%	35%

Because of the tax break, investors accumulate municipal bonds in their taxable portfolios. There is absolutely no point in investing in municipals in a tax-sheltered retirement account, as they are already protected from taxes.

Munis present a wide range of choices.

With more than 1.5 million bond issues outstanding, choices abound for even the most discriminating investor. In fact, the possibilities are so overwhelming that many people prefer to invest in munis through mutual funds.

Munis are creditworthy.

You may remember the largest and most infamous municipal bond collapse in U.S. history. In the mid-1990s, Orange County, California, declared bankruptcy and defaulted on hundreds of millions of dollars it owed to its bondholders. This stunning meltdown spooked a great many conservative investors.

Despite this scare, muni bonds have generally been exceptionally safe investments. What's more, in the new millennium, the muni market has been in better financial shape than it's been in past years. You can credit that with the nation's long economic expansion that only recently showed signs of weakening. Thanks to the boom, state and local government agencies from sewer districts to state highway departments found themselves flush with cash. In fact these civil servants were sitting on so much revenue that the bond rating services in the year 2000 busily upgraded muni bond ratings.

A self-insured investment

Of course, booms can always go bust. As an added incentive for anyone allergic to even an iota of risk, about half of the nation's muni bonds are insured. Those muni borrowers who can't manage to snag the highest "AAA" bond rating sometimes purchase insurance to boost their bonds' ratings up to that plateau.

Timing Your Muni Buys

Is there a bad time to buy munis? Some experts suggest there is. You may want to avoid purchasing munis from June to July and December to January. Why? Tons of bonds mature during those periods and those are heavy periods for coupon payments. All this cash creates a seller's market, as investors look to reinvest their coupon payments.

Before buying, find out whether munis are priced attractively. Since the 1980s, yields on municipal bonds have ranged from 70 percent to 105 percent of the yield on Treasuries, usually falling between 80 percent and 85 percent of the Treasury yield. (See Chapter 17 for an explanation of why bond yields are compared to Treasuries.) The closer the muni yield comes to matching the actual Treasury yield, the more excited muni investors get.

What does insurance mean to the investor? If a state or local government defaults on payments to its lenders, whether they are institutions or the average Joe investor, the insurer guarantees that the full interest payments continue to be mailed out without interruption. The insurance company also makes sure that the investors ultimately receive their principal back.

If you invest in an insured bond, there's no direct charge for the insurance, but you do relinquish a bit of yield. Typically, an investor gives up less than $5 in interest income a year on a $1,000 bond. In many cases, however, the yield on insured bonds is slightly higher than on uninsured ones that can also claim a Triple-A rating.

Note   Insurance on muni bonds doesn't protect bondholders from every possible financial disaster. Insurance can't shield lenders from fluctuations in bond price if a bond defaults or its credit rating is downgraded. However, for a buy-and-hold investor who keeps a bond until maturity, the ups and downs in a bond's value are irrelevant.

The fine print

Certain types of muni bonds are inherently riskier than others. The safest are general obligation bonds, which are approved by voters and secured by the full faith and credit of the issuer. Revenue bonds are a notch below in safety. They're dependent upon money generated by public projects, such as airports, bridges, low-income housing, hospitals, and water and sewage treatment facilities.

Before you invest in an individual bond, check the issuer's credit rating. You can do that by calling a bond rating service, such as Standard & Poor's and Moody's Investors Service, or visiting its Web site. (See the Resource Guide for contact information for both these organizations.) To be thorough, ask the bond issuer for its official statement or offering circular, which discloses details of its financial conditions. It's similar to a prospectus used for other types of securities, including mutual funds.

If you're investing in munis through a bond fund, call the fund's toll-free number and ask for a copy of its prospectus and annual or semiannual report. By doing so, you will find out what kinds of munis are in the portfolio, along with their credit quality.

Closed-end muni bond funds offer even better yields.

Most individuals buy municipal bonds through a mutual fund or individually, but there is another attractive yet relatively obscure alternative. You can often get an even better yield by investing in a *municipal bond closed-end fund,* a close cousin of mutual funds. Just as with traditional or "open-ended" mutual funds, a fund manager of a closed-end fund assembles a promising portfolio of stocks or bonds. But there is a key difference. Unlike its relatives, a closed-end fund is traded on the stock market, which presents opportunities to buy into these funds at a discount. (The closed-end variety got its name because there is a finite number of shares issued when the fund begins trading on the stock market. In contrast, shares of regular mutual funds are issued anytime a new investor comes aboard.) Can you imagine buying shares in the nation's most popular mutual fund, the Fidelity Magellan, at a 10 percent discount? It's never going to happen. But this kind of fire sale pricing occurs all the time with closed-end funds.

How is this possible? Because when these funds trade on the stock market, price discrepancies frequently result. That is, the price investors are willing to pay doesn't always match the value of the fund's underlying holdings, which is referred to as the *net asset value* (NAV).

Example

Suppose the NAV of a closed-end fund is $10 a share, but the shares are selling for $9 apiece on the stock market. In this case, you'd be buying shares at a 10 percent discount.

Of course, the opposite can be true too. A closed-end fund can also sell for a premium price, in which case you'd be paying more than the underlying fund share is actually worth. In contrast, if a traditional mutual fund's NAV is $20, it will sell for that same price; buying at a discount or premium is impossible.

The price discrepancies also can generate higher yields. Suppose the NAV of a closed-end muni fund is $10 and it pays out a yearly $1 distribution, which works out to a 10 percent yield. If the fund is selling at a discounted price of $8.50, your yield pencils out to 11.76 percent.

Tip

You can almost always obtain a higher yield with a closed-end fund than you can with an individual bond, plus you receive monthly dividends.

Timing closed-end fund purchases

The best time to buy a closed-end muni fund is typically in the fourth quarter of the year—traditionally the period when individuals are selling investments to lock in

tax losses for deductions next April. Selling a closed-end muni or any other investment at a loss can offset an investor's capital gains. And if there are no capital
gains, some of the money can be used to offset income.

Cross-Reference   You can learn more about bond tax strategies in Chapter 25.

A word of caution

Although taking advantage of price discrepancies can be a great way to squeeze out
extra yield, if you aren't careful you can get burned. If you buy a closed-end fund at
a premium and it later slips into discount territory, you can suffer staggering losses.
That's why you should never buy a closed-end fund at a premium. To exploit the
pricing inefficiencies, only purchase shares in a closed-end fund when they're on
sale. The deeper the discount relative to a fund's past average, the better.

The best performing closed-end municipal funds are typically leveraged. These
funds pledge some of their underlying portfolio as collateral to borrow money to
buy even more bonds. Just about 8 out of 10 closed-end bond funds leverage their
holdings. According to a study by Morgan Stanley Dean Witter, leveraged funds
have outperformed their peers during the past decade. While leveraging creates
more volatility, this may not matter if you're a buy-and-hold investor, who can sit
tight during rocky times. Table 19-1 demonstrates the historic performance of muni
closed-end funds.

Tremendous Resource for Closed-End Fund Buyers

Want to learn more about closed-end funds? The Closed-End Fund Association, a trade
organization that promotes this niche market, provides a wealth of information on its Web
site (www.cefa.com). You'll find fund stats, academic studies, and primers on closed-end
investing.

Also on this site is detailed information on more than 500 closed-end funds. While a dis-
proportionate share of these closed-end funds are devoted to muni bonds, other closed-
end funds specialize in domestic stocks, foreign stocks or bonds, corporate bonds, and
specific sectors, such as health care/biotechnology, energy, and financial services.
Information on each fund includes its daily net asset value (NAV), its yearly expenses, its
investment turnover rate, the tenure of its manager, the portfolio holdings, and a contact
number.

The site provides a huge service to investors by shedding light on each fund's current and
historic premium or discount. While it's best to avoid a closed-end fund unless it's selling
below its typical discount, finding this figure was a true challenge for individual investors
before this Web site came along.

Table 19-1
Track Record of Muni Closed-End Funds

Year	Discount or Premium	Total Return
1995	9.3% discount	23.74%
1996	4.9% discount	4.06%
1997	0.2% discount	10.46%
1998	3.9% premium	6.61%
1999	8.8% discount	–6.1%
2000	8.6% discount	15.75%
2001*	4.59% discount	1.56%

*As of May, 2001
Source: Lipper

Disadvantages of municipal bonds

Since everyone hates taxes, you might assume that munis are appropriate for any-one. But they aren't. Only investors in the top tax brackets should consider them; read on to discover why that is.

Their tax break makes for lower yields.

Keep in mind that a muni bond's yield is discounted because of the built-in tax break. If you're in a low tax bracket (10 percent or 15 percent), your tax savings in a muni are so puny that you're better off with a taxable bond offering a higher yield. For those in the next bracket up, which is 27 percent, it's often a coin toss. In con-trast, people in the top federal tax brackets reap the highest tax break.

Here's an example that illustrates the phenomenon. Say you are in the 35 percent tax bracket and you've got $30,000 to invest in bonds. You've narrowed your search to a muni yielding 5 percent and a taxable corporate bond yielding 7.5 percent. If you choose the muni, you'd earn $1,500 in interest (30,000 × .05). In contrast, you'd pocket $2,250 with the corporate bond, which on the surface seems like a much better deal. But look what happens at tax time. As a muni investor, you'd owe no federal taxes on the $1,500. However, you'd pay $787 in taxes (2,250 × .35) on the corporate income, which would drop your real income to $1,462—so your actual yield on that corporate bond is not quite 4.9 percent.

Now suppose you're in the 15 percent tax bracket facing the same choices. If you choose the muni, you'd get the same $1,500 in tax-free income. But if you selected the corporate bond, your federal tax bill would be just $337.50 (2,250 × .15). After federal taxes, you'd pocket $1,912.50. In this scenario, the muni is the worst choice.

Closed-End Funds Devoted to Single States

In the world of closed-end investing, municipal bonds represent the most popular investment category. There are 100 national muni funds that invest in muni debt across the country, while there are slightly more funds (113) that specialize in the muni bonds of just one state—again, allowing those investors to shield the income from state tax.

States with State-Specific Closed-End Municipal Bond Funds

Arizona	Maryland	New York
California	Massachusetts	North Carolina
Colorado	Michigan	Pennsylvania
Connecticut	Minnesota	Texas
Florida	Missouri	Virginia
Georgia	New Jersey	Ohio

Source: Lipper, a Reuters Company

 Note   Before buying a muni, compare the yield you'd get from a taxable bond with a municipal's typically smaller yield. Table 19-2 may help with that comparison.

Table 19-2
Taxable Equivalent Yield Table

If the Tax-Exempt Yield Is:			
	4%	5%	6%
Income Tax Bracket	The Taxable Equivalent Yield Is:		
15%	4.71%	5.88%	7.06%
27%	5.47%	6.84%	8.21%
30%	5.71%	7.14%	8.57%
35%	6.15%	7.69%	9.23%

In most cases, you're going to have to do your own calculations or, better yet, use the Bond Market Association's municipal bond calculator at www.investinginbonds.com.

If you don't have access to the Internet, you can do the calculations fairly easily. Say you want to compare a 9 percent corporate bond with a muni bond yielding 7 percent. Just follow these three steps:

1. Convert your tax bracket into a decimal. If your tax bracket is 30 percent, it would be .30.

2. Subtract the decimal from 1.00. (1.00 − .30 = .70).

3. Divide the tax-exempt yield of the muni by the figure in step 2. (.07 ÷ .70 = 10 percent).

As you can see in this example, the muni bond's tax-equivalent yield of 10 percent is superior to the corporate bond's 9 percent.

The tax break is worthless if they're in the wrong account.

You ruin the muni's tax advantages if you keep municipal bonds in a retirement account. Munis are always a terrible choice for an Individual Retirement Account. In fact, any self-respecting investment firm should talk a customer out of doing such a thing. Because you don't pay taxes while your investments are in IRAs, it doesn't make sense to put a tax-free bond into an already tax-advantaged account. Unfortunately, this happens all the time.

Munis are callable.

If you snagged a muni with a great yield, there's no guarantee that you'll get to hold onto it. Whether it's the Port Authority of New York, the California prison system, or the Denver school system, the vast majority of muni bond issuers have the right to ask for their bonds back. Bondholders hate this call option because, from their perspective, the debtor always calls the bond back at the worst time. It usually happens when interest rates have dropped. By canceling old debts, a borrower can issue IOUs at a lesser interest rate. You return the bond in exchange for a pre-established call price, but this cashout leaves you looking for a better deal at the worst possible time. Chances are excellent that even after scouring the bond universe, the replacement bond will offer a lower yield than what you were receiving.

Since the vast majority of munis feature call options, it's impractical to search for only ones that don't. Investors can pass up many excellent bonds by limiting themselves to the small universe of the uncallable ones.

Munis aren't immune from all taxes.

Munis aren't a magic tax elixir. Plenty of muni fans pay taxes. How can this be? Simple. If you sell your bonds for a profit, that capital gain will be taxed. Suppose you bought a $5,000 municipal bond and sold it later for $5,500. That $500 is subject to federal capital gains taxes. Whether you'd be hit with long-term or short-term capital gains depends upon how long you held the bond.

If you want to avoid taxes, it's better to hold onto a bond or stock for at least a year and a day to capture the long-term tax rate, which tops out at 20 percent. Short-term rates are taxed at your individual tax rate. So if you're in the 30 percent tax bracket, that's what your short-term gains will be taxed at.

Tip

You won't have to worry about capital gains taxes if you hold your munis until maturity.

Unfortunately, the buy-and-hold protection doesn't cover bond mutual fund investors. Bond mutual fund shareholders can get these capital gains distributions passed on to them if their portfolio manager sells bonds at a profit. You might think that getting distributions would increase the value of your investment, but it doesn't. The value of each share in your muni bond fund will drop in correlation with any capital gains distribution. So it's a wash. You, however, will be stuck on April 15 paying capital gains taxes on a distribution that did you no good at all.

Meanwhile, you definitely should avoid buying a bond (or holdings in a bond fund) that is subject to the much reviled alternative minimum tax (AMT). The AMT is intended to block the wealthy from claiming too many deductions on their tax returns, but its net can also snare middle-class folks. The AMT can apply to interest generated from "private activity" bonds. Proceeds form this type of muni bond benefits a business or other private entity, such as an industrial development or stadium construction. Aiming to tweak their yields, many muni bond funds hold this type of bond.

Muni junk bonds may be perilous.

Yes, there is such a thing as muni junk bonds. Not only are muni junk bonds less than investment-grade caliber, most of them aren't even rated by the rating agencies. (See this chapter's section on corporate bonds for a description of the investment-grade rating.) The vast majority of junk munis are issued by nonprofits, such as nursing homes and hospitals, as well as some public agencies, including power authorities and airports.

Rethink Munis in Retirement

If you're retired and still clinging to your municipal bonds, maybe you shouldn't be. All too often, muni investors who were paying high taxes during their working years slip to a lower tax bracket once they retire. It just never occurred to them to unload munis when the compelling tax reason for holding them evaporates.

There's a danger of holding munis during retirement as well: Munis can trigger an indirect tax. If a retired bondholder is receiving regular checks from a muni bond stockpile, the income, while tax free, could push him into a higher income tax bracket. And a higher tax bracket could force him into the distasteful prospect of paying taxes on his Social Security checks.

Considering Out-of-State Munis

If you're familiar with muni investing, you've probably memorized this rule: To get the biggest bang for your bucks, stick with munis in your own state. Single-state munis can be a boon to investors, who are shackled by high state taxes, such as the folks who live in New York or California. If somebody living on Long Island buys a New York muni, they skip state tax on the income. If a Georgia resident buys a New York muni, he or she wouldn't pay New York state tax either. But that wasn't going to happen anyway. He or she will, however, pay Georgia income tax.

Smart investors who are looking for high-yielding individual muni bonds will profit by occasionally forgetting this conventional wisdom. Sometimes the yield in another state's munis is so compelling that it's worth crossing the state line to get it. You won't get the state tax break, but the extra yield can more than compensate.

What's more, you may be lucky enough to live in one of the few states that won't tax you for income generated by another state's munis. These states include Pennsylvania and Ohio. And of course, residents of states where there is no state income tax, such as Washington, Nevada, Wyoming, Texas, and Alaska, are equally fortunate.

What's the attraction for this niche market? In general, these high-yield munis aren't as perilous as corporate junk. But investors are still assuming added risk, so they're rewarded with a higher yield. During the early 1990s, for instance, junk holders enjoyed yields that were two percentage points higher than their investment-grade counterparts. At other times, the difference has narrowed considerably.

Tip   The safest way to invest in muni junk is through a muni junk bond fund. It's best to let a professional cherry pick these more volatile bonds.

Without help from the credit rating services, it's even more of a hassle to evaluate these potential firecrackers. High-yield muni bond funds, however, may not be as volatile as you assume. That's because the supply of these bonds is not vast. To fill out the portfolio, a manager will typically add issues of investment-grade bonds that have the lowest credit quality.

Nonetheless, investors should be cautious if they invest in high-yield muni junk. It's probably better to invest in one of these funds through a major fund family. Play it safe with a fund that doesn't bet the farm on the riskiest munis, such as Vanguard High-Yield Tax-Exempt Fund, which has the bulk of its portfolio sunk into investment-grade munis.

Places to Bond on the Internet

While countless Internet forums are devoted to stock jocks, bond investors typically get short shrift. But take heart. There are a few fixed-income refuges online. One worthwhile place for both beginning and experienced fixed-income investors is TheStreet.com (www.thestreet.com). While the site devotes most of its ink to stocks, it does an excellent job of covering fixed-income basics, as well as advanced bond topics.

You may also want to check out Morningstar's Web site (www.morningstar.com) and head to the chat forum devoted to bonds (Bond Squad Forum), as well as the Investing During Retirement Forum, for intelligent discussions on a wide range of fixed-income issues from bond laddering to explanations of the inflation-fighting savings bonds. To make it easier for bond enthusiasts, Morningstar has consolidated its bond coverage and its bonds center. Meanwhile, on Vanguard's Web site (www.vanguard.com), you can download a helpful bond primer.

You need a lot of money to properly diversify.

Experts disagree on just how much money a muni investor needs to properly diversify. You can typically buy a muni bond for $5,000, but that doesn't necessarily mean you should. Some suggest that investing in individual munis is only practical if you can devote at least $50,000 to $100,000—or even more—to munis. Why is a large amount advisable? Because unless you have that much money to spread around, you can't properly diversify among different issuers.

An easy solution is investing through mutual funds. To get you started, here are a few nationally oriented muni funds that pass along minimal expenses:

✦ Vanguard Intermediate-Term Tax-Exempt at (800) 662-7447 or www.vanguard.com

✦ Fidelity Spartan Intermediate Municipal Income at (800) 343-3548 or www.fidelity.com

✦ USAA Tax-Exempt Intermediate-Term at (800) 382-8722 or www.usaa.com

Investment-Grade Corporate Bonds

Two types of corporate bonds coexist on the market—investment-grade and high-yield. The corporate crème de la crème issues the investment-grade debt, while those companies that don't make the cut—and most don't—peddle the high-yield bond stuff. Issuers of high quality corporate bonds run the gamut from well-respected retailers, such as the Gap, Home Depot, and Walgreens, to technology stalwarts like Intel and IBM, to automotive giants like General Motors and Ford Motor Co.

Whether a corporate bond receives the desirable "investment-grade" classification ultimately depends upon the opinions of the bond rating agencies. After analyzing such things as a corporation's financial statements, the quality of its management, and its business prospects, these independent agencies release what amounts to a grade for each borrower that ranges from an "A" all the way down to a "D." Just like on the school report cards, an A is cause for celebration, while a D is dreadful. Different variations exist for each letter grade. For instance, the "AAA" designation is the highest possible rating released by Standard & Poor's, but Moody's Investors Service classifies its top rating as "Aaa."

Bonds with a rating of BBB or higher are classified as investment grade. All the rest are lumped into the high-yield or junk category.

Cross-Reference For more description of credit ratings, see Chapter 17.

A heavy concentration of pharmaceutical stocks, as well as financial institutions with federal charters, has snagged the coveted triple A rating. As you can see in Table 19-3, a very small fraternity has earned this designation. The next highest designation, "AA" is also exclusive. Roughly five dozen corporations have received it, including Microsoft, Hewlett Packard, and Chevron, as well as a smattering of telephone, drug, and other oil stocks.

Table 19-3 Highest Rated AAA Corporate Bonds	
General Electric	Bristol-Myers Squibb
Exxon Mobil	Johnson & Johnson
Pfizer	Nestlé
United Parcel Service	Merck
Royal Dutch Shell	Imperial Oil
Toyota	Novartis
BellSouth	Automatic Data Processing
Abbott Laboratories	International Telecommunications Satellite Organization

Source: Standard & Poor's

Advantages of corporates

Here are the reasons you might consider investing in investment-grade corporate bonds:

Corporates have a stable credit history.

The chances of an investment-grade corporate bond defaulting are remote. The higher the rating within this category, the more minuscule the risk. These bonds can warm the hearts of conservative investors who place a premium on safety. After all, what are the chances of General Electric or General Motors going out of business?

Their yield is superior to Treasuries'.

An investment-grade corporate bond's coupon is more generous than a Treasury's because you sacrifice a smidgen of security. During the past 10 years, the average yield spread between a Treasury and a high-grade corporate bond has been 72 basis points. A basis point equals one hundredth of a percent. So, for example, 1 percent equals 100 basis points.

At times the yield spread is even wider. For instance, at one point in 2000, the yields of high quality corporate bonds were well over 1.5 percentage points more than Treasuries. That might not seem like a big deal to stock jocks, but the gulf is spectacular to fixed-income fans.

They provide opportunity for capital appreciation.

Not all investors gravitate to corporates for the yield. Investors of corporate debt, no matter what its quality, look for bonds that they suspect will be upgraded, kind of like a C or B student getting an A. When a corporate bond is upgraded, its value and hence its price can increase.

Caution   Making credit bets can be dangerous because generally bond prices slide down more easily than they move up. The bump a bond generally enjoys from a credit upgrade won't be as great as the body blow it absorbs if its rating is downgraded.

Speculative investors also get interested in top-notch corporate bonds when they believe the market has unfairly punished them. For instance, during periods when junk bonds are reviled, high quality corporates can be bludgeoned too. But some bond bargain hunters see this as an opportunity to snag high quality bonds. That's because even the most upstanding corporate borrowers must offer higher yields to attract willing customers.

Disadvantages of corporates

Factor in the disadvantages as well when looking at corporates.

Corporates don't provide a tax break.

One of the biggest knocks against these bonds, as well as the junk variety, is that they don't provide a tax break. The income generated by these bonds is fully taxable at the federal and state levels. Because of this drawback, consider stashing corporates in a tax-deferred retirement account. By doing this, taxes won't be an issue until the money is withdrawn.

Where Are the Corporate Bond Funds?

Interested in finding an investment-grade corporate bond fund? Good luck locating one. While you can invest in bond funds devoted to U.S. Treasuries, municipal bonds, foreign bonds, mortgage-backed securities, and even junk bonds, it's unusual to discover a fund devoted exclusively to high quality corporates.

There's a logical explanation for this black hole. Fund managers chafe at being pigeonholed into one type of bond. If corporates aren't a good value at one point, they want the freedom to gravitate to other types of bonds, aiming for the highest returns. This freedom isn't practical for many other types of funds. For example, if a muni manager adds taxable bonds to his portfolio, investors who depend on the tax protection will revolt. It's a similar story with a fund that invests in Treasuries or federal agency bonds. If a manager starts slipping corporates in the portfolio, that can understandably rattle ultra-conservative shareholders.

In contrast, a creature called an *intermediate-term bond fund* operates under a mandate to invest in whatever looks good, buying up promising bonds in any category. One of these funds can serve as the core bond holding in your portfolio.

If you're interested in a portfolio that mixes corporates and government bonds, you'll want to invest in a fund that's classified as an intermediate-term bond fund.

Need some ideas? You may want to consider the Harbor Bond Fund or the Fremont Bond Fund, which are both no-load funds, meaning they don't carry a sales charge. The pair is a cheap way to hire on Bill Gross, a well-known fund manager who has been widely regarded as one of the wizards of the fixed-income world. Gross oversees bond investing at PIMCO Funds, but those funds, which are primarily sold through stockbrokers and financial advisors, carry a sales charge. Another solid choice is Dodge & Cox Income.

✦ Harbor Bond Fund: (800) 422-1050 or www.harborfund.com

✦ Fremont Bond Fund: (800) 548-4539 or www.fremontfunds.com

✦ Dodge & Cox Income (800) 621-3979 or www.dodgeandcox.com

They are riskier than government bonds.

Even though corporate bonds are issued by instantly recognizable companies that produce such indispensable products as Colgate toothpaste, Tide laundry detergent, and Tylenol, corporate bonds are considered riskier than Treasuries or other government bonds because companies can fail, but the U.S. government cannot. Even a county government struggling to pay the interest on its muni bonds can always raise taxes as a last resort—not an option corporations have. Consequently, bond ratings are even more critical when you're shopping for corporate bonds.

Corporates are callable.

Just like muni bonds issuers, corporate debtors often insist on the right to call their bonds at a future date.

High-Yield (Junk) Bonds

Unlike most bonds, junk bonds claim a colorful pedigree. These bonds were dreamed up by Michael Milken, the flamboyant and controversial Beverly Hills bond trader. The former junk bond king, who later become known for his philanthropic work, correctly concluded that corporate America, as well as some adventurous investors, were starved for junk. Cash-poor companies without a sterling credit history would eagerly pay bondholders a premium for taking a chance on them. And sure enough the bonds thrived.

At the start of the 1990s, however, the fledgling junk bond industry ran into difficulties. At one point, an alarming 11 percent or so of the junk bonds on the market fell into default. Milken, junk's no. 1 salesman, was eventually hauled off to jail for federal securities violations. The financial press didn't hold back any invectives when describing the debacle. *The Wall Street Journal* called junk bonds a mediocre investment, while *Barron's* declared the whole affair a vast Ponzi of phony bonds.

Note   Junk bonds, despite the rocky beginnings, have survived since their initial crash more than a decade ago. What hasn't changed is the junk bond's inherent volatility.

Junk bond applications

At its inception, junk bonds were primarily used to finance corporate takeovers and mergers, such as the RJR Nabisco merger in the 1980s. The use of these bonds is now much more diverse. Some companies that resort to junk might be too small or have too short a track record to qualify for an investment-grade rating. You'll also find *fallen angels*—blue chip companies that have lost their coveted investment-grade rating—peddling junk. Finally, some enormous corporations could have debt rated as junk because they are highly leveraged with above-average debt loads.

With the majority of corporate bonds issued in this country classified as junk, it would be a mistake to assume that most borrowers are seat-of-the-pants startups. Within the junk ranks are such debtors as Apple Computer, Nextel Communications, Playtex Products, Vail Resorts, Bethlehem Steel, and Barnes & Noble. Telecommunications and technology companies are heavy users of junk bonds.

Tip   The best time to buy junk bonds is when the economy is expanding and consumer confidence is high. The worst time is usually during a recession when corporate earnings are struggling and investors grow nervous about holding risky bonds.

Advantages of junk bonds

Everyone knows junk bonds are volatile, but not everyone realizes the upside to these bonds.

They can provide higher returns.

Junk bonds enjoy the potential of generating higher yields and total returns than the more sedate Blue Chip corporates. When measured by total return, junk bonds have outperformed investment-grade corporates in 7 out of the last 11 years. (To obtain a bond's total return, you add together the interest it spins off plus any capital appreciation. A bond, despite its coupon rate, can register a negative total return if the value of its principal drops enough.)

Junk can spice up a portfolio.

Nobody can live on a diet of Tabasco and it's the same with junk bonds. Junk bonds aren't meant to serve as the main entrée but they can be used sparingly to add spice to a portfolio. Some experts suggest that investors, depending upon their tolerance for risk, allocate 5 percent of their portfolio to junk bonds. Aggressive investors may wish to allocate more—perhaps up to 15 percent.

Note   Anyone interested in these bonds should be prepared to hold onto them for at least five and possibly seven years because they are so volatile.

Junk doesn't follow the bond market in lockstep.

Junk doesn't quite behave like other bonds. Higher interest rates can devastate most bonds, but junk isn't as sensitive to escalating rates. Instead, these bonds tend to mimic stocks. When a company experiences an upturn, the good news can boost the value of a junk bond, just as it would a stock price. On the other hand, bad financial news can send the debt spiraling downward.

Tip   A company's junk bonds are less risky than its stock because if a business collapses into bankruptcy, bondholders line up in front of stockholders when the company's remaining assets are liquidated and distributed.

Disadvantages of junk bonds

Of course, you'll need to weigh the downside of junk bonds before buying into them.

They mean greater financial risk.

Junk bonds do go south. The companies issuing these bonds are far more likely to struggle in paying back their debts than the ones backed by corporate household names. The junk bonds' default rate is much greater than that of the higher grade corporates. Junk bonds' high yields merely reflect the precarious financial situation of a number of junk borrowers.

Note   When a bond issuer defaults, it means that it has failed to meet interest or principal payments. Usually, however, even bonds in default still retain some value.

Junk is less liquid.

Investors can experience difficulty finding buyers since junk bonds are less liquid (inherently less marketable). If you want to unload your junk bonds, others may be trying to do the same thing. You can obtain a lesser price than you expect if the market for used junk bonds is weak.

It's tough to evaluate corporate debt.

The real danger with buying individual corporate bonds is evaluating their credit worthiness. Will the telecom newcomer that just issued $500 million worth of debt honor its obligations? Frankly, most of us don't have enough time to pore through a company's financials to find out. Couch potatoes should invest in these bonds through a mutual fund.

Investing in junk bond funds

Since the junk bond terrain is lined with land mines, it's essential for all but the most experienced individuals to invest through mutual funds. Fund managers are better equipped to evaluate these bonds and find good values. By their very nature, these funds also provide the necessary diversification.

Note   Leaving the stock picking to a mutual fund manager doesn't mean you won't get burned. There are times, like the year 2000, when the entire junk bond market gets hammered. When that happens, it's very difficult for even the pros to hide.

Be sure to evaluate the track records of junk bond funds before selecting one. Fund managers vary tremendously in their investment temperament. Some are bungee jumpers, while others always wear a seat belt. More conservative managers will concentrate their portfolios on junk bonds rated "B" or "BB," which are high on the junk food chain. You can get a feel for how risky a fund is by looking at its annual or semiannual report. It will list the fund's holdings, along with their credit ratings. Morningstar also provides a summary of this information on many bond funds.

Tip   Be leery of any junk bond fund that dramatically overperforms or underperforms its peer group. A fund that skyrockets past the pack is probably assuming too much risk.

If junk bond funds intrigue you, here are some candidates to consider.

✦ Northeast Investors Trust: (800) 225-6704 or www.northeastinvestors.com

✦ Vanguard High-Yield Corporate: (800) 662-7447 or www.vanguard.com

✦ Janus High-Yield: (800) 525-8983 or www.janus.com

Multisector Bond Funds

Mutual funds stuffed with junk bonds aren't the only ones that can provide a wild ride. Just as volatile are what's called *multisector* or *strategic income funds*. These funds enjoy a wide latitude to invest in just about any kind of bonds under the sun. A portfolio can be stuffed with Treasuries, high-grade corporate, junk, foreign, and even emerging market debt. Some investors gravitate to these funds as a way to further diversify their portfolios.

Over the past few years, the funds that have invested significantly in volatile emerging market bonds have suffered. If you want a less volatile fund, you'll want to veer away from those containing a sizable amount of emerging market debt.

Here are two candidates to consider:

✦ Janus Flexible Income at (800) 525-8983 or www.janus.com

✦ T. Rowe Price Spectrum Income at (800) 638-5660 or www.troweprice.com

Summary

✦ Don't buy municipal bonds if you're in the lowest tax brackets.

✦ Tweak the yield of a municipal bond portfolio by investing in a closed-end bond fund.

✦ When considering the purchase of corporate bonds, check their spread against Treasuries.

✦ Lower your potential risk by investing in junk bonds through a mutual fund.

✦   ✦   ✦

Investing in Your Retirement

In the next three chapters, you'll learn what it takes to
retire in style. New federal laws now permit you to sock
away more money than ever before for your golden years, but
you need to know how to invest this cash wisely. You'll discover what your options are, including the latest IRA and
401(k) contribution ceilings, as well as the new catch-up provisions for retirement savings procrastinators.

Investing Through IRAs

In this chapter, you'll learn why the Individual Retirement Account is one of the very best ways to save for retirement. You will discover what your options are as well as which IRA is best for you. Also included in this chapter are the new IRA contribution ceilings that allow motivated savers, as well as procrastinators, to stuff far more cash into their IRAs and to even play catch up if your contributions have been lagging. Finally, you'll receive tips that can save you huge amounts of money if and when you inherit an IRA or would like to pass one on.

The Basics of IRAs

By now, Americans have probably gotten sick of hearing about their own personal ticking retirement clock. Every 24-hour news cycle brings each of us a day closer to the milestone we are all supposed to be diligently preparing for. According to many pessimistic media dispatches, though, our ability to focus on saving for retirement is no better than a third grader's attention span 10 minutes before summer vacation begins.

Surveys show that most people who are eligible to participate in a 401(k)—8 out of 10 workers—are doing so. But people are far less diligent about saving through another excellent vehicle—the Individual Retirement Plan. What's nice about the IRA is that it doesn't discriminate. Every worker, and in most cases their spouses, are eligible to stuff money into an IRA. In contrast, many companies, particularly smaller ones, don't bother implementing a 401(k) plan or other retirement plan. What's more, millions of workers aren't covered by corporate pension plans.

In 2001, Congress made IRAs even more alluring. The politicians scuttled the incredibly low $2,000 IRA contribution ceiling, which hadn't been changed in many years. Thanks to the legislation, individuals will eventually be able to stuff as much as $5,000 a year into an IRA. And anyone who is at least 50 years of age can toss in a little bit more thanks to new catch-up provisions; this chapter covers the specifics.

Rollover-a-rama

IRAs have become much more than a place to stuff spare change each year. Even before the sweeping legislation, the IRA had become the ultimate destination for a mother lode of money that Americans save at work. When employees leave behind the assembly line, the cubicle, the operating room, or a corner office, much of their workplace retirement savings that was methodically saved in 401(k)s, 403(b)s, pensions, and other plans ultimately flows into IRAs through rollovers.

Consequently, for most people, the biggest pile of their retirement money—no matter what its source—will eventually land in an IRA. It's no surprise, then, that trillions of dollars fill the nation's IRAs. No matter how the money got there, it's important to know the best way to use an IRA effectively.

Shelter from the tax storm

In the vast majority of cases, the IRA is the best place for orphaned retirement money. If it is deposited in an IRA, it continues to grow without the steady, drip, drip, drip of tax erosion. As long as money remains inside an IRA, it is not taxed. The IRA's Teflon-coated tax protection is a tremendous boon over time. Using the old contribution limits, Table 20-1 illustrates the potential growth of an IRA nest egg versus that of money placed in a taxable account.

Table 20-1
Annual $2,000 Contributions in an IRA Versus a Taxable Account

Number of Years Contributing	Taxable Account	IRA
10 years	$30,006	$37,123
15 years	$54,999	$76,380
20 years	$90,481	$142,530
25 years	$140,854	$253,998
30 years	$212,368	$441,826

* This table assumes an 11% return for an investor in the 28% federal tax bracket, who pays 6% in state taxes.

Getting started with an IRA

One of the biggest misconceptions about the IRA revolves around what it is. An IRA is not a type of investment. It's just a shell that allows you to invest in nearly anything you want without fretting about taxes.

You can establish an IRA at a bank, a mutual fund company, a brokerage firm, or other financial institution by opening up an account there and filling out a form that designates the account as an IRA. You will need to open an account whether you want to begin depositing money—up to the yearly ceiling—into an IRA or if you'd like to transfer any amount of money from your workplace plan after retiring or quitting. If you're moving money from a company plan or another existing IRA, you will have to fill out one extra piece of paperwork—the transfer form. The paperwork, however, can be easily filled out in a few minutes.

Once an IRA account is open, it's up to you to decide how you'll invest the money. If you're a refugee from a workplace plan and you liked your previous fund choices, you may want to explore establishing an account with a brokerage firm where you may be able to duplicate your investment lineup. Brokerage firms typically offer a menu of hundreds and, in many cases, thousands of funds, in addition to individual stock and bond choices.

Tip
You can avoid feeling overwhelmed by selecting an all-purpose mutual fund, which should carry you through rocky times as well as the most jubilant bull market. With this fund serving as your core holding, you can add other funds as desired to complement its investment style.

Steady sailing with an index fund

Where do you find this financial anchor? A stock index fund is a good place to start. Investing in an index fund is like buying everyday stoneware instead of fancy china. It's incredibly practical. Index funds seek to match the return of the stock benchmark to which their fate is tied. By far, the most popular index funds are linked to the Standard & Poor's 500 Index, which contains 500 of the biggest and best known companies, such as American Express, Home Depot, Boeing, Intel, and Hershey Foods. Over the years, large-cap index funds have routinely outperformed rival funds.

The undisputed indexing kingpin is Vanguard, which launched the first index fund a quarter century ago. That original fund—Vanguard 500 Index—has since grown to be the nation's second most popular mutual fund. Both it and the Vanguard Total Stock Market Index Fund (www.vanguard.com) are excellent starter funds. Other top candidates: Schwab 1000 Fund (www.schwab.com) and Fidelity Spartan Total Market Index Fund (www.fidelity.com).

Considering all the options

For those who can't get excited about an index fund, a solid alternative is a large-cap blend fund. One of these funds invests in major corporations that represent both the value and growth investing styles. You'll find fund recommendations in Chapter 7.

Meanwhile, don't feel rushed into putting your IRA money into play. If you invest in an IRA through a brokerage firm, consider stashing your cash into a money market until you devise a game plan. Major mutual fund companies also offer money markets.

Tip   Once you've decided how you'd like your money invested, you can move the cash all at once or gradually through dollar-cost averaging.

Know the new limits

As mentioned earlier, Americans will no longer be saddled with a miserly IRA contribution ceiling. To derive the maximum benefit from your IRA, you'll need to know the new limits, which are gradually being phased in over the next several years. Table 20-2 shows you the new ceilings.

Table 20-2 Maximum Contribution Limits for Traditional and ROTH IRAs	
Years	*Contribution Ceilings*
2001	$2,000
2002–2004	$3,000
2005–2007	$4,000
2008 and after	$5,000

What's also new is a way for Americans who are at least 50 years old to play catch-up by contributing more to an IRA than everybody else gets to. In the years 2002 to 2005, an older investor can sink an extra $500 per year into a IRA (admittedly not a princely sum.) In 2006 and thereafter, the annual catch up amount is $1,000.

Choosing from Three IRA Flavors

While your investment choices are unlimited when you invest in an IRA, just three types of regular IRAs exist.

- ✦ Deductible IRA
- ✦ Nondeductible IRA
- ✦ Roth IRA

The first two on the list are classified as traditional IRAs. The last is the newest IRA, which is named after a former U.S. senator from Delaware. What follows are the features of each one:

Deductible IRA

The deductible IRA is the only one that rewards you with an up-front tax gift. If you contribute to a deductible IRA, you'll receive a tax deduction on your federal income tax return. How big the write-off is depends upon your tax bracket and the size of the deposit.

Example   You invest $2,500 and you're in the 27 percent tax bracket. The tax deduction is $675 (2,500 × .27). In contrast, the tax savings for someone in the 15 percent bracket would be much lower—$375. Of course, if you deposit more into one of these IRAs, the tax break grows.

The best feature of this IRA is that the money grows tax-deferred for as long as it stays inside the account. As you learned from Table 20-1, allowing money to compound undisturbed for many years is an unbelievably valuable gift.

So far, this IRA sounds great, but there's a price to pay for the modest tax write-offs that individuals pocket over the years. When someone retires and begins tapping into his or her IRA, the IRS expects its share. Each time you pull cash out, you will owe income taxes, and where applicable, state taxes.

Example   Suppose you accumulate $300,000 in a deductible IRA and you want to withdraw $50,000. How much you owe in taxes will depend upon your tax bracket. Someone in the 27 percent bracket, for instance, would be liable for $13,500 (50,000 × .27).

Patience won't help you dodge this eventual tax burden. Uncle Sam won't allow you to postpone withdrawals forever. The government expects Americans to begin tapping into the two types of traditional IRAs shortly after reaching the age of 70½.

Note   If you're wondering if this IRA is ideal for you, agonizing might be unnecessary. Not everyone qualifies for the deductible IRA.

Look at Table 20-3 to determine whether the deductible IRA is even a possibility for you. Your gross adjusted income can't exceed the figures in the table to make a maximum yearly contribution. The eligibility ceiling, however, will continue to inch up for single people until 2005 and for married couples until 2007.

Table 20-3
Tax-Deductible Contributions to a Traditional IRA

Tax Year	Single Taxpayer	Married Filing Jointly
2001	$33,000	$53,000
2002	$34,000	$54,000
2003	$40,000	$60,000
2004	$45,000	$65,000
2005	$50,000	$70,000
2006	$50,000	$75,000
2007	$50,000	$80,000

Note: To qualify for a tax-deductible IRA, your adjusted gross income must not exceed these figures.

There are a few ways around these limits: It's possible to make a partial contribution if your adjusted gross income (AGI) is slightly higher than the limits shown in the table. A married couple or single individual can make up to an extra $10,000 in income and contribute partially. The only exception is in the year 2007, when a married couple can make up to an extra $20,000 and still make a partial contribution.

Even if you make too much money, you can still contribute to one of these IRAs if you don't participate in a company retirement plan. If you are married and just your spouse is covered by a plan, you can still sink the maximum into a deductible IRA if your combined AGI does not reach $150,000. You can make a partial contribution if your combined AGI doesn't exceed $160,000.

Nondeductible IRA

Unless you are rich and have no other IRA options, this IRA is the least attractive. The nondeductible IRA shares some of the same characteristics as the deductible variety. You can trade stocks with abandon or jump from fund to fund within an account, and your tax liability will still be zilch. The tax cocoon remains impenetrable until it's broken open. Just like with the other traditional IRA, once the money is withdrawn, taxes will be owed. So how is this IRA different from the deductible variety? You won't secure a tax write-off when you deposit cash into one. But this isn't a total negative.

Note   When you withdraw money during retirement, you'll only owe taxes on your investment gains. No taxes will be due on your original contributions since you received no up-front tax break for them.

What's Your AGI?

Because all but one of the IRAs have income limitations, it's important to know your gross adjusted income before deciding which IRA is best. Your AGI is listed on your federal tax return. It's calculated by adding all your income, including wages, tips, capital gains and investment income, and subtracting the deductions listed at the bottom of the first page of the 1040 tax form. Itemized deductions and deductions for children won't lower your AGI. But an oddball collection of deductions will, including:

✦ 401(k), 403(b), Keogh, SEP-IRA, and SIMPLE-IRA contributions

✦ Stock losses

✦ Alimony payments

✦ Student loan interest

✦ New deduction for higher education expenses

✦ Self-employment health insurance

✦ Rental real estate losses

✦ Self-employed business losses

✦ Moving expenses

Who should sink money into this IRA? The wealthy have no choice. If you make too much money, you are ineligible to invest in both the deductible and the Roth IRA. Only the nondeductible IRA doesn't care how wealthy you are. You can be a billionaire and still kick in the maximum each year.

Even though the nondeductible IRA isn't as compelling, if you are shut out of the other choices, this IRA makes a great deal of sense. After all, you will be able to see your money grow, without being shackled by an annual tax bill, for many years. And that's an invaluable gift.

Roth IRA

For many years, banks, mutual funds, and brokerage houses valiantly touted the wonders of IRAs, but few people listened. Americans ignored IRAs in droves. But the Roth IRA spurred taxpayers into thinking about IRAs. And it's no wonder since the Roth, with its tax goodies, is the best IRA yet.

Advantages galore

As with the other IRAs, the money sloshing around in a Roth remains immune from taxes. But here's the Roth's biggest virtue. If the rules are followed, the lucky Roth investor never has to pay taxes on this money. No matter how big the kitty grows, once the investor hits retirement age, the IRS can't get its mitts on it. You can take it out at once, nibble on it as needed, or pass the whole amount to your heirs, and you or your loved ones wouldn't pay Uncle Sam any income taxes.

Here's another plus: The Roth doesn't require yearly withdrawals later in life. Owners of traditional IRAs must take out a certain percentage of their account each year shortly after reaching age 70½. Unless they need the money, retirees hate pulling money out of their IRAs because taxes will be owed on the amount and the tax-deferral advantage vanishes.

The downside of a Roth

So what's the catch? First, not everyone qualifies to invest in a Roth. You can't fully fund a Roth if your adjusted gross income exceeds $150,000 (married taxpayers filing jointly) or $95,000 (single taxpayers). For people making slightly more than these levels, a partial contribution is possible.

Also, there's a trade-off, but arguably it's a minor one, for establishing a Roth. You can't deduct your yearly contribution to a Roth IRA on your tax return. That option is, of course, only available with the deductible IRA.

Tip
> Even without a tax deduction, the Roth IRA is an infinitely better deal for most people.

With a traditional IRA, after all, your immediate payoff is minimal. Saving hundreds of dollars on a tax return is not necessarily a compelling reason to reject the Roth IRA. That's especially true if the money is just going to get sucked into your checking account and disappear.

Penciling out the numbers

Need convincing? Look at two scenarios where one investor chooses a Roth and the other a traditional IRA. Both individuals are in the 27 percent tax bracket, and for 30 years each annually contributes $3,000 into their respective IRAs. After watching their accounts grow at an average 11 percent clip for three decades, both retirement savers have compiled nest eggs of $597,063. For the sake of comparison, say both investors cash in their windfall all at once and at the same time. Our Roth investor would owe a big fat zero in taxes. Investor no. 2, who had enjoyed a total of $24,300 worth of tax deductions over the years, would now owe federal tax of $161,207. Under the circumstances, tax deduction will now seem like a measly consolation prize. Table 20-4 lays out the numbers.

Table 20-4 Deductible and Roth IRA Comparison After 3 Decades of $3,000 Annual Contributions*		
Factors	**Deductible IRA Investor**	**Roth Investor**
Value after 3 decades	$597,063	$597,063
Federal tax	$161,207	$0
Total value of annual tax deduction	$24,300	$0
Bottom line	$460,156	$597,063

* Assumes each investor is in the 27% tax bracket and investments grow 11% a year.

The Roth advantage may seem clear cut, but you won't necessarily know it if you read the IRA materials distributed by financial institutions. The brochures make the choice between the Roth and the deductible IRS seem like a much closer call. And here's why: The calculations assume that the traditional IRA investor, who snags that nice tax deduction, doesn't spend the money. Instead, the investor tucks this money into a taxable savings account and does not touch it until retirement. Of course this reasoning defies human nature. Most taxpayers, who are eager for a tax write-off, probably aren't going to tie up this extra money in an investment account for decades. More than likely, the money will be spent many years earlier on credit card bills, a new sofa, spare tires, or a weekend getaway.

When the deductible IRA makes sense

In a limited number of scenarios, individuals will be better off snubbing the Roth and choosing the deductible IRA. Here are the exceptions:

✦ You plan to retire soon and will then drop down to a lower tax bracket.

✦ You're in your fifties and plan to take out the money at age 59½, which is the age when the early withdrawal penalty vanishes.

Considering an IRA conversion

Since the Roth IRA sounds so good, you may be wondering if you can transfer money from a 401(k) or other workplace plan directly into a Roth when you leave your job. That would be great, but it's impossible. When you move money from an employer's retirement plan into an IRA, it's considered a traditional IRA. That is, taxes will be owed when the money is removed from the IRA. It is possible, however, to convert the IRA rollover, once it's established, into a Roth, if you meet the requirements and can foot the up-front tax bill. No prohibition exists on how much money you can shovel into a Roth IRA conversion.

If you already have money stashed in a traditional IRA, whether funded by contributions or rollover money, you may wish to explore the possibility of converting this money into a Roth. Whether a conversion would be a shrewd move depends upon your circumstances. If you transfer your IRA money into a Roth, you won't have to pay taxes on this bundle when you retire. But there is one catch that has paralyzed some otherwise gung-ho investors. If you make the switch, you'll need to pay income taxes up front on the money that you move. If you want to convert a sizable chunk, this can create a huge tax bill.

Example   Suppose you have a $75,000 traditional IRA and you're in the 30 percent tax bracket. If you proceed with the conversion to a Roth, you'd owe $22,500 in federal taxes when you file your next annual IRS return.

Not every IRA investor will need to contemplate this move. If your adjusted gross income exceeds $100,000 during the year of the intended conversion, you won't qualify. The same income ceiling applies to married couples filing joint returns as well as single taxpayers. If you are married but file taxes separately from your spouse, you can't convert to a Roth IRA at all.

Reasons for converting to a Roth

Here are scenarios when converting to a Roth IRA can make sense:

✦ You won't need the cash during your retirement. Remember, only the Roth IRA won't force you to make yearly withdrawals after you're 70½ years old.

✦ You intend to leave your IRA to heirs. Many older Americans don't realize that the Roth IRA can be a great estate planning tool. Loved ones won't have to pay any income taxes on the money they receive in a Roth IRA. What's more, they will also be able to withdraw money from a Roth tax free over their lifetimes.

✦ You expect to be in the same tax bracket or higher when you retire.

✦ You're young. The more time the money will stay in an IRA, the more valuable the advantage of withdrawing the money tax-free later.

Reasons against converting to a Roth

Here's when a Roth conversion may not make sense:

✦ You're close to retirement. As a rule of thumb, the older you are, the less compelling a conversion is. (Unless you want to convert the Roth for estate planning purposes.) There won't be sufficient time to allow the Roth to accumulate enough tax-free earnings to outweigh the cost of the taxes owed up front.

✦ You believe you'll be in a lower tax bracket during retirement than you are now.

✦ You'd have to dip into the IRA to pay the conversion tax. If you do this, your portfolio loses momentum. The money you pull out for taxes never has the ability to steadily compound in value. What's more, if you are younger than 59½ years of age, you are hit with a 10 percent penalty.

Solid Source for Latest IRA Rules and Strategies

Got an IRA question? A Web site, `www.irahelp.com`, should be able to provide the answer. The online IRA source is maintained by Ed Slott, a CPA in frequent demand by journalists and financial professionals when they research IRA issues. Hundreds of his answers to common and esoteric IRA questions are archived on the site. You may also want to subscribe to Ed Slott's IRA Advisor newsletter; call (800) 663-1340. The 12-issue subscription is $79.95 a year, and will keep you up-to-date on changing IRA rules.

To convert or not to convert? Rather than agonize, consult a certified financial planner, a certified public accountant, or a tax attorney. If you think you can figure this out on your own, there are free sources of help. Just about any brokerage firm or mutual fund company can provide material to help you decide whether a conversion makes sense.

The following Web sites offer software that can help you make the conversion decision:

✦ Quicken.com (`www.quicken.com`)

✦ Fidelity Investments (`www.fidelity.com`)

✦ T. Rowe Price (`www.troweprice.com`)

✦ Charles Schwab (`www.schwab.com`)

✦ Financenter.com(`www.financenter.com`)

IRA escape hatches

Today's IRAs offer comfort to those who are petrified at the thought of tying their money up for decades. Because it's been a hard sell getting people to stuff money into IRAs, all three IRAs are now equipped with trap doors that allow investors to withdraw cash for a variety of reasons before retirement age without getting slapped too hard by the IRS. It's infinitely better, however, if you avoid the temptation to tap into your retirement nest egg no matter how worthy these other causes are.

Slipping out of a Roth IRA

Here's how to prematurely pull money out of a Roth:

For starters, the Roth allows someone to withdraw yearly contributions at any time or for any reason without financial repercussions. If you contribute $2,000 to a Roth in March and your roof needs to be replaced in November, the IRS won't blink if you pull the contribution out. No tax or penalty is owed and you have great flexibility: You can withdraw this money a few days or even a few years after making the contributions.

If the Roth is at least five years old, you can withdraw above and beyond the contributions, digging into an account's profits, without inflicting any tax pain in certain situations. Here are the circumstances in which you can siphon the earnings out of an older Roth without paying tax or penalties:

+ You're at least 59½.

+ You use the money, up to a lifetime maximum of $10,000, to pay for a first home for yourself or a family member.

+ You're disabled.

+ You die and your beneficiaries are receiving the money.

You can also skip the 10 percent penalty if you use your Roth earnings for any of the exemptions listed for traditional IRAs (next). For instance, if your Roth isn't at least five years old, you will owe taxes on money withdrawn for a first home or because of a permanent disability, but no penalty is triggered.

Siphoning a traditional IRA

It's harder draining money out of a traditional IRA before age 59½, which is considered retirement age. What follows are the instances when you can access your money without triggering a 10 percent early withdrawal period. In all these scenarios, however, you will still owe income tax on the money.

+ You withdraw up to $10,000 to buy a first home for yourself or a family member.

+ The money is used for college expenses.

+ The cash is used to pay medical bills that surpass 7.5 percent of your adjusted gross income.

+ You become permanently disabled.

+ You withdraw money in "substantially equal periodic payments" in what's called a 72(t).

Introducing the 72(t)

Have you ever dreamed about retiring before your name gets slapped onto an AARP mailing label? If you've built up a large sum in your Individual Retirement Account or workplace retirement plan, only Uncle Sam may be blocking your early exit.

The IRS punctures pipe dreams every day with its standing threat to impose a 10 percent penalty on much of the money that's prematurely withdrawn from retirement portfolios. Many people assume that the only way to escape this financial drubbing is to continue growing old, since once the age of 59½ is reached, the draconian penalty vanishes.

But hidden deep within the IRS's tax law is an escape hatch for the impatient. This obscure section of the tax code—specifically 72(t)—permits anybody, of any age, to withdraw money from an IRA penalty free. That's right, you can kiss that 10 percent penalty goodbye. It's also possible to duplicate the same feat with a 401(k) as long as you are no longer working for the company.

The fine print of a 72(t)

What's the catch? Once you raid your IRA, you've got to keep pulling money out, in what the IRS refers to as a "series of substantially equal periodic payments" for five years or until age 59½, whichever is further out. What's more, after a payment schedule is started, you can't tinker with it. Say you've agreed to drain $20,000 out of an IRA each year. The government expects you to keep withdrawing that amount for the required years even if you return to work, inherit a sizable estate, or become haunted by second thoughts. If you fail to withdraw the appropriate amount, a retroactive 10 percent penalty will be triggered on all the money you've already siphoned out over the years. Obviously, this could be a financial nightmare.

A 72(t) also can't help you dodge income taxes. No matter what your age, you'll owe income taxes on whatever you extract from an IRA, other than nondeductible contributions. The only exception, of course, is the Roth IRA, which, if all the conditions are met, permits tax-free withdrawals.

Who is the ideal 72(t) poster child? The most obvious candidates can be the truly desperate, such as someone in his or her 50s who is laid off and unable to find work. Plundering an IRA may be necessary to pay the mortgage and keep the lights on. But many people trapped in this predicament may not need a 72(t).

Tip Anyone who is at least 55 when leaving a job can begin drawing down a 401(k) account without getting tripped up by the 10 percent penalty. The penalty, however, will apply if the worker transferred the 401(k) money into an IRA rollover and then began siphoning it out.

In reality, the sort of people who are embracing the 72(t) are more likely to be affluent professionals who have built up sizable fortunes in their retirement plans. The 72(t) is a way to retire their alarm clocks, while still maintaining their comfortable lifestyles.

Who should avoid 72(t)s?

The 72(t) makes far less sense for those in their 30s and 40s. At first blush, the 72(t) can look tantalizing to somebody who wishes to take an extended sabbatical or retire at an age when friends are still changing their kids' diapers. But the commitment to stick with a 72(t) would be so long for younger people that in many cases it would be impractical.

A 72(t) also won't necessarily be a wise decision for someone nearing that 59½ milestone. Those in their late 50s might instead consider paying the 10 percent penalty on just the amount they need immediately. That way, they aren't tied into a rigid withdrawal plan for five years.

Caution   If a 72(t) sounds intriguing, don't try this solo. The theme of all the IRS's publications is that you can figure out your taxes by yourself, but in the case of 72(t)s, the IRS advises that you get professional help.

Not just anybody with an acronym on a business card will do. Grill your attorney, CPA, or financial planner on his or her experience in using the 72(t) section of the tax code. Like a heart surgery patient, you don't want to be the first or second client that somebody tries this out on.

IRA FAQs

Here are the answers to some frequently asked questions about IRAs.

What's the deadline for contributing to an IRA?

You have until April 15 to fund an IRA for the previous calendar year. You can wait, for instance, until April 15, 2003, to deposit money into an IRA in time for your 2002 income tax return.

When is the best time to fund an IRA?

To get the most bang for your buck, you should contribute as early in the tax year as possible. The first day you can contribute to a 2002 IRA, for example, is January 1, 2002. The cutoff would be April 15, 2003.

Do I have to contribute the maximum amount?

This is a common misconception. You don't have to contribute the maximum allowed each year. Actually, you can invest any amount into an IRA as long as it doesn't exceed the ceiling. Through automatic savings programs, many mutual fund companies allow individuals to invest monthly into an IRA with as little as $50 at a time. If you receive a bonus at work or a paycheck with lots of overtime, consider putting some of the extra cash into an IRA.

Note   There is no ceiling on the amount of money that can be rolled into an IRA from a workplace retirement account. The sky's the limit.

How do I establish an IRA?

It's easy. Contact a brokerage firm, bank, or mutual fund company for an IRA account application. You can also download the forms on the Web sites of many financial institutions.

Can I have more than one IRA?

Sure. There's no limit to how many accounts you can have. But don't let your IRA accounts pile up like mismatched socks. If you have IRAs scattered among, say, a brokerage firm, a couple of mutual funds, and a bank, it will be harder to keep track of them all. What's more, you may be required to pay annual maintenance fees. Consolidating accounts can save you money.

Note　If you have multiple IRAs, keep in mind that the yearly maximum contribution applies to *all* IRA contributions combined. For instance, in 2002, when the ceiling is $3,000, you can't contribute $3,000 to each IRA because the total can't exceed $3,000. (Or $3,500 if you are 50 or older.)

Once I establish an IRA, do I have to contribute to it every year?

No. You can skip any years you wish.

Can I move money from one IRA to another?

Yes, you can do this fairly easily. For instance, assume you have an IRA set up with the Janus Fund and you wish to transfer it to the Vanguard Primecap Fund. You'd call Vanguard's toll-free number and request an application and an IRA transfer form. (Or you can download the paperwork from the fund's Web site.) After Vanguard receives your paperwork, it contacts Janus and arranges the transfer. Once it's finished, Vanguard will notify you by mail.

Tip　When transferring your IRA to another financial institution, do not have the money sent directly to you. If you do not deposit the money into another IRA account within 60 days, you will owe income taxes on the amount and possibly a 10 percent early withdrawal penalty.

If your IRA is with a brokerage account, the transfer between funds or individual stocks will be even easier. By phone or online, it's possible to sell a fund or stock and direct the money into another investment within minutes.

Caution　If you do have the cash sent directly to you, don't do this more than once a year. If a second check is mailed to you within 12 months, you will owe income taxes and perhaps that pesky penalty.

Sep-IRA Versus Roth IRA

Self-employed individuals don't have to choose between a Roth and a SEP-IRA, which is a retirement plan popular with self-employed people. Because the federal government realizes that these workers won't enjoy a company pension, it allows freelancers, consultants, and anybody else who works for themselves to contribute to both plans. A self-employed person who otherwise qualifies for a Roth can contribute the maximum in the tax-free account and also contribute the top amount to a SEP-IRA.

Are some investments inappropriate for IRAs?

Absolutely. It makes no sense to include municipal bonds or muni bond funds in an IRA. Wealthy Americans gravitate to these bonds because the income they spin off is sheltered from federal taxes. Well, the income generated by any and all investments within an IRA is sheltered. Consequently, putting muni bonds in an IRA would be like using an umbrella in the house when it's raining outside. You'll get absolutely no benefit from doing this.

It's also not a good idea to invest in a variable annuity within your IRA. Variable annuities, which you'll learn more about in Chapter 22, are tax-deferred investments. Consequently, it's pointless to pay a premium for this tax protection when it's unnecessary.

Can a spouse who doesn't work outside the home contribute to an IRA?

It used to be that a nonworking husband or wife could only contribute a measly $250 a year into a spousal IRA. That unfair limitation was scrapped several years ago. Today, a spouse who files a joint tax return can also contribute the top amount. But the working partner must at least earn the amount that both the husband and wife are contributing. So if a husband and wife each sink $3,000 into an IRA, the working spouse must have earned at least $6,000 for the year.

How long can I contribute to an IRA?

You can keep feeding a traditional IRA until the year before you reach the age of 70½. And that assumes that you are still earning money. In contrast, Roth investors can continue making contributions at any age as long as they are generating a paycheck.

What if I can't afford to contribute to an IRA and my 401(k)? Which is better?

If your employer provides some kind of match to your 401(k) contributions, it's better to stick with your company plan. After all, the cash your employer contributes is free money. If your 401(k) doesn't kick in this extra cash, then you're generally better off contributing to a Roth IRA. The Roth IRA provides tax-free compounding for a lifetime. In contrast, taxes will be owed when money is ultimately withdrawn from a 401(k).

Making IRA Withdrawals During Retirement

If you own an Individual Retirement Account, you've probably got the drill memorized. You stuff as much money into an IRA as possible and then you sit on this cash until you're ready to retire.

But what happens next has bamboozled millions of people. The federal regulations governing the withdrawal process from IRAs were once so complicated that even financial institutions that oversaw these retirement accounts sometimes got confused. Withdrawal errors made by retirees and by their heirs, who receive what's left of these retirement accounts, in too many cases gutted these accounts.

Revised IRA regulations

Then in 2001, the IRS stunned tax professionals across the nation when it released dramatically simplified rules that affect how millions of Americans make withdrawals from their IRAs. In many cases, these rules allow elderly Americans to withdraw far less from their IRAs each year than was permitted previously. A retiree can now often withdraw 20 percent to 25 percent less than in the past. For affluent retirees, who hate touching their IRAs—and paying the resulting income tax—this is a terrific development. The new rules are also great for anybody who anticipates inheriting an IRA. Heirs are far more likely now to be able to stretch out the life of their inherited IRAs for decades.

 You can learn a great deal more about the revised inherited IRAs and IRA distributions rules in the *Retirement Bible,* a companion book to the *Investing Bible*.

User-friendly IRA distribution rules

Unless you've got your money tied up in a Roth IRA, someday you will have to start withdrawing money from your IRA. You must begin the withdrawals no later than April 1 of the year following the year you turned 70½. Obviously, the IRS prods retirees into doing this because it's tired of waiting around for its tax dollars.

Once the money is removed from the IRA, the federal government doesn't care what you do with it. You can spend it, put it into a taxable account, or give it away. It makes no difference. What the government cares deeply about is whether you are siphoning out at least the minimum required.

The rules that pinpoint the correct amount, as mentioned earlier, were once extremely intricate and unforgiving. Make the wrong decision and you often had to live with it for the rest of your life. Under the new regulations, the choices are now nearly mistake proof. The vast number of Americans will use the same IRS life expectancy table to determine what amount their mandatory yearly withdrawal must be.

Resource   You can order Publication no. 590, *Individual Retirement Arrangements,* which contains a supplement with the revised rules and the life expectancy table, by calling (800) 829-1040 or visiting the IRS's Web site (www.irs.gov).

When they reach the magic age for mandatory retirement account withdrawals, most people can use this simple formula: Each year, find your life expectancy figure in the IRS life expectancy table, and divide the value of your IRA(s) by that number.

Here's an example: Suppose that a retiree who has just turned 70½ can boast of a total of $100,000 in her combined IRAs at the end of the calendar year. To find the correct amount she must withdraw by the time she reaches age 71, she simply divides $100,000 by her official life expectancy of 25.3. The result: a minimum withdrawal of $3,953. Suppose that the next year her IRAs grow nicely and, despite last year's withdrawal, are now worth a total of $105,000. The next year's calculation will reflect the IRA's worth on the last day of each calendar year. This time she'll divide by the factor used by 72-year-olds.

Beware of Faulty Retirement Calculators

How much is enough when you're saving for retirement? Many people are turning to online financial calculators to help them answer this question. A lot of this software, however, is not worth your time. In fact, some of this online firepower can be downright dangerous because the numbers the calculators spit out are far too rosy. Simplistic calculators, which are mostly what you find on the Internet, are more likely to conclude that you won't die broke. It's not unusual for one calculator to estimate that an individual will die a millionaire, while a more sophisticated model will suggest instead that the same individual will wind up a pauper.

The vast majority of financial Web sites use the Stone Age approach. That is, the calculator assumes that your investment return and usually the inflation rate will be constant. Somebody sitting on a stock portfolio, for instance, might plug in 11 percent when the software asks for an investment return. (Eleven percent is the return that the stock market has averaged since the mid-1920s.) Leading financial experts, however, have discounted using a fixed number in retirement calculations.

Research has shown that depending upon a static return can be especially perilous for retirees. Researchers at T. Rowe Price illustrated this when they looked at how a hypothetical portfolio would have fared during a recent 30-year period. Based upon its asset allocation, the portfolio would have experienced a 11.7% annualized return. With this return, a retiree, withdrawing 8.5 percent a year (adjusted annually for inflation), wouldn't run out of money for 30 years. But in reality, this portfolio would have experienced erratic yearly returns, especially in the brutal bear market of 1973 to 1974. With the same withdrawal rate, the portfolio, using the actual fluctuating yearly rates of return, would have disappeared in less than 13 years. Other studies have generated similarly alarming results.

So what's the antidote to flawed calculations? Look for software that relies upon Monte Carlo simulations or upon vast amounts of historical data. Both methods produce remarkably similar conclusions. Instead of basing calculations on one average rate of return, Monte Carlo methodology can generate hundreds of computer simulations of what may actually happen to an individual's assets over a given period of time. Each simulation includes good and bad markets of various lengths and combinations over decades.

Ultimately, the Monte Carlo approach won't provide you with a pat answer on whether your portfolio will outlive you. Instead, you're presented with a portfolio's probability of success. For instance, you might discover that your portfolio has a 70 percent chance of succeeding. You'd then have to ponder whether that's too big of a gamble. If it is, you could change such things as your withdrawal rate and your investment mix.

The second type of probability analysis uses mountains of historical data to determine success rates. This software looks backward and relies upon what happened in the markets during overlapping historical periods. A statistician, for instance, who looks at investment returns during a 50-year period, may examine such periods as 1937 to 1987, 1938 to 1988, and so on.

Where can you find these calculators? Here are three sophisticated yet free online retirement calculators that have been praised by financial professionals:

Financeware.com Plan Audit Wizard	(www.financeware.com)
T. Rowe Price Retirement Income Calculator	(www.troweprice.com)
WAT$	(www.zunna.com)

Inherited IRA Survival Guide

Americans focus a great deal on investing their IRA, but they usually forget to contemplate what will happen to it at the end of the line. If your parents or grandparents expect to pass along their IRA to you, how they do it could mean the difference of tens or hundreds of thousands of dollars. This is true even if the IRA is only worth $20,000 to $30,000. If you expect to inherit an IRA or have recently inherited one, here's what you need to do:

Have a heart-to-heart with your parents.

This won't be the easiest conversation in the world, but it could save you and your parents a bundle of money. Most likely your parents haven't heard about the new IRA regulations. If they are grudgingly taking out mandatory yearly IRA distributions, they will be thrilled with the IRS move. They can calculate their new withdrawals, which most likely will be significantly lower.

Caution   While the new regulations are user friendly, they can't prevent every IRA from imploding. Warn your parents about one of the most common booby traps: naming their estate as the IRA beneficiary.

Designating an estate as an IRA recipient or simply failing to name anybody at all can be the quickest way to kill an IRA after the owner dies. If an estate is named as the IRA beneficiary, the IRA will often end up crippled. How long the IRA can be kept alive will typically depend upon the deceased's age. If the IRA holder died before facing mandatory IRA distributions, the entire IRA must be distributed no later than five years after the year of the death. If the IRA owner had already begun mandatory withdrawals, the IRA beneficiary actually gets a better deal. The person could preserve the IRA based on the time line that was already in place when the owner died.

What should be done instead? Every IRA owner should name primary beneficiaries and secondary beneficiaries on his or her IRA account applications. It's quite possible that your parents might not remember who they named on the paperwork, but they might figure that it's all taken care of with their wills.

Caution   A will doesn't matter when it comes to IRA beneficiaries. The document that counts is the paperwork you filled out when you established an IRA with a brokerage firm, fund family, bank, or other financial institution. Anyone who isn't sure who they named on this paperwork should contact their IRA custodian and find out.

Don't wipe Mom or Dad's name off the account.

Here's where being logical can cost you big bucks. Upon inheriting an IRA, you'd assume that the account, whether it's at Fidelity, Merrill Lynch, a bank trust department, or elsewhere, belongs to you. That's true, but you should never transfer the money into your own IRA account. If you substitute your own name, the IRS will conclude that you've cashed out of the IRA and you'll owe taxes on the full amount.

Tip   How can you protect against this fiasco? Keep the IRA in the original owner's name, but make sure the custodian adds your name and Social Security number to the account. The date of your benefactor's death should also be included on the account.

Decide whether you need the money.

When you inherit an IRA, you may be tempted to spend it. Remember, however, that cashing in an IRA, unless it's a Roth, will trigger income taxes. The IRA is infinitely more valuable if it's left alone to grow. As a general rule, an inherited IRA can mushroom to three to four times its original size over the years if someone isn't tempted to pull out more than the IRS legally requires each year.

Try to undo mistakes.

Previously, there was little that loved ones could do if their benefactors made mistakes when handing IRAs to the next generation. But beneficiaries now enjoy much more latitude to correct mistakes Mom and Dad or others committed.

The new rules, for instance, can come in handy if a parent leaves a single IRA to more than one child. The new rules permit a division of an inherited IRA that will allow each heir to use his or her own life expectancy in determining how long the tax protection can last. For some heirs, this will lengthen the life of an IRA considerably. That's because if children or grandchildren all share the same IRA, the life expectancy figure used for the calculation would be the oldest child's. Consequently, the youngest child would have to withdraw more money more quickly than he or she might like.

Anticipate your own mortality.

If you're lucky, you'll still be enjoying that inherited IRA by the time you begin contemplating the end of your own life. Ideally, you'll want to name your own children or other loved ones as the beneficiaries of the IRA you originally inherited. If you do this, your children could keep the IRA alive after your death. Not all IRA custodians, however, like their customers trying this. Some mutual funds and brokerage firms have balked at permitting clients to potentially extend the lives of their IRAs for another generation. If a financial institution refuses, you might want to involve your attorney or a financial advisor. Often it's the squeaky wheel that gets greased.

Luckily, this institutional reluctance is slowly beginning to evaporate. Some financial institutions are now developing special paperwork that allows IRA inheritors to designate their own beneficiaries.

Tip

When mailing in an IRA beneficiary form, request that the institution send back an acknowledgement that it received and accepted the form. This acknowledgement can come in handy if the paperwork is eventually lost during a bank merger or for some other reason.

Summary

✦ Among the three IRAs, the Roth is the superior choice for most Americans.

✦ If you're leaving a job, it's usually best to transfer the money from a company retirement plan into an Individual Retirement Account.

✦ While there are ways to pull money out of an IRA before retiring, it's almost always better to leave the money alone.

✦ Converting an existing IRA into a Roth can sometimes be a wise move, especially for the young or for estate planning purposes.

✦ When inheriting an IRA, be careful of picky IRS rules.

Squeezing the Most out of Your 401(k)

In this chapter, you'll learn why participating in a 401(k) plan is a great idea. You will also discover what it takes to manage your 401(k) like a pro. In addition, you'll learn how to evaluate your company's plan, and what to do if it's mediocre. Also included are the most common and the most profitable strategies for handling your 401(k) account when you leave a company. At least one of the tips might surprise you.

Discovering the 401(k) Advantage

It's hard to resist a 401(k). Those who remain immune to its charms are dwindling. More than 80 percent of eligible workers have already enrolled in a 401(k). And how many times do 8 out of 10 people agree on anything?

It's good that most of us are on the same page, because for more and more Americans, the 401(k) has become a financial life vest. Its importance has grown considerably as corporate America has begun to dispense with traditional pensions, which guarantee a lifetime of monthly checks for just about every worker in a company, from the chief executive to the person restocking the paper towel dispensers.

A 401(k), however, requires a great deal more work on your part than does a pension. The success of your account rests on your shoulders. And the stakes are extremely high. Picture two colleagues in adjoining cubicles stashing identical piles of cash into 401(k)s during their careers, but only one walking away a millionaire. It could easily happen. Suppose both invested $400 a month for 30 years. If one of the portfolios managed to generate 11 percent—the historic stock market return—the lucky owner would walk away with a cool $1.1 million. But suppose the other guy, through overly aggressive or conservative moves, managed only a 9 percent return, which is hardly shabby. That nest egg would be worth about $738,000.

Obviously, 401(k) accounts aren't meant to be put on autopilot. The exercise machine that so many people store in their basements is good for their health only if it's used. The same applies to a 401(k). Some care and attention is necessary to keep your retirement account in tip-top shape.

Understanding the nuts and bolts of 401(k) growth and maintenance, though, doesn't necessarily come naturally. We don't train people to be their own physicians or their own lawyers, but we expect people to be their own money managers. Luckily, mastering 401(k) mechanics doesn't have to be as taxing as you might think.

If you're not convinced that you should invest through a 401(k), read through this list of features that have made the 401(k) so popular:

Automatic savings

After signing up for your company's 401(k) plan, your contributions are automatically taken out of your payroll checks. Why is this so wonderful? This automatic withdrawal prevents those of us with little resolve from blowing the money. If the money's not there, you can't spend it. If it were up to you or me to save on our own without the discipline of a 401(k) account, it probably wouldn't get done, since there are too many competing interests for this money. With a 401(k), however, there's no agonizing about whether you can afford to contribute this week or next. It just happens. With any luck, most workers stop missing the money routinely siphoned out of their checks. They learn to adjust.

The Origin of the 401(k)

In 2001, the 401(k) observed its 20th birthday. Most people probably assume that Congress created the 401(k) with an ambitious and farsighted piece of legislation. Perhaps a Rose Garden ceremony ushered in the law with great fanfare. What really happened was far different.

Ted Benna, a consultant in Pennsylvania, dreamed up the idea after sifting through mind-numbing federal statutes. A bank, which was a client of his employee benefits consulting firm, was interested in revamping its retirement plan. In researching the issue, Benna concluded that using an obscure portion of the IRS Code—Section 401, paragraph (k)—might pave the way for a better plan. The client balked, but Benna's firm, which he co-owned, instituted its own 401(k) plan.

It took a while before this grand experiment caught on, but eventually the 401(k) exploded. Today, the 401(k) is the best hope for many Americans to secure enough money to afford a comfortable retirement. This is even truer today with a cloud of uncertainty hanging over Social Security.

Automatic savings is a plus for another reason. It forces us to save in good and bad times. The 401(k) doesn't accommodate market watchers, who time their investments based on what they think will happen on Wall Street. With a 401(k), your money is invested regardless of whether stocks and bonds are flourishing or floundering. This is a good thing. Countless academic studies have soundly concluded that market timing is a futile strategy.

Tax shelter

The 401(k) provides an irresistible tax break. You avoid paying federal and state income taxes on every chunk of money that you deposit in your 401(k). Your 401(k) contributions are not even reported as income on your tax return. And now, as you'll learn, it's possible to shelter more money than ever before into a 401(k)

Example

Say someone makes $50,000 and opts to direct 10 percent or $5,000 of that money into her 401(k). Her taxable income for the year will be $45,000, not $50,000. To put it another way: If she's in the 27 percent tax bracket, every dollar she puts in her 401(k) saves her 27 cents in taxes.

That's quite a deal, but the tax break doesn't end there. Your 401(k) is classified as a tax-deferred account because as long as the money remains in the account, the tax collector can't reach it. Consequently, your investment can grow phenomenally because taxes can be postponed on this money for decades. And your money remains in the tax-free zone regardless of how big the account balance grows. Only when you pull this money out at retirement will you owe income taxes on the withdrawals. By then, you could be in a lower tax bracket.

Caution

The ultimate tax on 401(k) money can be a financial blow to retired workers. Many people, in calculating their financial needs in retirement, never figure in the future tax obligations on their 401(k) withdrawals.

Greater contribution limits

While the federal government imposes limits on how much someone can annually squirrel away in these plans, the ceilings have never been higher. In 2001, Congress passed a massive tax package that increased the 401(k) ceilings beginning in 2002. (In 2001, a worker's maximum contribution couldn't exceed $10,500.) Table 21-1 lays out the new contribution limits.

Example

Suppose you annually save $4,000 in a 401(k) for 35 years, and the money earns 12 percent interest. After 35 years, the 401(k) would be worth $2.1 million. In contrast, if the same amount of money earned the same interest rate in a taxable account—subject to a federal tax of 28 percent and state tax of 4 percent—the account could easily be worth, at the 35-year mark, far less than half that amount.

Table 21-1
401(k) Contribution Limits

Tax Year	Maximum 401(k) Contribution
2002	$11,000
2003	$12,000
2004	$13,000
2005	$14,000
2006 and later	$15,000*

*After 2006, the maximum contribution only increases to account for inflation.

Even if you can afford to sock this much money away, however, your company may not permit you to do it. Corporations routinely limit contributions by placing a ceiling on the percentage of workers' salaries. The most common 401(k) contribution that's permitted by corporate America is 15 percent of a worker's salary. Your human resources department can tell you what the allowable maximum contribution is at your workplace.

Note The new federal 401(k) contribution ceilings also apply to 403(b) plans, which are retirement plans used by teachers and employees of charities, churches and non-profit hospitals.

Congress also paved the way for Americans who are at least 50 years old to stuff extra money into their 401(k) and 403(b) plans. The politicians created this catch-up mechanism in hopes that those who haven't saved enough will now start to do so. Table 21-2 spells out the amounts that older Americans can now contribute to their retirement plans, over and beyond the regular ceilings.

Table 21-2
Catch-up Contribution Limits

Tax Year	Amount
2002	$1,000
2003	$2,000
2004	$3,000
2005	$4,000
2006 and later	$5,000

401(k) Roths

When Congress was scrapping the old 401(k) contribution ceilings, it laid the groundwork for a new type of retirement plan—the Roth 401(k). Workers who sink money into a Roth 401(k) won't use pretax dollars as they would with a traditional IRA. Instead, the money will be deposited into a Roth 401(k) after it had been taxed. But the beauty of a Roth 401(k) is that the cash will grow tax-free and it never has to be withdrawn. If the money is pulled out during retirement, no income taxes will be owed. The Roth 401(k) could be ideal for those who expect to be in a high tax bracket during retirement or who want to leave money for their children or grandchildren. A worker will be able to contribute both to a regular and a Roth 401(k), as long as the maximum contribution ceiling is observed. What's more, affluent people who are ineligible for a Roth IRA would be eligible for a Roth 401(k).

If you're ready to sign up, relax. It's going to be awhile. The Roth 401(k) isn't scheduled to make its entrance until 2006.

Free money through matching funds

More than 9 out of 10 employers offer their workers some sort of contribution match. In other words, when you deposit money into your 401(k) account, so will your employer. The typical employer matches 50 cents of every dollar that a worker contributes, up to 6 percent of the worker's salary. Say you make $50,000 and you set aside 6 percent of your salary, which is $3,000. If your company meets the prevailing standard of 50 cents on the dollar, they will deposit an additional $1,500 into your account—that's free money. It's crucial, then, that you contribute enough each year to capture the full extent of your employer's match. If your employer will match up to 6 percent of your salary, for example, don't limit your contributions to 4 percent. Also, most plans have vesting periods that must be completed before the employee gets to keep the matching funds, a topic covered later in this chapter.

Current balances

In the Stone Age, workers had to wait for 401(k) performance updates that were issued quarterly or even less frequently. Now many corporations maintain 401(k) account information online. This arrangement allows participants to check on their investments at any time, as well as make changes to their portfolios. For those who aren't Internet savvy, companies typically maintain toll-free numbers that you can call to find out your account balances and make changes in your investment holdings.

Contribution Strategies to Match Your Needs

Ideally, you should plow as much money into your 401(k) account as your company allows. But many people, particularly those at the bottom of the salary food chain, won't be able to swing that. If you fit into that category, you'll want to put your money where it will do the most good.

Your best bet is to feed your 401(k) enough to at least guarantee the full company match. After you've secured the full extent of the match, the next best place for your retirement cash is in a Roth Individual Retirement Account. (See Chapter 20 for details on Roth IRAs.) While income eligibility requirements exist, the vast majority of Americans qualify to contribute to Roths. Ideally, you should put the maximum yearly contribution into the Roth. If you can kick in more after funding a Roth, put the remaining money into your 401(k).

Why is the Roth preferable to 401(k) money, after the match is met? It's simple. The Roth's tax advantage is phenomenal. At first glance, however, it may not seem that way. After all, the money you sink into a 401(k) is whisked from your paycheck before taxes. Obviously, that's a big plus. In contrast, the check you write to fund your Roth IRA is characterized as after-tax money. You enjoy no up-front tax break by tucking money in a Roth.

The true beauty of the Roth shines through at retirement. That's when the IRS is willing to reward you for denying yourself those initial tax deductions. When you withdraw money from your Roth during retirement, you'll owe absolutely no income tax on the windfall. In contrast, your 401(k) withdrawals will be taxed at your ordinary income tax rate. Imagine that a retired librarian accumulated $200,000 in his 401(k) and now wants to cash it out. If he were in the 27 percent tax bracket, he'd owe $54,000 in taxes if he withdrew it all at once. Somebody in the highest tax bracket—38.6 percent—would owe $77,200. In contrast, somebody who managed to amass a $200,000 Roth over the years would pay no tax on any withdrawals.

If you are married, you will have another decision to make. Ideally, you both should contribute as much pretax money as your employers allow. But if that's a financial pipe dream, scrutinizing both plans can really pay off. You should consider contributing the most money to whichever 401(k) offers the best employer match. If a husband's workplace offers a 50 percent match for his contributions, while the wife's stingy employer offers no match, funding his 401(k) to capture the match should be a high priority. What happens if both plans offer matches? Aim to capture the employer match in each one.

Seven Ways to Boost Your Investing Performance

Most people have already been sold on the virtues of 401(k) investing. They want ways to squeeze the best results out of their savings.

Some of the most influential people in the retirement field, including the consultant credited with creating the 401(k), are predicting that the 401(k) is on the verge of revolutionary change. In this new era, 401(k)s will become a la carte menus. No longer will you be confined to the typical 8 to 12 investment choices. Try multiplying that number by 1,000. This potential freedom excites many employees, who feel they are experienced enough to assemble a first-rate portfolio. Others find this potential freedom nerve wracking.

Regardless of potential 401(k) changes looming on the horizon, it's important to manage your account with the savvy of a Wall Street insider. Here are steps you should take to do just that:

Strategy no. 1: Pay attention to your asset allocation.

Asset allocation is a subject that can induce sleep faster than a drive across the Kansas plains. But if you dream about becoming a 401(k) millionaire, it's far too important to blow off. The purpose behind this strategy is to diversify your portfolio enough to maximize returns while at the same time minimizing risks during volatile markets. It's an easier concept to understand since the Nasdaq tech wreck in 2000. Someone who bet heavily on technology that year may have ended up with a 401(k) that looked like it had been hit by a bus. In contrast, a 401(k) with money spread across different types of stocks, as well as bonds, wouldn't necessarily be disabled by a gaping hole.

Asset allocation sounds simple enough, but even people who think they're doing it right often aren't. One study, co-authored by two preeminent researchers at UCLA and the University of Chicago, indicates that many people assume that asset allocation means spreading their money evenly among all their 401(k) choices. If 60 percent of a company's choices are stock funds and 40 percent are bond funds, sure enough, the typical 401(k) account will be divided about 60-40 among equities and fixed income. The professors documented this phenomenon when they examined investing patterns among University of California employees, TWA pilots, and other workers.

Caution
You should avoid automatically dividing your money among all the choices in your plan. Every fund won't necessarily be appropriate.

For instance, most thirtysomethings probably shouldn't direct cash into a money market or even a bond fund. These funds aren't necessary for someone with an investing horizon of thirty-plus years. On the flip side, somebody in their sixties might not want to put money into a technology fund. What you shouldn't do is mistake your company's lineup of 401(k) choices for divine guidance. The funds you choose, along with the percentages allocated to different types of investments, should hinge upon your individual goals.

Decide how you want to allocate your 401(k) only after developing a game plan. Review your time horizon, risk tolerance, and financial goals, and then pick among the various categories such as large-cap, small-cap, and foreign stocks, bonds, and cash.

> **Tip**
>
> When developing a game plan, look at the big picture of how your total retirement pot is invested, including the funds in taxable accounts, IRAs, your children's college funds, and elsewhere.

Looking at the bigger picture can also help if you feel hemmed in by an inadequate 401(k) menu. Say your firm has great large- and small-cap stock picks, but a lousy foreign fund choice. If you want to add a foreign fund to your overall portfolio, stick with the two superior funds for your 401(k) plan and invest in a better quality foreign fund through an IRA.

If you're married, you should also attempt to coordinate his-and-her workplace retirement accounts. Ideally, you can capitalize on each plan's strengths. Examine the quality and variety of the mutual fund choices in both plans. Suppose a husband has excellent large-cap stock fund choices, while his wife has solid small-cap and foreign funds. If their goal is to structure a balanced portfolio, the decision could be an easy one. The wife could put all or most of her contributions into her strongest funds in her 401(k) lineup, while her husband does the same.

Strategy no. 2: Think stocks.

Stocks should play an important part in just about anybody's 401(k). Traditionally, older workers have tended to shy away from stocks, but even people who qualify for AARP membership should not do that. The potential growth provided by stocks is crucial today with Americans living longer.

By now, most people appreciate that a heavier stock concentration in a 401(k) mix means a larger potential payoff. But you may be surprised at just how big the bounce can be, over the long haul, if you lighten up on bonds. To illustrate the phenomenon, here are statistics from Ibbotson Associates, the Chicago research firm. Ibbotson used as a hypothetical worker a 40-year-old man who had already saved $100,000 in his 401(k), is funneling 8 percent of his paycheck into a 401(k), and enjoys a 50 percent company match.

If our hypothetical worker kept his asset mix at 75 percent stocks and 25 percent bonds, he'd retire at age 65 with a $2.7 million windfall. In contrast, an evenly divided portfolio of stocks and bonds would decrease his payout to $2.1 million. But the account would take a severe hit if our guy adored bonds. The ending balance for his 401(k) with a 75 percent bond concentration: $1.6 million.

Strategy no. 3: Don't overdose on company stock.

Corporations love it when their worker bees invest in company stock. Corporate boards prefer that employees control large blocks of stock because they are considered friendly shareholders. But what's good for a board arguably isn't always good for the rest of the corporate food chain. Since your livelihood depends on the health of the company, it's best not to link your entire financial future to your employer as well.

Lifestyle Funds—One-Stop Shopping

If you don't have the energy or desire to devise a model 401(k) portfolio, consider an easy way out. Chances are your company's 401(k)'s lineup includes *lifestyle funds,* whose assets are automatically divided among stocks, bonds, and cash so you don't have to stress about figuring out your asset allocation. Also known as *life cycle* or *target* retirement funds, these accounts do the heavy lifting for you. These funds are meant to encourage one-stop shopping. If you invest in one of these, you may not need any others.

Some lifestyle funds rely upon a fund manager to determine a portfolio's mix of stocks and bonds. But many funds rely on formulas that make adjustments to the mix as you age. One of these formula-based funds will grow more conservative as the years go by. The closer your retirement date looms, the less volatile the fund will become as it embraces a bigger dose of bonds.

To make the job easier for you, 401(k) lifestyle funds are typically labeled conservative, moderate, and aggressive. Someone in their 20s and 30s, unless extremely phobic about risk, would invest in an aggressive fund. A conservative fund would be appropriate for much older workers.

Despite the lifestyle fund's simplicity, not everyone uses them wisely. One study suggests that the vast majority of people mix these funds with other 401(k) funds. What's the harm? The combination can torpedo someone's ideal investment mix. If a company offered a trio of lifestyle funds and a young employee put money in all three, his or her investment mix would be skewed too conservatively. In the study, the typical twenty-something investors who invested in multiple lifestyle funds actually had a 401(k) portfolio that contained nearly 40 percent bonds. For most people that age, that's terribly conservative. In contrast, an older worker who mixes and matches lifestyle funds may be sitting on a 401(k) that's too aggressive.

What's the bottom line? Lifestyle funds are most appropriate for less sophisticated investors, who want someone else to make decisions for them. If you intend to select a variety of 401(k) funds, strongly consider forgetting about the lifestyle funds.

Unfortunately, investing in employers' stock is wildly popular. According to one survey, company stock—in plans where it's offered as an option—represented 30 percent of workers' portfolios. It's easy to see how this happens: While most companies provide some kind of match for employee 401(k) contributions, that match is often made with company stock. Many companies also offer stock as a 401(k) option, along with typical mutual fund choices. What's more, nearly 8 in 10 corporations don't limit the amount of stock people can hold in their 401(k) accounts.

Professional money managers wouldn't dare stuff their portfolios with just one stock. A corporate pension plan can legally invest only 10 percent of its assets in its own company stock. But investors do it all the time. According to an annual survey conducted by *Pensions & Investments,* Pfizer employees have 88 percent of their retirement savings squirreled away in company stock. At Chevron it's 81 percent and at General Electric the figure is 73 percent.

The Average 401(k) Stash

How do you compare? A new study, issued by the Investment Company Institute and the Employee Benefit Research Institute, found that the average 401(k) account balance is $47,000, an increase of 26 percent from just two years earlier. Yet the average balance can be misleading. While 13 percent of 401(k) savers enjoy balances above $100,000, 45 percent have balances below $10,000.

Limit your company stock to 5 percent to 10 percent of your 401(k) stock holdings. If your company provides a 401(k) match in stock, see if it allows you to sell it. If the answer is no, don't put any of your own cash into company stock.

Tip   Also consider avoiding mutual funds that own a chunk of your company or other stocks in the same industry.

Strategy no. 4: Contribute more money.

The more cash you kick in your 401(k), the better. If you're the typical American, you're funneling 6.7 percent of each paycheck into your 401(k). While that certainly seems admirable, it's probably not going to secure a Carnival Cruise lifestyle during retirement.

To encourage 401(k) participation, about 90 percent of corporations provide a match for their employees' contributions. By now, most people are well aware of the financial press's mantra—"Capture the match!" That is, kick in enough of your own money to prompt your company to contribute the maximum. This is, after all, free money. Ironically, workers' fixation on scoring the full extent of their company's match may encourage many people to inadvertently short change their retirement prospects—too many younger workers, in particular, have been lulled into a false sense of security. They lock in the match, but don't toss in a dime more than that. If you stop there, you could be jeopardizing your retirement years.

So how much is enough? Researchers at the Vanguard Group made their own stab at answering that vexing question. For the sake of the study, the researchers assumed that workers would be relying solely on their 401(k)s and Social Security in old age and could live off 75 percent of their preretirement salary. Someone earning $50,000 a year, who can squirrel away money in a 401(k) for 30 years, should be okay saving 15 percent of his or her salary. In contrast, folks making $100,000, and saving for 30 years, would have to save 20 percent of their salary to maintain their higher standard of living. Someone making $75,000 would need to save 18 percent for 30 years.

Caution   Vanguard estimates that workers are saving only two-thirds of what they should.

Strategy no. 5: Start early.

The sooner you begin saving, the better your chances of reaching the finish line with enough cash. If you're a procrastinator, here's a cautionary lesson: Suppose two colleagues, Kevin and Diane, have 40 years to invest in a 401(k). Kevin plunges right in and invests $4,000 a year for 10 years and then never puts another penny into his account. If the money returned the stock market's average of 11 percent, at the end of 40 years he would enjoy $1.5 million.

In contrast, Diane waits 10 years before that first 401(k) contribution. Retirement seems so far away, she doesn't see the point. When she realizes that she should be socking something away, she invests $4,000 per year for the next 30 years. She ultimately contributes $120,000, which is whopping $80,000 more than investor no. 1. But even though Diane contributes for 20 more years than does Kevin, the tortoise never does catch up with the hare. At the end of the line, she's sitting on an account worth just $796,084. The point here isn't to encourage you to start early and then give up—someone who puts money away for 40 years will have far more than either of these folks—but to illustrate the power of compounding. Starting early provides investors with an unbelievable advantage.

Strategy no. 6: Scrutinize your choices.

You should analyze your 401(k) plan the same way that you analyze your other investments. The typical 401(k) menu consists primarily of mutual funds. Here's a checklist of what you should ask before making any decisions:

What is each fund's three and five-year track?

Pay the closest attention to the three- and five-year performance records. While a fund might have enjoyed a couple of great quarters or even a year, this is far less important than the long-term track record.

How volatile is the fund?

Unless you're a kamikaze investor, you won't want an entire portfolio packed with wildly volatile funds. While many investors focus exclusively on return, they also need to determine how much risk funds are assuming to obtain impressive returns.

Is the current fund manager responsible for that track record?

It's important that the manager who engineered a fund's sterling performance is still on the job. If someone else is now running the fund, think twice before investing unless this newcomer earned an excellent reputation at his or her previous fund.

Is the fund too popular?

This is a more subjective call. Funds frequently touted in personal finance magazines are deluged with millions of dollars in cash. Managers of multi-billion-dollar funds can sometimes find it difficult to invest this money quickly and wisely; small-cap funds in particular are more likely to be hurt with large infusions of new money.

You don't need to be a detective to determine whether a fund is too popular. You can start by reading the material your company furnishes on each mutual fund. In addition, check out Morningstar's evaluation of these funds. Many public libraries carry *Morningstar Mutual Funds,* a monthly publication that analyzes individual funds.

Resource   Morningstar's Web site (www.morningstar.com) has plenty of info. More detailed scoop is available to premium online subscribers, but you can sign up for a free one-month subscription, which is more than enough time to do your research online.

Strategy no. 7: Resist borrowing from your 401(k).

If you've got a 401(k), there's a good chance that some of your money is missing. Nobody stole it, you just borrowed it. More than 82 percent of companies offering the popular workplace retirement plan permit 401(k) loans. Nearly $2 trillion dollars have piled up in the nation's 401(k) plans, and frankly, all that cash has become irresistible.

Americans don't need much of an excuse to tap into their 401(k)s. Retirement money has been used to pay for college tuition, honeymoons, debt consolidation, fully loaded SUVs, and tummy tucks. According to the Profit Sharing/401(k) Council of America, nearly one out of every four people eligible for a loan has obtained one.

Anything wrong with all this debt? Borrowers don't think so. After all, they suggest, tapping into a 401(k) is better than getting a cash advance from a Visa card that's charging 21 percent interest. While a 401(k) loan does mean you have to pay some interest charges, you collect that interest instead of a bank. The interest payments are funneled right into your 401(k). Sounds like a great deal, right? Not necessarily.

Caution   Treat your 401(k) as a sacred cow. Don't touch it unless you absolutely, positively have to.

Before deciding for yourself, you need to know the lending guidelines. Most workplaces won't let you borrow rinky-dink amounts. The minimum loan is usually $1,000, while the maximum is 50 percent of your account's value, up to a maximum of $50,000. Some companies allow one outstanding loan, while others permit employees to take out multiple ones. Unless the money is earmarked to buy a home, a loan must be paid back in five years. Meanwhile, the interest rates are attractive. They are usually set at 1 percent or 2 percent above the prime rate, which is the rate the best corporate borrowers can expect.

Prompt repayment required if you leave

Here's one of the little known dangers of 401(k) loans: It can chain you to your cubicle. 401(k) plans generally require borrowers to repay the debt within 30 to 60 days of their departure if they leave the company—even if you are laid off or retire. If you've taken out a major loan for college, a car, or a home remodeling project, you may find it impossible to pay back the loans immediately.

Example Suppose you borrow $30,000 to buy a new SUV. Six months later, you get a tantalizing job offer. You're itching to bail, but you have this debt hanging over your head. Unless you can come up with $30,000 pretty quick, you'll have stay with your current employer.

What happens if you can't come up with the money? Brace yourself for a financial nightmare. The Internal Revenue Service will treat a delinquent loan as a cash-out of your 401(k). Consequently, you'll owe income taxes on the remaining loan balance and you'll probably get hit with a 10 percent penalty. Suppose you still owe $28,000 on that SUV loan. If you're in the 27 percent tax bracket, your federal tax on that amount would be $7,560. The 10 percent penalty, which most 401(k) workers under the age of 55 face, adds another $2,800 to the tab. If your state imposes an income tax as well, the total tax pain could exceed $11,000.

In desperation, many people who can't afford this kind of tax whammy raid what's left of their 401(k) to pay off the IRS. This poor strategy only extends the financial death spiral since taxes will be owed on this cash as well.

Opportunity for big returns lost

Need another reason to avoid these loans? Treating your 401(k) like it's a MasterCard or a credit union can ultimately jeopardize your retirement. Many borrowers don't feel any regret because all the interest they're paying gets dumped back into their 401(k) accounts. But borrowers aren't figuring in their lost investment opportunity. Sure you may be paying yourself interest at 8 or 9 percent, but you're foregoing the opportunity to potentially make even better returns, over time, on that money.

Caution What's more, people don't calculate a 401(k)'s potential dormant period. Many times, workers stop contributing to their 401(k) during the years when they're repaying their loans, forcing them to try to play catch-up later on.

Since 401(k) loans pose dangers, why do so many companies offer them? Corporate America created 401(k) lending as a way to entice the lower paid workers to participate. Understandably, it's the workers, who take home the smallest paychecks, who are reluctant to stash money away for the future when they are living on the edge today. But it wasn't a strictly altruistic move. Thanks to federal regulations, low participation in a company's 401(k) plan reduces the contributions that the higher paid executives can make into their own accounts. For example, if assembly-line workers enroll in a 401(k) because they realize they can borrow for emergencies later, their bosses can stuff more money into their own 401(k)s.

The Ideal 401(k)

Do you know how well your company's 401(k) plan stacks up? With more and more people relying upon 401(k)s for a big chunk of their retirement nest egg, nobody wants to be saddled with a mediocre one. If you're contemplating a job offer, it's important to know how a company's 401(k) and other employee benefits, which typically represent 30 percent of someone's pay, measures up.

Here, then, are the features of a dream 401(k):

Immediate enrollment

A new employee should be able to enroll in a 401(k) immediately. Typically, companies have forced workers to wait an unconscionable 12 months or even longer to sign up. With job-hopping an American way of life, imposing these waiting periods can jeopardize retirement dreams.

Note

To remain competitive, employers are being forced to drop the artificial time limit or scale it back.

Automatic enrollment

A growing number of companies are instituting automatic enrollments, in which workers are enrolled even if they don't get around to doing it themselves. This can be a blessing for frazzled new employees, who are too preoccupied with the new job to worry about enrolling in the 401(k) plan. After they get settled in, they can better turn their attention to making any changes to the default selections made for them.

Tip

Employees who have been enrolled automatically in a 401(k) plan must review the choices that the company made for them, to ensure that those selections are appropriate.

While this feature has resulted in greater participation, it isn't a panacea. Workers who are enrolled this way rarely change the default investment selection or savings rate. A company determines in advance what percentage of pay will be automatically extracted from the paychecks of employees who never fill out the paperwork, and that rate is probably much smaller than you might have chosen had you signed up yourself. Also selected for the employee is an investment from the 401(k) menu, which will often be the most conservative fund available. If you were enrolled automatically in a 40(k), you should be able to change the choices made on your behalf at any time.

Caution

The default savings rate may be a very modest 3 percent; if you sign up on your own, you can save much more aggressively right from the start. Also, the default investing choice is frequently a money market—a poor choice for most workers.

Generous match

The higher the company match, the better. As mentioned earlier, the typical company will kick in 50 cents for every dollar a worker invests up to 6 percent of his or her pay. But roughly 30 percent of corporations do better than the 50-cent contribution. Some companies match an employee's contributions dollar for dollar.

Immediate vesting

Workers understand the value of their company matches, but what most don't appreciate is that these matches can evaporate—some companies impose a vesting schedule for the matches. Many workers aren't entitled to a full or partial match unless they remain with a company for several years. Suppose a worker managed to accumulate $15,000 in her 401(k). Of that amount, $4,000 was the company match. If she leaves before she's vested, she loses all $4,000. If she's stayed long enough to be partially vested, she'd keep only some of that money.

When Congress boosted the 401(k) contribution limits, the politicians also made it harder for companies to withhold their matches. Beginning in 2002, matching employer contributions must be fully available to workers after three years of employment or after six years if the contributions vest gradually.

The best plans don't attach strings to their matches—no matter how long employees remain, they get to leave with the whole enchilada.

Tip

If you are contemplating a job switch, check to see if you have been at your job long enough to secure the entire company match. If you're close to vesting, consider postponing your career move until you are.

Plenty of investment choices

In the old days, the typical 401(k) offered just two or three mutual funds. Today, most workers face eight to 12 choices. Company stock is also frequently offered as an option. Despite the increase in choices, experienced investors still chafe at the limited menu. What they crave is unlimited freedom to invest in anything they please, from individual blue chip stocks and Nasdaq darlings to any mutual fund that strikes their fancy.

A small but growing number of these workers are getting their wish as trailblazing companies are turning their 401(k)s into a la carte menus. With at least a portion of their 401(k) assets, employees can invest in a self-directed brokerage account and trade however they'd like. Of course, many investors are paralyzed by all the choices. Ideally, then, this freedom should also be accompanied by investment guidance for the inexperienced and timid. For instance, a company can use an outside firm like Morningstar to offer premixed model portfolios of funds for aggressive, middle-of-the-road, and conservative investors.

Note

By and large, companies remain leery of giving employees too much freedom. They often limit their employers to devoting no more than 50 percent of their assets into a brokerage type account.

If your 401(k) doesn't offer a brokerage feature, it should at least provide top-flight mutual fund choices. The lineup should cover these investment categories:

✦ Large-cap growth fund

✦ Large-cap value fund

✦ Index stock fund

✦ Small-cap growth fund

✦ Small-cap value fund

✦ Mid-cap growth fund

✦ Mid-cap value fund

✦ Foreign stock fund

✦ Intermediate-term bond fund

✦ Money market

An alternative to offering both a growth and value fund in the various stock categories is to provide a blend fund that combines both investing styles.

Cross-Reference See Chapter 12 for definitions of and details on such investment categories.

Investment advice

The best plans will provide employees with access to investment advice—a revolutionary development because corporate America has traditionally hesitated to extend a hand. Why? In a word, lawsuits. Providing meaningful investing advice, they worried, could backfire. They fretted that a guy in the mailroom, after hearing that he should invest in blue chip stocks, would sue if his large-cap stock fund tanked. Consequently, companies were content for many years to impose an information blackout. If they did provide advice at workplace enrollment seminars, it was couched in such vague generalities that it did little if any good.

Ironically, litigation fears are fueling a change in sentiment in America's boardrooms. Now CEOs worry that they might be sued if they don't offer relevant investment advice. The best 401(k) plans provide that guidance through outside firms that can help employees make educated decisions on how to spread their money among the various investment choices.

Note Most of this advice is offered online. If your company hasn't made this move yet, it's certainly worth asking about.

How Does Your 401(k) Compare?

Every year, Hewitt Associates, a national employees benefits firm, conducts an ambitious survey of the nation's 401(k) plans. Here are the results of its latest survey:

✦ Average number of investment options: 11 choices

✦ Most common investment option: large-cap stock fund 78 percent

✦ Provides company match: 92 percent

✦ Most common ceiling on employee contribution: 15 percent of salary

✦ Permits 401(k) loans: 92 percent

✦ Does not disclose 401(k) fees unless asked: 57 percent

✦ Allows daily fund transfers: 86 percent

✦ Provides investment education: 86 percent

✦ Average employee contribution: 6.7 percent

If your company won't pick up the modest tab for investment advice, which is based on the number of plan participants a company has, you can consult with online advisory services for little money. These services are typically priced with a flat fee of under $100 or $200 for an entire year. Some of these high-caliber services were previously available only to institutional investors and the very wealthiest investors.

Here's a listing of the major online retirement advisory services:

✦ Financial Engines (www.financialengines.com)

✦ mPower (www.mPower.com)

✦ DirectAdvice.com (www.directadvice.com)

✦ Morningstar ClearFuture (www.clearfuture.com)

The software developed by these companies is designed to be brutally frank about your investment choices. They may not only provide specific recommendations based upon your 401(k) portfolio and other retirement holdings, but they also predict how your choices might perform in the years or decades ahead. Fancier software analyzes your specific retirement holdings and simulates how they'll perform in thousands of economic scenarios in the future.

The software behind Financial Engines, for instance, can estimate—with a percentage—your own chances of having enough income to retire. For instance, the program might conclude that your portfolio of company stock and bond and large-cap stocks funds gives you a 79 percent chance of reaching your annual retirement income goal of $120,000. It also provides a worst and best case scenario of what your portfolio could be worth the day you cut your retirement cake. The software won't strand you if the odds aren't so hot. You can tinker with several factors under your control, such as your projected retirement age, your yearly retirement contributions, and your risk tolerance. By plugging in different numbers, you can determine how to improve your chances of attaining your financial goal.

Despite the spate of advisory services, online 401(k) advice is still in the dinosaur age. For now, certain services are limited to providing guidance on the 401(k) funds at your workplace, which won't be as helpful if you want to coordinate your 401(k) holdings with your IRAs and other accounts. Some people never bother with the advice software because it requires typing in all your holdings (along with the correct ticker symbols), with the appropriate number of shares and other data.

Tip   Before biting, get a free taste of what these services can provide. Some of Financial Engine's advice is free, while Morningstar's ClearFuture can be taken for a spin if you sign up for free online trial Morningstar membership.

Getting the 401(k) you want

What happens if you've got a mediocre 401(k) plan? You and some of your colleagues may want to engage in some quiet diplomacy to lobby for changes. It may seem that companies make 401(k) policy decisions in a vacuum, but these decisions can be far more influenced by water cooler sentiment than you think. In fact, employee dissatisfaction is largely credited with shrinking the qualifying period: Companies routinely made their new hires wait an entire year before they could even participate. In many places now, the waiting period has dwindled to three months or has disappeared entirely.

Workers who approach this mission in an intelligent and nonconfrontational way can often trigger change. If you'd like to give it a try, here are steps to take:

Enlist help.

You'll be much more credible if you encourage other unhappy campers in the office to join you. Find out what the sentiments of others are and what they'd like to see improved.

401(k) Advice for the Boss

When a company is launching a 401(k) plan or seeking to replace a poor 401(k) provider, choosing among the crush of brokers, mutual fund companies, insurers, and banks clamoring for the business can be confusing. Two Web sites—www.401kExchange.com and www.Search401k.com—attempt to evaluate a large number of 401(k) providers. Employers can use these sites to identify better plans and providers.

Send a letter.

Direct a letter to your workplace's benefits director detailing the reasons you and colleagues think the 401(k) plan is inadequate. Include ways you'd like to see it improved. Also arrange a talk about these concerns with the person responsible for the company's plan.

Be constructive.

Don't just blast your 401(k) program as mediocre. When talking with company officials, be specific about how the plan doesn't measure up. For instance, if the fund choices are subpar, provide evidence showing how a fund has lagged the performance of other funds in the same category. You can obtain information like that from Morningstar's materials.

Don't get discouraged.

If your reasoned approach falls flat, consider soliciting the aid of employee or union groups and volunteer for a seat on your company's benefits committee. Another option is to buttonhole a top executive. Remember, company's top officers probably have more sunk into their 401(k)s than others. They might be too preoccupied to realize how lousy their plan is. Finally, be patient. Don't be disheartened if change doesn't happen quickly. Altering a 401(k) plan can take time.

Your 401(k) on Moving Day

Americans don't like to be chained to their jobs too long. A typical worker stays at a job for four years. But chances are when you empty out the contents of your desk into cardboard boxes, you give little thought to perhaps the most valuable possession you'll take away—your 401(k).

And you're not alone. While Americans have accumulated small fortunes in their workplace retirement plans, they often make poor choices about what to do with this cash when they leave their jobs. One recent study suggests that 68 percent of job hoppers, unable to resist the temptation of easy money, cash in their 401(k)s. The younger the worker, the harder it is resist the easy money. Twenty- and thirty-somethings are the most likely to raid their retirement accounts when they quit a job. Before you can appreciate why this is a disastrous move, you'll need to understand the other four alternatives:

✦ Deposit all the money in an IRA rollover.

✦ Put everything but company stock in an IRA rollover.

✦ Keep your 401(k) at your old employer.

✦ Transfer the money to your new workplace.

The alternative you choose depends upon the specifics of your situation, but making the right choice could save you a huge pile of money.

Establish an IRA rollover.

By selecting an IRA rollover, your money remains sheltered from taxes until you begin withdrawing the money at retirement. If you've got decades until that milestone, your cash can experience explosive growth. Once the money is in a rollover, you may want to convert part or all of the cash into a Roth IRA, which allows retirees to withdraw the money without paying income tax on it.

Cross-Reference   Details on the Roth and other types of IRAs are found in Chapter 20.

You can easily set up an IRA at any brokerage firm, mutual fund company, bank, and other financial institutions. For many folks, the best bet is a discount brokerage firm, where they can choose investments from a huge menu of mutual funds, as well as individual stocks and bonds.

Tip   If you crave the freedom to invest your 401(k) cash any way you like, establishing an IRA rollover account is ideal.

If you choose an IRA rollover for your 401(k) cash, proceed carefully. Congress, in a greedy moment in the early 1990s, made the rollover rules complicated in hopes of generating cash for the federal Treasury.

Tip   To avoid having 20 percent of the money held back by your employer, make sure that your company transfers the cash directly to your IRA rollover account rather than send a check to you.

So, for example, if you establish an account with Merrill Lynch, that's where your employer should send the check. If the money is mailed to your home, 20 percent of the cash will be missing. If your 401(k) plan is worth $120,000 when you leave the company, but the check is sent directly to you, it will total just $96,000. You can blame the disappearance on the federally mandated 20 percent withholding tax.

If you had intended to put the full $120,000 into a rollover IRA, you then have to come up with that missing $24,000 on your own. And you've only got 60 days to deposit the full amount. If you only put $96,000 into the rollover account by that deadline, you'll owe tax on the missing $24,000. The amount withheld by your old employer will be used to pay the tax and a possible early withdrawal penalty.

Note   If you do manage to invest $120,000 before the deadline, you can receive a refund of the 20 percent withholding tax after filing your next federal income tax return.

If you don't roll over all the cash or roll over only part of the money, you will owe income tax on any amount not rolled over. However, the $24,000 withheld by your former employer will be applied to the taxes generated by this windfall.

Put everything but the company stock in an IRA rollover.

While choosing an IRA rollover is almost always the superior move, sometimes it's better to keep company stock from your 401(k) out of the rollover. This strategy might sound counter-intuitive. Why would you want to pay taxes up front on the stock, when all taxes can be postponed, in some cases for decades, if it is stashed in an IRA?

Tip   Strange as it may sound, you could ultimately lower your tax bill by putting company stock from your 401(k) in a taxable account when you leave the company.

Usually, financial advisors will recommend that older employees—those at least 55—keep their company stock out of their IRA rollovers. That's the age when the 10 percent early withdrawal penalty disappears for 401(k) investors. But this strategy can also be a great option for younger workers who are sitting on greatly appreciated company stock.

Here's why: If you stick the stock in a rollover, no taxes are owed immediately, but when you begin pulling this money out, the money will be taxed at your ordinary income tax rate. You can lessen the tax bite, however, if you segregate the stock in its own taxable account, because then you'll owe up-front taxes only on the *cost basis*—the amount you actually paid for the stock during your years as a 401(k) investor (a figure your employer provides). At this point, you won't pay any taxes on the appreciation.

Example   Say you paid an average of $30 a share for your company stock over the years and now it's worth $200 a share. You owe no taxes on that fat profit until you sell the stock.

Once you begin selling the stock, you'll pay tax on this appreciation, but here's where keeping the stock out of the IRA will pay off. You will be liable for only long-term capital gains taxes, which max out at 20 percent. Remember, if you keep the stock in the IRA, the tax bill would be based upon your ordinary income tax rate, which could be significantly higher.

But if you're young, shouldn't the prospects of that 10 percent early withdrawal penalty discourage you from keeping stock out of an IRA? Actually, if your stock has a low cost basis, it's not a big deal. You would owe a 10 percent penalty, but it would be based on the stock's cost basis, *not* on your stock's actual current worth.

Example   If the cost basis of your company stock is $5,000 but it's worth $75,000 when you leave, you'd owe a penalty of only $500, not $7,500.

Still not convinced? Here's an example that compares the two strategies. Suppose you leave your company with 5,000 shares of company stock that was bought at various prices over the years. Today's share price is $40, so your stock is worth

$200,000. The cost basis is $20,000. Say you're in the 30 percent tax bracket and you put the stock in an IRA. A year later you sell it for $250,000 and withdraw it from the account. The withdrawal pushes you into the 38.6 percent bracket so your tax bill is $96,500 (38.6% × $250,000).

What if you had kept the stock in a taxable brokerage account instead and sold it a year later for $250,000? Up front, you would have paid income tax on the cost basis ($20,000 × 30% = $6,000), as well as a 10 percent penalty on the cost basis ($20,000 × 10% = $2,000). When you sold the stock, however, your profit would have been taxed at the more favorable long-term capital gain of 20 percent ($230,000 × 20% = $46,000). Your total tax bill—$54,000—wouldn't be nearly as painful.

Leave the money there.

Keeping your 401(k) at your old company can give you breathing room until you're ready to make investment decisions. For most people, leaving it there should be a temporary solution. Why not just leave it there forever? For starters, your old 401(k) will have a limited number of investment options. What's more, you never know what will happen to your former company. With mergers and acquisitions so common, you're leaving money behind with the knowledge that the company might be absorbed and disappear, making it difficult to discover where your cash is.

If you'd rather not disturb your 401(k), learn how flexible the plan will be once you're gone. Some companies impose arbitrary rules that dictate when ex-employees can dip into their 401(k)s. Ideally, the access to your 401(k) should be the same as you'd enjoy with an IRA rollover. Also, staying put may not be possible if you've got $5,000 or less in your 401(k) account. Employers are entitled to close out these modest accounts when workers leave. Plus, leaving behind a trail of small balances of $5,000 to $10,000 at former employers is not an efficient use of your money.

Escort your 401(k) to your new workplace.

In one recent study, only 6 percent of Americans chose to roll their 401(k)s into plans at their new companies. But if the prospect of establishing an IRA rollover and selecting your own investments leaves you cold, this tactic might work better for you. Moving your money to your next employer can make your financial life easier than leaving it with your old workplace or establishing a rollover IRA. If you move your 401(k) to the new employer, everything is together, you get one quarterly statement, and the money is in one place. You don't have to worry about keeping track of it.

Obviously, you're not going to want to transfer your 401(k) to your new company if its 401(k) plan offers a paucity of investments. Find out too whether your new employer is willing to accept your old 401(k). Some companies impose a one-year waiting period on 401(k) participation.

Cash out your 401(k).

Of course, most people just take the cash and run, using it to remodel their kitchens or buy new cars. If you follow the herd, you won't have the money when you really need it—during retirement. And by then, there won't be any more salary increases and job promotions to bail you out. But even if that grim prospect doesn't faze you, this might: The IRS is laying in wait.

Caution Most people must pay stiff taxes when they prematurely cash out—leaving that much less cash to live on during retirement.

Suppose you're 40 years old and in the 30 percent tax bracket when you cash out a 401(k) worth $75,000. Right off the top, the IRS will demand 30 percent of that money. Since you're under the age of 55, you'll likely be assessed that additional 10 percent early withdrawal penalty. Without figuring in the potential state income tax, your tax bill on the $75,000 will be $30,000! If someone had stuck a gun in your face and ran off with all the money in your wallet, much less $30,000, you'd never, ever forget it. Yet departing workers lose tremendous amounts of their retirement money every day without blinking.

Annuitize the 401(k).

If you're eager to get your hands on the cash once you've decided to leave a company, consider a compromise. You can tap into your 401(k) without incurring the 10 percent penalty—no matter what your age—if you *annuitize* it. By annuitizing, you agree to follow one of a variety of formulas that dictate the amount you need to take out of your old 401(k) each year.

When you annuitize through what's called a 72(t), you've got to keep pulling money out, in what the IRS refers to as a "series of substantially equal periodic payments," for five years or until age 59½, whichever is longer. After a payment schedule is established, it can't be adjusted. Say you've agreed to drain $20,000 out of the 401(k) annually. The government will expect you to keep pulling out that amount for the required time period even if you have second thoughts about spending it so soon.

 Cross-Reference You can also annuitize an IRA. For more on 72(t)s, see Chapter 20.

Summary

✦ Determine whether your 401(k) allocations mesh appropriately with the rest of your holdings.

✦ Start early and contribute the maximum amount to your 401(k).

✦ Avoid borrowing from your 401(k).

✦ If your company's 401(k) plan is mediocre, gently lobby for changes.

✦ When leaving a job, the best place for your 401(k) cash is usually in an Individual Retirement Account rollover.

✦ Consider keeping 401(k) company stock out of an IRA rollover.

The Truth About Annuities

After reading this chapter, you should know whether or not investing in a variable annuity is a wise move. For many Americans, recent tax changes in Washington D.C. have made these annuities a less attractive option than in the past. Those who remain interested, will learn where to find the best and cheapest annuities. The chapter also focuses on a promising annuity that very few individuals know anything about.

Don't Believe the Hype

If you own a variable annuity, do you know why? Without considerable hesitation, can you explain how an annuity works to somebody else? Do you know how much your annuity is costing every year?

If you're stumped by questions like these, it's no surprise. While people have poured billions upon billions of dollars into variable annuities, many have done so without really understanding why they are doing it. Many have a vague notion that annuities are a great way to shelter their money from taxes. But they don't realize that some annuities can be ticking tax bombs. Unfortunately, while many excellent variable annuities exist on the market, people often end up with mediocre and expensive ones because they don't know where to look.

Although investors can't always explain how an annuity snuck into their portfolios, the insurance industry knows why. Variable annuities have become the salvation of an industry that's encountered resistance from investors balking at buying expensive cash value life insurance policies. Variable annuities have also been a boon to insurance agents and brokers, who earn generous commissions with every annuity sale.

An Annuity Quiz That Could Save You Big Bucks

First ask yourself these questions:

✦ Do you usually skip contributing the yearly maximum to your workplace retirement plan and an Individual Retirement Account?

✦ Do you wish to invest in an annuity through a retirement account?

✦ Would you like to leave money in your annuity to an heir?

✦ Do you plan to withdraw money from an annuity within a few years?

✦ Are you in a high tax bracket?

✦ Do you expect to cash out or withdraw money from an annuity before age 59½?

✦ Are you in your fifties or sixties or older?

If you answered yes to any one of these questions, you probably should not be investing in a variable annuity. You will discover the reasons why throughout the chapter.

Caution   While variable annuities have experienced tremendous popularity, the sales figures obscure this uncomfortable reality: Many of the people who own variable annuities would have been better off without them. For most people, there are cheaper and more effective ways to invest for retirement.

Investing in variable annuities became even less desirable after Congress passed legislation in 2001 that increases the amount of money Americans can stuff into Individual Retirement Accounts and workplace retirement plans. It's better to sink as much money as the rules allow into these retirement accounts before turning to a variable annuity. The appeal of another kind of annuity, however, remains undiminished—the little-known but quite handy *immediate annuity,* which can provide a steady source of income during retirement. Ironically, while immediate annuities can be a tremendous source of comfort to many of the nation's retirees, who are living on fixed incomes, few annuities are used in this way.

Before you can decide whether an annuity makes sense for you, you'll need to learn how these investments really tick.

Variable Annuities 101

A variable annuity is a financial hybrid: part insurance policy and part mutual fund. Within an insurance wrapper, policyholders park their money in mutual funds that are referred to as *subaccounts.* The annuity is called variable because the return depends upon how the underlying mutual funds perform. Most Americans pour money into annuities during their savings years. Once they reach retirement, they tend to withdraw all or some of this cash.

Tip
Knowing how an annuity's subaccounts have performed historically is extremely important. You don't want to be saddled with a mediocre basket of funds. Before choosing an annuity, examine its subaccounts carefully.

Within an annuity, you should find a wide array of fund choices. A good annuity will be stocked with funds that specialize in small and large companies, overseas stocks and bonds. Within the fund menu, you should also be able to diversify with value and growth investing styles. While all variable annuities are created by insurance companies, the underlying investment choices in a single annuity can be provided by a variety of mutual fund firms, such as Janus, Fidelity, Vanguard, AIM, Putnam, and T. Rowe Price. Ideally, a variable annuity should offer enough fund choices so that an investor can be comfortably diversified among different types of stocks and bonds.

Cross-Reference
Because the variable annuity captures most of the attention, many people aren't even aware that another kind exists. Chapter 2 tells you about the fixed annuity, which can serve as an attractive alternative to a certificate of deposit.

Variable annuity strengths

Here are the reasons some people gravitate to variable annuities:

A variable annuity provides a death benefit.

Because annuities are a creation of insurance companies, they offer the promise that if you die, your heirs will at least get the amount of money that you initially deposited, minus any withdrawals that you made. Suppose someone invests $100,000 in an annuity and then the stock market crashes. The investor dies a short time later when her annuity is only worth $90,000. Thanks to the insurance, however, her survivors are entitled to the original $100,000 investment.

Your money grows tax deferred.

Contributions to a variable annuity are not tax-deductible, but while your money is in one, Uncle Sam can't touch it. Your money can happily compound for many years while you postpone paying taxes until the cash is withdrawn.

Note
When you eventually withdraw money out of the annuity, however, it is taxed at your current income tax bracket.

You can transfer cash between investments tax-free.

Variable annuities provide flexibility that you can't enjoy with investments outside a retirement account. You can transfer money among fund subaccounts within an annuity without getting slammed with taxes. Suppose your variable annuity offers 10 investment choices that run the gamut from a large-cap growth fund to a junk bond fund. If you want to rebalance your portfolio by transferring money from a technology fund to a small-cap value fund, for instance, no taxes are triggered.

In contrast, this tax benefit vanishes if you shuffle money in and out of taxable mutual funds. For instance, if you move cash out of the Fidelity Growth & Income Fund and direct it into the Vanguard 500 Index Fund, you'll have to pay taxes on any profit. This is often a shock for investors, who don't realize that switching from one fund to another, even within the same fund family, can trigger taxes.

You can swap annuities tax-free.

If you become disenchanted with your annuity, there's a way to move your money to a better annuity without generating taxes. When money is directly transferred from one annuity to another, no taxes are owed. At the end of this chapter, you'll learn more about these fund swaps, which are called 1035 Exchanges.

There's no limit on contributions.

As any eager beaver retirement saver can tell you, there is a cap on yearly contributions to an Individual Retirement Account. The federal government also keeps a lid on how much we can save in 401(k)s and other employer-sponsored retirement plans. But the variable annuity isn't shackled with any such restriction. Investors can stuff as much money into an annuity as they please.

Note   This option could be particularly appealing to some wealthy individuals who would like to shelter more money from taxes after they've maxed out their contributions to their other retirement accounts.

Learning About Annuities Online

Want to know more about annuities? Here are some sources:

✦ **Variable Annuities Online:** This site is a dream for anybody who's hunting for a high performance variable annuity. The site offers screening software that allows you to pinpoint best performing annuity subaccounts. You can also compare the performance of individual subaccounts with appropriate indexes, such as the Standard & Poor's 500. The Web site is www.variableannuityonline.com.

✦ **AnnuityNet.com:** A calculator on this site helps you assess whether you should invest in an annuity. You can also obtain information on some variable annuities. The Web site is www.annuitynet.com.

✦ **Morningstar:** *Morningstar Variable Annuity Performance Report* covers thousands of fund subaccounts and highlights the top performers. The report provides information necessary to compare different annuities. If someone wants to sell you a variable annuity, ask him or her for copies of the relevant Morningstar evaluations. Also helpful is Morningstar's Web site: You can see what ordinary investors are saying about annuities by typing "variable annuity" into the site's search engine. The Web site is at www.morningstar.com; phone number is (800) 735-0700.

Annuities have a more lenient withdrawal schedule.

The annuity enjoys another edge on 401(k)s and traditional IRAs, which require investors to begin withdrawing money shortly after reaching the age of 70½. In most cases, an annuity investor doesn't have to touch the money until age 85. (Among IRA options, only the Roth IRA permits savers to never touch their accounts no matter what their age is.) However, a variable annuity can be converted into a stream of income upon the owner's retirement, if need be.

Variable annuity weaknesses

Here are some of the major reasons why variable annuities have come under fire:

They cause greater tax pain at the end of the line.

Proponents love to tout the annuity's tax-fighting abilities: As long as the money stays inside the annuity, no tax is owed. But the IRS's patience doesn't last forever. It eventually expects to be paid. And so the tax protection evaporates when you withdraw money from a variable annuity. All the profits are taxed at your income tax rate. So if you're in the 30 percent tax bracket, close to one-third of all your gains will disappear. If you're in the top tax brackets, the tax bill hurts even more.

Okay, you might be thinking, taxes are inevitable for all investors, so why gripe about taxes on annuity profits? This is why: If you had invested cash in mutual funds or stocks outside an annuity, your tax bill would look puny in comparison. Why? Because the capital gains tax rates that apply to regular funds and stocks aren't so draconian. If you hold onto a stock or fund in a regular taxable brokerage account for more than a year, the highest tax you will face is 20 percent. Now 20 percent is a lot more palatable than 38.6 percent or even 27 percent.

> **Note**
>
> If you're in the 15 percent tax bracket, the tax on annuities might seem more advantageous, but that's not true either. For folks in this low tax bracket, the long-term capital gains rate is only 10 percent. What's more, if you've held an investment for at least five years, the rate drops to 8 percent.

So which sounds better to you—investing in stocks within an annuity, where you can postpone income taxes for many years, or in a taxable mutual fund, which may generate capital gains taxes each year? It might surprise you that in numerous studies, regular mutual funds have triumphed as the clear winner.

With the combined whammy of higher taxes and expensive costs, you'd have to remain loyal to your annuity for many years before your ultimate after-tax return could equal or exceed the one enjoyed by the typical mutual fund. In fact, you may have to hold onto an annuity for a couple of decades or more before you come out ahead. Of course, it's not realistic to expect somebody to hang onto any investment for that long. Because of this incredibly long holding period, variable annuities are generally not appropriate for people in their fifties, sixties or older.

Resource If you're unsure whether to buy a variable annuity, you may want to order free software developed by T. Rowe Price. The software compares the after-tax returns possible through an annuity versus regular mutual funds. Contact T. Rowe Price at (800) 638-5660 or `www.troweprice.com`.

Annuities are expensive.

Many variable annuities are price hogs. The fees that the typical annuity generates are far higher than regular mutual fund fees. Many people are unaware of the slew of fees being automatically deducted each year from their accounts. The high price tag can partly be explained by the traditional way these products are sold. Insurance companies must recover the costs of the commissions they pay to brokers, insurance agents, and planners, who pitch these products.

But another major reason why fees are so steep is that people haven't grumbled. Many customers, puzzled by this complicated product, do not comparison-shop. Unlike educated mutual fund buyers, they usually depend upon salespersons, who steer them to products with generous commissions. Also, some folks are so determined to shelter their money from current taxes that they never think to focus on the real cost of the annuity.

Here is the lineup of annuity fees:

✦ Mortality and expense risk charge (death benefit)

✦ Administrative fees

✦ Investment fee for underlying mutual funds

✦ Fees and charges for special features such as an enhanced death benefit

The most questionable fee of the bunch is arguably the mortality and expense risk charge, which compensates an insurer for providing the annuity's insurance coverage. The typical death benefit charge is 1.25 percent of the value of your assets. If someone's annuity was worth $50,000, the yearly fee would be $625.

Note Annuities work best for investors with lengthy time horizons, which makes it highly unlikely that the death benefit will ever be needed.

Suppose a 40-year-old, for instance, sinks $50,000 in an annuity for his retirement years. During the intervening years the market experiences its usual ups and downs. Shortly before he's ready to retire, however, the investor dies. What can his loved ones expect from the death benefit? Probably nothing. The typical annuity only ensures that the heirs will receive the lump of money that's been invested in the annuity. In this case, it's $50,000. But since more than two decades passed since that first investment, the account's value is probably far greater than $50,000. So in this example, the investor paid thousands and thousands of dollars in death benefit insurance for protection that became less and less important as time passed.

TIAA-CREF: A Glowing Exception to the Rule

There is one notable exception to the admonition that retirement plans and annuities don't mix. The nation's teachers have traditionally saved for their retirement through annuities. Fortunately, a major provider of these annuities is TIAA-CREF, which stands for Teachers Insurance and Annuity Association—College Retirement Equities Fund.

TIAA-CREF, which manages the world's largest private pension system, is fanatical about keeping expenses low. Unlike many insurers, it doesn't use surrender charges, nor does it offer a death benefit because it thinks it's a waste of customers' money. It also doesn't maintain a sales force, so commissions don't exist. Because of the penny pinching, the costs of a TIAA-CREF annuity are lower than the costs of most regular mutual funds. TIAA-CREF is in the same league as the Vanguard Group, the mutual fund firm known for its rock-bottom expenses.

Some academic researchers have concluded that the death benefit charges are extremely inflated. In a study done at York University in Canada with Goldman Sachs, researchers concluded that the insurance for a typical death benefit is only worth between 1 and 10 *basis points*. A basis point equals 1/100th of a percentage point. So a realistic charge on a $50,000 annuity would range from $5 to $50. In contrast, that $625 protection looks awfully steep.

It's expensive to cut the ties.

If you have second thoughts, walking away from an annuity can cost you dearly. If you wish to bail or withdraw just a portion of your money, most insurers will zap you with a surrender fee if you withdraw your money within the first 6 to 8 years and sometimes longer. The charge, which typically starts at 7 percent of your investment, often declines by one percentage point each year and eventually disappears for the long-term investor. So if someone sank $100,000 into an annuity and decided to pull the money out that same year, the tab for leaving would be $7,000. (In contrast, most mutual funds say goodbye to departing shareholders without charging anything.)

While many surrender charges eventually disappear, others are more insidious. Rolling surrender charges can keep the penalty alive for many more years. That is, every time an investor contributes more money into the annuity, the clock is reset and a new surrender period starts for the new cash.

Tax law has dimished their importance.

It's best not to invest in a variable annuity unless you've maxed out your yearly contributions to a workplace retirement plan, as well as an Individual Retirement Account. It's better to stuff money into these retirement options than a variable annuity. Why? For starters, those are pre-tax dollars you deposit into a 401(k), a 403(b) and other such workplace plans. The money gets siphoned out of your paycheck before it's hit with income taxes. Consequently, you lock in an immediate tax benefit that you can't get with a variable annuity, which is funded with taxable dollars.

Beware of Bonus Annuities

The annuity industry shares the same work ethic as Santa's elves. Insurers are busily trying to outdo each other by developing new features to attract greater foot traffic. What's the new hot product? The bonus annuity.

Bonus annuities, when explained by an agent or investment advisor, sound fabulous. By signing up, a customer can pocket thousands and sometimes tens of thousands of dollars. It certainly beats the old days when new savings and loan customers were presented with toasters. The fine print, however, reveals a different story. Here's how the bonus annuity typically works: Someone who buys an annuity is typically rewarded with a 3 percent to 5 percent bonus, which is deposited into a customer's account. So if someone purchases a $50,000 variably annuity, the customer can be entitled to a $2,500 bonus. At the start, the annuity's value would therefore be $52,500. That sure looks like a great head start, but in many cases it's a mirage.

Insurers aren't in the business of handing out wads of free cash. In reality, insurers often compensate for their apparent generosity by lengthening the annuity's surrender period by several years, increasing the death benefit charge, or adding other extra charges.

Even worse, sales forces are using the promise of bonuses to encourage investors to dump their current annuities for the bonus variety. This is a dangerous practice because customers, eager to grab the cash, may have to pay an onerous surrender charge to break their current contract. Even a long-time annuity customer, who doesn't face a surrender charge, can lose out. Purchasing a new annuity will start a new surrender fee schedule.

Bonus annuities have become popular because customers aren't aware of the quid pro quo—the free money isn't free at all. Concerned about how these annuities are being peddled, the U.S. Securities and Exchange Commission is investigating what it believes are questionable sales practices.

If you are tempted to buy a bonus annuity, look closely at the provisions of the contract and compare your current annuity with the new one. Chances are you'll be better off staying put.

Investing through IRAs is also preferable to using an annuity. With a Roth IRA, your investment enjoys tax-free growth; if you follow the rules, you or your heirs will never pay income tax on that money, ever. Meanwhile, the deductible IRA provides for an upfront tax deduction. Again, the annuity can't compete.

Only after all these retirement options have been maxed out should anyone even think about investing in an annuity. The federal tax legislation in 2001, however, made it less likely that people will even reach that point. That's because the contribution ceilings for IRAs and workplace retirement plans are being steadily raised. Consequently, investors can now put more money into these superior retirement plans. As a result, there will be less of a chance that any extra money earmarked for retirement will be left over.

Annuities can be used improperly.

Many people unwisely park their annuities inside Individual Retirement Accounts. What's wrong with this? IRAs and other types of retirement plans already provide protection against taxes. Money inside an IRA can grow without the threat of taxes for decades, so purchasing an annuity to put inside one of these accounts only results in unnecessary duplication. It's like opening an umbrella inside the house to keep dry.

Note   What's the harm of double protection? Remember, most variable annuities are expensive. You are paying a premium price for an annuity's tax benefits. Why pay extra for something you don't need?

The salespeople pitching these annuities don't always point out this consideration to their potential customers, so investors keep making this same mistake. The SEC has expressed concern about this practice, while some insurers have been sued for marketing annuities to IRA and 401(k) investors.

Americans are misusing annuities in another way. Many of the customers snatching up variable annuities are closing in on retirement age. As you've already learned, it could take decades before an annuity pencils out financially, but these folks won't necessarily have that much time on their side.

Annuities can be complicated.

Annuities can be difficult to understand, but unbiased advice is hard to find. The most common source of information on annuities is the investment advisors or agents who plug them. It's not hard to fathom how this can represent a conflict of interest. A typical customer knows little about annuities and so depends upon an agent, who will only earn a commission if he clinches the sale. Agents won't necessarily present an annuity's pros and cons, but rather will boast of a particular annuity's finest features. Don't expect an agent or broker to tell a customer that his or her annuity costs twice as much as another.

An annuity shopper is confronted with a dizzying array of features. The market is so competitive that insurers have felt compelled to continue offering new bells and whistles. Here are some of the extras that you might run across:

✦ Stepped-up death benefit

✦ Guaranteed minimum income benefit

✦ Long-term care insurance

Trouble is, you'll be paying extra for all of these options. If you do invest in an annuity, ask about the need for these features, and take the time to find out whether you can purchase such protection through separate and less-expensive policies.

Annuities are bad news for heirs.

If you die with money sitting in your variable annuity, your heirs will be in for a rude tax surprise. Your loved ones would have to pay capital gains taxes on any profit your annuity generated. So if you bought an annuity for $25,000 years ago and it's worth $55,000 when you die, tax will be owed on the $30,000 profit. And although you were paying for a death benefit the whole time, your heirs don't receive a death benefit payout—which might have offset the tax due—in addition to getting a check for the value of the account. Only if the value of the account dips below the original investment do heirs receive the death benefit sum.

The IRS treats other investments much more gently. Suppose you put that original $25,000 in a stock or mutual fund years ago and it too was worth $55,000 when you died. The kids sell the investment for the $30,000 profit, but they'll owe no capital gains tax at all. They enjoy what's called a *step-up cost basis*. Essentially, the IRS pretends the original investment was bought at $55,000 instead of the much lower price. You can't use the step-up cost basis loophole for annuities.

Sources for inexpensive variable annuities

Not all annuities are fee hogs. Some annuities keep expenses low and don't bother with surrender fees. Some refuse to pass along a death benefit fee. Ironically, these consumer-friendly annuities are largely ignored—the over-priced ones are far more popular. Why is that? Salespeople don't get paid to pitch the low-priced annuities, so they don't.

Economical annuities are typically offered by no-load mutual fund companies and discount brokerage firms, shutting out the middlemen by selling directly to the public.

Here are some sources of low-priced annuities:

✦ TIAA-CREF at (800) 842-2776 or `www.tiaa-cref.com`

✦ Vanguard at (800) 635-1511 or `www.vanguard.com`

✦ TD Waterhouse at (800) 745-6665 or `www.tdwaterhouse.com`

✦ T. Rowe Price at (800) 638-5660 or `www.troweprice.com`

✦ Fidelity at (800) 343-3548 or `www.fidelity.com`

✦ Schwab at (800) 838-0650 or `www.schwab.com`

✦ Ameritas Life Insurance at (800) 745-6665 or `www.ameritas.com`

✦ USAA at (800) 531-8343 or `www.usaa.com`

Ditching a Variable Annuity

Bailing out of an annuity can be as difficult as scraping gum off your shoe. Once you sign up, an insurer won't want you to leave. The trick is to plan your exit without losing a great deal of money in surrender fees and taxes. Here are some escape routes to consider:

Surrender the contract.

If you are dissatisfied with an annuity or you need the money, you can surrender your annuity for its cash value. What discourages some investors from acting is the surrender charge, as well as a looming tax threat.

When contemplating abandoning an annuity, compare the remaining surrender charge, if any, to the costs your investment is generating annually. The surrender penalty might not seem so onerous, when compared to the possible high cost of sitting tight. You will also want to factor in an annuity's performance. If the underlying investment funds are mediocre, this will provide even more incentive to move on.

Note When leaving, you also must consider the tax consequences. If you cash out, you'll owe income tax on your previously untaxed gains.

What's Your Beef?

If you've encountered problems with an annuity, here are three possible sources to contact:

✦ **U.S. Securities and Exchange Commission.** The SEC is interested in hearing from consumers with complaints about any type of investments. You can mail or fax your grievance or fill out an online complaint form. It has also produced an excellent publication entitled *Variable Annuities: What You Should Know,* that you can obtain either online or by contacting the SEC at its Office of Investor Education and Assistance, 450 Fifth St. NW, Washington, DC 20549; (202) 942-7040; www.sec.gov.

✦ **National Association of Securities Dealers.** You can contact the NASD, which regulates the securities industry, if you have a complaint about annuity sales practices. You may file the complaint online at www.nasdr.com or by contacting the nearest NASD regional office. You can find these phone numbers in the Resource Guide.

✦ **National Association of Insurance Commissioners.** This nonprofit organization represents insurance regulators in the 50 states and Washington, DC. Through the organization, you can find the contact number for your state's insurance commission. The address is 2301 McGee, Suite 800 Kansas City, MO. 64108; Web site is www.naic.org.

Many people will also be hit with an early 10 percent withdrawal penalty. The penalty kicks in for most individuals if they withdraw money before the age of 59½. There is a way, however, to postpone the taxes and sidestep the penalty. You can swap annuities.

Swap one annuity for another.

Taxes won't be a worry if you transfer your money from one annuity to another. You'll hear a planner or insurance agent refer to this as a *1035 exchange*. It gets its name from Section 1035 of the federal tax code. A 1035 exchange acts just like an Individual Retirement Account rollover. As long as the money is sent directly from one annuity to the next, no taxes or penalty apply.

Caution   If you swap annuities, make sure the money is sent directly from your original annuity insurer to the next. Do not instruct your old annuity provider to send you the check directly. If you get the check, your tax protection is blown to smithereens, even if you quickly re-shelter it.

Immediate Annuities: An Attractive Alternative for Retirees

Insurers have taken a lot of flak for making expensive and complicated variable annuities seem as indispensable as cold beer and hot dogs at a World Series game. But they could improve their reputations by becoming enthusiastic about immediate annuities, products that could make sense for many older Americans. A big reason these annuities aren't selling much is that they lack cheerleaders.

Immediate annuities are designed for retirees who'd like their money to generate a dependable monthly check. After depositing cash into an immediate annuity, monthly checks begin—and they can never run out. For instance, if you start collecting payments when you're 65 and you're still alive 30 years later, the insurance company continues to mail those checks, even if your original investment vanished long ago. When you purchase an immediate annuity, the insurer, using actuarial charts, bases your payment amount on how long you are likely to live.

Two options: Fixed and variable

Customers can choose between fixed and variable immediate annuities, depending upon whether they favor a conservative or aggressive investment style. Most of the immediate annuities that are being sold are the fixed variety, but more variable ones are being developed.

When you opt for a fixed annuity, you're guaranteed a set rate of return for your investment. The rate of return can never slip below the figure set when you signed up. While going with a fixed rate doesn't provide assurance that the annuity will keep up with inflation, a fixed annuity is suitable for folks desiring a sure thing.

Tip The fixed immediate annuities promise interest rates that are usually higher than a certificate of deposit's. What's more, the annuity owner enjoys a better tax break than a CD holder, because a portion of the monthly checks is considered a return of principal, which is not taxed.

In contrast, a variable immediate annuity behaves more like a mutual fund, but it offers an insured guarantee against losing even a fraction of your original investment (unlike mutual funds). The value of your annuity depends upon how well the underlying funds are performing; the heavy reliance on stock funds causes the fluctuations in rates and the accompanying fluctuation in your investment's value.

Who should consider an immediate annuity?

Immediate annuities can be ideal for a retiring worker who has received a lump sum from a 401(k) or other retirement plan and is uncertain how to invest it. It can also be a good idea for someone who has no pension to fall back on. Retiring with only Social Security providing a reliable stream of income can be a scary prospect.

If you have heirs counting on an inheritance, however, you might want to think twice about an immediate annuity. Why? Because once you annuitize with the traditional immediate product, called a *life annuity,* there's no retreating. If you put $150,000 into an immediate annuity and get hit by a bus a year later, that $150,000 belongs to the insurer, not your loved ones. Unlike with a variable annuity, there is no death benefit option with an immediate annuity.

Caution If you have second thoughts about choosing an immediate annuity after you have signed the paperwork, there's no getting your money back.

Policy options to take care of heirs

Knowing that the insurer keeps all the cash if they should die scares off plenty of investors. They are petrified by the hit-by-a-bus scenario. This risk, however, doesn't have to be a deal breaker. You can invest in an immediate annuity and still provide for loved ones. Here are some of the options:

✦ **Joint and life survivor:** This option is popular with couples. While both husband and wife are alive, they will pocket the full monthly checks. When one of them dies, the checks are reduced by either 25 percent or 50 percent. These smaller checks will continue until the widow or widower dies.

✦ **Life annuity with period certain:** With this option, the customer receives the annuity until death. If he or she should die before a predetermined period of time, which ranges from 5 to 20 years, the checks continue for a designated beneficiary. A 10-year period certain annuity, for instance, would not vanish if the client dies within a decade. So if a person bought this annuity in 2002 and died in 2006, the annuity would live on for another six years.

Caution   Annuities that last for more than one person's lifetime won't provide as much monthly income.

Quote sources for immediate annuities

If you'd like an immediate annuity, here are some sources for quick quotes:

✦ **Annuity Shopper.** At this Web site, you can plug in your age, state, and type of immediate annuity you desire and receive immediate quotes. Annuity Shopper also provides quotes for about two dozen insurers by phone. The Annuity Shopper doesn't supply quotes for some of the low-cost leaders, such as Vanguard and TIAA-CREF, so you'll need to contact them on your own (see those listings in the Resource Guide). Go to www.annuityshopper.com or call (800) 872-6684.

✦ *Comparative Annuity Reports.* This newsletter provides information on dozens of immediate annuity alternatives. Subscribers can also obtain brief consultations by phone at (916) 487-7863. Web address is www.annuitycomparativedata.com.

✦ **AnnuityRateWatch.com:** This Web site provides the top 25 quotes for a variety of annuities, including the fixed and immediate varieties. It also provides annuity product profiles.

Annuity Shopping List

Before buying an annuity, compare several policies, especially from sources known for their low costs. Here are questions to ask:

✦ How do the annuity's features work?

✦ Are extra features, such as long-term insurance, worth the price tag?

✦ What are the tax consequences of purchasing an annuity, particularly when it comes time to withdraw your cash?

✦ What fees does this annuity charge?

✦ Does the annuity have a surrender charge and how does it work?

✦ If a bonus credit is offered, will the bonus outweigh any higher fees or a longer surrender period?

✦ How many investment options does the annuity offer?

✦ What is the performance track record of the underlying mutual fund subaccounts?

Most annuities have a "free look" period during which a customer can change his or her mind without paying a surrender charge. The period usually lasts for 10 or more days.

Summary

✦ Don't invest in a variable annuity if you have not contributed the maximum to an Individual Retirement Account and a 401(k) or other workplace retirement plan.

✦ Variable annuities will often not make financial sense if you cannot afford to hold onto them for many years.

✦ Investing in an immediate annuity is a logical move for some retirees.

✦ Remain leery of investing in a bonus annuity.

✦ Fixed annuities can be a solid alternative to certificates of deposits and U.S. Treasuries.

✦ If you have trouble with an annuity provider, consider contacting a securities regulator.

All in the Family

In Part VI, you'll learn why saving for college is more rewarding now than at any other time. A wide variety of college investing choices exists, and there are more ways than ever to shield all this cash from taxes. You'll also learn how to instill in your children an appreciation of saving money with all sorts of tricks, including a kiddie 401(k).

Investing for College

✦ ✦ ✦ ✦

In This Chapter

Following smart
saving strategies

Understanding
Section 529 plans

Appreciating
Education IRAs

Considering taxable
accounts

Avoiding the worst
savings mistakes

Asking your child to
pitch in

✦ ✦ ✦ ✦

*I*n this chapter, you'll discover the best strategies for saving for college. In 2001, Congress approved dramatic changes to college saving rules that make some alternatives far more attractive than before. While more options exist than ever before, not all of them are appropriate. You'll discover which ones those are. Also included is a procrastinating parent's guide, for those who allowed college to sneak up on them. Other key topics include getting grandparents involved and exploring financial aid options.

Getting Past the Sticker Shock

Saving for college is no picnic. It can be downright numbing just contemplating it when you're also stuck with 300 more mortgage payments, an S.U.V. that spends too much time with your mechanic, and children who nickel and dime you with their dance lessons, summer camps, and soccer fees.

For some parents, the only thing scarier than trying to figure out where the money will come from is knowing what the tab will be. If you pencil out the numbers to determine how much it will cost to get all your kids through a private university, the tab might exceed the value of your house.

A light at the end of the tunnel

While the cost may seem to be multiplying faster than fruit flies, saving for college doesn't have to be as thankless a task as the figures suggest. Frankly, the grimmest predictions that parents hear about college costs are extrapolated from the tuitions of places like Harvard, Stanford, and Yale. A recent study, that you'll learn more about shortly, has even questioned whether an education at an elite private school is all that it's cracked up to be.

In comparison to the Ivy League, the state university two hours away from your house is offering a Blue Light special. In reality, the annual tuition and fees at the vast majority of public colleges doesn't even exceed $5,000. And if you look at the entire universe of American colleges and universities, more than two-thirds charge tuition and fees that are less than $10,000 a year. Meanwhile, for the price of a couple of Sony PlayStations, you can afford a semester at many junior colleges.

Running down some options

While you can't control what colleges charge, you can control how you prepare for this big-ticket item. Luckily, parents today are blessed with more investment choices than at any time in history. State college savings plans have exploded onto the scene and the federal government, as well as many state governments, have made things easier on parents by offering some incredible tax breaks. Meanwhile, the Education IRA, an option that has been traditionally snubbed by many parents for good reason has become a far more practical alternative. Many financial advisors are suggesting that the recent Congressionally mandated changes in Section 529 plans and Education IRAs, which take effect in 2002, have made traditional ways of saving, through custodial and taxable accounts, far less desirable. By the time you finish reading this chapter, you should have an idea of what strategies are worthwhile and which should be disregarded.

Here are the options that you'll learn more about in this chapter:

✦ Section 529 plans, state-sponsored college savings plans

✦ Education IRA

✦ Custodial accounts

✦ Index and exchange-traded funds

✦ Tax-efficient mutual funds

✦ Roth Individual Retirement Account

✦ Cash value life insurance

✦ Zero coupon bonds

✦ U.S. Savings bonds

✦ Hope Tax Credit

✦ Lifetime Learning Credit

Figuring out how much you need

In the good old days, you had to know how to use the kind of fancy calculators that CPAs carry around to figure out how much you need to save for college. That's not essential anymore. Countless financial Web sites now provide college cost calculators, and other sites help parents determine how much financial aid they may be qualified to receive.

These calculators, however, aren't miracle workers. You can't expect them to pro-vide definitive answers. Why? Here's a biggie—many of the numbers you plug in will be sheer guesses. For instance, you'll be asked to provide the growth rate for your investments, as well as how much you're capable of saving. Nobody can predict such things with pinpoint accuracy.

Tip

To guesstimate your investment's growth rate if you are invested strictly in stocks, it's probably best to use the historical stock market return of 11 percent annually. This figure is based on the market's performance stretching back to the 1920s.

In more recent years, the returns have been much higher, but it's unlikely they will continue at such a torrid pace. During the past two decades, an aggressive port-folio, devoted 95 percent to stocks, annually returned 17.3 percent. A moderate portfolio of 60 percent stocks, 30 percent bonds, and 10 percent cash provided a yearly return of 15.3 percent. No one can say whether your college fund will get those same returns, but history suggests that the figures won't be as high.

Despite drawbacks, these calculators can provide ballpark figures on what costs you face and how aggressively you'll have to save. Parents who use them are proba-bly more likely to develop a savings strategy.

Before using your calculator, pencil out some estimates for these costs:

- ✦ Tuition and fees
- ✦ Room
- ✦ Meals
- ✦ Books
- ✦ Transportation
- ✦ Personal items
- ✦ Phone
- ✦ Internet

Here are a few of the online sites where you'll find college calculators:

- ✦ **Student Loan Marketing Association (Sallie Mae):** Sallie Mae is an enterprise with ties to the federal government that provides funding and service for edu-cation loans. Go to `www.salliemae.com/calculators`.

- ✦ **College Board:** A nonprofit association of more than 3,800 colleges, universi-ties, and other educational institutions at `www.collegeboard.com`.

- ✦ **FinAid:** A comprehensive college financial aid site launched in the mid-1990s as a public service, located at `www.finaid.org`.

In addition, many mutual fund and discount brokerage firms offer free online col-lege planning software, including Charles Schwab, E*Trade, Fidelity Investments, T. Rowe Price, and Vanguard.

College Investing Survival Guide

Follow these investing tips and you'll probably emerge from your college-savings years in better shape than most of the parents you know.

Make saving for your retirement your first priority.

Banks will lend you cash for all sorts of worthy causes, whether it's a college education, a car, or your ultimate dream house. But lenders always balk at one request no matter how critically urgent the need. Nobody's going to loan you money for retirement. Consequently, most financial planners agree that it makes more sense to save aggressively for retirement than it is to subsidize a child's all-expense paid trip through college. After all, no one is going to give you a scholarship for growing older.

Funding retirement should come first. A child can always find a way to go through school even if you haven't saved enough. In fact, the sheer amount of financial aid available in this country is staggering. But if you want to retire comfortably, it's not going to happen if you haven't squirreled enough away.

Tip   Ideally, parents should contribute the maximum permittable each year into their IRAs and their 401(k)'s or other workplace retirement plans before tucking money into a college fund.

Don't disregard quality public schools.

Sure it's important that your toddler reach college someday. We've all read the statistics about what happens when a kid quits school after high school graduation. Odds are they won't earn nearly as much as their friends who kept going. In fact, studies show that a college grad can make double what a high school graduate will earn in a lifetime.

The trick is not going overboard. The obvious sacrificial lamb is a private education. The cost for a private school versus a public one can be tens of thousands of dollars more. In fact, you'd probably be able to send two children to a perfectly good state school for the price of a tony private one.

For those who believe you need an exclusive school on a resume, think again. A study done at Princeton and the Mellon Foundation concluded that graduating from an elite college does not necessarily boost a student's earning potential. The researchers suggested that the child's performance at school and not the pedigree makes the difference. (For purposes of the study, a school was considered elite if it had average SAT scores of 1,275 or higher, while schools were classified as second-tier if the average admission scores were between 1,000 and 1,099.) In other words, if you take two smart kids from the St. Louis suburbs and one goes to Yale and another to the University of Missouri, the one heading to Yale doesn't enjoy a built-in career advantage. The researchers did note one exception to the rule. For financially disadvantaged children, an elite education did bring greater rewards.

Resource If you want to see the results of research on public versus elite education, they are available online at www.princeton.edu/pr/news/00/q1/0126-krueger.htm

If pedigree is terribly important to you, consider a compromise. Let your child attend an in-state public school for a couple of years and then transfer to an expensive blue-ribbon institution for the junior and senior years. Or parents may skimp on the undergraduate bill but promise to help send their child to an A-list graduate school.

Start early.

For every five years that you delay saving for college, you may have to double the amount that you ultimately set aside to reach your goal. Saving for college doesn't have to be painful if you start early. You can thank the power of compounding interest for that.

Table 23-1 Contributing $150 a month starting at age:		
Age of Child	**Years Left to Invest**	**Value of Savings**
At Birth	19 years	$114,681
Age 8	11 years	$38,210
Age 12	7 years	$18,854
Age 15	4 years	$8,993

* Assumes 11% return

If you start early, you won't have to save nearly as much money. Here's an example of how dramatic a difference that can be: Suppose when your child was born, you began setting aside $200 a month. You did this for five years and quit. If that money sat in the college account for another 14 years, the balance, assuming an 11 percent return, would grow to $68,553. Not bad.

Contrast that with a couple who waited until their child entered kindergarten to start saving. These parents kicked in $200 a month until their child also reached age 19. Their account, earning the same interest rate, would reach $79,234. However, the second couple's financial sacrifice was much greater. They ended up making 168 monthly deposits into the account for a total investment of $33,600. But our first couple only sacrificed for 60 months and invested a total of just $12,000. As you can see, the early bird is truly rewarded.

Check under the sofa cushions.

You may think it's impossible to save another dime for college. If you examine how you spend money, however, you may be able to squeeze out even more. For instance, when your child stops wearing diapers, you're probably going to save at least $40 a month. It's not a huge sum, but it still presents an investing opportunity. Saving an extra $40 a month, at an 11 percent rate of return, will generate nearly $18,188 in 15 years. Another time to ratchet up the savings is when your child outgrows preschool. If he or she starts attending a public school, a great deal of money could be freed up.

Save automatically.

Vowing to save more is the easy part. Having the discipline to follow through is a whole other thing. If you have very little willpower, as do most of us, the solution could be to put yourself on a forced financial diet. You can do this easily by signing up for an automatic savings program through a Section 529 state-sponsored college saving plan. You can do the same thing if you establish an Education IRA or other college account with a discount brokerage firm or a mutual fund company. With these direct deposit plans, you decide the amount you want to automatically invest each month. Some Section 529 plans allow you to contribute as little as $15 or $25 a month, while brokerage or mutual fund firms typically require monthly deposits of $50 to $100. On the day you've specified, the money is whisked out of your checking or savings account and placed into a mutual fund.

Note   Parents who sign up for this service should occasionally review how much they are saving this way and ask themselves if they can squeeze out more.

Pay attention to investment costs.

Many parents invest in mutual funds for their children's education, but when shopping for a great fund, they often look exclusively at the performance figures. Obviously results matter and parents should narrow their search to funds that have produced above average returns for the past three to five years. But parents often forget to ask this most obvious question: "What is this fund going to cost me?" It's the first question that a car buyer would pose, but, alas, not college savers. Parents, who invest through a 529 state-sponsored plan, should also zero in on the costs. As you'll learn later, the costs of these programs are all over the board.

Annual investment fees can dramatically affect your college account's performance. (Most people have no idea how much these fees are because they're automatically deducted from your account.) At first glance the fees won't seem out of line. The average expense ratio for a stock mutual fund, for instance, was recently 1.4 percent. The expense ratio refers to the percentage of your account balance that is withdrawn yearly to pay the costs of running the fund. Expense ratios can be as little as .15 percent, while some charge 2.5 percent or higher. So, we're talking a difference of a few dollars, right? Hardly.

Cross-Reference To learn how to evaluate and select mutual funds, see Chapters 6 through 9.

The numbers do the talking

You might be amazed at what a difference one or two percentage points can make. First take a look at the Vanguard 500 Index Fund, an excellent choice for college savings. It charges a minuscule .18 percent a year. If you've got $2,000 in the fund, you'll pay $3.60 a year for professional management with an excellent track record. It's quite a bargain. In contrast, suppose you bought shares in the Boyle Marathon Fund, which charges 2.78 percent. Investing the same amount, your tab would be $55.60.

As your college kitty grows, the fees and the financial pain will widen too. Say you invested $2,000 into Boyle Marathon for a 15-year stretch and the fund grew 10 percent annually. By the end of the decade, your fees and the foregone earnings on those fees could cost you $2,881. In contrast, with Vanguard, the cost would be a mere $223.

The bottom line

So what's the bottom line? Never pay top dollar for a college investment. If you are investing in mutual funds through an Education IRA or a custodial or taxable account, find top-notch funds that charge expenses well below average. To find out what's average for different types of funds, take a look at Chapter 7. You can discover what a fund is charging by looking at its prospectus or by visiting Morningstar's Web site (www.morningstar.com). You'll want to be just as picky about costs if you are shopping for a 529 plan.

Invest appropriately for different ages.

Unless you plan to save for college through increasingly popular state-sponsored savings plans, you'll have to make your own investment decisions. The best way to tackle the huge college expense for children though the middle school years is to invest in the stock market. For most people, this means investing through mutual funds. Unless you are skilled at stock picking, your best bet is to select a stock fund that invests in America's largest companies. Ideally, this fund's portfolio will contain companies that are in both the value and growth category. Once you've accumulated several thousand dollars in that fund, you may want to diversify by putting additional money into a fund that specializes in medium or small companies. You can afford to embrace stocks at this stage, because you still have quite a few years to recover and rebound financially if the stock market takes one of its periodic dives.

Caution Unless you are a conservative investor, don't sink money into bonds or cash investments, such as certificates of deposit or money markets, before your child finishes eighth grade. When your children are young, it's far riskier to favor the "safe" investments because your portfolio runs the risk of failing to keep up with inflation.

Education Tax Credits

Uncle Sam understands how hard it can be to finance something as hefty as a college education. Consequently, the feds offer a variety of tax breaks—some old, some new. Here is the line up:

Hope Tax Credit and Lifetime Learning Credit

Under the Hope Tax Credit, you receive a credit on your federal income tax return up to $1,500 per student for each of the first two years of college. With the Lifetime Learning Credit, you can take a credit of $1,000 per year for qualified college expenses, and this one can be claimed for an unlimited number of years. It's good for undergraduate and graduate studies.

Income qualifications exist for these credits. The credits are phased out completely for joint filers who have an AGI above $100,000 and above $50,000 for singles.

College tuition deduction

Beginning in 2002, many families will be able to deduct up to $3,000 from their federal tax return for college tuition and fees. What's even better, this deduction is classified as an "above the line" deduction. That means it will directly lower your adjusted gross income, which is what determines your tax bracket. The maximum deduction rises to $4,000 for the years 2004 and 2005.

There are drawbacks to this tax break. First, it's not scheduled to last; the deduction will vanish in 2005. You also can't use this deduction in the same year that you claim a Hope or Lifetime Learning Credit.

Student loan interest deduction

There's also tax relief for parents and students facing college loan payments. The 2001 tax law change dramatically increases the ability of borrowers to deduct student loan interest. In the past, there was stiff income limitation that prevented a lot of people from taking advantage of a federal tax deduction. Those ceilings have been increased. Today, a single borrower can deduct the full amount of interest paid—up to $2,500—if his or her adjusted gross income doesn't exceed $50,000. For joint married filers, the ceiling is raised to $100,000. Partial deductions are also possible for some who don't make those cut offs. These income levels are adjusted annually for inflation. Once again, this deduction is classified as above the line.

Your decisions get trickier as your child approaches high school. At this point, your safety cushion of time is wearing thin. If the market hits the skids for an extended period, your college fund might not have time to recuperate. At this point, some parents pull all their education money out of stocks and put it into cash.

Tip   Once your child is in high school, you may want to stagger your move away from equities. After all, you won't be paying for four years of college all at once.

Consider pulling out money for your child's first year of college when he or she is just starting the freshman or sophomore year in high school. The next year, withdraw the cash for your child's second college year, and so on.

What should you do with this cash? You may wish to move it into a money market, a short-term bond fund, or an I Bond, which is an inflation-fighting savings bonds. Another choice is a zero coupon bond: The beauty of zero coupon bonds at this stage is that you can time the bond's maturity to your children's college years. You can do this by shifting your money into short-term zero coupons that come due in each of the years your child is in college. If she starts school in 2010, for instance, divide the money up into bonds that mature in 2010, 2011, 2012, and 2013.

If you purchase a zero coupon bond and hold onto it until maturity, there can be no nasty surprises. You'll know exactly how much money you can expect at the end. That's not true, however, if you get antsy and sell early.

 The price of zero coupons can be extremely volatile, based on changes in interest rates, so it's best not to buy if you might not hold onto them. (See Chapter 18 for more on zero coupon bonds.)

Don't get discouraged.

Kicking yourself for not saving enough is like getting discouraged because you can't purchase a home outright. Paying for college up front would be comparable to buying a house with cash, and we all know that very few people do that. Realistically, the most many can hope for is to save a big down payment for those college years. Scrimp the best you can, and then try to snare some of the billions in scholarship money and financial aid.

State-Sponsored Plans

If you're currently saving for college, chances are you've heard something about state-sponsored college plans, often referred to as Section 529 or just 529 plans. (The plans get the ugly name from a section in federal tax code.) It's impossible to pick up a parenting or personal finance magazine without reading breathless articles about the virtues of these savings vehicles. Thanks to Congress, these plans have gotten even more attractive, beginning in 2002.

These savings programs are a creation of state governments, which decided to help struggling parents by sponsoring their own college investment plans. Every state has rolled out one or more programs. These plans allow parents, grandparents, or any other kind souls to save for college without worrying about the yearly tax consequences. Each state either invests in-house the huge pools of money it gathers from parents or it hires an outside institutional money manager like Fidelity or TIAA-CREF to be in charge of the portfolios.

Caution While these plans are indeed promising, the media has perhaps been guilty of air-brushing the imperfections out. Before you enroll in one of these plans, critically evaluate them in the same way that you would any shiny big-ticket purchase.

One way to cut your research in half is to choose, at the start, which of two main types of state-sponsored plans you'd like—the prepaid tuition plan or the savings plan. The latter plans are the ones that are commonly referred to as 529 plans.

Prepaid tuition plans

The prepaid tuition plans are truly dinosaurs. When the prepaid plans, which were the first ones rolled out by the states, are compared with the newer models, they don't look very good. It's no wonder, then, that the prepaid plans have lost the popularity contest. What's the knock against them? They are extremely conservative and more rigid than the newer generation of plans.

Essentially, when you participate in a prepaid plan, your state guarantees that your investment will meet the costs of a public education in your state. And that's it. There is no chance of watching this money grow tremendously because the states shy away from riskier investments. They only have to invest the money to keep up with college costs, which lately were increasing 4 percent or 5 percent a year. What's more, prepaid plans only permit parents to use the money for tuition, which could represent just 50 percent of the college tab. Other costs such as books, living expenses, and transportation need to be figured in as well.

Caution If you decide not to send your child to a university in your state, you may get smacked with a huge financial penalty for withdrawal from the program. Additionally, your state may only return your original investments—minus the gains.

These plans may appeal to extremely conservative parents, who know their child will be attending an in-state public school. A survey of parents participating in Alabama's plan a few years ago indicated that 52 percent would have put their money in a savings account if the prepaid plan hadn't existed. Another 17 percent would have invested in savings bonds and only 6 percent would have chosen stocks.

Some states offer only a prepaid tuition plan, while others sponsor the more popular savings plan or both. You aren't limited, however, to investing through your state. Many other states will allow you to participate in their plans. For more information, go to either www.savingforcollege.com or www.collegesavings.org.

Section 529 plans: Advantages

Because the 529 savings plan is significantly more popular, here's a more detailed rundown of its features—both good and bad—starting with the reasons you may want to consider a 529 plan:

They provide a tax break.

The tax break is the biggie. Just like the prepaid plans, the 529 plans enable you to build up money in an account without triggering taxes. All this money grows within a parent's account without getting slapped by state or federal taxes. It used to be that when the money was withdrawn for college, it was taxed at a child's low tax bracket, not the parent's. But beginning in 2002, Congress eliminated the tax at the finish line. If the money is used for a child's college education, no federal tax is owed at all. In most cases, the cash is exempt from state income tax, too.

The wonderful tax breaks don't end there. Many states sweeten the pot even further by giving parents a tax deduction on their state income taxes for all their contributions. A couple in Missouri, for instance, can claim a tax deduction up to $16,000 a year for their contributions. New York offers its residents a tax deduction for up to $5,000 in contributions annually.

Here are some of the states that allow savers to claim a state tax deduction on their contributions:

Colorado	Mississippi	Ohio
Iowa	Missouri	Utah
Kansas	Montana	Virginia
Maryland	New Mexico	Wisconsin
Michigan	New York	Oregon
Nebraska	Louisiana	Idaho

These plans are run by well-regarded financial institutions.

You will recognize many of the financial powerhouses that are managing the investment portfolios for the states. For instance, Vanguard manages the money in Utah and Iowa's savings plan; Fidelity oversees the portfolios for Massachusetts, Delaware, and New Hampshire; Strong Investments handles the Wisconsin and Oregon programs; and T. Rowe Price manages Alaska's program. TIAA-CREF handles the programs in about a dozen states, including California, New York, Connecticut, and Missouri. Merrill Lynch, Salomon Smith Barney, Putnam, Alliance Capital, and Bank One also manage 529 money.

They give parents more control.

Parents who invest through a 529 never have to relinquish control of the money to their children. (As you'll learn later, this isn't the case with a custodial account.) So instead of Junior automatically being entitled to the cash after reaching the age of maturity, you continue to hold the purse strings.

Anybody can participate in a 529.

There is no income requirement for participating in these plans. No matter how wealthy parents or grandparents are they can shovel money into these plans. In contrast, the Education IRA, which provides similar tax breaks, imposes income limitations so the wealthiest parents or relatives can't participate.

In addition, there is no limit to how much you can contribute to a 529. Many plans allow contributions that reach into the six figures. In contrast, the annual contribution ceiling to an Education IRA is $2,000.

Section 529 plans: Disadvantages

Here are the drawbacks to be considered before signing up:

The options are intimidating.

There's no requirement that you participate in your own state's plan, and some states offer better programs than others do. If you're hunting for a 529 plan, do you know how well the portfolios in New Hampshire's plans have performed? Who is managing Colorado or Missouri's plan? When nearly every state is jockeying for your business, it's hard to get a handle on just what's available.

While many parents will automatically choose their own state plan, they don't need to be tied down to the program in their own state. A child can use the money in any state's 529 and go to any school in the country.

Many parents aren't even trying to locate a 529 on their own. Some hire financial planners to do the scavenging or rely upon a stockbroker. And some money management firms that are overseeing certain state plans are paying commissions to brokers and financial planners to drum up business.

Caution   If a broker or advisor is recommending a particular plan, ask whether he or she is receiving compensation for finding new clients. If that's the case, keep this potential conflict of interest in mind when making a decision.

Also find out how much experience the advisor has had with 529 plans. Ask, for instance, how many other families he or she has advised on this college savings approach.

Plans tend to be conservative.

Once you finally pick a state plan, the choices narrow considerably. Some states may only offer one investment choice. At the most, you'll encounter a handful. Many parents could find that the investing style is too conservative.

The most common investment choice is an age-based fund: The fund's investing style is based upon your child's age. For instance, in the California program, if a child was born in 2001, for instance, the money would be placed in a fund that is split 80 percent stocks and 20 percent bonds. This portfolio would progressively become saturated in bonds. A third grader would have 50 percent of his or her college money invested in bonds. California officials heard considerable grousing from parents that the bond allocations in these portfolios were too heavy for such young children. The Golden State's asset allocations, however, are very similar to many states.

The great tax break could eventually vanish.

What Congress gives, it can also take away. When Congress decided to abolish the federal income tax on 529 withdrawals for college, it put a time limit on its generosity. Current legislation dictates that the tax-free withdrawals will stop after 2010—an unnerving prospect for parents whose children will be attending college after that deadline. Of course, parents are going to want Congress to extend the tax perk in the future, but when it comes to politics, there is no sure thing.

You lose investing control.

If you invest in a regular mutual fund for your child, you can bail at any time. If you invest outside a 529, you can choose what mutual funds, stocks or bonds you'd like to invest in. Not so with a 529 plan. Most plans have just a handful of choices offered by one investment firm. And once you've selected a fund, you can't even switch the money to another fund within the same state's plan. Once you make your selections, they're intended to be permanent. It's crazy, but that's what federal law requires.

See how this can play out. Suppose a Los Angeles couple with a newborn signs up for the state of California's 529. They choose the plan's age-based fund, which is designed to grow more conservative as the child's college years approach. The parents, however, eventually conclude that the fund, which is managed by the highly regarded institutional money manager TIAA-CREF, is too stodgy. They want to move the money into a pure stock fund within the plan. But the L.A. parents are disappointed—and stunned—when they learn that the plan prohibits them from transferring money from one fund to another. As a compromise move, they stop contributing to the original fund and stash future cash in the stock fund.

 Caution   Because of federal law, all the states' plans are just as rigid. Consequently, some experts suggest that to maintain your ideal portfolio, you may have to invest in more than one fund within a state plan or in more than one state's program.

While it's convoluted, a solution exists to this lack of flexibility. If you no longer want money in a particular state fund, you can move the cash into a different state's program. This can be done without triggering any taxes. For instance, you could move money from the age-based fund in California to an all-stock fund offered by Missouri's plan. Ironically, both California and Missouri's stock fund is managed by TIAA-CREF, but of course the California plan participant can't just switch to the stock fund without heading out of state. There is a limit to how much switching is permitted. You can only transfer money from one state's plan to another once every 12 months.

This inflexibility can be troubling for parents as their children age. While a stock fund could be an excellent choice for young children, this kind of fund is going to be too risky for, say, a high school sophomore. Parents who chose an all-stock will probably want to transfer out of a stock fund and into an age-based fund sponsored by another state as their children get older.

Note   Financial institutions have been urging the Internal Revenue Service to liberalize its rules to allow money to be moved within a 529 plan. The IRS has acknowledged that it's considering this possibility.

The money must be used for college.

You can't use money in one of these accounts to pay for a child's high school expenses, a car or many other needs. The money must go towards qualified college expenses such as tuition, fees, certain room and board costs, books and supplies. If you ultimately don't use the money for college, for whatever reason, a 10 percent penalty will be assessed. What's more, both federal and state tax will be owed on the account's earnings at the parent's tax rate.

Tip   If the child for whom the account is established doesn't go to college, it is possible to use the money to pay for a brother or sister's education.

A 529 can jeopardize financial aid.

Stuffing money into a 529 plan can jeopardize a child's chances at financial aid. This problem occurs because money kept in one of these plans is counted as the child's income, not the parents'. Having a lot of cash in a child's name generally reduces a family's ability to receive aid.

Resources for 529 Plan Info

Want to learn more about 529 plans? Here are two sources:

✦ **Savingforcollege.com:** Undoubtedly, the most prominent cheerleader for these plans is Joseph F. Hurley, the author of *The Best Way to Save for College*. In addition to his book, the certified public accountant has devoted a Web site to the topic. On the site, you'll find articles written by the media on 529 plans, but the most helpful feature is Hurley's ratings of each state's program, using a five graduation cap designation for the best plans. The worst merit just one. Hurley also provides a Web link to each state's plan. At (800) 487-7624 or www.savingforcollege.com.

✦ **College Savings Plans Network:** This site, which is affiliated with the National Association of State Treasurers, provides links to every state's 529 plans. The association makes no attempt to evaluate any of the plans. Find it at P.O. Box 11910, Lexington, KY 40578-1910; (877) CSPN-4-YOU, (859) 244-8175; www.collegesavings.org.

Section 529 shopping list

If you're in the market for a 529, follow this checklist:

1. Explore you own state's program first. This will be the easiest one to check out. You may know other parents who have enrolled, and the local media has probably written stories about the plan. Request the plan's prospectus from your state. If you don't have a contact number, call or visit the Web site of the College Savings Plans Network. (See sidebar for contact information.) Your state program may look even more attractive if it offers a tax break for contributions.

2. Check out other state plans next. The creator of the Savingforcollege.com Web site has ranked the programs based on a variety of benchmarks.

3. When evaluating a plan, get the answers to these questions:

   - **Does the plan provide a state income tax deduction for contributions made by in-state residents?** This is a highly desirable feature since some of the money you sink into the plan will be offset by a tax break. If your state does offer a tax deduction, see if there is a maximum allowed.

   - **How many investment options are there?** The more choices, the better. You'll want to determine how conservative or aggressive the plan's asset allocations are as your child ages. In some plans, a child in second or third grade may have 40 percent of his college money in bonds. This is far too timid for most parents. You'll want to know if your choices include a 100 percent stock fund.

   - **Who is managing the plan?** As mentioned earlier, some big names in the fund world are overseeing these plans. But you'll want to check each fund's track record. SavingforCollege.com now lists the performance track records of individual state plans' funds.

   - **What are the yearly expenses?** Expenses are just as critical for these plans as they are for parents who invest in mutual funds. Yearly costs can take a significant bite out of your gains. Compare prices closely. As a general rule, no-load mutual fund companies, such as the Vanguard Group, Fidelity, TIAA-CREF, American Century and T. Rowe Price, will offer the lowest prices. State plans run by full-service brokerage firms tend to pass along higher costs.

   - **What are the minimum and maximum contributions?** Is there a penalty for transferring the money to another state's 529 plan? And what about an early redemption penalty? The fewer the penalties, the better.

   - **Are the deposit and withdrawal procedures easy or a hassle?** The more user friendly the program, the better.

   - **How long can the account stay open?** There can be age limits on use of this money. If you intend to save some of it for your child's graduate studies, you want to make sure that's okay under plan rules.

Education IRAs

While 529 plans are hot right now, it doesn't automatically mean that you should put all your college money into one. There is no one right way to save for higher education expenses. Whether a 529 plan or some other savings approach is best depends upon parents' individual circumstances. A tough competitor for the 529 plans, however, is the Education IRA.

Despite its misleading name, the Education IRA is not intended to pay for college courses for the elderly. The federal government created the Education IRA to encourage more people to stash cash away for college. Until recently, the 529 plans overshadowed the Education IRAs. But Congressional action that improved 529 plans also spiffed up the Education IRA. The new provisions take effect in 2002.

Strengths of an Education IRA

Two compelling reasons exist to consider establishing an Education IRA. First of all, just like a 529, you can save tax-free for college. Beginning in 2002, a parent, grandparent, or anyone else for that matter can put up to $2,000 a year in an Education IRA for any child under the age of 18. This money will grow tax-free as long as it remains in the account. If the money is used for college expenses, the earnings will never be taxed.

What's new is the contribution ceiling. Until the recent law change, parents, or anyone else for that matter, could only contribute a total of $500 per child per year into an Education IRA. The amount was so piddly that many parents didn't even bother. Financial institutions were also not wild about creating these accounts because they weren't profitable. In fact, some mutual fund companies that had established Education IRA accounts stopped taking in new customers. While the $2,000 ceiling is an improvement, the other types of savings approaches, such as 529 plans, allow limitless or nearly limitless investments.

Note   Under the tax laws passed in 2001, you can contribute up to $2,000 to an Education IRA annually for each child from birth until age 17. The law allows you to continue contributions for a special needs child who is 18 or older.

Unlike a 529 plan, the Education IRA is extremely flexible. You can invest in any mutual fund, stocks or bonds that you like by simply establishing an Education IRA at a mutual fund company, brokerage firm or some other financial institution. Once the money is deposited, you can decide how it should be invested. Because you control the investment, you can make changes to the account, such as switching from one mutual fund to another, without triggering any taxes.

The Education IRA is flexible in another way as well. If you've got an education IRA for a child and he or she doesn't attend college or doesn't use up all the cash, the money can be transferred to another child or grandchild. The uses for this money have also expanded. The cash in an Education IRA can be used to pay for elementary and high school tuition or expenses. Costs that are covered for these younger children include tutoring, computers, books, supplies, transportation, uniforms, room and board, and extended day programs.

Weaknesses of an Education IRA

Considering what college costs are, the $2,000 limit is still miserly. Realistically, if you want to save more than that each year, you may want to consider a 529 plan after maxing out an Education IRA. (Thanks to the recent legislation, you can now contribute to a 529 and an Education IRA in the same year without incurring a penalty.)

Caution   By the way, the $2,000 ceiling is per child, not per donor. Contributions from parents and grandparents, for instance, can't exceed a total of $2,000 per child per year.

Unfortunately, parents with more than one child might face some paperwork headaches: Each child must have his or her own Education IRA. You can't use one account to save for more than one kid.

Further, Education IRAs aren't an option for the most affluent. Potential donors must meet income restrictions. If a benefactor's gross adjusted income exceeds $95,000 (single taxpayer) or $190,000 (married taxpayers filing jointly), they can't make the full $2,00 contribution. Partial gifts are ruled out for anyone whose gross adjusted income exceeds $220,000 (married filers) and $110,000 (single filers).

And here's another zinger—the Education IRA may be considered the child's asset, which could reduce the amount of financial aid he or she is qualified to receive.

Mercifully, one of the nit-picky rules about Education IRAs that had the potential to drive parents batty vanishes in 2002. In the past, you couldn't withdraw money from an Education IRA during the same year that you claimed the Hope or Lifetime Learning credits. This no longer is true. However, the Education IRA cash can't be used to cover the same expenses for which the education credits are claimed.

Finally, if there's any money left in the account by the time an adult child reaches the age of 30, the IRS will lose its patience and will treat it as a distribution. (An exception is made for special-needs adult children.) All the earnings will be subject to income taxes and the account will be assessed a 10 percent penalty because the cash wasn't used for education purposes. What's more, if the money is spent on non-qualified expenses long before that cut-off age, you'll owe income taxes and face a 10 percent penalty.

Tip   The nation's tax schedules change fairly frequently. Before you base investment decisions on your particular tax bracket, make sure it's still the same or not about to change.

Custodial Accounts—Pros and Cons

Before the tax changes of 2001, investing for college through a custodial account was much more attractive. Now, however, there's no compelling reason to put new cash for college into one of these accounts because you will pay taxes on the money when it's withdrawn for college. (In contrast, the Education IRA and a 529 permit tax free growth.) These accounts, however, do provide a tax break—the cash is taxed at the child's presumably lower rate—so it can be worthwhile to save money for children this way for non-education reasons.

There are two types of custodial accounts that go by the unwieldy names of Uniform Transfers to Minors Act (UTMA) and Uniform Gifts to Minors Act (UGMA). They are very similar accounts; which one you end up with will depend upon the state you live in. These accounts can be set up at just about any brokerage firm, bank, or mutual fund company. Once the account is open, the custodian, who is typically a parent, oversees it. The custodian controls the assets until the child is legally considered an adult.

Here are some strengths and weaknesses of custodial accounts:

✦ **They provide a tax advantage.** A big reason many parents embraced custodial accounts in the past is for the tax break. If your child is under 14, the first $700 of yearly investment earnings is tax-free. The next $700 is taxed at 15 percent. Because the money is in the child's name, only annual gains above $1,400 are taxed at the parents' rate. After reaching the age of 14, the child gets to use his or her own tax rate, which presumably is lower.

✦ **They impose self-control.** Some parents like custodial accounts because they know the money can only be used for their child's benefit. If parents are saving for college in their own brokerage account, the money can easily get spent for other good causes, whether the furnace breaks down in January or Dad's car transmission has to be replaced. Custodial accounts, however, are flexible. The money doesn't have to be spent on education. You can pay, for instance, for your child's summer camp, cell phone bills, clothing, or a car.

✦ **They jeopardize financial aid.** Creating a kiddie account can ultimately interfere with your child's chance at grants and scholarship money. According to federal guidelines, students are expected to spend 35 percent of their savings each year for college. Yet the same formula only requires parents to part with 6 percent of their total assets. If you think none of this matters because you'd never qualify for financial aid, don't be so sure. Not all of a parent's net worth will be considered in the college's calculations. For instance, retirement assets stashed away in a 401(k) or IRA aren't included in financial aid calculations.

✦ **It's your child's money.** A custodial account can become a disaster if your "A" student decides to skip college and take up glassblowing instead. When your children become adults—age 18 or 21, depending upon individual state laws—the money in a custodial account is technically theirs. If your son withdraws his windfall to travel around the world, buy a sports car, or enrich a cult leader, you can't legally stop him.

Taxable Accounts

Until the advent of the 529 plan and the Education IRA, parents traditionally saved for college through taxable accounts. A taxable account refers to any account that you establish at any financial institution, from a passbook savings account to a mutual fund. A taxable account doesn't provide any tax benefits, but in exchange you enjoy absolute freedom to invest the money as you wish. You can also use the cash in any way you desire. If you wish to spend the cash on your children, that's fine, but if you decide to use it to remodel your house or buy a fancier car instead, that's up to you. You won't face any penalty.

Who might want a taxable account?

Taxable accounts were far more popular before 529 plans and Education IRAs became more desirable. These accounts can still be an alternative to parents who are worried about tying up money for college that they might need for other purposes later on. Some parents also might want to stick some money in a taxable account just to hedge their bets against future Congressional actions. Politicians, after all, find it very hard to resist tinkering with the nation's tax code. Consequently, there is a lot of uncertainty about whether the education tax perks will remain a permanent fixture. Tax-free withdrawals from 529 plans, for instance, are scheduled to disappear in 2011.

Parents who have already stashed money into taxable accounts may want to consider transferring the cash into an Education IRA or a 529 when their children reach the age when investment changes are required. For instance, a couple who invested for years in the same stock fund for their daughter will probably want to switch to a more conservative investment when she reaches the end of middle school or begins high school. Once the money is pulled out the parents will have to pay taxes on the gains, but then they can put the money into a conservative option through an Education IRA or 529 plan. When that cash is ultimately withdrawn for college, it can then be pulled out tax-free.

Look for tax efficiency

If you invest for your child through a taxable account, find a mutual fund that is extremely tax efficient. By avoiding tax hogs, you should greatly diminish your yearly tax bill.

Far more important than the raw performance statistics advertised by funds is each fund's after-tax performance. Just like overpriced funds, tax sloppy funds are hidden killers. In the past, it was nearly impossible to get this information. But the U.S. Securities and Exchange Commission recently began requiring funds to include the information in their fund literature.

Caution KPMG Peat Marwick estimates that the average mutual fund loses 2.6 percentage points of its yearly gains to taxes. Considering that stocks have historically returned 11 percent, a 2.6 percent tax bite represents an astounding 28 percent of the return.

What kind of funds are tax efficient? Index funds, such as the Vanguard 500 Index, Vanguard Total Stock Market Index Fund, Schwab 1000 Fund, and Fidelity Spartan 500 Index Fund, are typically quite tax friendly. That's because index funds, by their very nature, don't require a lot of stock trading, which tends to generate taxes as well as extra costs. (See Chapter 10 for more on index funds.)

Exchange-traded funds, a newer type of investment, are also usually tax efficient. Exchange-traded funds are a cross between a mutual fund and a stock. They are traded like stocks, but they hold a basket of individual stocks just like a mutual fund. As with stocks, you buy shares in ETFs through a brokerage account. Your best bet for college is to invest in an ETF that tracks a broad index, such as the S&P 500 or the Wilshire 5000 Index. See Chapter 11 for much more on exchange-traded funds.

Hope for long-term savers

Many of the parents who have struggled to save for their kids' college years in taxable accounts are shocked when they begin siphoning out this money. The IRS is first in line for its take. The profits earned thanks to Mom and Dad's smart investing are subject to capital gains taxes. Parents who had congratulated themselves on saving enough for college can now find themselves considerably short after paying off Uncle Sam.

Fortunately, the capital gains rate for long-term savers is slowly decreasing. Investments that were purchased in 2001 or later and held for more than five years will be subject to a top rate of 18 percent. (The current rate is 20 percent.) Meanwhile, the capital gains tax rate for folks in the lowest 10 or 15 percent tax brackets will slip from 10 percent to 8 percent. For this group, the reduced tax also applies to investments bought prior to 2001.

Bad Investment Choices for College Savers

Not every investment that you see touted for college savings is worthwhile. For long-term savers, here's a trio of dubious college investments:

Bad Choice no. 1: Savings Bonds

If you're a parent, you probably have savings bonds stashed in a desk drawer or safe deposit box. A savings bond is a thoughtful gift to bring to a baby shower, and grandparents love to buy them. What's nice about these bonds is they aren't budget busters. The purchase price of these bonds is always 50 percent of its face value, so for just $25, you can buy a $50 Series EE bond.

But don't depend on savings bonds to bankroll college. The returns percolating from these bonds just can't pack enough punch. If you wish to invest in savings bonds, the best choice will be I Bonds, which are designed to keep up with inflation. I Bonds are more appealing as a safe haven to stash money once a child is nearing college age.

 Cross-Reference You'll see a detailed description of the I Bond in Chapter 18.

Savings bonds do offer one tantalizing feature. While you never have to pay state and local tax on these bonds, you'll owe the Internal Revenue Service when the bonds are redeemed. However, if the bonds are used for a child's college tuition, the federal tax is waived if a laundry list of conditions is met.

First, parents must meet the federal income requirements at the time of the redemption. In 2001, a married couple filing a joint income tax return could skirt the tax if their modified gross income didn't reach $81,100. The tax break phases out entirely if the parents' adjusted income reaches $111,100 or higher. For single parents, the ceilings are $54,100 and $69,100. The income ceilings are adjusted annually for inflation, so you'll want to call the numbers listed shortly to get the most updated figures.

The tax-free bonus vanishes if the savings bond is in the child's name. The savings bond must be registered in the name of one or both parents. The child can't be listed as a co-owner.

Tip Fortunately, the common mistake of including the child as owner can be fixed. It's possible to retitle the bonds by contacting one of the Federal Reserve Banks designated to handle savings bond matters.

Savings bonds can only be used to pay for tuition and fees. Room and board, as well as books and supplies, are ineligible. Finally, here are a couple of other savings bond oddities to keep in mind. You can kiss the tax break goodbye if you bought savings bonds before January 1, 1990, or if—as a parent—you bought the bonds before your 24th birthday. Go figure.

Tip It's best to purchase savings bonds for education in small denominations. That way you won't have to cash in more bonds than you need to cover the tuition bill. Redemptions that exceed the tuition bill may be taxed when a federal tax return is filed.

If you have questions about savings bonds, here are two numbers to call:

✦ **Bureau of the Public Debt** at (304) 480-6112 or www.savingsbonds.gov

✦ **Federal Reserve Bank of Kansas City,** Savings Bond Customer Service Unit, at (800) 333-2919

Bad Choice no. 2: Roth Individual Retirement Account

It had become quite popular to hype the Roth Individual Retirement Account as the answer to just about any financial goal, whether it was financing a college education or paying for a tummy tuck or laser eye surgery. Liberal federal laws turned the Roth into a piggy bank rather than a pure retirement account.

Some people became excited about using the Roth IRA for college expenses because they could withdraw money for this purpose without triggering the 10 percent early withdrawal penalty. As long as the money has remained inside the Roth for at least five years, the penalty is waived. What's more, the actual contributions can be pulled without penalty or tax at any time.

Caution   What many parents don't realize is that when they withdraw the actual earnings—as opposed to the original contributions—they must pay tax on this money as income. So if a couple is in the 30 percent tax bracket, nearly $1 out of every $3 in earnings will disappear.

With tax-free ways to save for college through an Education IRA or a 529 plan, raiding a Roth is to pay for college is a bad idea.

Beyond the tax bite, using a Roth for college can jeopardize one of the best ways possible to save for retirement. If you don't disturb your Roth until retirement—or at least until age 59½—you will never pay a single dime in taxes. Without the threat of taxes, a Roth account can grow dramatically for many decades. If you raid your Roth, it's hard to play catch-up since Americans are limited in what they can contribute to one. Frankly, the retirement and estate planning advantages of a Roth shouldn't be wasted on financing a college education.

Tip   It's infinitely better to resist using the Roth for anything other than financing your golden years.

Bad Choice no. 3: Cash Value Life Insurance

Unlike term life insurance, which is strictly meant to insure someone's income, cash value (or permanent) life insurance doubles as an investment. With some policies, you can choose from a menu of underlying mutual funds that will determine the rate of return of the investment portion of the policy.

How are these policies supposed to be appropriate for college savings? When a child graduates from high school, a customer can borrow against the cash value of the policy to pay the tab. If it's done properly, the money won't be taxable. Insurance agents like to boast that the cash that builds up inside a policy won't hurt your child's ultimate chances for financial aid. That's because most college-financial aid formulas exclude life insurance and annuities when reviewing parents' net worth.

What's the downside? The premiums and sales commissions for these policies can be very expensive. Because of the cost, it could take many, many years for a policy to exceed the performance of a regular, taxable mutual fund—if at all. Meanwhile, if you die before repaying all that money you used for college costs, the death benefit will be reduced by the amount you owe. Some experts also warn that it would be reckless to assume that colleges will always exclude life insurance as an available asset to pay for tuition. The rules could change.

Tip   The bottom line: Run away if an insurance agent begins talking up the virtues of insurance for your future Harvard grad.

Your Child's Fair Share

All the scary tales that detail college costs leave out an important factor: your child's contribution. There's nothing wrong with expecting your kid to pay part of the bill. Instilling in your child the need to save for this big expense can start as soon as your little ones begin receiving allowances. By the time your child is working the takeout window at McDonald's, she can be turning over part of her paychecks.

Here are other ideas:

Get a head start on college classes.

In what could be a trend, more and more teenagers who took advanced placement (AP) courses in high school are zipping through college in three or 3½ years, which can go a long way toward easing parents' financial burden. In fact, skipping entry-level college classes can shave tens of thousands of dollars off parents' tab.

Fulfill basic requirements at a junior college.

A junior college doesn't carry the panache of a four-year institution, but it's a great way to save money for later. After two years, a child can transfer to a more prestigious school. In fact, by then you might be able to swing a more desirable school than if you had originally started at a four-year institution.

Get military assistance.

Letting Uncle Sam foot the bill is an age-old American tradition. If your child enrolls in the military, he or she will be able to take college courses during free time. The military pays for classes regardless of whether someone is currently serving or has been honorably discharged. Meanwhile, many states give veterans a price break on tuition. A former soldier just needs to ask.

The (Very) Generous Grandparents Guide

There have never been more opportunities for affluent grandparents to play Santa Claus. Here are three ways that grandparents can pitch in with college costs:

Direct tuition payments

This option rarely occurs to affluent grandparents, but it's a dandy. Grandparents can send a tuition check directly to their grandchild's college. By doing this, they know exactly where the money is going. There's no need to fear that some of the cash is being skimmed off to subsidize a Florida spring break adventure. By making the check out to the school, the grandparents don't have to report the gift—no matter how big it is—on their tax return.

Even better, sending the money directly to the school, rather than to the child or the parents, won't interfere with a grandparent's other serious gift giving. According to federal rules, a generous person is able to give $10,000 a year to whomever he or she wishes without triggering gift taxes. So if a grandmother wrote a $20,000 check for tuition and sent it to her grandchild, who cashed it to pay her college, only $10,000 would qualify for the annual gift-tax exclusion.

Section 529 Plans

Grandparents can help out with college costs and shrink the size of their taxable estate at the same time by contributing to a 529 plan. These plans allow grandparents to maintain ultimate control of the money.

Federal law allows a wealthy benefactor to contribute as much as $50,000 per year into a 529 plan without triggering gift taxes. The high contribution ceiling allows rich grandparents to make far more generous tax-free gifts to their grandchildren, nieces, nephews, and other favorite children, than is permitted by federal gift and estate laws.

If a grandparent does contribute $50,000 in one year, he or she will have to wait a total of five years before resuming annual $10,000 gifts, which are tax exempt, to a child.

Resource   To learn more about educational opportunities in the military, call the Department of Veterans Affairs at (800) 827-1000 or go to www.gibill.va.gov for a copy of the booklet *Summary of Education Benefits,* VA Pamphlet 22-90-2.

Another way to attend school courtesy of the military—albeit a harder way—is to snag a spot in one of the nation's military academies. Some have estimated that an admission to West Point or one of the other academies is worth $250,000.

Here's the admission contact numbers for the five military academies:

✦ Air Force   (800) 443-9266

✦ Army   (800) 822-USMA

✦ Coast Guard   (800) 883-8724

✦ Navy/Marines   (410) 293-4361

Look into financial aid.

Despite lectures from the financial media, most parents don't start saving for college until their kids are teenagers. If this sounds familiar, don't beat up on yourself; you and your college-bound kids just have to be more creative. Financial aid, which is now awarded to more students than ever before, is always a possibility.

One of your first contacts should be the U.S. Department of Education. Obtain a copy of the department's *The Student Guide,* which is updated annually. The free publication is the most comprehensive resource on federal student financial aid. In fact, about 70 percent of all student aid comes from programs covered in the guide.

 source   Call (800) 433-3243 for a copy of *The Student Guide.*

Also contact the financial aid administrator's office at the universities your child would like to attend. The staff will provide you with information about federal financial assistance and other aid programs. Also don't forget the high school guidance counselor's office.

Brace yourself, and your child, for the prospect of taking out student loans. While few of us are filled with joy by the prospect of our child taking on debt at such a tender age, for many families, student loans are inevitable. Here is a quick look at federal student loans:

✦ **Stafford loans:** These come with a low interest rate and are issued to college students if they meet the requirements of a financial aid formula. The federal government pays the interest on these loans while students are in school.

Students can also obtain unsubsidized Stafford loans regardless of family income, but they are responsible for the interest payments while in school. If they choose to postpone paying the interest, the amount is tacked onto the loan principal after graduation.

✦ **Federal PLUS loans:** These loans are actually assumed by the parents, and allow parents, who don't have to be financially needy, to borrow up to the full cost of their child's education. The borrowers must start making payments within 60 days of receiving the loan.

Don't forget scholarships and grants.

There are untold ways to qualify for scholarships and grants. Colleges and other public institutions may offer scholarships based on such criteria as grades, work experience, career interests, athletics, disability, and military service completed by students, parents, or grandparents.

Money for scholarships or grants is often available from private sources based on the applicant's religion, ethnicity, achievements, hobbies, and special talents. Places to contact include your church, local foundations, civic groups, and workplace. Your child's high school guidance counselor is another resource for scholarship leads as well as information on federal, local, and state programs.

> **Tip** *The Student Guide,* mentioned in the loan section, contains information on opportunities for work-study and grants as well.

Here are two federal grant programs to look into:

Pell Grant

These grants are geared toward the truly needy. While much of the financial aid available today takes the form of loans, the Pell Grants generate cash that doesn't have to be repaid. Unfortunately, the size of these federal grants has shrunk over the years. In the 1970s, for instance, the biggest Pell grants covered roughly 75 percent of the average cost of a four-year public education, but today's undergraduates are lucky if the grant pays for one-third of the expenses.

Federal Supplemental Educational Opportunity Grant

While these are federal grants, individual colleges can use their discretion in parceling out the money. If you're eligible for a Pell Grant, you should qualify for one of these too.

Scholarship scams

Not every scholarship is what it seems. Some are bogus. According to the National Association of Student Financial Aid Administrators, more than 300,000 people are the victims of scholarship scams every year.

Crooked scholarship services often offer no financial awards at all. The services exist just to collect application fees, which the crooks behind the facade pocket. Here are some of their favorite modus operandi:

✦ **Scholarship guaranteed.** Beware of any promoter that insists that you'll earn a scholarship or your money is refunded. There are no guarantees.

✦ **Scholarship redemption.** A bogus scholarship matchmaker may inform you that you've won a valuable scholarship. The service, however, won't release the source of this money until you've paid a redemption fee. Of course, if you pay the fee, you win nothing.

✦ **Invisible loan.** This scam notifies its victims that they've qualified for a low-interest college loan. Students, however, must pay a fee before receiving the loan. Once again, after the fee is paid, the con artists disappear. Student loans from legitimate financial institutions don't require an advance fee to apply for a loan. If the loan is granted, the fees are deducted when the check is cut.

Financial Aid Web Sites

When hunting for scholarships via the Internet, use more than one online database. Despite overlap, the extra effort will be worth it. Here are a few of the many financial aid sites on the Internet today:

✦ **College Board** at www.collegeboard.com

✦ **Scholarship Resource Network Express** at www.srnexpress.com

✦ **FastWeb** at www.fastweb.com

✦ **CollegeNet** at www.collegenet.com

Summary

✦ When saving for college, make your own retirement goals your first priority.

✦ Appreciate why investing in Education IRAs and 529 plans are now more attractive.

✦ Pay close attention to the expenses you pay while saving for college.

✦ Understand what your options are if you haven't saved enough money.

✦   ✦   ✦

Teaching Kids to Invest

In this chapter, parents learn tips on encouraging their children to save and invest; you'll discover what investment choices young investors face once they outgrow their piggy bank and how to encourage savings with a junior 401(k). The frightening reality of teen credit cards is also discussed, along with a more palatable alternative.

Kids Today: In the Investing Fray

In the past, the typical kid's idea of high finance was nagging mom or dad to bump up his or her allowance by 50 cents. Allowances are still with us, but many children are no longer content to scrounge for spare change under the sofa cushions.

Today, large numbers of kids seem to be grooming themselves to become future financial moguls. According to a survey by Stein Roe, 19 percent of children in grades 8 to 12 own stocks or bonds, a number that the mutual fund firm says has almost doubled since 1993. Merrill Lynch has estimated that 2.5 million children, ages 12 to 17, own stock, and another 2.3 million or so own mutual funds.

Along for the financial ride

While the statistics vary, the message is clear. Kids are far more interested in the stock market than previous generations were. Financial sites for children have sprung up like dandelions, stock-picking contests are hot, and children's growing interest in Wall Street compelled a national organization of investment clubs to begin offering child memberships. In an attempt to capitalize on this interest, dozens of mutual funds have been launched to specifically capture the kid market.

It's no surprise that pint-sized investors have infiltrated Wall Street. The longest bull market in history lured millions of first-time investors in the stock market, and their children tagged along for the ride. Just as with their parents, the Internet has made it easier for children to get hooked on investing. And investing small amounts, which is all most kids have to spend, is much more practical today with the price of many stock transactions now cheaper than a movie ticket.

More cash than know-how

Yet for all their fascination with money, kids are just kids. Their desire to emulate Bill Gates is at odds with their understanding of basic personal finance skills. Each year, for example, a sampling of 12th graders in public schools across the nation take a test sponsored by Jump$tart Coalition for Personal Financial Literacy. And sure enough, every year, the students flunk. Most recently, the average student test score was 51.9 percent, nowhere close to a passing grade. Curiously enough, kids who owned stock in their own name actually scored worse than those who didn't. So did children who had their own credit card.

What's alarming about these scores is this generation's easy access to money. Twenty years ago, even some college graduates experienced difficulty obtaining credit cards, but today bank issuers are enticing kids as young as 16 to sign up for fast cash. Unfortunately, teenagers have proven that they are no more responsible with plastic than their parents.

With kids exposed to money at an earlier age and quite capable of racking up huge debt, it's more important than ever that they learn good money management skills that follow them into adulthood. It's also crucial for children, who express an interest, to learn how to become educated investors. Even kid prodigies probably know less about stocks than they think.

The Making of a Millionaire

One of the biggest tasks you face as a financial role model is turning your child into a saver. If you can convince a kid with a bad case of the gimmes to squirrel a little away, you've won the biggest battle. A child who appreciates the wisdom of investing early in life will be less likely to spend irresponsibly later on.

How do you get your children to swallow the message? Start by explaining how lucky they are. Of course, your kids aren't going to feel very lucky. You're the one who makes money, buys cars, writes the checks, sets their allowance, and even controls the flow of candy into the house. Yet these kids don't realize the huge advantage they enjoy over their parents and grandparents. They've got time on their side.

Making the most of the biggest advantage: Time

Time is one of the biggest determining factors in whether someone will be a successful investor. Kids have many decades to sock money away. And if they start now they won't have to save nearly as much as a 40- or 50-year-old, who wakes up one day and realizes he's got only 10 or 20 years to stockpile enough cash to see him through 20 or more years in retirement.

What's the kid's built-in advantage? The effects of compounding. All that interest has time to turn a son or daughter's $10 and $20 contributions into a million bucks or more with very little effort on their part. Unfortunately, most people don't appreciate the magic of compounding until they reach middle age. That's when they want to slap themselves silly after realizing they'd now be millionaires if they had just started saving earlier. Of course, your kids aren't going to believe you. Perhaps Table 24-1 can make the case better than a half-hour lecture from Mom or Dad.

Table 24-1 Saving $2,000 Annually ($38.46 a Week)*		
Age at Start	**Years to Invest**	**Value of Investment at Age 65**
16-year-old	50 years	$3.7 million
18-year-old	48 years	$3 million
21-year-old	45 years	$2.2 million
30-year-old	36 years	$844,00
40-year-old	26 years	$284,000
50-year-old	16 years	$87,000

* Earning 11% a year

This chart clearly illustrates the value of getting started early. A 16-year-old who scrapes together $2,000 a year until he or she is 65 will be worth an astounding $3.5 million. What the chart doesn't show is that this enterprising teenager would be a millionaire in her 50s. Now that should get a kid's attention.

Note

Make sure your child appreciates what happens to middle-aged procrastinators, who start saving late. By the time a 40-year-old reaches 65, annual investments of $2,000 would result in a mere $268,650. The numbers look even worse for a 50-year-old.

Doubling for dollars—millions of them

The wonder of compounding is a hard concept to convey to kids. But this eye-opening example may help. Ask a child whether she'd rather receive $1,000 a day for a month or start with a penny and have it doubled every day during the same period. Chances are your child will pick the $30,000 answer instead of the right one. Table 24-2 shows the bottom line for that magical compounding penny.

Table 24-2 Compounding At Work			
Day	**Amount**	**Day**	**Amount**
Day 1	1 cent	Day 16	$327.68
Day 2	2 cents	Day 17	$655.36
Day 3	4 cents	Day 18	$1,310.72
Day 4	8 cents	Day 19	$2,612.44
Day 5	16 cents	Day 20	$5,242.88
Day 6	32 cents	Day 21	$10,485.76
Day 7	64 cents	Day 22	$20,971.52
Day 8	$1.28	Day 23	$41,943.04
Day 9	$ 2.56	Day 24	$83,886.08
Day 10	$5.12	Day 25	$167,772.16
Day 11	$10.24	Day 26	$335,544.32
Day 12	$20.48	Day 27	$671,088.64
Day 13	$40.96	Day 28	$1,342,177.28
Day 14	$81.92	Day 29	$2,684,354.56
Day 15	$163.84	Day 30	$5,368,709.12

Luring kids with a junior 401(k)

While these are all compelling numbers, your child might shrug it off and put his headphones back on. How do you get a kid to save? Pay him. That's right. Kick in money to get him started. This isn't as counter intuitive as it might seem. After all, we have to teach our kids all sorts of things. We teach them how to drive a car, braid hair, shoot a basket. You can teach kids how to save by providing them with cash to engage them in this important life lesson.

There are various ways to approach this. You may get the ball rolling by handing your child money to invest. You can give the money without attaching strings or have the child work for some or all of it.

Tip   If a child is using his or her own money to open an account, it's best to avoid mingling this cash with what's already stashed away in a college fund. Create a separate account instead.

Another option is matching the child's savings. If a child puts $25 in an investment account, for instance, you can provide a match of 100 percent or 50 percent or some other percentage. Children will be more inclined to set money aside if they know they'll receive an instant payoff. After all, that's the same incentive used by 401(k) plans. To encourage savings, most employers kick in a match when a worker invests money in a 401(k). So consider your generosity a junior 401(k) plan.

The Mechanics of Savings

Kids can't invest on their own. The government won't let them. Once a kid's money leaves a piggy bank, an adult must act as custodian. You can establish a custodial account for a child at just about any financial institution. That means you can invest directly with a mutual fund company, set up a brokerage account, or save through a bank or an insurance company. A parent, grandparent, or whoever creates the account has the power to make all investment decisions, but the money always belongs to the child. The child can erase Mom or Dad's name off the account upon reaching their state's age of majority, usually 18 or 21 (it varies by state).

Many custodial accounts are established by parents who are saving for their children's college years. Parents are often attracted to the tax advantages of saving through one of these accounts, but that may not be the best approach.

 Cross-Reference   Learn more about the pros and cons of custodial accounts in Chapter 23, which is devoted to college savings strategies.

Places for kids to park their money

If a child is old enough, he or she should play a major role in deciding where to invest the money. Here are the main choices:

Mutual fund company

Investing through a mutual fund is a great way for a kid to get started. A mutual fund provides immediate diversification so it's not as risky as placing a first bet on a solitary stock. It's also easier picking a solid mutual fund than analyzing and choosing a stock. Stick with a no-load fund, which is sold without a sales charge.

Getting Started for Peanuts

For cash-strapped kids, an ideal fund family to investigate is TIAA-CREF, which is best known as the money manager for the pensions of many of the nation's educators. TIAA-CREF's lineup of mutual funds requires an initial investment of only $250. Just as appealing to kids, subsequent deposits can be for as little as $25. And regular automatic deposits aren't required.

Custodial accounts often waive a high minimum for new customers. You typically can get started for as little as $1,000 or $500. Sometimes an initial deposit is waived altogether, if you sign up for automatic monthly investments. These can be as low as $25.

If your child is old enough, make the hunt for a top fund a family project. Simplify the task by using fund-screening software that's available at many financial Web sites, as well as brokerage Web sites. You can plug in qualities you desire in a fund, such as low expenses, better than average returns, and a veteran money manager, and the software matches up your criteria with the funds in its database. Here are four places to find these screens:

✦ Morningstar (www.morningstar.com)

✦ Quicken (www.quicken.com)

✦ Yahoo!Finance (http://finance.yahoo.com)

✦ Charles Schwab (www.schwab.com)

 Resource   Software is great for compiling a list of candidates, but further research is necessary. Visit the library with your child and check out *Morningstar Mutual Funds,* a bimonthly publication that includes a comprehensive analysis of 1,700 mutual funds.

Value Line also publishes a monthly mutual fund guide, but you're less likely to see that in libraries. You will also want to look through a fund's prospectus and most recent annual or semiannual report, which can be obtained free by calling a fund company's toll-free number or by visiting its Web site. You will learn the best ways to narrow your mutual fund choices by reading Chapters 5 through 8.

Discount brokerage account

This alternative is more practical for a child who has accumulated at least $2,000. Unlike investing directly with a mutual fund company, a brokerage account allows a kid to choose from a menu of thousands of mutual funds, as well as individual stocks. (The choices won't seem so staggering if you use fund and stock screeners.) A brokerage account can also substitute as a piggy bank. A child can tuck money away in the account, where it'll earn better interest than a savings account, until he or she decides where to invest it.

A brokerage account is even more practical once the child is sitting on several thousand dollars, which is enough to diversify into more than one fund or stock.

Tip   Avoid full-service brokerage firms for kids because the fees are generally stiffer than the discounters'. What's more, this is supposed to be a learning experience. With a full-service firm, you are paying a broker to share investment ideas. A child may feel less excited about the experience if someone else is doing the legwork.

If enough money piles up in a brokerage account, your youngster could qualify for what is sometimes referred to as *cash-management services.* This often includes the use of an ATM card, checking privileges, and a credit card. Obviously, this is better suited for a more responsible teenager.

Banks and credit unions

The bank or credit union option works best for little children who are making the transition from piggy banks to the financial world, since these institutions are basically huge piggy banks. A bank or credit union usually won't be an appropriate alternative for teenagers, who aren't going to get excited when their latest statement shows they've earned 25 cents in monthly interest.

Tip   Many banks waive fees for children's accounts because they treat them as loss leaders. If a bank does require a minimum balance or charges monthly fees for a kiddie account, look elsewhere. It's just not an economical alternative.

Account type: Taxable versus retirement

Once you've decided where to park your kid's money, you'll face another decision. Should the account be established as a taxable one or for retirement?

Both have their advantages and disadvantages. What a parent views as a plus, however, might be seen by a child as a drawback. For instance, it's easier to drain money out of a taxable account since no penalty kicks in if your child wants to cash out her savings. But the taxes can be painful with one of these accounts. Selling a fund or stock inside a taxable account can trigger taxes. What's more, mutual funds can generate yearly taxes even if your child's a buy-and-hold investor and never sells a single mutual fund share.

Note   Chances are, if yearly taxes are owed, you, not your son or daughter, will be the one writing the check to the Internal Revenue Service.

In contrast, it's much harder to pull money out of an IRA on a whim. Doing so may trigger a 10 percent federal penalty, and income taxes can be owed on the money. Obviously, from a parent's point of view, the more obstacles to withdrawing the cash, the better. After all, as long as the money stays inside an IRA, the account is incredibly tax friendly. No tax will ever be owed on money that remains in an IRA. That's true even if your child ends up hopping from one mutual fund or stock to another within an IRA. (This, by the way, is not recommended.)

Qualifying for a kiddie IRA

Not all children, however, will qualify for an IRA. The key factor here is whether the money in your kid's piggy bank is earned income. You can't open an IRA with allowance money. Instead, the child must use money he earned doing chores around the house, such as shoveling snow or washing the car. If you use the pay-for-chores route to contribute to a child's IRA, it's best to keep records just in case the IRS asks questions later. Keep track of what you pay your child for various chores and how much you'd pay outside labor for the same job.

Tip   Practically speaking, it will be the teenagers who can really take advantage of an IRA.

Obviously, a teen who is cramming for final exams won't be thinking about what a nursing home bed might cost her in 2060, but that's where the parental financial incentives, such as matching contributions, can come in. In fact, there is no rule that says the child has to use her own money to fund an IRA. A parent or grandparent may want to pick up the entire tab. The kind soul, however, must be careful not to contribute more than the child earned in a calendar year. For instance, if a child earned $1,600 working at the pretzel stand in the mall, the IRA contribution can't exceed that amount. The maximum yearly contribution to any IRA, regardless of age, was $2,000 in 2001. The annual contribution ceiling is scheduled to continue increasing until it reaches $5,000 in 2008 and after.

Nobody is suggesting that a 16-year-old begin saving energetically for retirement. But investing modest amounts at an early age can make it far easier for your children later when they won't have to struggle to save for retirement so vigorously.

Considering the great advantages of a Roth IRA

If you can talk your child into saving through an IRA, the best one by far for kids is the Roth. (See Chapter 20 for more info on the Roth.)

When you contribute to a Roth, which is named after a former U.S. senator from Delaware, you aren't entitled to a tax deduction. This perk is reserved for those who invest through a traditional deductible IRA. But realistically, this is not a big consideration for kids. After all, most of them are going to owe very little or no income taxes.

Tip   The Roth's real reward for kids: If the money is kept in the account until retirement, your child will be able to withdraw the money tax-free. That's right, if your kid ends up becoming a millionaire thanks to his Roth, the IRS will never be able to touch this loot.

The Roth is also flexible enough to be used for college expenses. When the money is withdrawn from a Roth for college expenses, the cash is not subject to a 10 percent early withdrawal penalty that many people are hit with when they touch their IRA before age 59½.

Tip In addition, the actual Roth contributions—as opposed to the earnings—can be withdrawn at any time, for any purpose, without triggering penalty or taxes.

Selecting starter investments

What's a great starter investment? If this money is intended for college expenses, you're probably going to want to exert more influence on how it's invested, than if it's the kid's lawn-cutting or baby-sitting money.

Tip A sensible first investment for a child is one that covers a vast swatch of the stock market. An ideal candidate is an index fund.

Proprietary funds

If your child is investing through a discount broker, it'll be more economical to choose from among your broker's own in-house index funds. For instance, a Charles Schwab investor may want to select Schwab 1000 or Schwab S & P 500. Fidelity, E*Trade and TD Waterhouse also have their own proprietary index funds.

If you are a brokerage customer, you'll have access to other index funds beyond your brokerage firm's in-house lineup, but it's quite likely a transaction fee will be triggered each time new shares of these other funds are purchased. That shouldn't happen when you buy a brokerage firm's own proprietary index funds.

Tip On the other hand, if you intend to invest directly with a fund company, consider one of the index funds offered by the Vanguard Group. Vanguard, the granddaddy of index funds, manages an excellent lineup of index funds.

Individual stocks

When kids are investing their own money, they'll probably be more excited about pouring money into an individual stock. Often kids prefer to invest in companies that make products they like, such as Coca Cola, Abercrombie & Fitch, Sony, Nike, and Tootsie Roll. Once again a trip to the library is a wise idea. At the reference desk, ask for a copy of *Value Line Investment Survey*, a weekly stock guide that includes ratings, analysis, and historical financial data on approximately 1,700 individual corporations. If your budding Wall Street tycoon is interested in smaller companies, see if the librarian has a copy of the *Value Line Investment Survey, Expanded Edition*, which covers 1,800 mostly small-cap stocks.

 Cross-Reference To learn more about analyzing stocks, see chapters 12 and 14.

Getting Kids Excited About Stocks

There are plenty of other ways to get your child involved in the stock picking experience. Here are some possibilities:

Stock market simulation games

Appeal to most kids' love of electronic games by introducing them to these pseudo-stock challenges.

✦ **Stock Market Game.** This popular stock simulation game allows students to invest an imaginary $100,000 in stocks during a 10-week period. Over the years, more than six million children have participated in The Stock Market Game, which is sponsored by the Securities Industry Foundation for Economic Education. Note: The games are played in classrooms, and only teachers can sign up kids to play; children cannot sign up solo. To learn more, visit www.smgww.org.

✦ **CNBC Student Stock Tournament.** This Internet-based contest gives students a chance to match their stock-picking skills against those of children throughout the U.S. and Canada. The competition, which also uses an imaginary $100,000 cache, is open to any student investment club or class in grades 4 through 12. The teams with the best records during the eight-week tournaments are eligible for prizes and a possible television appearance. You can discover more about the tournaments at http://sst.cnbc.com.

✦ **Investment Challenge.** In contrast, this stock simulation game allows individual students to play. To learn the rules for this contest, visit its Web site at www.ichallenge.net.

Other kid-friendly financial resources

The popularity of investing among teens is evident in the flurry of books, Web sites, and organizations that now provide a wealth of information to these young investors. Here are some solid resources to get a kid started:

✦ **National Association of Investors Corporation.** This national organization of investment clubs offers memberships to teenagers, as well as a home-study investing course for youngsters. Members receive a monthly newsletter. The NAIC's Web site contains links to numerous financial Internet addresses geared toward children. For more information contact the NAIC at (877) 275-6242 or visit its Web site at www.better-investing.org.

✦ **TeenAnalyst.com.** This Web site was developed by kids, for kids. It includes informational articles on investing in stocks, mutual funds, and bonds, as well as commentary on the favorite stock picks of the Web site's creators. You'll also be able to track the Young30 Stock Index, which the teenage founders compiled from corporations that affect children. Find it at www.teenanalyst.com.

Kid-Friendly Investments

The world of finance is trying to cash in on kids' increased interest in Wall Street. Mutual fund families and brokerage firms are appealing to them through catchy Web sites, kid-friendly newsletters, and investments with low minimums for customers investing their allowance and baby-sitting money.

Launched in 1994, Stein Roe Young Investor was the nation's first mutual fund that catered to children. The fund's mandate is to at least partially invest in stocks that appeal to kids, such as Walt Disney, the Gap, AOL Time Warner, and Johnson & Johnson. Today, according to the Mutual Fund Education Alliance, at least 70 other no-load funds that are oriented towards kids exist. Many more funds are sold through full-service brokerage firms and commissioned financial planners.

Stein Roe's special Web site for kids, www.younginvestor.com, offers puzzles and games to play. Pint-sized shareholders receive regular newsletters, and the fund company sponsors a financial essay contest with cash awards that any child who meets the age qualification can enter.

Of course, just because a fund is geared towards kids doesn't mean it's worth embracing. A mediocre fund can turn kids off on investing. Stein Roe Young Investor, however, has compiled an admirable record. But you will want to compare its performance with other choices before investing.

✦ ***Street Wise, A Guide for Teen Investors.*** This book demystifies Wall Street for teenagers. It explains how to evaluate stocks and mutual funds and shares anecdotes of famous money managers on how they got started investing. To its credit, the book, which was written by Janet Bamford, a senior editor at *Bloomberg Personal Finance* magazine, contains advice on how to survive a bear market. The book's Web site contains kid links, book excerpts, and a monthly e-mail newsletter. Visit it at www.streetwiseteen.com.

Raising Financially Responsible Kids

Developing the habits of responsible consumers will benefit children their entire lives; teaching them to handle money wisely is one of the greatest gifts you can give. Here are some key concepts to share with them:

Teach by example.

Kids soak up your attitudes about money like a paper towel. And it's easier to develop healthy money habits or change behavior when you're young. Perhaps the best way for parents to teach their children of any age about the value of saving is by example. Think about it. How much success can a chain smoker expect after warning his kids not to smoke? Badgering a child not to waste his money on the latest video game or sneakers will have little effect if a parent's second home is at the mall.

Use the 24-hour rule to avoid impulse buys.

If a child or teenager spies something in a store that she immediately must have, urge her to think about it overnight. Often a must-have item doesn't look so alluring 24 hours later. You might want to impose this rule for impulse items over a certain price, such as $20.

Get kids to comparison shop.

Smart adult shoppers hunt for the best deals and kids should too. A good way to get kids thinking about price differences is at the grocery store. Teach them how to read labels and compare unit prices. For instance, is a package of a pound of pasta selling for $1 a better deal than 8 ounces for 60 cents? Talk to them about using coupons when buying groceries and looking in the newspapers for store sales.

 To groom your junior shoppers to be discriminating, encourage them to log onto Consumer Reports Online for Kids (www.zillions.org), which was developed by the creators of *Consumer Reports.*

The Web site is devoted to making kids smarter consumers. The site, for instance, compares the prices and quality of different toys, such as scooters and video games. It also exposes misleading television commercials aimed at kids and explains how to find high quality clothes without the expensive name brands.

Teach them budgeting.

Give your children an allowance and explain to them what it must cover. For instance, you might expect a teenager's allowance to cover her clothing and entertainment expenses. As long as it's a reasonable amount, you should generally resist the temptation to bail your child out if he or she blows the budget. Allow older kids to make spending decisions, both good and bad, so they will learn from their mistakes. Encourage them to talk about the pros and cons of major purchases ahead of time.

Teach them to negotiate.

Whether they are buying used video games at a garage sale or a 10-year-old car from the classifieds, it's important that children learn the art of negotiation. Being able to negotiate will be a valuable skill later on when they find themselves trying to succeed in their personal and professional lives. Negotiating a raise or a promotion or dickering when buying a house can bring great rewards.

Dispel money misunderstandings.

Most kids harbor some crazy ideas about money. Try to tackle them as early as ages four or five by asking kids about their perceptions of your spending. You may find that your children don't think money grows on trees, but they do believe automatic teller machines spit out cash magically. It's the same story with credit cards. Your children see you handing plastic to a clerk and carrying home anything you want, as if that merchandise were a gift from the almighty credit card company rather than a financed purchase that may be carrying an exorbitant interest rate.

Use age-appropriate strategies.

Preschoolers aren't ready to understand the nuances of mutual funds, but children who are old enough to brush their own teeth are ready to start learning some basics. Here are some tips to get you started.

Little kids

When a child knows how to count, introduce him to money. Make it fun by asking him if he prefers a dime or nine pennies, or a quarter instead of two dimes. Put a pile of change in front of him and ask him to pick out the correct amount of his allowance.

Grade-schoolers

When your child is in grade school, help set financial goals for toys he or she wants. If a child is in love with the latest Barbie doll, she'll be more inclined to save up enough money if you make it clear that you won't pay for it.

Tip   Making kids save for toys rather than writing a check at Toys 'Я' Us on a whim should help instill the value of saving.

Once a grade-schooler has stuffed his piggy bank full, open a kiddie account with your child at a neighborhood bank. Let your child open the statement when it comes. Don't always talk your kids out of withdrawing money from the account, because it will discourage them from ever wanting to save.

Tip   Give children money in denominations that will encourage saving. Instead of giving your child a $5 bill for cleaning out the garage, pass out five ones.

To encourage saving, consider paying your child interest on the money she's managed to save. Borrow money from your child and pay interest just so she appreciates how she can earn money simply by not spending it. At an early age, a child can conclude that it's a much better deal to lend money than to borrow.

Tip   Use everyday transactions as learning opportunities. For example, when paying a restaurant bill by credit card, explain how the tip is calculated and show your child how you can verify if the bill is correct.

Preteens and teenagers

Explain to preteens and teenagers the virtues of stock investing. If you have a mutual fund established for your child's college education, show her how to calculate what it's worth by using the figures on the account statements. Talk to her about what kind of return she might expect from a stock mutual fund versus a low-interest bearing savings account. Have her track funds or stocks online at one of the many financial sites.

Get them a credit card with training wheels.

After expending so much time getting your children excited about investing, a thin piece of plastic can sabotage their best intentions. An increasing number of teenagers are walking around with a financial hand grenade in their pockets. That's right, a credit card.

Kids with credit cards: Recipe for disaster

No matter how often a parent reminds a child that a card isn't free money, the parent often goes unheard. Abusing card privileges is easy to do, but unfortunately it's much harder wiping away the mistakes. A poor credit history can haunt a teenager for many years in the future when they are shopping for a car, an apartment, or a home. It can even hurt their chances for a job. Quite a number of employers look at credit records before making hiring decisions.

Caution   According to a recent survey, two-thirds of college students own credit cards and a quarter of them got their first plastic in high school. So if you balk at authorizing a card, brace yourself for the inevitable protest.

Working with a stored value card

If your teenager is dying for a credit card, consider signing up for an innovative type of plastic referred to as a *stored value card.* It's called stored value because you activate the card by transferring money into it. So if you've deposited $150 into the card, a child can't buy a $300 Sony Playstation 2 with it. The concept is a lot like a prepaid telephone calling card, and it allows parents a tremendous amount of control over their children's spending.

When the cash in the card is depleted, a parent can transfer more money into the card by visiting the card's Web site or calling a toll-free number. The money can be moved from a checking or savings account, a credit or debit card. A child's spending is archived online, which allows parents to pinpoint precisely where the money is going.

Card issuers are marketing these pseudo credit cards to kids as young as 13 and as old as 22. The new generation of plastic goes by such names as Visa Buxx and American Express's Cobaltcard. These cards are accepted at nearly anyplace that now takes Visa and American Express. MasterCard is expected to unveil its own card shortly.

To learn more about how these cards work, visit these Web sites:

✦ Visa Buxx (www.visabuxx.com)

✦ Cobaltcard (www.cobaltcard.com)

✦ RocketCash (www.rocketcash.com)

Summary

✦ Get children in the habit of saving by providing a financial match.

✦ Establish a Roth Individual Retirement Account for a qualified child.

✦ Teach children the basics when investing in mutual funds and stocks.

✦ If a teenager wants a credit card, steer him or her towards one with training wheels.

✦ Be a financial role model for your child.

✦　　✦　　✦

Financial Fundamentals

Investing can certainly be rewarding, but a solid ground-work needs to be laid first. In this section, you'll learn how to vanquish your debt, as well as how to protect yourself and your livelihood with insurance. You'll also discover how to steer clear of unethical or incompetent financial help.

Defusing Your Investments' Tax Time Bombs

I n this chapter, you'll find ways to slash your tax bill whether you invest in mutual funds, individual stocks, bonds, or annuities. You will also learn strategies to better insulate your overall portfolio from taxes. While you can't control how well a stock or bond will do, with careful planning you can control your tax bill. As you'll discover, one way to reduce your taxes is to not automatically believe conventional wisdom.

The Insidious Effects of Taxes

Taxes. Just the mention of the word can cause heart palpitations. Elections across the country have turned on where political adversaries stand on taxes. Every April 15, television cameras show up at post offices to record disgruntled taxpayers mailing their IRS checks late into the night. Just as predictable are the media stories that calculate how many weeks we must work, as indentured IRS servants, just to pay off our yearly federal tax obligation.

For all the griping we do about taxes, however, as investors, we spend very little time doing anything about minimizing them. We've all heard the adage that death and taxes are the only certainties in our lives. That may be true, but our taxes don't have to feel like a deathblow. There are ways to keep the IRS's sticky fingers off our investments or at least limit what they take.

The Tax Rate Reductions of 2001

In 2001, Congress passed the biggest tax cut in 20 years. Among the hundreds of Internal Revenue Code changes was a ratcheting down of Americans' income tax rates. A new 10 percent tax bracket was carved out of the previously lowest rate of 15 percent. Except for the 15 percent bracket, all the other ones are scheduled to be scaled back through 2006.

Years	Tax Brackets			
	28%	31%	36%	39.6%
2001*	27%	30%	35%	38.6%
2002–2003	27%	30%	35%	38.6%
2004–2005	26%	29%	34%	37.6%
2006 and later	25%	28%	33%	35%

* Lower tax rate for 2001 began on July 1, 2001.

Before you can formulate a tax-wise investing strategy, however, you'll have to shake the mind set that so many of your friends, co-workers, and relatives cling to tightly. Americans love to treat their investments like a horse race. They cheer, for instance, if their mutual fund or stock pulls away from the rest of the pack. If you've got a mutual fund that's jumped 16 percent and your neighbor's ended the year up 11 percent, you're the one who can crow, right? Not necessarily. Here's what's hard to comprehend: Unless the money is protected in a tax-deferred retirement account, the raw performance totals don't mean much. In reality, the neighbor may have fared much better than you if your mutual fund is a tax hog.

Tip   The performance statistic that truly matters is an investment's after-tax return. That is, how much money you have left after paying taxes.

Investors' Tax Hit List

You can't possibly fortify your portfolio against a potential tax assault unless you know what you're up against. As investors, we face three different types of federal taxes on our investments. Here's the lineup:

Long-term capital gains tax

If you're going to owe taxes on your investments, this is the least objectionable one. Long-term capital gains tax rates are the lowest of the bunch. They are triggered when you sell your investment for a profit after holding it for at least one year and a day.

> **Note**   Investors in stocks and stock mutual funds typically encounter this tax far more frequently than do bond investors.

If your profit triggers long-term capital gains taxes, the rate that many investors pay is 20 percent. So if you earned a $10,000 profit on Home Depot stock, you'd owe $2,000 in taxes. This tax rate applies to everyone except those in the 10 percent or 15 percent income tax brackets, which are the lowest. For these investors, the tax shrivels to 10 percent.

Investments purchased in 2001 or later and held for more than five years will be subject to a top rate of 18 percent. The change is an even better deal for those sitting in the bottom brackets. These individuals will owe just 8 percent for investments that satisfy the five-year holding period. And for them, this reduced tax even applies to investments bought prior to 2001.

Short-term capital gains tax

Try hard to avoid this tax. It's aimed squarely at impatient traders, who dump an investment before that magical one-year period. Quick profits are taxed at whatever the investor's tax bracket is. So if your ordinary income is taxed at 30 percent and you sell that Home Depot stock for a $10,000 profit, after holding it for just a few months, the capital gains tax would be $3,000.

Cheat Sheet for Tax Weary Investors

Everyone hates paying taxes, but plenty of ways exist for investors to ease the pain. Here's a quick list of ideas that will be covered further in this chapter:

✦ Avoid short-term capital gains taxes.

✦ Use Morningstar and a mutual fund's own literature to determine your fund's tax efficiency.

✦ Seek out and invest in tax-efficient mutual funds.

✦ In a high tax bracket? Invest in municipal bonds.

✦ Offset investment gains by selling losers for a tax deduction.

✦ Handpick specific stock and fund shares to sell.

✦ Consider swapping your current bonds for better ones.

✦ Resist active trading in taxable accounts.

✦ Keep thorough investment records.

✦ Don't cash out your 401(k) or other workplace retirement plan before retiring.

Dodging short-term capital gains taxes is much easier if you hold individual stocks, because you are in control of the security's sale. As you'll learn shortly, mutual fund investors can get torpedoed with yearly taxes, even if they hold onto their shares for decades, because fund managers do the buying and selling for them.

Tax on interest income and dividends

Just like the short-term capital gains tax, this one is linked to your income tax bracket. The people who are most commonly ensnared by this tax are fixed-income fans. Most of these investors buy bonds for the interest income they generate. Individual bondholders, as well as bond mutual fund investors, must pay taxes on all that interest income.

Note   The tax is still owed by bond fund investors even if they automatically reinvest the interest payments back into a fund.

This same tax also covers dividends from stocks. If you hold a stock that generates dividends, here's how the tax works: Suppose you own 1,000 shares of JCPenney, which at one point had established a dividend of 50 cents per share. For the year, the department store chain pays you $500 in dividends. You may instruct your brokerage firm to reinvest this dividend payout, or the check might be mailed to your home. Either way, this $500 will be taxed just as your paycheck would. So if you're in the 27 percent tax bracket, you'd owe $135. If you're in the 30 percent bracket, the tax is $150. The higher your bracket, the bigger the tax bite.

Note   This tax also applies to interest generated by savings accounts and certificates of deposit that are parked at credit unions, banks, and other financial institutions.

Capital Gains Taxes on Home Sales

For many people, their home is their biggest investment. It's also the one investment where you can make a huge killing on the sale without sharing it with Uncle Sam. There is a limit to the IRS's largess, but the ceiling is so high that it won't matter for most. Here are the ground rules: If you are single, you can make up to a $250,000 profit on the sale of your home or condominium and owe the federal government nothing. A married couple who files their tax returns jointly can pocket a $500,000 profit and pay no taxes.

Some caveats, however, exist. To qualify for the tax exemption, you must have lived in your home at least two out of the previous five years before the sale. You also can't claim the exclusion more than once every two years. There are ways, however, for those who don't meet the criteria to at least eke out some tax protection. You can qualify for a partial tax break, for instance, if you're forced to sell a home because of health problems or a job transfer. In other words, don't assume it's hopeless without consulting a tax advisor.

Minimizing Mutual Fund Taxes

Not long ago, KPMG Peat Marwick raised eyebrows in the financial community by calculating just how badly taxes erode annual mutual fund returns. The number crunchers estimated that the typical mutual fund loses 2.6 percentage points of its annual performance to taxes. Considering that stocks have historically averaged annual returns of 11 percent, shaving off 2.6 percentage points means the return equals only 8.4 percent—which represents a 28 percent drop in performance.

What could possibly cause such tremendous erosion? Many fund managers don't care if their trading activities eventually cause an IRS feeding frenzy for their share-holders. They strive for eye-popping returns that their firm's marketing depart-ments can brag about in advertising. Since promotional materials have traditionally not mentioned this potential tax drag, they figured investors would remain clueless.

Obviously, fund investors don't deserve this kind of treatment. It is possible, how-ever, to fight back. While taxes are the single largest cost of mutual fund invest-ments, that cost can be controlled. Here are some of the best ways to stop the tax bleeding:

Strategy no. 1: Know why capital gains distributions are bad.

Before you can insulate your portfolio, you need to specifically understand why mutual funds can cause devilish problems at tax time that individual stocks don't present. If you hold individual stocks for years, you won't pay any capital gains taxes as long as you don't sell. With mutual funds it's possible to get slapped with capital gains taxes every year even if you hold on tightly to your shares.

Capital gains in action

What gives? The answer can be traced back to federal regulations. By law, every mutual fund must annually pass along capital gains distributions to its sharehold-ers. Here's the simplest way to explain what this is: Throughout the year, a portfolio manager trades stocks and or bonds in hopes of capturing a great return. At some point in the year, all the trades are tallied up. If the fund sold a lot of stocks for a considerable profit, but shed very few losing stocks, the fund, on balance, could have generated a very large capital gain or profit. On the other hand, a fund man-ager who tinkered very little with his or her portfolio or who balanced realized prof-its by selling some losers may have little or no gains to pass along.

Now remember, federal law requires that any excess profit—after subtracting the losses—must be proportionately passed along to each shareholder. On the surface, this probably sounds delightful. You share in the wealth. But this is not something to celebrate. Here's why: When you receive a capital gains distribution, you are taxed on this money. This is true even if you automatically reinvest this cash to buy more shares of the fund, which is what typically happens. Okay, so you must pay tax, but won't you still be ahead financially? Actually, no. That's because the price of each share of your fund will drop to compensate for the distribution. Say your fund's per share price is valued at $10 and every shareholder receives a capital gains distribution of $1.50 a share. When this happens, the value of each share now drops to $8.50.

So, as you can see, this entire transaction was a wash. If you received the capital gains and reinvested it, you now own more shares, but each share is worth less. And of course, Uncle Sam expects to be compensated for your phantom windfall. You can owe both short-term and long-term capital gains. Just how the distribution is divided between the two types of capital gains will be stated on a document called Form 1099-DIV. Your fund company or brokerage firm mails this to you at the start of tax season.

Interest and dividend taxes, too

Mutual funds can also trigger the tax for interest and dividend income. Any stock dividends and bond interest are passed on to shareholders each year. Once again, it makes no difference to the IRS whether you automatically reinvest this money or you instruct your fund company to send you a check. You'll owe annual taxes on these earnings.

Strategy no. 2: Stay away from tax hogs.

With thousands of mutual funds on the market, there's no reason to pick one that spews taxes like a broken fire hydrant. Keep your eyes open for these four warning signs of a potentially tax sloppy fund:

✦ High portfolio turnover

✦ High redemptions

✦ Portfolio manager change

✦ High percentage of unrealized capital gains

High portfolio turnover

If a fund trades stocks at a furious rate, it's more likely to be a tax guzzler. The tip off is a high *portfolio turnover rate,* which quantifies how long stocks stay in a fund portfolio. A turnover of 70 percent means that 7 out of every 10 stocks have been booted out of the portfolio within one year. A 100 percent turnover signals that the portfolio at the start of the year looks totally different 12 months later.

Note According to Morningstar, the average turnover rate for a stock fund is 112 percent. In the entire universe of funds, the rate ranges from an awesome 5,734 percent down to 0 percent.

There is some danger in making conclusions based solely on turnover. Some managers, who tend to flit in and out of stocks, actually do an admirable job of keeping down taxes. Bridgeway Aggressive Growth, for instance, recently generated a 203 percent portfolio turnover, but is as tax-friendly as Vanguard Tax-Managed Growth and Income, which sold only 4 percent of its portfolio within the past year. How is this possible? Managers at funds with rapid turnover can take fairly simple steps to minimize the tax pain; the managers at tax-sloppy funds just don't go the extra mile.

Tip   A fund's portfolio turnover rate is included in its annual report. You can obtain a free copy by calling a fund's toll-free number or by visiting its Web site.

High redemptions

Watch out if you bought into a fund at the height of a feeding frenzy. If your white-hot fund suddenly loses its heat, fickle friends will flee. It's happened plenty of times to such well-known fund families as Janus, Fidelity, PBHG, Firsthand, and Vanguard.

Regrettably, the fast money that darts in and out of a fund can cause tremendous tax headaches for the loyal shareholders left behind. When large numbers of investors bail, fund managers may be forced to unload stocks to pay off the departing customers. Selling stocks can, of course, trigger capital gains taxes.

It's not just the highest-flying funds that can suffer from significant redemptions. Investors are far antsier than in the past. According to a study by a think tank created by Vanguard's founder John C. Bogle, the average investor now owns a fund for just over two years. In contrast, funds used to stay in a portfolio for about 12½ years back in the 1950s and 1960s.

Manager change

A changing of the guard can also be a bad omen. Understandably, a new manager will be itching to run a fund his or her own way. That could mean a thorough spring-cleaning. Getting rid of stocks, once again, could trigger unwanted capital gains taxes. This is what happened to America's largest mutual fund, Fidelity Magellan, in 1996 when the manager was replaced. Shareholders paid dearly for the baton hand off.

High percentage of unrealized capital gains

This is the hardest one to appreciate. Just like an individual's stock portfolio, a fund builds up paper profits. A fund that was prescient enough to pick up shares in Cisco Systems or Wal-Mart many years ago would today have tremendous paper gains. This isn't a concern to shareholders unless a manager sells huge blocks of stock in the same year. The most likely reason to unload these stocks is if shareholders are panicking because of stock market turmoil or if a fund's performance is cratering. Either scenario could prompt shareholders to stampede for the door. When this happens, stocks may have to be sold to meet redemptions.

The Advantage of Sticking with the Biggest

A study done by *Mutual Funds Magazine* in the late 1990s suggests that the best-known fund families are usually the most tax-efficient. In the study, the fund families that did the greatest job of shielding customers from taxes were Vanguard, T. Rowe Price, Fidelity, Putnam, MFS, AIM, and Oppenheimer. Then again, other experts suggest that it's wise to find boutique fund shops where managers are very conscious of the tax ramifications of their trading because they have a great deal of their own money sunk into their funds. Funds that fit into that category include those offered by Mairs & Power, Torray, Muhlenkamp, and Bridgeway.

Resource To find out whether a fund is perched on a mountain of unrealized profits, check with Morningstar, the mutual fund rating firm at `www.morningstar.com`. You can subscribe to its publication, *Morningstar Mutual Funds,* or find it in many libraries.

Strategy no. 3: Consider tax-managed funds.

When tax-managed funds were launched in the 1990s, the skeptics howled. Why would anybody want to invest in a fund with a stated mission of saving taxes? The cynics argued that a fund manager who is preoccupied with dodging taxes would surely be distracted from making fabulous stock picks.

So far, the evidence suggests that the critics were all wet. (They originally laughed at index funds too.) Admittedly, tax-managed funds haven't soared to the top of the fund hit parade. And, as a result, they haven't drawn breathless front-cover treatment from the nation's personal finance magazines. Yet these revolutionary funds have quietly and consistently bested most of the field.

Note When Morningstar took a look at the performance of all the tax-managed funds with at least a five-year track record, they were declared an "unqualified success." On an after-tax basis, all of them outperformed their respective fund categories.

The tax efficiency of some of these funds has been just about flawless. The first three tax-managed funds that Vanguard launched in 1994, for instance, have never inflicted their shareholders with a capital gains distribution. That's right, never. And here's something even more impressive. In a footrace, the Vanguard Tax-Managed Growth and Income Fund has beaten the highly popular Vanguard Index 500 Fund. The tax-managed fund's five-year tax-adjusted return was slightly better than the Vanguard 500 Index, which just happens to be the nation's second biggest mutual fund.

How these funds tick

What makes this breed of funds so tax-efficient? When winning stocks are jettisoned from a portfolio, managers typically try to sell losing stocks to offset the profits. Managers are also careful about which stocks they sell—preferring to unload those with the highest original cost and thus the least tax liability. Some funds also avoid dividend-paying stocks since they generate yearly taxes. In addition, a redemption fee is sometimes imposed to discourage market timers, who jump in and out of funds and wreak tax havoc.

Nearly seven dozen tax-managed funds now exist, encompassing a wide variety of investment styles, including a focus on large and small corporations, value and growth plays, and the overseas market.

Tax-managed funds to consider

Many of the major fund families, including Fidelity, T. Rowe Price, Eaton Vance, Putnam, Dreyfus, Liberty, Van Kampen, and American Century now offer these funds. Brokerage firms have also jumped in with their own tax-managed funds. Those offering the funds include Charles Schwab, TD Waterhouse, Goldman Sachs, UBS PaineWebber, Prudential, and Morgan Stanley. Here are some tax-managed funds to explore:

✦ Fidelity Tax-Managed Stock: (800) 343-3548

✦ Schwab 1000: (800) 266-5623

✦ T. Rowe Price Tax-Efficient Balanced: (800) 638-5660

✦ Vanguard Tax-Managed Growth & Income: (800) 635-1511

✦ Vanguard Tax-Managed Capital Appreciation: (800) 635-1511

✦ Vanguard Tax-Managed Balanced: (800) 635-1511

✦ Vanguard Tax-Managed Small Cap: (800) 635-1511

Strategy no. 4: Consider index and exchange-traded funds.

Tax-managed funds aren't the only ones offering IRS relief. Index mutual funds and exchange-traded funds are inherently tax-efficient. Index funds captured investors' imaginations during the second half of the 1990s when the performance of the Standard & Poor's 500 Index, which is the benchmark for the nation's biggest corporations, was spellbinding. Because an index fund is mandated to hold the stocks that are contained in its corresponding index, little trading is necessary, which means taxes should be held to a minimum. Index funds are among the most tax-efficient funds available today.

Cross-Reference   Chapters 9 and 10 are devoted to index and exchanged-traded funds.

A much newer contender for the honor is the exchange-traded fund (ETF). These funds, which have exploded in popularity, borrow strengths from both mutual funds and individual stocks. Like index funds, the most popular ETFs track a specific benchmark, such as the S&P 500, the Nasdaq-100, or the Russell 2000. Consequently, an ETF should do nearly as well as its respective index.

Because these ETFs also don't require a lot of trading, they are inherently tax-efficient. The nation's most popular ETF, which is nicknamed the Spider (for its stock ticker SPY), hasn't made a capital gains distribution in four years. This ETF is linked to the S&P 500.

Caution   Not all ETFs are uniformly tax-efficient. In contrast, the S&P MidCap 400 Spider (stock ticker MDY) has made capital gains distributions every year since 1995, when it was launched.

Strategy no. 5: Rethink investing in a fund late in the year.

Adding a fund to your portfolio during the holiday season can turn out to be far more expensive than anything else on your shopping list. You may be thrilled at your new mutual fund, but what you may have unwittingly done is bought into somebody else's tax problem.

Here's why: Mutual funds typically make their capital gains distribution near the end of the year. This timing can be particularly disastrous for new shareholders because they must pay taxes on gains that they never got to enjoy.

Tip   Before you invest in a new fund at year's end, call the fund company and ask for its next *record date* (the day it plans to make its next distribution) and what the amount will be. If the fund isn't going to make a distribution that year, the timing of your purchase won't matter.

It also makes no difference if you are adding the fund to your retirement portfolio, because you don't pay taxes on money that remains in a retirement account.

Tip   Knowing a fund's release date is important for existing shareholders too. If you've been unhappy with a fund and have been toying with bailing, doing so before the record date can save you money.

With more investors becoming aware of late-year tax bombshells, however, fund companies have been getting sneaky. Some firms have pushed up the distributions to earlier in the year. A major reason for doing this is to stop a potential stampede of investors as the holidays approach. What's the logic of this? The firms hope that, with the bad tax news delivered early, investors will lose their incentive to leave in November and December.

How Tax-Friendly Are Your Mutual Funds?

Some types of funds are inherently more tax-efficient than others. Here's a run down:

Type of Fund	Potential for Dividend & Interest Income	Potential for Capital Gains Distributions
Taxable money market	High	None
Tax-free money market	Very low	None
Municipal bond	Very low	Low
Taxable bond	High	Low
Balanced (stocks & bonds)	Medium to high	Medium
Growth & income	Medium	Medium to high
Growth stock	Low	High
International stock	Low	High

Strategy no. 6: Know your funds' after-tax performance.

In the past, most people had no idea if they were invested in a tax hog until they were smacked with a nasty tax bill. There are now more ways to protect yourself from a ticking time bomb. The best defense is to keep tax-sloppy funds out of your portfolio. Don't worry—no one expects you to do your own analysis. Others have done the work.

In 2001, the U.S. Securities and Exchange Commission began forcing fund companies to provide after-tax returns in their prospectuses and annual reports. The after-tax figures are calculated using the top federal income-tax rate. These figures are displayed for 1-, 5-, and 10-year periods.

Mutual fund companies historically balked at providing after-tax performance numbers. They complained that there are no one-size-fits-all tax figures. That is true. Obviously, somebody in the lowest bracket won't face the same tax liability of someone in the highest. While the reporting can't precisely pinpoint your potential tax liability, it will give you a good idea of whether your fund is a tax nightmare.

Tip Morningstar is perhaps the best one-stop shop for the scoop on tax efficiency.

Know Your Cost Basis, Conserve Your Profit

When you sell a stock or fund for a profit, you may not owe as much tax as you think. Your tax bill will be based upon what's called the *cost basis,* which refers to the original purchase price. Suppose you bought $15,000 worth of fund shares and later sold your holdings for $20,000. On the surface, your cost basis would appear to be $15,000, so you'd be liable for a $5,000 profit.

But wait a minute. Many people don't realize that other factors can boost the cost basis. Included in the cost basis, for instance, are any sales charges or transaction fees you paid during your fund trading. Say you paid your discount broker a total of $60 to buy and later sell your fund shares. That adds $60 to your cost basis, which brings it up to $15,060. But here's the best news: Any reinvested capital gains distributions and dividends you received over the years are counted in the cost basis. In some cases, this can boost an investment's cost basis considerably and dramatically shrink your ultimate tax bill.

Morningstar assigns a tax-efficiency rating for 3-, 5-, and 10-year periods to every fund it evaluates. For example, the Muhlenkamp Fund, which invests in mid-cap value stocks, enjoys an impressive three-year tax efficiency of 95 percent. This means that an investor kept 95 percent of the fund's returns. In contrast, look at Berger Small Company Growth, which has a three-year tax efficiency of less than 61 percent. That means that a big chunk of an investor's gains were swallowed up by taxes.

 Resource Another source of quick tax information are some of the brokerage firms. Fidelity Investment and Schwab, for example, list the after-tax returns of the funds they offer on their Web sites.

Strategy no. 7: Sell the right fund shares.

Realistically, you can't keep the IRS at bay forever. At some point, you're probably going to want to sell a chunk of your mutual funds or stocks. There is a way, however, to shrink the tab. You may be able to save a great deal of money by being choosy about which shares are sold.

Most investors calculate the average cost of their shares and use that figure to determine the gains. If you are selling all your shares, that can be an acceptable approach. But if you're only unloading a portion of your shares, you should consider specifying the ones you wish to sell. Ideally, you would sell the shares that you bought at the highest price. You shouldn't take this approach, however, if the highest priced shares wouldn't qualify for the long-term capital gains tax treatment.

 Note If selling only a specific portion of shares, you must identify which shares you want to sell before the sale. It won't count if you do this after the sale.

Strategy no. 8: Look out for fund swap taxes.

Don't get tripped up by this common mistake. Many investors believe that capital gains taxes aren't triggered in their taxable accounts if they switch their money from one fund to another within the same fund family. Say you own shares of Fidelity Contrafund and you wish to transfer the money into Fidelity Blue Chip Growth. If you've made a profit by investing in Fidelity Contrafund, you will owe taxes. It makes no difference if the money stays within Fidelity.

Using Six Strategies for Stocks

Here are ways to reduce the taxes on your stock portfolio.

Strategy no. 1: Buy and hold stocks.

Stocks are one of the most tax-efficient investments you can buy. That's because you control when you pay capital gains taxes. If you don't sell any of your stock, you won't owe Uncle Sam for capital gains taxes. This is true even if your stock has escalated dramatically in value. A lot of elderly widows, who have IBM, Coca-Cola, and other blue chip stocks, are sitting on vast fortunes, but they haven't had to worry at all about capital gains taxes.

Strategy no. 2: Avoid short-term capital gains.

If you trade stocks frequently, it's best to do so within a retirement account. Why? Stocks, which aren't held for more than a year, will be hit by those draconian short-term capital gains taxes. If you move in and out of stocks within a retirement account, however, no taxes are triggered.

Strategy no. 3: Sell the losers.

Need a tax write-off? You might have one sitting in your taxable portfolio. If you've got a stock—or a mutual fund—that has lost ground since it was purchased, consider selling it. You don't have to banish the investment from your portfolio forever—just long enough to lock in a tax deduction. If you sell a loser, you can use the loss to offset realized profits in your portfolio.

Caution When selling a losing stock, you can't repurchase shares of that stock or fund within 30 days. If you do ignore the deadline, the tax deduction vanishes.

Some investors might find the month-long moratorium nerve-wracking. What if your stock soars while you're sitting on the sidelines? If you don't want to assume that risk, one solution is buying a similar stock in the same industry. Or you may prefer to buy additional shares with the stock price depressed and then wait 30 days to sell your original block of stock for a loss.

Strategy no. 4: Sell the right shares.

When selling stock, pick the right shares to cash in. For instance, if you want to reduce your exposure in General Motors, sell those General Motors shares you acquired for $75 each rather than ones scooped up for $45. By doing so, the capital gains hit won't be as painful, because you haven't made as much profit. If you don't specify the shares to sell, the Internal Revenue Service will assume you've used the first-in, first-out method and expect you to pay tax on your oldest (and probably cheapest) shares.

Strategy no. 5: Pass stocks along to heirs or charities.

One way to avoid capital gains taxes is to never sell your stock. Instead leave the shares to loved ones or to a charity. When someone inherits a stock, he or she receives a true tax gift. Suppose a grandchild inherits a block of stock worth $100,000 that her grandmother originally bought for $10,000. If the grandmother had sold the stock before dying, she'd have owed taxes on a huge profit. But when the grandchild inherits the stock, the IRS essentially pretends that the $90,000 gain never happened. The cost basis is adjusted to $100,000. The tax savings on this posthumous transfer of ownership is invaluable. If she ultimately sells the stock when it reaches $125,000, for example, she'd only owe capital gains taxes on $25,000, not on $115,000.

You can also benefit by donating valuable stock to a favorite charity. Say you bought $20,000 worth of American Express shares years ago and they're now worth $50,000. If you give the shares to charity, you claim a tax deduction based on their current rather than original value.

Strategy no. 6: Consider using a privately managed account.

While individual stocks are more tax-friendly, assembling a stock portfolio can be hard work. Not everyone has the time or the inclination to research stocks and remain vigilant once they've been selected. You can, however, hire someone to pick your stocks. It's possible to do this through what's called an individually managed account. These accounts have become quite the rage among the Volvo and BMW set, who feel they've outgrown mutual funds.

Putting a manager on your payroll

With one of these customized accounts, you're essentially hiring your own professional money manager to oversee your portfolio. Many of these managers handle investments for pension funds, endowments, and multimillionaires. One of the biggest draws is the potential tax protection. At least in theory, these managers are exquisitely mindful of their wealthy clients' tax concerns and try to limit them as much as possible.

Tip

Because of this promise of tax protection, most investors limit their use of these customized portfolios to taxable accounts. Once again, taxes aren't an issue in a retirement portfolio since trading activity doesn't trigger taxes.

Customized stock portfolio management is no longer just an option for people blessed with vast wealth. The investment minimums have been plummeting. Hiring a money management firm directly can still require a few million dollars, but if you go through an intermediary, such as a brokerage firm, the admission price is vastly lower.

But are fees better than taxes?

Whether one of these accounts is a tax panacea is debatable. Detractors, for instance, suggest that the highly touted tax sensitivity is just hype. What is undeniable is that these accounts aren't cheap. Each year, you could have anywhere from 1 percent to 3 percent of the value of your portfolio drained away for expenses. That's a stiff price for tax efficiency when a tax-efficient index fund charges just a fraction of that amount. You'll need to decide for yourself whether the privately managed account is an expensive ego play for the wealthy or a legitimate tax saver.

Beating Bond Taxes

One of the biggest knocks against bonds is that they trigger the worst kind of investment tax. A healthy chunk of the interest generated by bonds can get eaten up by income taxes. Bond fans should use every tax tactic at their disposal.

Strategy no. 1: Consider municipal bonds.

One way to loosen the tax tourniquet is to invest in municipal bonds (munis). Municipal bonds are issued by state and local government to pay for such big-ticket items as bridges, prisons, and hospitals. The interest generated by muni bonds isn't subject to federal income taxes. Some munis also avoid state income taxes. The higher a person's tax bracket, the greater the incentive to invest in munis, which are also called tax-free bonds. Granted, the pre-tax yield for most bonds will trump a muni because they don't offer any tax perks. Muni holders are willing to swap a little yield for the tax protection, and as long as they keep their munis in taxable accounts, they'll get what they pay for.

Caution

Be careful where you park your muni bonds. Munis are only appropriate for taxable accounts. Putting muni bonds in a retirement account is an absolutely dreadful idea. A retirement account already provides tax protection.

Cross-Reference

To learn much more about municipal bonds, see Chapter 19.

Strategy no. 2: Sell bond losers.

If you own a bond that has lost its value, consider a bond swap. With a swap, you capture a loss that you can use as a valuable deduction on your income taxes.

Here's how the swap can work: Suppose interest rates climb, and your bond fund experiences a substantial loss. You can capture that loss by selling the fund, which makes your paper loss a real one. You can use this loss to offset other capital gains in your portfolio. Your next step is to purchase another bond fund.

 Caution   The tax code's so-called wash-sale rule governing stocks also applies to bond transactions. If you sell a bond fund and then buy shares in the same fund within 30 days, you aren't entitled to claim the loss on your tax return. It's the same with individual bonds.

Realistically, bond swapping works best with bond funds. That's because it's possible to move in and out of bond funds for little or no charge. Individual bond transactions are more expensive so the financial incentive to do this may not be compelling.

Steering Your Portfolio Away from Taxes

One of the tricks of investing wisely is knowing how to protect your overall portfolio from taxes. Here are some tips:

Strategy no. 1: Reconsider conventional wisdom.

If you've read a lot of personal finance magazines, you probably think you know where to stash your bonds. Traditional wisdom dictates that bonds should be sheltered in retirement accounts. Why? Because they are tax pigs. Bonds mostly generate interest income. All that money is taxed the same way as your paycheck. So if you're in the 35 percent tax bracket and your Treasury bonds spun off $10,000 in interest this year, more than a third of it would be swallowed by federal taxes.

In contrast, stocks aren't such tax hogs. If a stock appreciates and then you sell it, you'll only owe capital gains taxes. As mentioned earlier, the tax pain for a stock you've held for more than a year tops out at 20 percent and can be much lower. Dividends are taxed the same way as a bond's coupon payments, but dividends, at historically low levels, are not the way investors are getting rich in the stock market.

Rethinking the parking places for stocks and bonds

Two recent studies have undermined the conventional wisdom. Researchers at T. Rowe Price, the mutual fund family, suggest that the potential for stock gains is so significant that equities, in many cases, should be sheltered in retirement accounts. In other words, the gains that stocks enjoy over time can cause greater tax pain—despite lower tax rates—than bonds.

The other study, conducted by three professors at Stanford University and the Massachusetts Institute of Technology, examined how an investor would have fared if bonds were segregated in a tax-deferred account and stock mutual funds were kept in a taxable one during a 37-year period, ending in 1998. They also looked at what would happen if the investments were flip-flopped in the two types of accounts. In both scenarios, $1,000 was invested annually in the hypothetical accounts, with the money evenly split between stock funds and bonds. By the end of the experiment, the investor who put the bonds in a tax-deferred account had a portfolio worth $83,010. But the portfolio that kept bonds in the taxable account was worth 8.8 percent more, or $90,290.

Looking further at the research

You can obtain both studies on the Internet. T. Rowe Price's study is available at its Web site (www.troweprice.com) in the section devoted to tax planning. The academic study is available at the National Bureau of Economic Research's Web site at http://papers.nber.org/papers/w799111.

Strategy no. 2: Use your retirement account to rebalance your overall holdings.

Is your portfolio unbalanced? Even a model portfolio becomes lopsided. Your ideal proportion of stocks, bonds, and cash can get out of whack when market conditions change. When Wall Street is enjoying a long spell of prosperity, for instance, a portfolio originally divided between 60 percent stocks and 40 percent bonds can become overly dominated by stocks, as the equities appreciate.

Bond and stock mixes aren't the only allocations that can get out of whack. During the 1990s, large growth stocks behaved as if they were on steroids, while large-cap value stocks performed anemically. A portfolio that wasn't readjusted could have been brutalized when value became the big winner again.

What does all this have to do with taxes? Plenty. Rebalancing often means selling holdings. Of course, selling winning positions will make Uncle Sam happy. The solution is to try to limit your tinkering to your retirement account.

Tip

You can make as many changes as you'd like to the holdings in a 401(k), a 403(b), an Individual Retirement Account, a SEP-IRA, or another retirement plan without paying any taxes for profits on sales.

Strategy no. 3: Don't cash out workplace retirement accounts.

When you leave your job, resisting the temptation to cash out your 401(k) or other workplace retirement account can be as hard as passing up a chance for a second piece of pumpkin pie at Thanksgiving. According to one survey, 57 percent of workers cash out their 401(k) when leaving a workplace. They might purchase an SUV, remodel the house, take a vacation, or spend the windfall in countless other ways.

Caution   If you cash out your retirement accounts, the money will be gone when you really need it in retirement, and you'll have lost the benefit of years of potential compounding.

But even if the prospect of retiring broke doesn't scare you, remember this: The IRS will expect its share. You will face onerous taxes if you dip into a 401(k) prematurely. Suppose you're 30 years old when you leave your job with a 401(k) worth $20,000 and that you're in the 27 percent tax bracket. Right off the top, the IRS will demand 27 percent of that money. That brings you down to $14,600. Since you're under the age of 55, you'll be assessed a 10 percent early withdrawal penalty. This reduces your windfall to $12,600. Actually, the tax and penalty bite for many people will be even worse because state income tax will also nibble away at this money.

Cross-Reference   Chapter 21 gives more detailed information on 401(k)s.

Many people have no idea how severe the tax pain can be. Employees frequently believe that they only have to pay a 20 percent withholding penalty, because their former employer is obligated to withhold 20 percent of the money when sending a check directly to an ex-worker. True, that money will be applied to the amount of income tax that will be owed if the cash isn't placed in an IRA rollover account. But more income tax could be due, as well as a 10 percent early withdrawal penalty.

Tip   Save yourself some fiscal heartache by instructing your former employer to send your 401(k) assets directly to an IRA rollover account.

Eluding Annuity Taxation

If you value investing tax-efficiently, you may need to reexamine how you feel about annuities; other investment options already covered in this chapter may provide better alternatives for you and your portfolio.

Rethink annuities

If you own a variable annuity, you probably know a stockbroker. Most people would be unable to explain what an annuity is, but if they've crossed paths with an ambitious broker or financial advisor, they might believe they desperately need one. Sadly, this is often not the case. While the financial industry promotes the annuity as a bonafide tax fighter, investors usually only hear half of the story. (This phenomenon is covered in Chapter 22.)

Here's the good news: As long as you don't touch the money in an annuity, it remains happily shielded from taxes. Even if your annuity spins off dividends and capital gains, it's not going to matter one whit. If your annuity is in a taxable account, it could grow for decades without you owing a dime in taxes. Many investors, after hearing this sales pitch, can't believe their good fortune in stumbling across such an ironclad tax shelter. But here's the bad news: The ironclad tax protection is a mirage. Investors will pay dearly when they withdraw their money from an annuity.

Caution The tax burden for annuity investors is greater than it is for those who choose to invest through mutual funds and individual stocks in a taxable account. That's because variable annuity profits are taxed at an investor's own tax bracket.

Here's how both scenarios can play out. Suppose someone in the 35 percent tax bracket made a $10,000 profit from his annuity. He'd owe the IRS 35 percent of his windfall, which pencils out to $3,500. Now suppose his neighbor, in the same tax bracket, made a $10,000 profit on a fortunate stock pick from a couple of years back. The neighbor would owe just $2,000. If the annuity investor were in the highest tax bracket, the tax difference would be even more dramatic. Someone in the 38.6 percent bracket, for instance, would watch nearly $4 out of every $10 of his annuity windfall disappear.

Note Because of taxes, variable annuities are impractical unless you can hold onto one for many years, even a couple of decades. It can take that long, or longer, before the investment can grow tax-deferred long enough to overcome high fees and the potentially high tax bill.

The U.S. Securities and Exchange Commission was so concerned that Americans weren't aware of annuity pitfalls, including the tax surprise, that it issued a publication called *Variable Annuities: What You Should Know.* You can obtain a free copy by calling the SEC or going to its Web site. Contact the Office of Investor Education and Assistance, 450 Fifth St. NW, Washington, DC 20549; (202) 942-7040; www.sec.gov.

Summary

- ✦ Avoid triggering short-term capital gains taxes by holding onto your stocks at least one year and one day whenever possible.

- ✦ Choose tax-friendly mutual funds for your taxable accounts.

- ✦ Even though stocks are extremely tax-efficient, it can make more sense to keep them in a tax-protected retirement account.

- ✦ You can offset taxes triggered by profits in your portfolio by selling other investments for a loss.

- ✦ Be leery of investing in variable annuities for tax protection; the strategy can backfire.

✦   ✦   ✦

Troubleshooting for Investing Scams

Investing is challenging enough without encountering troubles with an unethical financial pro. But this happens more than you might think. This chapter explains what you can do if you experience difficulties with your brokerage firm, financial advisor or insurance agent. You can learn how to minimize potential problems with these folks up-front by playing detective. You will also learn to identify the telltale signs of financial scams. And you will appreciate why you should be careful if an insurance agent wants to sell you something beyond an insurance policy.

Be Careful Out There

Investing in today's financial markets can often feel like an excursion into the twilight zone. Complaints from investors who trade through both traditional and discount brokerage firms have risen dramatically in recent years. An increasing number of con games are being played on the Internet, but investors who don't even own a computer are just as vulnerable to financial chicanery. Where there is money, there are crooks and the kind of unethical people your mother used to warn you about. But these bad guys don't wear ski masks and you won't see their mugs on the FBI's most wanted lists. They might dress in $1,000 suits and keep photographs of their children's Little League teams on their desk. When a burglar visits your home, you know you've been robbed. But if you've been swindled in a financial deal, you might not even realize it. And that's where the danger lies.

Some of the scams are old hat. We've all heard the stories. A widow, who doesn't know the difference between a zero coupon bond and a grocery store coupon, depends on her stockbroker to put her money in a Teflon-coated portfolio stuffed with safe investments. The suave stockbroker assures the grandmother that she needn't worry. But her seat in the broker's office is barely cold before he starts investing her money into limited partnerships, initial public offerings, and other high-risk investments that generate fat commissions for him. The widow, of course, loses her nest egg.

There are more sophisticated twists to this woeful tale. Shifty stock promoters, as well as unethical financial publications and Web sites, are paid to hawk stocks that may have nothing behind them except a name and stock ticker symbol. Investors, eager to strike it rich, are unwittingly duped into buying stock in nonexistent companies. And it's not just cynical con artists who are yanking investors' chains. Even college and high school students have been caught promoting obscure stocks on the Internet in hopes of making a fast buck. Not long ago, federal investigators arrested for stock manipulation a couple of recent UCLA grads working out of the school library, as well as a New Jersey teen who wasn't even old enough to drive.

Caution   While teenage hackers tend to grab the headlines, investors are much more likely to be victimized by their own brokerage firms.

Complaints of botched trades, accounts transfers, and other procedural mistakes have been increasing in recent years. The complaints are due not only to intentional swindling but also to simple human (or computer) error. A delayed trade execution or an error in processing an order can be just as financially devastating for the investor as being the victim of a scam.

The U.S. Securities and Exchange Commission (SEC) receives thousands of complaints each year regarding brokerage firms. Here are the latest top 10 complaint categories:

1. Account transfer problems

2. Failure to process or delays in executing orders

3. Unauthorized transactions

4. Misrepresentation

5. Errors in processing orders

6. Mistakes or omission in account records

7. Failure to follow customer's instruction

8. Margin account problems

9. Problems receiving funds after selling an investment

10. Trade execution problems

A Scam a Minute

While a great deal of attention has been focused on bad brokers and scam artists, state regulators across the country have pinpointed a new and disturbing source of swindles—insurance agents. According to the North American Securities Administrators Association (NASAA), which represents state regulators, insurance agents are increasingly selling fraudulent investments to unsuspecting clients. This is an especially alarming trend, because many people, particularly older Americans, implicitly trust their insurance agents. You'll learn more about how to combat this growing problem later in the chapter.

While no one can determine how extensive financial frauds are in all arenas of the financial world, the projections are disturbing. The NASAA estimates that losses from inappropriate high-risk investments and scams are costing investors about $1 million an hour. Meanwhile, the SEC receives a flood of e-mail complaints every day.

If you feel you've been wronged, either intentionally or through somebody else's mistake, there are ways to fight back. By the end of this chapter, you should know what your rights are.

Playing Detective

You'll reduce your chances of encountering trouble with your investments if you seek out the best help. This is true whether you depend on a full-service or discount broker or a financial advisor. Before signing up, check the track record of an individual planner or a broker. If the regulatory record is spotty, walk away.

Tip   Save yourself a lot of grief by sticking with well-established, well-respected brokerage firms, whether it be a traditional or discount broker.

The firms with national reputations to protect are likely to handle disputes in an honorable way. That's not always true with obscure brokerage firms. Even when investors win a case against a little-known brokerage firm, they are likely to walk away empty-handed. According to a recent U.S. General Accounting Office report, nearly half of the awards investors won against brokerage firms were not paid. Most of these delinquent firms were no longer in existence.

Tip   You should devote as much time to selecting a broker and a firm as you would to the purchase of a car or home.

It's easy to play detective once you know where to look. Here's what you need to know, and where to find it:

Looking into brokers and brokerage firms

Before signing on with a traditional broker, read the broker's Central Registration Depository (CRD) report. These reports are stockpiled in a massive computer database jointly overseen by the North American Securities Administrators Association (NASAA), which represents each states' financial watchdog departments, and the National Association of Securities Dealers (NASD), which regulates the brokerage industry. Dirty laundry should show up in this report. Here is some of what you will find:

✦ Disciplinary actions taken by federal or state securities offices

✦ Broker's work history

✦ Felony charges and convictions and investment-related misdemeanors

✦ Civil judgments involving securities

✦ Arbitration with clients

✦ Consumer complaints settled for $10,000 or more

✦ Written consumer complaints, filed within the past two years, alleging sales practice violations and damages of more than $5,000

✦ Outstanding judgments and liens

✦ Terminations after investment-related violations

You can obtain the CRD, which is free, after contacting either one of these associations:

✦ North American Securities Administrators Association, 10 G St. NE, Suite 710, Washington, DC 20002; (202) 737-0900; www.nasaa.org. NASAA won't provide the report itself, but it will give you the phone number of your state's securities department, which will mail it to you.

✦ National Association of Securities Dealers, P.O. Box 9401, Gaithersburg, MD 20898-9401; (800) 289-9999; www.nasdr.com.

Always Snub Cold Callers

Don't hire a broker who dials your number out of the blue. A cold-calling broker, who could be hundreds of miles away at a tiny firm, can make a great living by reeling in investors with a confident, friendly demeanor. But you are just asking for trouble if you agree to turn over your money to a smooth talking telephone caller. Although not all the brokers dialing for dollars are up to no good—it's a rite of passage for greenhorns at brokerage houses to make cold calls to build up their client lists—you should just say no to whoever is on the other end of the phone. After all, you wouldn't accept medical advice from a physician who called you out of the blue, so why would you put your financial health on the line when an unknown broker calls?

Resource   You can also contact one of the NASD's district offices. A list of these phone numbers is in the Resource Guide.

You should also check the background of a brokerage firm, especially if the firm isn't well known. By contacting the same resources, here's what you can find out about a brokerage firm:

✦ Actions triggered by the Securities and Exchange Commission or other regulatory body

✦ Criminal charges within the past 10 years

✦ Civil judicial actions, including injunctions, that occurred within the past decade

✦ Bond company denials

✦ Unsatisfied judgments or liens from previous legal actions

Examining investment advisors

The term *investment advisor* is a broad one, describing nearly anyone who gives advice about securities to clients. Investment advisors may also manage clients' portfolios. Most financial planners fall into the investment advisor category. Brokers, however, aren't classified as investment advisors, because they are considered salespeople. Any advice that a stockbroker provides is considered incidental to his job of selling investments.

Brokers' records are listed on their CRDs, but you need to look at a different document when checking out the background of an investment advisor: the ADV Form (ADV is simply short for "advisor"). Before hiring a planner, always take a look at the ADV Form, which must be filed with either the SEC or a state. If an advisor manages more than $25 million in client assets, the form is filed with the SEC. You can obtain the ADV Form from the SEC by contacting its Office of Public Reference, 450 5th St. NW, Room 1300, Washington, DC 20549; (202) 942-8090. If a professional manages less than $25 million, the document is filed with the appropriate state securities department. If you aren't sure how to reach your state regulatory agency, contact the North American Securities Administrators Association (see previous section for NASAA contact information).

You can also request a copy of the ADV from your potential advisor. The ADV Form consists of two parts, but any juicy stuff is in Part I. Ironically, an investment advisor is legally obligated only to provide you with Part II.

Tip   If the advisor hesitates or balks at providing you with both parts, find someone else.

Here are some of the things an ADV Form can tell you about an advisor's background:

✦ Education

✦ Professional history

✦ Types of investments the planner recommends

✦ Method of payment

✦ Potential conflicts of interest

✦ Disciplinary record

✦ Lawsuits and arbitration proceedings

If you are a client of a Certified Financial Planner or are considering hiring one, there is one more place to check. Contact the Certified Financial Planner Board of Standards. The organization sets strict qualification standards for CFPs and can strip a planner of the CFP designation if an individual commits a crime or acts unethically. By contacting the board, you can discover whether the person is a CFP in good standing. You should also touch base with this group if you experience trouble with a CFP. Here's how you can reach the board: 1700 Broadway, Suite 2100, Denver, CO 80290; (888) CFP-MARK; www.CFP-Board.org.

Watching Your Back

Here are steps to take to detect potential troubles before things have gone too far:

Don't ignore the fine print.

When opening an investment account, read the paperwork carefully. Don't just blow it off as a formality. The fine print may ultimately come back to haunt you if you don't understand what you are agreeing to. Before opening an account, make sure your broker or financial advisor understands your level of investing experience (this isn't a time to exaggerate), your tolerance for risk, and your investment objectives. All of this information should be put into writing. This documentation can be invaluable evidence if you end up alleging misconduct or incompetence later on.

Read all correspondence from a brokerage or investment firm.

The best way to head off trouble is to read all correspondence from a brokerage and or investment firm. Regular statements can tip you off if there's something fishy going on in your account. Pay special attention to the opening value of your account and its ending value. The opening balance is how much your portfolio was worth at the end of the previous month. The ending value is what it is worth 30 or 31 days later. If your account has suddenly gained or lost a great deal of money, check the statement to find out why.

Your statement also describes each investment, its quantity, and its value on the monthly closing date. By comparing your holdings with previous statements, you can see which investments did well and which might be lagging. Lastly, you'll see what activity your account generated for the month. If you bought or sold securities, received dividends, or transferred money from one mutual fund to another, all those moves will be listed. If you notice a strange transaction, there could be something wrong. For instance, a broker might have picked up shares of a stock that you never authorized.

One way to double check on your account activity is to file all transaction slips you receive by mail. When a trade is made on your behalf, the brokerage firm sends you a piece of paper that lists the name of the investment, sale price, number of shares bought or sold, and date of the transaction. It also lists just how much your brokerage firm charged in fees and commissions.

Tip
Save all the documents you receive from your brokerage firm. If you're embroiled in a dispute in the future, you'll never know what you'll need to fight back.

Monthly account statements are not known for being user-friendly, but many brokerage firms have booklets that explain how to interpret them. If that doesn't work, ask your broker for an explanation. Do the same with an investment advisor. If you are unsatisfied with the explanation, you should probably find another firm.

Ask questions and listen carefully.

Many of us tend to clam up when we feel out of our element whether we're in the office of a doctor, lawyer, or financial planner. Nonetheless, when a planner or broker is recommending an investment, make sure you thoroughly understand the rationale behind the recommendation. Ask the broker to justify the sale.

Tip
Don't worry about whether your questions sound sophisticated. What's important is asking them.

Before you agree to a new securities purchase, request supporting documents, such as a stock or mutual fund's annual report, a Morningstar fund analysis, or a stock report from Standard & Poor's or the brokerage firm's own research department. Look through the material at your leisure at home before making a decision.

Take notes.

When talking to your broker or financial advisor, take notes during the conversations and keep a log. When you instruct your broker or advisor to make any changes in your portfolio, follow up with a letter detailing your instructions, particularly if you gave them over the phone. All these documents could be invaluable if problems develop later.

Tip It's easy to keep records of conversations with a broker by using the NASAA's Investor Notepad, which is a form you can download from the NASAA web site. The form reminds you to jot down such things as the date of the broker's call, the nature of the investment and the broker's CRD number.

Spotting the Big Broker Offenses

Of course, even the most diligent investor occasionally runs into trouble. Your best line of defense is to spot any problem with your account quickly. Here are some telltale signs that a stockbroker may be more interested in generating commissions rather than client profits:

Churning your account

Consider this scenario: Your broker buys shares in a mutual fund and pockets a commission for the sale. Two months later, the broker dumps the mutual fund and buys shares in one that could be its twin sister. Once again, your broker enjoys a generous commission. Emboldened, he picks up the pace. He buys shares in Coca-Cola and then dumps it for PepsiCo stock. Then he picks up shares in Merck, the pharmaceutical giant, but he sells them quickly to buy a position in Pfizer, another drug company kingpin. For every transaction, he collects a commission. Does this sound fishy to you? It should.

What he's been doing is a big no-no. Even if he calls you for your okay before every trade, it's still not acceptable because he's churning your account to make himself richer. In other words, he's making trades simply to generate commissions. A broker shouldn't switch you from one investment to another when there is no legitimate reason for the switch.

Tip Ask yourself whether your broker frequently advises you to dump securities after less than a year. A buy-and-hold investor should wonder about a broker who recommends investments that can't be held in a portfolio for years.

To prove churning has occurred, you'll have to show that the trading was excessive. One method: Calculate the rate of return that would be necessary just to cover the commissions that all the trading generated. If your portfolio has earned nowhere near that rate of return, you may have a strong case against the broker.

Trading without permission

Imagine looking at your monthly brokerage statement and noticing that you bought 500 shares in a company you've never heard of. You are astounded. When your broker bought that stock, it was an unauthorized trade, which is prohibited.

Sometimes a broker tries to backtrack by calling the customer after the trade, but it's still not a legal trade.

Promising guaranteed stock winners

Your broker is on the phone just bubbling with good news. He's promising that the stock he wants you to buy is a guaranteed winner. Caught up with his enthusiasm, you approve the deal. If you regret your decision later, you might have grounds to recoup your money. While seasoned investors should know that no stock can be a certified moneymaker, a less-sophisticated investor might not understand that an aggressive broker's claim is outlandish.

 Caution

If your broker promises that a stock will soar 30 percent in the next year, 15 percent within 60 days, or some other boast, he's lying. No one knows for certain what the price of *any* stock will do in the future.

Recommending unsuitable investments

Say you've made it clear to your broker that you are a conservative investor. What if he doesn't let your wishes get in the way of his trading? For example, recommending a limited partnership, which is a risky, very long-term investment, wouldn't be appropriate for an 80-year-old retiree. Knowingly making investments that are unsuitable for a client's comfort level is unethical.

A seriously lopsided portfolio is another variation of this bad broker behavior. If a broker devotes a very large part of your portfolio to one type of investment, such as junk bonds or technology stocks, you may rightfully have a case against that broker. Why? A portfolio that is too concentrated in one area can dramatically increase your risks.

Note

A broker has a responsibility to factor in the risks a client can—or shouldn't—assume, the potential tax liabilities of certain investments, the client's risk tolerance, and his or her time horizon.

Acting with negligence

Some brokers shouldn't even be in the business. They might have trouble following instructions, executing trades, and providing competent advice. If a broker can't demonstrate a minimal amount of competency, he might be guilty of broker malpractice. A broker is supposed to act with at least "reasonable care." While this phrase is open to interpretation, it essentially means that a reasonable person in the same position would probably follow a certain course of action. Deviating wildly from actions that indicate reasonable care can indicate negligence of duties.

Pushing margin accounts

Investment clients can also get into trouble when a broker creates margin accounts for them. With this type of account, investors use money borrowed from their brokerage house to put more cash into play. The collateral for this type of loan are the investments in an investor's brokerage account. If an individual can't repay the loan, which can happen when stocks are getting pummeled, the brokerage firm can recoup its money by forcing the sale of securities in the person's portfolio.

This sort of leveraged account, however, is appropriate only for sophisticated investors who thoroughly understand the risks. While some customers might complain that they never authorized a margin account, most of the time people did give their okay. They just didn't understand what they were agreeing to.

Caution　Again, you must read the fine print before agreeing to open a margin account—or any kind of account—and ask pointed questions, even if you're afraid they'll make you look stupid. Better to look unsophisticated up-front than feel taken later.

Online trading complaints

Certain offenses, such as churning and trading without permission by individual brokers, generally occur only at full-service brokerage firms. But discount brokerage firms can generate plenty of their own difficulties. Online trading has exploded in popularity: An estimated 7.8 million people have online accounts today, while back in 1995, there were none. Keeping pace with the popularity is the increase in complaints—the SEC receives thousands of complaints each year from customers of firms trading online, and the numbers keep rising.

The biggest complaint the SEC hears? A broker fails to execute or delays a trading instruction. An online brokerage firm may be unable to process huge amounts of orders during extreme market volatility due to the limits of its computer infrastructure. This can obviously lead to customers' inability to trade, which can cause financial losses.

Caution　A discounter may also allow investors with little to no experience and limited financial resources to access extremely risky activities such as investing on margin.

Through their advertisements, discounters have also been faulted for creating false impressions of what their services can do. Here is a list of the most common online trading complaints that the SEC receives:

1. Failure or delay in processing orders

2. Problems with margin accounts

3. Difficulty accessing accounts

4. Account transfer problems

5. Errors in processing orders

The Inevitable Bad Advice

Did your broker tell you to sell, when you should have held on? You'll hear variations of this complaint a lot. You buy a stock your broker recommends, and then it climbs. It's what we all dream will happen. Eventually, the broker calls and urges you to get rid of it for a modest profit. You agree. But then you notice that the stock keeps soaring. In fact, it doubles not long after you authorized the sale. Sorry, but you won't get much sympathy if you complain that your broker is an idiot. In hindsight, your broker made the wrong call, but bad judgments happen every day in the markets.

Fighting Back When Brokers Stray

If you spot a problem with a brokerage account, act quickly. The clock could already be ticking since there can be time limits to taking action. A brokerage firm could use any procrastination to insist that you really didn't have any problem.

If you've concluded that your broker has behaved unethically, your first instinct might be to sue. But think again. The brokerage industry, concerned about its own bottom line, has made it extremely difficult for anybody to litigate. When you open up an account, you might not make it through all the fine print, but there's no doubt that the brokerage houses' legal eagles have inserted a provision stating that any customer signing this application will agree to arbitration if a dispute arises.

When trouble strikes, here are the steps you should take:

1. Call your broker and discuss the problem. Be ready to explain how you'd like the matter resolved. Send a follow-up letter to the broker detailing all your grievances.

2. Contact the branch manager if the broker doesn't help. With any luck, your problems will end there. But watch out if the supervisor sends you a "comfort" letter. This letter will make you want to scream. Rather than addressing your complaints, the letter will note that you are satisfied with the trading done in your name. Don't ignore this goofy letter, since it could provide the firm with future legal ammunition. Instead, move ahead quickly with the next step.

3. Going up the chain of command, write to the compliance division of the brokerage firm. Once again, clearly state what your grievance is and how you'd like it to be resolved. Ask the compliance office to respond in writing within 30 days.

4. Send a copy of all the correspondence to your state securities agency. State agencies typically try to investigate every complaint. If you don't know where to locate it, call the NASAA for the contact number and address in your state. At the same time, file a complaint with the National Association of Securities Dealers. You can send an electronic complaint by visiting the association's Web site at www.nasdr.com.

5. Consider mediation, in which a neutral party attempts to bring both sides to a mutually agreed upon outcome (the process is detailed later in the chapter). If mediation fails, go to the next step.

6. Enter the final stage: arbitration (detailed later).

Going with mediation

If your complaint remains unresolved, mediation could be your next best bet. During this process, an outside mediator brings the warring parties together and tries to help them formulate their own solution. A mediator does not decide a case's outcome and can't force the sides to settle. Thousands of claims are handled every year this way.

Note   Unlike arbitration, which is a more serious, costly, and formal step, mediation isn't binding. If you don't like the outcome, you don't have to accept it.

The NASD has been running a successful mediation program for several years. While there are hundreds of mediators across the country, you can find a list approved by the NASD, along with a great deal of information on the mediation process, at its resolution dispute Web site (www.nasdadr.com).

Tip   You can represent yourself in mediation or you may opt to hire a lawyer. The more money that's in dispute, the more advisable it may be to seek legal help.

Entering arbitration

If a dispute can't be settled any other way, you might want to consider arbitration. With arbitration, a third party makes the final decision in the dispute. Thousands of cases are filed by disgruntled investors across the country each year. Your first step is to dig out the form that you signed when you opened your account. The brokerage house could have designated the arbitration forum that it favors. Contact that body and request an arbitration packet, which explains how to get the process started.

Legal Lockout

Americans settle a lot of disputes in court, but rarely can they sue their stockbroker. You can blame this legal no man's land on the 1987 U.S. Supreme Court case Shearson v. McMahan. The justices essentially said that a client who signs a contract with a brokerage house that requires all disputes to be handled through arbitration can't file a lawsuit. In very limited cases, investors can sue, but the vast majority of people are denied that option.

How arbitration works

While arbitrators are chosen differently in each forum, typically the panel that hears your complaint will be composed of one to three people. If the amount in dispute is under $10,000 through the NASD, there won't be any hearing at all. In this case, a single arbitrator reviews all the paperwork without any of the parties present and makes a decision. The arbitrators, who have all been trained to do this specialized work, aren't all picked from the financial industry. In fact, you are shown the names in advance and have an opportunity to reject a potential arbitrator.

Arbitration is far from the People's Court. You won't know the verdict by the end of the day. In fact, it could take a while before you hear anything. For most people, the entire arbitration process will take about a year from the time the paperwork is initially filled out. You'll receive the verdict in the mail.

Caution Once you choose arbitration, there's no turning back. You must agree to accept whatever the outcome is. If the panel sides with your opponent, you are out of luck. You may also be required to pay for the other side's legal bills.

Is arbitration worth the effort? Many people who won their cases through arbitration probably don't think so. An alarming percentage of awards are never cashed. Unfortunately, losing brokerage firms don't always honor their obligations. This travesty doesn't happen with the well-known firms, such as Merrill Lynch, Schwab, E*Trade, and Salomon Smith Barney. The obscure outfits are the derelicts and most of them are no longer in business.

A report from the federal General Accounting Office (GAO) released in 2000 determined that 49 percent of the awards in 1998 were unpaid—that's $129 million of $161 million awarded in that year.

The GAO could not determine whether the arbitration process itself was fair. But it did note that investors from 1992 to 1998 won anywhere from 49 percent to 57 percent of the cases in a given year. This was a decrease from earlier years, but the GAO noted that more firms are settling the disputes before they reach arbitration.

Sources for arbitrators

The National Association of Securities Dealers handles the vast majority of arbitration cases. Trailing far behind is the New York Stock Exchange. A big reason why the NASD attracts most of the arbitration business is because virtually all brokerage firms have to belong to the NASD. In contrast, many firms are not members of the New York Stock Exchange. Investors file their cases with a body that has jurisdiction.

✦ NASD Dispute Resolution, 125 Broad St., 36th floor, New York, NY 10004; (212) 858-4400; www.nasdadr.com

✦ New York Stock Exchange, Arbitration Department, 20 Broad St., 5th floor, New York, NY 10005; (212) 656-2772; www.nyse.com/arbitration

Arbitration is not free. Just how much it will cost depends in part on how much money you hope to recoup. If you were pursuing a $100,000 claim, for instance, you'd have to pay a $225 filing fee and another $750 for a panel of three arbitrators.

Using a securities attorney

If you're tired of battling a brokerage firm alone, your next best step could be finding an attorney experienced in securities law to handle either mediation or arbitration. Find an attorney who typically represents individual investors like you. Stay away from attorneys who specialize in defending brokerage firms.

Rather than start from scratch, contact the Public Investors Arbitration Bar Association, an organization of attorneys who specialize in representing individuals in securities cases. If you visit the association's Web site or call its toll-free number, you can obtain contact information about attorneys near you. Approximately 350 attorneys in 44 states belong to the group. Most of the attorneys in this association won't charge you for a 15 or 20-minute initial consultation.

 Resource   You can reach the Public Investors Arbitration Bar Association at 2241 W. Lindsey, Suite 500, Norman, OK 73069; (888) 621-7484; www.piaba.org.

After contacting the organization, you will still have to do some footwork, because the organization abstains from making attorney recommendations. However, to become a member, an attorney has to be in good standing with his or her state bar association and must have represented at least one investor in the last year. In addition, 80 percent of a member's securities cases must entail representing individuals.

Once you've got a list of names to start with, seek out an attorney who'll accept the case on a contingency-fee basis. That is, the attorney takes a cut from any money you are awarded. Even with a contingency case, though, you will probably have to pay some out-of-pocket legal expenses.

Tip   Before retaining an attorney, always check with the appropriate state body to see if he or she has a disciplinary record.

You can also find a lawyer by contacting your state bar association or visiting the American Bar Association's Web site at www.abanet.org. Another source is Martindale-Hubbell's lawyer locator at its Web site at www.martindale.com.

Legal help for smaller cases

Be forewarned that not every worthy case will spark an attorney's interest. If your claim is for less than $40,000 to $50,000, many lawyers won't bite. An alternative is to seek help from the handful of law school clinics in New York State that assist investors. Law students work on the cases under the supervision of law professors. You don't have to be a resident of New York to receive help, but each school has its own client eligibility guidelines.

Investor Protection in Name Only?

Anyone who keeps cash in a bank probably knows about FDIC (Federal Deposit Insurance Corp.) insurance. The insurance protects customers from losing up to $100,000 if a bank fails. The brokerage world offers its own protection through the Securities Investor Protection Corp. (SIPC), which was established by Congress back in 1970. This protection is supposed to kick in if your brokerage firm fails and you are unable to recoup all or part of your money. Ostensibly, the SIPC covers you for up to $500,000, of which $100,000 can be cash rather than securities.

However, the SIPC has been the target of bitter criticism from investors, some state securities commissioners, and investor attorneys, who allege the nonprofit corporation too often disallows claims. According to an investigation by the *New York Times,* the SIPC has paid out of its own coffers $233 million to investors during nearly three decades, but attorneys, acting as trustees assigned to the cases, received nearly 37 percent more.

The GAO, which is examining whether the SIPC treats investors fairly, is expected to release a study on the issue shortly.

Here is a list of the schools:

✦ Brooklyn Law School, Securities Arbitration Clinic, 1 Boerum Place, Room 300, Brooklyn, NY 11201; (718) 780-7994

✦ University of Buffalo, School of Law, Room 507, O'Brian Hall, Buffalo, NY 14260; (716) 645-2167

✦ Fordham University, School of Law, Securities Arbitration Clinic, 33 West 60th St., 3rd floor, New York, NY 10023; (212) 636-7231

✦ Pace University School of Law, John Jay Legal Services, 80 N. Broadway, White Plains, NY 10603; (914) 422-4333

Keeping Alert for Con Artists

Lousy brokers aren't the only hazards you could encounter. Scam artists are thriving as Americans ignore their common sense and chase after promises of great riches.

The Internet, however, has made it more complicated to detect fraud. The potential for shenanigans on the World Wide Web is boundless, what with Internet technology making it so much easier for swindlers to set their traps. Scamming innocent people used to be incredibly time-consuming: A con artist often needed to pay people to make telephone calls to hundreds and hundreds of potential victims, and had to rent a space big enough to fit all these telephone solicitors. Interrupting people with cold calls when they were eating dinner didn't help business. Going door to door looking for hapless victims was even more tedious. But with a computer equipped with a high-speed modem, a crook can single-handedly manipulate a stock price or send a pitch to thousands of people almost instantaneously.

Anybody with a modem and larcenous instincts can create havoc. For instance, not long ago a college student, who was looking to scoop up some stocks at a deep discount, managed to get a bogus press release distributed on the Internet, which claimed that the CEO of a fiber optic company was resigning in the midst of an accounting scandal. None of the information, which was picked up by the wire services, was true, but the stock quickly plunged by 62 percent before trading was halted. The stock lost $2.5 billion in value and many panicky investors, who unfortunately dumped the stock, lost a bundle. Obviously, investors who thought they were reacting to a legitimate source of financial news were snookered.

Tip   It's best not to act in a knee-jerk manner to bad stock news. Select solid stocks that you can feel good about holding for a while, despite bad (and possibly untrue) press.

In most cases of potential fraud, ways exist to protect yourself. Here are a few of the most common investment scams you want to stay away from.

Penny stock or micro-cap fraud

The price of these stocks may seem incredibly cheap. While you can't always pick up shares for pennies, often shares in penny or micro-cap stocks can be bought for less than $5 apiece. These stocks can be traced back to tiny outfits with brief, erratic, and even nonexistent histories of sales and earnings. While some of these companies are legitimate, others are not, and it is hard for many to tell them apart. Investors should avoid these stocks.

Promoters for an unethical company bring in new shareholders by misrepresenting a stock. They may assure potential shareholders that they'd be buying into the next Cisco Systems on the ground floor. But if you stop and think about it, some of their claims will sound absolutely ridiculous.

Federal Scam Watchdog

Have you been the victim of a financial scam, or do you have reason to suspect you have? If so, the Securities and Exchange Commission wants to know about it. The SEC's Division of Enforcement investigates all sorts of potential violations of federal securities laws. Write down the specifics of your complaint in a letter and then mail or fax it to the SEC Complaint Center at 450 Fifth St. NW, Washington, D.C. 20549. The fax is (202) 942-9634. Even easier, you can use one of the SEC's online complaint forms, which are located at the agency's Complaint Center at www.sec.gov.

Tip   You might hear that a tiny company is on the verge of making fossil fuel obsolete or developing a sure-fire cure for cancer. But wouldn't advances of this dimension be trumpeted on the front pages of the *New York Times* or *The Wall Street Journal?*

Priming the pump and dump

Here's how small-stock scams sometimes work: A thinly traded penny stock outfit hires outsiders, such as a public relations firm, a financial radio show host, or some Internet financial sites, to hype the stock. When the price of the stock jumps thanks to the good press, the insiders, who paid little or nothing for their shares, bail out and make a tidy sum. The stock inevitably deflates, leaving innocent investors with potentially big losses. This kind of scam is called a *pump and dump.* The stock is pumped up, and then all the players quickly cash in their shares.

A pump-and-dump operation, however, doesn't need to be that elaborate. Somebody with a computer can pick a penny stock and hype it to high heavens. Using a variety of aliases, someone can praise the stock in Internet chat rooms, where active stock traders hang out. Unsuspecting investors may never guess that one person can be behind a glowing public relations assault.

On the other hand, unscrupulous investors can make just as much money by bad mouthing a thinly traded stock. Someone can *short* a stock—that is, bet that a stock is currently overvalued and will lose its value—and then begin spreading the word through cyberspace that a stock is in trouble. When you short a stock, you borrow stock shares from a brokerage firm and hope that the price plummets. If it does, you buy new shares and return the cheaper borrowed ones for a profit. If the price of the borrowed shares increases, however, a loss results.

The OTC Bulletin Board: Approach with caution

You'll find thousands of penny stocks trading on the OTC (Over The Counter) Bulletin Board, which unfortunately a lot of people confuse with the Nasdaq Stock Exchange. Investors believe these penny stocks carry the imprimatur of the Nasdaq, so the companies must be on the up and up, but the assumption is wrong. The OTC Bulletin Board is not part of the Nasdaq. In fact, it's often the stocks that can't manage to qualify for inclusion on the Nasdaq that end up on the Bulletin Board.

Caution   Unlike Nasdaq stocks, OTC stocks don't have to meet rigorous financial requirements, nor do they have to file annual or quarterly updates with the Securities and Exchange Commission.

Affinity schemes

Even if you hang up on telephone solicitors and you never troll the Internet, you won't necessarily be completely safe from financial shysters. You can be victimized at your own church or synagogue, as well as at professional and cultural organizations. Con artists join groups just so they can acquire legitimacy. Wouldn't you be more comfortable with a pitchman if he belonged to your own political club or church group?

People who have fallen for affinity scams include political conservatives in Southern California; Chinese-American business owners in San Francisco; physicians in Utah; affluent Indian and Polish immigrants in New York; and Catholic parishioners, along with their priest, in Illinois.

Prime bank investment schemes

Some investment scams sound so outrageous that you might think that you'd never be trapped by such oily scam artists. But not all the fraudulent deals appear so patently exotic and bogus. For example, promoters may offer something called a *prime bank security,* creating sophisticated-looking documents that appear official and insisting that highly regarded financial institutions are connected to these investments. Often victims are told that they are gaining access to an investment that is normally only reserved for elite financiers on Wall Street, London and other money centers, or for such fabulously wealthy people as Saudi royalty. In response, investors have pumped millions upon millions of dollars into these securities after receiving assurances that they would double their money in fairly short order. Trouble is, there is no such thing as a prime bank security.

The promoters have been incredibly bold. They have even been known to advertise these fraudulent prime bank investments in *The Wall Street Journal* and *USA Today.* Amazingly, charities and municipalities, as well as individuals, have fallen for the pitch.

Limited partnerships

A limited partnership is one of the most abused investments you could possibly stumble into. Brokers love them because they provide juicy, ongoing commissions and are packaged with plenty of expenses and fees. After all those costs are deducted, you could very well end up with just 70 to 80 percent of your money or less devoted to a limited partnership.

Learning More About Fraud

Two sources for more information about financial fraud are the Investor Protection Trust at www.investorprotection.org, as well as the National Consumer League's National Fraud Information Center at www.fraud.org.

Many limited partnerships are involved in real estate, equipment leasing, and oil and gas. These ventures are usually made up of a general partner who manages the project and the limited partners who invest money—usually a minimum of $5,000— but aren't involved in the daily management. Typically, these investors receive a share of capital gains, income, and tax benefits.

Caution If you need to bail out of a limited partnership, you'll find few takers. Consequently, you might be able to unload it only at a fire-sale price.

Beyond the expenses, a common rap against limited partnerships is that you can't follow them by simply opening up the daily newspaper. Unlike stocks and mutual funds, limited partnerships are frequently not listed on any of the stock exchanges. Investors rely on their brokers to keep them informed about how the limited partnership is faring. After assurances over the years that an investment is doing well, an investor can learn that a limited partnership is worth a fraction of the original price or maybe worth nothing at all. Your natural instinct might be to retaliate legally, but you might have to contend with statute of limitation issues.

Tip As with all investment complaints, it's best to act quickly if you'd like to take legal action to try getting your money back.

Ponzi schemes

Ponzis are one of the oldest investment frauds around. In these pyramid schemes, people are promised fabulous returns on investments in real estate, gold mines, and anything else you can imagine. Early investors are paid off with the money from people lured into the scheme later. When the rush of new victims slows, the money dries up and the Ponzi collapses. In this scenario, many investors lose their money.

Insurance agent shenanigans

What's notable about the NASAA's latest Top 10 scam list is that it spotlights the growing problem of rogue insurance agents. Insurance agents, who illegally peddle investments beyond the insurance arena, are a fairly new phenomenon. Most of the insurance agents who push questionable investments are independent agents. Those agents attached to a particular insurance company pose far less of a problem.

Regulators strongly suspect that more independent agents are selling fraudulent or unsuitable securities; it's become harder for agents to make a decent living now that the cheaper and more practical term life policies have become far more popular than traditional cash value insurance policies, which have generous built-in commissions. Filling the income void for some unethical agents are bogus investments like promissory notes and pay phone sales. Agents are attracted to these scams because the sponsors offer extremely high commissions. One way that scam artists hook up with agents is by advertising high-commission opportunities in insurance trade publications. In some cases, insurance agents are promised commissions of 30 percent or so.

Top 10 Investment Scams

Every year, the North American Securities Administrators Association releases a new list of the most common investment scams that state regulators are combating. The current top ten most popular scams include:

1. **Insurance agents and other unlicensed individuals selling securities.** To verify that a person is licensed to sell securities, contact your state securities regulator.

2. **Affinity group fraud.** Many crooks use their victims' religious or ethnic identity to gain their trust and then scam them of their life savings.

3. **Pay phone sales.** Independent insurance sales agents and others are leasing coin-operated pay phones to individuals, promising annual returns from these phones of up to 15 percent. These are often Ponzi schemes.

4. **Promissory notes.** These IOUs, which are issued by obscure or non-existent companies, promise high returns—upwards of 15 percent a month. These worthless pieces of paper are often sold by insurance agents.

5. **Internet fraud.** Internet scams include a variety of bogus investments, including the previously mentioned pump and dump operations.

6. **Ponzi/pyramid schemes.** These scams promise investors high returns, but the only people who consistently make money are their crooked creators.

7. **Callable CDs.** These typically higher-yielding CDs can be recalled by the bank if the interest rate becomes too favorable to the investors. When investors redeem a callable CD early, they may suffer a tremendous loss.

8. **Viatical settlements.** Originally created as a way to help the terminally ill pay their bills, investing in the death benefits of these patients' insurance policies is risky and sometimes fraudulent.

9. **Prime bank schemes.** Unsuspecting individuals are promised very high returns for sinking money into the investment portfolios of the world's elite banks.

10. **Investment seminars.** The only people prospering from get-rich seminars, which are often marketed through infomercials on television, are the promoters who charge admission fees and sell expensive tapes and books.

Insurance agents aren't supposed to sell any securities for which they do not have a license. To be licensed, an agent must pass certain government-mandated competency tests. You can easily find out if an agent is licensed to sell investments by calling your state securities department. Do not buy anything from an unlicensed agent. By the way, the vast majority of agents are not authorized to sell investments.

Tip   Also ask your state regulator whether a proposed investment is registered in your state. If it's not, don't even consider it.

Some of the investments that insurance agents are pushing can seem far-fetched, but victims are plentiful. For instance, regulators in Colorado are prosecuting an agent who was selling interest in a company that claimed it was melting down old mufflers and extracting precious metals. He was promising 42 percent returns. The same agent allegedly stole money from a nun and then explained that he was helping her keep her vow of poverty.

Know the telltale signs of scams

Luckily, there are ways to protect yourself from unscrupulous deals, whether you are approached on the phone, on the Internet, or by somebody in your own church. Here are clues that something is amiss:

✦ You are promised a rate of return for your money that is higher than a bank CD, Treasury bill or money market.

✦ You are pressured to make an immediate decision or one within a short period of time, on the premise that other people are signing up quickly.

✦ The promoter promises that it's impossible for you to lose money. Claims that the investment is risk-free are a sure sign of trouble. No financial investment is risk-free, and a high rate of return will mean greater risk.

✦ The promoter offers to share "inside information." Watch for buzzwords like "limited offer," "safe as a certificate of deposit," and "IRA-approved."

✦ The opportunity is located in another country. When you send your money abroad and something goes wrong, it's difficult to determine what happened, much less get your money back.

✦ The promoter is on the Internet. Pseudonyms are common online, and some salespeople hide their true identity.

Defend yourself with documentation

To protect yourself from crooks, never agree to anything until you receive written documentation, even if an investment seems tantalizing. Ask for an organization's prospectus, a financial statement, and any other documents that are available. Also ask your state securities regulation office if it has more information on the company and the people behind it. The agency can tell you whether the company or individual has broken any securities regulations in the past and whether they are authorized to do business in your state. It's also a good idea to contact your local Better Business Bureau to see if any complaints have been logged.

 You can read a wealth of financial material at the U.S. Security and Exchange Commission's Web site at www.sec.gov.

In addition, never assume that anything you read in an Internet chat room is true. Assume everyone has their own ulterior motives for posting messages. Also view skeptically any financial advice you get from many Web sites or from unsolicited e-mails.

Tip

Lessen your chances of running into trouble by consulting only well-known and respected Web sites.

Today anybody can publish official-looking stock research reports and stock newsletters on the Internet. The chances of getting into trouble is less if you only visit well-known and respected Web sites, such as the ones on this list:

✦ CNBC on MSN Money (`www.money.msn.com`)

✦ Yahoo!Finance (`http://finance.yahoo.com`)

✦ CBS MarketWatch (`www.cbsmarketwatch.com`)

✦ Motley Fool (`www.fool.com`)

✦ Morningstar (`www.morningstar.com`)

✦ National Association of Investors Corp. (`www.better-investing.org`)

✦ American Association of Individual Investors (`www.aaii.org`)

Summary

✦ It's easy to run a background check on a prospective broker or an investment advisor; get the appropriate form from regulatory bodies.

✦ To avoid getting hurt, know the signs of bad broker behavior.

✦ Keep meticulous records in case you eventually run into trouble with your brokerage firm.

✦ Consider mediation and ultimately arbitration if your broker misbehaves.

✦ If an investment seems too good to be true, walk away.

✦ Watch out for cleverly disguised cyberscams.

✦ ✦ ✦

Dealing with Debt

I t's hard to get serious about investing if you're deeply in debt. In this chapter, you'll find out what your options are if your debts are seriously endangering your sanity and financial health. You'll learn how to avoid common credit card traps and review two dozen ways to save money. You'll also discover what can booby-trap even the most well-intentioned plans for consolidating debt. Meanwhile, those who are debt-free will find out why they should examine their own credit report. And those with a spotty credit report will learn how to fix it.

Americans Leading the Charge

Look around next time you're at the mall and you'll see an awful lot of people who owe about $7,500 on their credit cards. Why $7,500? According to CardWeb.com, that's the average credit card balance for the typical American family. But the mountainous debt isn't discouraging many to cut up their plastic. Consumers are charging more than $1 trillion a year on their cards.

Americans used to reserve their credit cards for the big-ticket purchases: furniture, computers, airline tickets, and a new fridge. Those days, however, are long gone. Today, you'll see people pulling out plastic to pay for groceries or even a cup of coffee. According to one industry publication, Americans are charging nearly 17 percent of everything they pay for, from movie tickets and speeding citations to school tuitions and income taxes.

Facing the reality of plastic

It's easy to appreciate Americans' love affair with plastic. The convenience is hard to beat, and the cards essentially give users interest-free loans for nearly a month. Plus, many consumers love accumulating frequent flyer miles with certain cards. None of this would be alarming if Americans simply charged what they could afford. But study after study shows that many consumers are seriously overextended, and that they seriously underestimate how long and how much they'll actually be paying for items charged.

 Example

Say you owe $10,000 on a VISA with a 17 percent interest rate, and each month pay only the minimum payment of $200. At that pace, it will take you *50 years* to eliminate the balance. In the process, you'll shell out a total of $33,447—essentially spending $167 for every $50 purchase. That's quite a penalty for the convenience of carrying plastic.

Telltale signs of trouble

How do you know if your debt is serious enough to require drastic action? Here are some warning signs:

✦ Your debt payments, without including a mortgage, exceed 20 percent of your pretax income.

✦ You only make the minimum payment on your cards.

✦ You're at or near the limit on your credit cards.

✦ You are borrowing from one card to pay another.

✦ You skip payment on some bills to pay others.

✦ You argue a lot with a spouse about money.

✦ You're afraid to total up how much you owe on your plastic.

Seven Strategies for Credit Card Containment

If you've just concluded that you're in trouble, perhaps you can take some comfort knowing that you are not alone. Millions of people are in the same predicament. Luckily, there are steps you can take to climb out of the hole. Here are some strategies to get you started:

Try shock therapy.

We've all heard horror stories about how credit card debt can take decades to pay off. But these doomsday scenarios may not seem real when they are somebody else's example. Internet financial calculators, however, now allow you to plug in your own numbers to determine your personal cost of carrying credit card balances. The calculators pinpoint how long it will take to erase your debt, based on your payment schedule. But perhaps what is most shocking is how much interest you will owe. The interest can far exceed the original cost of all the stuff you bought.

Here are Web sites that can do the analysis for you:

✦ FinanCenter.com: www.financenter.com

✦ Nolo: www.nolo.com

✦ Bankrate.com: www.bankrate.com

✦ Myvesta.org: www.myvesta.org

Limit your plastic.

The typical American family owns more than a dozen credit cards, which is definitely overkill. Consider keeping just two cards, a MasterCard plus a VISA or perhaps an American Express card. Funny as it might seem, creditors become suspicious if you carry only one card. Banking institutions want to make sure you can handle more than one card at a time.

Tip If you know that, realistically, you're going to keep a balance, put all that debt on the card with the very lowest interest rate. Find a no-fee card for all the purchases you expect to pay off each month when the bill arrives.

Renegotiate your card's interest rate.

People know they can haggle with a car salesman, but not many realize that they can—and should—ask their card issuer for a lower interest rate. If you carry a balance, the bank issuing your card certainly doesn't want you to look elsewhere for a cheaper one. Keeping you happy is important. Call your card's toll-free number— you might be surprised at the rate you get.

Get It in Writing

When you cancel any credit card, don't just cut it up. To officially close your account, you must call each issuer. While on the phone, ask each card issuer to send you a letter stating that it was your idea to end the relationship. Why is this important? You can use these letters as evidence if all the card cancellations are interpreted the wrong way by credit-reporting agencies. For example, you wouldn't want to get turned down for a car loan because the dealer, reviewing your credit report, read that four department stores had terminated your cards.

Tip If you receive offers for cards with very low introductory rates, use these offers as leverage when you call your current credit card company to negotiate.

Cut up department store plastic.

If you think the interest rate on your MasterCard is ridiculous, have you checked what your favorite department store is charging? You might be getting gouged to the tune of 24 percent or 25 percent. Since major department stores accept other plastic, there's no reason to use these cards.

Find the best credit card rates.

The Internet has made it easy to find the best deals on credit cards. CardWeb.com (www.cardweb.com) and Bankrate.com (www.bankrate.com) provide listings of a variety of attractive card offers. You can specify what type of card you are interested in, whether that's a no-fee gold card, a high-limit card, or cards geared towards students or those with poor credit.

Money-Saving Tips for Tight Budgets

There's another sure-fire way to reduce your debt. Don't spend as much money. Here are a few tips to help you do just that.

✦ When purchasing a new or used car, use Internet-based car buying price guides, such as Edmunds.com, to find the best rates out there.

✦ Increasing your automobile insurance deductible can save you a bundle.

✦ Request auto insurance discounts. Air bags, anti-lock brakes, anti-theft devices, a safe driving record, or any one of these may cut a policy's price.

✦ Find a cheaper telephone plan. Obtain a long-distance comparison guide by contacting the nonprofit Telecommunications Research & Action Center at P.O. Box 27279, Washington, DC 20005; www.trac.org.

✦ Improve gas mileage by tuning up your car and maintaining the correct tire air pressure.

✦ Bring your lunch to work.

✦ Stop buying lottery tickets.

✦ Brew your own coffee.

✦ Refinance your mortgage with a no-points loan if interest rates are down.

✦ Swap babysitting duties with friends rather than hire a teenager.

✦ Pay off credit cards with the highest interest rates first.

✦ Avoid investing in vacation time-shares.

✦ Try consolidating multiple student loans into one with a lower rate. Call (800) 4FED-AID for details.

✦ Don't watch the Shopping Network on television.

✦ Put your household on a budget.

✦ Stop buying on impulse. Go home and think about it first.

✦ Clip coupons and buy generic food brands.

✦ Skip the theaters: Wait until movies come out on video.

✦ Reduce your taxes by taking advantage of a medical savings account.

✦ Bargain for a cheaper hotel price. Don't accept a quote from a chain's toll-free number—call the hotel directly too. Ask for any discount you might be entitled to for membership in AAA, AARP, and military service.

✦ When selling a house, offer less than the agent's standard 6 percent commission.

✦ Shop for items off-season: swimsuits in September, furnaces in July.

✦ Schedule vacations off-season when airfares and hotels offer better deals.

✦ When shopping for appliances or electronics, look for closeouts or last year's models.

✦ Buy energy efficient appliances.

✦ Save on your energy bill by lowering the setting on a hot-water heater to 120 degrees.

✦ Scrutinize your itemized hospital bill. Studies have shown that an amazing number of these bills contain errors favorable to the hospital.

✦ Consider banking at a credit union; the fees are often fewer and lower.

Here are questions to ask when you're shopping:

✦ What is the card's annual percentage rate?

✦ Is the interest rate fixed or variable?

✦ If the rate is variable, under what conditions will it change?

✦ Is there an interest-free grace period?

✦ How is the interest calculated on balances?

✦ Is there an annual fee?

✦ Is there a fee for exceeding the credit limit?

✦ If there is a late charge, what is it?

✦ What is the interest rate for cash advances? Is there an additional fee?

✦ Does the card offer benefits such as airline or hotel frequent purchase programs, insurance, or special discounts?

Restrict your credit.

Limit your total credit lines to no more than 10 percent or 15 percent of your annual income. This way, you'll put a ceiling on your potential debt load.

Tear up blank checks.

Card companies love to bombard people with invitations to charge, charge, charge. A favorite ploy is to mail you blank checks that are tied to your plastic. These unrequested checks often land in mailboxes during the Christmas holiday and tax seasons. What's the harm in using one? Maybe for a weekend in Palm Desert or to splurge on a new suit? For starters, you can be dinged 2 percent of the total just for the privilege of writing the check. Then of course, you're stuck paying the interest, which can be astronomical.

The Pros and Cons of Debt Consolidation

Budget-trimming suggestions are fine, but what if you already have enough bills sitting on your desk to fill a recycling bin? Many people believe debt consolidation is the answer. The idea is simple. Instead of having a dozen or more creditors pestering you for your payments, you transfer all the debt to one place. You'll then have one bill every month, perhaps at a lower interest rate.

Before exploring your consolidation options, do some soul-searching. All too often, squeezing your debt into one payment fails to fix the real problem—uncontrolled spending. Somebody with great intentions can end up as deep in debt as before. And the consequences can be dire. For instance, if a couple taps into their equity when they obtain a loan against their house, they could lose the home if they fall behind in their payments.

Caution   Debt consolidation won't work for people who continue to spend more than they earn.

There are several ways to consolidate your debt. Here are the main options:

Credit counseling agencies

For most people, these agencies provide the very best way to consolidate debt. A nonprofit credit counseling agency can intercede with a debtor's creditors, draw up a reasonable budget, and provide a client with the tools to avoid getting into paralyzing debt again.

After enrolling in a credit counseling program, you essentially put your creditors in a time out. The card issuers usually stop assessing late charges and other penalties and often eliminate or reduce the interest on your plastic. The counselor works directly with your creditors and can help devise a repayment program to keep the creditors happy. After settling on a payment plan, you'll write one check a month to the counseling service, which will distribute the money to your various creditors. The counselor also evaluates how you are spending your money and recommends changes to pull your finances out of the red.

What's the catch? When you enroll in one of these programs, you're expected to stop using plastic until your bills are paid. Some agencies keep a bowl of cut cards in their office lobbies. Many people, however, are actually relieved to get rid of the cards.

While there are a variety of credit counseling services, here are two organizations to consider:

✦ **The National Foundation for Credit Counseling.** The nonprofit organization oversees a network of 1,448 offices scattered across the U.S. and Canada. You can seek help from counselors in person or receive assistance over the Internet. To find an office near you, call (800) 388-2227 or go to www.nfcc.org.

✦ **Myvesta.org.** This nonprofit debt-counseling organization helps clients by phone and over the Internet. Formally known as Debt Counselors of America, Myvesta also publishes downloadable publications on such things as credit scoring, improving credit ratings, bankruptcy, and strategies for erasing debt. The site maintains a forum where visitors can discuss their own financial predicaments. Contact Myvesta at (800) 680-3328 or www.myvesta.org.

Nonprofit debt counseling groups are funded by creditors, such as card issuers and department stores, as well by as the United Way and state and local governments. Depending on what you can afford, the service is free or modestly priced.

These voluntary programs don't promise a quick fix, but the debt experts who run them observe that just about anybody's financial problems are solvable. In these programs, many people can walk away with their debt under control in two to four years.

Credit card balance transfers

Credit card companies are always urging customers to transfer their debt onto their cards. If you prefer this route, find one that offers a low rate for as long as possible. A lot of the card offers clogging your mailbox come with an introductory teaser rate. When your teaser rate is about to expire, you can switch to another card with another lower introductory rate, but this can get tiring.

Caution   Credit card issuers hate card surfers and will stop sending offers to individuals who churn through too many cards. Playing hot potato with the plastic for too long and too often can hurt your credit rating, too.

Before applying for a new card, contact your current card issuers and explain your desire to consolidate your debts. Ask each card issuer if it will lower the rate so this can be financially feasible. If this doesn't work, apply for a new card advertising the best terms. If you do transfer your balance to a better card, cut up the original card and close out the account.

Home equity loans

With a home equity loan or a line of credit, you borrow against whatever equity you have in your house. Equity is the portion of the home that you actually own. For instance, if your house is worth $175,000 and there's a $100,000 balance on the mortgage, your equity is $75,000. Banks will often loan you 80 percent of your equity, which in this case is $60,000. Some financial institutions will approve a loan that equals 100 percent of your equity and sometimes even 125 percent.

Home equity loans are a big hit with consumers who need help paying their bills, and banks love them. Of course, the banks aren't really risking anything. Since you'll use your home as collateral, the banks can legally confiscate your house if you can't make the payments. For this reason, you have to consider the consequences before you make this move.

Caution   If you have trouble controlling your spending, borrowing from your home's equity can be as dangerous as waving a lit stick of dynamite.

With one of these loans, you're essentially draining away your home's value. Unless you change your spending habits, chances are you will end up accumulating more debt, as well as jeopardizing your house. That said, there is a compelling reason why homeowners gravitate to these loans.

Note   Unlike many other types of loans, the interest is tax-deductible. This tax break, however, can only be used for those who file itemized tax returns.

The traditional home equity loan works like a traditional second mortgage. You borrow for a set number of years, and the loan is usually offered at a fixed rate. You repay little by little every month for a preset number of years. Your other option is a home equity line of credit, which is sometimes referred to as a HELOC. This type of loan works a lot like a credit card. A bank approves you for a certain amount of credit up to a ceiling. You don't have to use that money all at once or ever, but it's there if you need it. Say you have a $50,000 line of credit, but you use only $30,000. You're still entitled to borrow the remaining $20,000 any time you want. As you repay what you owe, the amount available to borrow increases.

Avoiding Home Equity Scams

If you do shop for home equity loans, watch out for unscrupulous lenders. To be safe, stay away from any unfamiliar lenders, such as those sending you all that irritating junk mail. They could try to entice you into a high-cost loan that could ultimately become a financial nightmare. While you might not fall for these slick come-ons, perhaps your mom, dad, or a grandparent would. These shady companies typically prey on homeowners who are elderly, as well as those who are experiencing credit problems.

Here are some home equity scams that the Federal Trade Commission says consumers should watch out for:

✦ **Equity stripping:** The lender issues a loan based on the equity of your home, not on your ability to pay. If you can't make the payments, you can lose the house.

✦ **Loan flipping:** You are urged to refinance over and over again. Each time you refinance, you pay extra fees and interest points that only increase your debt.

✦ **Bait and switch:** The lender offers you one set of loan terms when you apply and then pressures you to accept higher charges when you sign the final papers.

✦ **Credit insurance packing:** The lender adds unnecessary credit insurance.

✦ **Deceptive loan servicing:** You fail to receive accurate or complete account statements, making it almost impossible to determine how much you've paid or how much you still owe. You might end up paying more than you should.

Home equity lines of credit are usually offered with variable interest rates. The rate is tied to the prime rate—the rate the best corporate customers receive—or some other index. Lenders often generate business by offering a temporary teaser rate. Don't be snookered by these offers. Ask what will happen to the interest rate after the introductory offer expires. Financial institutions will be glad to quote their rates over the phone. The process is quick and a loan officer can usually tell you by phone if you qualify.

Tip

Before choosing a lender, scour the marketplace. There is tremendous competition among lenders, and rates and terms can vary widely even in your local neighborhood.

Don't forget to include in your calculations what you'll have to pay in fees for such things as credit and title reports and your home's appraisal. But don't assume you must agree to all these costs. Due to competition, many lenders are willing to shave some fees and eliminate closing costs.

source

To learn more about home equity loans, consider ordering *Home Equity: A Consumer's Guide to Loans and Lines* from HSH Associates, a major publisher of consumer loan information. Phone (800) 873-2837 or go to www.hsh.com.

Loans from family and friends

You've probably heard the standard advice, "Never borrow from relatives." There are probably good reasons this admonition has survived so many years, but in some cases, turning to a rich uncle, your parents, or a friend might be worthwhile. First, however, ask yourself if there will be strings attached or if you can emotionally handle a loan from someone so close. Also consider whether the person willing to bail you out should be lending money at all. If he or she is on a fixed income, think twice about taking the money.

401(k) loans

Most employees allow workers to borrow from their 401(k)s. By law, you can borrow no more than 50 percent of your 401(k) assets up to a maximum of $50,000. Typically, you are expected to pay off the loan within five years unless it was used to buy a house. In that case, the repayment term is extended.

The interest rate you pay is often only one or two points above the prime interest rate (banks charge their best corporate customers the prime rate). Your employer is prohibited from offering you a rate that is below the prevailing market interest rates. As you repay the loan, the interest you are charged is added to your 401(k) account.

Caution   You're better off not touching your 401(k) money. With the money temporarily withdrawn from the plan, your retirement nest egg can't grow.

Keep in mind that, historically, the stock market has increased an average of 11 percent a year, which is a lot of potential growth to pass up. Just as bad, many people stop contributing to their 401(k)s while they are paying back their loans, which can jeopardize their retirement plans. Finally, people are often shocked when they learn that they must pay off the entire loan all at once if they leave the company for any reason. If a departing employee can't come up with the money, he or she will have to pay income taxes on the amount and possibly pay a 10 percent IRS early withdrawal penalty too.

 Cross-Reference   See more on 401(k) borrowing in Chapter 21.

Examining Your Credit Report

Whether you enjoy sterling credit or your financial life is in a shambles, make it a point to know what's in your credit report. You might be amazed at what you find. Perfect strangers' credit problems, for instance, could be listed on your report. This can happen when two people have similar Social Security numbers or identical names.

To play it safe, check your credit report every year. It's also crucial to obtain copies if you're contemplating a major purchase such as a house, a condominium, or a car. You should also take a look if you're in the job market. Potential employers will sometimes examine these records.

Once you have the report, here are potential problems to watch for:

✦ Inaccurate or incomplete name, as well as wrong address, Social Security number, and marital status.

✦ Closed accounts that look open.

✦ Closed bankruptcy cases older than a decade.

✦ Credit cards you've never owned.

✦ Lawsuits you've never heard about.

✦ Accounts you have closed that don't have the notation "closed by consumer."

✦ Paid-off accounts that still report a balance due.

✦ Erroneous late payments.

Each of the three major credit bureaus has a file on most American adults. Here's how you can reach them:

✦ Equifax: (800) 685-1111 or www.equifax.com

✦ Experian: (888) 397-3742 or www.experian.com

✦ TransUnion: (800) 888-4213 or www.transunion.com

The cost to obtain your credit report is minimal, while residents of a few states can receive a free annual copy.

Tip   If you've been rejected for credit (whether a credit card, a mortgage, a car loan, or something else), you are entitled to a free report. You must, however, ask for it within two months of the rejection.

It used to be that spotting an error in a credit report was easy compared to getting it erased. Now the process is easier. If you find a mistake, write to the agency and ask that the error be removed. The agency must investigate your complaint and share what it has learned within one month. If you need this done quickly because of a pending car or home loan, the agency should be able to speed up the process. If you are right or the creditor has no records of the disputed item, the bureau is obligated to erase it.

Cleaning up your credit record

Do you have justifiable black marks on your credit history? Erasing the smudges won't be fun, but it is doable. There are proven ways to rehabilitate yourself. Here are four tips:

✦ **Try damage control.** If there are understandable reasons your credit is fouled up, explain them. By law, you are entitled to attach a 100-word letter to your credit report. In the note, you should explain to any potential creditors why your credit history looks bad. Be as direct and concise as possible. If you were conscientious about paying your bills up until a divorce, a job layoff, or a hospitalization set you back, be sure to mention that. A credit bureau has the right to summarize your statement when it sends out your report to others.

✦ **Make sure you receive credit for any good news.** If your credit report fails to include accounts that you pay on time, try to get that information mentioned. Write a letter to the credit bureaus and attach a copy of a couple of recent statements that show your payment.

✦ **If possible, keep a couple of credit cards and cancel all others.** Then do everything in your power to make sure your payments are timely. Losing these cards could make your troubles worse. To play it safe, try to write a check the day your bill arrives.

✦ **If your resolve to live within your means is slipping, consider joining Debtors Anonymous.** Just like Alcoholics Anonymous, this support organization uses a 12-step recovery program with branches throughout the country. For more information, contact the group Debtors Anonymous, General Service Office, P.O. Box 920888, Needham, MA 02492-0009; (781) 453-2743; www.debtorsanonymous.org.

Negotiating with Creditors

When you feel overwhelmed by your bills, another strategy is to negotiate directly with your creditors. Many creditors allow you to reduce your payments temporarily if you just ask. You might feel awkward calling a credit card issuer to ask for this favor, but remember they take calls like this all day, every day. Know what you're going to say before you dial the number. Be prepared to discuss what payments you'd like to make, as well as how long you want the reduced payments to continue. Get the name of the person with whom you talked and take notes during the conversation. Follow up by sending a letter explaining why you are requesting the leniency and what you propose.

Even if your uncollected debt gets shipped to a collection agency, you still have an opportunity to negotiate. Sometimes you will be able to clear up 50 to 80 percent of what you owe simply by paying a lump sum. If that's out of the question, see if the creditor will take the past-due notation off your credit report if you start paying monthly installments again.

Resource To learn much more about resolving credit problems, consult these two books, written by attorney Robin Leonard and published by Nolo (go to www.nolo.com or call 800-992-6656): *Money Troubles: Legal Strategies to Cope with Your Debt* and *Credit Repair: Quick and Legal.*

Building up good credit again

Once your debt is under control (perhaps due to the intervention of a credit counselor), it can be time to start using credit cards again. Ironically, the only way creditors will respect you again is if you show you can use plastic responsibly. But if you've had delinquent accounts in the past, you may have problems getting a credit card now.

Tip If you lost your credit cards during financial troubles, try obtaining a new card through the more lenient issuers, such as a local department store or a gasoline station chain. Once you have established a good repayment record, aim for a MasterCard or VISA.

If you get turned down for a gas or department store card, one way to redemption can be through a secured credit card. These are credit cards with training wheels. Bank-card issuers take a chance on you because the risk for them is minimal. To qualify, you must deposit an agreed-upon amount of money into a certificate of deposit or a savings account with the bank. If you fail to pay your bills, the bank can use your money to cover the debt.

Expect to pay more for these second-chance cards. Typically, the annual fee and the interest rates are higher. And you also might be dinged for an application fee. Despite the greater interest rates and annual fees, secured cards provide a valuable steppingstone. Many people find they can graduate to an unsecured credit card within a year or 18 months.

Tip One way to avoid the stiffest fees is to shop for a card at a credit union first. Credit unions generally offer more reasonable terms for their plastic.

Don't be surprised if you don't qualify for a secured card that offers the lowest interest rate. Secured card issuers all have their own specific requirements. Some, for instance, won't issue a card to anyone who has a bankruptcy listed on her credit report. Or they might reject an applicant whose bill payments have been delinquent during the prior six months or who hasn't held a job for one year.

Protecting yourself from irritating bill collectors

Bill collectors are famous for being rude, sneaky, and bullheaded. They might be the only workers in America who are rewarded for acting like jerks. But believe it or not, debt collectors legally aren't supposed to behave like that.

Beware of Credit Repair Clinics

When rebuilding your credit, avoid credit repair clinics. These outfits promise to polish your tarnished credit reputation, but you could end up paying $500 to $1,000 or much more and be no better off. The tactics many of these outfits use on your behalf are questionable at best. For instance, they might flood credit bureaus with countless letters refuting the black marks on your credit report. By overwhelming a credit bureau, the clinic hopes that some of the negative entries will be erased at least temporarily. Some of these companies even suggest that their clients assume other identities to escape their bad credit histories.

Under federal law, one of these for-profit outfits is prohibited from accepting any money from a customer until it has fulfilled its contract. That means a clinic is breaking the law if it demands money up-front. Even if a clinic follows the rules, there is no reason to use one. Everything one of these companies can legally do, you can accomplish yourself. For instance, a clinic might give you a list of banks issuing secured credit cards, but you can obtain these names by visiting the Web sites listed in this chapter. You can also contact credit bureaus about mistakes on your credit report.

Thanks to federal law, collectors can't threaten to break your legs or any other parts of your body. (This isn't a joke.) And they can't let curse words slip into the conversation. Calling too early or too late is also unacceptable—calls must be made between 8 a.m. and 9 p.m. These guys can't pretend to be your long-lost uncle or an old college chum when they contact friends and acquaintances to dig up dirt on you. In fact, they aren't supposed to call anybody else, other than your lawyer, unless it's to simply locate your current residence. When they call you, they must always identify themselves as bill collectors.

Note   If a collection agency has broken these rules, you can write a letter requesting not to be contacted again. By law, the debt collector must honor your request.

Your request to be left alone, however, won't prevent the agency or the original creditor from suing you to recoup the money. But you will have every right to sue the agency yourself if it has flagrantly harassed you. The low-cost way is to file in small claims court.

Summary

✦ You can reduce your debt by following smart credit card strategies.

✦ Use Internet calculators to discover the true price of carrying a credit card balance.

✦ Debt consolidation often backfires for those debtors who can't spend less than they earn.

✦ If you're seriously in debt, consider contacting a nonprofit debt counseling service or possibly joining Debtors Anonymous.

✦ Even if your credit is immaculate, order a credit report to check for errors.

✦ Stay away from credit repair clinics.

✦   ✦   ✦

Insuring Your Investing Future

Being inadequately protected by insurance is a quick way to endanger your hard-earned investment portfolios. In this chapter, you'll discover why term life insurance is the best and cheapest option for most people. You'll also learn where to find the most reasonably priced cash value life insurance. How to evaluate disability and long-term care needs and policies is also included. For those who desire to learn even more about insurance, this chapter directs you to handy resources.

The ABCs of Life Insurance

Few financial transactions can be more mind-numbing than purchasing a life insurance policy from an agent. Many an American has spent a long evening on the couch listening to an agent discuss the merits of various insurance policies with glossy charts, computer-generated illustrations, and other props.

If an insurance agent has ever made you squirm in your own house, you appreciate that there are no easy escape routes. Navigating through whitewater in an inner tube would be easier than just saying, "Look, I'm confused and I'm not prepared to buy any insurance right now." Instead, maybe you've opted for Plan B. You bought a policy.

You don't need this book to tell you that buying insurance to please a stranger is worse than a bad idea. Anytime you are pressed into buying, it is most likely not a good deal for anyone but the salesperson. But scenes like these are played out in living rooms and around dining room tables every day. That's because many of us have never taken the time to learn some insurance basics. Once you have, you'll be surprised at how you can make better decisions.

Insurance 101 on the Web

Need a crash course on insurance basics? Insure.com (www.insure.com) is an excellent place to bone up on insurance. This Web site, which provides exhaustive coverage of the insurance industry, is packed with consumer-oriented articles about a variety of insurance, including life, health, auto, and property. If you encounter a problem with your insurer, Insure.com provides links to state insurance departments. Another good place to get immersed in the basics is *Kiplinger's Personal Finance* magazine's Web site (www.kiplinger.com). Also visit Insurance.com (www.insurance.com), which provides primers on a variety of insurance. Finally, you may want to check out a Web site from a California life insurance analyst, Anthony Steuer, who maintains some sophisticated insurance tools on his Web site, as well as in-depth reports on such topics as undoing an insurance policy loan and analyzing your own policy. You can reach his Web site at www.tonysteuer.com.

Sorting out the nuances of life insurance policies can make untangling wet spaghetti noodles look easy. But it doesn't have to be an impossible task. Simplify the decision-making process by getting answers to these essential questions:

Question no. 1: Do I need life insurance?

Not everybody does. If you're single, it could be a huge waste of money. If nobody, such as an elderly parent or grandparent, is dependent on you, then it can make little financial sense. Some agents argue that young singles should buy insurance so they can lock in cheap rates while they are young. Unless you've got some genetic disposition to contract a serious medical condition later in life, this is usually not advisable. Instead, invest the money you would have sunk into a premium. Coverage can be prudent, however, if you're in a committed long-term relationship and would like to leave something behind for your partner.

Tip   Some married couples without children may also not see any compelling need to buy life policies, particularly if both husband and wife are making about the same salary.

But the picture can change once a couple buys a house. Paying a mortgage is usually dependent upon two paychecks, so if a widow or widower would have trouble meeting the mortgage or paying off debts, insurance is warranted. Even without a house, if one spouse earns considerably less than another, insurance can be wise.

Parents with dependent children typically have the greatest need for life insurance. A death would cause not only emotional but financial turmoil as well. Insurance for single parents can be even more essential.

Caution   Too often, couples make the mistake of not insuring a stay-at-home parent, but they're not figuring in the cost of providing childcare if that parent should die.

Once children are grown, however, the urgent need for life insurance fades. (Parents with a special-needs child, however, could need insurance indefinitely.) Usually by this time, people have built up considerable assets and are possibly entitled to a pension. Life insurance also is much pricier as people age. Older, affluent Americans are more likely to require life insurance for estate planning purposes, such as to pay any estate taxes owed upon their deaths.

 Note Massive federal tax legislation in 2001 made it even less likely that individual Americans will ever realistically need to face estate taxes, as the estate tax exemptions were substantially increased. Paying the tax, however, is still a possibility for the very wealthiest. The estate tax is scheduled to die in 2010, but Congress would have to reauthorize the repeal for any years following that.

Question no. 2: How much is enough?

No one right answer exists to this question. Some insurance advisors suggest that coverage should provide anywhere from five to eight times your yearly income. Some individuals buy enough coverage to pay off their debts, such as a mortgage and college tuition. Still others decide on coverage based on how much they expect to make between now and their retirement.

Tip Generic guidelines are too inexact for most situations—follow them and you may end up with too small or too large a policy. It's better to spend a little more time evaluating your needs.

Use the following guidelines to calculate a more realistic figure:

Short-term expenses

This category includes the expenses generated by someone's final weeks and months. You'll need coverage to pay for hospital and physician bills, funeral costs, and expenses generated by settling an estate, including attorney fees. Also under this heading are debts left behind, such as credit card and utility bills, car or student loans, and any other outstanding bills.

Long-term needs

Debts in this category include a home mortgage and college tuition. If your children are nowhere close to being in college, you'll need to project what the costs might be in the future. Recently, the inflation rate for college has been about 5 percent.

 Resource To find the latest inflation rate and private and public college costs, visit The College Board's Web site at www.collegeboard.com.

You'll also need to calculate how much income your loved ones will need to maintain their same standard of living. From that yearly amount, you'll want to subtract survivor benefits they would receive through Social Security.

Insurance Calculators

Obviously, calculating insurance needs is difficult, but Internet tools can help. Keep in mind, though, that these calculators have their own limitations. Many of them crunch just 10 to 20 variables, while the typical person may need to consider a hundred or more variables to come up with an accurate coverage amount.

Here are some insurance calculators to experiment with:

✦ **Insurance.com:** www.insurance.com

✦ **Kiplinger's Personal Finance:** www.kiplinger.com

✦ **CNBC on MSN Money:** www.money.msn.com

✦ **InsWeb.com:** www.insweb.com

 Resource You can get an estimate of survivor benefits by filling out and submitting a form. Contact the Social Security Administration at (800) 772-1213 or www.ssa.gov.

You have to plug in even more "what ifs," such as the effect of inflation and the stock and bond market on your insurance proceeds. For inflation, use 4 percent. Consider playing it conservatively and using a return of 8 percent for a mixed portfolio of stocks and bonds.

 Tip Once you've figured out the total amount of life insurance you need, check with your workplace's human resources department to see whether they provide any life insurance. Companies often provide a limited amount in employee benefit packages.

Keep it current

One mistake that many consumers make after purchasing insurance is not periodically reevaluating their insurance coverage. Once they buy a term policy, it usually doesn't occur to them to occasionally explore whether they need the full coverage anymore. For instance, suppose you bought a $1-million, 15-year policy when a child was 7. The child is now a freshman in college with a partial scholarship. Do you still need that $1 million coverage? Perhaps college costs aren't as high as you expected and your net worth is higher than it was when the policy was selected. If you've got more cash in the bank, it makes sense to evaluate whether you can scale back on the insurance. Rather than focusing strictly on whether or not you still require coverage, consider what amount is now necessary.

Question no. 3: What type of policy do I need?

Once you determine the amount of coverage you need, you should explore the types of policies available. You've got two basic choices: term insurance policies and cash value policies, the latter of which can be broken down into whole life, universal life, and variable life.

Term life insurance: The simplest way to go

Term is the life insurance industry's version of a stripped-down new car that comes without any extras. With a term policy, you buy insurance that pays a benefit to your survivors if you die. And that's it. Term insurance offers no investment component. You pay a premium based on your age, health, and other factors.

Tip   Term insurance is the most straightforward and easy to understand of all life insurance on the market. For the vast majority of people, it's all they really need.

Here are reasons you might want term insurance:

✦ You need insurance for a fixed period of time, such as the period between your child's birth and his or her college graduation.

✦ You want to spend as little as possible on a policy.

✦ You are not interested in using insurance as an investment tool.

For families raising children, term is the cheapest way to go. However, the older you are, the more a policy costs. Term insurance is usually financially prohibitive once you reach the age of 60 or so. For older Americans who need insurance, cash value policies are realistically the only option.

While term policies are fairly straightforward, there are a few decisions you have to make. Here are the biggies:

How long do I want the insurance to last?

You can insure your life for various amounts of time—1 year, 5 years, 10 years, even 30 years. When the time period (or term) ends, most policies can continue, but often with higher premiums that are subject to increases each year.

Do I want a policy with a level premium that stays the same until the policy expires or one that has a lower initial rate but increases over the years?

With the latter kind of policy, your premium increases as you get older, although it's priced lower initially. If you stick with your policy until the end, the level premium policy costs you less money. Consequently, a level premium is the preferable option.

Evaluating Insurance Carriers

You purchase insurance to protect your family from catastrophe, but many people, whether they are purchasing term or cash value policies, forget that they need to protect themselves from their own insurer's demise. If an insurer goes out of business, a policyholder can suffer financially.

Insurer insolvency happens more often than you might think. In 2000, for instance, 56 insurers went belly up—the most since 1993 when Hurricane Andrew flattened parts of Florida. The latest crop of insurance casualties included about a dozen life insurers.

How do you protect yourself? Buy policies only from financially secure insurers. Fortunately, independent rating companies have done the footwork to evaluate a company's soundness. Each of the rating services uses somewhat different criteria so don't rely upon one single rating. Instead, choose a company that has an excellent rating from at least two of the sources. Don't do business with an insurer who fails to secure—at a minimum—a rating service's fifth or sixth highest ranking. The only exception to this rule would be when a person, with a health problem, is forced to use a lower-ranked insurer.

Here are the major rating services and the top three ratings they award:

✦ A.M. Best at (908) 439-2200 or www.ambest.com

   Three best ratings: A++, A+, A

✦ Fitch, IBCA, Duff & Phelps at (800) 853-4824 or www.fitchratings.com

   Three best ratings: AAA, AA+, AA

✦ Standard & Poor's at (212) 438-2400 or www.standardandpoors.com/ratings

   Three best ratings: AAA, AA+, AA

✦ Moody's Investors Service at (212) 553-0377 or www.moodys.com

   Three best ratings: Aaa, Aa1, Aa2

✦ Weiss Ratings at (800) 289-9222 or www.weissratings.com

   Three best ratings: A+, A, A-

With most of the services, you can obtain the ratings for no charge either by calling or visiting a service's Web site.

Do I want to buy term insurance through an insurance agent or through an insurance quote service?
There shouldn't be a price difference between the two options. However, don't expect all insurance agents to embrace term policies.

Caution

Sales of term policies generate small commissions, so many agents prefer to steer people toward cash value policies.

Cash value insurance

Unfortunately, cash value or permanent insurance is more complicated than the cut-and-dried term policies. That's because these policies provide more than just a simple death benefit. They double as a tax-deferred investment as well. Part of your annual premium pays for the death benefit, and the rest—after expenses and commission are deducted—goes into the investment side of your policy. Cash value policies cost more than term policies.

Here are reasons you might be interested in cash value insurance:

✦ **You desire life insurance coverage after age 60.** For older Americans, term insurance can be prohibitively expensive.

✦ **You want insurance to pay for future estate taxes.** Older persons, who have sizable estates, typically use cash value policies as a way to pay estate taxes so their heirs won't be forced to sell off assets when they die. As mentioned earlier, the estate tax is being whittled down, but it isn't scheduled to vanish until 2010. It's possible, thanks to the way the legislation was written, that the estate tax will reappear in 2011.

✦ **You want your savings to grow tax-deferred through an insurance policy.** Some people who already have maximized other tax-deferred investment plans also use cash value policies as a way to shelter even more money. The interest generated by this cash stockpile grows without being encumbered by taxes through the duration of a policy. It's now less likely, however, that Americans will have extra retirement cash that they want to stuff into a policy. Why? The tax-deferred feature isn't as compelling since Congress passed its meg-tax package in 2001. That's because individuals will now be able to siphon greater amounts of money into Individual Retirement Accounts, 401(k)s and other retirement plans. The investments that you can choose for these retirement plans, such as mutual funds and individual stocks, are less costly and therefore more attractive than saving through an insurance policy.

✦ **You'd like to be able to borrow against your insurance policy.** Although the amount of any unpaid portion of the loan is subtracted from your heirs' payout, you can borrow from the cash accumulated within the policy.

✦ **You want the flexibility to change your premium payments (within certain limitations).** This feature is found in some cash value life policies.

✦ **You are a small business owner.** Family businesses also rely on these policies to preserve the company after one of the partners dies. Policy proceeds can buy out a deceased partner's share of a business. This is an effective way of spinning off a portion of the company's wealth to heirs who have zero interest in its operations.

As a general rule, there is often little reason for people who are not approaching retirement age to sign up for one of these traditional cash value policies. However, this hasn't dissuaded some persistent insurance agents from pressuring customers in their twenties, thirties, and forties from buying them. What's the rationale? Agents insist it's a foolproof way of forcing people to save despite spendthrift tendencies.

Caution · Using a cash value policy as a conservative investment is rarely a smart move, because of the high commissions. There are plenty of cheaper ways to invest in stocks and bonds.

Here's a look at the three major types of cash value insurance:

Whole life

Whole life is the oldest type of cash value policy on the market today. If you buy a whole life policy, you won't be surprised by your future premiums because they typically stay the same throughout the lifetime of the policy. Since your payments remain level even as your life expectancy shrinks, insurers charge you more than the actual cost of the insurance in the early years of a policy. This surplus is invested so there will be sufficient money when a policyholder dies and a big check is cut. When someone dies, the beneficiary receives the policy's face amount.

There is nothing risky about how your cash is invested in one of these policies. The insurance company puts your money into fixed-income securities, such as corporate bonds and mortgages. Usually the insurer guarantees a minimum return on your money, such as 4 percent.

Unlike term insurance, you don't have to die to unleash the benefits of whole life insurance. You can, for instance, take out a loan against the money you've already accumulated in your policy. If the loan remains unpaid when you die, the insurer subtracts that amount from your heir's payout.

Caution · Agents like to tell potential customers that they can also use the cash built up in their policies to cover their premiums. Beware, however, of any promise of vanishing premiums. In most cases, it's not a realistic option.

Universal life insurance

In some respects, universal life insurance acts like its whole life brethren—a portion of the premiums is directed toward the death benefit, while the rest is stashed in the investment side. A universal life policy, however, is more flexible than a whole life one. And that's what attracts many people. You can adjust the amount of the annual premium, withdraw cash, and increase or reduce the death benefit. (Fattening the death benefit usually requires that you undergo another medical exam.) You could conceivably pay a reduced premium or none at all on occasion and kick in additional money at other times.

As with whole life, you can divert money from the policy's cash account to pay the premium, and you are given a guaranteed rate of return up-front. It'll usually be low, but there is potential for the return to be higher than with whole life policies.

Caution · You can't assume that your coverage will outlast you when you borrow money from a cash value policy or use the cash value to reduce your premiums. Policies can expire even before you die, when the cash value is used up prematurely.

Amazingly, your policy can cash itself out even if you continue to faithfully write checks for your full premium amounts. How could this be? An insurer's mortality charges could climb over the years, while the interest rates that an insurer is generating on the cash could fall.

Anyone with a cash value policy should find out whether his or her coverage is in any danger. You can do this by requesting what's called an *in-force illustration* or *in-force ledger* from your carrier. They are obligated to provide you with this documentation. You can mail a standard request form to your insurer that can be obtained at this insurance analyst's Web site, www.tonysteuer.com.

Many universal life policies held by Americans today are most likely underfunded and will terminate before the customers die. Interest rates used to sell these policies were not realistic, while at the same time insurers have increased their mortality charges.

Variable life insurance

This kind of cash value policy isn't as tame as universal or whole life; its investments are tied to the ever-unpredictable stock market. The rate of return depends on how well the underlying investments do. You get to decide where you want your money to go. You can typically choose from among stock, bond, and money market mutual fund accounts. Sometimes a minimum death benefit is guaranteed no matter how badly the stock market performs, but you won't hear the same kind of assurances about your cash investment.

Caution If your policy's stock and bond holdings don't do well, you might be forced to increase the premium payments to protect your insurance coverage.

Unlike the other types of cash value policies, you receive a prospectus before signing any papers. Read it carefully. Variable, as well as universal life policies, can generate higher fees than the simpler whole life alternative.

Shopping for the Best Term Insurance Policies

Compared to cash value insurance, searching for an ideal term policy is a breeze. You can either use a quote service or an insurance agent. Agents and electronic quote providers are compensated by an insurance company for serving as go-betweens. Rates are set by an insurer, so they will be the same no matter how you hear about them. If you receive a different price on the same policy from the same insurer, the quote is probably based on a different rate category (for example, if you mentioned on one application that you have high blood pressure, but not on the other).

If you feel you need advice and hand-holding before making a decision, you might as well consult an agent. Just make sure that he has access to the quotes of many insurance companies. An independent agent, who works with many insurance companies, will probably be your best bet. (As a precaution, consult some quote services on your own and see how the agent's quotes compare.) On the other hand, if you hate dealing with agents and like the convenience of finding insurance on the Internet, stick with the quote services.

Working with quote services

You can contact quote services by phone or through their Internet sites. You indicate the amount and length of coverage you want. You also provide a cursory background of such things as your medical history, age, height, weight, and whether you smoke or fly in private planes. The quote service tries to find the cheapest policies available and provides a list with prices from a variety of insurance companies. These referrals are free.

> **Tip**
> Some quote services survey many insurers for you. Others check only a handful. To thoroughly cover the bases, obtain quotes from more than one place.

Here are some quote sources to check:

✦ Accuquote at (800) 442-9899 or www.accuquote.com

✦ QuoteSmith.com at (800) 431-1147 or www.quotesmith.com

✦ QuickQuote at (800) 867-2404 or www.quickquote.com

✦ InstantQuote.com at (888) 223-2220 or www.instantquote.com

✦ Answer Financial at (800) 233-3028 or www.answerfinancial.com

✦ InsWeb at www.insweb.com

✦ SelectQuote at (800) 289-5807 or www.selectquote.com

Qualifying for the best rates

If you're not careful with quote services, you can get ensnared in what may feel like a bait-and-switch operation. You're quoted one price, but you're asked to pay a lot more when the bill arrives.

That's because the services often give out quotes based on their best rates, which you may see referred to as "preferred-plus" rates. Some insurers, however, only give this exclusive rate to about 5 percent of their applicants, who are in excellent health. About 60 percent of applicants qualify for the next best rate category, "preferred." Applicants who still can't qualify end up in the standard or even a substandard category. Someone paying the standard rate may have minor health problems, such as high cholesterol, or may be noticeably overweight. So while you may be quoted the best rate, you may later be offered a less desirable one.

Blue Light Specials

In recent years, term life insurance rates have dropped dramatically. Consequently, if you bought a term policy—even just a year or two ago—you may want to obtain new quotes. Chances are today's policies are cheaper than the one you've got, for a variety of reasons. For starters, Insurers are demanding that people be healthier to qualify for the best rates. Americans are also living longer, which helps the industry's bottom line. Plus, insurance rates are instantly available to anyone who wants to spend a few minutes on the Web, which puts tremendous pressure on pricing. What's more, less than 1 percent of all term policies actually pay a death benefit.

Never cancel a current policy before you've officially purchased a new one. Typically, you have to undergo a medical screening process before you receive another policy. If the new insurer ultimately turns you down, you don't want to be stranded without protection.

Tip   Before seeking a quote, be honest with yourself about your health. Since securing the best available rate is a long shot for most people, ask each insurer its preferred (second best) guidelines to see if you would qualify.

Here are the qualifications you must typically meet to snag the very best rates:

- ✦ Nonsmoker
- ✦ Stringent weight/height requirements
- ✦ Low cholesterol level
- ✦ No heart disease or cancer deaths in parents or siblings before age 60
- ✦ Blood pressure below 140/90 without medication
- ✦ No more than three moving traffic violations during the past three years
- ✦ No drunk-driving convictions
- ✦ No serious illnesses
- ✦ Does not travel in private planes

Tip   Because different insurers use slightly different criteria to rate applicants, you should check rates with a variety of insurers. While one insurer may put someone in the standard rate class, another insurer will give the same applicant a preferred rate.

Shopping for the Best Cash Value Policy

Whether you are buying a new cash value policy or shopping for a replacement, it is extremely difficult to analyze competing policies. There are no meaningful tools to evaluate whether the policy your former college roommate is pressuring you to buy from him is any better than another agent's favorite. There is no unit cost pricing of cash value life insurance, no annual percentage rate (APR) to scrutinize. In fact, it's because of the gobbledygook factor that there are still hundreds of insurers in this country—the lousy ones can hide behind the confusion.

Get professional advice

You are obviously going to need help. Plenty of people will be glad to guide you through the process, but you sure don't want to rely on an insurance rookie. Instead find an experienced agent who has completed extra training. Consider sticking with an agent who is a Chartered Life Underwriter (CLU) or Chartered Financial Consultant (ChFC). Of the two, the ChFC designation is the more prestigious one. A CLU candidate's course work is primarily centered on insurance, while someone with a ChFC has successfully completed classes that involved a more holistic financial planning approach.

 To find an agent with the CLU or ChFC designations, contact the Society of Financial Service Professionals at 270 S. Bryn Mawr Ave., Bryn Mawr, PA 19010-2195; (888) 243-2258; www.financialpro.org.

Another option is consulting a certified financial planner (CFP) or a certified public accountant (CPA) that specializes in financial planning. (See Chapter 5 to learn more about working with CFPs and CPAs.) They can look at your entire financial picture before counseling you on what cash value coverage, if any, you need. Seeking help from one of these professionals can eliminate a potential conflict that agents face. If an agent doesn't sell a policy, he won't pocket a commission. Consequently, an agent is highly motivated to peddle insurance, whether it's appropriate or not. A fee-only advisor, who does not accept commissions, won't face the same temptation. Advisors avoid traditional policies with built-in commissions and choose "low-load" policies instead, which are stripped of commissions.

Why can low-load policies beat the policies that agents sell? It's simple—blame it on high commissions. It's not rare for your entire first-year premium to be swallowed by the commission. So if your premium is $3,000 the first year, your assets 12 months later will be zero. Your second year's premium could get gobbled up by commissions as well. Unfortunately, there aren't many of these newer low-load products on the market, but this could change.

Another alternative for professional advice is a life insurance analyst, who can work on a fee-only basis, rather than strictly on commission. You can pay one of these insurance advisors to evaluate your insurance needs. The name given to these insurance professionals will vary by state. For instance, in Texas they are called insurance counselors. Unfortunately, the number of these insurance experts is small. In California, for instance, there are less than 40.

Getting a Trusted Second Opinion

Finally, here's a cheap resource to help you analyze any cash value policy: the Consumer Federation of America. The not-for-profit organization has developed an effective way to evaluate all types of cash value policies and compare one to another. James H. Hunt, an insurance actuary, who is a former insurance commissioner of Vermont, determines the value of a policy's death benefit, as well as the rate of return on the savings portion. After estimating the true investment returns on any policy, the consultant compares that figure to the alternative of buying a term policy and investing the money you'd save in a hypothetical alternative investment, such as a bank account or mutual fund.

The cost of the analysis is $50 for the first policy and $35 for each additional one that is submitted at the same time. You can contact Hunt at this address: 8 Tahanto St., Concord, NH 03301-3835. To learn more about the service visit the Consumer Federation's Web site at www.consumerfed.org.

The federation's research also might help you decide whether you want to buy a policy through an agent—and pay a stiff sales commission—or buy what's called a low-load policy from insurance companies that do not employ agents.

Resource To find an insurance analyst, call your state Department of Insurance. (Not all states license these professionals.) To obtain the number of your state's insurance department, contact the National Association of Insurance Commissioners, 2301 McGee, Suite 800, Kansas City, MO 64108; (816) 842-3600, www.naic.org. Two other resources are the Life Insurance Advisers Association at (800) 521-4578 and Financial Advisors Insurance Resources, Inc. at (877) 411-FAIR; www.lowloadinsurance.com.

Switching cash value policies

If you already own a cash value policy, don't expect persistent insurance agents to leave you alone. Why? Because they can make another handsome commission if you agree to switch policies.

Caution Most of the time, replacing one cash value policy with another is a monumental financial mistake—if you switch policies, you incur those exorbitant up-front sales charges all over again.

Say you buy a whole life policy that comes with an annual $3,500 premium. The first year, your investment is worth nothing because the entire premium goes toward the commission. Two years later, an agent convinces you that a universal life policy is offering more generous terms. You agree and drop your old policy. Once again, however, your first year's premium gets gobbled up by the commission. So far, you've paid $7,000 and have little or nothing to show for it.

Life Insurance Checklist

Here's a cheat sheet for buying life insurance:

✦ Determine how much life insurance you need. Using an online calculator may be helpful.

✦ Comparison shop. Term insurance is a highly competitive market so you'll want to check a lot of rates. Quote services can speed up the process.

✦ Check an insurer's financial soundness. Most rating services provide this information free of charge.

✦ After narrowing your search, ask for a copy of actual policies and compare.

✦ Make sure your medical history is completely accurate when filling out an insurance application.

✦ After receiving a policy, read it carefully to make sure there aren't any errors. Ask for an explanation if something isn't clear.

One argument you will hear from agents is that your type of cash value policy no longer makes the most sense financially. And that could be true. When economic conditions such as interest rates change, the attractiveness of your policy might diminish. In the 1980s, for example, universal life policies were popular because high interest rates allowed them to offer better returns. But a lot of people who rushed to sign up were later disappointed with their returns when interest rates slumped. Trading in a policy every time economic conditions change only makes your insurance agent wealthy. That said, there are times when abandoning a policy in favor of another makes sense.

Here are three major reasons to bail out:

✦ Your insurer is in danger of going out of business.

✦ If you're more affluent, solid estate-planning reasons can necessitate a change. Your estate-planning attorney can advise you on this.

✦ Your policy is dramatically overpriced, and you're considering a low-load policy.

Here are some questions you should ask an agent if he is pushing you to replace your policy:

✦ If I replace my current policy, how soon will I have access to the same amount of cash value that I currently have?

✦ What is the difference in guaranteed values between the two policies?

✦ If interest rates go down, how will the proposed policy perform? How would my existing policy perform?

✦ Can the payment of a death claim be challenged if I die within two years of buying the new policy?

If a policy is at least two years old, the insurance company has less right to snoop around in the private life of a dead customer. Assuming there's no fraud, the insurer must simply pay up. If the policy is a newer one, however, the insurer has the right to deny a claim or reduce the benefits if it determines that the deceased customer fibbed in any way on the application. What's more, if the policyholder commits suicide within the first two years, the beneficiaries don't receive the death benefit.

✦ Are there any tax consequences when considering a replacement?

When a cash value policy is surrendered, a calculation must be made to determine if there was a taxable gain. There also might be a loss of other income-tax benefits, such as the deductibility of interest payments and "grandfathered" benefits that newer policies can't offer.

✦ Are there features in my policy that would be lost if I replaced it?

Your old policy might have a low, fixed loan rate, while the new one may have a variable loan rate that can conceivably become prohibitively expensive. Also, some policies sold in the 1980s have an interest-rate guarantee as high as 6.5 percent, while today's policies might only guarantee 4 or 4.5 percent. A new policy might not be underwritten on as favorable a basis as the old one.

Don't Forget Disability Insurance

You no doubt appreciate the importance of insuring your income, your home, your health, and the cars in your garage. But you may not have given much thought—if any—to insuring your very ability to earn a living.

Note   Just look at the odds: If you are 40 years old, the likelihood of becoming disabled for at least 90 days is a staggering 67 percent. If you just turned 30 years old, the chances of becoming incapacitated for at least three months is 70 percent.

A disability policy bails you out if you can't perform your job because of a temporary illness or a permanent one. Although the maladies triggering the biggest claims are back problems and mental and nervous conditions, the reasons somebody might need one of these policies are limitless. Back surgery might keep a carpenter off the job for several months. A nagging carpal tunnel problem in the wrist might sideline a software programmer. A serious car accident with a drunken driver might leave an innocent passenger critically injured for the rest of her life.

Could you survive without your salary for a year, two years, maybe longer? What would happen if your spouse couldn't work? If you can handle this financial nightmare without trouble, then you won't require this insurance. But for everybody else, read on.

When shopping for a disability policy, this checklist should make the task easier.

Check your employer's benefits package first.

If you work for a large or medium-size company, you may already enjoy some type of freebie coverage as part of your benefits package. Find out what the policy covers. Usually, a corporate policy only provides coverage for a short period of time. If that's the case, you need additional protection.

Consider your needs carefully.

When shopping for a policy, insurers will ask how long of an *elimination period* you want, meaning the length of time it takes before you start receiving disability checks (your deductible, essentially). Elimination periods range from 30 days to as long as two years. A policy with a short waiting period usually costs more. You'll also need to determine a policy's *benefit period,* or length of time a policy pays once a claim is made. The benefits can last for as little as a year, or they can continue until you die.

Tip Most policyholders choose a disability period of 60 to 90 days, which is usually a wise decision, and most ask for coverage that ends when they reach 65, to coincide with retirement age.

Make sure you and the insurer are on the same wavelength: Know what an insurer's definition of disability is. When somebody complains bitterly about a policy's payout, it's usually due to misunderstanding the policy's definition of disability. There are three definitions:

✦ **Own occupation:** This is the Cadillac of policies that kicks in if you can't perform your specific job, even if you could make the same income in a different occupation. For example, if an orthopedic surgeon loses several fingers in a car accident, she can no longer work in an operating room—but she starts teaching at a medical school and also working as a medical consultant. With this policy, she's still entitled to disability checks since she can no longer perform surgery.

✦ **Any occupation:** Under this definition, you don't qualify for disability payments if you can still work at a job that is appropriate for your level of education and training. In this scenario, the surgeon can't expect any checks.

✦ **Income replacement:** This is the cheapest of the three policies. It guarantees your old salary level if your disability forces you to work at a lower-paying job.

Disability Insurance on a Budget

Disability insurance can be costly, but there's hope for penny pinchers. The best way to slash premium costs is to buy a policy through an organization that obtains a group rate. Check with alumni associations or professional organizations that you might be able to join.

Obtaining coverage through a group can be even more critical for women because their individual rates are higher. Why? Women file more disability claims, though no one is certain why. Through a group policy, women may be able to find a unisex policy that charges the same rates for men and women.

Which policy should you buy? Own-occupation policies are increasingly difficult to find and the cost can be prohibitive. Some policies, especially the ones you can obtain through professional organizations, may use an own-occupation definition for several years but then stop payments if you can hold onto a job that fits the any-occupation category. Income replacement could be your best bet since it does guarantee your old salary while costing the least.

Most often, insurers only provide coverage for 60 to 70 percent of your gross earned income. Realistically, you won't find better coverage. Why? Insurers don't want you to live as well as you did before your setback, because any incentive to return to work may evaporate.

When calculating what you'd need to cover all your monthly bills, keep in mind that, unlike with your regular salary, you won't owe taxes on your disability payments. But there is one big exception: If your employer paid for your premium, then you'll owe Uncle Sam taxes for those payouts.

Tip Also find out if a disability policy takes into account more than your base salary—a critical consideration if commissions and bonuses represent a sizable amount of your yearly compensation.

Looking for Long-Term Care Insurance

If you are approaching retirement and you've been contemplating buying long-term care insurance, it's no wonder. Studies have suggested that close to half of all Americans who reach the age of 65 will spend time in a nursing home. Ending up in a nursing home can destroy a nest egg that took a lifetime to build—unless you are insured against those expenses.

Long-term care policies provide coverage in cases where a person is suffering from a chronic disability or illness so debilitating that they can no longer take complete care of themselves. These policies can provide for more than just nursing home coverage. They can also cover the costs of such services as home health care and an adult day care center, possibly allowing a policyholder to remain longer in his or her own home.

These policies aren't cheap. Like any other kind of insurance, the rates can vary depending on such factors as your age, health, and whether you want a fancy policy. Your premium will be steeper if you demand coverage that kicks in shortly after you need help. The length of your coverage also matters. A policy with lifetime coverage, for instance, costs a lot more than one that expires after a few. Consumers often pick a coverage period that lasts three to five years.

Who needs long-term care insurance?

Some older Americans assume they don't need long-term care insurance because Medicare would pay their freight if they ever required nursing home care. But that's a dangerous misconception. Medicare won't pay for a long stay in a nursing home, and neither will *Medi-Gap* policies (insurance offered by private insurers to cover expenses that Medicare doesn't pay). And to qualify for Medicaid, the state-run welfare program, you have to be nearly impoverished. You can keep a car, a small amount of cash, your home, a prepaid funeral, and some jewelry (you won't have to sell your wedding ring), but often just about everything else must go. When you die, you can't even be assured that your heirs will hang onto the family home—a state can seize it to pay your old bills. Rather than become impoverished, plenty of people have shifted anything of value to their children or other relatives. But even that trick is hard to pull off. If you transfer your estate to others, Medicaid can make you wait three to five years before it begins picking up your nursing home tab.

Tip

Explore buying long-term care insurance once you are nearing retirement if you are middle or upper middle class and have accumulated a significant amount in assets during your lifetime. Recently, the average age of a policy purchaser was 67.

The very rich and the lower middle-class won't need to bother. If you're barely scraping by, it doesn't make sense to purchase a policy, since Medicaid will come to your rescue fairly quickly. On the other end of the spectrum, a millionaire may be able to foot his or her own nursing home bill. The Consumers Union has suggested that long-term care isn't necessary for someone who can set aside $160,000 to cover four years of nursing home care and still have enough money to leave behind to a spouse or dependent child. The nonprofit group used the four-year figure because that's the average amount of time someone remains in a nursing home.

Agents often encourage people in their 40s and 50s to buy policies by suggesting that they will secure policies when the rates are cheaper. It is true that the premiums are dramatically lower for younger customers, but unfortunately there is no guarantee that the rates will remain low. It's true that an insurer can't raise the premiums just because customers are now older, but that's not much of a problem for the industry. An insurer can hike rates as long as it's done for an entire class of customers in a state. Significant numbers of customers have seen dramatic price increases.

Tip Contact your state insurance department to see if an insurer has a history of raising long-term care insurance premiums.

Well over one hundred insurance companies would love to sell you a long-term policy. Of these, a dozen companies sell the vast majority of policies. Stick with a company that has a track record in this relatively new field.

Caution Don't buy a policy from a company whose rates are significantly cheaper than other insurers. These lowballers could go out of business or they might have to increase their rates significantly to survive if they priced their premiums poorly.

Consider inflation protection

We've all heard those spooky warnings about how inflation can rip the best-laid retirement plans to shreds. Well, consider this scenario: A 50-year-old man buys a long-term care policy that provides for $45,000 worth of coverage a year. He doesn't need the policy until he's 80 years old and he breaks a hip. A year in a nursing home, by that time, however, costs $235,000. (This figure assumes a 5.8 percent inflation rate, which is realistic for this industry.) Obviously his policy will only cover a fraction of his costs.

Insurers calculate inflation protection two ways: by a simple or compounded method. With the simple method, interest is calculated strictly on the original amount of money invested. A pricier feature, compound interest, is calculated upon the original investment plus the accumulated interest so it provides more protection.

Tip If you can afford it, select the compounded inflation protection. This protection, however, can be prohibitively expensive for older customers. Instead consider buying a policy with higher coverage and no inflation protection. For instance, suppose you really wanted an inflation-protection policy that provides for $150 a day nursing home costs. You may be able to get a cheaper policy that provides $200-a-day coverage with no inflation protection. That extra $50 in coverage could be considered your inflation hedge.

Coverage for Your Parents

Too young for long-term care insurance? You might want to buy coverage for your parents or in-laws. Some insurers suggest that you spring for the premium so you won't have to subsidize their costly care later. Interestingly, an increasing number of employers are now offering, as a benefit, long-term care insurance for employees' parents, as well as to employees themselves.

Coverage for older parents can be especially important for middle-aged women. In one study published in the *Journal of Gerontology* in the 1990s, 23 percent of middle-aged female caregivers left their jobs, while 43 percent cut back their hours to care for aging relatives.

Before selecting a policy, it's best to learn as much as you can about long-term care insurance. Here are some resources:

✦ *A Shopper's Guide to Long-Term Care Insurance.* This guide includes a worksheet that lists the important questions that any potential buyer will want to ask an insurer. National Association of Insurance Commissioners, 2301 McGee, Suite 800, Kansas City, MO 64108; (816) 842-3600; www.naic.org.

✦ *Long-Term Care Planning: A Dollar & Sense Guide.* Published by the not-for-profit United Seniors Health Cooperative, 409 Third St., Suite 200, Washington, DC 20024; (202) 479-6973; www.unitedseniorshealth.org

✦ The American Health Care Association, which is a federation of health care providers, has posted a detailed explanation of long-term care insurance issues on its Web site. Contact this organization at 1201 L St. NW, Washington, DC 20005; (202) 842-4444; www.ahca.org.

Summary

✦ If you require life insurance, a term policy is usually the best bet.

✦ Using quote services can cut down on the time necessary to find an ideal term life insurance policy.

✦ Consult an unbiased source to evaluate cash value insurance policies.

✦ Know an insurer's definition of disability before buying a disability policy.

✦ If you are nearing retirement age, you should explore whether you need to buy long-term care insurance.

✦   ✦   ✦

Glossary

8-K A corporation must file this document with the U.S Securities and Exchange Commission if it experiences a "material" (significant) event that should be shared with investors. The news can be good or bad.

10-K A corporation's yearly financial report, which is filed with the U. S. Securities and Exchange Commission. It provides more in-depth information than an annual report.

10-Q A company's quarterly financial report, which must be filed with the U.S. Securities and Exchange Commission.

12b-1 A fee that allows a mutual fund to pass along to its shareholders the costs of its marketing efforts.

401(k) An employer-sponsored retirement plan that takes its name from a section of the federal tax code. Workers can contribute pretax money to this plan, and the money grows tax-deferred until it is withdrawn.

403(b) An employer-sponsored retirement plan for persons who work for tax-exempt organizations such as schools, health care facilities, and charities. Employees contribute pre-tax dollars, which grow tax-deferred until they are withdrawn.

accounts receivable ratio This financial ratio, which is used to analyze a stock, attempts to pinpoint how fast a corporation collects its money from its customers. The higher the number the better.

ADV Form Investment advisors must file this form with either their state securities department or the U.S. Securities and Exchange Commission. The document includes such information as the advisor's professional background, method of compensation, and whether he or she has faced any disciplinary actions.

aggressive growth fund A mutual fund that typically invests in small or fast-growing companies. These funds are very risky.

analyst An expert who evaluates corporations and makes conclusions about whether a stock should be bought or sold. Analysts typically specialize in a particular industry, such as semiconductors, drugs, or beverages. They are primarily employed by investment, brokerage, and mutual fund firms.

annual report A corporation's yearly accounting of its financial status. The U.S. Securities and Exchange Commission requires all publicly traded companies to issue one.

annuitant A person covered by an annuity contract.

annuity A series of payments made until someone's death, either received from a company pension plan or from a private annuity, which is an insurance product purchased to provide monthly payments during retirement.

ask The price at which a security is offered for sale.

asset allocation The process of deciding how to diversify your portfolio among stocks, bonds, and cash.

asset allocation fund A mutual fund that maintains a mix of stocks, bonds, and cash in order to provide instant diversification. Some of these funds adjust the mix to capitalize on economic changes, while others become more conservative as their shareholders age.

assets Possessions that have monetary value, such as stocks, bonds, real estate, cars, and jewelry.

back-end load A sales commission charged when a mutual fund investor sells shares. If the shares are held long enough, the back-end load may disappear, but it's common for this type of fund to charge higher annual expenses.

balanced fund A more conservative mutual fund that attempts to provide current income as well as growth with a portfolio of stocks, bonds, and cash.

balance sheet A portion of a corporation's annual filing with the Securities and Exchange Commission, which shows the status of its liabilities, assets, and shareholder's equity on a specific date.

basis A security's purchase price plus commission or other expenses. It's used to calculate what taxes, if any, are owed when the stock is sold.

bear market Describes the stock market during a period of prolonged decline, specifically a period in which stock values decrease at least 20 percent or more.

bequest Property left to an heir according to terms of a will.

beta A figure used to measure a stock's volatility in relation to the overall stock market. For example, a beta of 1 indicates that a particular stock will be no more volatile than the market. A beta greater than 1 suggests the stock will be more volatile. Stocks with betas less than 1 are considered less so.

bid The price the buyer is ready to pay for a security.

bid-ask spread The difference in the buy and sell prices of securities.

blue-chip stock Stock of a widely recognized corporation that possesses a long record of growth. The term comes from the blue chips used in poker, which are the most valuable.

bond A type of IOU issued by corporations and government bodies from the federal to the local level. The issuer makes regular interest payments to the lenders and ultimately pays back the entire amount in a specific number of years. If a company is liquidated, bondholders enjoy a greater chance of retrieving some of their investment than stockholders do.

bond ladder A bond strategy in which a portfolio is constructed to have approximately equal amounts invested in various maturities within a given time horizon.

bond rating A letter grade given to a bond that signifies the creditworthiness of the issuer. A high rating indicates that a rating service believes that the bond issuer is likely to pay off the debt as promised.

book value Calculated by dividing the net worth of a company by the number of shares outstanding. Book value is one tool used by investors when they evaluate whether a stock is underpriced.

broker Someone who charges a fee or commission for trading stocks, bonds, and other securities.

brokerage commission A fee paid to a broker for executing a security transaction.

bull market Describes the stock market when stock prices have increased for an extended period of time.

buy and hold A long-term investing strategy of investors who purchase stocks or mutual funds and keep them despite ups and downs in the financial markets.

call An option that gives an investor the right to buy a specific number of shares in a stock at a certain price by a fixed date.

callable bond Bonds that the issuer has a right to redeem (or call) prior to maturity at a specified price.

capital gain The profits you make when selling assets such as stocks, bonds, and real estate for more than you paid.

capital gains distribution Distribution made by a mutual fund to its shareholders for the profits it made on the sale of stocks or bonds in its portfolio. Investors are liable for the taxes generated by these gains even if they don't sell their shares.

capital gains tax The tax on profits from the sale of securities.

capitalization The market value of a company, which is determined by multiplying the price per share of its stock by the number of shares outstanding.

certificate of deposit (CD) An interest-bearing deposit at a bank that locks up an investor's money for a preset period. CDs usually pay a higher rate of interest than a regular bank account.

Certified Financial Planner (CFP) A financial advisor who possesses a wide knowledge on a variety of personal finance issues. A CFP has passed a rigorous exam administered by the Certified Financial Planner Board of Standards in Denver, as well as met other requirements.

certified public accountant (CPA) An individual who specializes in accounting, auditing, and preparing tax returns for individuals or corporations.

churning Excessive securities trading by unethical brokers to generate more commissions from their clients.

closed-end fund Shares in this type of mutual fund are sold on the stock exchanges. They may be purchased at a premium or a discount. These funds aren't as popular as traditional or open-end mutual funds.

commission The fee you pay a broker for completing a trade for such securities as stocks, bonds, and mutual funds.

common stock A fractional share in a publicly traded corporation. Common stock shareholders are entitled to certain rights, such as voting on the company's directors and receiving any dividends.

compounding Growth that results from income and gains on the original investment as long as the reinvested income and capital gains are not withdrawn but are left to grow.

conference call A corporation's management discusses the results of its most recently completed quarter on a telephone call hook-up with analysts.

confirmation A written acknowledgment from a broker that a trade has been completed.

Consumer Price Index (CPI) An index calculated by the U.S. Bureau of Labor Statistics that measures the cost of buying a certain assortment of consumer goods. This index is supposed to represent realistic purchases by Americans. Social Security payouts are tied to changes in the CPI.

corporate bond A taxable bond issued by a company. Corporate bonds issued by less financially secure companies are referred to as junk or high-yield corporate bonds.

cost basis Represents the original cost of an investment, such as a stock or mutual fund, which is used to determine an investor's profit when the holding is sold. It's necessary to pinpoint the profit or capital gain to establish what tax is owed.

crash A dramatic drop in the stock market, such as the 1929 crash that triggered the Great Depression.

current ratio This financial ratio, which is used when analyzing a stock, takes a company's current assets, which includes cash, inventory, and accounts receivables, and divides it by current liabilities, such as outstanding bills and expenses. The ideal ratio is around 1.5, but the range will differ among corporations and industries.

cyclical Describes industries such as oil, paper, and manufacturing whose fate is closely tied to the nation's economy.

defined benefit plan Another name for a pension plan that guarantees a certain benefit based upon a formula that includes years of service and salary history.

defined contribution plan A workplace retirement plan, such as a 401(k) or profit sharing arrangement, that depends upon employee contributions and, in many cases, employer contributions.

Diamond Nickname for an exchange-traded fund that encompasses the 30 corporations in the Dow Jones Industrial Average.

disability insurance Insurance that provides a policyholder with regular payments if he or she can't perform his or her job because of a temporary or long-term illness.

diversification Owning different types of investments in order to reduce risk.

dividend A company's distribution of earnings to investors who own stock or mutual fund shares.

dividend-reinvestment plan (DRIP) DRIPs enable investors to automatically reinvest dividends that are generated by stocks they own.

dollar-cost averaging Systematic way of investing a set amount of money monthly or quarterly. With this strategy, an investor tries to reduce the risk of investing a large sum of cash all at once.

Dow Jones Industrial Average This is the nation's most closely watched and oldest index. The 30 major corporations in the average include American Express, Disney, DuPont, Intel, J.P. Morgan, and Wal-Mart.

duration A measure of the sensitivity of a bond or bond fund prices to interest rate changes.

early withdrawal penalty A penalty charged by the bank if you cash out a certificate of deposit early. Also, a 10 percent penalty you usually must pay if you withdraw your money from a tax-deferred retirement account before the age of 55 or 59½.

earned income Any money you earn in making a living, including salary and self-employment income.

earnings per share A key way to evaluate a stock's profits. If a company's profit is $1 million and 500,000 shares are outstanding, the earnings per share are $2 ($1 million divided by 500,000 equals $2).

EDGAR (Electronic Data Gathering Analysis and Retrieval) The electronic depository for all the public filings a corporation must provide to the Securities and Exchange Commission. EDGAR (www.sec.gov) is a popular research tool for stock investors.

education IRA A tax-advantaged way for parents or others to save for a child's education. The contributions, which are limited to $500 a year per child, grow tax deferred.

elimination period This is essentially a disability insurance policy's deductible. It refers to the length of time it will take before you begin receiving disability checks. The average waiting period is 60 to 90 days.

emerging market fund A mutual fund that invests in stocks of companies located in less-developed countries.

enrolled agent A professional tax preparer who must typically undergo a rigorous test administered by the Internal Revenue Service.

equity The value in something you own after deducting all liabilities related to the asset. For instance, if you own a home worth $225,000 and your mortgage is

$125,000, your equity is $100,000. This term is also used to refer to stocks because holding those shares essentially grants a stockholder a small piece of the company.

estate tax A federal tax imposed on some large estates after a person dies.

exchange-traded fund This tax-efficient investment acts like an index fund, but it trades like an individual stock. Just like an index fund, an exchange-traded fund holds a stake in companies that make up a given benchmark.

expense ratio What you annually pay a mutual fund, which is expressed as a percentage of your total investment. The expense ratio includes management and administrative fees and any 12b-1 fees.

Federal Deposit Insurance Corporation (FDIC) A federal agency that guarantees that a customer's money in a bank will be protected (up to a certain ceiling) if the institution fails.

Federal Reserve Board The governing board of the Federal Reserve System. Its members are appointed by the president of the United States and confirmed by the U.S. Senate.

Federal Reserve System A system created in 1913 to regulate the nation's monetary and banking network.

fee-based planner A financial advisor who is compensated through a combination of fees and commissions.

fee-only planner A financial advisor who does not accept commissions. Some fee-only planners charge a percentage of assets; others charge by the hour or by the project.

financial advisor Generic term used broadly by many professionals, including financial planners, insurance agents, and brokers.

financial consultant Generic term commonly used by many professionals, including insurance agents and brokers.

fixed annuity Payment of a set sum of money to a person at regular intervals for a specific period of time or for life.

front-end load An upfront sales commission that is paid when shares of certain mutual funds are purchased.

global fund A mutual fund that can invest in foreign corporations as well as American ones.

good-till-cancelled order An order to buy or sell stock that remains in effect until the trade is completed or the request is canceled.

growth-and-income fund A mutual fund that invests in corporations that expand at a decent clip and also generate dividends.

growth fund A mutual fund that invests in companies that have the potential to grow handsomely over time and provide fat returns.

high-yield corporate bond fund A mutual fund that invests in the bonds of corporations that do not enjoy the best financial reputations.

HOLDRS® An investment product created by Merrill Lynch. Each HOLDR contains a basket of stocks in a particular industry, such as telecom, semiconductors, and biotechnology.

immediate annuity Used primarily by retirees, who desire a steady stream of income. A lump sum is invested in an immediate annuity and in return an insurer sends monthly checks to the customer.

income statement Contained in annual and quarterly reports, the income statement is a summary of a corporation's revenues, costs, and expenses.

index fund A mutual fund that seeks to match the returns of whatever stock or bond benchmark or index it is linked to. The most popular index funds are tied to the Standard & Poor's 500.

Individual Retirement Account (IRA) A retirement savings vehicle created by the federal government. Every year, individuals are allowed to deposit up to $2,000 into one of these accounts. The accounts can be established at a mutual fund firm, a brokerage house, a bank, or other financial institution.

inflation index bond This bond, offered by the U.S. Treasury, is linked to the Consumer Price Index. The bond's principal rises if inflation does. For instance, if inflation jumps 4 percent one year, the $1,000 face value of the bond rises to $1,040. The Treasury Department uses that figure, not $1,000, to determine what the annual interest payment will be.

initial public offering (IPO) The first time a company makes the purchase of its stock available to the public.

insiders Directors and senior officers of a corporation, who obviously have inside information about their company.

institutional investors Refers to major investors, including insurance companies, endowments, pension funds, mutual fund companies, and investment firms.

inventory turnover ratio This ratio shows, on average, how often a company sells and then replaces its inventory each year. The higher the inventory ratio, the better.

investment club A group of people who pool their money to build a stock portfolio. Many investment clubs belong to the nonprofit National Association of Investors Corp. in Royal Oak, Michigan.

investor relations department The division of a company that answers stockholder questions and sends them regular updates about the company's performance.

joint-and-survivorship pension A pension covering two people and paying benefits until both have died. The benefit often drops to 50 percent after the first partner dies.

junk bond Nickname for high-yield corporate bonds that are rated below investment grade.

Keogh plan A retirement savings program for small-business owners or the self employed.

large-cap stock Stocks belonging to the nation's biggest corporations. The capitalization of these companies exceeds $10 billion and can go much higher.

limit order An investor's instruction to buy or sell stock at a specific price or better. There is no guarantee that the order will be filled.

liquidity Ability to trade large amounts of a stock easily without greatly impacting the price. Major corporations are considered very liquid, while small publicly traded companies are not.

load fund Load refers to a mutual fund's sales charge. The fee pays a stockbroker or financial advisor's commission.

long-term care insurance An insurance policy that pays for nursing home and/or home care expenses if the policyholder can no longer care for himself or herself.

low-load fund Usually sold directly by a mutual fund firm, a fund of this type typically charges an up-front fee of 2 to 3 percent.

management's discussion & analysis In this narrative portion of its annual 10-K, a company is supposed to provide a candid portrayal of the company's successes and failures in the previous year. This section must also discuss where executives hope to take the company in the next year and what difficulties they foresee in reaching their goals.

market order Instructions to trade stock at the best available price. Most orders executed on the stock exchanges are market orders.

market timing An investment strategy used by people who try to outsmart the stock market. They attempt to anticipate trends by buying when they think the market is on the verge of advancing and selling before they expect a market downturn.

maturity The date a bond matures, which is the point when the bondholder gets back the face value of the bond.

micro-cap stock Stocks belonging to very small companies, by Wall Street standards. The capitalization of these companies is below $1 billion.

mid-cap (capitalization) stock Stocks belonging to medium-sized companies. The capitalization of these companies ranges from $2 billion to $10 billion.

money market fund The safest type of mutual fund. Some investors use money markets instead of bank savings accounts or certificates of deposit.

Morgan Stanley Capital International EAFE (Europe, Australasia, and Far East) Index This index tracks the performance of stocks in developed markets overseas.

Morningstar A well-known mutual fund ratings firm in Chicago. Morningstar is best known for its five-star designation for what it considers to be the nation's best mutual funds. You can usually find Morningstar's mutual fund publications in libraries.

municipal bond Debt of state and local governments (essentially IOUs) that is issued to fund capital projects such as schools, roads, and water treatment plants. It's often called a muni.

mutual fund A pool of money from thousands of shareholders that is invested in stocks, bonds, and/or cash. As a shareholder, you can own a tiny piece of dozens or hundreds of individual stocks or bonds just by holding a few shares of the mutual fund.

Nasdaq Acronym for National Association of Securities Dealers Automated Quotation system. This system handles trades for thousands of stocks.

Nasdaq-100 Contains the biggest and most popularly traded companies on the Nasdaq. The index is dominated by technology companies.

National Association of Investors Corp. The nonprofit investment club organization that has helped thousands of clubs around the nation get started.

National Association of Securities Dealers (NASD) Brokerage firms belong to this nonprofit organization, which operates the Nasdaq. It also sets ethical guidelines for the industry and investigates violations of its rules.

net asset value (NAV) The value of one share of a mutual fund's investments. The NAV is adjusted daily and is reported each day in a newspaper's financial pages.

net income A corporation's profits after taxes, depreciation, interest, and other expenses are deducted.

net worth What's left when a person subtracts his or her debts from his or her assets.

New York Stock Exchange Started in 1792 on Wall Street, it's the nation's oldest stock exchange.

no-load fund A mutual fund that does not impose a sales charge.

noncallable bond A bond that cannot be redeemed by the issuer prior to maturity.

option The right to buy or sell stock at a specified price during a certain period of time.

par value The face value of a bond. When the bond matures, the issuer must pay back the bond's par value.

PEG ratio The PEG ratio is obtained by dividing a stock's P/E ratio by its projected earnings growth rate. The PEG ratio is used to assess the potential value of a stock.

penny stock These stocks got their name because they can usually be bought for under $5 a share, and sometimes the price is less than what you'd pay for a candy bar. Penny stocks are extremely volatile and are too speculative for almost all investors.

pension plan A fund established by a company for the payment of retirement benefits. The number of American companies offering pension plans has been shrinking.

personal finance specialist (PFS) Designation used by certified public accountants who specialize in personal financial planning.

portfolio All the securities held by an investor.

preferred stock A hybrid equity that behaves more like a bond than a stock. Some conservative investors buy shares in preferred stock to generate income. If a company is liquidated, preferred stockholders enjoy a greater chance of retrieving some of their investment than common stockholders do.

prepaid tuition plan A tax-deferred method of saving for college that is sponsored by many individual state governments.

price-to-book value A figure that essentially tells investors how much the company would be worth if it sold all its assets for cash.

price-to-cash flow ratio Current stock price divided by cash flow per share. Cash flow is defined as income after taxes minus preferred dividends, plus depreciation, depletion and amortization.

price-to-earnings ratio (P/E ratio) The current market price of a share of stock divided by the company's annual earnings per share. A trailing P/E is obtained by dividing the current price by the latest year's reported earnings. This number is the P/E found in newspapers. A forward P/E is based on analysts' forecasts of next year's earnings.

principal The amount of money you originally put into an investment.

profit-sharing plan A workplace retirement plan in which contributions, based on each participant's compensation, can be varied and no minimum contribution is required.

prospectus A legal document containing important information about a mutual fund, including its risks, costs, and past performance.

pump-and-dump scam Scam artists hype a mediocre stock on the Internet, radio call-in shows, or other media in hopes of pumping up the price so they can then sell, or dump, the stock for a profit.

put option This contract allows an investor the right to sell a certain number of stock shares at a specific price by an agreed-upon deadline.

Qube Nickname for exchange-traded fund that encompasses the 100 top companies in the Nasdaq.

quick ratio This financial ratio is supposed to give a realistic idea of what kind of cash resources a corporation can draw upon in an emergency. A quick ratio of 1 or better is usually okay.

real return The return on an investment after factoring in the rate of inflation. If an investment returns 10 percent and inflation is 3 percent, the real return is 7 percent.

registered representative An employee of a brokerage house who has acquired a background in the securities business and has passed required tests. Another name for stockbroker.

required minimum distribution The amount of money that federal law requires that you withdraw from a retirement account after reaching the age of 70½.

return-on-equity ratio (ROE) Essentially ROE indicates the rate that investors are earning on their shares. A company that has a ROE of 20 percent, for instance, is creating 20 cents of assets for every $1 that was originally invested.

revenue A company's sales.

risk The potential of losing money or not making an expected rate of return on an investment.

rollover A tax-free transfer of money from one retirement plan to another.

Roth IRA Named after a former U.S. senator from Delaware, this is arguably the best IRA for the vast majority of Americans. The contributions are not tax deductible, but you won't have to pay any taxes on this money when you withdraw it at retirement.

Russell 2000 This best-known small-cap stock index is composed of 2,000 companies.

sales load A commission charged by some mutual funds on new purchases of shares. A typical commission, or load, is 4 or 5 percent.

Sector A broad grouping of stocks by category, such as utilities, transportation, and consumer cyclicals. Each sector is composed of many smaller industry groupings. Within the consumer cyclical sector, for instance, are such industries as casinos, advertising, and restaurants.

sector fund A mutual fund that invests only in stocks in a particular sector or industry, such as wireless communications, healthcare, or energy.

Section 529 plan These state-sponsored college savings plans allow parents to shelter money from taxes as they save for their children's college education.

securities A catchall name for stocks, bonds, and other types of investments.

Securities and Exchange Commission (SEC) A federal agency created in 1934 to oversee the securities industry. Its prime goal is to protect the investing public from abuses in the industry.

SEP-IRA Short for Simplified Employee Pensions-Individual Retirement Account. A retirement plan geared toward the self-employed that allows for tax-deferred savings.

separately managed accounts Professional money managers oversee the portfolios of affluent individuals with these accounts. Some investors who dislike the tax inefficiency of mutual funds are turning to these accounts.

Series EE savings bond Savings bond issued by the federal government in denominations that range from $50 to $10,000. Issued at a discount, they are redeemed for face value at maturity.

share price The price of a solitary share of stock.

shareholder A person who owns shares of stock in a company.

shareholder equity What's left after subtracting a company's debt from its assets.

simple interest Interest calculated on the original amount of money invested.

short-term capital gains tax The tax that applies if an investment, which is sold for a profit, is held for exactly one year or less.

SIMPLE-IRA Short for Savings Incentive Match Plan for Employees-Individual Retirement Account. A tax-deferred retirement plan geared toward firms with fewer than 100 employees.

small-cap (capitalization) stock Stocks in companies whose market value is less than $2 billion. Small-cap companies as a group have historically grown faster than large ones, but they are also more volatile and fail more frequently.

socially responsible fund A mutual fund that only invests in companies that are considered good corporate citizens and that do not produce such things as alcohol, weapons, and tobacco.

Spider Short for Standard & Poor's Depository Receipts. Nickname for exchange-traded fund that contains all the stocks in the Standard & Poor's 500 Index.

spousal IRA An Individual Retirement Account for a nonworking spouse. In the 1990s, the federal government raised the maximum contribution from $250 to $2,000.

spread The difference between a stock's bid and ask price.

Standard & Poor's 500 Index (S&P 500) An index of the stocks of 500 very large American corporations. The index is widely regarded as a barometer of the overall health of the U.S. stock market.

Standard & Poor's MidCap 400 Index An index created in 1991 to monitor the investment performance of medium-sized companies.

Standard & Poor's SmallCap 600 Index An index that serves as a barometer of the health of small American corporations.

stock A share of ownership in a corporation.

stock split When a stock splits, the number of shares held by an investor generally goes up, but the price is reduced accordingly, so the transaction is a financial wash. However, a stock split is seen as a positive move that the company believes its stock price will continue escalating.

stop order An order to sell a stock when its price falls to a certain level. This order is intended to limit an investor's losses.

tax-deferred Any earnings on a tax-deferred investment remain untaxed until you make a withdrawal.

tax-free bonds Another name for municipal bonds. These tax-exempt bonds are free from federal income tax and might be free of state and local taxes as well.

tax-managed mutual fund A mutual fund that strives to obtain high returns, while at the same time keeping an investor's yearly tax burden low if nonexistent.

technical analysis Refers to a method of analyzing stock by looking at patterns in a stock's historic price movements.

term life insurance Life insurance that provides a cash benefit to survivors if a policyholder dies. This insurance provides no investment value.

ticker symbol Letters that identify a company for trading purposes. These symbols can be located in a newspaper's stock tables or on many financial Web sites.

total return A measure of an asset's performance. It includes the income an investment has generated as well as any capital appreciation.

Treasury bill Also called a T-bill, this is a short-term obligation of the federal government with a maturity of 13 or 26 weeks.

Treasury bond A federal government obligation that matures more than 10 years after it's issued.

Treasury note A federal government obligation that matures from 2 to 10 years after it's issued.

turnover Can refer to how often a mutual fund manager buys and sells stocks in the fund's portfolio.

universal life insurance A cash value life insurance policy that provides a death benefit as well as an investment component.

value stock Stocks that have a low market price relative to their earnings.

variable annuity A variable annuity is part insurance policy and part mutual fund. Within an insurance wrapper, policyholders invest their money in mutual funds. The annuity is called variable because the return depends upon how the mutual funds perform. The insurance guarantees that if the investor dies, the heirs will at least receive the amount of the original investment.

variable life insurance This type of policy provides a death benefit but also serves as a tax-deferred investment vehicle. The rate of return on the investment depends upon what underlying securities are chosen.

vesting Refers to the right to receive workplace retirement benefits. An employee often isn't entitled to a pension or employer contributions to a 401(k) plan until he or she has been at a company for a certain period of time.

Wall Street The financial district at the lower end of Manhattan in New York City. Many brokerage firms, as well as the New York and American stock exchanges, are located here.

whisper numbers A company's rumored earnings numbers. These numbers, which are formulated outside the official analyst community, can hurt a stock's price if they are not met.

whole life insurance An insurance policy that provides a death benefit to the survivors as well as a tax-deferred investment. Part of the annual premium pays for the death benefit; the rest is invested for you.

Wilshire 5000 Index The broadest stock market index. Despite its misleading name, the index encompasses more than 7,000 companies.

yield Income received from an investment, usually expressed as a percentage of the market price of the security.

yield to call Yield on a bond, assuming that the issuer will redeem the bond at the first possible opportunity.

yield to maturity The yield an investor will receive if a bond is held until its maturity date.

zero coupon bond A bond sold at a deep discount to its face value. It can be extremely volatile unless it's held to maturity.

Resource Guide

401(k) and 403(b) Plans

mPower Cafe
http://401k.mpower.com

Annuities

Annuity.com
www.annuity.com

AnnuityNet.com
(877) 569-3789
www.annuitynet.com

Comparative Annuity Reports
(916) 487-7863
www.annuitycomparativedata.com

Fisher Annuity Index
(800) 833-1450

Morningstar Variable Annuity Performance Report
(800) 735-0700
www.morningstar.com

National Association for Variable Annuities
11710 Plaza America Dr., Suite 100
Reston, VA 20191
(703) 707-8830
www.navanet.org
www.retireonyourterms.com

TIAA-CREF
(800) 842-2776
www.tiaa-cref.org

U.S. Securities and Exchange Commission
Office of Investor Education and Assistance
450 Fifth St. NW
Washington, DC 20549-0213
(202) 942-7040
www.sec.gov

WebAnnuities.com
(800) 872-6684
www.annuityshopper.com

Arbitration & Mediation

National Association of Securities Dealers Dispute Resolution
125 Broad St., 36th floor
New York, NY 10004
(212) 858-4400
www.nasdadr.com

New York Stock Exchange
Arbitration Department
20 Broad St., 5th floor
New York, NY 10005
(212) 656-2772
www.nyse.com

Public Investors Arbitration Bar Association
2241 W. Lindsey, Suite 500
Norman, OK 73069
(888) 621-74484
www.piaba.org

Bonds

Bond Market Association
www.investinginbonds.com

Bondsonline
www.bondsonline.com

Bureau of the Public Debt: Savings Bonds
(304) 480-6112
(800) 4US-BOND (Automated)
www.savingsbond.gov

TreasuryDirect
U.S. Treasury Department
(800) 722-2678
www.publicdebt.treas.gov

Certificates of Deposit

Bankrate.com
www.bankrate.com

BanxQuote
www.banxquote.com

iMoneyNet.com
imoneynet.com

Estate Planning

American College of Trust & Estate Counsel
3415 S. Sepulveda Blvd., Suite 330
Los Angeles, CA 90034
(310) 398-1888
www.actec.org

Heirs, Inc.
P.O. Box 292
Villanova, PA 19085
(610) 527-6260
www.heirs.net

Nolo.com
www.nolo.com

Exchange-Traded Funds

American Stock Exchange
(800) THE-AMEX
www.amex.com

Barclays Global Investors
(800) 474-2737
www.ishares.com

Nasdaq
www.nasdaq.com

Financial Planners

American Institute of Certified Public Accountants
Personal Financial Planning Division
Harborside Financial Center
201 Plaza Three
Jersey City, NJ 07311-3881
(888) 999-9256
www.aicpa.org.

Financial Planning Association
(800) 282-7526
www.fpanet.org

National Association of Personal Financial Advisors
355 W. Dundee Rd., Suite 200
Buffalo Grove, IL 60089
(888) FEE-ONLY
www.napfa.org

Government and Industry Regulators

Certified Financial Planner Board of Standards
1700 Broadway, Suite 2100
Denver, CO 80290-2101
(888) CFP-MARK
www.cfp-board.org

North American Securities Administrators Association
10 G St. NE, Suite 710
Washington, DC 20002
(202) 737-0900
www.nasaa.org

Securities and Exchange Commission
450 Fifth St. NW
Washington, DC 20549-0213
(800) 732-0330
www.sec.gov

National Association of Securities Dealers (NASD)
125 Broad St., 36th floor
New York, NY 10004
(800) 289-9999
www.nasdr.com (a resource for investors and the securities industry)
www.nasdadr.com (a forum for securities dispute resolution)

NASD District Offices

District 1
525 Market St., Suite 300
San Francisco, CA 94105
(415) 882-1234

District 2
300 S. Grand Ave., Suite 1600
Los Angeles, CA 90071
(213) 627-2122

District 3
Republic Plaza Building
370 17th St., Suite 2900
Denver, CO 80202
(303) 446-3100

Two Union Square
601 Union Street, Suite 1616
Seattle, WA 98101
(206) 624-0790

District 4
12 Wyandotte Plaza
120 W. 12th St., Suite 900
Kansas City, MO 64105
(816) 421-5700

District 5
1100 Poydras St.
Suite 850, Energy Centre
New Orleans, LA 70163
(504) 522-6527

District 6
12801 North Central Expressway, Suite 1050
Dallas, TX 75243
(972) 701-8554

District 7
One Securities Centre, Suite 500
3490 Piedmont Rd. NE
Atlanta, GA 30305
(404) 239-6100

District 8
10 S. LaSalle St., Suite 1110
Chicago, IL 60603
(312) 899-4400

Renaissance on Playhouse Square
1350 Euclid Ave., Suite 650
Cleveland, OH 44115
(216) 694-4545

District 9
581 Main St., 7th floor
Woodbridge, NJ 07095
(732) 596-2000

11 Penn Center
1835 Market St., Suite 1900
Philadelphia, PA 19103
(215) 665-1180

District 10
33 Whitehall St.
New York, NY 10004
(212) 858-4189

District 11
260 Franklin St., 16th floor
Boston, MA 02110
(617) 261-0800

Index Funds

Indexfunds.com
www.indexfunds.com

Vanguard Group
(800) 871-3879
www.vanguard.com

Individual Retirement Accounts

Ed Slott's IRA Advisor
(800) 663-1340
www.irahelp.com

mPower Cafe
http://ira.mpower.com

Insurance

Consumer Federation of America
1424 16th St. NW, Suite 604
Washington, DC 20036
(202) 387-6121
www.consumerfed.org

Insure.com
www.insure.com

National Association of Insurance Commissioners
2301 McGee, Suite 800
Kansas City, MO 64108-2604
(816) 842-3600
www.naic.org

Society of Financial Service Professionals
270 S. Bryn Mawr Ave.
Bryn Mawr, PA 19010-2195
(610) 526-2500
www.financialpro.org

Insurance Ratings Services

A.M. Best
(908) 439-2200
www.ambest.com

Fitch IBCA, Duff & Phelps
(800) 853-4824
www.fitchratings.com

Standard & Poor's
(212) 438-2400
www.standardandpoors.com/ratings

Moody's Investors Service
(212) 553-0377
www.moodys.com

Weiss Ratings
(800) 289-9222
www.weissratings.com

Investor Education

American Association of Individual Investors
626 N. Michigan Ave.
Chicago, IL 60611
(800) 428-2244
www.aaii.org

Investorama
www.investorama.com

Investment Clubs

bivio.com
www.bivio.com

Motley Fool
www.fool.com

National Association of Investors Corp.
P.O. Box 220
Royal Oak, MI 48068
(877) 275-6242
www.better-investing.org

Mutual Funds

Morningstar
(800) 735-0700
www.morningstar.com

Mutual Fund Education Alliance
www.mfea.com

Online Retirement Advice

DirectAdvice
www.directadvice.com

Financial Engines
www.financialengines.com

www.MonteCarloSimulations.org
www.montecarlosimulations.org

Morningstar's ClearFuture
www.morningstar.com

mPower
www.mpower.com

Quicken 401k Advisor
www.quicken.com

Options

Chicago Board Options Exchange
(877) THE-CBOE
www.cboe.com

The Options Industry Council
(888) OPTIONS
www.888options.com

Real Estate Investment Trusts

National Association of Real Estate Investment Trusts
1875 Eye St. NW
Washington, DC 20006
(800) 3-NAREIT
www.nareit.org

Social Security

Social Security Administration
(800) 772-1213
www.ssa.gov

Women and Social Security Project
National Council of Women's Organizations
www.women4socialsecurity.org

Stock Indexes

Indexfunds.com
www.indexfunds.com

Nasdaq-100 and composite
www.nasdaq.com

Russell 2000
www.russell.com

Standard & Poor's 500
www.spglobal.com

Wilshire 5000
www.wilshire.com

Morgan Stanley Capital International indexes
www.mscidata.com

Barra indexes
www.barra.com

Stock Research

Big Charts
www.bigcharts.com

CBS MarketWatch
www.cbsmarketwatch.com

CNBC on MSN Money
www.money.msn.com

Edgar
U.S. Securities and Exchange Commission
www.sec.gov

Morningstar
www.morningstar.com

Motley Fool
www.fool.com

Multex Investor
www.multexinvestor.com

TheStreet.com
www.thestreet.com

Value Line Investment Survey
(800) 634-3583
www.valueline.com

Yahoo!Finance
http://finance.yahoo.com

Zacks Investment Research
www.zacks.com

Taxes

Internal Revenue Service
(800) 829-3676 (publications)
(800) 829-1040 (tax questions)
www.irs.gov

Internal Revenue Service: Office of the Director of Practice
1111 Constitution Ave. NW
Washington, DC 20224
(202) 694-1891

National Association of Enrolled Agents
200 Orchard Ridge Dr., Suite 302
Gaithersburg, MD 20878
(800) 424-4339
www.naea.org

✦　　✦　　✦

Index